NEW CONSUMERISM: SELECTED READINGS

Edited By

WILLIAM T. KELLEY

THE WHARTON SCHOOL
DEPARTMENT OF MARKETING
UNIVERSITY OF PENNSYLVANIA

Second Printing

To

Ralph Nader

INTRODUCTION

Interest in consumerism is growing at a tremendous rate in America. In the academic field alone, the author knows of more than 220 colleges and universities now studying the consumer movement in special courses established for the purpose, or as a part of other courses in such subjects as welfare economics, home economics, and social welfare. The general public, too, is very interested in this area. Books by and about Ralph Nader sell like the proverbial hotcakes. Program chairmen can assure themselves of packed houses for the Rotary Club, Lions, PTA, etc., if they choose speakers expounding the new consumerism. Teachers know that students in courses concerning quite remote subjects turn often turn the discussion around to this exciting new social movement.

The author has conducted several research courses or seminars on consumerism, both undergraduate and graduate, at the Wharton School. He can testify as to the keen interest and enthusiasm displayed by his students on consumeristic questions. Several of the papers coming from these research seminars were of such high quality, in their instructor's opinion, as to be worthy of publication. This led him to realize there were many other worthy papers and monographs which were very up-to-date, significant, and either had not been published at all or had been published in media of relatively restricted circulation. Other current and choice articles in widely circulated papers and journals, such as *Wall Street Journal, Journal of Marketing, Business Week* and *Harvard Business Review*, came to hand and seemed to fit with materials available.

As the author pondered these materials, they appeared to fall into a pattern which seemed to afford a logical and comprehensive coverage of the entire field of consumerism. So, these are the means by which this book of readings came to be.

It is emphasized that these readings are drawn from the whole subject matter of the new consumer movement. Therefore, they fit in very well with extant textbooks in the field. They especially complement *Social Issues in the American Economy* by Y. Hugh Furuhashi and E. Jerome McCarthy, another Grid book which became a best seller shortly after its introduction in 1971.

The general reader will find these articles unique and most timely. More than one-half of them have not heretofore been widely read, and it would be nearly impossible to secure copies of them. The remainder are significant papers already well known, which are likely to become classics in the literature of consumerism. The author is especially proud to introduce to a wider audience two meritorious collections of papers: one presenting the business side of the story, originating in DuPont's *Context;* the other collection exhaustively examining the new social responsibilities of American business, which came from the White House Conference on The Industrial World Ahead: A Look at Business in 1990 (1972)."

In every case where possible, the author tried to present both sides of a debate. Indeed, many facets of the social responsibility of business are disclosed in the White House Conference collection. Contrasting articles concerning the pros and cons of advertising are also there for that purpose.

Some of the articles may annoy or even enrage the reader. At least, the reader may differ with many of the positions taken by the various authors. This is as it should be. A subject as vital as consumerism should evoke controversy. But we hope the gentle reader will remember that it is all in the interest of getting at the truth. In a rapidly changing and developing field such as this we know of no other way of achieving that purpose. We solicit the reader's forebearance in this matter.

In our acknowledgments we thank the many people who contributed to this collection: renowned deans and professors, noted social scientists, business leaders, members of the working press and government officials. But we also thank those who still have to make it in life — our undergraduate and graduate students who achieved such a fine level of research excellence in their respective studies. We are proud of them.

Any work that aspires to be scientific should begin with a definition of terms. What do we mean by the "consumer movement"? By "consumerism"? By "social welfare"?

Alas, no simple, concise definition of these terms is available. To answer these queries, we must turn to experts who *should* be able to render a definition within their own field of interest.

The following are some definitions of consumerism propounded by leaders in the area.

FOOTNOTE

1. Adopted from *Context,* No. 1, 1973, pp. 1-3.

SENATOR CHARLES H. PERCY
(R., Ill.)

To me, the consumer movement represents a broad public reaction against bureaucratic neglect and corporate disregard of the public.

It is a repudiation of misleading advertising, empty warranties and guarantees, deceptive packaging, anti-competitive conduct, unfair pricing and bait-and-switch merchandising.

It is a check on sham, misrepresentation, deceit and fraud. And it is a control against monopolistic behavior by some corporations and

ii

the abuse of authority or discretion by certain agencies of government.

The fight for consumer protection is a battle for quality in goods and services, for fairness in advertising and promotion, for honesty in the marketplace. In its broadest sense, I believe that the consumer movement amounts to a yearning for an improved quality of life — for an America that works again, for people, products and governmental institutions that support the society rather than tear it apart. It is an affirmation of the interest of the many over the interest of the few, of a broader public interest over special interests.

What's good for the consumer is good for business. Most businessmen know this and build their businesses on this philosophy. And there is no better foundation than insuring that the product or service produced is worthy of public acceptance.

SIDNEY MARGOLIUS
Author and Columnist on Consumer Affairs

If I had to define the common denominator in the many aspects of this movement, I would define it as a protest and attempt to solve the problem of waste and diversion of family — and thus national — resources from urgent public needs. The protest often centers on waste which occurs because of poor design and undependable or unsuitable quality, or wastefully high marketing costs.

JAMES BISHOP, Jr.
Deputy Bureau Chief — NEWSWEEK
Washington, D.C.

"Consumerism" is neither the creature of the "radic lib" nor a passing fad. America's newest "ism", conservative at bottom, represents the strong grass-roots demand for a new marketing ethic in America — an ethic which seeks nothing less for every American than a secure physical environment and a just economic one.

Because millions of Americans have been exposed to such futures for decades by advertising, their expectations are high — so are their frustrations and, lately, their fears.

The widespread discovery of hazards has destroyed the 20th Century myth that the consumer is an omniscient, sovereign king who can protect himself in the bewildering marketplace of 1973.

By codifying the rights of every individual to truth, health and safety in the marketplace, the forces of consumerism are also signalling to industry the existence of a highly profitable new future — one in which profit will be based on performance, quality and disclosure. In sum, consumerism will be a major new form of competition for the rest of the century.

SEN. WARREN G. MAGNUSON
(D., Wash.)

"Consumerism" is a word used to describe the phenomenon whereby purchasers of goods and services are trying to attain a marketing system which makes the consumer sovereign — which guarantees to him the right to safety, the right to be informed, the right to choose, and the right to be heard.

Consumerism is based upon that basic tenet of the free enterprise system which says that the consumer (rather than government) should control, through rational purchasing decisions in the marketplace, which goods and services are produced. But consumerism looks to government to control producers who would interfere with rational choice and thereby destroy the free enterprise system.

For example, "consumerism" asks that government require producers to make products which do not contain hidden dangers; it asks that government require producers to give consumers certain information; it asks that government adjust the laws so producers live up to their warranties and other promises; it asks that government facilitate the settlement of disputes between consumers and producers; and, where necessary, it asks that government require the production of certain products that would not be available to the consumer but for such governmental requirements.

DAVID A. AAKER
Associate Professor of Business (University of California, Berkeley) and Author on Consumerism

Consumerism is an evolving set of activities of government, business, independent organizations, and concerned consumers that are designed to protect the rights of consumers. It is an evolving, dynamic movement with an enlarging scope and changing spokesmen and issues. It is action oriented and therefore more than an analysis of problems.

The activities are not confined to consumer activists. Indeed, government and business are involved in developing and implementing innovations which are part of consumerism today.

Consumerism is concerned with the rights of the consumer to safety, to be informed, to choose and to be heard. Although the meaning of these four rights has been broadened considerably and their focus altered since President Kennedy put them forth in 1962, they still form the core motivation for consumerism activity. A fifth right must be added, however: the right to an environment which will enhance and not detract from various life styles.

LEO BOGART
Executive Vice President and General Manager
Bureau of Advertising, American Newspaper
Publishers Association

Consumerism is a catchword in current vogue among marketers to describe a variety of distinct phenomena. These include (1) the long-term evolution of a more sophisticated and better educated buying public; (2) public skepticism about business practices, a reflection of deeper malaise with all established institutions in the aftermath of the Vietnam war; (3) organized activism (led by a handful of articulate advocates with a following among university students) to correct product deficiencies and advertising claims, and (4) legislative moves to increase consumer protection and an intensification of actions by government regulatory agencies.

ROBERT E. BROOKER
Chairman of the National Business Council
for Consumer Affairs

When the President formed the National Business Council for Consumer Affairs, we concluded that the answer to the problems that arise with consumers was to provide goods or services which meet the consumer's expectations.

In other words, a consumer is one who uses goods or services to satisfy his needs. Consumerism is the system, which may be either voluntary or regulated, which hopes to assure the consumer of being satisfied according to his expectations at the time the goods were acquired or the services contracted.

It is our feeling on the Council that it is the responsibility of business to satisfy the consumer's expectations on a voluntary basis by providing standards of performance which are fair and understandable to the consumer.

HERBERT S. DENENBERG
Pennsylvania Insurance Commissioner

Consumerism is not merely putting safety into cars or taking fat out of hot dogs. It is much more than improving the physical environment, creating safer products, and protecting the public from fraud and other consumer abuses.

Consumerism should have more basic purposes. Consumerism should aim for government and institutions "of, by, and for the people" instead of government and institutions "of, by, and for special interest groups."

Consumerism has been focused on some of the obvious symptoms of lack of responsiveness to the public interest. But consumerism is moving toward a more fundamental definition which is in fact a reaffirmation of our basic democratic concepts: Consumerism seeks to give representation to all interests, especially the individual buyer, consumer, and citizen who now has no adequate voice in the power structure.

BETTY FURNESS
Former Special Assistant to President Johnson
for Consumer Affairs

"Consumerism" is a word originally coined by industry to make the burgeoning consumer movement sound like a dangerous threat. Business loved the word. Consumer advocates didn't, but they were too busy doing their work to bother about it.

Today, the movement by any other name would smell as sweet. We'll take the title.

Consumerism is an effort to put the buyer on an equal footing with the seller. Consumers want to know what they're buying. What they're eating. How long a product will last. What it will and will not do. Whether it will be safe for them and/or the environment.

That's consumerism.

Consumers do not want to be manipulated, hornswoggled or lied to. They want truth, not just in lending, labeling and packaging, but in everything in the whole vast, bewildering marketplace.

ERMA ANGEVINE
Executive Director
Consumer Federation of America

Industry spokesmen coined the word "consumerism." It's their label for the rising tide of consumer self-awareness. It vaguely implies some philosophical connection with communism, socialism, or other "ism". Actually, we have no philosophy — except that "the sole aim of production is consumption" (Adam Smith). Because the word (consumerism) has no meaning, I abhor it.

This consumer self-awareness rose in the early New Deal days, ebbed during World War II, and turned to flood with President Kennedy's historic statement of the rights of consumers.

Instead of debating "consumerism," let's discuss those real, meaningful matters that affect consumers.

Now, having enlightened (or perhaps hopelessly confused) our readers as to what the book is all about, we shall turn to a short analysis of its specific coverage.

We first look into the history of consumerism. We examine what the fathers of economics had to say about the position of the consumer within the market. Dr. Eugene Beem traces the two earlier 20th Century movements, muckraking and the era of protest in the 1930's. Then, we look at the revival of interest in consumerism in the late 1960's and early 1970's. We read of the influence of Ralph Nader and his followers. Professor Kotler gives us an overview of the contemporary significance of the new consumer movement. He certainly concludes that it is not a flash-in-the-pan, but will be a part of the American scene for a long time.

Next, we consider the role traditionally ascribed to the consumer within the market place. Is he a king, dictator, supreme court, or a mindless automation, moulded at will by the hidden persuaders? What are the implications of "consumer sovereignty" for our society?

After this we analyze certain market segments, looking into the problems of the poor, the black, and the ghetto dweller. Are the hapless poor abused by greedy merchants? Do they pay more for common goods? Why?

A probe of the parties most often accused of exploiting the consumer follows. We evaluate the frequently raised questions about advertising morality and ethics, role conflict, and the impact of television on our children. A close-up examination of one line of business frequently under attack, the drug industry, is made.

Then, we consider two early cases in which the impact of consumerism was felt, the cigarette and the cereal industries. By evaluating these impacts, we hope to be able to predict the effect of consumer attacks, and consequent industry reactions, for other industries in the future.

What has business done to meet the threat of aroused consumers? The ombudsman system is explored; we see how business firms have established offices of consumer relations to deal more effectively with consumer complaints. The new idea of the company social audit is described by the *Business Week* "Special Report."

The next section deals with new departures in regulation (government reaction to consumerism). We have articles on class action suits, remedian advertising, unit pricing, and the Federal Trade Commission's (FTC) attempt to require advertisers to substantiate their claims with hard data filed with the Commission. The author and Mr. Gorse analyze the 1966 Packaging Act to discern if it aids at all in reducing the buyer's confusion and informing him better.

The other side of the question is covered in the next section. Is business abused by consumers? Does it try to protect the buyer by testing the products? Does business think that, after all, consumerism may not be all bad?

Much attention is now being paid to the social responsibilities being thrust on business. What action should the firm take to enhance public welfare? How far should it go? How much can business do? What are the future impacts on the corporation? Will the corporation be altered greatly? What new priorities must it accept?

Finally, we conclude by looking at two proposals bearing weighty future impact. These are examples of the sort of social planning being done by concerned parties in our land. Mr. Yohalem competently gives us a peek into the shape of things to come in 1990. Does he predict an Orwellian world or a paradise? This, the reader must ascertain for himself.

William T. Kelley
Philadelphia
May, 1973

ACKNOWLEDGEMENTS

Sincere thanks are rendered to the following editors and publishers for permission to use materials from their respective publications:

William M. Alrich, Editor, *Wharton Quarterly* — several articles from the Fall, 1972 edition.

John McCafferty, Editor, DuPont *Context* — five articles from Vol. 2, No. 1 (1973) edition.

Robert W. Miller, Executive Director of the White House Conference Staff on the Industrial World Ahead — nine papers presented February 7-9, 1972, in Washington, which afford us a deeper understanding of the social responsibility of business in the years ahead.

Time — the excellent *Time* profile of Ralph Nader.

Royal Bank of Canada — short, incisive study of the Ombudsman system.

Business Week — article on the "Social Audit".

New York Times — Consumers Spur Industry Response; Capitalism Lives in Naderland".

Wall Street Journal — "More Consumers Press Lawsuits".

Advertising Age — "Thirty Three Ways Marketers are Coping".

Heartfelt appreciation is expressed to the following authors without whose valuable contributions this book could not be:*

Eugene R. Beem, Ph.D. in Economics, University of Pennsylvania, Vice President, Corporate Planning and Economics, Sperry and Hutchinson, New York.

Philip Kotler, A Montgomery Ward Professor of Marketing, Northwestern University, author of a best seller book, *Marketing Management*, analysis, planning and control.

Graham Bannock, British business economist, consultant, and author.

E. B. Weiss, feature writer for *Advertising Age*.

Leonard Sloane, writer for the *New York Times*.

Richard A. Shaffer, writer for the *Wall Street Journal*.

Charles S. Goodman, writer for the *Wall Street Journal*.

Charles S. Goodman, Professor of Marketing, Wharton School.

Robert W. Nason, Assistant Professor of Marketing, Wharton School.

J. Scott Armstrong, Associate Professor of Marketing, Wharton School.

Thomas S. Robertson, Associate Professor of Marketing, Wharton School.

Thomas F. Schutte, Associate Professor of Marketing and Assistant Dean, Wharton School.

Elisha Grey III, Chairman, Better Business Bureau Councils, Inc.

Bess Myerson, Director of Consumer Affairs, City of New York.

Virginia Knauer, Special Assistant to the President for Consumer Affairs, Washington.

Rose de Wolf, columnist for the *Philadelphia Bulletin*.

A. Clinton Collins, writer for the DuPont *Context*.

Robert Choate, consumer advocate and Sloan Fellow at the Wharton School.

John Hobson, British advertising agency director.

Peter F. Drucker, Professor of Management, New York University.

G. Cameron, reporter for the Newark (N.J.) *Evening Times*.

Last but not least, it is with great pride that we thank the following students and graduate assistants from the Wharton School for their respective research monographs:

Harold J. Ashby, Jr.
Dennis Bechara
Susan A. Garland
Robert A. Goodman
Etienne Gorse
Keith Hansen
Robert Silverstein
Albert Zanger

* Only the most recent connection or affiliation is given.

TABLE OF CONTENTS

PART I

HISTORICAL ORIGINS OF CONSUMERISM

EARLY ECONOMISTS VIEW OF SOCIAL WELFARE

WILLIAM T. KELLEY AND DENNIS BECHARA

When we examine the works of the early economists, we are awed by the near absence of concern about the consumers position within the marketplace.

Adam Smith *seemed* to assign a very central position to the consumer, as seen from this oft-quoted excerpt from the *Wealth of Nations:*

"Consumption is the sole end and purpose of all production: and the interest of the producer ought to be attended to only so far as it may be necessary for promoting that of the consumer. The maxim is so perfectly self-evident, that it would be absurd to attempt to prove it."[1] But then, Smith, following his own advice, says no more about consumption, and hurries on to discuss other matters.

Throughout the period from 1776 until the early 20th Century, principles of buyer behavior on the demand side of the market were not analyzed, beyond the development of a simplistic assumption of complete rationality within the market on the part of all buyers. Later, the value of a good on the demand side was thought to depend upon an estimation of the "utility" or usefulness of a good to the prospective buyer. Writers spoke of a kind of calculus in which the relative utilities of the various products offered and available within a given market at a given time were weighed by the buyer. A rank ordering, or scale of preferences, was formulated. Scare purchasing power was rationed out according to the priorities thus established.

But the very early economists, such as Smith, Mill and Ricardo, did not really tackle the problem of consumer behavior. They made certain assumptions about the nature of consumer behavior, completely untested by evidence, somewhat along the following lines: (1) Buyer and seller stand at arm's length, each attempting to get the best deal he can; (2) the buyer is as knowledgeable about the goods in question as is the seller, (3) the buyer could, using his own senses, judge very well the quality, quantity, and value in pounds or dollars of the goods; (4) the buyer expects the seller to flatter the goods, to put them in their best light, even to misrepresent the products somewhat. Any reasonable person would discount heavily the seller's "puffing" of the goods and would use his own judgment. If he is deceived, it is his own fault for being a careless buyer, and his associates would have little sympathy for his plight. If he allows his emotions to rule him rather than his reason, or is credulous about buyer's claims, that is just too bad.

So, for a proper economic system *vis-a-vis* the consumer, all one has to do is allow maximum freedom for economic forces and interests to work themselves out, and all will be well. Adam Smith's famous theory of the "invisible hand" comes to mind at this point:

> As every individual, therefore, endeavours as much as he can both to employ his capital in the support of domestic industry, and so to direct that industry that its produce may be of the greatest value; every individual necessarily labours to render the annual revenue of the society as great as he can. He generally, indeed, neither intends to promote the public interest, nor knows how much he is promoting it. By preferring the support of domestic to that of foreign industry in such a manner as its produce may be of the greatest value, he intends only his own gain, and he is in this, as in many other cases, led by an invisible hand to promote an end which was no part of his intention. Nor is it always the worse for the society that it was no part of it. By pursuing his own interest he frequently promotes that of the society more effectually than when he really intends to promote it. I have never known much good done by those who affected to trade for the public good. It is an affectation, indeed not very common among merchants, and very few words need be employed in dissuading them from it.[2]

Note in the above quotation, the proviso: "By pursuing his own interest he *frequently* promotes the interest of society. . . " This caveat, we think, indicates that Adam Smith had some reservations on the matter: Sometimes, he implies, social welfare will *not* be promoted. But, alas, he does not further explore this intriguing byway, nor does he elsewhere in the book. However, Smith definitely has further observations to make about other aspects of the social welfare.

It must be remembered that Adam Smith wrote *The Wealth of Nations* at a time when manufacturers had a tremendous control over the economic policies of Parliament. Viewing the tremendous influence that these people exerted over the government, he argued these privileges were wrongful to society at large, hoping these laws would be eliminated. One of these acts was the Settlement Act. This, according to Smith, provided that ". . . every parish should be bound to provide for its own poor; and that overseers of the poor should be annually appointed, who, with the church wardens, should raise by a parish rate competent sums for this purpose".[3] The ill effect of this act was that villages prevented poor people from moving in, because these villages did not want to support more poor people. A necessary condition for the allowing of people to enter and live in other villages besides their own was that they have a residence of at least 40 days in that village. The overseers could expel these new inhabitants any time within the 40 days period "unless he either rented a tenement of ten pounds a year, or could give such security for the discharge of the parish where he was then living, as those justices should judge sufficient".[4] Thus, the mobility of labor was prevented, allowing the workers to only remain in their own villages without any opportunity to better themselves. Adam Smith wanted to eliminate this act because, by doing so, the workers would have benefited. Yet the law, when it was finally repealed, was done so as to benefit the employers and not the workers. The result was that "the law was flouted because it proved profitable to the property owners".[5]

Another of these acts was the Apprenticeship Act, which provided that nobody "should for the future exercise any trade, craft or mystery at that time exercised in England, unless he had previously served to it an apprenticeship of seven years at least".[6] The masters of the guilds would then obtain the free service of the apprentice for a period of seven years, and all they had to do was to feed the apprentices. Smith opposed this act because it made the prices of the goods produced by these people higher by preventing free competition between craftsmen. When this act was finally eliminated, it was done because it was more profitable for the craftsmen to let the apprentices go because machines had made labor cost very little. "The obvious is frequently overlooked; 1776 was not 1815. It was one thing to advocate the abolition of apprenticeship regulations at a period when they insured monopolistic privileges to a small group; it was an entirely different matter to suggest their abrogation when they formed one of the few remaining safeguards against the complete pauperization of a large portion of the labor population".[7]

Many of these laws were finally eliminated under the pretense that Adam Smith's ideas coincided with the elimination of controls which would prove to be obstacles to the workings of a free economy. Adam Smith was portrayed to be the master defensor of laissez-faire, and it was under these arguments that the laws were finally eliminated.

Yet, one cannot but wonder that perhaps Adam Smith's ideas were taken too far in order to achieve ends of which he would have disapproved had he been alive. Certainly his intention was to help mankind, not to hinder it. Perhaps an explanation for his doubt of the good in governmental interferences may be due to the condition of the governments of the era in which he lived.

The governments in Smith's era were not controlled by high conscientious motivation; corruption reigned. Powerful minorities were able to exert so much influence on the policies of the governments that it came as no surprise to see that Smith was very skeptical governments could ever accomplish anything that would prove beneficial for society at large. Yet, Smith was not totally blind to the possible outcomes the future could bring. Indeed his flexibility even showed to include governments, for Smith felt (as Viner said): "Government, by improving its standard of competence, honesty, and public spirit, showed itself entitled to wider possibilities".[8]

Before this took place, however, Smith was willing to allow the governments to assume a triple role in society. First of all, governments should have provided for the defense of a nation by having a specialized armed forces that could perform this task in the most efficient way. The second function governments ought to have performed was to maintain what is now commonly called "law and order". A major assumption here was that the laws that were to be implemented should have been laws that were beneficial to society at large, not laws that benefited only a minority of the population. The third and final function that Smith saw for governmental interference was in the field of public works. The construction of such things as highways, parks, sewer systems — in short, aspects that would prove to be unprofitable for an individual or for a group of people to undertake. Education, as Professor Freeman has pointed out, is another public enterprise that Smith felt governments must pursue.

Indeed, Adam Smith was a strong proposer for education that should be spread to all members of society, because he felt all of us had the potential to be educated. "The difference between the most dissimilar characters, between a philosopher and a common street porter, for example, seems to arise not so much from nature as from habit, custom, and education".[9] An educated public would have the advantage of being able to judge what policies were best for the nation, and at the same time, there would be no room for demagoguery, because it would be much harder — if not impossible — for irresponsible leaders to deceive the general public.

Indeed, Smith attributed the corruption in government to the fact education was not available to all members of society. "An instructed and intelligent people ... feel themselves, each individually, more respectable, and more likely to obtain the respect of their lawful superiors and they are therefore more disposed to respect those superiors. They are more disposed to examine, and more capable of seeing through the interested complaints of faction".[10]

Education played such an important role in Smith's assumption that to disregard it would be to alter his theories. He even criticized universities, especially Oxford, because "in the University of Oxford, the greater part of public professors have, for these many years, given up altogether even the practice of teaching."[11] Once the public has been educated, and once the government has proven itself willing to be more responsive to the needs of society at large, then, Smith felt, governmental functions could be expanded to include such things as the control of monopolies and the protection of the consumer. In order to permit self interest "to operate more effectively",[12] Smith felt that regulations should be made to make sure buyers obtained what they were told they were getting. As Freeman points out, Smith felt there were two areas where governmental interference may be required "wherever it appeared as though monopoly would develop in spite of competition and thus lead to a misallocation of capital and wherever the consumer needed protection if his self-interest was to work effectively in maximizing satisfactions."[13] This interference on the part of the government would be beneficial to society, according to Smith, for if the laws were made to satisfy the needs of the entire society — and not of a powerful minority — competition would be increased.

Adam Smith's concern for the issues that affect society did not end here, however. He felt wages should be relatively high so that the workers would be able to ameliorate their social position and provide their children with opportunities for advancement. Besides providing for better social conditions, "the liberal reward of labor . . . increases the industry of the common people. The wages of labor are the encouragement of industry, which, like every other human quality, improves in proportion to the encouragement it receives".[14]

Adam Smith also felt that although the division of labor proved to be very effective in increasing productivity, other social aspects were involved as well. "The man whose life is spent performing a few simple operations . . . has no occasion to exert his understanding, or to exercise his inventory in finding out expedients for removing the difficulties which never occur. He naturally loses, therefore, the habit of such exertion, and generally becomes as stupid and ignorant as it is possible for a human creature to become".[15] As a solution to this problem, Smith envisaged yet another possible function for government: to provide for cultural activities that would counterbalance the effects of the division of labor.[16]

Adam Smith, as we have seen in this short exposition of the economic ideas that he expounded, was not fanatical about free trade. He believed that in order for the economy to function most effectively, the least amount of controls should be exerted; but this, however, did not mean that no controls should be exerted. Economic welfare did not necessarily coincide with social welfare because, as Skinner has pointed out, Smith believed that "economic advance might erode those faculties and propensities by virtue of which we are capable of attaining some degree of moral existence; qualities such as reason, imagination, sympathy, and fellow feeling". [17]

The great John Stuart Mill seemed to have had less to say about social welfare than did Adam Smith. He and Ricardo concerned themselves almost exclusively with working out the principles governing the supply or seller side of the market-price determination, costs of production, division of wages, rents, interest and profits. These complicated questions certainly gave them enough to occupy their minds. They, as did Smith, assumed the consumer could protect himself rather well, given a free market, a minimum of government interference, and a heavy rivalry amongst the sellers for his custom. Inexorably, the theory went, sellers who did not offer fair value for the money would be found out by the buyers, as would those who cheated the consumers. They would be driven from the market once buyers perceived their deficiency, so that the vigorous, honest businessmen would survive. Thus, the market was in a sense self-cleansing.

Although they would minimize the role of the government, these early economists did recognize situations in which state intervention would be desirable. Mill sanctioned governmental intervention in the following cases. [18]

1. **Education.** Mill recognized that private enterprise could not afford adequate education for the masses who could not pay for it. Therefore, Mill advocated that the state provide schools for the people, at least at the elementary level.

2. **To protect and aid** those who could not help themselves — chidren, women left with infants, the insane.

3. **Public works,** such as canals, roads, harbors, waterways, and the like, which might result in a monopoly, and which are beyond the powers of private concerns to organize, finance, and administer fairly.

4. **Regulations** affecting broad classes of people who cannot organize themselves for beneficial regulation, e.g. maximum hours to allow women and children to work per day. But Mill did not recommend group action to achieve better conditions (such as unions).

5. **Colonization, voyages of geographic and scientific exploration.** Mill would have the state subsidize scientific investigation which would benefit society, yet not supply a profitable return for private endeavor. He recognized that great enterprises, such as establishing new colonies, needed vast resources and direction far beyond the abilities of private enterprise.

6. **Finally, the enforcing of contracts,** keeping the peace, and prohibiting and punishing conduct injurious to others. [18]

Note that Mill *carefully excludes* consumer protection from the admissible functions of government. He does recognize that consumers do not have perfect judgment, as is shown by the following quotation. But, he says that better consumer education is the key to the situation, rather than measures to keep the consumer from being misled, making poor purchases, and thereby misallocating resources of society.

Now, the proposition that the consumer is a competent judge of the commodity, can be admitted only with numerous abatements and exceptions. He is generally the best judge (though even this is not true universally) of the material objects produced for his use. These are destined to supply some physical want, or gratify some taste or inclination, respecting which wants or inclinations there is no appeal from the person who feels them; or they are the means and appliances of some occupation, for the use of the persons engaged in it, who may be presumed to be judges of the things required in their own habitual employment. But there are other things of the worth of which the demand of the market is by no means a test;

things of which the utility does not consist in ministering
to inclinations, nor in serving the daily uses of life, and
the want of which is least felt where the need is greatest.
This is particularly true of those things which are chiefly
useful as tending to raise the character of human beings.
The uncultivated cannot be competent judges of
cultivation. Those who most need to be made wiser and
better, usually desire it least, and if they desired it, would
be incapable of finding the way to it by their own lights.
It will continually happen, on the voluntary system, that,
the end not being desired, the means will not be provided
at all, or that, the persons requiring improvement having
an imperfect or altogether erroneous conception of what
they want, the supply called forth by the demand of the
market will be anything but what is really required. Now
any well-intentioned and tolerably civilized government
may think without presumption that it does or ought to
possess a degree of cultivation above the average of the
community which it rules, and that it should therefore be
capable of offering better education and better
instruction to the people, than the greater number of
them would spontaneously demand. Education,
therefore, is one of those things which it is admissible in
principle that a government should provide for the
people. The case is one to which the reasons of the
non-interference principle do not necessarily or
universally extend. [19]

Thus, by education, Mill would protect the consumer, making him
more knowledgeable, and raising his cultural level and tastes, so that a
higher order of goods would be evoked in the market, but, note well,
through the free market mechanism. John Stuart Mill probably
would have deplored the British Broadcasting Corporation!

So this is the pattern of classical economic thought right up to the
early 20th Century, when the "muckrakers" exposed the widespread
abuses of the machine age in America. One looks in vain for
evidences of real consumerism in the writings of the physiocrats,
Utopian Socialists and communists.[20] Even those outside the
mainstream of conventional economic theory lent little light to the
subject. Karl Marx, like the classical economists, devoted his
attention to analyzing the ills of capitalism from a production and
distribution of production proceeds point of view. Henry George got
hung up on his single tax scheme. Simon N. Patten was indeed the
first economist to recognize the implications of mass production, and
to analyze the radical changes that would attend the coming of the
affluent society. But even these perceptive men had little inkling of
the gravity of the problems that the new society would create for the
consumers. Curiously enough, it was two literary figures, Ida Tarbell
and Upton Sinclair, rather than trained social scientists, who jolted
the American public into an awareness of the great costs and

penalties incurred by the comfort economy. It was a government man, Dr. Harvey Wiley, who agitated for a whole generation before the first, feeble legislation was passed by the Congress to protect the consumer, the first Federal Pure Food and Drug Act of 1906.

We shall now turn to a consideration of the genesis of the first round of consumerism in America during the early part of our century.

QUESTIONS FOR REVIEW

1. What did Adam Smith, the father of economics, believe about the position of the consumer?

2. Why did Adam Smith pay so little attention to analyzing the demand side of the price equation? To looking into the dynamics and psychology of consumer demand?

3. What simple model of consumer behavior did these classical economists develop? To what degree was that model true in the 18th Century? Is it more or less applicable today?

4. Given the state of knowledge of human psychology in the late 18th and early 19th Centuries, *could* these writers have developed a better theory of buying behavior?

5. Why did Karl Marx and early communist writers pay little attention to the position and functions of the consumer in their system?

6. What is meant by *laissez faire?* According to Smith and Mill, was there ever justification for government intervention in the "free" market?

7. Why do you think the early welfare economists such as George and Petten paid so little attention to the consumer's position within the market?

FOOTNOTES

1. Adam Smith, *The Wealth of Nations* (New York: The Modern Library, 1937), p. 625.

2. *Ibid.* p. 423.

3. *Ibid.* p. 240.

4. *Ibid.* p. 241.

5. Eli Ginsburg, *The House of Adam Smith* (New York: Octagon Press, 1964), p. 17.

6. *Ibid*, p. 224.

7. *Ibid.* p. 181.

8. R. D. Freeman, *History of Political Economy*, p. 173.

9. Smith, *op. cit.*, p. 120.

10. *Ibid*, p. 178.

11. *Ibid.* p. 179.

12. *Ibid.* p. 181.

13. *Ibid.* p. 182.

14. *Ibid.* p. 184.

15. Freeman, *op. cit.* p. 175.

16. Smith, *op. cit.* Introduction, p. 80.

17. *Ibid.* p. 79.

18. John Stuart Mill, *Principles of Political Economy* (New York: D. Appleton and Company, 1892, Vol II), pp. 574-603.

19. *Ibid.* pp. 573-4.

20. If you assume that an all-wise planning commission would decide what was best for the people under communism, and would produce precisely the best goods for the least costs, social and material, then there obviously would be no problems of consumer protection. Nor could the consumer mislead production by purchasing poor or worthless goods. There would not be any!

THE BEGINNINGS OF THE CONSUMER MOVEMENT

EUGENE R. BEEM

The Consumer Movement Defined

The expression, the *Consumer Movement*, may be used provisionally in either of two ways. In its more inclusive sense, the term refers historically to the efforts of individuals and groups, acting more or less in concert, to solve consumer problems. In this sense, the Consumer Movement refers to activities from the earliest time to the present, and includes the organized activities of consumers themselves, and of other groups and individuals such as teachers, writers, private business, and government agencies that have worked in the consumer interest. In a second sense, the Consumer Movement refers more particularly to the great burst of activities in behalf of consumers that began in the 1930's and has continued at an accelerated pace.

The present chapter reviews the earlier attempts to help solve consumer problems. Chapter 3 describes the Consumer Movement beginning with the 1930's when the pianissimo of consumer discontent swelled into an anvil chorus.

Consumers' Cooperatives

Consumers' cooperatives were an early effort by consumers to solve their buying problems without outside help. "Consumer cooperation is merely an attempt to substitute joint efforts of consumers in supplying their needs for those of private enterprise."[1] Consumers must inevitably perform, in part, certain of the marketing functions, such as storage of goods, some types of risk bearing (spoilage, for example), and, as a rule, transportation of goods from store to household. Consumer cooperation is but an extension beyond the normal sphere of consumer activity.[2] Because of its substitution of mutual benefit for profit gain, a consumer cooperative has no incentive to charge exorbitant prices, to misrepresent goods, or to hold back information concerning quality.

Credit for establishing the principles of modern consumer cooperation is usually given to the Equitable Pioneers Cooperative Society, which was formed in 1844 by 28 poor weavers in Rochdale, England. The Rochdale pioneers laid down basic rules to assure democratic control as well as sound financial and market practices. In addition to the provision that the "co-op" be collectively owned by its members, there were the following requirements:

1. Open membership.
2. One vote per member regardless of the amount the member invests in the co-op enterprise.
3. A limited return on the capital invested by members.
4. Sales at market prices to avoid price wars with private business.
5. Patronage refunds paid out of net income at the end of the year in proportion to each member's volume of purchases.
6. Sales for cash only.
7. The establishment of reserve funds to be used for expansion and for promotion of cooperative education.

An early effort to apply the Rochdale principles in the United States started in a buying club set up by a Philadelphia labor union in 1862. The co-op failed after four years, but it aroused an interest in the Rochdale methods in the United States. Depression after the Civil War in the Agricultural West led the National Grange and later the Farmers' Alliance to try their hand at cooperative organization — for the purpose of marketing as well as purchasing. After the panic of 1873, two labor groups, the Sovereigns of Industry and the Knights of Labor, encouraged their members to establish cooperatives. Most of the union-sponsored co-ops passed out of existence before 1900, but many of the farm co-ops with their dual role of marketing and purchasing were solidly implanted. Failing co-ops were often the victims of inexperienced management and inadequate capital.

Co-ops sprang up again during the period of rising prices accompanying and following World War I. In 1916, the Cooperative League appeared as a clearing house of information on how to run co-ops, and as a promotional agency. Co-ops in the credit field, called credit unions, became popular in this era. The merchant philanthropist, Edward A. Filene, played an important role in their development. A few co-op petroleum associations also sprouted, mainly in the Middle West. The latter continued to expand during the 1920's, but the co-op movement as a whole made only moderate progress. By 1929, there were 1,476 retail distributive associations including stores, petroleum associations, and a few miscellaneous organizations, such as creameries and bakeries doing a business of approximately $63,000,000 a year, and 85 service associations in such fields as laundries, restaurants, housing, burial, and room and board associations doing a business of about $1,500,000. There were also nine wholesale associations servicing co-op stores which did a business of about $11,000,000, and 974 credit unions doing a business of about $54,000,000.[3] There was little in these statistics over which private business had cause for concern.

Other Self-Help

In addition to the consumer cooperatives several other organizations appeared, in the century preceding the 1930's, whose interests were devoted primarily to the problem of improving the technique of consumption. The most significant was the American Home Economics Association, founded in 1908 under the leadership of Mrs. Ellen H. Richards (1842-1911), instructor of sanitary chemistry at the Massachusetts Institute of Technology. The A.H.E.A. grew from a series of nine summer conferences held at Lake Placid beginning in 1899, to bring together those interested in promoting better consuming habits. The emphasis at first was on the wiser use of purchased goods. During World War I, the Association became interested in the standardization of consumer goods and in more informative labeling to simplify the complexity of buying. A textile committee was set up in 1919 to secure the cooperation of business in promoting this end. The committee also worked with the National Bureau of Standards to perfect performance tests for judging textiles. In 1927, the Association appointed a standing committee on the standardization of consumer goods, and in 1928, became a member of the American Standards Association, an organization of business and other groups seeking to promote standards for industrial goods. Since the beginning the A.H.E.A. has published the *Journal of Home Economics* to keep its members posted on developments in the field of consumption, and has appeared before congressional committees to testify on issues related to the consumer interest. The membership in the association has never been large, but it has been drawn primarily from the influential ranks of home economics teachers.

Pressure Groups for the Consumer Interest

Another consumer organization was the Chicago Housewives League, started in 1910 with the establishment of study groups to accomplish wiser buying techniques. A campaign to "read your labels" was the first step undertaken in self-help. A few similar organizations in other cities were set up. In a small way, these associations attempted to represent consumers before legislatures. One of the two witnesses appearing on behalf of consumers at the 1921 tariff hearings on the Fordney-McCumber Bill was a representative of a housewives' league. After World War I, some of the leagues organized buyers' strikes in protest against the mounting cost of living. Spontaneous consumer organizations sprang up throughout the country during this inflationary period. They are remembered for their parades, meat strikes, and rent strikes. There was talk of a nation-wide middle class union to represent consumers' interests, but all of this died with the price drops in 1920-1921 and the prosperity which followed.

Organizations with primary interests in labor conditions, social affairs, or civic matters occasionally turned their attention to consumer problems. The National Consumers' League, founded by Florence Kelley in 1899 to organize consumer boycotts against enterprisers who exploited their laborers, occasionally broadened its scope to include matters of more direct concern to consumers. For example, the League actively supported the drive for pure foods and drugs which culminated in the 1906 Act. The General Federation of Women's Clubs fought hard for the same cause. The Federation was holding its biennial convention at St. Louis in 1904 at the same time Dr. Harvey W. Wiley was displaying his spectacular exhibit of adulterated foods and injurious drugs at the St. Louis World's Fair. The club women were so impressed with Dr. Wiley's exhibit that they appointed a national committee to educate their members all over the country on the importance of food and drug legislation. They distributed leaflets, made speeches, and submitted petitions. When the bill was held up in committee, the clubs organized a telegram campaign, flooding Washington congressmen with demands for immediate action. The federation deserved no small measure of credit for the eventual passage of the act.

Pioneers in Consumer Education

Some individual authors and educators are important as antecedents of the Consumer Movement because of the stimulus which they exerted on the development of consumer education and consumption theory. Perhaps Benjamin Franklin keynoted the whole development of consumer education by popularizing his slogan, "a penny saved is a penny earned." The home economists, however, were the first to become actively interested in consumer problems. The founder of this movement was Benjamin Thompson (Count Rumford) who made some of the earliest researches into cooking, heating, and other matters of domestic concern near the close of the 18th century. The first course in household arts appears to be that offered by Mrs. Emma Willard in the Troy Female Seminary in 1821. The first texts in home economics were Catherine E. Beecher's *Treatise on Domestic Economy* (1841) and her *Domestic Receipt Book* (1842). Edward L. Youmans, a chemist, published *Household Science* in 1857, a scientific study of food, air, heat, and light from the standpoint of the consumer. Many public school and college teachers were offering courses in domestic science by the end of the 19th century. From their ranks came the home economists who, under the leadership of Mrs. Ellen H. Richards, established the American Home Economics Association in 1908.

With few exceptions, economists, beginning with Adam Smith, have paid lip service to consumption as the sole end of production, and then have proceeded to neglect the subject or treat it as an afterthought or as incidental to a fuller understanding of production. The first prominent American economist who made consumption a primary interest was Simon N. Patten, who published his *Consumption of Wealth* in 1888. He is remembered for his pioneer efforts to establish a theory of consumption, although this theory is best left to the obscurity in which it now reposes. Patten also proposed that consumer education be taught to school children — not as domestic science, but as a general program of economic education.

Herbert J. Davenport, in his *Outlines of Elementary Economics* (1898), and even more so in his teaching, used a consumer approach to economics subject matter. "The schools," he wrote, "should teach us how to use the wealth which we may later gain . . . Education must indeed be a preparation for life, but a preparation in the art of living it . . . "[4]

Considerable impetus toward broadening the scope of economics to include consumer education resulted from the writings of America's Thorstein Veblen, and England's John A. Hobson. Veblen's widely-read *Theory of the Leisure Class* (1899) ridiculed the futility and irrationality of consumer choices. His *Theory of Business Enterprise* (1904), *Engineers and the Price System* (1921), and *Absentee Ownership* (1923) made vituperative attacks upon the wastes of salesmanship and advertising. Hobson decried the overemphasis in economics texts on production, urging in *Work and Wealth* (1914) that economists give equal consideration to consumption.

Wesley C. Mitchell's paper on "The Backward Art of Spending Money", read at the 1912 meetings of the American Economics Association, aroused the interests of many economists in consumer problems.

Five important books appeared in the 1920's, which tried to integrate consumption into the economics curriculum. Benjamin Andrews' *Family Economics* (1923), Hazel Kyrk's *Theory of Consumption* (1923), Elizabeth Hoyt's *The Consumption of Wealth* (1928), Warren C. Waite's *Economics of Consumption* (1928) and Paul Nystrom's *Economic Principles of Consumption* (1929) became textbooks or collateral reading for college courses in the economics of consumption. Dr. Nystrom's text was intended primarily as a guide for producers, rather than education or counsel for consumers.

Specialists in education were pioneers in the effort to integrate consumer education with the regular curricula of the public schools. An early leader in this effort to base the teaching of subjects such as mathematics, business, and general science upon real life problems was Frederick G. Bonser. This movement, which began about 1910, received a great stimulus from Henry Harap's *Education of the Consumer* (1924). Dr. Harap offered quantitative evidence of present habits of purchasing such products as food, housing, fuel, and clothing, and contrasted these habits with what he considered efficient practice. Conclusions from these comparisons were presented as objectives of consumer education. A wealth of suggestions was made for integrating this study material with the regular curriculum.

The Muckrakers

Some of the muckrakers of the Progressive Era called dramatic attention to the problems of the consumer through their vicious exposes of monopoly, graft and corruption. The popular magazines, *Ladies Home Journal* and *Colliers Weekly*, were especially vehement in their condemnation of patent medicine frauds. Upton Sinclair, in his best-seller, *The Jungle* (1905), ruined the appetites of many a meat eater with his revealing decription of the filth and fraud in the meat packing industry.[5]

Dr. Harvey W. Wiley

The leader in a 26-year crusade for a Federal Pure Food and Drugs Law was Dr. Harvey W. Wiley, chief of the Bureau of Chemistry in the Department of Agriculture. Through his speeches, writings, exhibits of injurious and adulterated foods and drugs, and his famous "poison squad," he helped to arouse the public indignation which eventually forced Congress to take action. Prior to the 1906 Act almost 200 pure food and drug bills had been introduced into either the House or the Senate, but each one had been killed by the organized opposition of the affected business interests. Dr. Wiley continued as chief of the Bureau of Chemistry until 1912. By then the continued pressure from vested interests upon the chief executive and the Department of Agriculture had resulted in so restricting Dr. Wiley's authority that effective administration of the Pure Food and Drug Law was impossible. He resigned from his government office in disgust and began another vigorous crusade, preaching, with publications and from the rostrum, the ineffectiveness of current food and drug protection. His protesting voice was an impetus toward the expanding Consumer Movement.[6]

Help from Private Business

Alarmed by the widespread criticism of advertising during the Progressive Era, the Associated Advertising Clubs of the World organized a National Vigilance Committee in 1911 to protest abuses in their trade. They adopted "truth in advertising" as a slogan and tried through moral suasion to raise the standards of advertisers. *Printers Ink* contributed a model statute to outlaw misleading and fraudulent advertising, and with the aid of local Vigilance Committees throughout the country, campaigned successfully for its passage in many states. The Vigilance Committees soon changed their name to Better Business Bureaus and expanded their purpose to include the purging of dishonest business practices of all types.

The Hughes life insurance investigation in 1906 led to "house-cleaning" in that industry. Under the inspiring leadership of Dr. Solomon S. Huebner, a program of insurance education was inaugurated in colleges and universities, and a "Chartered Life Underwriter" designation was established for salesmen in 1927. The "C.L.U." program, administered by the American College of Life Underwriters, and still in effect, involves the establishment of educational standards for insurance agents in such fields as insurance principles, economics, finance, American government, social problems, investments, trusts and taxes, and business law. The purpose is to raise the competence of agents in the counselling of consumers as to their life insurance needs. Rigorous examinations are drawn up in the fields noted, and the agent who passes the examinations and has served three years in the industry is awarded the "C.L.U." degree.

Another business group which contributed significantly to the consumer interest in this period was the American Medical Association. Its publications exposed the worthless nostrums and quackery of the Patent Medicine venders.[7]

Caveat Emptor

One of the earliest efforts by organized government to protect consumers against fraud was the adoption of a uniform system of weights and measures and its enforcement by state and municipal governments. The so-called English system of weights and measures, which dates from a law passed in England in 1266, was adopted by the English colonists who migrated to America. With few exceptions, to be noted presently, little else was done by governmental units specifically to aid or protect consumers until the 1930's. The prevalent doctrine, derived from the intensely individualistic Roman law, was *caveat emptor* (let the buyer beware).[8] The problem of developing the vast potential wealth of the American continent was considered paramount. Producers were aided with grants, subsidies, tariff protection, and the dissemination of information on markets and scientific production, while consumers were left to shift for themselves. The philosophy was that of the Scotchman who bought only one spur for his horse, figuring if one half would go, the other half would go too. If only production could be steadily increased, the gains would trickle down to all of the consumers. Recognition that the "invisible hand" which had protected consumers in Adam Smith's day was no longer adequate dawned slowly among legislators. The oil, which made Smith's economic system function smoothly, was the presence of competition and enlightened consumers. The weakening of these checks against business abuse in the late 19th and 20th centuries threw the consumer open to flagrant exploitation.

The first notable exception at the federal level to this policy of *caveat emptor* was the Pure Food and Drug Act of 1906, which made it unlawful to manufacture in any territory or the District of Columbia, or to transmit between states adulterated or misbranded foods or drugs. The bill excluded advertising and cosmetics, however, and required only that drugs and their derivatives be identified on the label in a non-misleading manner. As previously noted, the pprotection which this law provided was weakened by curbing the authority of Dr. Wiley through executive edict. A few of the states had food and drug legislation before the turn of the century, and many more followed the federal lead after 1906.

As noted earlier, a number of states passed "truth in advertising" laws following 1911. There are, however, relatively few instances in which these state laws have been used to curb advertising abuses, noble though their intent may have been. What improvements there were up to 1929 resulted primarily from the pressure of honest business interests.

Consumers were protected to some extent by federal meat inspection (when interstate commerce was involved) after legislation was passed shortly before 1900. The real motive, it has been alleged, was not to protect consumers but to meet a prerequisite for getting American meat into foreign ports.[9] By 1929, some of the states and municipalities were also providing for meat inspection, and some of the municipalities were inspecting milk and grading it according to butter fat content.

In addition to the limited protection provided through sumptuary laws, a trickle of information was available to consumers through the research activities of various echelons of government. As far back as 1847, the Patent Office in its annual report added some data on proper nutrition. In later reports farm houses and the consumption of milk were discussed. When the Department of Agriculture was established in the federal government in 1862, a Bureau of Home Economics was included to take over the work in the household arts which the Patent Office had begun. In 1894, an Office of Human Nutrition Investigations was added to the Agriculture Department and $10,000 was appropriated for this work. The Smith-Lever Act in 1914 provided for a rural extension service, through the Agriculture Department, which brought training in home management to a limited number of housewives in rural areas.

Some of the states had agriculture departments which furnished comparable services to consumers who took the trouble to use them. In the early 1870's, the land grant colleges in Iowa, Kansas, and Illinois were giving instruction in the household arts. Some of the public colleges and universities followed this lead in later years. The state which furnished the most aid to consumers appears to be North Dakota. Its laboratories were testing consumer goods and publicizing the information on comparative qualities *according to brand names* by the 1920's.

No illusion is held that the foregoing discussion of the government aid to consumers prior to the 1930's is a complete one. No mention has been made, for example, of laws such as the Sherman Act and the Federal Trade Act or the laws to regulate the rates and service of railroads and public utilities, or the Public Health Services in the field of promoting sanitation (except insofar as the latter relate to food inspection). To some extent, these provisions protected consumers in their buying, but the intent was to serve a much broader purpose. This survey has been directed at the question, "What did government agencies in the United States do specifically to further the consumer interest in the years preceding the 1930's?" The paucity of aid was even greater than what is indicated in the foregoing discussion, for very often consumer activities were financed by the meagerest scrapings from the budget barrel, or were administered through groups controlled by producer interests.

The "Guinea Pig" Books

Many consumers who were unaware of their plight, or who passively accepted the labyrinth into which they had been drawn by the complex factors discussed in Chapter IV were jarred out of their complacency by a book which appeared in 1927 entitled *Your Money's Worth*. Written by Stuard Chase and Frederick J. Schlink, this publication was termed by Robert S. Lynd "the *Uncle Tom's Cabin* of the consumer movement." *Business Week* summed up the impact of *Your Money's Worth:*

> Simon Legree and Eliza — crossing-the-ice in Harriet Beecher Stowe's classic may have roused grandma's crusading zeal back in 1852, but grandma's desire to do something about it pales into insignificance alongside mother's when Mr. Chase (who had been on the staff of the Federal Trade Commission) and Mr. Schlink (who had been with the National Bureau of Standards) first told her that the soap which made her so popular at the dance was made with "a little creosol, a common and cheap disinfectant recommended by the government for disinfecting cars, barns and chicken yards;" that the Journal of the American Medical Association had said that $495 worth of Listerine had the antiseptic action of a cent's worth of corrosive sublimate and that its effect was mainly to "cover one smell with another;" . . . that the best and safest mouthwash was a little warm water with salt.[10]

The theme of the book is that the consumer is like Alice in a Wonderland. The market place is a veritable "wilderness in which we consumers wander without chart or compass".[11]

> We buy not for the value of the product to meet our specific needs but because the story told on every billboard, every newspaper and magazine page, every shop window, every sky sign, every other letter we receive — is a pleasing, stimulating and romantic story . . . But whether or not it is a fairy story we do not know save through the bitter and wasteful process of trial and error.[12]

Your Money's Worth was offered as a "Book of the Month" selection and became a best seller with estimated sales of 100,000 copies.[13]

The success of *Your Money's Worth* led to a wave of books debunking advertising and portraying the plight of the consumer. Mr. Schlink collaborated with Arthur Kallet in 1933, to turn out *100,000,000 Guinea Pigs*, the most popular consumer book ever written with estimated sales of over 250,000 copies.[14] The readers are told that they and their fellow Americans are "guinea pigs" because they offer themselves for experimental testing by purchasing all sorts of pernicious and doubtful products. Citing a wealth of illustrations, the book bitterly indicts commercial interests, the inadequacy of the 1906 Food and Drug Law, and the deficiencies of the Agricultural Department officials who were currently administering the law. The authors conclude with a challenge to the consumers to—

> Give your congressmen and senators, and your state legislators no rest until they sit in judgment on the work of the National Food and Drug Administration and the local health and food control authorities.
> Above all let your voice be heard loudly and often, in protest against the indifference, ignorance, and avarice responsible for the uncontrolled adulteration and misrepresentation of foods, drugs, and cosmetics. [15]

The "guinea pig" metaphor caught the public imagination, and soon became the appelation for a whole group of debunking books.

The third largest seller among the "guinea pig" books was *Skin Deep* by Mary C. Phillips, the wife of Mr. Schlink.[16] Mary Phillips placed under the microscope soaps, lipsticks, rouges, cold creams, hair dyes, fat reducers, and other beauty aids, and concluded that many women were wasting their money and endangering their health with these preparations. She urged women everywhere to work for stringent laws governing the sale of cosmetics and fat-reducing nostrums.

Other debunking books, although not reaching the popularity of the big three, were nevertheless important in stimulating interest in consumer problems during the 1930's. Another book by Mr. Schlink, *Eat, Drink and Be Wary* (1934), exposed food adulteration and dietary deficiencies.[17] Our Master's Voice: Advertising, by James Rorty, (1934) was a confession of the abuses in this trade by a former advertising copy-writer. He maintained that advertising cost was—

> The tax which business levies on the consumer to support the machinery of its super-government — the daily and periodical press, the radio, the apparatus of advertising. . . By this super-government the economic, social, ethical, and cultural patterns of the population are shaped and controlled into serviceable conformity to the profit-motivated interests of business.[18]

Counterfeit, by Arthur Kallet (1935), pictured the consumer as duped by manufacturers, advertisers and retailers of many well-known brands of commercial products. He found a paucity of avenues over which consumers could escape.[19] *Partners in Plunder*, by Joseph B. Matthews and Ruth E. Shallcross (1935), paraded some 750 cases by the reader to illustrate the authors' contention that consumer exploitation was a by-product of the profit system as it was then operating.[20] Mr. Matthews' *Guinea Pigs No More* (1936) continued the expose of business mal-practices, but concluded with a constructive plan for organizing consumer resistance to such evils through passage of a bill (given in the book) creating a Federal Department of the Consumer. Through consumer education and organization Mr. Matthews contended that U.S. capitalism could be converted from business dictatorship to consumer dictatorship. [21]

A final "guinea pig" book, important in arousing consumers, was Ruth de Forest Lamb's *American Chamber of Horrors* (1936). Miss Lamb, a member of the staff of the Food and Drug Administration, wrote the book in a crusade for federal legislation controlling the sale and advertising of cosmetics and for more effective food and drug legislation. Miss Lamb ranked with the most effective of the debunkers, as the following passage shows:

> It is all too true that a pretty young woman was blinded by an eyelash dye. It is also true that scores of others suffering from paralysis and impared vision have been sent to hospitals for long expensive treatment as the result of using a rat poison to banish superfluous hair. A prominent business man really was killed by radium-charged drinking water that dissolved the bones of his skull instead of curing the ailment for which it was advertised. Three sisters, one after another, rubbed horse liniment on their cough-racked chests in the pathetic belief that it would cure them — and died of tuberculosis. At this very moment, men and women all over the country are literally burning their tissues to death in trying to reduce their weight with deadly dinitrophenol. [22]

These "guinea pig" books set afire the accumulation of consumer discontent which had been piling up in previous decades, and led directly to the establishment and rapid growth of consumer financed testing and rating agencies. They aroused, from apathy, numerous individual consumers, women's clubs, religious associations, civic groups, labor unions, and educational agencies which set their sights on an attempt to solve the serious problems of the consumer.

QUESTIONS FOR REVIEW

1. What is meant by the "consumer movement"?
2. Why were consumer cooperatives given as an early effort to help the consumer? Why did they fail to do so?
3. Would the extension of producer and consumer cooperatives be the answer to better consumer protection now? Why or why not?
4. Many early pioneers in consumerism pinned their hopes on better education for the consumer in buying? Do you think this was a good idea? Where did it fall down?
5. What is "muck raking"; Who were the "muckrakers"? Why did these early critics seem to originate from the literary area rather than from the professional social scientists of the time?

6. Evaluate the contribution of Dr. Harvey W. Wiley to the first round of consumerism in America.

7. What is meant by "caveat emptor"? What made this doctrine increasingly inappropriate during the 20th Century?

8. What were the "guinea pig books"? What influence did they have on the consumer movement of the 1930's?

FOOTNOTES

1. Harold H. Maynard and Theodore N. Beckman, *Principles of Marketing* (New York, Ronald Press Co., 1946) p. 211.

2. The difference between the consumer cooperative and the profit-seeking business is set forth clearly by Donald F. Blanknertz, "Consumer Actions and Consumer Nonprofit Cooperation," in *Theory in Marketing*, edited by Reavis Cox and Wroe Alderson (Chicago, Richard D. Irwin Co., 1950), pp. 163-177.

3. Bulletin # 531, *U.S. Bureau of Labor Statistics* (February, 1931), p. 6.

4. Herbert J. Davenport, *Outlines of Elementary Economics* (New York, MacMIllan Co., 1898) p. 280.

5. The following passage from *The Jungle* describes the ingredients which it is alleged the Chicago meatpackers customarily put into their sausage:

It was the custom ... whenever meat was so spoiled that it could not be used for anything else ... to chop it up into sausage ... There would come all the way back from Europe meat that had been rejected, and that was moldy and white — it would be dosed with borax and glycerine, and dumped into the hoppers, and made over again for home consumption. There would be meat that had tumbled out on the floor, in the dirt and sawdust, where the workers had tramped and spit uncounted billions of consumption germs. There would be meat stored in great piles in rooms; and the water from leaky roofs would drip over it, and thousands of rats would race about on it. It was too dark in these storage places to see well, but a man could run his hand over these piles of meat and sweep off handfuls of the dried dung of rats. These rats were nuisances, and the packers would put poisoned bread out for them; they would die, and then rats, bread, and meat would be shoveled into carts, and the man who did the shoveling would not trouble to lift out a rat even when he saw one — there were things that went into the sausage in comparison with which a poisoned rat was a tidbit. . . Upton Sinclair, *The Jungle* (New York, The Viking Press, 1946, reprinted from the original manuscript, copyrighted 1905) p. 134-135. When this book was first published, President Theodore Roosevelt sent two commissioners to Chicago to investigate stockyard conditions. The commissioners then turned in a report which sustained Sinclair's charges. They told the author later that the only point on which they could get no proof was his statement that men had fallen into the lard vats and gone out to the world as pure leaf lard. (p. 1x author's preface to 1946 edition).

6. See Harvey W. Wiley, *An Autobiography* (Indianapolis, Bobbs-Morill Co., 1930) and Harvey W. Wiley, *History of the Crime Against the Pure Food Law* (Washington, D.C., H. W. Wiley, 1929).

7. See Arthur J. Cramp, *Nostrums and Quackery* (Chicago, American Association, Bureau of Investigation, three volumes published 1911, 1921, 1936).

8. While the exploited consumer had the power under common law to sue the producer who utilized fraud and misrepresentation, this legal protection was an empty shell inasmuch as suits would, as a rule, be more costly and time consuming than consumers could afford, and in addition, might easily be lost by the inability of the consumer to prove intent to defraud or misrepresent.

9. Robert S. Lynd, "The Consumer Becomes a 'Problem,' " *Annals of the American Academy* (May, 1934), p. 2.

10. "The Consumer Movement," *Business Week* (April 22, 1939), p. 40.

11. Stuart Chase and Frederick J. Schlink, *Your Money's Worth* (New York, MacMillan Co., 1927), p. 254.

12. *Ibid.*

13. R. A. Robinson, *Advertising the Consumer Movement* (Crowell Publishing Co., 1937), p. 22.

14. R. A. Robinson, *op. cit.,* p. 22.

15. Arthur Kallet and Frederick J. Schlink, *100,000,000 Guinea Pigs* (New York, The Vanguard Press, 1933) pp. 302-303.

16. Mary C. Phillips, *Skin Deep* (New York, The Vanguard Press, 1934).

17. Frederick J. Schlink, *Eat, Drink and Be Wary* (New York, Covici-Friede Co., 1935).

18. James Rorty, *Our Master's Voice: Advertising* (New York, John Day Co., 1934), p. 30.

19. Arthur Kallet, *Counterfeit — Not your Money But What It Buys* (New York, Vanguard Press, 1935).

20. Joseph B. Matthews and Ruth E. Shallcross, *Partners in Plunder* (New York, Covici-Friede Press, 1935).

21. Joseph B. Matthews, *Guinea Pigs No More* (New York, Covici-Friede, Inc., 1936).

22. Ruth de Forest Lamb, *American Chamber of Horrors* (New York, Farrar and Rinehart, 1936) p. 4.

EUGENE BEEM

Consumer Revolt in the 1930's

The propaganda of the "guinea pig" books was the most important reason for the awakened interest in consumer problems in the 1930's, but there were other factors also playing a part. Perhaps the major reason so many consumers reacted strongly to the disclosures of the "guinea pig" books was the simultaneous onslaught of the Great Depression. A whole generation of Americans had grown up in an era of rapidly increasing national product and living standards. The typical individual likened himself to the heroes of the Horatio Alger novels who rose from "rags to riches." The prospect of rapid gains from his producer interest left little inclination to dwell upon the less dramatic gains which might be possible by furthering his consumer interest. The Great Depression shattered, for many, this notion that one's producer role alone would suffice to gain him a high standard of living. The shrinking money incomes of the 1930's made more people tractable to the notion that living standards could best be increased, or maintained by the wiser use of existing income, and by protective consumer legislation rather than through expanded earnings.

The depression also aroused resentment against business enterprise for its failure to keep the economy operating at a high productive level. Consumers, unable to understand the paradox of intense wants alongside idle plants and manpower, were ready to accept the indictments of the "guinea pig" authors. The widespread attitude of cynicism, which was a legacy of the post World War I years, likewise helped to put consumers in a receptive mood for this literature.

Other reasons, too, played a part in bringing the Consumer Movement to fruition in the 1930's. Increased leisure afforded housewives by the time-saving mechanical inventions of the 20th century, and by a reduction in the size of families, gave them more time to devote to problems of wiser consumption. The steady growth of literacy and the higher level of average sophistication, resulting from widening dissemination of college and secondary school education, facilitated the comprehension of consumer problems and cooperation toward their solution.

The possibility of more scientific consumption was a final factor which stimulated the Consumer Movement in the 1930's. Wesley C. Mitchell told his economics colleagues, at the 1912 American Economic Association Convention, "progress in the arts of consumption ... waits upon progress in science."[1] Considerable progress in the scientific testing of consumer goods had been made by 1929. General Motors had a proving ground for testing its own and its competitors' products. Sears-Roebuck and Macy's, among other retail stores, had laboratories for testing the merits of goods before selling them to customers. Good Housekeeping had a laboratory where the products of its advertisers were subjected to analysis as a check on the accuracy of advertising claims. The Educational Buyers' Association had an arrangement with the Engineering Department of the University of Chicago, whereby competing brands of supplies bought by E.B.A. members were tested and reported upon. The Hospital Bureau of Standards and Supplies was testing and reporting on competing brands of supplies for its member hospitals. The U.S. Testing Company and the Electrical Testing Laboratories were testing a wide range of products for manufacturers and large scale buyers on a *fee* basis. The American Medical Association was testing proprietary drugs and certain food products. Perhaps the most comprehensive testing agency was the National Bureau of Standards, whose secret reports to government purchasing agents on the merits of competing goods were said to be saving the American taxpayer $100,000,000 a year.[2]

Commenting upon the development of scientific product testing procedures, Chase and Schlink wrote:

> It is evident that the United States contains today a series of outposts which are doing sound work in the direction of substituting the scientific method for rule of thumb. The outstanding difficulties with the exhibit are lack of coordination, and a failure to pass on results to the consumer in a form he can use ... In the accumulated research of these outposts, sufficient technical information is now on file to deflate and destroy the great majority of selling games; the bulk of poetic advertising; the massed magic of salesmanship.[3]

The developments in the scientific testing of consumer goods opened a new vista to consumers — the possibility of a way out of the maze of conflicting quality claims by the testing and rating of competing product brands. They made feasible the establishment of the product rating agencies which have been described as the "dynamos of the Consumer Movement."[4]

The Consumer Movement was an inevitable development, made thus by the magnitude of the plight into which a highly developed and complex economy had plunged the consumer. The forces discussed above reacted interdependently to bring consumer problems to a vivid focus in the 1930's, and to awaken an urge by millions of consumers for immediate corrective action.

Participating Groups

The groups, which have been active in the Consumer Movement, may be classified into those whose interest in consumer problems was a sideline to a broader purpose, and into those whose primary purpose was the alleviation of the consumers' plight. Quantitatively, the former type of organization has been more important than the latter. This type included such groups as the women's clubs, labor unions, settlement houses, religious organizations, educational bodies, some government agencies and certain private business interests. Those groups with a primary concern for consumer problems included the product rating agencies, consumer cooperatives, The American Home Economics Association, consumer committees and councils, and national associations formed to coordinate and represent politically the consumer interest of individuals and all of the previously mentioned groups of both types.

The remainder of this chapter will describe briefly the activities of these various organizations with the exception of the product rating agencies which will be treated in later chapters.[5]

Organizations with Secondary Consumer Interests

(1) WOMEN'S CLUBS. Many of the women's clubs have played a major part in the Consumer Movement. Organizations with civic, political, and multifold purposes having an aggregate membership of over five million have had study programs in their individual chapters on consumer problems, and have supported legislation to protect and further the consumer interest. Their interest has been sporadic rather than persistent, but was particularly forceful in the decade, 1937-1946. Among the major organizations which emphasized consumer programs were the American Association of University Women, the National League of Woman Voters, the General Federation of Women's Clubs, and the Y.W.C.A. Thirteen national women's groups united in support of the Federal Food, Drug and Cosmetic Act enacted in 1938. Various clubs have urged the enactment of such measures as increased appropriations for federal agencies engaged in consumer protection, compulsory grade labeling of canned foods, a Federal Department of the Consumer, and the repeal of the Miller-Tydings Act.

(2) LABOR UNIONS. Labor unions have shown a steadily increasing concern for the consumer interest. Since the 1930's the International Ladies Garment Workers Union has included lectures and courses on consumer problems in its welfare program for members. During World War II years many unions established consumer information centers in their meeting halls to distribute government pamphlets and materials on price control, rationing, and efficient consumption. Some unions held informational meetings at which problems of conservation and wise buying were discussed. Representatives of both the C.I.O. and the A.F. of L. participated in a committee of The American Standards Association which aimed to promote minimum standards for consumer goods. The A.F. of L., the C.I.O., and several of the national unions composing these organizations urged their union members to join consumer

cooperatives, and helped their local unions to establish consumer cooperatives where no existing ones prevailed. Of the non-farm cooperatives reporting to the Bureau of Labor Statistics in 1947, 31 percent said that half or more of their members belonged to unions.[6]

Over 150 union newspapers now publish a syndicated column by Consumers Union entitled, *Your Dollar*. This release, which appears monthly, digests the four leading product ratings contained in the current issue of *Consumer Reports*.

(3) MISCELLANEOUS GROUPS. Miscellaneous groups have intermittently sponsored consumer programs. The Federal Council of Churches has distributed literature and aided churches in establishing consumer cooperatives, the National Congress of Parents and Teachers has encouraged consumer study programs in its local chapters and has supported legislation in the consumer interest. The National Federation of Settlements has organized mothers' clubs which have studied better buymanship techniques and have supported local and national legislation for consumer protection.

An insight into the nature of the study programs, sponsored by the several dozen organizations which have approached consumer problems as a sideline, was provided by an analysis of consumer meetings reported in the press. Among 4,141 meetings between 1940 and 1946, the most popular topics (excluding those which related primarily to the war effort) were: 1) commodity buying information, 2) consumer education, 3) the care and use of consumer goods, 4) the Consumer Movement in general, and 5) health and nutrition.[7]

(4) EDUCATIONAL INSTITUTIONS. Educational institutions have been one of the most significant elements contributing to the Consumer Movement. At the high school level a great upsurge of courses in consumer economics began in the middle 1930's. At the same time, a consumer approach began to win increasing favor in such courses as social studies, economics, sociology, arithmetic, and natural science. A poll of high schools enrolling 300 or more pupils by Dr. Thomas Briggs for the National Association of Secondary School Principals in 1946, showed that 26 percent of the schools responding were offering separate courses in consumer education, exclusive of home economics.[8] Consumer education was being taught as a part of one or more other courses by 87 percent of the schools replying.[9] In 1942, the National Education Study" which led to the publication of 11 text pamphlets, averaging about 100 pages each, on such topics as "Learning to Use Advertising," "Money Management," "Consumer Credit," "Buying Insurance," and "Effective Shopping." The units were suitable for use in either a separate consumer course, or in a consumer approach to other subjects of the secondary school curriculum. About 500,000 copies of these pamphlets were in use during 1949 in more than 2,000 schools.[10] At least one state, Wisconsin, made instruction in consumer cooperatives compulsory in all public high schools.

Public school systems have also furnished teaching personnel and sometimes facilities for adult education in consumption. Evening school classes of this type — most of them paralleling the home economics courses of the secondary schools — had an enrollment of about 326,800 adults in 4,000 adult centers and 500 schools during 1940-1941.[11]

A phenomenal increase in the number of courses in consumer economics has occurred at the college level during the last 20 years. Unfortunately the latest study of such courses appears to be that completed before World War II by Alpheus Marshall. He found 920 separate courses, exclusive of home economics, being given in 451 colleges and universities. His survey covered the catalogue offerings of 1,249 of the 1,709 institutions of higher learning in the United States and outlying territories, in 1939.[12]

A substantial increase in the number and enrollment of these courses has taken place since 1941. A trend may be developing toward the use of a consumer approach in the introductory economics course at the college level. Paul Samuelson's *Economics, An Introductory Analysis* (1948) lays great emphasis upon the importance of the consumption function in maintaining an economy of full employment. His text includes material on problems of personal finance. Leland Gordon's *Elementary Economics* (1950) orients the whole subject matter of economics around the consumer. His goal is to teach consumers how their economic system acts or fails to act to meet their needs. Elizabeth Hoyt's *The Income of Society* (1950) is a more standard treatment of principles, but contains a wealth of material on consumer living standards, buying motives, and consumption problems. A text, *Economics, Experience and Analysis* (1950) by Broadus Mitchell and others, contains three chapters on using the national income.

From 1937 to 1941, the Institute for Consumer Education at Stephens College, Columbia, Missouri, acted as a clearing house for gathering, organizing and testing consumer education materials. The Institute was financed by a generous grant from the Alfred P. Sloan Foundation, and was headed by Professor John M. Cassels. A monthly newsletter, *Consumer Education*, and occasional pamphlets and books kept educators informed of the latest developments in the consumer field. The three national conferences, which were held from 1939 to 1941, brought together several hundred consumer educators, club leaders, government workers, labor representatives, and scientific workers, and gave a stimulus and a coordination to the Consumer Movement as a whole.

(5) BUSINESS AGENCIES. The early reaction of private business interests to the Consumer Movement has been characterized as "watching, wishing, and witching."[13] The "watching" involved a careful analysis of the objectives of the movement by retailing interests and the advertising trade journals in particular. The "wishing" was the conclusion that there was no Consumer Movement at all — only professional agitators. The "witching" was an attempt to smear the movement as subversive. Demands for honest advertising, grade labeling, and consumer cooperatives were termed "doctrines of Moscow." Women's clubs were "transmission belts." By 1941, a significant number of business leaders had recognized as

legitimate many of the demands of the Consumer Movement, and were attempting to meet them. The activities of these progressive business groups have furthered consumer education and protected the consumer in his buying.

The Better Business Bureaus have been the most important business agency in the Consumer Movement. Their program of fraud fighting and consumer protection has increased significantly in the last 20 years. In 1937, the National Better Business Bureau began the publication of a "Facts You Should Know" series for consumer education. Pamphlets on 25 subjects have been published on such topics as "Buying Used Cars", "Cosmetics", "Health Cures", "Jewelry", "Securities", and "Advertising". About 680,000 "Fact" booklets are distributed in a typical year.[14]

In addition, 91 local Bureaus reached consumers through radio programs, newspaper advertising, news items, pamphlets and posters. Since 1942, the National Bureau has sponsored the Consumer Education Study of the National Association of Secondary School Principals, which has been discussed previously. Each of 64 American Business Firms has contributed $6,000 through the National Bureau toward the support of this program. The financing does not appear to have affected the objectivity of the pamphlets.

Another business-sponsored organization which furthered the consumer interest was the National Consumer-Retailer Council. Established in 1937, its purpose was "to promote cooperation between consumers and retailers to the end that problems of mutual concern could be solved in a way advantageous to both".[15]

Consumer members are the American Home Economics Association and the National Board of Young Women's Christian Associations. Seven trade associations of retailers are members of associate members in addition to the National Better Business Bureau. An outstanding project of the Council has been its work in encouraging informative labeling and advertising. Its Sales Promotion Package Program offers complete instruction to retailers on what information should be included in advertising and labeling specific products, such as men's shirts. Guidance is given in planning programs to educate sales personnel and customers in the value of such informative selling. The Council also distributes a series of pamphlets informing consumers how to get the most for their money in purchasing vegetables, bathing suits, dry cleaning service, and the like. A transcribed radio program, entitled "Keys to Wise Buying," furnishes buying tips to consumers over 22 stations reaching 30 states. The NCRC News covers developments in the Consumer Movement, and is distributed to consumers — primarily teachers — in 2,473 communities throughout the country.

A few business groups have simplified the buying problems of consumers by their promotion of consumer good standards on an industry-wide basis. Consumer standards are specific criteria by which quality, quantity, performance, or terminology may be judged, or to which they conform. Standards enable a meeting of minds between seller and buyer. Where standards prevail, a can of corn labeled "A", size "38" in a topcoat, or a certification by the American Gas Association on the label of a gas stove, provides in each case an understandable basis for consumer selection.

Standardization of consumer goods by individual firms has been practiced for many decades. All this means is that merchandise under a given brand is uniform in quality, that size "7" hats of a particular manufacturer have the same dimensions, that "Fancy" as a particular canner's label for a certain type of peas denotes a uniform quality for *that* canner. Such standards are of limited aid to the consumer when competing firms use different standards. The developments in consumer good standards, which have been a part of the Consumer Movement, were, formerly, on an industry-wide rather than on an individual firm basis.

Foremost among business agencies which have promoted consumer standards is the American Standards Association. The A.S.A., established in 1918, is a clearing house for coordinating the standardization work of private business and governmental agencies. Its membership at present includes more than 100 national, technical, and trade organizations. Several hundred other national organizations are cooperating in A.S.A. standardization work. The primary interest of the A.S.A. has always been in the standardization of producer goods and industrial production methods, but in 1936, an Advisory Committee on Ultimate Consumer Goods organized to coordinate and direct standardization work on consumer goods in particular. The membership of this committee embraces trade associations representing consumers such as the American Association of University Women, Congress of Industrial Organization, American Federation of Labor, American Home Economics Association and Consumers Union. Among the standardizing projects which have been studied are body measurements for children, quality and labeling of bedding and upholstery, shoes, sheets and sheeting, boys' clothing, hosiery, household refrigerators, silver-plated tableware, waterproof and water repellant fabrics, color permanence, and performance criteria for rayon fabrics. Only a few of the 1,124 standards approved, up to July, 1949, by the American Standards Association are in the field of consumer standards. One reason for this is the necessity for support from a consensus of industrial members concerned before promulgation of standards may be undertaken. This limitation is not so serious with industrial goods in which members profit directly from the standards adopted. In the field of consumer standards, producer gains are less direct, and are by no means certain to be shared by all producing units.

A number of commercial agencies grant a seal of approval for use in labeling products which are found to meet specific standards as to safety or quality. The American Gas Association has developed 36 sets of national standards for various gas appliances designed to insure their safety in use. The seal of approval which is granted to manufacturers who conform to the A.G.A. standards is found on more than 95 percent of the gas burning equipment being marketed.[16] Underwriters' Laboratories, Inc. has 150 different sets of standards designed to insure the safety of such products as electrical cords, fuses, fans, lamps, flat irons, radios and television sets, heating appliances, roof-covering materials, electric blankets, and toys. The U.L. seal of approval is displayed on more than 475,000 products manufactured by over 7,500 producers.[17] Fabrics which meet certain tests for shrinkage, color fastness, or tensile strength may exhibit approval seals of the American Institute of Laundering, the Better Fabrics Testing Bureau, or the U.S. Testing Company. The Electrical Testing Laboratories issue a Certification Tag for lamps which meet the specifications of the Illuminating Engineering Society.[18]

The American Medical Association and the American Dental Association have pursued programs to enlighten and protect the consumer. The A.M.A.'s Council of Foods and Nutrition, which had its origin in 1929, makes a systematic analysis of food advertising and labeling, and awards a seal of acceptance to foods which are advertised and labeled informatively and honestly, and which meet the Council's standards for safety and nutrition.[18a] Pamphlets on foods, nostrums, and quackery are distributed to interested consumers. The A.M.A.'s Council of Pharmacy and Chemistry publishes the names of "acceptable" proprietary drugs. A monthly magazine, *Hygeia*, contains material on health education, which is written for the understanding of the layman. The American Dental Association supplies interested consumers with information on dental products such as toothpastes and powders, denture cleaners and mouth washes.

At one time the Association publslihed a list of "accepted" dentifrices which included those meeting standards of safety plus honest and informative advertising labeling. Such products were permitted to carry the A.D.A. seal of acceptance on their label. In 1950 a new policy was adopted restricting acceptance to dentifrices which demonstrated ability to *prevent* tooth decay. As of July, 1950, no product had qualified for the new standard of acceptance. Dentifrices containing urea and ammonium salts, fluorides, and chlorophyll derivatives were under study by the A.D.A. Council on Dental Therapeutics, but test results were inconclusive.[19]

The focusing point for a large amount of business activity in the Consumer Movement is the Committee on Consumer Relations in Advertising, financed by the American Association of Advertising Agencies and leading advertising media.

The Committee was organized in 1940 for the primary purpose of interpreting the Consumer Movement for advertising interests, and interpreting advertising for the Consumer Movement. A continuing study of consumer meetings in the United States, as reported in the press, was made between 1940 and 1946, and a study of consumer attitudes toward advertising was undertaken in 1946.

The *Consumer News Digest* is a monthly bulletin which reports objectively the important developments in the Consumer Movement. It is mailed without charge to interested producers and consumers. A series of seven pamphlets entitled The *Consumer-Buyer and Distribution*, has been published for use in consumer education studies of adult groups. Catalogues of business-sponsored educational materials and films are published for the guidance of teachers of consumer education. About 250 sources of pamphlets and leaflets are given, and over 1,000 motion pictures and film strips are described. Many of these materials are primarily promotional in nature, but a number offer very objective and valuable aid to consumers.

The Household Finance Corporation has an outstanding consumer education program which originated in 1932. Its series of Better Buymanship pamphlets offer counsel in budgeting and in buying food, clothing, home furnishings, health, and other commodities and services. About 1,000,000 of these booklets are distributed every year at $.05 each to homemakers, schools, adult education groups, women's clubs, and libraries. Charts and filmstrips are furnished to teachers of consumer education.

The "Chartered Life Underwriter" program of the American College of Life Underwriters, which was discussed in the preceding chapter, has grown steadily in stature. In 1950, about 17 percent of all life insurance agents either had a "C.L.U." degree, or were studying for the degree.[20]

(6) GOVERNMENT AGENCIES. A considerable increase in the incidental consumer activities of federal government departments has taken place in the last 20 years. Consumers won *de facto* recognition from the federal government in the 1930's when consumer representatives were placed in several governmental agencies. In the National Recovery Administration a Consumer Advisory Board participated with a Labor Advisory Board and an Industry Advisory Board in approving Industry Codes designed to put the economy back on its feet. The primary significance of the C.A.B. was a beginning of consumer representation in the government, for the Board lacked the well organized constituency which supported the Industry advisors, and was woefully weak.[21]

Advisory Consumer Counsels were provided in the Agricultural Adjustment Administration (1933) and in the National Bituminous Coal Commission (1937). The effectiveness of both in guarding the consumer interest against abuse in the planning programs of those producer-dominated agencies was slight. The A.A.A. Counsel published a *Consumers' Guide*, which campaigned for compulsory grade labeling and consumer cooperatives, and published a wealth of home economics material. Both Counsels and the *Guide* were discontinued.

During the World War II period the Office of Price Administration contained consumer representation in an advisory capacity. The consumer unit encouraged, and to some extent, coordinated the work of the consumer committees on the local Defense Councils which were established in all parts of the nation. The only consumer representation in the federal government as of June, 1950, was the

Consumer Advisory Committee to the President's Council of Economic Advisors.

The Committee includes 25 individuals representing consumer, church, educational, negro, welfare, and women's organizations. The significance of this representation is minimal since consumers are only an advisory group to an advisory group for the President, who in turn can merely advise and recommend legislation to Congress. Consumers have been consistently thwarted in their attempt to secure *de jure* recognition in the President's cabinet with a Department of the Consumer which would parallel the type of representation accorded labor, business, and agricultural interests.

Various departments of the federal government have contributed to consumer protection against exploitation and to consumer education in general. Prior to 1938, the Federal Trade Commission could take action to halt deceptive or unfair business conduct *only* when injury to one or more competitors resulted. The Wheeler-Lea amendment to the Federal Trade Act in that year gave the F.T.C. power to initiate action to protect consumers specifically against fraudulent and misleading advertising of foods, drugs, devices, or cosmetics. The F.T.C. made up an exhibit of its work on behalf of consumers which it displayed during 1947, and part of 1948. The display included examples of articles falsely advertised, against which the F.T.C. had acted. A few of the items included suntan lotaion advertised as destroying germs, moth spray which attracts rather than repels moths, and "Pure Raspberry Preserves" found to be a complete fake except for the seeds.

The F.T.C. shares with the Anti-Trust Division of the Justice Department the responsibility of ferreting out monopolistic abuses. The F.T.C. also conducts trade practice conferences at which agreements are established standardizing labeling terminology, promulgating standards of identity, and guarding against consumer deception of other types. The agency also administers the Wool Labeling Act, which became effective in 1941, requiring producers to state the wool content of garments on the label, including the percent of re-processed or re-used wool. The Anti-Trust Division of the Justice Department in the immediate years before World War II, and since the end of that war, has crusaded vigorously against monopolistic restraints such as those in the building trades, which have been especially abusive of the consumer interest.

The Food and Drug Administration and the Office of Education in the Federal Security Agency of the Interior Department have increased in significance for the consumer in the last two decades. Some of the worst defects of the 1906 Food and Drug Act were corrected in the Food, Drug, and Cosmetic Act of 1938. For example, cosmetics and mechanical health devices were brought under control, and more information concerning ingredients and quality of foods and drugs was required. Enforcement provisions were also strengthened. The U.S. Office of Education has distributed bibliographies of readings on consumer economics and has published suggestions for teaching methods in home economics.

The Bureau of Human Nutrition and Home Economics of the Department of Agriculture is devoted to research on homemakers' problems and the dissemination of its findings. The Bureau is currently distributing at a minimum price, about five million copies a year of its 100 or more different bulletins. Advice is offered on such subjects as "Meat for Thrifty Meals," "Money-saving main dishes," "Slip covers for furniture," and "Housecleaning management and methods." The Extension Service of the Department of Agriculture is reaching more than 3,000,000 rural homemakers a year in its program of general consumer education. A great increase in the use of the Department of Agriculture's voluntary food grading plans has taken place in the last 20 years. Although a large part of this grading is used only in wholesale marketing, a steadily growing volume of graded food products is available in consumer markets.[22]

The Board of Governors of the Federal Reserve System has carried on a continuing study of the spending patterns of various income groups since 1946.

The Bureau of Labor Statistics of the Department of Labor studies living standards and reports on living costs. Progress reports are made on consumer cooperatives in the United States and abroad, and information on the establishing and managing of cooperatives is distributed.

From 1935 to 1938, a Consumer Project Division in the Labor Department undertook research on consumer standards and related problems. The Division was the outgrowth of work which was previously being done by the Consumer Advisory Board of the N.R.A.

The National Bureau of Standards of the Commerce Department has cooperated with consumer groups and others in the standardization and simplification of consumer goods. The Department of Commerce contributes to the consumer interest in a second way — through the distribution of educational pamphlets on such subjects as "Care and Repair of the House," and "Safety for the Household."

An increasing concern for the welfare of consumers has also developed at the level of state and local government in ways which parallel to a varying extent, and supplement the activities of the federal agencies discussed above.

Organizations with Primary Consumer Interests

(1) CONSUMER COOPERATIVES. Among organizations dedicated primarily to alleviating consumer problems, consumer cooperatives were, and still are, of major importance. Kenneth Dameron estimated that 0.37 percent of all retail business in the United States was done by co-ops in 1929.[23] *Business Week* estimated that co-ops handled slightly more than one percent of retail sales in 1939, and slightly more than two percent of the $129 billion of retail sales in 1949.[24] The total number of retail

distributive associations grew from 1,476 in 1929, to 3,985 in 1947, and the number of service co-ops in fields such as housing, burial, room and board associations, hospital and health associations, and cold storage lockers grew during the same years from 85 to 793. The number of credit unions increased almost tenfold from 974 to 9,040. The number of wholesale associations servicing co-op stores jumped from 8 to 36.[25]

An indication of the growing significance of consumer cooperatives has been the establishment of the National Tax Equality Association by certain business interests to protest the alleged tax favoritism accorded consumer cooperatives. The net receipts of consumer cooperatives, which are paid out in patronage refunds to members, are exempted from the corporate income tax. The increasing interest of labor unions in consumer cooperatives and the promotional activities of governmental agencies for co-ops have already been recounted. The campaign of the National Tax Equality Association has led the Cooperative League to establish a Washington Office and a Congressional lobby. This lobby not only campaigns for the cooperative cause but also testifies, for what it considers the consumer interest, at hearings on various types of questions affecting consumers.

(2) AMERICAN HOME ECONOMICS ASSOCIATION. Membership in the A.H.E.A. increased from 10,000 in 1929 to 19,345 as of April 30, 1949,[26] and the scope of consumer activities increased significantly. The organization participated actively in the work of the National Consumer-Retailer Council, and the Advisory Committee on Ultimate Consumer Goods of the American Standards Association. From 1936 to 1948, the *Consumer Education Service* was published as a monthly bulletin to report progress in standardization, grade labeling, consumer protective legislation, and other aspects of the Consumer Movement. Occasionally, representatives have testified at Congressional hearings on legislation affecting consumers. The Association has repeatedly urged larger appropriations for the Bureau of Human Nutrition and Home Economics of the Agricultural Department, with which it cooperates in numerous research programs. The "Consumer Speaks Project", initiated in 1946, serves as an information channel between the manufacturer and the consumer. Discussion groups are held throughout the country to determine the qualities women want in various commodities. The votes of the women are tabulated, and standards and specifications are drawn up to express for manufacturers the technical points stressed by the homemakers. Up to June, 1948, 3,942 groups representing 100,000 consumers in 40 states had participated in projects for such products as pots and pans, refrigerators, washing machines, irons, ironing boards, cotton and rayon blouses, and house dresses.[27] The A.H.E.A. reports great interest in these reports on the part of manufacturers.

(3) CONSUMER COMMITTEES AND COUNCILS. During the N.R.A. period about 200 local consumer councils were established

throughout the nation to provide support and a sounding board for the Consumer Advisory Board. A number of the councils continued after the demise of the N.R.A., providing a meeting place for discussing the mutual problems of producers and consumers, and representing the consumer interest before city councils and state legislatures. During the life of the O.P.A. these veteran councils and many additional consumer committees, which were affiliated with local defense councils, attempted to educate consumers in conservation habits, and tried to secure vigorous enforcement of the price and rationing controls. Some consumer groups such as the one in Newark, New Jersey, established consumer information centers in prominent locations to advise consumers on buying problems, and to receive and check complaints of OPA violations.

A leading consumer council is that in Cincinnati, Ohio, which includes 63 cooperating organizations and many individual members. The conference represents consumers at legislative hearings, publishes a monthly bulletin on wise buying, and presents frequent radio programs. An average of 200 attend the monthly meetings.

The St. Louis Consumer Federation conducted a three-day milk strike in 1948, in protest against high milk prices. In 1947, the New York City Consumers Council held a mock trial to denounce the rising cost of living. The Washington, D.C. Committee for Consumer Protection called a meat strike in October, 1946, About 37,000 housewives signed pledges not to pay more than 60 cents per pound for any cut of meat, and many of them set up picket lines in front of butcher shops and groceries.

(4) NATIONAL CONSUMER ORGANIZATIONS. Several attempts were made to coordinate the activities of groups with a primary or secondary consumer interest through a national organization, but most of the efforts have proved abortive. The latest effort was the National Association of Consumers, established following the dissolution of the OPA around a nucleus of groups and individuals which were active in fighting for the maintenance of price controls. Miss Helen Hall, head of the Henry Street Settlement House in New York City, and a veteran leader in the Consumer Movement, was chairman of the N.A.C. Its long range objectives were:

1. To promote the organization and education of consumers.
2. To gain consumer representation in agencies of government — city, state and federal.
3. To secure recognition of consumer interests in programs of business, agriculture, and labor designed to shape and direct the American economy.
4. To gain official consumer representation in the United Nations and its constituent councils and commissions which deal with consumer welfare.[28]

With respect to day-to-day activities, the N.A.C. spoke for consumers at legislative hearings in Washington. The chairperson, Miss Hall, was a member of the Consumer Advisory Council to the President's

Council of Economic Advisors. A representative acted in an advisory capacity to the United States Delegation at the United Nations Food and Agriculture Organization meetings. Consumers received aid in establishing local chapters of the N.A.C. in their own respective communities. Finally, a four-page paper, *Consumers on the March*, kept members informed on pending legislation and its significance for the consumer, and on other information of interest to consumers. The membership in January, 1950 included 3,000 group and individual members in 960 communities throughout the nation. Like

FIGURE 2
THE CONSUMER MOVEMENT – 2nd Round

GOAL: "To further the consumer interest"

METHODS: (indicated in diagram below)

A Few Groups Would Add	Some Groups Would Add	General Agreement On Proposals Listed Below	Some Groups Oppose	A Few Groups Oppose
A program of evolutionary socialism or a program leading to a "cooperative commonwealth"	Extension of welfare state. Promotion of consumer co-ops.	Programs of consumer education (including product testing). Protective legislation against fraud and misrepresentation. More effective anti-monopoly legislation. More factual buying information. Standardization of consumer goods. Compulsory grade labeling. Federal Dep't. of the Consumer. Consumer political pressure groups.	Compulsory grade labeling.	Federal Dep't. of Consumer. Consumer political pressure groups.

PARTICIPATING GROUPS:

Consumer Rating Agencies
Consumer Cooperatives
Consumer Committees and Councils
Educational Groups
Settlement Houses

Women's Clubs
Government Agencies
Professional Associations
Religious Groups
Labor Unions
Certain Business Groups.

the national consumer groups which preceded it, the N.A.C.'s chief problem was obtaining financial support to carry on its ambitious program.

A second national consumer group was the Consumer Clearing House, composed of group representatives having a primary or a secondary consumer interest. Under the direction of Miss Caroline Ware, the representatives met for the purpose of exchanging information on consumer issues and planning action. The Clearing House, itself, did not act as a body, but rather recommended action, and provided a means for the member groups to cooperate in programs when they wished to do so.

A Panoramic View of the Consumer Movement

The previous pages have presented a piecemeal view of the Consumer Movement during the 1930's and 1940's, describing briefly the major participating groups with the exception of the rating agencies. The central goal of all participants was to further the consumer interest, but there was a divergence of opinion as to the best way of accomplishing this objective.

The Consumer Movement has been likened to Stephen Leacock's horseman who "jumped on his horse and rode in all directions". Table I shows those methods upon which there is general agreement with a brief indication of the expanded aims of the left wing groups and the restricted proposals of the right wing. Bitter feeling exists between some of the leftist and rightist groups because of their opposing economic philosophies.

The Consumer Movement of these two decades appeared to be predominantly a revolt by a minority of the middle and upper income groups. A study made in 1940 by Dr. George Gallup (parts of which are summarized in Table II) showed that only about 12 percent of the lower income families had even heard of the Consumer Movement. About 32 percent of the middle income group had heard of the Movement, and about 48 percent of the upper income group were aware of the Movement. Among the upper income group, 15 percent had attended meetings for the purpose of discussing what products consumers should or should not buy. Among the middle income group, 10 percent had attended such meetings, while among the lower income group only 4 percent had done so. The same poll showed that the middle and upper income groups were more critical of advertising than the lower income groups, and were more interested in compulsory grade labeling. Subscribers to the services of the consumer rating agencies were likewise concentrated in the middle and upper income groups.

During the period of post-war recovery and unexampled affluence of the 1950's and 1960's, the consumer movement, so vigorously founded in the early 1900's and revived in the 1930's, may be said to have "run down". True, it was never really missing from the American scene during this time. For example, the consumer rating

TABLE II
PUBLIC OPINION POLL ON CONSUMER MOVEMENT, 1940*

Response to Question: "Have you heard of the Consumer Movement?"

All income groups:	yes — 27%	no — 73%
Upper income group:	yes — 48	no — 52
Middle income group:	yes — 32	no — 68
Lower income group:	yes — 12	no — 88

Response to Question: "Have you ever attended a lecture or meeting held for the purpose of discussing what products consumers should or should not buy?"

All income groups:	yes — 9%	no — 91%
Upper income group:	yes — 15	no — 85
Middle income group:	yes — 10	no — 90
Lower income group:	yes — 4	no — 96

Response to Question: "Have you any criticisms of advertising?"

All income groups:	yes — 41%	no — 59%
Upper income group:	yes — 56	no — 44
Middle income group:	yes — 47	no — 53
Lower income group:	yes — 30	no — 70

Response to Question: "Are you in favor of having ABC grade labeling made compulsory by the government?" (Asked only of those interested in grade labeling)

All income groups:	yes — 48%	no — 52%
Upper income group:	yes — 60	no — 40
Middle income group:	yes — 54	no — 46
Lower income group:	yes — 39	no — 61

* "Survey of Public's Buying Habits," Ballot 703 C, *A.I.P.O.*, Sept. 29, 1940, pp. 16, 27, 29, 31.

agencies, such as the Consumers Union, continued to grow and flourish; the circulation of *Consumer Reports* grew from about 100,000 just after World War II to more than one million in 1963 (covering about two percent of the nation's families).[29] But, it is fair to say that a substantial hiatus developed in these two decades. As many have noted, the typical American was much more interested in earning money effectively than spending it wisely. Few in the "good old days" of Eisenhower and Johnson perceived that the consumer was not spending very wisely, nor that he needed protection from the rising tide of those "quick buck artists" who were out to exploit him (and not all of this number were counted amongst the "fly-by-night" outfits).

In this affluent, self-satisfied sky a brilliant new rocket rose and exploded, shattering the complacency, and launching a new round of consumerism that made the previous two rounds seem pale by comparison. In the next section we examine the origins of this bright new force, Ralph Nader, and examine his influence, try to apprise whether the third round will be a flash-in-the-pan, as many say, or will become a permanent part of life in our time.

QUESTIONS FOR DISCUSSION

1. Why did the Great Depression, 1930-1939, stimulate the second round of consumerism so strongly?

2. How much protection to the consumer was afforded by the establishment of testing laboratories for products by mass merchandisers such as Sears, Roebuck and Macy's? How about the Good Housekeeping seal of approval?

3. Would it have been a good thing to open up to the public the results of tests on goods done by the National Bureau of Standards? Why, in your opinion, were these valuable reports not released for general dissemination to the public?

4. What influence did the following organizations have during the second round of consumerism:
    (a) Women's clubs
    (b) Educational institutions
    (c) Labor unions
    (d) Better Business Bureaus
    (e) Trade associations and professional societies

5. A number of people were appointed to governmental agencies during the 1930's to represent the interests of the consumers, e.g., NRA, Coal Board, etc. Why did the author feel that their influence was "weak"?

6. It looks as though a great many government agencies in the 1930's were carrying on education and protection programs for the consumers. Why were these less than successful?

7. Why did consumer cooperatives fail to develop very well in the 1930's and 1940's? Were they well adopted to the American marketing environment?

8. Why in your opinion did the consumer movement "run down" in the 1950's and 1960's? What or who revived it?

FOOTNOTES

1. Wesley C. Mitchell, "The Backward Art of Spending Money," *American Economic Review* (1912, Vol. 2), p. 275.

2. Stuart Chase and Frederick J. Schlink, *Your Money's Worth* (New York, MacMillan Co., 1927), p. 5.

3. *Ibid.*, p. 238.

4. "The Consumer Movement", *Business Week* (April 22, 1939), p. 41.

5. The descriptive material in this chapter has been obtained from the following sources, in particular, in addition to those cited in later footnotes:
   a. Personal interviews with representatives of many organizations discussed.
   b. Helen Sorenson, *The Consumer Movement* (New York, Harper & Bros., 1941).
   c. Werner K. Gabler, *Labeling the Consumer Movement* (Washington, D.C., American Retail Federation, 1939).
   d. "The Consumer Movement — Some New Trends," *Consumer Education Service* (March-April, 1947).
   e. Caroline F. Ware, *Consumer Goes to War* (New York, Funk Co., 1942).
   f. Helen Hall, "Consumer Protection," *Social Work Year Book* (1949), pp. 142-150.

6. "Consumer Cooperatives: Operations in 1947" *Bulletin #948, Bureau of Labor Statistics* (1947), p. 8.

7. Kenneth Dameron, "Consumer Meeting Agenda, A study in Consumer Interests," (April, 1948), p. 102.

8. Thomas Briggs, "Consumer Education in 1946-47" *Bulletin of the Department of Secondary School Principals* (May, 1947), p. 137.

9. *Ibid.*

10. *Consumer News Digest,* (October, 1949), p. 3, (June, 1949), p. 3.

11. Esther C. Franklin, in *Consumer Education,* edited by James E. Mandenhall and Henry Harap (New York, Appleton-Century Co., 1943), p. 210. The author knows of no later statistics, but a great increase in this type of training appeared during the war years.

12. Alpheus Marshall, "920 Courses in Consumption Economics," *The Educational Record* (January, 1941), p. 27-38.

13. Donald E. Montgomery, Talk to American Association of Advertising Agencies in May, 1940.

14. *Facts You Should Know About Your Better Business Bureau* (no date) p. 13.

15. From the masthead of the *NCRC* News.

16. Jessie Coles, *Standards and Labels for Consumer Goods* (New York, Ronald Press, 1949), p. 493.

17. *Ibid.*, p. 490.

18. The reader who wishes more than this cursory examination of the present status of consumer standards is referred to Part VII in Jessie Coles' *Standards and Labels, op. cit.*

18a. The American Medical Association ceased granting seals of acceptance in the late 1950's. It still carries on the evaluative studies described. The American Dental Association still grants such seals, e.g., see Crest toothpaste.

19. "Revised Procedure for the Evaluation of Dental Products," *Journal of the American Dental Association* (June, 1948), pp. 489-495.

20. Information supplied by Davis W. Gregg, President, American College of Life Underwriters.

21. William N. Loucks, "Price Fixing: The Consumer Faces Monopoly", *Annals of the American Academy* (May, 1934), pp. 113-124.

22. Coles, *op. cit.*, Chapter 22.

23. Kenneth Dameron, *Consumer Problems in Wartime* (New York, McGraw-Hill, Co., 1944), p. 358.

24. "Co-op Growth Faces Hurdles", *Business Week* (December 10, 1949), p. 48.

25. "Consumer Cooperatives: Operations in 1947", *B.L.S. Bulletin #948* (U.S. Department of Labor, 1947), p. 2.

26. Keturah E. Baldwin, *The AHEA Saga* (Washington, A.H.E.A., 1949), p. 101.

27. *Ibid.*, p. 50.

28. *Consumers on the March* (May, 1947), p. 3.

29. Edward L. Brink and William T. Kelley, *The Management of Promotion* (New York: Prentice-Hall, Inc., 1963), p. 358.

PART II
THE NEW CONSUMERISM
OF THE 1960'S AND 1970'S

Having traced the early manifestations of the consumer movement in the 19th Century, and the character of the first two rounds of consumerism in the 20th Century, we now turn to an appraisal of the third round.

It may be said that one man, Ralph Nader, was really responsible for setting off the new consumer movement in 1966 with the publication of his study of the safety of automobiles. His concept of the consumer advocate, of a man well trained in the law, devoting his time and great energies to the public interest was indeed unique. Initially it inspired cynical disbelief, especially in the corporate boardrooms (what's Nader's angle?) which gave way in time to grudging admiration, if not acceptance (he seems for real!). Indeed, amongst the teen age population and college crowd, Nader took on the dimensions of a folk hero, and his penache and influence was strong and persistant, and is to this day.

So, in the now classic *Time* profile we examine Ralph Nader as a person, and see the directions of his endeavors and his accomplishments as the virtual leader of this new social movement.

Then, an article by Marlyn Bender brings the Nader story up-to-date. She points out that a toleration or living together was evolved between the Nadarites and most of business, and that Nader's campaigns have been by no means adverse to the interests of business itself.

Philip Kotler furhter traces the effect of the new consumer movement on business, particularly as concerns the marketing segment. This well-rounded review ends with the opinion, well supported, that consumerism is not a flash-in-the-pan but will become a permanent countervailing force on the American business scene. He warns business men that they had better learn to live with this new force. He gives some useful guidelines as to how this accommodation may be effectuated by the business firm.

TIME

*"The U.S.'s Toughest Customer, *Time* (December 12, 1969), pp. 89-98. Reproduced by permission.

Midway through lunch at a fashionable Washington restaurant not long ago, a young man named Ralph Nader stopped suddenly and gazed down in disgust at his chef's salad. There, nestled among the lettuce leaves, lay a dead fly. Nader spun in his chair and jabbed both arms into the air to summon a waiter. Pointing accusingly at the intruder on his plate, he ordered: "Take it away!" The waiter apologized and rushed to produce a fresh salad, but Nader's anger only rose. While his luncheon companions watched the turmoil that had erupted around him, Nader launched into a detailed indictment of sanitation in restaurants. He pointed out that flies killed by insect spray often fall into food, thereby providing customers not only with an unappetizing bonus but also with a dose of DDT — or something even stronger.

Restaurant owners had better take heed. Nader is by now an almost legendary crusader who would — and could — use a fly to instigate a congressional investigation. As the self-appointed and unpaid guardian of the interests of 204 million U.S. consumers, he has championed dozens of causes, prompted much of U.S. industry to reappraise its responsibilities and, against considerable odds, created a new climate of concern for the consumer among both politicians and businessmen. Nader's influence is greater now than ever before. That is partly because the consumer, who has suffered the steady ravishes of inflation upon his income, is less willing to tolerate substandard, unsafe or misadvertised goods. It is also because Nader's ideas have won acceptance in some surprising places. Last week, for example, Henry Ford II went farther than any other automobile executive ever has in acknowledging the industry's responsibility for polluting the air and asked — indeed, prodded — the Government to help correct the situation. The auto companies must develop, said Ford, "a virtually emission-free" car, and soon. Ford did not mention Ralph Nader, but it was not really necessary. Nader is widely known as a strong critic of the auto industry for, among other things, its pollution of the atmosphere.

Nader was able to force off the market General Motors' Corvair, which was withdrawn from production this year. Corvair's sales had plunged by 93% after Nader condemned the car as a safety hazard in his bestseller, *Unsafe at Any Speed*. That influential book, and Nader's later speeches, articles and congressional appearances, also forced the Department of Transportation to impose stricter safety standards on automobile and tire manufacturers.

Advocate, muckraker and crusader, Nader has also been almost solely responsible for the passage of five major federal laws. They are the National Traffic and Motor Vehicle Safety Act of 1966, the Wholesome Meat Act of 1967, the Natural Gas Pipeline Safety Act, the Radiation Control for Health and Safety Act and the Wholesale Poultry Products Act, all of 1968. This week Congress will almost certainly pass the Federal Coal Mine Health and Safety Act, which Nader and a group of insurgent mine workers supported against the wishes of complacent union leadership. The act contains stiff preventive measures against working conditions that can cause black lung.

Nader was the first to accuse baby-food manufacturers of imperiling the health of infants by using monosodium glutamate, a taste enhancer that medical research shows can cause brain damage in some animals. The three largest producers of baby food have since stopped using it. In addition, Nader's repeated warnings about the dangers of cyclamates and DDT helped to nudge the Department of Health, Education and Welfare to press research that led to recent federal restrictions on their use. From witness chairs and podiums, he has also taken aim at excessively fatty hot dogs, unclean fish, tractors that tip over and kill farmers, and the dangerous misuse of medical X rays. He has revealed that some color-television sets were recalled for leaking excessive amounts of radiation. (The Federal Trade Commission has publicly warned viewers to sit at least six feet away from color tubes.)

The Erosion of Life

To many Americans, Nader, at 35, has become something of a folk hero, a symbol of constructive protest against the status quo. When this peaceful revolutionary does battle against modern bureaucracies, he uses only the weapons available to any citizen — the law and public opinion. He has never picketed, let alone occupied, a corporate office or public agency. Yet Nader has managed to cut through all the protective layers and achieve results. He has shown that in an increasingly computerized, complex and impersonal society, one persistent man can actually do something about the forces that often seem to badger him — that he can indeed even shake and change big business, big labor and even bigger Government.

"My job is to bring issues out in the open where they cannot be ignored," says Nader, chopping his hands, as he often does when he speaks. "There is a revolt against the aristocratic uses of technology and a demand for democratic uses. We have got to know what we are doing to ourselves. Life can be — and is being — eroded." To prevent that erosion, he unmercifully nags consumer-minded U.S. Senators, pushing them to pass new bills. When their committees stall, he phones them by day, by night, and often on Sundays. "This is Ralph," he announces, and nobody has to ask, "Ralph *who*?"

Nader today is widening his sights. A lawyer by training, he is investigating the affairs of Covington & Burling, the Washington law firm headed by former Secretary of State Dean Acheson. At one time or another, Covington & Burling has numbered among its clients 200 of the nation's 500 biggest corporations, and Nader wants to determine just how much influence the firm has inside the Government. Most of all, he is probing into the affairs of ossified federal bureaucracies. "We hear a lot about law and order on the streets," he says, with a mischievous twinkle in his eyes. "I thought we ought to find out how law and order operates in the regulatory agencies." How does it? "It doesn't."

Most Outstanding Man

He issued a report (now in hard-cover) that scaldingly criticized the FTC and called for its reorganization; recently several FTC officials have agreed with him. He is examining laxity within agencies as diverse as the National Air Pollution Control Administration and the Federal Railroad Administration, which he says shares the blame for the fact that U.S. railways have 100 accidents a day, accounting for 2,400 deaths a year. "Regulatory agencies have failed by the most modest of standards," Nader contends, in great part because their top men are too cozy with the industries that they oversee and often use their Government jobs as stepping-stones to lucrative private careers in the same field. By his count, 75% of former commissioners of the Federal Communications Commission are employed or retained by the communications industry. This, he charges, amounts to a "deferred bribe." Agency officials who resign their jobs, Nader contends, should be barred from accepting immediate employment in the industry that they were supposedly policing.

To multiply the manpower for his campaigns, Nader has enlisted the help of vacationing students for the past two summers. Their Zola-like zeal for investigating bureaucracies has earned them the name "Nader's Raiders." Last year there were only seven Raiders, but this year the number grew to 102 law, engineering and medical students. The Raiders, who were paid a meager living allowance ($500 to $1,000 for ten weeks), delved energetically into the Department of Agriculture, the Food and Drug Administration, the National Water Pollution Control Administration, occupational health agencies, the Interstate Commerce Commission and several other fiefdoms.

In anticipation of their findings, which are due to be released beginning early next year, at least one ICC official has already resigned. Meanwhile, Nader and his Raiders have accused Government authorities in general of "systematically and routinely" violating the 2½-year-old Freedom of Information Act, which is supposed to entitle public access to much federal information. "If Government officials displayed as much imagination and initiative in administering their programs as they do in denying information about them," he says, "many national problems now in the grip of bureaucratic blight might become vulnerable to resolution." In line with that philosophy, one group of Raiders last month filed a suit in federal court to force the Civil Aeronautics Board to release findings on passenger complaints. Nader expects similar suits to be filed soon against the Departments of Labor and Agriculture.

Over the long run, the inspiration that Ralph Nader is providing for young Americans may prove as important to the country as his own lone battle. The Harvard Law School newspaper has somewhat generously called him "the most outstanding man ever to receive a degree from this institution," which has counted among its graduates Oliver Wendell Holmes and Felix Frankfurter. Nader is a major hero in most law schools. Two of last summer's Raiders canvassed Texas colleges and returned with 700 applications for next summer.

Critics and Champions

Nader is not universally loved for his efforts. New Left revolutionaries condemn him because he wants to improve the economic system rather than tear it down. Businessmen complain that he is a publicity-seeking gadfly and that he can be self-righteous to the point of arrogance. His most obvious weakness is that he sometimes exaggerates for effect, as when he said that frankfurters are "among the most dangerous missiles this country produces." But many businessmen, whatever their feelings about Nader's methods, applaud his accomplishments and concede that he is an important and often valuable critic. Last month a study committee of the U.S. Chamber of Commerce deplored "the tardiness of business in responding constructively" to consumers' criticism. The committee called on sellers to "expand information regarding safety, performance and durability of products." Nader insists that he is not "anti-business" but simply "pro-people." He often jokes that he is as much a foe of the funeral industry as Jessica Mitford but that while she only wrote a book, "I'm trying to reduce the number of their customers."

Occasionally the people whom Nader is trying to help seem more resentful of his efforts than do his corporate targets. On his taxi rides through Washington, cabbies regularly berate him because they must now pay for seat belts and 28 other pieces of mandatory safety equipment. Nader sympathizes with them but argues that the automakers could reduce prices by at least $700 per car if they would do away with costly annual style changes. Even Lyndon Johnson, who signed the 1966 auto-safety bill into law, has found some Nader innovations irritating. On a drive across his Texas ranch, L.B.J. noticed a spot on the windshield of his new Chrysler and groped for the washer and wiper knobs. Still unfamiliar with the Nader-inspired safety feature of non-protruding knobs, Johnson pawed at the dashboard in vain while he continued to drive. Utterly frustrated, he turned to a passenger and muttered: "That goddamned Nader."

The Origins of Discontent

Paradoxically, many U.S. consumers are discontented even while they are the envy of contemporary civilization — the best-fed, best-clothed, most pampered people in histroy. Most companies have a self-interest in promoting product safety and performance, if only to induce customers to buy and buy again. Since the large majority of consumers do exactly that, businessmen understandably believe that they are producing the kind of merchandise that the nation wants. The average buyer probably gets more value for $1,000 spent in a current mail-order-house catalogue than in an edition of 50 years ago.

Nevertheless, many low-quality and hazardous goods find their way into the marketplace; too much is overpriced, and too little works right. Consumer protest groups, often led by women, have been organized in many states. Longtime consumer activists profess amazement that the public has waited so long to fight back. Until lately, amateur, part-time buyers have felt unequal to challenging professional, full-time sellers. Says Peter Drucker, author of *The Age of Discontinuity:* "We have been a very patient people by and large. Now people are fed up, and I do not blame them."

The movement that Nader fostered goes by the awkward name of "consumerism." It belongs to an age of discontent that has roiled campuses and ghettos, subjected old certitudes to new doubts and stimulated individual assertiveness. Economist Walter Heller says: "People are much more questioning of authority, including the authority of the marketplace."

Today's consumer is better educated than his forebears and thus less willing to accept the exaggerated salesmanship, misleading advertising, shoddy goods and even bits of deceit that buyers once considered natural hazards of commerce. He is justifiably confused by product guarantees written in incomprehensible legalese, by conflicting claims for chemical additives in gasoline and toothpaste, by food and soap that are packaged to defy easy comparison with the prices of competitive products. Though the poor and the uneducated are more systematically bilked than other groups, the current upwelling of consumer protest comes primarily from the comfortable middle class. The anger rises from the irritation of the telephone caller who cannot get a dial tone, the commuter whose dilapidated train runs 45 minutes late, or anyone at all who tries to get his auto, dishwasher or TV set properly repaired.

The Most Serious Theft

It is almost impossible to estimate the dollar loss to consumers through unscrupulous practices. The chairman of the Senate

Commerce Committee, Washington's Warren Magnuson, argues that deceptive selling is the nation's "most serious form of theft," accounting for more dollars lost each year than robbery, larceny, auto thefts, embezzlement and forgery combined. An idea of its scope comes from the case of some major drug manufacturers, which have admitted entering into a long-term price-fixing scheme that netted them at least $100 million before they were caught. Three large plumbing-fixture manufacturers were convicted not long ago, and twelve others pleaded "no contest" in a similar conspiracy involving $1 billion worth of sinks, tubs and toilets.

The human costs of unsafe products and practices are even harder to measure, though Nader can almost endlessly cite alarming statistics. "Do you realize that there are 2,000,000 needless cases of salmonella food poisoning a year?" he says. "Just think of it. And that's only one aspect. Do you realize that more Americans died on the highways by mid-October of this year than have been killed in all of the Viet Nam War? Consumers are being manipulated, defrauded and injured, not just by marginal businesses or fly-by-night hucksters but by blue-chip business firms."

The bulk of complaints against business falls into four broad categories:

DECEPTIVE PROMOTION. The U.S. Food and Drug Administration has reported that commercial mouthwashes — a $212-million-a-year business — are useless for curing "bad breath," and that more than 300 other patent drug items are useless for the purposes for which they are advertised. Chicago officials recently fined 121 service-station operators who had put out curbside signs advertising gasoline at one price but charged more at the pump. Another advertising abuse involves the "bait and switch" routine. Salesmen lure customers by advertising an extremely low-priced product; but when the time comes to buy, the product is "not available" and the customer is induced or coerced to accept a costlier one. In California, the attorney general's office has found this practice used by swimming-pool contractors, home-freezer-and-meat-supply operations, and by a dealer who specialized in collecting advance payments from G.I.s serving in Viet Nam.

HIDDEN CHARGES. A subtler method of parting consumers from their dollars is to tack on additional, often vaguely named charges. Lenders, for example, collect "service charges" and "points" that add substantially to borrowing costs. Often such charges would amount to usury under state laws if they were labeled as interest, which they simply supplement. Some retailers who mail out unsolicited credit cards try passing on the high costs of collection and theft loss to their customers. Until protests from three states prompted revisions in the plan, Montgomery Ward billed charge-account customers for credit life insurance on themselves to avoid the expense of settling with the estates of deceased buyers. Unless customers specifically requested not to be enrolled in the plan, they were billed 10¢ a month on each $100 owed. Although the charge amounted to pocket change for most persons, it was designed to pass on a major expense of Montgomery Ward's to the customers.

SLOPPY SERVICE. Consumers Union, a nonprofit, private testing organization of which Nader is a board member, distributed 20 deliberately broken TV sets to New York City homes and asked neighborhood repairmen to fix them; only three of the 20 were properly serviced. Television, air-conditioner and many other repairmen commonly refuse even to look at a cantankerous appliance until they collect a substantial "estimate fee." Texas authorities have forced finance companies to return $1,900,000 to victims of unscrupulous and outrageously sloppy home-improvement firms. Automobile repairing has broken down so badly that automakers have instituted training programs for mechanics, and are developing new gadgetry for electronic diagnosis of engine troubles.

UNSAFE OR IMPURE PRODUCTS. Consumers can get information about the nutritive value and ingredients of dog food more easily than about some forms of canned meat; the chairman of the Senate Consumer Subcommittee, Utah's Frank Moss, likes to point out this discrepancy by reading the can labels to his audiences. When Consumers Union analyzed federally inspected pork sausage, inspectors found that one-eighth of the samples contained "insect fragments, insect larvae, rodent hairs and other kinds of filth." Investigators for the National Commission on Product Safety have found many potentially lethal toys on the market. Eleven Philadelphia children recently had to have tiny toy darts, which they accidentally inhaled from a plastic blowgun, removed from their lungs. Other hazards include a child's electric stove that produced temperatures of 600° and a baby's rattle that was held together with spike-like wires. Under a law signed last month, the Government can ban the sale of toys that present electrical, mechanical or heat hazards. But the law does not become effective until after the Christmas buying season, and Congress disregarded a commission recommendation that the Department of Health, Education and Welfare pretest some kinds of toys for safety. By the estimate of the Product Safety Commission, about 100,000 persons each year are injured when they walk through safety glass; yet builders have repeatedly refused to make it stand out better by marking it clearly. Nader has charged over nationwide TV that complex electronic medical equipment causes large numbers of unreported electrocutions in hospitals; doctors have estimated, he said, that anywhere from 1,200 to 12,000 patients per year are electrocuted. Official safety regulations, where they do exist, are often loosely enforced. Last month the Department of Transportation announced that one-quarter of the tires that it has tested this year failed to meet a significant test: standards originally devised by tire manufacturers themselves.

Politicians at every level of government recognize that consumerism has become a vote-catching issue. There has been a surge of activity to protect the consumer from fraud in the marketplace, and sometimes from his own bad judgment. Under a new law in Massachusetts, people who are fast-talked by door-to-door salesmen into signing contracts for unwanted goods can now cancel the deal within ten days. California's Department of Professional and Vocational Standards has instituted a television-repair inspection system that has trimmed $15 million a year from fraudulent fixit bills. The department tests the honesty of any suspicious repair outfit by planting deliberately broken sets in private homes; if the repairman makes unnecessary charges, his license is lifted.

The Belated Protectors

Nearly all major cities and about 22 states have created offices of consumer affairs, many of them headed by attractive and energetic women with whom housewives identify easily. The national prototype is Mrs. Virginia Knauer, 54, a Philadelphia grandmother who served as Pennsylvania's consumer adviser and last April was chosen by President Nixon to head the federal consumer program. Bess Myerson Grant, the 1945 Miss America who is now New York City's commissioner of consumer affairs, recently sent inspectors out to test restaurant hamburgers. When nearly one-third of the burgers failed to meet the city's all-beef standards, Mrs. Grant complained loudly about "shamburgers," 156 people were subpoenaed, and those found guilty were fined. During her first year as Chicago's commissioner of consumer sales, Jane Byrne issued 1,144 tickets and collected $58,000 in fines. Some supermarkets were caught placing "cents off" labels on items that were selling at the regular price or even higher.

All too few consumer watchdogs, however, are effective. The limp performance results partly from austerity budgets and from the reluctance of many juries to convict businessmen under criminal codes. The appointees to consumer-affairs jobs frequently have little experience in government. California's Kay Valory, consumer counsel to Governor Ronald Reagan, has not testified in three years before any committee considering consumer legislation. She recently made the extraordinary recommendation that buyers shun the "very narrow" testing reports of Consumers Union in favor of the handbook of the National Association of Manufactuers.

Winning in Washington

It has been left to the Federal Government to provide most of the protection for U.S. consumers. Congress has already enacted at least 20 major pieces of consumer legislation despite strenuous efforts by most industry lobbyists to defeat them. The lobbyists have been considerably more successful in keeping enforcement of the new rules to a minimum. The favorite lobbyist tactic is to persuade Congress to provide only token funds to administer new laws. Enforcement of the 1966 Fair Packaging and Labeling Act, adopted over vigorous objections from the food industry, has been all but abandoned by the FDA: it has funds to pay only two employees to do the job. The FTC initially received enough money to inform retailers of the new truth-in-lending law, effective last July 1, but not enough to enforce it.

Six weeks ago, President Nixon called on Congress to enact a "buyers' bill of rights." The President declared: "Consumerism is a healthy development that is here to stay." Among other things, he proposed the establishment of a new consumer division in the Justice Department and expanded powers that would enable the FTC to seek injunctions against unfair business practices. As Nader and other consumer activists have long been demanding, the President also asked Congress to allow consumers to join together in "class action" damage suits in federal courts against errant manufacturers or merchants. If found guilty of deceptive trade practices, manufacturers would have to bear all legal fees and pay damages to all who sue. Nixon disappointed consumer advocates, however, by proposing that suits be limited to eleven specified offenses, including worthless warranties and false claims for a product. Moreover, consumers would be unable to go to court until the Justice Department had first established fraud through a lawsuit. Even Mrs. Knauer, the Administration's own adviser, wanted much broader measures. "Timid tiptoeing," complains Nader. "Politics turned the message into Swiss cheese."

Still, U.S. consumers stand an increasing chance of winning in Washington. The Veterans Administration recently agreed to make public its comprehensive test data on hearing-aid performance. Nader wants the General Services Administration, the principal federal purchasing agent, to release its vast store of product information, which includes test results on goods as varied as bed sheets and flatbed trucks. Legislation is now in preparation to 1) require producers of household poisons to render their containers "childproof" by making bottles and packages harder to open, 2) set up more stringent health rules in fish-processing plants, and 3) force manufacturers to guarantee the adequate performance of their products and live up to all claims that they make for them. A farther-reaching piece of legislation, being drafted by Senator Moss's Consumer Subcommittee, would set up an independent "consumer council" to act as the buying public's ombudsman. Nader has advocated the idea of a Cabinet-level consumer post for years.

What makes Nader so effective today? Much of the answer lies in his lawyer's dedication to hard facts. He makes accusations almost daily that would be libelous if untrue; yet no one has ever sued him on his charges against companies or products. He collects facts everywhere — from his audiences on campus speaking tours, from obscure trade journals and Government publications, from interviews with high officials, from secret informers in public office and private industry, from thousands of letters addressed simply to "Ralph Nader, Washington, D.C." Nader receives more mail than the

majority of U.S. Senators and Congressmen, reads all the letters —
but can answer few.

His first inkling that all was not well with the Corvair's suspension
system came from a disgruntled General Motors auto worker who
wrote him a letter. In *Unsafe at Any Speed*, Nader went on to single
out the sporty car's rear-suspension system as an example of
hazardous compromise between engineering and styling. At certain
speeds and tire pressures, or in certain types of turns, he charged, the
rear wheels could "tuck under," causing a driver to lose control.
G.M., which eventually redesigned the system, at first did not even
recall the model for checking. But executives were disturbed enough
by Nader's charges to hire a Washington law firm to look into the
matter. The lawyer, in turn, engaged the Vincent Gillen private
detective agency to trail Nader. Purely on a fishing expedition that
was to find nothing, the agency's head urged his men to uncover
what they could about Nader's "women, boys, etc." Tipped by
friends that investigators were looking into his private life, Nader
charged publicly that he was being harassed. G.M.'s use of grade-B
spy-movie tactics was fully exposed when its president, James Roche
(now chairman), was summoned before a Senate subcommittee and
twice apologized to Nader for the company's investigation.

In his battle for pipeline-safety legislation, Nader secured
important technical data from an engineer who was fighting the
installation of a gas main near his home. He first learned of the
damage that pipeline explosions could cause from a professor whom
he met at an M.I.T. conference. "Sometimes the things these
professors casually drop at conferences send me up the wall," says
Nader.

Influence On the Law

Typical of Nader's battle style was his campaign for more stringent
federal meat inspection at packing plants. While speed-reading the
small print of a House report on Agriculture Department
appropriations, Nader noticed that it urged "further studies" of the
U.S. meat-inspection program. Did that mean that here has been
earlier studies showing that the U.S. had a meat problem? Indeed it
did, as Nader found out when he requested a copy of the
little-known study at the Agriculture Department. "Nobody ever
asked for this before," said the employee who handed it to him. The
study gave graphic descriptions of conditions in some meat plants.

Now Nader had his ammunition. He sent a summary of the study
to the House Agriculture Committee, which was about to hold
"clean meat" hearings for the first time in eight years. He quickly
wrote an article for *The New Republic* titled "We're Back in the
Jungle" — a title that echoed Upton Sinclair's classic indictment of
the meat industry 60 years ago, *The Jungle*. He sent press releases to
newspapers located near the worst plants. As a result, Nader was
deluged by letters from meat handlers, meat buyers and anonymous
Agriculture Department officials. He gave tips and new evidence to
the Senate sponsor of the meat bill, Minnesota's Walter Mondale.

What Nader's activity produced was the Wholesome Meat Act, which brings small, intrastate meat-packing plants under federal interstate jurisdiction.

One campaign leads to another. Many doctors who wrote Nader about meat urged him to investigate the steadily rising fat content of the venerable hot dog, which they said was contributing to heart disease. Nader found that average frank fat had increased in 15 years from 17% to 33% of the total content. The "fatfurter" campaign was on, and he now emphasizes it frequently in his speeches. Nader cultivates mutually helpful friendships among Congressmen, offering to let them take credit for his digging and even drafting legislative proposals for them. His chief contacts in the Senate are Magnuson, Moss, Teddy Kennedy, Wisconsin's Gaylord Nelson and William Proxmire, Texas' Ralph Yarborough, Connecticut's Abraham Ribicoff and Indiana's Vance Hartke.

As a result of Nader's indictments, the Government is making many changes. "When Nader issued his report on the Federal Trade Commission, my first feeling was irritation," says an FTC commission, May Gardiner Jones. "But I feel now that the commission has pulled itself together more, and faster, than if it had not come out." Though the FTC still has a long way to go, it has lately begun to take more vigorous actions. Sample: after nearly a decade of indecision, the commission in August ordered gasoline stations and food stores that use giveaway games for promotion to inform customers as to just how infinitesimal are their chances of winning.

Though Nader has rarely done his fighting in the courtroom, he has exerted a profound influence on the law. Before his auto-safety crusade, accident injuries were blamed on faulty drivers — not faulty cars. In order to collect damages, an accident victim was usually required to prove negligence on the part of a manufacturer. But Nader contended that automakers should build "crashworthy" cars that would not cause bodily injury in a "second collision" after the accident itself. The second-collision concept is now recognized by many courts. A 22-year-old Pennsylvania college student, who suffered permanent injury when the roof of a car buckled in an accident, recently won the right to use the "second-collision" principle in a damage suit against General Motors. U.S. District Judge John A. Fullam ruled that the roof should have been built to withstand the car's roll-over and that automakers are required "to provide more than merely a movable platform capable of transporting passengers from one point to another." Since the second-collision principle could be applicable to other products as well, manufacturers may become more safety-conscious and design their products to avoid injury in case of mishap.

The New Citizenship

The entire legal profession must be reformed. Nader maintains, if society is to alleviate its ailments. "The best lawyers should be spending their time on the great problems — on water and air pollution, on racial justice, on poverty and juvenile delinquency, on the joke that ordinary rights have become," he says. "But they are not. They are spending their time defending Geritol, Rice Krispies and the oil-import quota."

That is changing, in no small part because of Nader. Of the 39 *Harvard Law Review* editors who will be graduated next June, not one intends to join a high-paying Wall Street law firm. Instead, most plan to enter neighborhood agencies or government service — and represent the individual against the institutions. Nader believes that the rise of the youthful protester, which began in the '60s, will accelerate into the '70s. "You watch," he predicts. "General Motors will be picketed by young activists against air pollution."

Student demonstrators, he believes, will increasingly choose to become student investigators. Many of them will move to Washington and, like Nader, spend their early careers prowling among the Government filing cabinets, searching for examples of abuse and seeking means of reform in the existing system. "This is a new form of citizenship," Nader says. At heart, he is teaching the oldest form of citizenship: that one man, simply by determined complaining, can still accomplish a great deal in a free society.

APPENDIX
The Lonely Hero: Never Kowtow

His suits are shiny, his shoe heels generally worn. The nation's No. 1 consumer guardian is a conspicuous nonconsumer. Ralph Nader does not care much about goods or appearances, and his income rules out luxury. He earns nothing from most of his work and supports himself by writing magazine articles and making public speeches for fees of $50 to $2,500. He refuses to divulge how much he earns, lest corporations find out how many investigators, if any, he can afford to hire. He turns down occasional six-figure offers from law firms and regularly shuns pleas for product endorsements. Partly because he knows that his personal purchases might be interpreted as a stamp of approval, Nader owns no major appliances, no television set, no car. Yet he refuses to acknowledge sacrifice or unusual achievement. At a recent award ceremony in his honor, Nader gently scolded sponsors in his speech: "I should not be given an award for doing what I should be doing."

Like a man possessed, Nader has forsworn any semblance of a normal life. His workdays last 16 to 20 hours, often seven days a week. He has no secretaries, no ghostwriters, no personal aides other than his summer volunteers. Nader operates from two little-known Washington addresses and two unlisted telephones — one in the hallway outside the $80-a-month furnished room that has been his home for the past five years, the other in his one-room office in the National Press Building. He rarely answers knocks on the door and sometimes lets the telephone ring; the surest way to reach him is to send a telegram.

Nader's feeling for duty and constant study grew out of his family upbringing in Winsted, Conn., a gracious town of 8,000. His mother Rose used to ask friends all about films showing at the local movie house and would send her four children only to the few that had useful messages. Nightly dinner was more a course in forensics than food: it often lasted four or five hours, and everyone was expected to contribute his opinions to the topic of the evening. Nadra Nader, now 77, a Lebanese immigrant who built up a moderately prosperous restaurant business, presided over these Kennedy-like sessions, and he urged the children to stand up for their rights. "Never kowtow," he taught — and they learned the lesson.

As student at Princeton, Ralph settled into his lone, irregular life-style. Always a late-night worker, he was given a key to Woodrow Wilson Hall so that he could study after hours. He righteously refused to lend that key to envious friends who wished to visit the dark, vacant study hall with their dates. On weekends, Nader hitchhiked out of town — just to see the U.S. — and learned, among many other things, that trucks were not built the way he and truck drivers thought they should be. For instance, a coat hanger in some truck cabs could puncture a driver's skull in case of an accident. He graduated *magana cum laude* and won a Phi Beta Kappa key.

Later, at Harvard Law School, Nader was passed over for the staff of the prestigious *Law Review*, but became editor of the school's issue-oriented newspaper. One of his articles was "American Cars: Designed for Death." After graduation, he pursued his growing interest in highway safety while working as an aide to Daniel Patrick Moynihan, then an Assistant Secretary of Labor, and he later expanded his law-school article into *Unsafe at Any Speed*. The book, published in 1965, was dedicated to a friend who had been crippled in an auto accident. It is a shocking indictment of the auto industry, engineering groups, governmental agencies and traffic-safety organizations for failing to make automobiles more "crash-worthy." Written by an unknown 31-year-old, the book did not make much of an impression at first. But G.M.'s investigation into Nader's life — and the public apology to him by the president of the company — made Nader famous overnight.

A lanky six-footer who is constantly behind schedule and late for appointments, Nader can be painfully shy among strangers. When asked to give his name in hotels and on planes, he often tries to avoid recognition and replies, "Nader, initial R." He even keeps his birthday secret lest admirers send him cakes or other gifts. His driving intensity about work can sometimes trap him into hasty accusations. When economists in the Johnson Administration once met with auto industry leaders in an effort to win voluntary price restraint, Nader was too quick to accuse the Administration of "acquiescing" to Detroit. In fact, L.B.J.'s emissaries had stood their ground.

Intimates relish his flashes of dinnertable wit, which are nearly always aimed at one of the establishments he is bucking. "The people at regulatory agencies are utterly confounded when we come to investigate them," he says. "They have forgotten what citizens look like." On rare evenings out at a party, he usually leaves early to get in a couple more hours of reading, writing or phoning at his office. Though Bachelor Nader has no antipathy to girls, he rarely has the time or inclination for dates. Says his father: "We're very proud of Ralph. But we wish he would get married soon."

CAPITALISM LIVES —
EVEN IN NADERLAND *

MARYLIN BENDER

* Marylin Bender, "Capitalism Lives — Even in Naderland," *New York Times* (Sunday, January 7, 1973), pp. 50,63. Reproduced by permission.

A row of neckties in blinding prints is strung against a wall in the modest offices of The Center for Study of Responsive Law in Washington, D.C., which is more or less the headquarters for the elusively ubiquitous Ralph Nader. What do they signify in the cause of consumerism, a visitor wonders.

Only that capitalism lives in Naderland, a staffer replies with a knowing smile. Mr. Nader has been attacked from left to right and some conservatives fear that he is out to destroy the capitalist system and substitute Socialism, Communism or some other dread collectivism. In fact, Mr. Nader is a reformer who merely warns in dire tones that if the system is not made responsive to citizen interests, it will be replaced.

Those neckties are made by a center volunteer who asked for display space for her wares in the think tank of one of the nation's drabbest dressers. The center is the tax-exempt foundation from which Mr. Nader's so-called Raiders, that eager army of young lawyers and researchers, have produced some two dozen reports documenting wrongs from the pollution of streams to the segregation of the aged in nursing homes.

The book-length reports represent copious research, sometimes flawed in fact, but always packaged in language that catches newspaper headlines. Few in the age of mass communication have used the medium of the press and legislator-intermediaries more skillfully than the 38-year-old lawyer with the mumbled diction and rambling prose.

In the months to come, Mr. Nader and Naderism will move increasingly from rhetoric to action, from study to litigation and legislation. The flashier topics affecting consumer safety and pocketbooks, like unsafe automobiles and poor-quality meat, will not be discarded but emphasis will go to the knottier questions of constitutional and corporate law that could seriously alter corporate activities and relations with stockholders, the Government and the public.

His optimistic concept of an aroused citizenry will spread to the grass roots. He will be "distributing the movement around the center," he said during an interview held on a plane and in a taxi. Like the Kennedys, Mr. Nader has not attained pop celebrity status by fawning over reporters. He keeps them on the run, often leaving them to pick up the tab for cab fares and telephone calls.

Two examples of the new direction of Naderism:

Consumers Union has opened a public-interest law firm in Washington, inspired by Ralph Nader, a member of the Consumer Union board, and headed by Peter Schuck, a Nader alumnus.

It has already intervened in proceedings before the Federal Power Commission on natural gas prices, has filed suit against the Food and Drug Administration on toy-safety regulations and plans to monitor the operations of the Price Commission.

Student-run law firms, known as Public Interest Research Groups and financed by $3 membership fees, are operating in 14 states with a total budget of more than $1-million. They employ recently graduated lawyers, accountants and economists to litigate regional consumer and environmental issues.

Peering down the road of the next 12 months, Mr. Nader ticked off "unfinished business." First, there is the massive study of Congress, financed out of his own earnings. So far, profiles of Senate and House members have been published.

Nader forces will have "another round" of trying to extract a Consumer Protection Agency from the 93d Congress. A bill setting up such an independent agency died during the last session, though a Product Safety Commission was created. Like the National Highway Safety Bureau and other agencies Mr. Nader sired, it can expect to be kept on its toes by watchful Naderites.

The most ambitious charge up the Hill will be the introduction of a bill for the federal chartering of corporations. The opening gun of that campaign, which will probably be protacted and bloody inasmuch as it strikes at the vital aspects of corporate America, will be sounded next month with typical Nader strategy, the publication of a book.

"Corporate Power in America" states his case for federal chartering, which he regards as the only efficient way to control large national and multinational corporations.

The legalistic emphasis does not mean that the stream of reports will dry up. Scheduled for publication in 1973 are reports on: the Communications Satellite Corporation; the National Institute of Mental Health; Think Tanks; the American Automobile Association; Veterans Affairs; Brown Lung Disease; Pollution in Maine; Food Marketing to Children (in which the connection between advertising and nutritive content is analyzed), and Monopoly Makers (a study of regulated industries and regulatory agencies).

The report on the First National City Bank, issued in draft form in 1971, will be updated and published with a separate section analyzing its trust department (to what extent funds are commingled and lesser investors sacrificed to the performance of wealthier accounts).

The Citibank report prompted Chairman Walter Wriston to compare Nader with a fried-chicken franchiser. Mr. Wriston was casting aspersions on the supervision Mr. Nader gives to the work of his disciples, to which his major-domo, Theodore Jacobs, countered, "Ralph has more personal oversight than [Mr.] Wriston does."

In the seven years since Mr. Nader burst into public view, a diffident young lawyer and journalist being apologized to before a Senate subcommittee by the chairman of General Motors, he has ranged far beyond the automobile and the highway. He has become a generic synonym for consumer. No industry or institution seems to escape his scrutiny or his righteous indignation, including Congress, some of whose members believe he has bitten the hands that fed his acceptance.

The most orchestrated criticism against him is that he is spreading himself too thin, building an unwieldy organization that he cannot supervise and that is not subject to the kind of checks he demands of business and Government agencies.

Response to the criticism depends partly on how much of Naderism should properly be charged to Ralph Nader and how much of his power is exerted through tenuous lines of influence rather than formal control.

At present, the Nader organization consists of no more than 50 people. "We try to keep the organization small," said Mr. Jacobs, director of the Center for Study of Responsive Law and the only one who consistently knows Mr. Nader's whereabouts. "We've resisted efforts to open branch offices in Los Angeles and New York. We don't want a large franchise operation. The future of the consumer movement must not depend on Ralph doing it."

Mr. Jacobs runs the research hub of Naderism on a budget of $300,000 a year. It is financed mostly by grants from foundations — such as the Stern Fund, the Field Foundation and the Midas-International Foundation of Midas Muffler origin, which has been the most magnanimous angel — individual contributions and royalties from the Nadar Task Force Reports which, disappointingly, have yielded no more than $30,000 a year.

The center holds a copyright on the reports — the researchers and writers receive only their center salaries — that are published mostly by Grossman Publishers and Bantam Books.

Mr. Nader is a trustee of the center but draws no salary or expenses from it or from any of the units in his organization. A meager consumer, he lives abstemiously on the income from his speeches and writings — (speech fees range from zero to $3,000).

He has dipped into his personal income and much of the $425,000 settlement of his suit against G.M. for invasion of privacy to finance the Congress project and three other groups.

He supports a public-interest law firm, the Washington Public Interest Research Group, which has spawned independent, publicly funded groups in a dozen states as well as the student-run public-interest research groups.

The starting salary for Nader lawyers has been raised to $5,000 from $4,500 with step-ups soon bringing them to the $8,000-$12,000 level. No one in Mr. Nader's organization has yet crossed the $20,000 divide.

Mr. Nader also finances the Corporate Accountability Research Group, directed with a $60,000 budget by Mark Green, who wrote the Nader study on antitrust enforcement. This group is the center of the Federal chartering campaign, as well as of the Clearinghouse for Professional Responsibility to which employes are encouraged to report bad practices by their corporations or Government agencies. In the Nader world it is called "Whistle Blowing." Others term it snitching on the boss.

The $30,000 budget of the Aviation Consumer Action Project has been provided mostly by Mr. Nader. But increasingly, it is hoped, contributions will help. This group champions the cause of the air passenger and goads the Civil Aeronautics Board and the Federal Aviation Agency.

Mr. Nader's pocket is not bottomless. Last year, he formed Public Citizen, Inc., to raise funds for his citizen advocates on a broad base. More than $1-million in contributions (average $15) was received in response to three mailings and paid advertisements in 13 publications. Out of that, and with minimal, Nader-style administrative and fund-raising costs, nearly $800,000 was left to support new groups devoted to tax reform, health research, small claims courts, retired professionals, public citizen litigation and state citizen action groups.

Renewals have been running up to expectations — about 50 per cent — and a wider appeal will be conducted soon.

An independent affiliate is the Center for Auto Safety, started by Mr. Nader in 1968 and now run by Lowell Dodge, a 32-year old lawyer, with the help of Consumers Union and royalties from "What to Do With Your Bad Car: An Action Manual for Lemon Owners." Its offshoots, Professionals for Auto Safety and the Center for Concerned Engineering, are staffed by volunteers.

Among groups that are simply encouraged by Mr. Nader or run by alumni of his organization are: Fishermen's Clean Water Action Project; Scientists in the Public Interest; Consumer Action for Improved Foods, and the Center for Law and Social Policy, a public-interest law firm. On the international side, he has given advice and addressed consumer groups in Britain, Japan and Australia.

The Project on Corporate Resplnsibility, which ran two proxy battles knows as Campaign G.M., is generally assumed to be affiliated with Mr. Nader, although it is not. The only link is the blessing he conferred on Campaign G.M. Round I by announcing it at a news conference in 1970.

The project will also enlarge its activities against corporate targets with litigation and research as well as proxy fights.

PHILIP KOTLER

* Philip Kotler, "What Consumerism Means for
Marketers," *Harvard Business Review* (May-June, 1972),
pp. 48-57. Reproduced by permission.

In this century, the U.S. business scene has been shaken by three
distinct consumer movements — in the early 1900's, the mid-1930's,
and the mid-1960's. The first two flare-ups subsided. Business
observers, social critics, and marketing leaders are divided over
whether this latest outbreak is a temporary or a permanent social
phenomenon. Those who think that the current movement has the
quality of a fad point to the two earlier ones. By the same token,
they argue that this too will fade away. Others argue just as strongly
that the issues which flamed the latest movement differ so much in
character and force that consumerism may be here to stay.

In retrospect, it is interesting that the first consumer movement
was fueled by such factors as rising prices, Upton Sinclair's writings,
and ethical drug scandals. It culminated in the passage of the Pure
Food and Drug Act (1906), the Meat Inspection Act (1906), and the
creation of the Federal Trade Commission (1914). The second wave
of consumerism in the mid-1930's was fanned by such factors as an
upturn in consumer prices in the midst of the depression, the
sulfanilamide scandal, and the widely imitated Detroit housewives
strike. It culminated in the strengthening of the Pure Food and Drug
Act and in the enlarging of the Federal Trade Commissions's power
to regulate against unfair or deceptive acts and practices.

The third and current movement has resulted from a complex
combination of circumstances, not the least of which was
increasingly strained relations between standard business practices
and long-run consumer interests. Consumerism in its present form
has also been variously blamed on Ralph Nader, the thalidomide
scandal, rising prices, the mass media, a few dissatisfied individuals,
and on President Lyndon Johnson's "Consumer Interests Message."
These and other possible explanations imply that the latest
movement did not have to happen and that it had little relationship
to the real feelings of most consumers.

In this article, I shall discuss the current phenomenon and what it
protends for business. In so doing, I shall present five simple
conclusions about consumerism and largely focus my discussion on
these assessments. Consider:

1. *Consumerism was inevitable.* It was not a plot by Ralph Nader

and a handful of consumerists but an inevitable phase in the development of our economic system.

2. *Consumerism will be enduring.* Just as the labor movement started as a protest uprising and became institutionalized in the form of unions, government boards, and labor legislation, the consumer movement, too, will become an increasingly institutionalized force in U.S. society.

3. *Consumerism will be beneficial.* On the whole, it promises to make the U.S. economic system more responsive to new and emerging societal needs.

4. *Consumerism is promarketing.* The consumer movement suggests an important refinement in the marketing concept to take into account societal concerns.

5. *Consumerism can be profitable.* The societal marketing concept suggests areas of new opportunity and profit for alert business firms.

These assessments of consumerism are generally at variance with the views of many businessmen. Some business spokesmen maintain that consumerism was stirred up by radicals, headline grabbers, and politicians; that it can be beaten by attacking, discrediting, or ignoring it; that it threatens to destroy the vitality of our economic system and its benefits; that it is an anti-marketing concept; and that it can only reduce profit opportunities in the long run.

What is consumerism?

Before discussing the foregoing conclusions in more depth, it is important to know what we mean by "consumerism." Here is a definition:

Consumerism is a social movement seeking to augment the rights and power of buyers in relation to sellers.

To understand this definition, let us first look at a short list of the many traditional rights of sellers in the U.S. economic system:

Sellers have the right to introduce any product in any size and style they wish into the marketplace so long as it is not hazardous to personal health or safety; or, if it is, to introduce it with the proper warnings and controls.

Sellers have the right to price the product at any level they wish provided there is no discrimination among similar classes of buyers.

Sellers have the right to spend any amount of money they wish to promote the product, so long as it is not defined as unfair competition.

Sellers have the right to formulate any message they wish about the product provided that it is not misleading or dishonest in content or execution.

Sellers have the right to introduce any buying incentive schemes they wish.

Subject to a few limitations, these are among the essential core rights of businessmen in the United States. Any radical change in these would make U.S. business a different kind of game.

Now what about the traditional *buyers' rights?* Here, once again, are some of the rights that come immediately to mind:

Buyers have the right not to buy a product that is offered to them.

Buyers have the right to expect the product to be safe.

Buyers have the right to expect the product to turn out to be essentially as represented by the seller.

In looking over these traditional sellers' and buyers' rights, I believe that the balance of power lies with the seller. The notion that the buyer has all the power he needs *because he can refuse to buy* the product is not deemed adequate by consumer advocates. They hold that consumer sovereignty is not enough when the consumer does not have full information and when he is persuasively influenced by Madison Avenue.

What additional rights do consumers want? Behind the many issues stirred up by consumer advocates is a drive for several additional rights. In the order of their serious challenge to sellers' rights, they are:

Buyers want the right to have adequate information about the product.

Buyers want the right to additional protections against questionable products and marketing practices.

Buyers want the right to influence products and marketing practices in directions that will increase the "quality of life."

Consumer proposals

The "right to be informed," proposed by President Kennedy in his March 1962 directive to the Consumer Advisory Council, has been the battleground for a great number of consumer issues. These include, for example, the right to know the true interest cost of a loan (truth-in-lending), the true cost per standard unit of competing brands (unit pricing), the basic ingredients in a product (ingredient labeling), the nutritional quality of foods (nutritional labeling), the freshness of products (open dating), and the prices of gasoline (sign posting rather than pump posting).

Many of these proposals have gained widespread endorsement not only from consumers but also from political leaders and some businessmen. It is hard to deny the desirability of adequate information for making a free market operate vitally and competitively in the interests of consumers.

The proposals related to additional *consumer protection* are several, including the strengthening of consumers' hands in cases of business fraud, requiring of more safety to be designed into automobiles, issuing of greater powers to existing government agencies, and setting up of new agencies.

The argument underlying consumer protection proposals is that consumers do not necessarily have the time and/or skills to obtain, understand, and use all the information that they may get about a product; therefore, some impartial agencies must be established which can perform these tasks with the requisite economies of scale.

The proposals relating to *quality-of-life* considerations include regulating the ingredients that go into certain products (detergents, gasoline) and packaging (soft drink containers), reducing the level of advertising and promotional "noise," and creating consumer representation on company boards to introduce consumer welfare considerations in business decision making.

The argument in this area says that products, packaging, and marketing practices must not only pass the test of being profitable to the company and convenient to the consumer but most also be life-enhancing. Consumerists insist that the world's resources no longer permit their indiscriminate embodiment in any products desired by consumers without further consideration of their social values. This "right" is obviously the most radical of the three additional rights that consumers want, and the one which would constitute the most basic challenge to the sellers' traditional rights.

Consumerism was inevitable

Let us now consider in greater depth the first of the five conclusions I cited at the outset of this article — namely, that consumerism was inevitable. Consumerism did not necessarily have to happen in the 1960's, but it had to happen eventually in view of new conditions in the U.S. economy that warranted a fresh examination of the economic power of sellers in relation to buyers.

At the same time, there are very good reasons why consumerism did flare up in the mid-1960's. The phenomenon was not due to any single cause. Consumerism was reborn because all of the conditions that normally combine to produce a successful social movement were present. These conditions are structural conduciveness, structural strain, growth of a generalized belief, precipitating factors, mobilization for action, and social control.[1] Using these six conditions, I have listed in *Exhibit I* the major factors under each that contributed to the rise of consumerism.

Structural conduciveness refers to basic developments in the society that eventually create potent contradictions. In the latest consumer movement, three developments are particularly noteworthy.

First, U.S. incomes and educational levels advanced continuously. This portended that many citizens would eventually become concerned with the quality of their lives, not just their material well-being.

Second, U.S. technology and marketing were becoming increasingly complex. That this would create potent consumer problems was noted perceptively by E.B. Weiss: "Technology has brought unparalleled abundance and opportunity to the consumer. It has also exposed him to new complexities and hazards. It has made his choices more difficult. He cannot be chemist, mechanic, electrician, nutritionist, *and* a walking computer (very necessary when shopping for fractionated-ounce food packages)! Faced with almost infinite product differentiation (plus contrived product virtues that are purely semantic), considerable price differentiation, the added complexities of trading stamps, the subtleties of cents-off deals, and other complications, the shopper is expected to choose wisely under circumstances that baffle professional buyers."[2]

Third, the environment was progressively exploited in the interests of abundance. Observers began to see that an abundance of cars and conveniences would produce a shortage of clean air and water. The Malthusian specter of man running out of sufficient resources to maintain himself became a growing concern.

These developments, along with some others, produced major *structural strains* in the society. The 1960's were a time of great public discontent and frustration. Economic discontent was created by steady inflation which left consumers feeling that their real incomes were deteriorating. Social discontent centered on the sorrowful conditions of the poor, the race issue, and the tremendous costs of the Vietnam war. Ecological discontent arose out of new awarenesses of the world population explosion and the pollution fallout associated with technological progress. Marketing system discontent centered on safety hazards, product breakdowns, commercial noise, and gimmickry. Political discontent reflected the widespread feelings that politicians and government institutions were not serving the people.

Discontent is not enough to bring about change. There must grow a *generalized belief* about both the main causes of the social malaise and the potent effectiveness of collective social action. Here, again, certain factors contributed importantly to the growth of a generalized belief.

First, there were the writings of social critics such as John Kenneth Galbraith, Vance Packard, and Rachel Carson, that provided a popular interpretation of the problem and of actionable solutions.

Second, there were the hearings and proposals of a handful of Congressmen such as Senator Estes Kefauver that held out some hope of legislative remedy.

Third, there were the Presidential "consumer" messages of President Kennedy in 1962 and President Johnson in 1966, which legitimated belief and interest in this area of social action.

Finally, old-line consumer testing and educational organizations continued to call public attention to the consumers' interests.

Exhibit I. Factors contributing to the rise of consumerism in the 1960's

---

1. STRUCTURAL CONDUCIVENESS
   - Advancing incomes and education
   - Advancing complexity of technology and marketing
   - Advancing exploitation of the environment

↓

```
┌─────────────────────────────────────────────────────────────┐
│ 2. STRUCTURAL STRAINS                                         │
│    • Economic discontent (inflation)                          │
│    • Social discontent (war and race)                         │
│    • Ecological discontent (pollution)                        │
│    • Marketing system discontent (shoddy products, gimmickry, │
│      dishonesty)                                              │
│    • Political discontent (unresponsive politicians and institutions) │
└─────────────────────────────────────────────────────────────┘
                              ↓
┌─────────────────────────────────────────────────────────────┐
│ 3. GROWTH OF A GENERALIZED BELIEF                             │
│    • Social critic writings (Galbraith, Packard, Carson)      │
│    • Consumer-oriented legislators (Kefauver, Douglas)        │
│    • Presidential messages                                    │
│    • Consumer organizations                                   │
└─────────────────────────────────────────────────────────────┘
                              ↓
┌─────────────────────────────────────────────────────────────┐
│ 4. PRECIPITATING FACTORS                                      │
│    • Professional agitation (Nader)                           │
│    • Spontaneous agitation (housewife picketing)              │
└─────────────────────────────────────────────────────────────┘
                              ↓
┌─────────────────────────────────────────────────────────────┐
│ 5. MOBILIZATION FOR ACTION                                    │
│    • Mass media coverage                                      │
│    • Vote-seeking politicians                                 │
│    • New consumer interest groups and organizations           │
└─────────────────────────────────────────────────────────────┘
                              ↓
┌─────────────────────────────────────────────────────────────┐
│ 6. SOCIAL CONTROL                                             │
│    • Business resistance or indifference                      │
│    • Legislative resistance or indifference                   │
└─────────────────────────────────────────────────────────────┘
```

Given the growing collective belief, consumerism only awaited some *precipitating factors* to ignite the highly combustible social material. Two sparks specifically exploded the consumer movement. The one was General Motors' unwitting creation of a hero in Ralph Nader through its attempt to investigate him; Nader's successful attack against General Motors encouraged other organizers to undertake bold acts against the business system. The other was the occurrence of widespread and spontaneous store boycotts by housewives in search of a better deal from supermarkets.

These chance combustions would have vanished without a lasting effect if additional resources were not *mobilized for action*. As it turned out, three factors fueled the consumer movement.

First, the mass media gave front-page coverage and editorial support to the activities of consumer advocates. They found the issues safe, dramatic, and newsworthy. The media's attention was further amplified through word-of-mouth processes into grass-roots expressions and feelings.

Second, a large number of politicians at the federal, state, and local levels picked up consumerism as a safe, high-potential vote-getting social issue.

Third, a number of existing and new organizations arose in defense of the consumer, including labor unions, consumer cooperatives, credit unions, product testing organizations, consumer education organizations, senior citizen groups, public interest law firms, and government agencies.

Of course, the progress and course of an incipient social movement depends on the reception it receives by those in *social control*, in this case, the industrial-political complex. A proper response by the agents of social control can drain the early movement of its force. But this did not happen. Many members of the business community attacked, resisted, or ignored the consumer advocates in a way that only strengthened the consumerist cause. Most legislative bodies were slow to respond with positive programs, thus feeding charges that the political system was unresponsive to consumer needs and that more direct action was required.

Thus all the requisite conditions were met in the 1960's. Even without some of the structural strains, the cause of consumerism would have eventually emerged because of the increasing complexity of technology and the environmental issue. And the movement has continued to this day, abetted by the unwillingness of important sections of the business and political systems to come to terms with the basic issues.

It will be enduring

As we have seen, observers are divided over whether consumerism is a temporary or a permanent social phenomenon: some people argue that the current consumer movement will pass over; others argue that it differs substantially from the two earlier movements. For example, the ecology issue is here to stay and will continue to fuel the consumer movement. The plight of the poor will continue to raise questions about whether the distribution system is performing efficiently in all sectors of the economy. There are more educated and more affluent consumers than ever before, and they are the mainstay of an effective social movement. The continuous outpouring of new products in the economy will continue to raise questions of health, safety, and planned obsolescence. Altogether, the issues that flamed the current consumer movement may be more profound and enduring than in the past.

No one can really predict how long the current consumer movement will last. There is good reason to believe, in fact, that the protest phase of the consumer movement will end soon. The real issue is not how long there will be vocal consumer protest but rather what legacy it will leave regarding the balance of buyers' rights and sellers' rights.

Each of the previous consumer movements left new institutions and laws to function in behalf of the consumer. By this test, the victory already belongs to consumers. Sellers now must operate within the new constraints of a Truth-in-Lending Law, a Truth-in-Packaging Law, an Auto Safety Law, an Office of Consumer Affairs, an Environmental Protection Agency, and a greatly strengthened Federal Trade Commission and Federal Food and Drug Administration.

It is no accident that such laws and institutions come into being when the demonstration and agitation phase of the consumer movement starts to dwindle. It is precisely the enactment of new laws and creation of new institutions that cause the protest phase to decline. Viewed over the span of a century, the consumer movement has been winning and increasing buyers' rights and power. In this sense, the consumerist movement is enduring, whether or not the visible signs of protest are found.

It can be beneficial

Businessmen take the point of view that since consumerism imposes costs on them, it will ultimately be costly to the consumer. Since they have to meet more legal requirements, they have to limit or modify some of their methods for attracting customers. This may mean that consumers will not get all the products and benefits they want and may find business costs passed on to them.

Businessmen also argue that they have the consumer's interests at heart and have been serving him well, and that customer satisfaction is the central tenet of their business philosophy. Many sincerely believe that consumerism is politically motivated and economically unsound.

The test of beneficiality, however, lies not in the short-run impact of consumerism on profits and consumer interests but rather in its long-run impact. Neither consumerism nor any social movement can get very far in the absence of combustible social material. Protest movements are messages coming from the social system that say that something is seriously wrong. They are the body politic's warning system. To ignore or attack protest signals is an invitation to deepening social strains. Protest movements are social indicators of new problems which need joint problem solving, not social rhetoric.

The essential legacy of consumerism promises to be beneficial in the long run. It forces businessmen to reexamine their social roles. It challenges them to look at problems which are easy to ignore. It makes them think more about ends as well as means. The habit of thinking about ends has been deficient in U.S. society, and protest movements such as consumerism, minority rights, student rights, and women's rights have a beneficial effect in raising questions about the purposes of institutions before it is too late.

Beyond this philosophical view of the beneficial aspects of protest movements may lie some very practical gains for consumers and businessmen. Here are four arguments advanced by consumerists:

1. Consumerism will increase the amount of product information. This will make it possible for consumers to buy more efficiently. They may obtain more value or goods with a given expenditure or a given amount of goods with a lower expenditure. To the extent that greater buying efficiency will result in surplus purchasing power, consumers may buy more goods in total.

2. Consumerism will lead to legislation that limits promotional expenditure which primarily affects market shares rather than

aggregate demand. Consumer games, trading stamps, and competitive brand advertising in demand-inelastic industries are largely seen as increasing the costs of products to consumers with little compensating benefits. Reductions in the level of these expenditures, particularly where they account for a large portion of total cost, should lead to lower consumer prices.

3. Consumerism will require manufacturers to absorb more of the social costs imposed by their manufacturing operations and product design decisions. Their higher prices will decrease the purchase of high social cost goods relative to low social cost goods. This will mean lower governmental expenditures covered by taxes to clean up the environment. Consumers will benefit from a lower tax rate and/or from a higher quality environment.

4. Consumerism will reduce the number of unsafe or unhealthy products which will result in more satisfied, healthier consumers.

These arguments are as cogent as contrary arguments advanced by some business spokemen against responding to consumerism. This is not to deny that many companies will inherit short-run costs not compensated by short-run revenues and in this sense be losers. Their opposition to consumerism is understandable. But this is not the basis for developing a sound long-run social policy.

It is promarketing

Consumerism has come as a shock to many businessmen because deep in their hearts they believe that they have been serving the consumer extraordinarily well. Do businessmen deserve the treatment that they are getting in the hands of consumerists?

It is possible that the business sector has deluded itself into thinking that it has been serving the consumer well. Although the marketing concept is the professed philosophy of a majority of U.S. companies, perhaps it is more honored in the breach than in the observance. Although top management professes the concept, the line executives, who are rewarded for ringing up sales, may not practice it faithfully.

What is the essence of the marketing concept?

The marketing concept calls for a *customer orientation* backed by *integrated marketing* aimed at generating *customer satisfaction* as the key to attaining long-run profitable volume.

The marketing concept was a great step forward in meshing the actions of business with the interests of consumers. It meant that consumer wants and needs became the starting point for product and market planning. It meant that business profits were tied to how well the company succeeded in pleasing and satisfying the customer.

Peter F. Drucker suggested that consumerism is "the shame of the total marketing concept," implying that the concept is not widely implemented.[3] But even if the marketing concept as currently understood were widely implemented, there would be a consumerist movement. Consumerism is a clarion call for a *revised marketing concept.*

The main problem that is coming to light rests on the ambiguity of the term *customer satisfaction*. Most businessmen take this to mean that *consumer desires* should be the orienting focus of product and market planning. The company should produce what the customer wants. But the problem is that in efficiently serving customers' desires, it is possible to hurt their long-run interests. Edmund Burke noted the critical difference when he said to the British electorate, "I serve your interests, not your desires." From the many kinds of products and services that satisfy consumers in the short run but disserve or dissatisfy them in the long run, here are four examples:

1. Large, expensive automobiles please their owners but increase the pollution in the air, the congestion of traffic, and the difficulty of parking, and therefore reduce the owners' long-run satisfaction.

2. The food industry in the United States is oriented toward producing new products which have high taste appeal. Nutrition has tended to be a secondary consideration. Many young people are raised on a diet largely of potato chips, hot dogs, and sweets which satisfy their tastes but harm their long-run health.

3. The packaging industry has produced many new convenience features for the American consumer such as nonreusable containers, but the same consumers ultimately pay for this convenience in the form of solid waste pollution.

4. Cigarettes and alcohol are classic products which obviously satisfy consumers but which ultimately hurt them if consumed in any excessive amount.

These examples make the point that catering to consumer satisfaction does not necessarily create satisfied consumers. Businessmen have not worried about this so long as consumers have continued to buy their products. But while consumers buy as *consumers*, they increasingly express their discontent as *voters*. They use the political system to correct the abuses that they cannot resist through the economic system.

The dilemma for the marketer, forced into the open by consumerism, is that he cannot go on giving the consumer only what pleases him without considering the effect on the consumer's and society's well-being. On the other hand, he cannot produce salutary products which the consumer will not buy. The problem is to somehow reconcile company profit, consumer desires, and consumer long-run interests. The original marketing concept has to be broadened to the societal marketing concept:

The societal marketing concept calls for a *customer orientation* backed by *integrated marketing* aimed at generating *customer satisfaction* and *long-run consumer welfare* as the key to attaining long-run profitable volume.

The addition of long-run consumer welfare asks the businessman to include social and ecological considerations in his product and market planning. He is asked to do this not only to meet his social responsibilities but also because failure to do this may hurt his long-run interests as a producer.

Thus the message of consumerism is not a setback for marketing but rather points to the next stage in the evolution of enlightened marketing. Just as the *sales concept* said that sales were all-important, and the original *marketing concept* said that consumer satisfaction was also important, the *societal marketing concept* has emerged to say that long-run consumer welfare is also important.

It can be profitable

This last assessment is the most difficult and yet the most critical of my five conclusions to prove. Obviously, if consumerism is profitable, businessmen will put aside their other objections. It is mainly because of its perceived unprofitability that many businessmen object so vehemently.

Can consumerism be profitable? Here my answer is "yes." Every social movement is a mixed bag of threats and opportunities. As John Gardner observed, "We are all continually faced with a series of great opportunities brilliantly disguised as insoluble problems." The companies that will profit from consumerism are those in the habit of turning negatives into positives. According to Peter F. Drucker:

"Consumerism actually should be, must be, and I hope will be, the opportunity of marketing. This is what we in marketing have been waiting for."[4]

The alert company will see consumerism as a new basis for achieving a differential competitive advantage in the marketplace. A concern for consumer well-being can be turned into a profitable opportunity in at least two ways: through the introduction of needed new products and through the adoption of a companywide consumerist orientation.

New opportunities

One of the main effects of consumerism is to raise concerns about the health, safety, and social worthiness of many products. For a long time, *salutary criteria* have been secondary to *immediate satisfaction criteria* in the selection of products and brands. Thus when Ford tried to sell safety as an automobile attribute in the 1950's, buyers did not respond. Most manufacturers took the position that they could not educate the public to want salutary features but if the public showed this concern, then business would respond.

Unfortunately, the time came but business was slow to respond. Consumer needs and wants have been evolving toward safety, health, and self-actualization concerns without many businessmen noticing this. More and more people are concerned with the nutritiousness of their foods, the flammability of their fabrics, the safety of their automobiles, and the pollution quality of their detergents. Many manufacturers have missed this changing psychological orientation of consumers.

Product reformulations

Today, there are a great many opportunities for creating and marketing new products that meet consumer desires for both short-term satisfaction and long-term benefits.

Exhibit II suggests a paradigm for thinking about the major types of new product opportunities. All current products can be classified in one of four ways using the dimensions of immediate satisfaction and long-run consumer interests. As this exhibit shows, *desirable products* are those which combine high immediate satisfaction and high long-run benefit, such as tasty, nutritious breakfast foods. *Pleasing products* are those which give high immediate satisfaction but which may hurt consumer interests in the long run, such as cigarettes. *Salutary products* are those which have low appeal but which are also highly beneficial to the consumer in the long run, such as low phosphate detergents. Finally, *deficient products* are those which have neither immediate appeal nor salutary qualities, such as a bad tasting patent medicine.

The manufacturer might as well forget about deficient products because too much work would be required to build in pleasing and salutary qualities. On the other hand, the manufacturer should invest his greatest effort in developing desirable products — e.g., new foods, textiles, appliances, and building materials — which combine intrinsic appeal and long-run beneficiality. The other two categories, pleasing and salutary products, also present a considerable challenge and opportunity to the company.

EXHIBIT II

Classification of new product opportunities

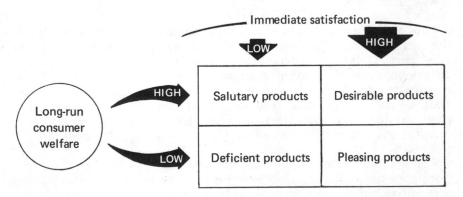

The challenge posed by pleasing products is that they sell extremely well but they ultimately hurt the consumer's interests. The product opportunity is therefore to formulate some alteration of the product that adds salutary qualities without diminishing any or too many of the pleasing qualities. This type of product opportunity has already been seized by a number of companies:

• Sears has developed and promoted a phosphate-free laundry detergent which has become a big selling brand.

• Pepsi-Cola has developed a one-way plastic soft drink bottle that is degradable in solid waste treatment.

• Various automobile manufacturers are redesigning their engines to reduce their polluting levels without reducing their efficiency.

• Various tobacco firms are researching the use of lettuce leaf to eliminate the health hazards of tobacco leaf in cigarettes.

Not all of these product reformulations will be successful. The new product must incorporate the salutary qualities without sacrificing the pleasing qualities. Thus new low-phosphate detergents must continue to wash effectively, or almost as effectively, as the former high-phosphate detergents. New low-lead or no-lead gasolines must continue to give efficient mileage and performance.

In addition, the company must be skilled at marketing the new products. The company faces difficult questions of what price to set, what claims to make, and what to do with the former product. In the case of low-lead gasoline, initial sales have been disappointing because of several factors, not the least of which is that it was priced at a premium and discouraged all but the most devoted environmentalists from buying it. The environmental appeal is strong, provided that the new product performs about as well as the old product and is not priced higher.

Salutary products, such as noninflammable draperies and many health foods, are considered "good for the customer" but somehow lack pleasing qualitites. The challenge to the marketer is to incorporate satisfying qualities in the product without sacrificing the salutary qualities. Here are examples:

• Quaker Oats has been reviewing desirable nutrients and vitamins, and formulating new breakfast cereals around them.

• Some food manufacturers have created new soybean-based products, in each case adding pleasing flavors that appeal to the intended target groups.

• Fabric manufacturers are trying to create attractive draperies out of new synthetic noninflammable materials.

Thus new product opportunities may be found by starting with appealing products and trying to add salutary qualities, or starting with salutary products and trying to add appealing qualities. This will become more important as more people show a concern for their environment and demand desirable products. There is already a sizable market segment made up of environmentalists who are ready to buy any product that has a salutary stamp. The alert company can even specialize in this market by committing itself to creating and assorting products of high environmental appeal.

Consumerist orientation

A second way to respond profitably to consumerism is to become one of a growing number of companies that adopt and implement a thoroughgoing concern-for-the-consumer attitude. This goes beyond the occasional introduction of a few new products that combine pleasing and salutary qualities. It goes beyond an enlarged public relations campaign to appear as a "we care" company. To be effective, it involves management commitment, employee education, social actions, and company investment. A few companies have moved into a total consumerist orientation and have earned high consumer regard in the process. Here are two illustrative examples:

• Giant Food, Inc., a leading supermarket chain in the Washington D.C. area, actively introduced unit pricing, open dating, and nutritional labeling. According to a spokesman for the company, "These actions have improved Giant's goodwill immeasurably and have earned the admiration of leaders of the consumer movement."

• Whirlpool Corporation has adopted a large number of measures to improve customer information and services, including a toll-free complaint service and improved product warranties. According to Stephen E. Upton, Whirlpool Vice President, "Our rate of increase in sales has tripled that of the industry. Our interest in the consumer has to be one of the reasons."

Obviously, such companies believe that these measures will increase their consumer goodwill and lead in turn to increased profits. The companies in each industry that adopt a consumerist orientation are likely to earn the early advantage and reap the rewards. If the profits are forthcoming, others will rush in and imitate the innovators. But imitation is often not as effective as innovation. Consumerism may well turn out to be an opportunity for the leaders and a cost for the laggards.

Conclusion

Consumerism was born for the third time in this century in the middle 1960's as a result of a complex combination of circumstances, not the least of which was increasingly strained relations between current business practices and long-run consumer interests. To many businessmen, it came as a shock because they thought the economic machinery, creating the highest standard of living in the world, was beyond consumer complaint. But the movement was inevitable, partly because of the success of the economic machinery in creating complex, convenient, and pleasing products.

My assessment is that consumerism will be enduring, beneficial, promarketing, and ultimately profitable. Consumerism mobilizes the energies of consumers, businessmen, and government leaders to seek solutions to several complex problems in a technologically advanced society. One of these is the difference between serving consumer desires efficiently and serving their long-run interests.

To marketers, it says that products and marketing practices must be found which combine short-run and long-run values for the consumer. It says that a societal marketing concept is an advance over the original marketing concept and a basis for earning increased consumer goodwill and profits. The enlightened marketer attempts to satisfy the consumer *and* enhance his total well-being on the theory that what is good in the long run for consumers is good for business.

As some day it may happen that a victim must be found,
I've got a little list — I've got a little list,
Of society offenders who might well be underground,
And who never would be missed — who never would be missed.

William Schwenck Gilbert, 1836-1911
The Mikado, Act I

FOOTNOTES

1. These conditions were proposed in Neil J. Smelser, *Theory of Collective Behavior* (New York, The Free Press, 1963).

2. "Marketers Fiddle While Consumers Burn," HBR July-August 1968, p. 48.

3. "The Shame of Marketing," *Marketing/Communications*, August 1969, p. 60.

4. Ibid., p. 64.

PART III

POSITION OF THE CONSUMER ON THE MARKET PLACE

Having looked at the historical origins of consumerism, and having analyzed what Kotler calls the "third round" of the movement, we are now ready to examine the position of the consumer on the market place.

A debate for a long time has taken place among economists and others as to what influence the consumer really has in a "free, competitive, capitalistic" enterprise system. Some economists have ascribed a very important place to the consumer: The consumer is visualized as being a king; indeed, dictator would be a better word in this day of constitutional monarchies. He[1] is considered as being at the apex of the market system. He calls forth supplies of goods when he wants to do so, and inhibits the production of others that he does not want by the means of his dollar votes, his expenditures on the market. He is the king whom all enterprisers must please, be they manufacturers, renderers of services, or middlemen. His role is thought to be highly creative: If he wants a product, say a satisfactory electric automobile, his wants will be catered to by the auto manufacturers. Attracted by the possibility of good profits, electric cars will be put on the market.

Other thinkers view the consumer not so much as a dictator as a supreme court. They say that enterprisers are never very certain of the shape of consumers wants. They try out numerous kinds and variations of products. From this plethora the consumer picks and chooses, judging the relative values, utilities, and want satisfying qualities to be obtained from the alternative offerings continually brought before him by the market. Thus, as a judge in court evaluates the merits of the cases brought before him, so the consumer acts as a court of last resort[2], putting his money behind his judgments of the worthiness of the goods and services in question. The process is democratic[3]: If sufficient dollar votes are cast for a new product, it survives and flourishes; but the item which receives insufficient votes perishes.

This is inherently a quite wasteful process. It is said that nine out of ten consumer products introduced to the market fail to make it. But defenders of the system point out that this waste of capital, materials and manpower is fully justified, for it is the price we collectively pay to assure that we shall have an innovative, dynamic, freely working economic system.

Finally, another group of observers say that the system is not as free as it looks and that the consumer is no king. For they charge that producers and distributers of products have powers, well used[4], to influence the wants and shape the demand patterns of the consumers. They heavily influence the buyers through advertising and promotion to want particular products which *they* choose to put out, and these are often shoddy, inferior and of poor value for the money. Due to monopolistic influences on the market, moreover, goods in certain fields tend to become quite uniform and undifferentiated. The choice is really between Boggs soap and Moggs soap with little discernable difference in price, quality, shape or functions between the two brands.

Eugene Beem examines the role of the consumer in the more conventional terms. He clearly attributes a most important influence to the consumers. Graham Bannock, on the other hand, presents a more critical analysis: He examines in depth oligopolistic influences on our modern markets and comes to some disturbing conclusions as to the influence of the consumers over what is produced and marketed.

Then, Dr. Beem analyses the plight of the consumer and the reasons for the predicament described. He shows how little consumers really know about the products they buy, and analyzes the consequences of this situation to social welfare.

Next, two large minority markets are examined, the black and the latino. Harold Ashby goes beyond the consumerism question, and analyzes the black consumer from the standpoint of his psychology, and how to appeal to blacks through advertising. His article, with its fresh viewpoints, has been printed in its entirety. The editor provides a short look at the interesting Latin market, which has many unique characteristics.

We end the section with two sharply contrasting articles — one by Cameron, representative of many which seek to prove that "the poor pay more", the other by Goodman which shows this is not necessarily so in all ghetto areas. Why were Goodman's people better off, obviously, than those described by Cameron? Does the difference yield a clue to what the social planner might do to improve the ghetto situation? We leave the answer to the reader.

FOOTNOTES

1. Hereafter the consumer will be referred to as "he" so as to eliminate the awkward and boring term, "he or she". The reader should realize that the consumer might be of either sex.

2. There is no appeal to a higher court. Once the consumers turn your product down, you have "had it".

3. Of course, in a true democracy, each voter has but one vote. On the market, differences in wealth and income amongst buyers means that some consumers have many votes, others few.

4. About 22 billion dollars were spent for advertising in 1972; Probably four times this amount was spent for personal selling functions in the United States that year.

EUGENE BEEM

Fundamental Decisions of an Economic System

In all economies there are a multitude of consumer wants ranging from food, clothing and shelter, to the wants found in commercially advanced nations for such things as television sets, air conditioning and maid service. At the same time, there are resistances to the satisfaction of these wants because of the limited quantities and qualities of available productive resources.

It is necessary in any type of economy for decisions to be made with respect to which of the many wants will be satisfied, who will produce the desired goods, whose wants will be satisfied, and how the scarce resources will be harnessed to accomplish this production. The complexity of this undertaking is enormous. Literally billions of decisions must be coordinated continuously regarding production in the varying stages of a countless number of complex goods. A smoothly functioning economic system is the solution to a supendous and dynamic jig-saw puzzle. Ideally, millions of interlocking parts fit together so that at any given time the right amount and quality of each type of productive resource is at the point where it is needed in the production process. The typical automobile, for example, has about ten thousand parts which are brought together along an assembly line. With perfect coordination the correct quantities of tires, glass, ignition parts, headlights, radios, horns, and other parts flow in from the outside at the necessary speed; the right quantity and quality of labor are on hand where needed. The manufacturers of parts and the growers and extractors of raw materials perform similar problems of coordinating manpower and material flow, and the coordinating process continues as the completed goods move through the marketing channels to the final consumer.

How the Decisions are Made in Modern Capitalism

In a modern capitalistic economy, such as the United States, these fundamental decisions regarding what goods to produce, who is to produce them, who is to get them, and how to produce them are made with limited government intervention. The nature of the institutions is relied upon, for the most part, to coordinate economic decisions as the spontaneous result of economic liberty itself. The pieces of the jigsaw puzzle are expected to fall into place without central over-all guidance as the result of the totality of individual and private group decisions. The principal institutions of modern capitalism are private property, freedom of enterprise, freedom of consumers' choice, and the profit motive. The price-cost structure is the mechanism through which this quartet of institutions operates. In addition to these characteristic features, modern capitalistic economies embrace a great many facilitating institutions such as the corporation, advertising, the factory system, and markets for establishing and maintaining contacts between buyers and sellers, but these institutions evolve from those named previously.

Institutions of Modern Capitalism

Private property means the freedom to own, use, and dispose of consumer goods or producer goods rather much as one wishes, subject to certain restraints imposed for the protection of others. *Freedom of enterprise* signifies an open door for workers into any occupation which they wish to enter so long as it be lawful and a similar open door for private business firms into any field which they choose. Such a freedom by no means implies equality of opportunity. It connotes only that the gateway on the road to economic success is open in each industry. Some individuals or groups easily reach their goal through such means as superior ability, financial resources, predatory activities, fortuity or merely getting onto the road early, while others less richly endowed, or handicapped in other respects, drop by the wayside. Many times certain industrial highways are so clogged with traffic or the conditions of travel are so hazardous as to discourage entry onto the road. At times entrance to the road is not feasible for individuals as such, but necessitates their combination in corporate or union organization. Freedom of enterprise, then, does not imply equality of opportunity, nor does it require continuous entrance and exit from an industry. It may operate through groups rather than individuals. It *does* necessitate an absence of collusive or otherwise arbitrary roadblocks erected by the vested interests in an industry to choke off potential competition.[1]

Freedom of consumers' choice means that consumers may buy whatever goods are available in market places without rationing restrictions. It means also that consumers share with producers the role of co-director of economic activity. At any given time demand pressures exist among consumers for each type of goods which producers have to sell. The pressures are determined by such forces as the following: (1) preferences of consumers, (2) current and prospective consumer incomes, (3) the present and anticipated future price of the good, (4) the present and anticipated future price structure of other goods. These pressures guide producer decisions. It is fallacious, however, to conclude that the consumer is absolutely or necessarily a sovereign. Producers often influence individual preferences through a combination of control over quality and conditions of sale coupled with advertising and personal selling tactics. Producers likewise exert a partial control over cost factors, and over the quantity of merchandise offered for sale — factors which determine, in part, the level of prices. It is best to say that consumers share with producers the function of directing a modern capitalistic economy.

The textbook concept of consumer demand is in a sense misleading. It suggests producers have precise information about consumer choice for their products at various price ranges, but as a matter of fact, demand, *ex ante*, is seldom more than an informed guess. Advertising media and producers themselves frequently make surveys of buying habits which give an insight into consumer choice within narrow price ranges. The Federal Reserve System makes an annual survey of consumer buying intentions which foretells prospective demand *at existing prices.* The usefulness of such aggregate demand studies is weakened by the limitations of the sampling technique, the whimsical nature of consumer choice, and the workings of the business cycle. The most serious limitation, however, is that for most producers an estimate of total demand is not sufficient. They must discern what share of the over-all market they can capture, and this is a very difficult task, indeed. Most producers are in the position of a tennis player whose every move is conditioned by the actions of his opponent. A price drop or an advertising campaign by a competitor may throw askew the most scientifically determined market share estimate of a particular producer. It follows, therefore, that producers are guided by *their* estimates of consumer demand, which may or may not prove accurate. It is through the trial and error approach that consumer choices exercise their influence over production.

The *profit motive* as the principal motivating and coordinating force in business decisions is the very heart of capitalism. It is the prospect of profit which induces production and the prospect of loss which discourages production. The nature of the profit motive is best seen through a description of the manner in which it operates.

Coordination of the Institutions

The mechanism through which the profit motive operates is the price-cost structure of individual goods. The classical function of price is to equate demand and supply, rising to choke off purchasing and encourage selling when demand at the existing price out-strips supply being offered — falling to encourage buying and dissuade selling when supply at the existing price is greater than demand. Swelling profits in the former case lead through the profit motive to greater production. Falling profits in the latter case cause a contraction in future output. When price is not sufficiently flexible to perform its classical function, a change in profits, caused by fluctuations in sales and production and recorded through costs, performs the production-controlling function. The degree of responsiveness of price to changes in demand or supply depends largely upon the type of market involved. The greatest responsiveness is in an "automatic" market where there are so many buyers and sellers of a homogeneous product that no one buyer or seller can by his policies influence the market price. When buyers and sellers act independently, such rivalry is termed "pure" competition. It is usually accompanied by organized trading centers to bring together buyers and sellers. Price may change numerous times a day in effecting a constant equality between quantities demanded and supplied. "Automatic" markets are found in the sale of a number of raw materials — in particular, agricultural products.

Overhwelmingly more important in the U.S. economy is the "administered" market characterized by sellers acting independently or in concert who are able to control, more or less, the price at which their particular commodity will sell through control of supply.[2] Nearly all manufactured goods are sold in this type of market. Because the seller sets the price himself without the seller-buyer bargaining characteristic of automatic markets, "administered" markets seldom reflect at any given time a perfect balance between amounts demanded and amounts supplied. Sellers of manufactured products typically hold in inventory, and offer for sale at an "administered" price a stock in excess of sales at any particular time. The immediate result of changes in demand is reflected in the size of inventory — in other words, in quantity sold rather than price, whereas in an "automatic" market both price and quantity move. An unplanned rising inventory reflects falling consumer demand; an unplanned falling inventory mirrors rising consumer demand. These inventory changes *could* lead retailers to drop their price to stimulate sales in the first instance, or increase their price to absorb maximum profits in the latter case. Sometimes such price changes occur, but mark-ups in the retail trade are traditional and accordingly vary but little. The "fair-trade" laws in 45 states, and the Miller-Tydings Act, legalizing this resale price maintenance in transactions between states have furthered the tendency toward rigid retail mark-ups. The typical retailer reaction to inventory changes, either up or down, is, apparently, to pass the problem back to wholesalers, who, likewise are inclined to pass it back to the manufacturers for a solution.

Manufacturers with one eye on public good will and the other on the cash register are inclined to make the adjustment to demand shifts, in so far as is feasible, by a shift in production policies rather than by a shift in price policies. Manufacturers — particularly large ones — hesitate to raise prices *unless* they can be justified in part by wage increases or other cost increases, for such action incurs the ill will of the public. When prices are increased, they are often "inched up" at a rate which may keep them considerably below the level which would prevail if the market were of the "automatic" type. Price decreases are likewise postponed by many producers so long as it is practical to do so. Where the demand elasticity for a commodity or the cross-elasticity of demand for close substitute goods is less than one, or little more than one, as might be the case for gasoline, the policy of lowering prices encounters the danger of a price war. If the elasticity or cross-elasticity of demand is considerably greater than one, as might be the case for television sets in 1950, price deflation is more likely. Still, a price decline conveys the impression that prices may fall still lower, and for a short period, may actually cause a decrease in consumer demand. The downward inflexibility of the wage structure is another reason for maintaining price in industries which have strong labor unions and in which wage costs are a substantial fraction of total costs. Also, a fall in prices creates inventory losses at each stage of the marketing channel in which title to goods is taken. A final deterrent to price declines is the growing attitude taken and propagandized by trade associations that price cuts are not an ethical way of eliciting additional business. There are at least two more reasons that account, in part, for the tendency toward both up and down price inflexibility. First, there appears to be a feeling among producers that buyers will protest less against a stable price structure, than one which is constantly moving up and down. Second, it is expensive for a firm with a nation-wide market to make price changes, for it must distribute -new price schedules to all of its suppliers.

As a consequence of the above factors, manufacturers tend to react to demand shifts primarily through production policies — expanding output, if possible, to absorb demand increases, contracting output to absorb demand decreases. The manufacturers' prices are typically set to provide a break-even point at somewhat less than capacity output.[3] Hence, when demand permits the industry to go at full speed, the optimum utilization of the plant enables average total costs to fall and abnormal profits to be earned. Even a small drop in average total costs proves a powerful stimulant to profits if the turnover of goods increases appreciably. The effect of the abnormal profits may be to entice additional enterprises into the field or to induce some of the existing firms to expand capacity if the demand boost appears sufficiently lasting.

Manufacturers tend to meet the main effect of a demand decrease by curtailing their operations. With only a fraction of capacity in use, average fixed costs rise, pulling up average total costs, and creating losses for many firms. Even a small increase in average costs when coupled with a sharp drop in the volume of turnover, may lead to a drastic decline in profits. Firms will continue production for a while to the extent that they are able to meet their average variable costs, but if the demand shrinkage continues, depreciated equipment will not be replaced, and bankruptcies in the industry will mount.

No mention is made in the foregoing discussion of the manner in which demand pressures guide production in the service trades. Here again prices are typically "administered," and "sticky". That is to say, they fluctuate relatively little. Enterprises in the service field usually operate with a fairly rigid price at less than capacity output. A movie theater, for example, will normally have only a fraction of its total seats occupied. A sustained decrease in the demand for movie tickets in a given market will force up costs per customer, and either reduce profits or cause losses. If the decrease in demand is of long time duration, bankruptcies among some movie houses are likely, and some of the facilities may be converted to other purposes. Some facilities may be permitted to depreciate without replacement.

No claim is made that the analysis pictured above is applicable to all administered markets at all times. It is believed, however, that this behavior is *typical.* Actually there is no sharp dichotomy in the universe of markets. "Administered" markets shade off into the "semi-automatic" variety, and the latter shade off into the more of less "automatic" type. Sometimes price rigidity in "administered" markets is more apparent than real. As a substitute for outright price reduction in a declining market sellers may offer higher trade-in allowances in the case of durable items. Free merchandise or extra services may be "thrown in" to speed up sales of slow moving goods. The phenomenon of "red" markets may appear in which discounts from list prices are made to consumers willing to bargain for them, and in which more than the customary discounts are made available to marketing middlemen. When manufacturing costs rise, price may be held rigid at the expense of quality degradation. A drop in manufacturing costs may lead to improved qualtiy or the addition of "frills" to a product while the price remains relatively constant. In a market where effective demand is running ahead of effective supply less attractive conditions of sale may be offered to consumers. "Gray" markets may develop in which buyers pay more than list price to obtain prompt delivery. Manufacturers' discounts to middlemen may be cut. As a general rule, the greater the number of sellers and the more equal the size of the sellers, the more "automobile" the market will be and the more sensitive prices will be in making adjustments to demand fluctuations. The fewer the sellers and the greater the concentration of strength in an industry, the more rigid prices will probably be and the more likely that alterations in production will compensate, in the main, for shifts in demand.

The primary coordinating mechanism in a modern capitalistic economy is, then, the profit motive operating through the price-cost structure of individual goods. Profits are determined jointly by consumer and producer decisions through the interaction of price, cost, and sales volume. The prospect of abnormally high or increasing profits is usually a signal for expansion; the prospect of declining profit is usually a signal for contraction. Sometimes independent consumer decisions will be the more dynamic element governing profit prospects while at other times producer decisions will be the more active factor.[4]

Some concrete examples will show how consumer and producer decisions are constantly interacting through the profit motive to cause expansion and contraction in varying sectors of the economy. From 1929 to 1939, the production of animal fats went down 9 percent, the output of butter up 10 percent and the output of vegetable oils up 4 percent. Cotton consumption went up 5 percent, rayon-yarn deliveries up 178 percent and silk deliveries down 38 percent. Bituminous coal sales went down 27 percent while electric power went up 36 percent and fuel oils up 10 percent.[5] The profit motive likewise governs expansion and contraction within given industries. An example of this, spectacular in the $80 million dentifrice field, was the rapid growth of ammoniated tooth powders and pastes in 1949. The promise of a 40 percent reduction in tooth cavities proved such a great stimulus to consumer demand that "Amident," first into the field with this new product, jumped its sales 135-fold between November, 1948, and March, 1949. Though relatively unknown four months earlier, "Amident" ranked with the leading brands by the spring of 1949.[6] The surge of "Amident's" profits from the production of ammoniated dentifrices caused competitors to revamp their powders and pastes to include this new drug.

In the cigarette industry "Chesterfield" increased its domestic sales in 1948, 6.3 percent as compared with 1947. "Phillip Morris" jumped 17.4 percent, "Old Gold" climbed 13.8 percent and "Lucky Strikes" 2 percent. "Camel" suffered a 4 percent decline, and "Raleigh," a 25 percent drop.[7] In the automobile industry in 1936, "Chevrolet" had 27 percent of the market, "Ford," 22 percent, and "Plymouth," 10 percent. By 1948, "Chevrolet" had 20 percent of the market, "Ford," 14 percent, and Plymouth," 10 percent.[8]

In the process of co-directing the production of final goods, the consumer also influences the allocation of productive resources between and within industries. His demand for television sets, for example, gives rise to a derived demand for land, labor, and capital of varying types needed in the different stages of producing the sets. The derived demands for these agents of production arc equated in whole or in part to the supply of agents offered again through the price-cost mechanism. The consumer, as suggested in the introductory chapter, is like a Janus head; his other face is as a supplier of a productive factor. His influence as a consumer helping to guide production depends in part upon his role in the production process, and this, as indicated above, is considerably affected by aggregate consumer preferences. For example Joe Dimaggio, New York Yankee baseball star, earned a salary of $100,000 in 1949, and accordingly had 100,000 votes (minus taxes) in directing the allocation of society's resources in that year. The demand for his services was derived from the demand of consumers to watch professional baseball games. It was this demand, together with the shortage of players of comparable ability, which accounted for his high income.

The previous discussion has shown how a modern capitalistic economy solves the basic questions of what goods to produce, who is to produce the goods, and who is to get them. The fourth major decision in any type of economy, that of organizing the natural resources to produce the goods, is made in a capitalistic society by the business enterprisers or their managerial assistants. The drive for profits furnishes a powerful incentive toward maximum efficiency in this task. Per capita real income of the U.S. people has tripled from

1850 to 1950 while hours worked per week have decreased from 70 to 40, and advocates of capitalism affirm that this type of economy is responsible, at least in large part, for this happy result.

Government and the Economy

Not all of the expenditures which influence the flow of economic activity are initiated by individual consuming units. The percentage of the U.S. national income spent collectively through government agencies has increased greatly in the last twenty years primarily because of national defense needs, international responsibilities, and the expanding welfare programs of federal and state governments. Collective expenditures are not inconsistent with a basically capitalistic economy so long as they represent a minor proportion of total expenditures. Government agencies, of course, also influence the direction of economic activity by the laws they pay and enforce. While consumers have the direct power to influence private enterprise economic activity by their dollar votes, they have an *indirect* power to guide the economic policies followed by their political votes for public officials. Inasmuch as every voter is a consumer, the potential political power of consumers is greater than that of any other interest group in the economy.

Conclusion

It has been shown that the consumer possesses considerable power in the major decisions of a modern capitalistic economy. To a large extent he has the power to guide production toward his own interests by his choices in the market place. He is responsible, in part, for the allocation of resources between and within industries, and he influences to a considerable extent the determination of income shares. He possesses this power directly when he, himself, spends his income — indirectly when his elected representatives spend it for him, and when they pass and enforce legislation of an economic nature.

QUESTIONS FOR DISCUSSION

1. Under capitalism, who makes the decisions as to what and how much shall be produced? How are these decisions made under communism?

2. What postulates do we make under a free market economy?

3. How "automatic" is the free market process?

4. What is meant by an "administered" or "sticky" price?

5. Does the government seek to promote freedom of pricing?

6. In your opinion does government intervention in the market ever reduce free market forces?

FOOTNOTES

1. For a stimulating development of the concept of opportunity, see Reavis Co., "Quantity Limits and Economic Opportunity", in *Theory in Marketing*, edited by Reavis Cox and Wroe Alderson (Chicago, Richard Irwin Co., 1950), pp. 225-244.

2. A third type of market is the "authoritarian" market found with government operated or regulated enterprises in which the government sets the price or controls the output (or both). Since authoritarian markets are, strictly speaking, a departure from capitalism, they are not elaborated in this chapter which is concerned primarily with the role of consumers in capitalistic markets. This three-way classification of markets was suggested by Edwin G. Nourse, *Price Making in a Democracy* (Washington, Brookings Institute, 1944), Ch. 1.

3. Capacity output is defined in this paper as that scale of operation using existing plant equipment after which there is a pronounced rise in average total costs.

4. The author's discussion of "administered" markets has been suggested by the following sources, in particular: Saul Nelson, *Price Behavior and Business Policy* (TNEC Monograph #1, 1940), pp. 1-161.
Gardiner C. Means, "The Consumer and the New Deal," *Annals of American Academy* (May, 1934), pp. 7-17.
Industrial Prices and Their Relative Inflexibility (Senate Document #13, 74th Congress, 1st session 1935).
Wilford J. Eiteman, *Price Determination,* Business Practice Versus Economic Theory (Ann Arbor, University of Michigan, 1949).
Edwin G. Nourse, *Price Making in a Democracy*, (Washington, Brookings Institute, 1944).
Willard L. Thorp, "Price Theories and Market Realities," *American Economic Review Supplement* (1936), pp. 15-22.
Frederick J. Mills, "Discussion", *American Economic Review Supplement* (1936), pp. 62-64.

5. *Survey of Current Business* (February, 1940), p. 5.

6. *Printers Ink* (April 22, 1949), p. 25.

7. Harry M. Wooten, in *Printers Ink* (January 7, 1949), p. 29.

8. *Automotive Industries* (February 13, 1937), p. 210; (March 15, 1949), p. 86.

GRAHAM BANNOCK

* Graham Bannock, "Consumer Sovereignty," *The Juggernauts* (Indianapolis: The Bobbs-Merill Co., Inc., 1971), Chapter 4, pp. 53-78. Reproduced by special permission.

Economic advance is not greater satisfaction of old needs and wants. It is above all new choice. It is the widening of the horizon of expectations and aspirations. This is largely a function of marketing which, therefore, is needed to make technological change economically productive, that is, result in the satisfaction of human needs and wants.

Peter F. Drucker, The Age of Discontinuity

The quality of life is being diminished. Even bread doesn't taste as good — I don't care how much advertising they spend on it, you're eating bathmats.

Bryan Forbes, quoted in the Sunday Express,
31 August 1969

In Part One I have argued that the economic organization of the advanced countries is in the process of transformation from one where there are relatively large numbers of competing firms to one where a small number of enormous corporations, which do not compete in the traditional sense, dominate private industry and commerce. In this second part it will be shown that in this process of change much of the crude but effective mechanism for reconciling the interests of owners, managers, consumers and employees has been destroyed by the separation of ownership from control, by the decline in competition and by the unnecessary size of the industrial monsters that have been created. Much of this discussion is inevitably theoretical but more flesh will be put on the bones of the ideas in this part in the remainder of the book.

The conventional wisdom is that the largest corporations have attained their size because they have consistently given a better and more efficient service to the customer. The fittest have survived by offering original, cheaper and better-quality products and by ensuring their ready availability. It is also the conventional view that the mature corporations retain their position because they are better managed and because they can afford the latest techniques and the best equipment. The justification for this is, quite simply, that the consumer, being both free and rational, will choose the better of the alternatives open to him. Competition, therefore, ensures that the giant corporation will remain large only as long as it remains more efficient than the rest. Were it not so, other corporations would move in and take its business away by offering a better service. They would be motivated to do this by the opportunity for profit that this action would provide. It is recognized that there will often be temptations for corporations to conspire together to eliminate competition by agreements on prices and other means, or for corporations to exclude new competitors by preventing them access to retail outlets or raw materials. These and other abuses of the rules of the game are, in the conventional view, susceptible to control by the state, which acts as a referee to ensure that the competitors fight clean!

It is, in. fact, recognized by many economists that in concentrated or oligopolistic industries, price competition will be muted by the general knowledge that in the face of a few powerful competitors price warfare would be ruinous for all concerned. Price agreements are illegal but are not necessary. In mature concentrated industries prices rarely fall and if one manufacturer increases his prices the others usually follow.*

This situation is now part of the industrial scenery and passes unremarked in the daily press. The following three examples taken at random from *The Times* on three successive days in August 1969 illustrate this:

Du Pont UK Lycra plant starts up . . . . A spokesman for the United States chemical giant Du Pont said yesterday that there would be no immediate price reductions although Courtaulds' spanzelle elastomeric fibre would now face a United Kingdom rival.

Du Pont has been paying as much as 25 per cent duty on imports of Lycra from its plants in the Netherlands and in the United States. 'We shall use the money we save to give ourselves a better margin on this operation from now on,' said the spokesman.

Bakelite polythene prices up . . . Bakelite Xylonite, Britain's second largest supplier of polythene film, yesterday announced price increases of between 4 and 6 per cent.

This follows the announcement last week by British Visqueen, the wholly-owned Imperial Chemical Industries subsidiary, that it is to raise the price of its best selling polythene by a similar amount.

Pirelli workers warned of 'drastic relapse' . . . Rising production costs forced all tyre manufacturers to increase prices earlier this year, but warning of a further round of rises. . . .

---

* Some economists, including myself, believe that oligopolistic pricing has much to do with persistently rising price levels in all the industrialized countries. Note that before a stable oligopolistic situation is reached the big corporations often do compete in price either to establish leadership or to drive smaller companies out of business. IBM does not need to compete on price but Boeing still does.

It is recognized that competition is diverted into other channels: 'Oligopolists love to shift rivalry and competition into dimensions other than price: to advertising, to changing the wrapping of their product and the size of its replacement parts, to quick and reliable service'.

Some economists, like Paul Samuelson, who wrote this, appear to think that some of this non-price competition, or 'rivalry', is wasteful. Others think it is beneficial to the consumer and that, on the whole, state monopoly regulation is sufficient to contain the worst abuses. Others, like Samuelson's American colleague, George Stigler, believe that the state should intervene more vigorously to restore genuine competiton, if necessary by reversing the process of concentration.

Galbraith, however, has poured scorn on the whole belief that 'the heartland of the economy', as he calls it, is in any sense competitive. He maintains, and quite rightly in my view, that the managers of the mature corporations, or technocrats, bear no resemblance in behaviour or motivation to the traditional entrepreneur figure. Nevertheless, he mistakenly believes that the giant non-competing mature corporations are a necessity of modern technology and that to break them up would be to destroy the economy.

While there are at least some reasons for thinking that modern technology often requires substantial organizations and hence concentration in some industries, there are none for assuming that competition among the mature corporations is any more genuine than the wrestling matches enjoyed by television viewers, although it is frequently as vigorous and dramatic. And yet the concept of competition is deeply embedded in current thought. The following passage, for example, occurs in the 1969 edition of L.W. Rodger's text-book, *Marketing in a Competitive Economy*:

The approach adopted in this book assumes conditions of competition since these are the conditions that apply in our economy. These conditions of competition imply freedom of independent action on the part of business firms to increase profits by offering customers incentives to do business with them. These same customers are free to accept alternative incentives offered by rival firms.

All serious expositions of the subject, such as that quoted, cannot ignore the obvious fact that much of the economy consists of heavily concentrated markets, nor of the necessity for the regulatory role of the state. A few of the more sophisticated works also recognize that profit maximization is not always consistent with the other (implicit) objectives of management. These recognitions are illustrated from the following further passages from the same source:

A competitive economy does not necessarily mean a free-for-all economy. Certain rules must be observed in order to preserve the best elements of competition and to protect society from harmful or noxious activities, cut-throat practices, fraud and misrepresentation. For such purposes the State's role should be one of purposive intervention. . . .

Firms engaged in 'monopolistic' are not in *exclusive* control of the market. . . . it is stretching the use of language a bit far to say that because one firm produces an expensive car which no no other firm can make, it is therefore in a monopoly position. It has to compete with other expensive and uniquely designed cars, with smaller cheaper cars, and with other forms of personal and public transport.*

These statements are especially interesting because the book from which they are taken is a very successful management textbook and can therefore be expected to reflect the assumptions of the technocracy. It will be noted that oligopolistic concentration is realistically accepted as a fact of life, so too is state intervention. The relatively minor role of profit is admitted in almost Galbraithian language:

It seems likely, however, that in most real life business situations, the maximum or optimum long-term rate of profit is not discoverable as a basis for policy making. Drucker has suggested that 'the guiding principle of business economics is not the maximization of profits, it is the avoidance of loss'. According to this view, there is a minimum level of profit for each firm which is vital for its survival, but this does not imply any compulsion to maximize profit.* Firms may deliberately avoid maximum or optimum profit for several reasons, such as fear of attracting new competitors, fear of being charged with unreasonable profiteering, and the abuse of excessive market power, fear of damaging the company's public image and fear of antagonizing its workers and the Trade Unions. [See[5].]

Nevertheless, despite all this, profit and competition have to be retained as powerful forces. Once they are dropped altogether very awkward questions arise about how the consumers' interests are safeguarded and what check there is on the power of the technocracy. Thus, it is asserted in the second of the three passages quoted above that motor cars in one price range experience competition from cars in other price ranges and from other forms of transport. This is not a very convincing argument. If Cadillac or Rolls Royce were the only expensive cars available, within very broad limits a rich man is hardly likely to be deterred from paying through

---

* This is a reference to Chamberlin's revision of the theory of competition to allow for the fact that in the modern economy producers differentiate their products. In the original Marshallian theory it was assumed that all products of competing producers were identical as the wheat of farmers today. Confusingly enough, what actually happens in mature oligopolistic markets is that producers strive to make their products more and more alike while giving an impression of differentiation.
The italics are Rodger's.

* Fine arguments are possible about the difference between maximizing profit, in the medium term and the long term. It is arguable that a corporation could aim to grow in size and to achieve modest dominance so as to be in a position to maximize profits at some distant point in time. Where this point is beyond the working life of the executive, however, this argument has little force.

the nose for one by the thought that he can travel by train or, even if price were important in this class of product, that he could turn to a cheaper car.

More convincing but just as unrealistic is the notion frequently put forward that the giant corporations police one another. Professor McFadzean of Shell, for example, said in a lecture published in 1968:

The competitive position that exists today is only one of the factors to be taken into consideration—potential competition is also important. Thus Procter & Gamble and Unilever dominate the detergent market today. If one of them acted as market leader by raising the price, the other may or may not follow suit. If it did, and the return in our judgment on the capital involved became more attractive than the alternatives open to us, we as large producers of the basic raw materials, would probably push into the retail side of the business. We would equally consider doing so if we thought that the managements had fallen asleep and that we could do a more efficient job.

General Motors made a similar claim in a statement for the 1968 US Senate hearings, *Planning, Regulation and Competition:*

Automobile Industry:

The continuing challenge of innovation is another constant potential source of competition. Large electrical equipment manufacturing firms, such as General Electric and Westinghouse, have been mentioned prominently as possible entrants utilizing electric power for the cars they would build. These firms have expended substantial research efforts on prototype vehicles.

GE and Westinghouse could conceivably produce electric cars as GM suggests, and it will be helpful if we look at this possibility and see why it is unlikely that either they, or GM, will do so unless or until pushed into action by some third party.

If the problem of devising a smaller, lighter and cheaper battery could be overcome, an electric motor would provide an attractive alternative to the internal combustion engine for motor cars; it would also be particularly suitable for a specialized town vehicle.* General Motors or General Electric, or for that matter several other corporations, should all have the technical resources to overcome the problems that remain in developing an electric city car. It is not improbable that some of the problems have already been solved. In any event, although GE may or may not have some advantage in developing the power unit, GM certainly ought to have an advantage in developing the chassis and manufacturing and marketing the vehicle. Neither corporation (nor Ford nor Chrysler) has any obvious incentive to take such an important and risky step, however, and

* An electric motor requires no gearbox, can be placed anywhere in the wheels, it is silent, safe and non-polluting. The principal difficulty at the moment is that batteries that would provide sufficient power and range, would be very large and costly.

both have several reasons for not doing so. Unless action is forced by the government either to solve problems posed by further anti-pollution legislation or by new regulations governing the use of vehicles in cities, or unless a foreign competitor introduced a successful product, the market leaders are unlikely to act.* In any event, it is as improbable that GE would choose to enter GM's preserve of motor cars as GM would be to embark on the production of electrical generating plant in direct competition with GE.

In the first place, a great deal of money would have to be spent to develop and tool up for such a car, expecially since neither the engine nor the body could be built with existing plant and equipment. There could be no guarantee that, in the absence of government intervention, car buyers in sufficient numbers would be willing to pay a substantial sum for an electric car with smaller range, inferior performance and luggage capacity, as well as less grandiose appearance, than the standard American automobile, despite its considerable advantages in cities. Should the project prove unsuccessful, profitability would be temporarily quite significantly affected.

In the second place, the sales of such a car would inevitably be at the expense of a proportion of GM's existing full-sized (and highly profitable) cars, especially in cities and in the blooming second and third car market. GM might calculate that it could sell a million electric cars at a price that gave a profit per unit about one-third less than on its full-sized cars. On this basis the corporation could persuade itself that it would actually lose net income from the venture and that the more electric cars it sold the more it would lose.†

Finally, if the new electric car were successful and profitable, Ford and Chrysler would follow suit. These corporations, which share the oligopoly with GM, are quite capable of emulating anything that GM can do and would follow GM's initiative as soon as it was clear that it was going to be a success. In this event, GM would lose city car sales

---

* There can be little doubt that in a truly competitive market a city car to meet the requirements of urban areas would already have been put on the market. A number of small non-motor manufacturers have already produced prototypes but they face enormous obstacles. The first successful city car may well come from a state-aided or non-Juggernaut-dominated industry, for example in France or Japan. It is interesting to note that the British government has given the Lucas group substantial financial assistance for battery research work in this field. A city car need not be electric-powered, of course, and the argument here is equally applicable to a conventionally powered city car. In fact a conventionally powered city car, the 'Bug', was introduced by Britain's small independent car company, Reliant, in June 1970.

† The lower absolute profitability of small cars is one of the reasons why the US owned manufacturers in Europe do not compete in the mini-car market. This is not to say that they, unlike their competitors, are trying particularly hard to maximize their profits, but that they are strong enough to abstain from competing with them. It is also the result of their belief that market conditions will soon approximate to those in the United States. (See Chapter II).

to its competitors and most of these sorts of calcuation the whole exercise would look just too risky to attempt.

I have explained why GM is unlikely to enter the electric car market. I have not, however, explained why GE or Westinghouse should not do so, but the reasons are very similar. If GE entered the market, it would do so at a disadvantage, for it has no reputation for passenger cars and no suitable manufacturing, distribution or service organization. The capital cost of a GE entry would be greater than that for GM for this reason and yet, if GE's venture proved successful, GM would be forced to follow and so would other motor manufacturers. No doubt GE have prototype electric cars, so have Ford and GM, but these essays in research are made for defensive and prestige reasons; they do not signify an intention to enter the market. It is possible, of course, that GE might develop a suitable battery and motor and offer them to the motor manufacturers under a licensing agreement. For the reasons given, however, the motor manufacturers would still not be enthusiastic in introducing the car and, even if they were, they would prefer not to have to pay license fees to GE for such important components as the motor and battery. In the unlikely event that GM developed and patented its own highly original battery (which it has no incentive to do) GE would, however, probably follow with another of its own design and offer it to the remaining motor manufacturers. GE would not want to see GM too well established in the general field of electric power: this would threaten its own security.

As I will show later on, there are reasons why the larger firms in concentrated industries are less able to innovate than those in more freely competitive ones, even if they wished to do so. It has not been generally recognized by economists, however, that just as there are forces in an oligopolistic situation to discourage price compeition, there are also forces discouraging product competition, so that there are no incentives to innovate.* Although General Motors (no. I) earning rather more on its capital employed than General Electric (no. 4), the latter is not likely to embark on price or product competition with GM unless its growth and security are threatened by GM or unless GM's market offers a relatively risk-free opportunity which, in view of the strength, resources and undenied vigilance of GM, it definitely does not. This is equally true of the competitive relationship between Shell (no. I) and Unilever (no. 5) in Britain and all the other permanent corporations around the world.

---

* Economists have argued that whilst price cuts can be matched at once, it is possible to acquire a substantial lead with a technical innovation and cash in on it while competitors are helpless. This is often unrealistic under modern conditions, where industrial espionage provides considerable lead time, and research laboratories especially suited to imitative invention exist in all mature corporations. In other cases, such as the transistor, licensing rights are made available to other corporations because more can be gained that way and with less risk than in straightforward product competition.

Since the mature corporations do not compete on price, or on product, but devote whatever competitive spirit they can summon up to more superficial matters, it follows that the products themselves are likely to become more and more alike. When product characteristics do diverge through genuine competition from a smaller company they soon come back together again. When Wilkinson introduce a stainless steel blade, Gillette follow with the same thing at about the same price, not with something better but different or substantially cheaper: if one corporation successfully introduces an Indian-type freeze-dried beef curry, then so will the others. So far there are no industries in which all forms of competition have disappeared completely, so the full effects of conformity have yet to be seen. The American motor industry is probably the nearest complex example, but simpler examples are to be found in other consumer durables and not merely in products but in marketing methods as in cigarettes, detergents and petrols. In mature concentrated industries in almost all the developed countries the products of the different companies are not only priced alike, they look alike and *are* alike.

None of the reasons so far provided for expecting both price and product competition in concentrated industries to be muted is inconsistent with the traditional view that earnest managers are doing their best to maximize profits in the interests of shareholders. One of the characteristics of the mature corporation, however, (most mature corporations are active in one, or several, concentrated industries) is that its shareholders are so numerous and dispersed that they have very little opportunity to influence the objectives of the business they own. Since, at the same time, the directors and senior staff of a mature corporation are typically remunerated by salary and fringe benefits and have no, or only very small, shareholdings in the business, they do not have a strong incentive to maximize the return on equity capital. They will, of course, have fairly strong incentives not to let this return fall below a certain minimum level — probably somewhere around the average for their industry — because they cannot afford to let their share prices fall very far.* If profits are consistently below average, share prices will fall so as to bring yields in line with that average. Once share prices have fallen, then the corporation is open to a take-over bid and its own acquisition (that

---

* This perfectly rational desire to keep share prices within limits does not apply only to year-to-year profitability, but also to shorter periods. On 15 December 1969 *The Times* revealed some of the contents of an internal Unilever document implying 'that Unilever is anxious, if possible, to maintain its share price in the short term', and was prepared to adopt a policy of 'profit smoothing'. *The Times* expressed shocked concern 'that in an extreme case there could be a danger of sacrificing long term commercial considerations for the sake of propping up the share price in the short term'. Unilever, who had lost an opportunity of a bumper merger with Allied Breweries earlier in the year (see p. 319) through an adverse movement in its share price, clearly had an incentive to adopt such a policy, although they shortly afterwards claimed that *The Times* report was misleading.

is, growth) programme will be seriously impaired. Much less important, the corporation will also find it difficult to raise more capital on reasonable terms if it needs it. They have no reason, however, to maximize profits if this would conflict with their own security or growth or job-satisfaction, and even less reason to maintain high dividends.

When it is recognized that the mature corporation is aiming at a 'normal' profit and not maximum profit, it is clear that there are further reasons for expecting the quality of competition and particularly of innovation to diminish in concentrated industries. Profit has its origin in risk-taking: the last thing a technocrat wants to do is to take risks, although sometimes he is forced to do so. If a shareholder takes a risk by speculating on a chancy share, he stands to gain perhaps 100% on his investment in the share or to lose, say, 80% of it. If the managing director of a mature corporation takes a major risk, he stands to lose his job and even his career. He may stand to gain very little. Motivations are quite different: there is nothing theoretical about this, it is the real stuff of daily life. The captain of a great passenger liner running late would not run the risk of putting his ship on the rock by taking a short cut through some uncertain waters, where an owner of a private yacht might not hesitate, either for personal gain or merely for the thrill of pitting his skill against the elements.

Professor Galbraith is quite aware of all this; indeed he has made the best, if not the first, analysis of the growing dichotomy between the interests of the shareholder and the corporate manager.* He has not, however, seen that the interests of the consumer and the corporate manager are also diverging and that this is a much more dangerous schism. His argument is that the technocracy are driven on to innovate by their desire for growth and by the sheer fascination of the technical challenge of the job. Furthermore, he maintains that modern innovation is so capital-intensive as to require the virtual elimination of risk that occurs in heavily concentrated industries with high promotional expenditures. The necessary research he maintains is also so complex and costly as to rule out the small and medium-sized concern. So great are these demands that government support of the oligopoly in some form is also normally necessary. Boeing would never have committed the enormous capital required to develop the 747 Jumbo Jet, for example, if there were a number of other aircraft manufacturers doing the same thing: uncertainty on this scale would block progress. His argument, if true at all, is only true of a very small proportion of capital-intensive economic activity, notably in aerospace where the spur to innovation is often not

---

* This dichotomy can only arise because of the diminishing power of the shareholder over the corporate manager. The shareholder's power is not limited simply by the fact that typically he owns only an insignificant proportion of the corporation's stock, but also because the modern corporation is so complex that he is debarred from credible comment or criticism.

technocracy but government initiative. In the case of Boeing it is difficult to see why they should have developed the 747 if there were not potential competition. Certainly Boeing's interest in an SST was not spontaneous. The vast majority of industry is far more concentrated than is justified by the capital requirements of a truly competitive market structure and, as I shall show later on, there is overwhelming practical evidence that concentration and sheer size inhibit not only innovation but invention also. To take Boeing as an example again, its aircraft have all been ultra-conventional.

The reader, while finding it relatively easy to accept the potential evils of concentration, may find it difficult to accept the weakness of profit maximization as a motive in the mature corporation — after all, great emphasis is put on profits by all businessmen. In the light of what has been said, one would expect the technocracy to place emphasis on profit as shareholders' meetings, but they also never cease to refer to its importance where they do not need to do so, both in private meetings in the corporation and in public. Lord Beeching, ex-deputy chairman of ICI, for example, has said with obvious conviction that the fundamental difference between private and nationalized industry is that:

. . . in the case of the first there is a single and clear primary objective, namely, the maximizing of profit which management can pursue, whereas in the case of a nationalized industry there are numerous objectives, one being profitability and others being of varying nature, often ambiguous, sometimes incompatible.

Now, although ICI are the fourth largest corporation in Britain and enjoy a near monopoly in several products in fast-growing markets, the reader will find that their net profit before interest and tax on capital employed was not particularly high — it was between 10% and 13% during the last four years. This is less than the average return for the Top 500 as a whole. It is, in fact, substantially less than many of ICI's Juggernaut competitors. Did Lord Beeching and his colleagues fall down on the job? Not at all. On the contrary, Lord Beeching was so successful in the private sector that he was invited to take on the formidable task of making British Railways profitable. The board and senior executives of ICI who, perhaps, have faced more competition than the other giants at the top, were not able to catch up their neighbors in terms of profit, but they kept up with them in growth of assets and turnover. ICI did not do as well as some of its competitors; it would, no doubt, have liked to have higher profits but it probably could not do this and get growth too.

It is not what people say they do that is important — it is the priorities that are apparent in their actions that count. This is not to accuse the technocracy of dishonesty; they do want to maximize profits, but not at the expense of their own livelihood, nor do they wish to do so at the expense of anti-social action, such as the overt exercise of monopoly power. This is perfectly honest and rational action. As Galbraith has pointed out, the objectives of the technocracy are well recognized by society. Except under monopolistic conditions large profits are technically supposed to be a sign of efficiency. In fact, they are often seen simply as a manifestation of greed or excessive market power. Sir Peter Runge wrote: 'We refer to a "nice little profit" in one breath and in the next will run someone down with some such expression as "He's a quick profit man," or be downright abusive by calling him a profiteer.'* (See [8].)

Profit is less ambiguously regarded in America than in Europe, but in both places the chairman of a small, highly profitable corporation would be much less highly regarded than the chairman of a giant corporation that merely broke even. Like the notion of competition, however, that of profit is deeply embedded in current thought about economic motivation, and for a very good reason: a capitalist industrial society in which profit plays a minor part no longer has a 'hidden hand' to safeguard the interests of the consumer and the community.

Fortunately, profit figures are among the most easily available information on corporations and we can turn again to the 500 listings for some (fairly) solid evidence on the subject.

If it were true that the managers of the largest or mature corporations were more interested in growth and security than profit, we should expect to find that the larger corporations tend to have more rapid growth and more stable profits than smaller corporations, prepared to take risks to satisfy the consumer, would be rewarded by much higher profits when they were successful although, because some would fail, they would not necessarily make higher profits on average. Finally, since managers have no reason to be averse to making profits, but are simply reluctant to sacrifice security or growth in the attempt to *maximize* them, we should expect profits to be higher in highly concentrated industries than in the more freely competitive ones. The available evidence, in fact, confirms all these expectations.*

The last chapter showed that the largest corporations are increasing their share of economic activity and this, of course, means that as a group they are growing faster than the smaller ones. Rigorous academic studies have demonstrated the remaining tendencies beyond reasonable doubt, but the reader himself can, with patience and a little knowledge of such special factors as

---

* Like those of Dr. Beeching, the corporations with which Sir Peter Runge is connected are notable more for their size and rate of growth than their profitability. He is joint vice chairman of Tate & Lyle (no. 36, 1968 pre-tax return 11%) and a director of Vickers (no. 51, 1968 return 6.4%).

* The prevalence of relatively low but stable profits among larger corporations does not, in fact, prove that mature corporation managements are not trying to maximize profits in the medium term. However, if, for example, large corporations are too large to be run at a high profit through administrative frictions or for other reasons, then theoretically the management should propose reducing them in size.

mergers and major strikes (that can temporarily distort financial results), verify this for himself. The profits of the larger firms at the top of the 500 list tend to fluctuate less and vary less from firm to firm than those at the bottom of the list. The other tendencies — for profits to be higher in concentrated industries and to be smaller for large firms — are more difficult to verify because these two tendencies work in opposite directions: bigger firms tend to be in the more highly concentrated industries. Nevertheless, in the USA, for example, only one of the ten highest returns on invested capital among the 500 largest corporations was to be found among the Top 100 in 1969, the 8th highest (no. 94). Of those in the Top 200 most, such as Avon and Gillette, were in highly concentrated industries. In Britain, the highest profit earners tended to be even further down the list and profit performance also appeared to be more variable — both what one would expect given the lesser maturity of British industry.

The consumer is not concerned only with innovation and with low selling prices, however. He wants the industrial system to give him a wide choice of goods and services; he wants high standards of quality; and also, of course, he wants security and continuity of supply.

In security and continuity at least the interests of consumer, shareholders and technocrat are united. The shareholder need not fear that in normal economic conditions the value of his investment in GM or ICI will fall to nothing overnight as a result of rash behaviour by its managers, nor need the consumer fear that, while the present economic system continues, a Ford dealer will not be found nearby, or that he will not be able to purchase an IBM computer or enjoy a Coca-Cola, Nescaffe or Johnny Walker if he has the money to pay for them. Genuine freedom of choice and quality are quite different matters, however. It must follow that, as the number of firms diminishes and concentration increases, genuine choice diminishes. This remains true, even if the diminishing number of corporations offer an increasing number of products.

There are three distinct ways in which consumer choice is reduced as industries become more concentrated. The first one is obvious: the fewer the firms the fewer firms' products there are to choose from. The second one is the less obvious way, already discussed, in which firms under oligopolistic conditions tend to avoid product competition and eschew innovation so that while, paradoxically, sales promotion makes products appear to differ more and more, they are actually becoming more and more alike. The third way in which consumer choice is reduced in concentrated industries is even less obvious: it is a consequence of the increasing absolute *size* of corporations. Not only are there strong economic reasons why a corporation should reduce the number of its products to a minimum — so as to achieve economies of scale in production or purchasing of components and raw materials — but the management problems of large organizations are such that there is always a need to simplify everything as much as possible so as to economize on management time. Product decisions are invariably high policy decisions and must be reduced to a minimum.

So, in the relatively rare case where an established producer goes into liquidation and in the now more usual case where no new firms are entering the industry and existing firms do not increase their product offerings, consumer choice will be diminished to the extent of the entire product range of the liquidated firm. In the much more usual case where a producer is acquired by another, the new owners will have three choices as far as products are concerned. First, they can continue to market their own product lines and those of the acquired firm alongside one another. Second, they can eliminate the production and sale of uneconomic, overlapping, or directly competing products which may, in some instances, amount to dropping one product line altogether. Third, they can drop the acquired firm's product range or their own but continue to market virtually identical products under the two different brand names. This last course of action is very widespread, especially in markets where consumers are ill-informed, such as pharmaceuticals, electrical products and motor cars. It also occurs in a different form where chain stores, like Sainsburys or Boots, sell their own, often unadvertised, brands of tinned foods, washing-up liquids or sun oils which are identical or virtually identical with higher-priced, heavily advertised branded goods of the manufacturers who supply them. These identical products may lie, differently priced, side by side on the shelves. When a product line is dropped, the greater power of the vested interests of the management of the acquiring corporation usually ensures that it is their product and not that of the acquired corporation that continues although, of course, both brand names may continue to be used. Thus, the least successful of the two products may survive.

The forces in favour of offering identical products under different brand names are very strong, since the reduction in the number of products may often produce economies in production and will always produce immediate economies in other directions, such as stocking, administration, purchasing and design and development. At the same time, consumer loyalty to well established brands and the desire for variety are such that it is often well worthwhile bearing the additional costs of packaging and advertising to differentiate otherwise identical products. A higher total sales volume can usually be obtained with two brands than with one brand alone.

Even in the first case where a firm decides to continue two parallel product lines it will often be found, in the short run, that individual bits and pieces of the two products are, or readily can be made, interchangeable. When the time comes for a re-design or improvement in the product this interchangeability will usually be extended. Even where it is decided to retain the separate identity of the two products, internal forces in the corporation will tend to frustrate that objective. It is almost impossible for a corporation to design and market two completely original and independent solutions to a single market requirement. Design teams meet and influence one another, corporate traditions are a powerful unifying force and are, of course, rigorously fostered for other purposes and, equally important, the man at the top can hardly ever resist fostering one idea to the exclusion of others.

The sheer size of the mature corporation with its staff, equipment, factories, depots, work force, in short its large overhead costs, is so great, the sheer arithmetic of accounting is such, that everything it does must be a success and must sell in volume. If a product line does not sell in volume, it cannot bear its share of overheads and will make a loss. We shall see in a moment that this has other implications, but for the moment it is yet another factor working to reduce consumer choice. The mature corporation cannot afford to satisfy minority requirements. In many cases a small company will produce and sell a product in low volume at a profit. When that company is absorbed by a larger corporation this product will no longer be economic and consumers will have to make do with something designed for a much wider span of tastes.

In this and other respects, the mature corporation will concern itself more with illusion than with reality. It will endeavour to create the impression that its products are different from one another and from its 'competitors' by packaging, advertising and other promotional devices. It will also introduce superficial differences among what are basically the same products. Thus, there will be three or more versions of an electric razor: a standard model, a de luxe model with a device for clipping moustaches; and a super de luxe model with dual voltage control, padded sides and an elaborate carrying case. This approach is highly developed in the motor car industry. The term 'personalization' is used to describe the way motor cars can be embellished by consumer choice of optional items, thus diverting attention from the fact that choice between largely non-functional optional items is a most inadequate substitute for the expression of personal preference among alternatives that really are different.

Unfortunately, the only remaining concern of the consumer, quality, also tends to suffer in the mature corporation and under conditions of oligopoly. Just as the technocracy has an incentive to aim at a minimum standard of profitability, so too will it aim at a minimum standard of quality. The mature corporation does not put rubbish on the market: that would bring it into disrepute. But just as the mature corporation has no incentive to compete in price or in innovation, nor does it compete in quality. That, too, would be potentially ruinous; moreover, it involves complicated managerial problems, and the mature corporation wishes to avoid complication. Again, the only pressure on the technocracy at a personal or social level is to divert attention from the whole question of quality of product, or where it is appropriate, quality of service. No single individual can normally expect to influence the quality of a product nor can any individual be identified with the product or take any real personal pride in it. The president of Standard Oil or the chairman of ICI would not, of course, like to come under attack for spectacular breaches of minimum standards of product quality. The technocracy ensures as far as possible that this does not occur: ICI paints do not discolour and their fertilizers do not kill domestic animals; motor cars do not explode when run on Esso petrol — on the contrary they run very well. However, especially in those cases where very considerable technical knowledge, and probably apparatus, is required to detect differences in quality, such as in petrol or cigarettes, it is usually not difficult to show that standards of quality among oligopolists do not differ much and are sometimes even below the standards of smaller manufacturers who may be working under very considerable disadvantages.

The inferior quality of Juggernaut products, like the existence of growing concentration, is something which, although self-evident to some people, is not at all obvious to others. Diminishing choice and inferior quality (in the widest sense of the word) result partly from a technocratic obsession with organizational efficiency and corporate growth. These preoccupations mean that the modern producer is not really interested in the product for its own sake, although there are other contributing reasons. In any event, artists, writers and most of those members of the upper middle classes who have not profited by the emergence of the new industrial order, are well aware that progress has not always been accompanied by improved product choice, quality and durability, and also that the technocracy seem to be very efficient at some things but not at others. The fact is that a neat and outwardly tidy organization and the continued growth of an already large corporation raises management problems that are apparently insuperable. Eventually something has to give and in the technocratic scheme of things it is usually genuine efficiency, quality, originality and variety. Giant organizations can do big things and even do them effectively under an exceptional stimulus, but there is always a price for someone to pay.

The striking, even ludicrous, contrast between the efficiency of the Saturn V moon rocket and the Apollo spacecraft and that of the New York telephone or electricity systems has not, for example, gone unnoticed by many.* Norman Mailer wrote at the time of the moonshot:

If many, too many, an American product was accelerating into shoddy these years since the war, if planned obsolescence had all too often become a euphemism for sloppy workmanship, cynical cost cutting, swollen advertising budgets, inefficiency and general indifference, then in one place at least, and for certain, America could be proud of a product.

Or, to take another example, this time from Patrick Goldring's protest *The Broiler-House Society*, which appeared in Britain in 1969: 'For in almost all the aspects of life which make up the dignity of the human condition, we are retreating from standards and qualities we know to be good towards the comfortable second and third rate or to some mass produced inferior substitute . . . we are passing through a new dark age of the shoddy. . . . .'

---

* *Time* magazine for 23 March 1970 had a special section, 'Inefficiency in America — why nothing seems to work any more'.

Some of the nostalgia now being expressed in England for Victorian and Edwardian times is not simply a yearning for the days of Britain's imperialist power; it is also, clearly, a yearning by some for some of the lost fruits of the industrial revolution, fruits which television, tape recorders and medical drugs do not entirely make up for. Here, for example, is an extract from a wistful review in the *Times Literary Supplement* of a reprint of the Army and Navy Stores catalogue for 1907:

But half an hour with this fascinating volume, which needs a lectern for comfortable reading, suggests that what made 'The Stores' a legend was much more than good business sense. It was an attitude of serving, of providing, rather than persuading. The Edwardians, we are led to feel, knew what they wanted, and the Stores supplied it. Paradoxically this seems to have given them a range of choice that would bewilder us today .... The Army and Navy's [catalogue] has shrunk from 1,200 pages to some pamphlets totalling 142.

The reasons for these changes, which are, of course, the subject of this book, bewilder commentators. Goldring, however, is in no doubt that the diminishing quality of life for the mass of the population is the result of a sacrifice of their interests for the benefit of the *managers* of society. He says, on the fact that goods and services are becoming inferior: 'When anybody points out this fairly obvious fact of present day life he is quickly reminded of his ignorance. For to make the point involves a value judgment.' This is right. The standard technocratic reply, for example, to Bryan Forbes' complaint about bread at the heading of this chapter is something as follows: 'The centralization of bread manufacture and distribution produces enormous economies and pre-packed, sliced bread has enormous advantages — it keeps longer, it is attractive in appearance and hygienic and it is much more suitable than ordinary bread for your automatic toaster,' and so on. If the consumer persists that it still tastes like bathmats and, furthermore, that it isn't much cheaper than traditional bread, he is told: 'But it is what the public wants; you do not have to buy it; you are just expressing your own and, if I may say so, rather sophisticated, personal view' (that is, you are making a value judgment). The hidden flaw in the technocratic argument is that the public have not expressed their preference for packaged, mass-produced bread and continued to express it. Baking is a highly concentrated industry and it is becoming increasingly difficult to buy anything else but mass-produced bread in most places.

The inferior quality of many products made on a large scale is often assumed, at least in part, to be an inevitable outcome of the techniques of mass production and the choice between cost and quality. This is not necessarily so, although things like poor assembly can sometimes be attributed to the understandable lack of personal interest on the part of assembly line operators in their work. The durability, fit, regularity and finish of components made by mass production, however, ought to be, and sometimes are, superior to those of hand-made products. This is simply because the machine is more accurate than the human hand, does not get tired, or, if properly designed and maintained, make mistakes. Almost nothing nowadays is made entirely by hand in the advanced economies, but the mature corporation can afford and indeed has to use better-quality tools than the smaller organization producing in smaller quantities. The tools for the mature corporation normally have to produce more products during their lives than those of smaller firms and costs are accordingly spread over a large number of units. The largest-scale producer can also use quality control techniques and test methods that ensure a very high standard of quality and reliability. It is again a question of incentive; capability in this instance is not important.

The technocracy of the mature corporation has only a negative incentive to maintain high standards of quality — it will lose out if its products drop below certain *minimum* standards. The mature corporation does, however, have very great incentives to reduce costs. To quote Professor McFadzean again:

But the factor to which we pay most attention, and the one probably over which we have most control, is the effect of a particular investment decision on our costs. The constant endeavour to improve costs relative to those of competitors is not the only, but certainly the main way of achieving maximum profitability . . . .

From a competitive viewpoint the cost angle is of prime importance. If any company can reduce its costs relative to its competitors the *status quo* in the market place is threatened.

These passages implicitly recognize that the mature corporation tries to improve its profitability, not by selling more through improved quality or reduced price, but by reducing cost. The reason for this is that although price adjustments can and will be met immediately and product innovation or increased sales promotion will also be met, cost reductions cause no ripples on the surface of the market; they may even for a considerable time remain secret; they enhance the security of the technocracy in an absolutely safe way. If they are matched nothing is lost; if they are not matched then the mature corporation's security is relatively enhanced.

For these reasons very considerable ingenuity is exercised in the search for new sources of cost reduction. Costs can be reduced by improving the general efficiency of the organization — by raising the productivity of office staff, for example, by reducing stocks, or by other means. Costs can also be reduced by the adoption of more efficient, perhaps more capital-intensive, methods of production or by the adoption of entirely new processes, such as forging instead of casting and machining. All this is, of course, in itself normally socially beneficial. Another fruitful line of approach which is of much more recent origin and which is characteristic of the mature corporation, at least in systematic and scientific form, is that of 'value engineering', i.e., cutting cost out of the product. This is a particularly good source of savings when a mature corporation looks at the products of an acquired company. Products can often be re-designed so that lower-cost materials can be employed or so that they can be produced more cheaply. When this involves the substitution of a non-corrodible material, such as nylon, for another, such as steel, or when totally unnecessary weight, and hence cost, is reduced, this is to the consumer's advantage as well as to the corporation's. In other cases where packaging is re-designed to give less protection, or when strength or durability is sacrificed to save weight, or where hardboard is substituted for steel, or in thousands of other detailed and unnoticed instances of the substitution of welds for bolts, stampings for castings, clips for screws, two coats of paint for three, the consumer suffers.

Economists have neglected the subject of product quality because these things are difficult or impossible to measure.* Yet it is a matter of common observation that many particular products are neither better nor cheaper than they were many years ago. Most people with more specialized knowledge know that many other products are not as good as modern technology enables them to be. It has been unkindly said that some of the best brains in industry are in advertising: certainly many of the best engineers are engaged in calculating what can be left out of next year's products. In their own eyes the most admirable achievements of the modern technocracy are thinner throw-away bottles, peppermints with holes and motor cars without chassis.

In markets dominated by a small number of large corporations, both price and product competition decline. Such products as are on offer tend increasingly to resemble one another, and scope for consumer choice diminishes. Such competition as remains is mainly in the form of packaging, advertising and other forms of sales promotion.

It has been widely observed that since before the war in the United States and the early 1960s in Europe there has been a major shift in emphasis from the production of goods to distribution and sales promotion.* The technocracy have given these (in their extreme forms) essentially wasteful and unnecessary activities of selling and

---

* And, of course, because the necessary information is not available. Snippets sometimes appear in the press. The *Sunday Express* for example on 12 July 1970 reported on the results of a 5-year check on the quality of ingredients of hundreds of consumer goods by the Warwickshire weights and measures office. The results of these measurements had been recorded by computer and analysis showed 'that the quality of many consumer goods is tending to deteriorate even though it may appear to be improving. For example it was found that 'bigger loaves of bread had been blown up by adding moisture during baking . . . . A cheaper bottle of washing-up liquid was found to have been diluted . . .' The report quoted the chief weights and measures officer as saying that manufacturers 'know they will lose sales by putting a price up . . . whereas they can boost profits by reducing quality.'

* Oliver Marriott in his book *The Property Boom*, for example, attributes increased demand for office space in central London in the early 1960s to 'the change in emphasis from making goods towards designing and marketing them, the tendency towards the amalgamation of industry into larger units . . .' . (p. 16).

sales promotion respectability by re-naming them 'marketing'. Prodigious intellectual effort has gone into the development of new 'marketing-techniques' and in justifying the devotion of large amounts of resources to them. The origin of this new 'science' is firmly rooted, according to the technocracy, in the needs of the economic system:

The degree to which marketing has been studied or felt to have been a worthwhile subject for separate study has depended to a large extent on the relative strength of prevailing economic forces. So long as the basic economic problem was . . . 'how to produce enough' marketing was assumed to be an automatic process. [See[3].]

Originally, marketing laid great emphasis on such worthy practical issues as the persuasion of introverted chemists or engineers in charge of corporations to leave their laboratories and workshops, to go out into the market place and find out what customers really wanted, to increase production capacity where profitable products were in short supply and perhaps less profitable products were not, and to make more customers aware of the products available. Elementary and obvious sales-orientated management measures of this kind, however, are no longer the pre-occupation of the marketing expert. The nature and significance of the change is well brought out by the way the British Institute of Marketing's definition of its subject was changed in September 1966. Prior to that date, L.W. Rodger notes, it read as follows:

The creative management function which promotes trade and employment by assessing consumer needs and initiating research and development to meet them; it co-ordinates the resources of production and distribution of goods and services; determines and directs the nature and scale of the total effort required to sell profitably the maximum production to the ultimate user.

After September 1966 the definition of marketing became more confidently:

Marketing is the management function which organizes and directs all those business activities involved in assessing and converting customer purchasing power into effective demand for a specifc product or services and in moving the product or service to the final customer or user so as to achieve the profit target or other objectives set by a company.

Note that the reference to consumer needs has been deleted, that the existence of objectives other than profit have been recognized and that 'selling' has been replaced by the much more sinister 'converting customer purchasing power into effective demand'. The addition of the words 'profit target or other objectives set by a company' is of even greater significance. These terms bring in the issue of corporate growth and survival. The most important element in the marketing approach is the need for awareness of the relationship between corporate growth and survival and the orientation of the corporation towards consumer purchasing power. This comes down to the fact that if the corporation cannot sell one thing it must switch its resources to something else. Selling is selling something in particular for the benefit of the consumer; marketing is absorbing purchasing power for the benefit of the corporation.

Economists have played little or no part in the development of modern marketing theory. In fact, Rodger writes:' . . . businessmen have put principles swiftly into practice in advance of academic exploration into the subject.'* When academic exploration fully penetrates the fog that surrounds marketing, however, it is likely to find that on balance it works powerfully against economic efficiency rather than for it. Provided that consumers have sufficient purchasing power and confidence and are kept informed about an increasing number and quality of products available, there is no evidence to suggest that their purchases will falter, especially when increasing education is widening and intensifying their tastes. It is probably true that persuasive advertising and other means of sales promotion are necessary to stimulate the demand for a diminishing variety and quality of products. It is no coincidence that the increased respectability of sales promotion and its new name of marketing have coincided with the rise of the technocracy. In other words, the shift in emphasis to marketing is largely the result of increased concentration rather than affluence and is just as unjustified as the concentration itself.

Galbraith obviously takes a poor view of the moral and aesthetic desirability of the more extreme forms of marketing technique, and it is clear from *The New Industrial State* that he sees them as inevitably associated with the prevalence of the mature corporation:

There is an insistent tendency among solemn social scientists to think of any institution which features rhymed and singing commercials, intense and lachrymose voices urging highly improbable enjoyments . . . as inherently trivial. This is a great mistake. The industrial system is profoundly dependent on commercial television and could not exist in its present form without it.†

Nevertheless, Galbraith, who appears to see technology as the master, not as the servant of man, believes that the control of demand by advertising and sales promotion is an imperative of this technology. If demand could not be controlled by these means then the large capital commitment required for any modern productive venture would never be made: the risks would be too great. Sales promotion is, in his view, an indispensable tool of the technocracy and a vital means for maintaining the demand for ever-increasing

---

* Rodger attempts to justify marketing by association with Keynes and implies that marketing has a role to play in maintaining full employment.

† Galbraith is referring partly here to the belief of some economists that under oligopolistic conditions advertising largely cancels itself out so that all firms have about the same share as they would if they did not advertise. He argues that these firms increase the total demand for their industry's products at the expense of other industries that do not advertise. This may well be true: my contention is not that advertising is irrational for the large corporation, but for society.

amounts of both essential and inessential goods. Heavy advertising expenditure, like the mature corporation, is, for him, a consequence not of concentration but of technological necessity. Advancing technology need not render the manipulation of consumers necessary (although it does provide the means to do it) but even if it did, then we should try to find some way of avoiding this. Fortunately, more plausible as well as logical explanations are possible.

Very briefly, it should now be clear that, like the decline in price competition, increased advertising is principally a consequence of concentration, just as conventional economic theory would suggest. Greater marketing effort is also made necessary by the need for the technocracy to simplify its management problems, reduce risk and increase growth. Furthermore, marketing is itself an important force in increasing concentration because it is itself the subject of what economists call increasing returns to scale. Whilst there are limits to the economies of large-scale production, there are no apparent limits to the 'economies' of marketing. Small firms cannot survive against large corporations in some markets simply because they cannot afford the advertising expenditure to neutralize that of their larger competitors. General Motors has 47% of the market, but it does not need to spend more than twice as much per car as Ford, which has 24%, to maintain that position.* One big advertisement per week in the Sunday colour supplements costs GM the same as it costs Ford. Advertising costs, therefore, can become a barrier to the entry of new competition. The need for marketing strength, as I shall try to show in later chapters, is one of the most important elements in the pursuit of concentration. Firms need to merge together so as to acquire the resources to market their products against those of larger groups which, in turn, need to get bigger for the same reason. Once the consumer is dethroned and the discipline of competition eliminated, the vicious circle of Juggernautism requires more and more concentration.

---

* The economies of scale in advertising are very substantial. Between 1954 and 1957 GM spent, on average $26.6 per car on advertising, Ford spent $27.2, Chrysler $47.8, Studebaker Packard $64.0 and American Motors $57.9.[17]

QUESTIONS FOR DISCUSSION

1. Why, do you think, has non-price competition increased on the American market? Is it likely to grow even further in the next decade?

2. Does the development of new products (innovation) promote oligopoly or inhibit it? Why? Do oligopolistic firms promote innovation?

3. Is the consumer really "king" in our economy? If so, how does he exert his powers? If not, why is the concept inaccurate?

4. Dr. Beem argues that the consumer cannot make good choices on the market because he has such a wide choice of merchandise; now, Professor Bannock seems to say the choice is ever narrowing. Who is correct?

5. Do you think that things were better back in the Victorian or Edwardian times? In what ways might things have been better? In what ways worse?

6. Does Professor Bannock approve of advertising and promotion? What does he object to?

7. How do you feel about the role of advertising in our economy?

EUGENE R. BEEM

Unfortunately, consumers have been unable to exercise with maximum effectiveness the considerable power which they possess in the direction of the U.S. economy because of the plight in which they find themselves. The great material gains which consumers have made are much less than they might have been. Disguised under the cloak of aggregate production have been countless billions of dollars worth of inferior, worthless, dangerous, and exorbitantly priced commodities and services. In many cases the consumers' power has been ineffectual because it has not been used with the alertness and knowledge which is required in a modern capitalistic economy. In other instances the potential power of consumers has been thwarted by producer activities. The manifold predicament of consumers is considered in the present chapter. The scope of discussion is somewhat arbitrary. In a sense *all* economic problems are consumer problems. Business cycles, inequality, public finance, inflation, industrial warfare — all these are perplexing problems affecting living standards. The author includes in the "plight of consumers" only those problems arising from the lack of knowledge or alertness of consumers with respect to choosing and using goods, and from the exploitive practices with which household buyers are confronted. The more basic reasons for the problems discussed are treated in the next Chapter.

The Multitude of Goods and Brands

One author has estimated that there are 250,000 distinct types of consumer goods being marketed.[1] The Sears-Roebuck and Company catalogues, alone, described between 90,000 and 100,000 types of commodities. On top of this baffling assortment of goods from which to choose, consumers are confronted with a myriad of competing qualities for most every product which they wish to buy. Philadelphia families in a recent year, were using 64 brands of packaged coffee, 86 of butter, 39 of fresh milk, 52 of laundry soap, 122 of face powder, 49 of safety razor blades, 32 of automobile tires, 71 of electric toasters, and 51 of vacuum cleaners. The differences among brands may be in content, package, or merely label — but which, the typical consumer does not know. The brand selection problem is further complicated by the fact that qualities are constantly changing — allegedly for the better, but the uninformed buyer can never be sure. Do flouride toothpastes reduce the prospect of dental decay as claimed? Does "Dial" soap with its "amazing ingredient" really "keep you fresh around the clock?" Does "Shell platformate" gasoline actually give the automobile driver something he cannot get in other fuels?

When it comes to buying personal services, the problem is equally bewildering. The Philadelphia phone directory lists about 900 enterprises offering plumbing services by registered master plumbers, about 450 enterprises offering roof building or repairing services, about 250 carpentry enterprises, over 3,600 physicians and surgeons and over 1,800 dentists.

A consumer is entitled to the best quality good available for the money he wishes to spend, but the uninformed buyer has little more chance of finding it than he has of winning the prize in a lottery contest. He may, through trial and error, or the word of a friend, find a satisfactory product or service, but even when he does there is often available a better product or better service for the money he has to spend if he only knew where to find it.

Advertising and Personal Selling as Guides for Consumers

Advertising and personal selling are major sources of guidance for most consumers. At their best, these instruments may inform consumers fully as to the *merits* of a given product. Unless there are industry-wide standards or grades, these selling devices usually reveal nothing of the product's defects, and nothing as to how the product may be inferior to goods of competing firms. The purpose of advertising and personal selling is to make sales, and the producer, accordingly, presents only the complimentary aspects of a product, much as an attorney presents in court only the aspects of a case which are favorable for his client.

Unfortunately, much advertising and personal selling falls short of informing consumers fully and truthfully about the merits of even a single product. The Federal Trade Commission spot-checks advertising in newspapers, magazines, mail order catalogues, and radio and television broadcasts. Among 238,000 advertisements examined during the 1970 fiscal year, 8,000 plus appeared to untruthful.[2] Among the catalogues of 50 mail order houses, 178 advertisements were marked for investigation. While the percentage of misleading advertising indicated above is small, (3.4 percent), it must be remembered that the F.T.C. checks only what *appears* to be *seriously* misleading claims. F.T.C. studies probably underestimate the extent of deceit in advertising, since even reasonable claims made in an advertisement may prove unwarranted when they are checked against the producer's product. A great deal of advertising, of course, is truthful but not informative. Its purpose is merely to create good will by keeping the name of a particular brand or producer before the public. Unwarranted claims are probably found more often in personal selling than in advertising, but this statement is not susceptible of proof.

Labels and Containers

Labels, another major source of guidance for consumers, are subject to the same limitations with respect to usefulness as advertising. When fully informative, they may guide purchasers as to the merits of a particular brand, but except in those few instances in which there is some sort of grade labeling based on industry wide standards they can do no more than this. Despite considerable progress during the last 20 years, many labels fall short of providing adequate information about the product to which they are attached. Many contain only the trade mark of the producer, or the trade mark and name of the manufacturer. Quality designations on labels are far too often puffed or meaningless. The packers of rice designate quality as medium, choice, extra choice, fancy, and extra fancy. Mushrooms are labeled stems, pieces, choice, first choice, extras, small extras, sur extra, petite, sur extra petite, and extra miniature. Olives are designated standard, medium, large, extra-large, mammoth, giant, jumbo, colossal, and super-colossal. Many terms used in labeling indicate different things when used by different producers. Much ambiguity is attached to such words as "waterproof," "pre-shrunk," "color fast," "mothproof," "guaranteed," "genuine," and "pure." Where goods are produced in different sizes, as in clothing, size standards sometimes vary between producers.

Labels sometimes give inaccurate information — especially when legal regulations have not been imposed. A study made shortly before the Wool Labeling Act of 1939 became effective revealed that of 133 fabrics containing one fiber, only 12 percent were labeled accurately. Of 135 fabrics containing two or more kinds of fibers not a single one was labeled adequately. The majority of the fabrics in both studies contained no fiber label at all.[3] The National Better Business Bureau has reported widespread mislabeling of non-woolen garments. A chief element of deception is the use in large type of the word, "nylon" on labels attached to clothing items which contain as little as seven percent of nylon, and in some cases, only nylon thread in the stitching. Jack Johnston, manager of the Chicago Bureau, described this deception as "one of the rankest frauds ever carried on in merchandising in recent years."[4]

In a number of food products for which quality standards have been established on an industry-wide basis, the absence of standards for terminology make these quality standards very confusing. Of the various grades established by the U.S. Department of Agriculture, U.S. #2 identifies second grade Bermuda onions, tomatoes, and honey-dew melons, third grade cucumbers and pears, fourth grade lettuce, cheese, peaches and grapefruit, and sixth grade honeycomb sections. U.S. #1 refers to first grade pears, second grade cucumbers, third grade cheese, and fourth grade honeycomb sections. In many instances Department of Agriculture grade labels are used in wholesale trading, but not in retail markets.

Buying problems are complicated by a needless multitude of container sizes. Before World War II canned fruits and vegetables were packed in 258 sizes of cans, many of them very similar in size.[5] The product ratings of *Consumers Union* indicate the endless variety of container sizes for other products. CU shoppers attempt to buy the competing brands to be tested in uniform sized containers, so the following figures underestimate the profusion of container sizes. Among 31 brands of muffin and biscuit mix there were 13 sizes of packages.[6] Among 10 brands of insect repellant there were 6 sizes of containers.[7] For 44 brands of toothpaste there were 23 sizes of tubes.[8] For 82 brands of cleansing creams there were 20 sizes of jars.[9] It appears that producers seeking a profit advantage are tempted to sell their product in a container which is microscopically smaller than that of competitors. Most shoppers will see no difference between a can #303 and a can #2, but #303 holds 16.88 ounces of distilled water while #2 holds 20.55 ounces. While food containers must give the quantity of contents, hurried consumers may not read this information, and those who wish to buy on the basis of price need a slide rule to compare the cost per ounce of competing brands. Efforts are currently being made under the leadership of the National Bureau of Standards to reduce the number of can sizes for fruits and vegetables to 32, but even this seems unreasonably high.

Substandard, Dangerous, and Worthless Goods

Many products and services being marketed are substandard, dangerous, or worthless. Just before the Great Depression, a committee of 50, representing private medical practice, public health, medical institutions, social sciences, and the public, made a study into the economic aspects of medical care. The author believes that the conclusions of the committee are still useful, although the magnitude of the problem has probably diminished since the passage of the Food, Drug, and Cosmetic Act of 1938. It was found that of $3,647 million paid out each year for medical services, 3.5 percent was being spent for the services of naturopaths, faith healers, and similar groups, and about 10 percent for patent medicines. The committee concluded that much of the former and virtually all of the latter was wasted.[10]

The patent medicine field has no monopoly on dangerous, worthless or sub-standard products. When *Consumers Union* made laboratory tests of 93 dentifrices, it found 13 pastes and powders which were so abrasive that there was danger of harming the enamel on the teeth of many users.[11] The same agency found all 50 rayon blend blankets tested to be highly flammable: burning time ranged between 2½ seconds and 21 seconds, making 100% "not acceptable."[12] Four of 32 AM radios in the under $30 line were found to have a short circuit hazard.[13] Among 26 pressure cookers tested 8 had dangers of burning, scalding, or exploding which made them of questionable safety.[14] In tests of 28 canister vacuum cleaners, 9 were rated ineffective due to low suction and 7 other

brands had "service deficiencies" of one part or another.[15] Tests of
48 variations of sunburn preventatives showed that 30 afforded very
poor protection.[16] When *Consumers' Research* tested golf balls, it
found that 5 of 23 types had very poor driving or putting qualities,
or a too-ready tendency to become lopsided.[17] Of 13 varieties of
undershirts tested, 3 had excessive shrinkage.[18] Among 14 automatic
irons, 6 models were found with defective thermostat controls.[19] In
tests of 13 electric toasters, 4 involved danger of burns, or were
defective in other respects.[20] CR has listed 28 gasoline "dopes" or
"savers" being marketed which are worthless.[21] The same agency
claims there are at least 29 products sold as additives to the regular
crankcase oil for reputedly better motor performance. There is no
proof that any of these improve the operation of a motor. Many
contain graphite, which may do more harm than good by separating
and blocking critical points in the lubricating system.[22]

TABLE I

ENFORCEMENT STATISTICS OF THE FOOD AND
DRUG ADMINISTRATION FOR FISCAL YEAR
ENDING JUNE 30, 1970

Type of product	No. of factory inspections	No. of Samples collected or shipments inspected	Seizures	Legal actions taken
Foods	15,432	34,666	267	56
Drugs and devices	9,807	25,337	285	10
Cosmetics	644	494	4	0
Hazardous substances	1,392	801	44	0

* Adapted from tables presented in the *Annual Report of Department of Health,
Education and Welfare,* 1970, pp. 273-274. The number of actions taken is
smaller than the number of seizures since several samples representing shipments
at different times, or a variety of articles contained in a single shipment may be
combined into a single libel action.

The annual reports of the Food and Drug Administration in the
Department of Health, Education and Welfare indicate a persistant
problem with respect to food products, drugs and devices, vitamin
and health foods, and cosmetics and food colorings. Table I, shows
the number and kind of interstate samples of these products
collected or inspected by the F.D.A. during the 1970 fiscal year the
seizures, and the number of actions taken, prosecutions and
injunctions. About two-thirds of the food seizures which led to
action against 945 producers were based on filth and decomposition.
The other samples were defective for such reasons as short weight,
misbranding, and presence of dangerous chemicals. Action was taken

against 178 drugs and 117 therapeutic devices.[23] With respect to drugs, several deaths and hundreds of ill effects resulted from mix-ups in pharmaceutical plants due to inadequate inspection and testing methods. The F.D.A. issued the following warning in its 1948 annual reports:

> It is essential that the strictest type of control be maintained by pharmaceutical plants at every step in their operations, and this is recognized by most manufacturers. Some firms, however, attempt to economize by eliminating laboratory examination of finished products. . . When mix-ups occur under these circumstances they are revealed only after injuries or unfavorable reactions. . .
>
> Too many reports of incidents of this type were received during the year, some from manufacturers, others from physicians and consumers. Routine regulatory operations of the Food and Drug Administration uncovered other mix-ups and faulty controls before the product reached the market. In most cases the recall was superficial both in coverage and because of failure to disclose to the consignee the dangerous nature of the product until they are required to do so by the Food and Drug Administration.[24]

Most of the drug seizures were for misbranded proprietary remedies which claimed unwarranted curative powers. Among the 41 worthless therapeutic devices against which action was taken were the following: a plastic dumbell containing water with "expanded hydrogen atoms" claimed to give off atomic energy and cure all diseases when held in the hands; several gas generating devices claimed to cure sinus trouble, hay fever, asthma, nervous disorders, and the like; ultraviolet lamps with unwarranted claims as a germicide; a colonic irrigator claimed to be effective in treating high blood pressure, arthritis, and other ailments; a helmet-shaped hair drier said to emit thermomagnetic rays which would give the user more energy, strike at the underlying cause of disease, and control asthma, arthritis, sinusitis, colds, bronchitis, pleurisy, high blood pressure, male and female troubles, and other ailments. Most of the twenty actions taken against vitamin and health foods were for unwarranted claims. One product, for example, was nothing but seaweed which its promoter had extolled at health lectures throughout the nation as a cure for stomach ulcers, apoplexy, arthritis, rheumatism, diabetes, and other disorders. Action was also taken against fifteen cosmetics and five food colorings. Most of the cosmetic cases involved mislabeling. For example, seven seizures were of "egg shampoos" containing little or no egg. One case involved a dangerous eye shadow. The food coloring cases involved the use of possibly harmful dyes.

Since the passage of the Food, Drug and Cosmetic Act of 1938, drug products have been required to meet certain criteria for safety.

However, the Kefauver-Harris Ammendments passed in 1962 provided for more stringent standards of safety and efficacy. This calls for an evaluation of the risk-benefit ratio of a pharmaceutical item: some drugs are quite effective but entail a high risk of inducing harmful side effects and damage to the body; others are both ineffective and low risk; still others lie in-between. Hardly any have good effectiveness and no risk — even the ubiquitous aspirin tablet occasionally harms the taker.

In 1970, the Food and Drug Administration asked the National Academy of Sciences/National Research Council to examine drugs on the market to determine if they in fact were not efficient for their purpose, or were unduly dangerous, or both. In November, 1970, the FDA published a list of 350 drugs with the names of their producers.[25] Nearly all of these were subscription drugs, many in the antibiotic category. *Consumer Reports* advised readers to avoid these drugs, but it is patently impossible for a layman to determine whether his physician prescribes these items. Meanwhile, the FDA has been preparing to investigate the safety-efficacy of patent medicines; since there are more than 100,000 of these preparations on the market, and it will take a great deal of time to do this. Under the review program, panels of nongovernmental scientists will review the effectiveness of various classes of nonprescription drugs, such as antacids, pain relievers and cold remedies. Eventually, they will establish criteria of efficacy for each class of drugs; those criteria will become binding on the producers. After this, the manufacturer either must comply with the standards, submit tight evidence that an alternative product formulation is effective and safe, or withdraw from the market. This overwhelming task of drug evaluation will take at least three years.[26]

Meanwhile, at the end of 1972, the FTC was proceeding against the manufacturers of eight over-the-counter analgesics. In the complaints, the FTC asked that, in addition to refraining from false statements, the companies include in all advertising relevant "affirmative disclosures". For example, *Anacin* and other products incorporating aspirin would have to reveal its presence in their advertising.

The FTC complaint also proposed that "corrective advertising" be run to offset the false impressions engendered in the public mind by years of deceptive advertising. In the case of *Bufferin*, for example, the manufacturer would be required to spend 25 percent of its brand advertising budget on corrective advertisements saying that:[27]

> (a) It has not been established that *Bufferin* is more effective than aspirin for the relief of minor pain
> (b) It has not been established that *Bufferin* will cause less gastric distress than will aspirin
> (c) *Bufferin* will not relieve nervous tension or irritability
> (d) *Bufferin* will not enable persons to cope with the ordinary stresses of daily life.

Twenty-five percent of the advertising budgets of the other seven pain-killer remedies would also have to be devoted for two years to corrective advertising, under the complaint.

At present writing, it is uncertain as to the outcome of either the FDA's program to evaluate drugs, or the FTC's drive against false and misleading claims of the patent medicine producers. These are certainly steps in the right direction although past history gives one little reason to expect too much.[28]

Price as a Guide to Quality

Many are the consumers who, amid a swelter of multiple brands and conflicting claims, rationalize to themselves, "after all, you only get what you pay for!" This "rule of thumb" is not a very good guide for consumers who want to get the best quality available for the money they wish to spend.

When Macy's put out cold cream, the equivalent of $1 jars of well-known brands, and offered it for 49 cents, demand was unresponsive. When the price was raised to 54 cents, and later to 69 cents, sales climbed sutstantially.[29] Table II, taken from Ruth deForest Lamb's *American Chamber of Horrors*, reveals a typical mark-up over the cost of the ingredients in the selling price of cosmetics of between 500 percent and 1,000 percent.

A group of 11 drugs sold under brand names at an aggregate wholesale price per ounce of $28.95, but at the same time they could

TABLE II

COST-PRICE SPREAD FOR A REPRESENTATIVE
SAMPLE OF COSMETICS*

BRAND NAME AND PRODUCT	COST OF INGREDIENTS	SELLING PRICE
Coty face powder	$00.1195	$00.75
Coty rouge refill	00.0370	00.38
Elizabeth Arden face powder	00.3381	03.00
Elizabeth Arden Venetian Lip Paste	00.0240	01.00
Harriett Hubbard Ayer Cream Rouge	00.3823	00.55
Harriett Hubbard Ayer face powder	00.0656	00.60
Max Factor face powder	00.1183	00.75
Max Factor dry rouge	00.0823	00.38

* Items selected at random from Ruth deForest Lamb, *American Chamber of Horrors* (New York, Farrar and Rinehart, 1936), Appendix, pp. 338-349.

be bought under their chemical names for an aggregate wholesale price of $4.59 per ounce.[30] All aspirin is required by law to conform to the same standard, but in its most recent analysis Consumers Union found the price per 100 tablets varying from 17 cents for a private brand of aspirin to 59 cents for the leading national brand.[31]

A doctoral dissertation by Charles W. Hauck, involving the grading according to U.S. Department of Agriculture standards of nine unprocessed and six canned fruits and vegetables which were purchased in Columbus, Ohio stores revealed that with the exception of canned beans and canned peas, there was very slight, if any, association between price and quality. In these two cases the degree of correlation was only moderate.[32]

The food items covered are listed below:

Unprocessed foods	Canned foods
Jonathan apples	beans (snap)
Rome beauty apples	cherries
carrots	corn
onions	peas
peas	sauerkraut
potatoes (sweet)	tomatoes
potatoes (white)	
tomatoes	
turnips	

Mr. Hauck concluded that some producers may make "a deliberate effort. . . to disguise low quality with high price, on the theory that if a high price is asked the customer is likely to assume high quality and be more willing to purchase".[33] Canned fruits and vegetables are graded for Consumers Union by the U.S. Department of Agriculture. As a rule six cans of each brand are tested. Figure #1, shows the price ranges for the various grades of 116 brands of canned peaches. Note that Grade "A" Clingstone peach halves could be bought for a cheaper price than some brands which were graded "C". For Freestone peach slices a grade "A" brand was cheaper than some grade "B", "C", and "D" brands. In tests of Turkish Towels, based on strength and rate of absorption, a leader in quality among 17 brands examined by Consumers' Research was the Marshall Field model, "Fieldcrest" ($1.25). Inferior to the "Fieldcrest" were the "Callaway Absorbenized" ($1.49), the "Pacific Supersorb" ($1.98), and one of the Sears-Roebuck "Harmony House" brands ($1.89). The latter towel was "not-recommended" because of low breaking strength and poor rate of absorption.[34]

Among 30 of the leading brands of sun glasses rated by Consumers Union, one of the best in optical quality was the "Fosta" ($1.98). Some of the more expensive brands were rated "not-acceptable" — "American Polaroid," for example, ($1.95 and $2.69) because of bad distortions, and "Rockglas Naviex" ($4.98) because of differences between the lenses in light transmission of 20 to 33 percent.[35] Among nine electric refrigerators, all featuring an across-the-top freezing compartment, Consumers Union rated the "General Electric NH8-F" ($399.75) the best in over-all quality. Yet, the "Kelvinator

MM," selling for only a few dollars less ($389.95) was considered "non-acceptable" because its freezing compartment failed to maintain a temperature low enough for efficient storage.[36] Consumers' Research tested a half-dozen samples of each of six brands of flashlight batteries, type D. Each brand sold for ten cents, but the average life of the different brands varied from 900 minutes for the "Burgess No. 2" samples to 475 minutes for the "General Leakproof" samples.[37] These illustrations of the unreliability of price as a guide to product merit appear to be typical of nearly all goods which consumers buy.

Method of Stating the Cost of Consumer Credit

Much confusion exists over the true cost of credit to consumers who borrow money or purchase on the installment plan. Interest charges are often stated as a percent of the original amount borrowed, but repayments are made at regular intervals. An accurate statement would show the interest rate in relation to the unpaid balance. Dr. Ruth Ayers presented the results of an interest rate study made in Massachusetts at the T.N.E.C. Hearings. Of 106 cases in which the stated interest rate was six percent, only 2 cases were actually below nine percent, seven were over 100 percent and the rest were somewhere in between.[38] *Business Week* has reported what it considers a typical abuse in the installment selling of automobiles. A Cleveland, Ohio, dealer was advertising new cars for "$100 down and $40 a month." Taking the advertised price of a new car at $1,795, it was found that such extras as heater, tax, and title transfer would bring the total cost to $1,918. Assuming a down payment of $118, the balance to be financed would be $1,800. Insurance for two years, plus six percent interest and carrying charges would bring the total amount due to $2,263. After two years of paying $40 per month, a balance due of $1,343 would remain. If the loan were renewed for another two years on a comparable basis, at the end of that time the buyer would still owe $920. After a third 2-year renewal expired the buyer would have paid in, all told, $2,878, and would still owe $151.60 — more than the car would be worth on the basis of normal depreciation.[39]

Honesty in the Service Trades

Another problem facing consumers is the possibility that they will be cheated by unscrupulous producers. The *Readers Digest* made an analysis of the honesty of automobile, radio, and watch repairmen in 1941. The investigation covered 347 auto garages, 304 radio repair shops, and 462 watch repair dealers selected at random from large and small communities in every state. The investigators were a man and a woman who traveled around the country in a second-hand Lincoln Zephyr coupe, which was also used for the automobile repair tests. The man was an expert mechanic who kept the coupe in flawless condition. The radios used were two new portables in perfect working order. The watches were widely known brands also in flawless operating condition. The general plan for each of the three types of investigation was identical — a simple and obvious defect was introduced into the product which was shortly afterwards submitted to a repair man for correction. In the case of the auto, a wire was disconnected which caused the engine to operate on only six of its twelve cylinders. In the case of the radios, a tube was loosened or a snap-on wire disconnected. In the case of the watches a small screw fastening down the crown wheel was loosened, disengaging the gears so that the watches would no longer wind. About 37 percent of the auto repairmen saw the loose wire at once, fixed it in a few seconds, and either asked a reasonable sum or made no charge. The rest (63 percent) gave all together 74 different explanations of what was wrong, and charged bills as high as $24.60.[40] In the radio repair experiments the investigators were cheated 64 percent of the time,[41] and 68 pseudo-diagnoses were made.[42] In the watch repair cases the investigators were cheated 49 percent of the time, and 54 fake defects were given.[43] Dishonesty was considerably greater in large communities than in small. For example, in New York City, only two of sixteen garage men were honest.[45]

Ignorance of Proper Nutrition

Another consumer problem is the ignorance of homemakers with regard to the nutritional needs of their families. Fewer than one-fifth of the families in the country had diets in 1936 that met the recommendations of the Food and Nutrition Board of the National Research Council with respect to desirable nutritional content. While one-quarter of the farm families met the standard, only one-seventh of the non-farm families were at this level. The Council regards these figures as optimistic because they do not take into account wastes or nutritive loss in food preparation.[46] At the National Nutrition Conference in 1941, Brigadier General Lewis B. Hershey, Deputy Director, Selective Service System, declared that probably one-third of the 40 percent of the men of the nation who had been rejected as unfit by the Selective Service were suffering from disabilities directly or indirectly connected with nutrition.[47] A Better Business Bureau booklet on vitamins points out that "Those suffering from malnutrition are not confined to the under-privileged, but include a high percentage of the population that can well afford to and does spend considerable money for food."[48] Statistics cited by Dr. Ouida Abbott at the 1949 National Dietary Food Association Convention reveal that only one family in ten has a good diet, four in ten have passable diets, and of the remaining five families over half have poor diets. Dr. Abbott maintained that these statistics were valid for wealthy and middle classes as well as the poor.[49]

Monopoly

Workable competition in modern capitalistic industries requires the freedom of entry into industries, discussed in Chapter II. It requires also such rivalry among sellers that if any enterprise were to raise its price, without altering quality or the conditions of sale, it would be unable to maintain its former share of the customer market.[50] Competition, however, does not necessitate continuous competing upon the basis of price. Rivalry may vary between price, quality, and conditions of sale so long as there is the potentiality of price competition. It may exist between firms producing identical or differentiated goods in the same industry, between entire marketing channels established to move particular commodities from an early producing stage to the consumer, or between industries producing substitute goods. It is consistent with markets in which there are many or few sellers so long as the tests noted above are met.[51]

Conversely, monopoly is present (1) when freedom of entry is arbitrarily restricted; (2) when an enterprise is able to raise its price, while maintaining previous quality and conditions of sale, without loss of its share of the customer market; (3) when an enterprise may maintain its price and share of the market, while offering poorer quality or less favorable conditions of sale; or (4) when the possibility of price competition is absent.

Consumer welfare in a capitalistic economy is a sort of by-product of the profit motive. Without the protection of workable competition among sellers, consumers may be exploited in any or all of the following ways: (1) restriction of output; (2) exorbitant prices; (3) delay or prevention of quality improvements; (4) quality deterioration or induced obsolescence in order to speed up replacement sales; (5) a drying up of consumer options as to the conditions of sale.

While monopoly is customarily discussed in relation to business enterprises, it may prevail in labor unions as well when unions have such bargaining strength with management that they are able to enforce their demands without appreciable loss of employment for their members.

Some examples of monopoly and attempted monopoly should illustrate the nature of this consumer problem. Few industries are more infested with monopolistic restraints than the building industry. Some of the cases in which the Anti-trust Division of the Justice Department were involved during 1949 were the following: (1) Action was taken against three firms manufacturing water-thinned and water-mixed paints who were charged with conspiracy to fix and stabilize prices.[52] (2) A case was brought against four manufacturers of sand-paper and others, charged with price fixing through patent pools to eliminate competition.[53] (3) Another suit involved the National Wall Paper Wholesalers' Association of Philadelphia and others, charging a conspiracy to fix discounts, allowances, and other terms and conditions of sale for wall paper throughout the United States.[54] (4) Another action was against the National Lead Co., Titan Co., Inc., E.I. du Pont de Nemours and Co., and others with respect to titanium pigments used principally in the manufacture of paints. Defendants were accused of engaging in an international cartel which had divided the world into exclusive non-competitive areas, each assigned to a certain member of the conspiracy. It was alleged that patents were pooled and that restrictions were imposed upon small producers of titanium pigments in the United States.[55] (5) Action was taken against the Seattle Electrical Contractors' Association and members, charged with price fixing and refusing to supply labor to install electrical equipment unless the same was purchased from the defendants.[56] (6) Another case involved the Besser Manufacturing Co., makers of machinery for the production of concrete blocks. The charge was combination through stock purchases, some of it secretly, leading to the control of 80 percent of the market. The defendant was accused of attempting to eliminate competition from the rest of the industry by the illegal extension of patent rights and the harassment and oppression of small competitors by threats of suit against them and their customers.[57] (7) Another suit was against 14 building material dealers and one individual in the Cleveland area, charging that defendants had eliminated competition through the use of a uniform price list for some 90 hard building materials used in home construction.[58] (8) Another action was against the Northern California Plumbing and Heating Wholesalers Association, 16 of its members, and others, charging a conspiracy to fix prices in the sale of plumbing supplies.[59] (9) Still another action was against four kitchen equipment manufacturing corporations and others charging that a bid depository was maintained, the use of which enabled the defendants to take turns in obtaining contracts at excessive prices.[60] Labor unions in the building industry have likewise been guilty of monopolistic practices. Exorbitant initiation fees and discriminatory membership rules have restricted entry into unions, and through this artificially induced scarcity, increased or maintained high wages for workmen. "Make work" rules, unofficial in many instances, have forced the use of more labor than necessary in construction projects, and have retarded the introduction of cost-reducing building methods such as pre-fabrication.

The building trades are by no means alone in their futherance of monopolistic restraints. Several additional cases in which the Justice Department was involved during 1949 are illustrative. (1) Action was taken against 19 linen supply corporation and others doing business in Philadelphia, Pennsylvania, Southern New Jersey, and Northern Delaware, charging a conspiracy to fix prices and allocate customers in this market area.[61] (2) A case was brought against the Univex Lens Co., and others who were accused of combining with wholesale optical dealers throughout the United States to fix the resale prices of multifocal eye glass lenses.[62] (3) Another suit involved Austenal Laboratories, Inc., makers of dental alloy used in dentures. The charge was an illegal use of patent license agreements with 175 dental laboratories by which the defendant required these laboratories to purchase all chromium-cobalt alloys from Austenal.[63] (4) Another action was against two Chicago corporations and others, makers of a newly developed plastic eye. The defendants were accused of threatening competitors with patent infringement suits, and of falsely claiming patent rights which they did not have.[64] (5) One suit involved the Tri-State Retail Dealers Association of Pittsburgh and others, charging price fixing of records sold to the general public, churches, schools and music-box operators. The defendants were accused of boycotting manufacturers and distributors of low-priced records.[65] (6) Still another case was against the Stern Fish Co., of Philadelphia and others charging that potential competitors in the Philadelphia market were paid to refrain from competing with the defendants in the live fish business with the result that the defendants were able to control 90 to 95 percent of the annual wholesale live fish business in this market, and to charge unreasonably high prices.[66]

A somewhat different type of limited monopoly power is often obtained by promotional techniques. The good will attached to a given brand name may permit the seller of that brand to raise his

TABLE III

Number of Consumers in Boston and Washington, D.C. Who
Would Buy by Brand Regardless of Price for Certain
Prepared Food Products*

Prepared Food Product	Total Number of Consumers Reporting	Number of Consumers Who Would Buy by Brand Regardless of Price
fresh meat	54	10
American cheese	53	12
soda crackers	52	13
corn flakes	41	13
canned pineapple	51	11
dried raisins	41	10
salt	55	16
butter	53	16
evaporated milk	36	14
white bread	56	18
rolled oats	41	12
bacon	53	14
ginger ale	45	15
cocoa	46	15
family flour	53	22
canned baked beans	50	17
canned salmon	50	18
tomato soup	51	14
tea	54	21

* Adapted from Saul Nelson and Walter Keim, *Price Behavior and Business Policy* (Washington, D.C., T.N.E.C. Monograph #1, 1940), p. 79.

price without appreciable loss of patronage, and maintain a premium price over other goods of comparable or even higher quality. In the T.N.E.C. investigation some of the staff members circulated a questionnaire among a small group of consumers in Washington, D.C. and Boston. Consumers were asked to specify on a list of 60 prepared foods the degree to which their purchasing was determined by brand preference. Table III, which includes 19 of 60 foods, shows that a large number of consumers buy by brand, regardless of price for certain food products. A Gallup Public Opinion Poll in 1940, showed that about 72 percent of consumers, as a general rule, were willing to pay more to obtain a product with a nationally-known brand name.[67] The lack of association between price and quality, noted earlier in the chapter, likewise suggests the monopolistic value of certain brand identifications. Further proof is indicated in the fabulous prices sometimes paid for the purchase of established brand names.[68]

The Forgotten Man in Politics

A look at the record makes it clear that the consumer interest is not a major factor influencing the voting in legislatures. High import tariffs on such unessential domestic products as green olives, oriental rugs and laces, perfumes, pepper, cheeses, and epsom salts, to name only a few, result in higher-than-necessary consumer prices. Interstate trade barriers such as discriminatory inspection laws against goods and trucks moving across state lines produce similar results. Liberal patent laws protect monopolies. Likewise, 12 states have anti-chain store taxes which protect independent merchants at the expense of consumer pocketbooks. Many cities have antiquated building codes and cost-padding regulations which protect jobs for those in the building trades. So-called "unfair trade" laws in 25 states fix price floors below which merchants cannot sell their goods. "Fair trade" laws permit manufacturers to set a minimum retail price for their branded goods.[69] The McGuire Act legalizes this price fixing in interstate commerce. "Fair trade" laws are like an umbrella, protecting inefficient retailers from competition by the efficient. In the late 1940's statutes appeared in many states outlawing self-service gasoline stations which were able to sell fuel oil five cents a gallon cheaper than full-service outlets, and were threatening to drive out existing vested interests.

Federal farm legislation has enforced scarcity and high prices for food products, adding billions of dollars to the food costs of U.S. consumers. The exemption of labor unions from prosecution under the Sherman Anti-trust Law enables a strong union by strike action, to paralyze some sector of the economy, causing great inconvenience and sometimes danger to the consumer. This exemption also fosters monopoly by enabling handicraft enterprises such as barbers, plumbers and carpenters to establish legally a uniform price for their services on a city-wide basis.

The Food, Drug, and Cosmetic Act of 1938, wangled through Congress after five years of delay tactics led by certain vested interests, contained many loopholes. Soaps, for example, were excluded. The ingredients of cosmetics did not have to be indicated on the labels. There was no provision for official testing to assure the safety of new cosmetics before release to the public. Food labels did not have to give the amount or percent of various ingredients contained.[70]

In 1946, Congress emasculated price controls although the National Opinion Research Center reported April 11, 1956, that 82 percent of the U.S. consumers wanted their full preservation.[71] At the hearings on the extension of price controls before the House Banking and Currency Committee, oil producers were given a whole morning to testify. Real estate representatives had four and one-half hours. The National Association of Manufacturers received an entire morning. Twenty consumer organizations representing ten million consumers were given one and one-half hours one afternoon after 5 P.M., when no more than five members of the House Committee were present.[72]

Demands by consumer leaders for positive aids such as compulsory grade labeling and a Federal Department of the Consumer, which would parallel the representation accorded business, agriculture, and labor, have steadily been ignored.

How true it is, as Stacy May had pointed out, that "In the world of politics, the consumer is a blind beggar of gigantic stature, who stands on the corner of Paradox Street and Pressure Group Lane with nothing to sell but his woe. . . *Consumers'* claims have a universality that makes them the most respectable of all the economic interests, but the smaller, and tougher, and better coordinated pressure groups run off with all the prizes."[73]

Consumers May Not Recognize Their Plight

It is sometimes argued that the majority of consumers are well satisfied with their existing position in the economy, and that there is, therefore, no consumer plight of the nature discussed in this chapter. Such reasoning appears seriously fallacious to the author. Many "satisfied" consumers are merely unaware of their problems, while others are possibly profiting in their role as producers from the exploitation of consumers in general.

Certainly ignorance of a problem does not justify the conclusion that there is no problem, for to argue this would mean that a person with cancer has no problem unless he is aware of the cancer, that malnutrition is not serious unless people are aware of it, that fraudulent patent medicines are no problem if consumers believe the claims and die after their usage, that dishonesty is of no concern if it is carefully concealed. The philosophy that "ignorance is bliss" must be rejected as completely barren.

QUESTIONS FOR REVIEW

1. What sort of "plight" is referred to?
2. What are the main reasons for the consumers' plight?
3. One authority has estimated that there are 30,000 actively advertised brands of goods on the American market. Of what significance is this to the plight of the consumer?
4. Some observers criticise our economy for making a bewildering choice of goods available on the market place, while at the same time, others castigate it for monopoly, stating that business is in too few hands in some industries. How can this be? Who is right?
5. Since the Federal Trade Commission in a recent year set aside a little more than 3 percent of the hundreds of thousands of advertisements examined for falseness, how can critics pillory advertising? After all, the FTC found 97 percent of American advertising to be O.K.
6. Why do you think the FDA and FTC gave first priority to examining the drug industry? Was this a case of discrimination?
7. "You only get what you pay for," True?
8. Dr. Beem feels that many consumers do not recognize their plight. They live in a "fool's paradise". Would you think that this would apply more to the rich or to the poor? The whites more than the blacks? The poorly educated rather than the well educated?
9. It has been argued that really the consumers' plight is his or her own fault. For if the consumer wanted objective facts about goods he or she could easily obtain them from *Consumer Reports*, government bulletins, home economics pages in the newspapers, etc. Do you agree? If not, what is wrong with this argument?

FOOTNOTES

1. Charles Wyand, *Economics of Consumption* (New York, MacMillan Co., 1937), p. 117.

2. *Annual Report by the Federal Trade Commission*, for the final year ending June 30, 1970, p. 8.

3. Hazel Fletcher and Lois Denhardt, "Adequacy of Labeling of Certain Textile Fabrics with Regard to Fiber Content," *Journal of Agricultural Research* (June 15, 1939), p. 901.

4. Reported in *New York Times*, May 7, 1950, p. F-11, col. #4. Since the passage of the Wool Products Labelling Act, Textile Fiber Products Identification Act. Fur Products Labelling Act, and the Flammable Fabrics Act, much better protection of the consumer has come about. For example, the Federal Trade Commission in 1970, made more than 10,000 inspections under the four acts; of these, 4,776 alone were under the Flammable Fabrics Act. The Bureau of Textiles and Furs turned up about three million misbranded items valued at some $40 million. (*FTC Annual Report*, 1970, p. 33).

5. "Containers at the Crossroads", *Consumers' Guide* (March, 1946), p. 12.

6. *Consumer Reports* (August, 1948), p. 356-357.

7. *Ibid.* (July, 1949), p. 311.

8. *Ibid.* (August, 1949), pp. 349-351.

9. *Ibid.* (February, 1950), pp. 61-63. The new Packaging and Labelling Act, 1966, has had some effect in reducing this proliferation of container and package sizes. But, it is still a weak law, and the situation outlined above unfortunately still prevails for the most part.

10. William T. Foster, "Dollars, Doctors, and Disease," *Atlantic Monthly* (January, 1933), p. 92.

11. *Consumer Reports* (August, 1949), p. 351.

12. *Ibid.*, (April, 1971), pp. 238-239.

13. *Ibid.*, p. 516.

14. *Ibid.* (February, 1949), p. 59.

15. *Ibid.* (April, 1971), pp. 246-248.

16. *Ibid.* (July, 1948), p. 303.

17. Consumers' Research Bulletin (May, 21, 1949), p. 10.

18. *Ibid.* (January, 1949), p. 17.

19. *Ibid.* (Sept., 1949), p. 13-14.

20. *Ibid.* (June, 1949), p. 18-19.

21. *C. R. Annual Cumulative Bulletin* (1949-1950), p. 172.

22. *Ibid.*, p. 345.

23. *Annual Report, H.E.W.* (1970), p. 250.

24. *Annual Report, Federal Security Agency* (1948), p. 552.

25. *Consumer Reports* (February, 1971), pp. 114-117.

26. *Consumer Reports* (August, 1972), p. 542.

27. *Ibid*, p. 543.

28. The FTC instituted a complaint against *Excederin* and several other brands in 1961. In 1965 it withdrew its complaint against *Excederin* altogether, having accomplished nothing. It took the FTC sixteen years to get the word "liver" out of *Carter's Little Liver Pills. Ibid.*

29. Ruby T. Norris, *Theory of Consumer's Demand* (New Haven, Yale University Press, 1941), p. 185.

30. Saul Nelson and Walter G. Keim, *Price Behavior and Business Policy* (TNEC Monograph #1, 1940), p. 81.

31. *Consumer Reports*, (August, 1972), p. 541.

32. Charles W. Hauck, *Tests of Reliability of Brands and Retail Prices as Guides to the Quality of Selected Fresh and Canned Fruits and Vegetables* (Columbus, Ohio, unpublished, typewritten doctoral dissertation presented to the faculty of Ohio State University, 1939), pp. 50-53.

33. *Ibid.*, p. 54.

34. *Ibid.* (October, 1949), p. 9-10.

35. Consumers Reports (July, 1948), p. 306.

36. *Ibid.* (October, 1949), pp. 451-452.

37. *Consumers' Research Bulletin* (April, 1950), p. 24.

38. Ruth Ayers, "Problems of the Consumer," *T.N.E.C. Hearings, Part 8*, (1940), p. 3356.

39. *Business Week*, "Easy Auto Credit Returns," (October 29, 1949), p. 21. This case would be less likely to happen today in view of the Truth in Lending Act, 1969. But people for the most part still do not pay attention to the actual rate of interest revealed in the installment contracts. See "The 1970 Survey of Consumer Awareness of Finance Charges and Interest Rates" in *Annual Report to Congress on Truth in Lending for the year 1970*, (Board of Governors of the Federal Reserve System, January 4, 1971).

40. Roger W. Riis, "The Repair Man Will Gyp You If You Don't Watch Out." *Readers Digest* (July, 1941), pp. 2-3.

41. Roger W. Riis, "The Radio Repair Man Will Gyp You If You Don't Watch Out," *Readers Digest* (August, 1941), p. 6.

42. *Ibid.*, p. 8.

43. Roger W. Riis, "The Watch Repair Man Will Gyp You If You Don't Watch Out," *Readers Digest* (August, 1941), p. 11.

44. *Ibid.*, p. 12.

45. *op. cit.* (July, 1941), p. 3. The research project is written up in greater detail in Roger W. Riis and John Patric, *Repair Men Will Get you If You Don't Watch Out*, (Garden City, New York., Doubleday, Doran & Co., 1942).

46. *Bulletin of National Research Council #109*, (November, 1943). "Inadequate Diets and Nutritional Deficiencies in the U.S."

47. Lewis B. Hershey, *Proceedings of the National Nutritional Conference* (Washington, D.C., May, 1941), p. 64.

48. Better Business Bureau, *"Facts You Should Know About Vitamins"*, p. 15.

49. *Consumer News Digest* (October, 1949), p. 8.

50. This test was suggested by Professor Simon W. Kuznets in a lecture given in his course in Economic Development, 1948.

51. For a complementary development of the concept of workable competition see John M. Clark, "Toward a Concept of Workable Competition," *American Economic Review* (June, 1940), pp. 241-256; John M. Clark, *Alternative to Serfdom* (New York, Alfred A. Knopf Co., 1948), pp. 68-72; Clair Wilcox,

Competition and Monopoly (T.N.E.C. Monograph #21, 1940) pp. 8-9; Reavis Cox, *op. cit.* Jesse W. Markham, *"Alternative Approach to the Concept of Workable Competition,"* *American Economic Review* (June, 1950), pp. 349-361. The concept is discussed more fully in the treatment of monopoly in the following chapter.

52. *Department of Justice press release*, January, 1949.

53. *Ibid.*, January 28, 1949.

54. *Ibid.*, 1949 (no month and day given).

55. *Ibid.*, (March 1, 1949).

56. *Ibid.*, (March 14, 1949).

57. *Ibid.*, (April 28, 1949).

58. *Ibid.* (May 3, 1949).

59. *Ibid.* (June 22, 1949).

60. *Ibid.* (July 13, 1949).

61. *Ibid.* (April 25, 1949).

62. *Ibid.* (May 24, 1949).

63. *Ibid.* (June 10, 1949).

64. *Ibid.* (June 23, 1949).

65. *Ibid.* (November 2, 1949).

66. *Ibid.* (December 7, 1949).

67. ,,*Survey of Public Buying Habits*, A.I.P.O. (Ballot 703 C, September 29, 1940), p. 23.

68. For additional illustrations of the monopoly problem see: Thurman Arnold, The Bottlenecks of Business (New York, Reynal & Hitchcock, 1940); David Lynch, *The Concentration of Economic Power* (New York, Columbia University Press, 1946); Corwin Edwards, *Maintaining Competition* (New York, McGraw Hill Co., 1949); *The Federal Anti-trust Laws*, with Summary of Cases Instituted by the United States (New York, Commerce Clearing House, Inc., 1949).

69. Once existing in as many as 45 states, these laws have been eroded in recent years by adverse court cases and lack of enforcement. At their height, it is estimated that no more than five to ten percent of retail sales have ever been covered by fair-trade contracts — these were mainly in drugs, patent medicines, liquor, and photographic equipment. See: William J. Stanton, *Fundamentals of Marketing* (New York: McGraw-Hill, 1971), p. 471.

70. The Labelling Act of 1966 changed this in certain cases. See pp.

71. Reported in *Public Opinion Quarterly* (Summer, 1946), p. 278.

72. Chase G. Woodhouse, "The Consumer and Congress," *Journal of Home Economics* (September, 1946), p. 389.

73. Stacy May, "The Work Most Needed in the Next 5 Years," *"Next Steps in Consumer Education* (Proceedings of 1st Conference of Institute for Consumer Education, Columbia, Missouri, 1939), pp. 179-180.

EUGENE R. BEEM

Much of the predicament of consumers is rooted in their own apathy, and in their lack of buying skill, but one must not blame consumers alone for this situation. They are the legatee of a whole complex of forces.

Reasons for the Consumers' Plight

The reasons for the predicament of consumers are pointed out by the evolution in production and distribution activities during the last century. About 150 years ago families were largely self-sufficient. There were craftsmen in the towns ready to produce for those rich enough to pay the price — silversmiths, shoemakers, butchers, bakers and candlestick makers, but on the whole, production and consumption were organized around the family unit, and the problem of spending the family income wisely seldom presented itself. Being skilled craftsmen themselves, the family heads, when they did make purchases, were experts at wise buying.

What are the changes to be noted as the focus shifts to a later era? The Industrial Revolution introduced the economies of specialization, mechanization, and large scale production, and was the godfather not only of high living standards, but also of the consumers' plight. Let us look at the forces — most of them growing out of the Industrial Revolution which account for the present predicament of consumers.

(1) A rapidly rising standard of living has, in itself, created a consumer problem, for it has meant a tremendous widening in the scope of possible goods and services among which buyers may choose, and this, as noted in the last chapter, has made the task of wise selection exceedingly complex.

(2) A high plant investment, and the need in many industries for mass production or steady output to achieve economies, leads to production in anticipation of demand. Under pressure to find a mass market to absorb goods, producers may resort to exaggerated claims, pseudo-product differentiation, high pressure selling, and sometimes to outright fraud.

(3) A high living standard aggrevates consumer problems in another way. Many of the goods produced are non-essentials for which demand is notoriously fickle. In an effort to achieve stability in their operations, producers are tempted to use aggressive selling and advertising to manipulate this demand in their own interests.

(4) The mechanization of production coupled with the growth of fancy packaging and trimming has made it much harder for buyers to discern real quality. When manufacturers put an attractive "front" on their product, consumers may be misled as to what is really inside.

(5) Vast improvements in communication and transportation facilities during the last century have also aggravated the consumer's predicament, while at the same time making possible an enormous increase in his well-being. Great inequalities in living standards, less noticed in earlier times, have become apparent to the poorer households. As a result the preference scales of the poor have been revamped by their vision of abundance enjoyed by the rich. This has led some producers to debase their products in any way necessary to reach the low income families.

(6) Less of the personal contact between producer and consumer, which characterized the era of handicraft production, has increased the likelihood of producer misrepresentation. It is much easier to exploit an unknown customer than one the producer knows and constantly meets fact to face. This gulf also increases the difficulty of determining buyers' preferences in advance of production, and thus becomes another tendency impelling the producer toward aggressive methods to sell what has already been produced.

(7) The spirit of specialization and mechanization have invaded the home as well as the factory. The knowledge of foods, cloths, and woods, which was second nature to craft-minded forefathers, was lost as succeeding generations made less and less goods themselves, and bought more and more from the stores. In the last century of growing divorcement between production and consumption the science of wise buying has atrophied like a muscle which gets little use. More physical therapy in the form of consumer education is badly needed.

(8) While specialization and mechanization in production were followed by large scale producing units, their entrance into the home has led to no appreciable change in the small scale nature of consuming units. This small scale operation is a serious barrier to intelligent consumption. Learning objective tests for quality and their application often appear to be a waste of time and energy, particularly since the scope of buying encompasses so many different products. So, many consumers fall back on the very unsatisfactory rule of judging quality by price with the result that sometimes producers hesitate to ask low prices for fear of discouraging sales.

(9) The growth of gargantuan enterprises with nation-wide markets has made profitable the extensive use of newspaper, periodical, and radio advertising. About two-thirds of newspaper and periodical receipts, and a large percentage of radio and television income comes from commercial sponsors. The effect has naturally been to ally these powerful instruments of persuasion with the vested interests of the producers. As a result, the press and broadcasting tend to hold back information which might weaken the confidence of citizens in business enterprises, and the consumer is lulled into a

false sense of security in his buying. Action taken by the Food and Drug Administration against adulteration and by the Federal Trade Commission against misleading advertising ought to be page one news when the indicted are nationally known firms, but frequently such news is suppressed or hidden away on a back page where few will find it.

(10) Another explanation for consumer apathy is the presence of higher than subsistence living standards among most families. The prospect of what is erroneously forseen as "small savings" makes it "too much bother" to learn wise consumption habits or to urge legislators to vote for consumer interests.

(11) Still another reason for consumer apathy lies in the nature of the family unit. The ability to manage a home efficiently is not a primary attribute which most men require when they select a mate, nor are divorces commonly granted for bungling the family finances. Most women relegate the art of home economics to a minor importance beneath their husbands, their children, and their social and recreational interests. Perhaps it is this factor which has given rise to the definition of a consumer as "a person of sluggish intellect who doesn't know what he wants."

(12) The organization of business interests into pressure groups such as the National Association of Manufacturers, the Chamber of Commerce, and 2,000 national trade associations, the organization of farm interests behind national spokesman such as the National Farmers Union and American Farm Bureau Federation, the organization of laboring groups into the Congress of Industrial Organization and the American Federation of Labor — all these represent groups which stand between the consumer and the market, and between the individual and his government. They are the components of an evolving feature of our society, rule by pressure groups. By contrast, consumers, until the last few years, have been almost entirely unorganized. Lacking both articulation and buying information, they have been prey to mulcting by these powerful groups in the legislatures as well as in the markets. Business and labor groups bargain for wage increases which are paid for by consumers in higher prices. Monopolistic conspiracies raise prices, cheapen quality, and stifle progress. Legislatures pass laws which protect certain business, farm, or labor interests at the expense of consumers. Bills in the consumer interest die in pigeon holes or pass in weakened form, for as David Lynch has suggested, "When substantially all the pressure, suasion, duress, and publicity is in one direction, legislators often willingly or unwillingly yield."

(13) There are certain difficulties involved in organizing a sizable group of consumers as a competing pressure group. As Caroline Ware points out,

> Consumers lack a point of focus, for their interests are
> spread over the whole range of goods and services, and
> are directed toward particular products only for the short
> period when a particular purchase is being made.

Moreover, since benefits reach consumers by devious routes — not directly like wage increases negotiated by workers with employers — it is hard to show results. Consequently, it is difficult to enlist sufficient interest and inspire sufficient confidence among people who have little in common except their buying to provide an adequate economic base in membership payments. It is hard to envisage, say a million consumers paying "union dues" of a dollar a month to provide a treasury such as that with which the United Automobile Workers — CIO, can operate for its members.[2]

(14) The rise of monopoly power is explained, for the most part, by the following factors: economies from large scale production, inelastic demand, insecurity, patents, control of the supply of a productive agent, and consumer ignorance. In some industries the size of enterprise necessary to achieve maximum efficiency in production is so large in relation to the size of the market that there is room for only one or a few enterprises in the industry. Federal and regional governments have established regulatory commissions over this type of industry in some fields, notably public utilities and railroads — an admission that without competition the unregulated market is intolerable.

When there are a limited number of business units producing a homogeneous product in an industry confronted with inelastic demand, there is a powerful incentive toward collusion or merger. No single enterprise can increase its market appreciably except at the expense of competitors who are likely to retaliate if price is cut. A policy of "live and let live" may evolve to avoid the costly incidence of price wars. It is no accident that some of the earliest U. S. monopolies were in such fields as salt, sugar, oil, matches, and steel.

Sometimes the purpose of monopoly is not so much inflated profits as it is market stability. Collusion or merger is a threat, for this reason, in industries manufacturing durable producer goods, for downward movements of the business cycle are greatly magnified in these industries, contributing to great insecurity. Loopholes in the patent laws have been an entering wedge for many monopolistic enterprises which have used their patent protection to the detriment of consumers as well as fellow producers. Control of a source of supply, whether it be raw materials, land area, labor, or some other productive agent, has sometimes given the power to extort a payment limited only by what the traffic will bear.

Often consumer ignorance makes possible monopolistic power based upon promotional techniques. In the absence of adequate knowledge about competing goods consumers are prone to rely upon heavily advertised goods, and to trade with sellers who have long been established in the community. As a result rivalry from small, relatively unknown firms sometimes fails to have a salutary effect upon the price, quality, or selling conditions of the giants in the industry. Although exorbitant profits prevail in an industry, new firms are frequently unable to get a foothold because of their inability to overcome the "good will" advantage of the established enterprises. Jerome Ephraim, a small scale manufacturer of toothpaste and other chemical goods, related the nature of this problem at the T.N.E.C. Hearings. He pointed out that it cost about $100,000 just to *test* the possibility of selling a toothpaste in the national market. He concluded that a product, however, meritorious, cannot reach consumers unless the manufacturer can afford the huge advertising outlay necessary to create demand.[3] One author contends that consumer ignorance is one of the leading reasons for the growth of oligopoly in consumer good industries.[4]

Consequences of the Consumers' Plight

The consequences of the consumer problems which have been discussed are a possible endangering of the health and safety of some consumers; a great waste of consumers' income, time, and effort; and a great waste of society's resources. Sumner Slichter has discerned in the inadequacy of consumer knowledge "undoubtedly the greatest source of industrial waste".[5] Among the wastes and dangers which originate in whole or in part from the plight of consumers are the following:

(1) The waste of national resources in the production of illth — positively harmful goods such as some patent medicines and defective merchandise.

(2) The possible endangering of health and safety which results from the consumption of illth.

(3) The production and consumption of health — worthless goods which neither benefit nor harm, such as motor oil dopes or certain therapeutic devices.

(4) The failure of consumers to get the maximum real income out of their spending because (a) they fail to find the quality of product desired, (b) they spend more than is necessary for the quality wished, (c) they are over-charged or short-weighted by dishonest sellers, or (d) they are exploited by monopolistic practices.

(5) The wastage in time and effort of consumers who do not know where to find what they want to buy.

(6) The wastage of food which results from foolishly cooking or cutting away much of its nutritional content, and the health and energy deficiencies which result from a failure to properly balance family diets.

(7) The higher than necessary marketing costs which are due, in part, to the following: (a) a high rate of returned goods by consumers, many of whom did not know the quality of the goods they were buying; (b) the high expense of competitive advertising for products having only superficial differences; (c) those crossfreights which are profitable because of pesudo-differentiation; (d) the excessive number of brands (many representing only pseudo differentiation) which retailers must carry in stock, the effect of

which is to slow down average turnover of inventory and accordingly increase unit costs; (e) a fickleness of consumer demand which accelerates the risks in marketing; (f) the increased number of sales persons needed to counsel prospective customers.

(8) The waste of the nation's resources which results from keeping inefficient producers in business as a result of uninformed buying practices, and as a result of anti-consumer legislation protecting the inefficient from price competition.

Commenting on certain of the types of waste illustrated above, Edwin Nourse suggests that "at the present stage in our business evolution, we seem to have reached something of an impasse between mass production and individual consumption. In a very real sense gains in productivity so ingeniously and industriously 'saved at the spigot' are blindly or improvidently 'wasted at the bunghole'."[6]

Although much remains to be done, progress has been made — especially in the last two decades — in alleviating the plight of consumers. The action on behalf of consumers, which has been termed the Consumer Movement, is an important factor in this picture.

QUESTIONS FOR DISCUSSION

1. What are the historical reasons for the plight of the consumer?

2. Is consumer ignorance responsible for the rise of monopoly influences. Why?

3. What serious consequences result from the ignorance of the consumer and poor buymanship?

4. What can be done to better the position of the consumer and to reduce the attendant waste in our economy?

FOOTNOTES

1. David Lynch, *The Concentration of Economic Power* (New York, Columbia University Press, 1946), p. 300.

2. Caroline F. Ware, *The Consumer Goes To War* (New York, Funk and Wagnalls Company, 1942), p. 33.

3. Jerome W. Ephraim, "Problems of the Consumer," *T.N.E.C. Hearings* (Part 8, 1940), pp. 3396-3412.

4. Tibor Scitovsky, "Ignorance As a Source of Oligopoly Power," American Economic Review (May, 1950), pp. 48-54.

5. Sumner Slitchter, *Modern Economic Society* (New York, Henry Holt and Company, 1931), p. 542.

6. Edwin G. Nourse, *Price Making in a Democracy* (Washington, D.C., Brookings Institute, 1944), p. 244.

HAROLD J. ASHBY, JR.

INTRODUCTION

Background

Among advertising's many purposes is making the consumer aware of a particular product's existence. Whether he ultimately purchases the product is another matter. To make the consumer notice the advertising has been the age old problem. Hundreds of artistic techniques, advertising philosophies, copies, lay-outs, etc. have been proposed. Selecting the right combination of these that capture the consumer's attention is the real challenge.

In the past, advertising agencies had a conception of whom the "average American" was and directed their ad campaigns to him. Assuming Mr. Average American had certain characteristics, ideals, values, concerns, needs, and aspirations; the agencies incorporated these feelings into the campaigns. This was in an effort to make the advertising more appealing. It was further assumed that if Mr. Average America's attention was captured, then the entire American market had been won. However, this has not been the case.

Until recently when advertisers have begun to appreciate the various sub-markets, Mr. Average American was the one to whom advertisers directed their campaigns. But studies have shown there are multitudes of people who do not necessarily fall into Mr. Average America's category. The various ethnic and minority groups who, due to their diverse backgrounds and distinct heritages, cannot be expected to be like Mr. Average America. Although everyone is an American — living and working within the system, an individual is first a member of his particular ethnic group. Instilled within him are certain values and beliefs that are based upon his background. Some groups find themselves closer to the mainstream of American life than others. In fact, some share a heritage that is directly related to the "American culture". However, due to specific circumstances, other groups are more isolated.

One such group is the Black American. As a direct result of his servitude position, the Black has been ignored by the rest of society and left to care for himself in any way that he could. For decades, white America ostracized him from the mainstream of life through discrimination, segregation, and force; she put him outside the fold. In vain attempts to sever him from her community, she forced him to live in concentrated ghettos and forgot him. As the years passed, tremendous changes occured within the Black areas. These ghettos, located in major urban centers, have grown in economic importance. A new large market — the Black Market — has come into existence and is growing faster than the market as a whole. Although they are not comparable to whites, Blacks are slowly beginning to climb the economic ladder. In 1947 the aggregate income of non-whites in the United States (92 percent of non-whites are Black) was $7.2 billion. By 1957 non-white income had more than doubled to $15.3 billion, and by 1963 had more than tripled to $23.6 billion. Non-whites were getting a larger share of the income dollars. In 1947 non-white income was 4.9 percent of white income; by 1963 it was 6.4 percent.[1]

Because of this growth, many national advertisers are eager to tap the Black Market through advertising. White America is suddenly in a hurry to learn more about this market in order to capture it. But advertisers, like the rest of the white society, are lost because Blacks have been ignored for so long that little is known, and even less understood, about the Black and his motivational desires. To complicate the issue, the Black population is not a homogeneous group; what applies for one segment, is not necessarily true for others. Like the rest of America, it is full of variation.

> It is a fallacy that there is a 'Negro market' which is composed of a 'homogeneous' group of people who all listen to the same media, read the same publications and respond as an amorphous man to advertising and market stimuli.[2]

Like the rest of America, the Black community has been affected by the present social revolution. Within the Black community there are hundreds of forces that are reshaping it. The emergence of concepts like "Black Power" and "Black Consciousness" has altered the thinking of many Blacks. Therefore, previous studies made of the Black masses have very little relevance for those attempting to understand it today. Current findings are proving previous studies to be all out of date. An example is the highly praised 1961 Bullock article that was considered as the definite study on Black motivation.

> . . . Just as Negroes reject radio stations beaming only to them, so do they reject advertising copy that has been given a black tone. . . . . Negroes are highly sensitive to what other Negroes buy, but are even more sensitive to the patterns of white consumers. They do not want to be Negro, but they do not want to be white either. They want to be *like* white people — to be able to live the way whites do, own the things whites have, enjoy the same privileges.[3]

But according to John H. Johnson, publisher of *Ebony*, "The Negro is increasingly responsive to advertising oriented toward him."[4], and to Robert Bell, general manager of WVON, Chicago, "Negroes no longer want to be white. They are proud to be Negroes and recognized as such".[5] Leonard Evans, publisher of *Tuesday*, sums it up:

The first blunder of advertising and marketing people in assessing the Negro market is assuming that the Negro wants to be white. He doesn't want to be white or act white. If anything, he is getting more nationalistic and prouder of his color all the time.[6]

The problem before white business firms and white advertising agencies is how to attract Black America's attention. As advertising is the main tool to make the consumer aware, how does one get the Black's eye? Ad agencies have planned elaborate campaigns that they thought would appeal to Blacks, but later find them ineffective. In other cases, ad agencies used the same ads that were designed for the general public in black media and call themselves directing it to Blacks by substituting Black models for white ones. And still other firms indiscriminately integrate their advertising, hoping that this is the answer. But at present, no one really knows the answer.

Scope of the Study

The Black consumer is a relatively new target. And as such, advertisers are not quite sure how to approach him. Many agencies have their own particular philosophy and own approach to the question. But these techniques have not been adequately tested to determine their effectiveness. At the same time many marketing journals are now publishing results of scholarly studies conducted on the Black Market and on all aspects related to it, including advertising. As this author sees it, there is beginning to develop a substantial amount of material on advertising directed towards Blacks, but few are making the effort to collect and analyze it and then applying their findings to the problem. Therefore, this paper is a broad survey of the background behind, and the current thinking in this area. To be more specific, it will study the various communicative techniques used by ad agencies in visual advertising aimed at Blacks through national magazines.

Definition of Terms

The following terms are used throuthout the reading according to the definitions here supplied:

Black stereotypes — the representation of the Black in an unflattering manner; as an undesirable, despicable character; or as typically lazy, ignorant, servile, or inherently inferior to whites.

General advertising — advertising that is directed to the masses with a general target in mind; advertisments appearing in national media distributed to the general public.

All-Black advertising — Black themes, life styles, or all Black models in non-stereotyped roles in the pictorial

portions of advertisements in media distributed to the
general public or in media directed to Black audiences.

Integrated advertising — the inclusion of Blacks (or other
identifiable non-white ethnic groups) in non-stereotyped
roles in the pictorial portions of advertisements in media
distributed to the general public as opposed to media
directed to ethnic audiences.

There are two types of Black portrayals that might be excluded
from this definition of integrated advertising. First, the appearance in
an advertisement of a well-known Black personality, athlete,
entertainer, or the like, who appears because of his fame or
popularity. As such, he does not represent the ordinary person, but is
unique. Second, the appearance of Blacks in scenes representing
foreign countries where customs and racial relationships may be
different from the United States. For example, an advertisement
showing white American tourists sightseeing in a country populated
predominately by Blacks cannot be considered as integrated
advertising.

Section II HISTORICAL BACKGROUND

How The Black Image Developed In This Country

The treatment of the Black in fiction and non-fiction has varied
with changes in social, economic and political conditions over the
years. During the post-Reconstruction period of the late 19th
century, writers and editors, particularly in the South, vilified the
Black in print. Slavery had been abolished but most Southern writers
were intent upon keeping the Black "in his place".

Southern editors used such terms as nigger, coon, burr head,
ginger cake, and darky when referring to Blacks. The context in
which such terms were used often amplified their sting. As Thomas
Clark observed, "Seldom did this word (nigger) appear in print
without a suggestion of bitter vengeance or scrutiny behind it".[7]
And it was not just Southern editors who ridiculed the Black with
such derisive terms; many Northern newspapers used them as well.

Even leading literary magazines in the 1880's and 1890's used
derogatory reference to Blacks in stories, poems, anecdotes, and
cartoons. Terms such as nigger, darky, coon, pickaninny, and yaller
hussy appeared regularly in *Harper's*, *Century*, and *Atlantic Monthly*.
The Black was depicted as being "superstitious, dull and stupid,
ignorant, suspicious, happy-go-lucky, lazy, immoral, criminal; he was
a liar, a thief, and a drunkard".[8]

The treatment of the Black by the media in the North changed
between 1890 and 1910. While Southern writers and editors
continuously degraded the Black to keep him "in his place", the
Northern media largely turned their backs on him. Newspapers that

formerly reported activities of prominent Black groups and leaders reduced such coverage. News about Black communities turned to growing social problems such as crime. The stereotyped view of the Black as a "problem" emerged.

The year 1915 brought a devastating blow to the Black image. The motion picture, *The Birth of a Nation*, was released. The film was critically acclaimed as a masterpiece. But despite its artistic and technical merits, the film did more to promote anti-Black feeling than any other thing, before or since. The film served to magnify the emotional reaction of whites to Blacks as vile, fearsome brutes.

The film industry never really emerged into the "social realism" era of the twenties. With the exception of the films that pictured the Black as an immoral brute or uncivilized savages, most of Hollywood's movies stereotyped the Black as the faithful family retainer or the ignorant clown. The latter was standard from the beginning of commercial film making, through the 1920's, and well into the 1930's, and included the early "Rosters" and "Sambo" pictures, the "Our Gang" series, and the many pictures that featured the shuffling antics of "Stepin Fetchit".

Although the 1954 Supreme Court decision, *Brown v. Board of Education*, was a milestone in the Black's quest for equality and full citizenship, equality under law did not mean he had gained equal status in the minds of many whites. The slowness with which civil rights court decisions and civil rights legislation have been implemented is testimony to the fact that changing laws cannot wipe away personal prejudices and long established predispositions.

Most whites in America had had little, if any, personal contact with Blacks; and so the traditional Black stereotypes that had been perpetuated for centuries served as the primary means for understanding what the Black was really like. To those whites the typical Black was the carefree, hand-clapping darky or the docile white man's servant. He spoke an exaggerated dialect; he was laughed at, tolerated, or pitied, but never admired or respected. He was descended from Harriet Beecher Stowe's Uncle Tom, Joel Chandler Harris' Uncle Remus, or Stephen Collins Foster's Old Black Joe, or from the entertaining Black caricatures perpetuated by the early minstrel shows, then by vaudeville, and in the 1930's and 1940's by the popular radio series, "Amos and Andy".

Blacks In Ads

The Black Image that developed in the arts was the image that most whites had of Blacks. Therefore, it is easy to see how Blacks earned their particular servitude status in advertising. Traditionally the Black shown in advertising was either the broad grinning, watermelon eating, comic buffoon type used to capture attention; or the servant type, such as maids, butlers, or porters. Some advertisers clearly associated such Black stereotypes with their products — the black mammy with Aunt Jemima pancakes, the courtly black waiter with Maxwell House coffee, the black butler with Uncle Ben's rice, and the black chef with Cream of Wheat cereal. These stereotypes were not used as a means of appeal to Black customers; they simply expressed the advertiser's views of how their white customers pictured the Black.

Years later this same Black stereotyped image was further developed in illustrative ads in magazines. A study was conducted by Kassarjian to determine the Black's status in advertising in the late 1940's. The magazines examined represented the spectrum of national media, *Life*, *Good Housekeeping*, and *Atlantic Monthly*.

> In 1946, 78 percent of the American Negro actors or models were depicted in the ads as having laborer or service jobs: maids, waiters, slaves, field hand, personal servant, the Aunt Jemima, or the Uncle Tom. The higher status occupations (including police and firemen) shown in the ads constituted 3 percent of the American Negroes; an additional 15 percent were entertainers or sports participants.[9]

Another study was made for the period between 1949-1950. The magazines studied were *Life*, *Saturday Evening Post*, *Time* and *The New Yorker*.

> .... Negroes occupy a relatively lowly position in the advertisements, in that they are nearly always portrayed in the semi-and unskilled laboring group, the great majority of them being cast in the roles of servants, porters, and waiters. Where the persons being waited upon are pictured, they are uniformly white.[10]

Kassarjian continued his original study to include advertising in the mid-1950's. He used the same magazines, *Life*, *Good Housekeeping*, and *Atlantic Monthly*. Apparently the civil rights movement had made an impression upon the advertisers.

> By 1956 the number of Negroes depicted as sports heroes or entertainers increased to 36 percent, and the number of occupations in the service and laborer categories dropped to 52 percent. The number of Negroes shown as members of white-collar or professional occupations remained constant at one per year.[11]

The CORE Campaign

Since the fall of 1963, the Black has become increasingly visible in the mass media. Advertisements and editorial content in magazines and newspapers now include pictures of Blacks as a matter of course. Prior to 1963, in general magazines, a black face was seldom seen unless it was that of a famous entertainer or Black personality, or unless the Blacks shown were "in the news" and appeared often because of their connection with the civil rights movement. But this has changed. The black face in advertisements is no longer inconspicuous due to an industry-wide campaign conducted by the Congress Of Racial Equality (CORE). Although their efforts were mainly directed towards integrating television commercials, CORE's fight also increased the number of Blacks appearing in national advertisers' magazine ads.

In early August 1963, Lever Brothers "asked all of its ad agencies for suggestions on greater use of Negroes and other minority groups in its advertising".[12]   Although Lever Brothers issued a press statement saying their move was guided by a desire for better community relations, it was generally known that CORE helped them reach that decision. Their first integrated ads appeared later that month. There was no question that the appearance of Blacks in Lever Brothers' commercials was a breakthrough in the campaign to integrate advertising. Lever Brothers was the fifth-largest user of national television advertising in the United States. This was the first time a major network advertiser showed Blacks in its commercials as ordinary people.

As soon as Lever Brothers' commercials appeared, CORE sent letters to the Colgate-Palmolive Company, and demanded that Colgate immediately begin using Blacks in television and print advertising. It responded to CORE's letter immediately saying Colgate had been considering integrated advertising for some time and that the firm already had two integrated television commercials in production.

Encouraged by the favorable response, CORE promptly sent a letter to the Proctor and Gamble Company, the largest national television advertiser. Like Colgate, P&G expected it would soon be approached by CORE and had already scheduled an integrated television commercial for one of its products.

Since three of the nation's largest television advertisers had begun to use Blacks in commercials, CORE broadened the approach of its campaign. It sent letters to 14 major advertisers and asked them to attend a meeting. The letter said that three large national advertisers already agreed to CORE's demands and were integrating their commercials. It also explained that the purpose of the meeting was to obtain commitments from those who intended to begin using Blacks immediately in television commercials and in other advertising aimed at the general public.

The CORE officials met with the advertisers as scheduled and presented their demands. They emphasized the readiness of CORE's selective purchasing committees (a euphemism for boycotting). While some who attended the meeting felt CORE's attitude was presumptuous, none disagreed with the goals. One company representative said:

> We think they are going to be successful. Their requests
> are not unreasonable. This (integrated advertising) is
> coming, and you didn't have to go to that meeting to
> figure it out. The soaps have shown us the way; now for
> us it is a matter of when and how.[13]

In less than a week CORE received signed agreements from three firms.

By this time it was clear that CORE's campaign was succeeding and that no major advertisers intended to resist the demands. The meeting indicated that CORE would expand its campaign and contact many advertisers quickly. It was only a matter of time before CORE contacted almost all major national advertisers. Therefore, it was not surprising that some advertisers who were not even invited to the meeting began to integrate their advertising.

Section III THE BLACK MARKET

Description

To a business man, the market is "all persons or business units who buy or may be induced to buy a product or service".[14] People displaying certain characteristics may be grouped into a market due to that similarity. Black people are a market because as a group, they follow certain behavioral approaches and adhere to certain marketing patterns. The common heritage is incidental. Lynn Preston, Data Analyst for *Ebony*, remarked:

> Yes, there is a Black Market. Black Market means buying patterns among Blacks as a whole which are different from the rest of the nation.[15]

In the past, large manufacturers rarely distinguished their products or methods of marketing for the Black consumer. Since in the past Blacks had been ignored, nothing was known about them. Businesses assumed the Black Market was too small and since Blacks composed such a small percentage of the total population and their earnings were not large, the Black's low purchasing power did not warrant special attention. Even special market segmentation policies were ignored. All effort was devoted to white America.

But it has been found that the Black Market is large, both in numbers and in purchasing power. In 1960, there were almost 19 million Blacks, more than the entire Canadian population, in the United States. They comprised almost 11 percent of the total population, and the numbers are growing at a rate more rapid than that of the population in general.[16] From 1960 to 1966, the Black population climbed 14.2 percent compared with 8.6 percent for whites; in the same period, the number of black youth aged 14 to 17 increased 40 percent compared with 26 percent for whites.[17] Migration from the South to Northern urban centers put more than 70 percent of the Black population within the nation's major marketing areas.[18]

In terms of wealth, the Black Market has about the tenth highest income among all nations in the world. In a recent *Time* article, it spoke of the "45 billion-a-year Negro consumer market".[19] Most of this money is found in large urban centers with large Black populations. For example, in 1963 Baltimore Blacks spent an estimated $61.2 million a year for food, Chicago Blacks spent $34.3 million a year for house furnishings, New York Blacks spent $60.6

million on automobiles and servicing.[20] The black urban income is
slowly catching up to the whites. As larger cities approach the 25
percent Black population level, the consumer income of non-whites
(92 percent of them Black) show steady gain. In most urban areas,
black incomes now average 60-80 percent of white families income,
and, in some cities, Blacks equal and exceed white family incomes.[21]

Do White Firms Believe In It?

The major problem with the Black Market concept is that there
has not been any in-depth study to evaluate it or give it proper
dimensions. What is available are a number of population statistics
and income comparisons that only lead to estimated gross figures.
There is nothing positive to give concrete evidence of a Black Market.
Leonard Evans, Editor & Publisher of *Tuesday* Publications, Inc.,
(and indidentally a Black) thinks that Blacks can be separated out of
the general market only because they are concentrated in the larger
cities, and because of their lowly economic position. In other words,
Evans believes that if Blacks were dispersed throughout the market
on an equal basis, the Black Market would cease to exist.[22]

Clearly, there are reasons for a number of firms not to believe in
the Black Market. It naturally follows that there would be no reason
for them to aim specifically at the Black as a special consumer. Their
advertising policy would probably reflect this. In these cases, the ad
campaign would probably be directed toward Mr. Average American.
If it were willing to experiment, it might run this ad in a black
publication. But according to William Capitman, president of the
Center for Research in Marketing, "Those companies that economize
by using the same plate of ads which use white models in Negro
publications display their lack of interest or understanding in this
market and risk offending potential purchases".[23]

Of Those Who Believe, How Many Understand It?

This author spoke to two advertising directors from different
insurance companies. Both felt they understood the Black Market.
The first said he had made attempts to study the market. At the
beginning — nine or ten years ago — before it was even thought of as
a Black Market, he thought he could reach it through using the black
media. He was called upon by an *Ebony* representative and was
convinced that Blacks read *Life* but the only time they saw
something that related to him was a negative image and nothing
positive. He was further convinced that Blacks did not identify with
white magazines and if he wanted to communicate with Blacks, he
should use the black media. Therefore, his company uses *Ebony*,
Tuesday, and *Black Enterprise.* However, further questioning
revealed there was no study; his "understanding" was based upon

personal experience. Actually, the firm felt their ad agency had the expertise in this area and was advised by them on matters relating to it.[24]

The second executive agreed there was a Black Market and felt that the fact that his firm advertises in *Ebony* indicated they had given it some thought. Some of the sales personnel told him years ago that they should advertise in the black media because they could sell there. He had also talked to some Blacks in the marketing and communications fields — that was the extent of his study. The second company also relied upon its ad agency for information of this type.[25]

Carl McMasters, vice president and Account Supervisor at Zebra Associates, Inc. did not feel that white firms, nor anyone for that matter, understood the Black Market because there are no statistical figures on it.[26] Vernice McGriff, a product manager at Beech-Nut, Inc. said:

> Not really because they don't understand Blacks. In most cases they have Blacks around so they can give them some guidance. Whites only know what they read about Blacks in the newspapers. They don't know what makes them tick.[27]

And Miss Preston again commented:

> There is a wall between the races. Much of what whites think or think they know is hear-say. The old myths are perpetuated among themselves. For example, all Blacks own Cadillacs. There are too many whites who are eager or over-eager to say 'But they're just like us. Why treat them differently?' . . . . There are still many whites in ad agencies whose attitude toward Blacks is patronizing and they read about Blacks from sociology books. They don't understand the subtleties in the Black consumer market. . . . Whites are slow to understand that Blacks sometimes speak a different jargon that is purposely used to confuse his white brother. . . . Whites can't throw in a black jargon in the middle of an ad and then think he has understanding.[28]

However, there are a few firms that do understand the subtleties and that there is a high correlation between their direct participation in the Black Market and sales. P. Ballentine & Sons, a Newark, New Jersey brewery, is among the more successful companies in the Black Market. Ballentine has been using Black models in some of its advertising for more than 18 years. The company has been active in Black community affairs, sponsoring civic dinners, providing tournament trophies and holding a largely black golf tournament annually. The firm says it is good for company relations with the community. But all the same, industry sources say that Ballentine beer is highly popular in black neighborhoods and that the popularity helps make Ballentine the biggest seller in most parts of its marketing area in the Eastern states.[29]

Do Ad Agencies Have a Particular Expertise In This Area?

Although agencies are advising their clients on how to reach the Black Market, the reliability of their counseling is quite questionable. There is no concrete evidence to indicate that they understand the market any better than their clients. This author contacted a reputable New York agency in an effort to interview someone about integrated advertising or about the Black Market. The director of personnel informed this author that there was *no one* in the agency who handled anything of that nature; all their advertising was directed to everyone. What seems to be occurring is that a number of the larger agencies are hiring a few Blacks to work in non-decision making positions. Rather than consulting a black marketing expert, the agency asks the Black his opinion whenever there is a question in this area. And more than likely, the agency will base its campaign on his opinion. Predictably, a number of these campaigns have failed because they were based upon one man's subjective opinion and not on facts.

There is further comment by Leonard Evans, publisher and Editor of *Tuesday:*

> I don't think the advertising agencies accept the fact that there is a Negro market because they have never utilized or employed the proper personnel who know what it was all about in the first place. Their decisions have been based on the fact that the Negro market is a mere selection of media, or the substitution of a Negro market for a white market.
>
> The fact that there is a need for special creativitiy in copy, layout, sensitivities in the use of products, and in the type of construction and reality does not accrue to the advertising agencies.[30]

Section IV GENERAL ADVERTISING

Ads That Are Aimed At Everyone

Until quite recently, advertising agencies never considered addressing themselves to the question of national advertising aimed at minority groups. To their way of thinking, the white majority set the norms for the whole society and there was no substantial data to indicate otherwise. It was just assumed that everyone naturally shared similar beliefs, needs, values, aspirations and desires. Therefore, it was relatively simple to devise a general advertising campaign that incorporated everyone and that was aimed at the masses. A number of appliance and retailers told *Electrical Merchandising Week*: "Negroes can read and listen, so they are exposed to my ads in general media like anyone else".[31] So in effect, the general-oriented ads were advertising at and not to Blacks.

Advertisers rationalized that so long as the advertising business was the matter of selling products to the masses, and so long as the majority of the country could most readily be reached by making no particular point of racial differences, the tendency should be to use predominately white themes in national advertising rather than introducing anything for the minorities. Various studies reinforced this viewpoint. Bullock's motivational study is an example. Bullock reasoned that it was more expensive, and unnecessary, to devise special advertising or illustrations to reach the Black Market. He advocated the use of illustrations with a "common denominator". This would not alienate either white or black consumers. And advertisers could render their ad so unstructured that consumers could read into it their own words.[32] Many agencies heeded this counseling.

An often overlooked aspect of general advertising is that many firms who use it have restricted budgets. To finance an elaborate campaign can cost an advertiser quite a huge sum. Unless it is a profitable organization, the company has budgeted itself only limited funds for general advertising. Ads for any particular groups other than the general market is out of the question.

> . . . . Those whose budgets do not permit use of ethnic advertising claim they can reach the Negro just as well with mass media ads. For you don't need costly research to prove that Negroes watch television, listen to general as well as Negro-programmed radio, read the *New York Daily News* as well as the *Amsterdam News, Life,* as well as *Ebony.*[33]

Although these "white" ads were continuously run, the advertisers conducted few tests to determine their effectiveness. When questioned about his firm's advertising attracting black attention, one insurance executive said he did not know how effective it was. But he was quick to add that his company was the first major insurance firm to advertise in *Ebony*. His company had never conducted any tests and *Ebony* does not provide this service. In spite of this lack of information, the company continues its present advertising policy and there is no indication that it is being questioned.[34] However, Mrs. McGriff commented:

> They must have worked. Many things Blacks express a desire for were inspired long before the use of Black models or integrated ads.[35]

Black vs. White Norms

> Although the Negro has obviously been a part of American life for years, he has not been recognized by Madison Avenue media planners until recently. As with

color TV, the advertising industry's interest in the Negro market came about almost overnight.[36]

The recognition of a Black Market did not change the general advertisers approach to Blacks. Mass media ads were still beamed at him. Basically, the problem was centered around the fact that ad agencies did not know how to approach the Black. The type of things that concern Blacks were never included in the general advertisements. Even though advertisers were aware that the Black Market was distinct and had its own unique life style, white middle-class values and norms were still blared into the Black Market. But today Blacks are just not receptive to general ads that naturally are aimed at the white majority.

> Unlike other groups, the Negro remains a Negro despite his position, income and achievements. Effective advertising must be believeable and realistic in terms of his experience and his comprehension.[37]

And John H. Johnson feels:

> Advertisers will continue to find it increasingly difficult to influence black people with ego ideals and ego models that are exclusively white. [38]

Henry S. Clark Jr., staff member of Fry Consultants, points out that the concepts of "Black Power" and that of "Black Consciousness" have had tremendous effects on the black community.

> The psychology and sociology of the black community today works against the categorical acceptance and emulation of the interests, norms, and standards of middle-class white America.[39]

The following sums up the contemporary Black's feelings:

> A recent issue of *Ebony* magazine contained a tire manufacturer's ad picturing a couple on a beach gazing into each other's eyes. Nearby was an auto and the advertised tire. The ad referred to the product and to a commonly accepted Occidental hero — Columbus. The copy tried to show a relationship between Columbus' discovery and the product. . . .
>
> The ad was the subject of a tape-recorded interview held not long ago to measure Negroes' reactions to the advertising they encounter. A local militant best summarized the feelings expressed at the session in regard to the tire ad.
>
> 'Man', he said, 'the ad is ridiculous. It doesn't do a thing for me.' He itemized his objections thus: 'I want to see black people in ads aimed at me. I reject the ad on the basis of its hero — Columbus. I'm an exponent of black history, and there were plenty of black explorers. I reject it on the basis of the beach scene. We just don't go to the beach. In fact, we hardly ever get out of town. Finally, no one in this community is going to pay $40 a piece for

sporty tires when we don't have enough money to feed our families."[40]

The Black Is An Individual

General advertising ignores two elementary human needs — recognition and identification. After years of being ostracized by society, the Black needs to have recognition as a person. The very fact that an advertiser will undertake a special campaign directed toward the Black Market is interpreted as a form of recognition to the Black. Those businesses who generally advertise and expect this to satisfy the Black will find themselves at a competitive disadvantage.

Identification is equally important and should be of great concern to advertisers. Due to his particular situation, the Black cannot identify with or relate to all aspects of the American culture. His color, for example, makes him stand out and be highly distinctive in this society. Most personal product ads use copy or phrases in their general advertising that causes the Black to be reminded of his distinguishing feature and also causes him not to identify with the ad. No matter how much he tries, the Black cannot identify with ads that promise "lovelier, whiter hands with ABC soap" or that "blondes have more fun".

Edward Wallerstein, executive director for the Center for Research in Marketing, Inc. explains:

> When we consider that the Negro approaches advertising in all media with a question that does not occur to the white population, namely 'Do they really mean me?', it becomes clear that the advertising which is not specifically inclusive of Negroes does not reach large segments of the Negro population in any effective manner, even among those who will see the advertising.[41]

Dr. G. Franklin Edwards, Chairman, Department of Sociology, Howard University, believes:

> . . . . the Negro response to TV commercials on a general market TV station is blocked by 'functional illiteracy'. The Negro sits, but he does not experience the TV message because he feels the message is 'not for him'.[42]

Eventhough an ad may meet the recognition and identification requirements, if it is not placed in the proper medium, it will not be effective. John H. Johnson feels advertising must be put into an atmosphere where Blacks can readily accept it.

> For maximum impact on the Negro market, the ad must be placed in media which are oriented to the whole of Negro existence. Unless the ad is supported by an atmosphere geared to or oriented to meet the needs of all consumers, it will not — it cannot — have the most efficient and effective selling power.[43]

Section V INTEGRATED ADVERTISING

An Alternative

As can be seen, the general advertising campaigns needed some reinforcing in the Black Market. Their message was supplemented through the use of "split-run" ads. These were identical ads prepared for the white and black press. The black version was a duplicate of the white except it was adopted for the black media by substituting black models for white ones. The copy was the same. However, this process was extremely expensive because it meant the advertiser had to finance the preparation of duplicate plates used in each media. Only the more financially stable companies could afford to do this. As a result, of the $12 billion spent for U.S. advertising in 1963, advertisers were spending less than $12,000,000 in ads addressed to Blacks.[44] Advertisers plagued by the controversial and dollar-loaded question of how to reach the Black Market were offered a new solution: the integrated ad.

Response to the solution was slow. One excuse offered by large firms was that although they were strongly in favor of using more Blacks and other minority groups in advertising, their ad agencies were reluctant to use them when it came time to develop campaigns. Actually the clients never told the agencies not to use Blacks. However, they approved for use those advertisements that they thought would appeal to the mass audience. The agencies' response to integrated advertising was somewhat ambivalent. This difference between the attitudes of advertisers and agencies was explained by one unidentified advertising man who said:

> Naturally, the advertisers are going to say 'Darn right we ought to have more Negroes in ads.' They are not going to say anything that would displease minority groups. They want the people to buy their products. But the agencies are the ones faced with the actual problem of putting Negroes in the ads, so their replies would, of course, be more guarded. If the agency put a minority-group member in there on its own initiative, the client would be the first to scream. If the advertiser wanted Negroes in there, don't worry they'd by there. The agency would do anything to please the client.[45]

While readily agreeing that Blacks should be represented in advertising, firms hesitated to take the step for fear of adverse reaction by white customers. The attempt to appeal to two distinct market segments in one advertisement might result in a form of white "backlash".

> Some of the 89 New York corporations and 17 agencies contacted by Mayor Robert F. Wagner's committee on job advancement intimated they couldn't risk losing

customers to a competitor by showing a Negro in a national ad.[46]

What caused the change in attitude was when the big giants, Lever Brothers, Colgate, and P&G, began integrating their national ads. Smaller firms saw it was the trend of the future and actually had little bearing on their sales. They found that use of Black models antagonized only insignificant elements of the white population, but in many instances, gained the loyalty of a large new market.[47] It was found that use of a Black model in an ad triggered a Black's decision to purchase one brand in preference to another than used only white models. William Hardy, of the Davidson Hardy Agency, commented:

> Statistics have shown that when Negroes and whites are used in advertising programs, sales of the particular product go up; they do not decline. This destroys an age-old myth accepted by many major advertisers.[48]

Preparation

> Many restrictions are still placed on how far integrated advertising can go and be both effective and believable. Because of that and because of the formulas and quotas with which many advertisers and agencies work, they can only represent a small portion of the majority of advertising created in the United States.[49]

The over-riding restriction in integrated advertising is the social conditions within this society. Advertising that attempts to mirror society must be influenced by it. The well established polarization in this country does not lend itself to much mixing of the races in ads. The fact that the races do not socialize off the job, do not live in the same neighborhoods and that their life styles, in many instances, are so different that it keeps them "worlds apart". The intermingling that does exist is kept sparse. So, therefore, when it comes to integrating ads, agencies are forced to create strained situations that do not exist. The plain fact is that today when advertising moves into integration of whites and Blacks, the risk of offense proves to be greater than when no people are shown at all. For example, one advertiser ran an ad picturing two couples, white and Black, socializing and fishing on a Carribean beach. When the ad appeared, this type of mixing was not common and especially on this particular beach because it was known to be segregated. The criticism from the Black community was extremely harsh.

As illustrated with the beach scene, the main problem with integrated advertising is that it creates non-existent social relationships. Blacks are less comfortable with ads that focus on social and status situations. They are very sensitive about how they are portrayed in such settings. For example, sometimes an ad may feature a Black "model — smoking, drinking, modeling clothing, etc. — with a number of white models. Although the intent of the advertiser is to establish empathy, Negroes respond primarily with a sense of loneliness and alienation and become uncomfortable".[50] In certain unbelievable situations, advertisers offend Blacks and whites and make it more difficult for Blacks to identify with the ad. Joe Black, vice president of special markets, the Greyhound Corp., remarked:

> Most of the commercials you see on television are flimsy because they depict no realism. It is a commitment, an obligation to the F.C.C. So they are going to say 'We are using blacks' . . . . Ad agencies have to consider that if you are trying to motivate everyone, you have to depict them in realistic scenes. Their main defense is that you alienate the majority. Ad companies have to be sold.[51]

To be effective, an integrated ad must be within reality — i.e., believable. John H. Johnson also commented on this:

> To be believable, you should not contrive an ad, you should not show an integrated something that is not. If it is normally integrated, then show it; if it is not integrated, then don't show it as such. Tell the truth. It's that simple.[52]

H. Naylor Fitzhugh, vice president for special markets, Pepsi-Cola Co., said:

> To be effective, however, integrated ad scenes must be realistic. . . . not contrived or over-drawn. . . . a picture Negroes will react to, not resent.[53]

Black Response To Integrated Ads

As with whites, there has been very limited testing done to determine Black response to integrated advertising. However, of the available material, the results are predictable. A study published in 1969 tested how NAACP leaders viewed it. The study suggested there may be an important difference between the definition of "integrated" advertising used herein and that understood by NAACP officials. The latter's conception of integration in advertising may well have social interaction at its core rather than the mere appearance of a Black in an ad not aimed specifically to a Black audience. Ads showing Blacks segregated from whites, or standing near but not interacting with whites, or engaged in implausible situations of interaction may be worse than ads showing no Blacks at all.[54]

Another test studied how Black and white women reacted to integrated advertising. Ads placing Black models in a subservient position received more negative response from black respondents than other ads. Ads using clearly identifiable Black models seem to gain more favorable responses from Blacks than ads with Black models who were only marginally different from white models.

But the study, based on interviews with 395 women (209 white, 185 black), reveals that black women are far more likely than whites (36 percent to 11 percent) to mention spontaneously that an ad includes a black model. Black women, by 30 percent to 18 percent margin, also were able to prove their recall of an ad with a black model. Approximately equal proportions of blacks and whites (15 percent and 16 percent) proved recall of ads with only white models.[55]

In another, Blacks were shown three sets of identical ads, one with all white models, with an integrated mixture, and an all-Black group. The Black subjects tended to evaluate both the integrated ads and the Black model ads rather similarly and showed slightly less relative preference for the white model treatment. The same test was used on a group of whites. The results revealed a decidedly favorable response to ads which pictorially combined white and Black models. Even racially integrated advertisements which depicted a socially intimate scene was scored quite well by whites as well as by Blacks.

Last year an interviewer questioned a group of Blacks concerning their feelings about selected integrated advertisements. Of the variables used, age seemed to be the most significant. Respondents under the age of 30 were more likely to express negative feeling than those who were 30 or older. The interviewer interpreted the results as the following: The older people were accepting because integrated ads were visible evidence of social changes which they had long awaited. Younger people, he felt, were waiting to see the evidence of a more thorough going society than as reflected in the institution of advertising.

Section VI THE CURRENT SITUATION

Black Advertising

We cannot overemphasize the weakness of beaming special advertising to Negroes and the strength of including them in the main stream. Using Negro models to push a product through Negro magazines and white models to push it through white magazines accumulates an undesirable attitude that grows in direct ratio to the Negro's integration aspirations. Showing that this attitude is already rising in ascendancy, one Negro consumer said the dual model policy looks like the seller is ashamed to be caught with Negroes.[56]

Before the appearance of general and integrated advertising aimed at Blacks, there was a phenomenon known as Black Advertising.

These were ads that appeared in the black media only. For those firms that even bothered to advertise in thie medium, it was at first merely the same ads that appeared in the white media. From the illustrations, these ads suggested that the Black population consumed no milk, used no toothpaste, ate no food nor washed body or clothes. But after a time, Black models appeared in them and this began the use of "split-run" advertising. The advertisers still used the same themes for both markets, but merely substituted Black models in the same setting for whites. In effect, the agencies were using the white ad with Black faces to capture the Black Market. However, this approach was extremely expensive. The use of integrated advertising that included both black and white principals allowed the advertisers to use one ad to reach the black and white markets, thereby avoiding separate preparation costs for the two markets. In addition, it was possible for some companies to run an integrated print advertisement in one general medium only, rather than in both general media and black-oriented media.

As previously noted, the more or less integration that occurs in advertising is closely related to the racial situation in society. As the strides for integration in this nation have tapered down since the mid-1960's, so has it tapered in advertising. The Kerner Report indicated that this country is slowly becoming two separate nations — one black and the other white. Racial polarization could be interpreted as the unofficial U.S. internal policy for the 1970's. As the races become more polarized, integrated advertising becomes less believable and in effect, less acceptable to both races.

In recent years, research has shown that "one of the safest ways to reward from the black audience is to use advertising which show Negroes exclusive".[57] Therefore, in order to still compete for the Black Market, advertisers seem to be returning to the practice of all-black ads in the Black medium.

> True, Negroes do read and listen to the general media, perhaps more than many are willing to admit. However, the point being made by Negro leaders is that while Negroes may be sold by a product advertised in the general media, they could be easily unsold by a competitor's ad or commercial in a special Negro medium.[58]

In fact, the "split-run" ads have returned. If one thumbs through a general media magazine like *Life*, or *Look*, and then look through several issues of *Ebony*, one will encounter the same ads, but with different face colors. Both insurance companies that this author contacted use "split-run" ads. An executive for the first company said they used Black models in the black media because the black audience identifies with other Blacks. In all three black publications, they use Black models. He argued that the reason they did not run the black ad in the national magazine was that although whites would not be offended, they would likely pass it over because they do not identify with Blacks. However, he had done no testing to

determine if this were true.[59] The second executive said his firm had
struggled with the question of "split-run" ads and the answer had
been to use models with whom they thought most readers of the
publication associated themselves. Their black ad did not appear in
the national media because in their opinion since 85 percent of the
readers were white, they could not associate with the ad.[60]

An ethical question in the minds of many firms is the possibility
of a black-oriented ad campaign being misinterpreted as "pandering".
Roy Wilkins, executive director of the NAACP, was asked about this
issue. He replied that if one makes an obvious play for the Black in
advertising at a time of high emotional disturbance, it could be
interpreted as cheap pandering. The solution, he said, is in the
"natural" use of Blacks in advertising. He cited a campaign by the
New York Telephone Co. which pictured an attache-carrying Black
about to use a sidewalk phone booth.

> He looked so much a part of the landscape that I'm sure
> many Negroes didn't notice the ad until it was called to
> their attention. If you use a Negro model in that sense,
> you can avoid the problem you described.[61]

Mrs. McGriff responded to that question also:

> Yes, it's exploiting the Black. And that is the name of the
> game, advertising. One should not criticise them anymore
> than one would for the use of white models.
> Black-oriented ads and the use of Black models are just
> an extension of the advertising game.[62]

Black Models

When surveys were still being taken to inquire if Blacks wanted
integrated advertising, the answer was obviously affirmative. Blacks
wanted to see someone in the ads with whom they could identify
and recognize as being somewhat like them. The models represented
someone who resembled him and typified his life style. As Eddie T.
Arnold of Johnson Publishing Co. put it, "The most effective avenue
to communicating with black people is other black people".[63]

However, there was another side to the issue. How would Black
models affect the company image that was projected to whites? In
the last several years, there has been a substantial increase in the use
of Blacks as models in mass media advertising. There was probably a
reluctance on the part of some agencies and clients to employ Blacks
because they feared negative consequences. As a result of this,
therefore, the use of Blacks in advertising may have been more a
result of pressure than of conviction that their use would not
adversely affect marketing instincts. Use or non-use of Blacks may
not have reflected the personal views of agency personnel or clients,
but rather a belief in the effects of such a decision on a product or
service. Actually, until recently when a study was conducted by Dr.
Guest, there was little or no data that showed the affects of using
Black models in advertising illustrations. Guest's results were:

On the basis of this study, even with its limitations, it appears that advertisers need not be fearful of adverse effects through the use of Negro models, either by themselves or integrated with whites, especially in view of the expanding market of young and educated consumers. From a long range of theoretical viewpoint, it seems that previous suggestions that there is hostility toward blacks by whites when status position is threatened, especially when a woman is in a lower deference position, is not universal. The advertisement picturing the superior status role of the executive being occupied by a black man, and the inferior status role of a white woman secretary fared better, or at least not significantly different, than the situation where the roles were reversed, or where both roles were occupied by whites.[64]

Apparently, the use of Black models by advertising agencies for use in displays and TV commercials has made tremendous strides over the previous years. One Chicago agency reported that Blacks appeared in over 20 percent of its recent TV commercials that used models; a year ago, no Blacks were used.[65] However, agencies are facing a new problem — which type of Black model best represents the Black community. The various philosophies being argued within the community makes it extremely difficult to select one model as being representative. One insurance executive was honestly confused about the issue. He and his ad agency did not know what standard to use as a basis for selecting models for his company's ads. He did not know whether to use light, fair, or dark models, or ones with Afros or without. This problem seemed to have caused him considerable concern because he did not want to offend anyone.[66]

Trying to gauge the Black community's attitude on a question like this one is almost impossible. Charles H. Sterling, associate general sales manager, P. Lorillard Co., remarked that "today's Negro is increasingly aware of his heritage. This should be related to your over-all approach to Negro models".[67]   Kelvin Wall, vice president, Coca-Cola Co., added:

> Choice of models can be just as crucial as choice of settings. You've undoubtedly heard of the identity crisis. One of its subtler ramifications is that there is little consensus among Negroes as to which Negro characteristics are desirable and which are not. Care must be taken in the presentation of Negro models, because there are few idealized or standard types of persons for Negroes to identify with than in the clearly structured white society. Negroes apparently prefer to see models representing a spectrum of Negro skin shades. . . . [68]

The Black Advertising Agency

In addressing the American Association of Advertising Agencies, Kevin Wall, vice president, Coca-Cola, remarked:

> If agencies do not act to solve the communications
> problem of reaching the Negro market, either new
> agencies will be formed to meet these corporate needs, in
> a manner similar to the media buying service, or
> American industry will establish in-house capabilities.[69]

As stated, white advertising firms were making no headway with the
Black Market. The ideas they hurled into the market were not
received well by Blacks. Insufficient data, and even more so, a basic
misunderstanding of Blacks prevented ad agencies from reaching
them. Madison Avenue and the Black Market were "worlds apart".
As Charles Sterling said, "It's awfully hard for white people who
have been white people all their lives to understand how black people
think".[70]

Out of a need for a rapport between white businesses and the
Black Market, Black advertising agencies appeared. In the beginning,
their main selling point to white business was their ability to relate to
the Black and their ability to gain him entrance into the Black
Market. The black firms were merely an extension, according to
white thinking, of Blacks communicating with Blacks. The more
black consumers got, the more they wanted, and the more critical
they became of advertising that denied them acceptable images.
Whites hoped that the black agencies would succeed where the
whites had failed. Vince Cullers, president, Vince Cullers, Inc., a
black Chicago agency, said:

> There is an important place for the black advertising
> agency today, because, by thinking and speaking black, it
> can do the best job of communicating with black
> America.[71]

From the start, Black firms approached advertising differently.
They dismissed automatically white concepts and accepted the Black
as a person with particular needs, concerns, and interests. Their
approach was to appeal directly to these needs and concerns as they
understood them. At first they used the "jive hip-talk" approach
creating the type of advertising message that communicated with the
community. But now, they are shying away from the hard driving,
jive sales approach to more subtle ways. Firms are tailoring
campaigns that apply the unique tools needed to capture the Black
Market through the Black consumer's unique life style and language
patterns. There is a trend away from the straight use of Black
models. Some advertisers are finding inventive ways to suggest the
Black milieu and idiom. They are making symbolism — in dress, in
surroundings, in the still life of an ad — perform the ethnic
identification job.

The different approach used by Black ad agencies has been
credited for their success in the Black Market. Mr. McMasters from
Zebra, a black agency, felt black firms follow either of two patterns.

> There are two types of approaches. The hip jargon and
> phrase approach. Or the second which we use that is the
> new and more sophisticated one. It focuses in on life

styles and marketing information that you have to dig out if it's not available. White agencies don't go into life styles; they focus only on buying habits.[72]

And Mrs. McGriff remarked:

Their input is different. It's based on their personal experiences. However, which agency's ads, white or black, are more effective is not known. There is no evidence. But, I'd imagine that black agencies are more effective because they have a better understanding.[73]

In the future, there will still be friction among the races, but perhaps there will also be considerably more integration. Black firms will have to appeal to something other than "Black Is Beautiful". They will have to demonstrate that they have something significant to say to the general market as well as the Black community. They will have to prove to the white business establishment that they can do ads better than white firms. Some black advertising men have already shown their talent by creating extremely successful campaigns in the general market.

Section VII CONCLUSION

Before the modern civil rights movement began, the use of Blacks by advertisers was limited to the comics or black stereotypes. As the civil rights movement evolved, however, advertisers realized it would be unwise to continue using their stereotypes. As a result, the Black in advertising virtually vanished. A few of the old Stereotypes remained, such as Aunt Jemima, Uncle Ben, and Cream of Wheat's black chef. But even these have been restricted to pictures on the product packages and were no longer featured in advertisements.

The year 1963 brought the Black back into advertising, but this time he appeared in non-stereotyped roles. He was no longer the comic inferior or the white man's servant; he was shown as a human being. At the same time, this new portrayal clearly showed that the Black was not the advertiser's customer. The traditional stereotypes in advertising were never meant to appeal to the black consumer; they were simply attention-getting and product-identifying symbols for white customers. But the new image of the Black shown by advertisers conferred on him equal status as a customer — one who spends $45 billion annually.

In 1967, Ramon S. Scruggs, a senior vice president of the National Urban League, criticized the advertising industry for continuing to discriminate against Blacks and other minority groups. He said, "No segment in America has done so much to make Negro Americans the invisible men as the advertising industry."[74] This author interviewed Mr. Scruggs and asked him if he thought the situation had changed.

He responded:

> Yes, it's changed. But it seems more in an area of being a symbolic thing rather than a regular channel of commercial advertising. If you examine past issues of *The New York Times* magazine section and look for ads with minority group members, you's probably find them in about 10 percent of the ads. When I made the same study in 1967, of 187 ads with people, only one had the possibility of a non-white individual. . . . We've come a long way.[75]

Yet, in spite of this optimistic thinking, the situation appears to be reversing. More than any other communicative instrument, advertising closely patterns itself after the social developments within the country. In this respect advertising is a mirror that reflects society. Presently, this nation is experiencing a racial polarization that is keeping people apart. Advertising must reflect this separation. The main society would not notice the effect. However, for the black community it means Blacks are appearing less frequently in national advertising and companies are using more "split-run" ads. Any quick thumbing through past issues of any national magazine will verify this.

While many advertisers — mainly the big "liberal" organizations — individually have increased their efforts to provide more minority group representation, on the whole there has not been much progress. Excluding the racial polarization issue, there seems to be at least two other reasons for the lack of progress. The first is that the advertising industry's reaction in the fall of 1963 was somewhat impulsive, and constant pressure had been needed to keep the effort going. There is no evidence that either CORE or the NAACP have aggressively followed up what they started.[76] The second is that it is quite obvious that the current black public is not actively involved in the integration movement. It seems that Blacks are less interested in the number of their group who appear in advertising. Their attention is now aimed towards matters that directly effect them and their pocket.

But even if social conditions were ignored, advertisers would still be unable to relate to their new target, the Black Market. It is a basic fact that they do not understand it nor the Black. So, businesses look to their ad agency for counseling. They, in turn, show less understanding than their clients. This merely demonstrates how whites continued to ignore Blacks until they became an economic force, and now when they need to, they do not even know what motivates him. The ad agency's real failure in this area has been to ignore all the available data on the Black Market and all aspects of it that are being reported in the marketing and advertising journals. Few agencies are making the effort to collect and analyze it and then apply their findings to the problem.

There is no simple answer to the problem faced by the advertising industry. However, beyond making intensive studies and analyzing the data, the agencies could begin to approach one aspect of a final solution on a very basic level — employment. Very few Blacks are working for major advertising firms. An even smaller number are occupying top executive positions. What needs to be done is to hire Blacks and other minority group members and give them a meaningful role in the organization. What is more important is to give them training for decision making positions — i.e., put Blacks in jobs where they can say more than no when questiond. Miss Preston observed:

> It is a vicious cycle. White firms need to start on the employment level. They need to promote people from within to positions where they have some authority. Firms need to give them some decision making experience. . . . Whites have to come out of their Ivory Tower settings on Madison Avenue and stop making decisions based on their West Chester existence. . . . The white man can't make a decision about the Black Consumer without the aid of Blacks to translate what is going on in the Black Community.[77]

FOOTNOTES

1. U.S. Bureau of the Census, *Current Population Report*

2. "Ways of Reaching Negro Market are Changing, AMA Told", *Advertising Age*, (May 26, 1969), p. 98.

3. Bullock, H.A. "Consumer Motivation in Black and White: 11", *Harvard Business Review*, (July-August 1961), p. 110.

4. "Adman's guide to Negro Media", *Sponsor* (July 1967), p. 42.

5. *Ibid.*

6. "The Negro Market — Two Viewpoints", *Media/Scope* (November 1967), p. 70.

7. Clark, T.D., *The Southern Country Editor* (Indianapolis: Bobbs-Merril Co., 1948), p. 200.

8. Logan, R.W., *The Negro in American Life and Thought: The Nadir 1877-1901* (New York: Dial Press, 1954), p. 242.

9. Kassarjian, H.H., "The Negro and American Advertising, 1946-1965", *Journal of Marketing Research* (February, 1969), p. 29.

10. Shuey, A.M., "Stereotyping of Negroes and Whites: An Analysis of Magazine Pictures", *Public Opinion Quarterly* (Summer, 1953), p. 281.

11. *Op. Cit.*, Kassarjian.

12. *Wall Street Journal* (August 19, 1963), p. 1

13. "Integration Drive Gains Momentum in TV Industry", *Advertising Age* (September 30, 1963), p. 105.

14. Kotler, P. *Marketing Management: Analysis, Planning and Control*, (Englewood Cliffs: Prentice-Hall, Inc. 1967) p. 13

15. Interview with Miss Preston (November 5), 1971

16. Bauer, R.A. and Cunningham, S., "The Negro Market", *Journal of Advertising Research* (April 1970), p. 3

17. "The Negro Market: 23 million consumers make a $30 billion market segment", *Marketing Insights* (January 29, 1968), p. 9

18. *Ibid.*

19. "Black Capitalism: The Rarest Breed of Women", *Time* (November 8, 1971), p. 102.

20. *Wall Street Journal* (August 19, 1963), p. 1

21. Oldipupo, R. "The Urban Negro Separate and Distinct", *Media/Scope* (July 1969), p. 10.

22. "The Negro Market — Two Viewpoints", *Media/Scope* (November 1967), p. 70

23. "Advertiser's guide to marketing 1965: Negro Market", *Printers' Ink* (August 30, 1963), p. 47.

24. Interview with Mr. X, November 4, 1971

25. Interview with Mr. Y, November 4, 1971

26. Interview with Mr. McMasters, November 12, 1971

27. Interview with Mrs. McGriff, October 28, 1971

28. *Supra.* Preston

29. *Wall Street Journal* (August 19, 1963), p. 1

30. "Black Is Beautiful But Maybe Not Profitable", *Media/Scope*, August 1969, p. 31

31. "The Negro Consumer", *Electrical Merchandising Week* (April 27, 1964), p. 13.

32. "Some Ads, Intelligently Done, Can Sell to Both Whites, Blacks: Bullock", *Advertising Age* (June 12, 1960), p. 23.

33. "Courting the Black Billionaire", *Media/Scope* (August, 1969), p. 41.

34. Interview with Mr. Y, November 4, 1971.

35. Interview with Mrs. McGriff, October 28, 1971.

36. "Media decision: integrate or segregate?", *Sponsor* (July 25, 1966), p. 29.

37. "New tactics are pinpointed on special needs", *Sponsor* (October 22, 1962), p. 13.

38. "Use of Negro Models in Ads Won't Reduce Sales to Whites, Johnson Advises Workshop", *Advertising Age* (December 9, 1968), p. 24.

39. "Ways of Reaching Negro Market Are Changing, AMA Told", *Advertising Age* (May 26, 1969), p. 98.

40. Clark, H.S., "Black *Is*", *Sales Management* (September 15, 1969), p. 64.

41. "Negroes Respond Negatively to Ads", *Editor & Publisher* (October 5, 1963), p. 22.

42. "Media decision: Integrate or Segregate?", *Sponsor* (July 25, 1966), p. 29.

43. "Integrated Ads Misfire in White-Only Media, John Johnson Tells WSAAA", *Advertising Age* (April 27, 1964), p. 2.

44. "Despite Integration, Negro is Separate Market, Grayson Says", *Advertising Age* (June 3, 1963), p. 104.

45. "Minority Groups May Get More Ad Notice", *Printers' Ink* (January 25, 1963), p. 10.

46. "Ads Sans Minorities Distort U.S. Image, Says N.Y. Committee", *Advertising Age* (March 4, 1962), p. 28.

47. "Negroes Desire 'Integrated Ads', Researchers Find", *Advertising Age* (November 12, 1962), p. 28.

48. "All-Negro Davidson Hardy Agency Creates 'Multi-Ethnic' Advertising", *Advertising Age* (May 20, 1968), p. 54.

49. Gibson, D.P., "View From The Top", *Media/Scope* (August, 1969), p. 63.

50. Wall, K.A., "The Great Waste: Ignoring Blacks", *Marketing/Communications* (February, 1970), p. 42.

51. "Black Is Beautiful But Maybe Not Profitable", *Media/Scope* (August, 1969), p. 31.

52. "Don't Contrive 'Integrated' Ads, Johnson Advises", *Advertising Age* (September 23, 1963), p. 1.

53. "The Negro Market — Two Viewpoints", *Media/Scope* (August, 1969), p. 70.

54. Schmidt, D.C. and Preston, I.L., "How NAACP Leaders View Integrated Advertising", *Journal of Advertising Research* (September, 1969), p. 13.

55. "Use of Black Models in Ads Doesn't Alter Sales Patterns, B of A Reports", *Advertising Age* (November 9, 1970), p. 52.

56. Bullock, H.A., "Consumer Motivation in Black and White: 11", *Harvard Business Review* (July-August 1961), p. 110.

57. Wall, K. "The Great Waste: Ignoring Blacks", *Marketing/Communications* (February, 1970), p. 42.

58. "The Negro Consumer", *Electrical Merchandising Week* (April 27, 1964), p. 13.

59. Interview with Mr. X, November 4, 1971.

60. Interview with Mr. Y, November 4, 1971.

61. "Help Negro in Image Effort via Ads, Wilkins Asks", *Advertising Age* (November 11, 1963), p. 1.

62. Interview with Mrs. McGriff, October 28, 1971.

63. "Be Honest in Ads Addressed to Negro Market, Ad Club Told", *Advertising Age* (September 30, 1968), p. 64.

64. Guest, L. "How Negro Models Affect Company Image", *Journal of Advertising Research* (April, 1970), p. 29.

65. *Wall Street Journal* (January 28, 1969), p. 1.

66. Interview with Mr. X, November 4, 1971.

67. "Ethnic Ads Should Not Be 'Contrived', Lorillard Exec Tells Negro Market Seminar", *Advertising Age* (February 19, 1968), p. 50.

68. *Supra.* Wall.

69. "Kanter, Wall Blast Advertising to Black, Mexican-Americans", *Advertising Age* (March 16, 1970), p. 3.

70. "Black Agencies Should Be Used To Reach Black Market, Wright Says", *Advertising Age* (February 3, 1969), p. 87.

71. "Marketing to Blacks Still Mystifies Whites, Speaker Advises Conference", *Advertising Age* (June 2, 1961), p. 19.

72. Interview with Mr. McMasters, November 12, 1971.

73. Interview with Mrs. McGriff, October 28, 1971.

74. "Admen Rapped for Keeping Negro 'The Invisible Man' ", *Editor & Publisher* (November 18, 1967), p. 16.

75. Interview with Mr. Scruggs, November 12, 1971.

76. Boyenten, W. H. "The Negro Turns To Advertising", *Journalism Quarterly* (Spring, 1965), p. 227.

77. Interview with Miss Preston, November 5, 1971.

GLENDHILL CAMERON

* Glendhill Cameron, "Shopping Plight of the Poor,"
(Trenton, N. J.) *Evening Times*, (January 9, 1968).
Reproduced by permission.

Highest prices were found in slum areas in a recent *Evening Times* survey of grocery costs in individual stores located in lower, middle, and upper income neighborhoods.

Comparison shopping showed also that if a woman living in any one of three city slum areas investigated was able to go to the nearest supermarket, her savings would be from 18 percent to a whopping 60 percent on food bills.

Comparison was made item by item with 16 staples chosen from a list of 37 on a "Shopper's Guide" available from the New Jersey Office of Consumer Protection, 1100 Raymond Street, Newark.

No sales prices were included. Saving would be even greater if a shopper took advantage of weekly sales, bought in bulk, or, in some cases, bought the store's own brand.

In the shopping survey, however, known brands and identical weights and sizes were compared.

But the small neighborhood store with the highest total price for the 16 items, for instance, sold bacon only in half-pound packages for 59 cents, so a pound cost $1.18.

Prices for bacon in other low-income area stores ranged from 59 to 89 cents a pound. Individual stores in upper-income neighborhoods charged 89 cents to $1.15. In the supermarkets it was 59 to 89 cents.

Small stores also often stock only the very small or the very large sizes of common items, such as bleach or detergent, for example.

Prices for a 20-ounce "regular" popular size box of detergent ranged from 30 cents in supermarkets to 33 to 41 cents in all areas. But one store in the poorest neighborhood displayed only two sizes, smallest 7½ ounces, and largest, 84 ounces.

If a woman always bought the small one, she would pay eventually 54 cents for 20 ounces of the detergent. And even if she bought the box marked in large letters "economy size" as a "bargain" for only $1.49, simple arithmetic shows that even this way she would pay slightly more than 35 cents for each 20 ounces.

A 5-pound bag of a well-known brand of sugar is 59 cents in supermarkets and costs a top of 89 cents in better neighborhood stores. But one slum area store offered sugar only in 2-pound (27 cents) or 10-pound ($1.35) bags. Thus 5 pounds here would cost 65½ cents in either small or large quantity.

The most popular size in cornflakes, 12 ounces, costs 30 cents in supermarkets and up to 39 cents in some small establishments. But four out of five stores in poorer neighborhoods carried only an 8-ounce size for 23 to 26 cents. It was difficult to distinguish the 8-ounce from a 12-ounce box, especially without the other size there for comparison. It was necessary to check the label to be sure of the weight.

A woman buying for a large family with small children might easily use three or four boxes of cornflakes a week; she would pay $1.20 for four 12-ounce boxes (48 ounces) of the cereal at the supermarket. The poor woman shopping in some neighborhood stores would have to pick up six 8-ounce boxes and her 48 ounces of cereal would cost $1.56.

Bread—one full pound—which ranged as low as 18½ cents for [the market's] own brand in supermarkets to 30 cents for a known quality loaf in higher priced stores—was hardly found at this weight in poorer neighborhoods.

Some loaves even looked like more than other one-pound loaves. They were longer in size but were only 14 rather than 16 ounces in weight and cost 17½ to 21 cents.

While rich and poor alike are aware of certain foods as low-cost items, there was another significant fact noted in the survey. Spaghetti, peanut butter, and pork and beans were priced highest in just those neighborhoods where they might be expected to be a steady part of the diet.

True, a one-pound box of a popular brand of spaghetti was only 2 or 3 cents more than the low 26½ cents of the supermarket. But it is a food bought constantly and in quantity by the poor family and represents a proportionately higher cost on the food bill.

Peanut butter was one item which cost more in most slum stores than anywhere else. Pork and beans, 14 cents at a supermarket and a uniform 16½ cents at upper-income stores, cost 17 to 19 cents in slum areas.

"It is a naked economic reality" that small groceries must charge more for merchandise, one supermarket spokesman has said, since such stores cannot buy in bulk or count on fast turnover.

But there is a difference between the individual grocer who charges enough to make a fair profit and the venal* merchant who charges what the traffic will bear—and often with no regard for the quality he offers.

For example, in a mixed racial neighborhood, one small store was found to have the highest prices of any in this survey. The owner ingeniously admitted his method of operation. While serving desultory customers, usually buying only one or two items, he discussed one of the little-known brands on his shelves.

"Some items in this line will go in this store, but some won't—like mayonnaise." But in another store he owned in an all-Negro neighborhood, he carried all items of this low-cost brand. Customers there, he said, would take whatever was available. What then is the answer for the woman with a low income trying to feed her family as well as she can?

The Essex County Youth and Economic Rehabilitation Center is going to add a new weapon to the war on poverty arsenal—a course on how to shop economically.

Director Marti Lordi announced plans for the course. "We find that the poor people, the ones least able to afford it, are paying more for the necessities of life than their affluent neighbors," he said.

He noted that poor people are sometimes ineffective shoppers because of their limited education and unfamiliarity with practices like comparison shopping.

"Our poor don't have the time or the inclination to do any comparison shopping, and even if they had both, they have never learned how," he said.

"We want to change that," he added. "We want to show them how to read advertisements in newspapers and understand them, and we want them to learn how important it is that they read any sales contract carefully so they do not end up being victimized by paying exorbitant interest rates or carrying charges to conscienceless merchants."

QUESTIONS FOR DISCUSSION

1. Mr. Cameron argues that the poor do pay more. Do you agree with him?

2. What evidence does the author present to show the ghetto buyers pay more?

3. Can you see why prices might be higher in a ghetto area than in, say, a middle class suburban shopping center? What risks are assumed by the ghetto merchants that are not encountered to the same degree in more affluent shopping areas?

4. What solution(s) do you see for the problem?

5. Why do the ghetto dwellers not engage in comparison shopping?

DO THE POOR PAY MORE? *

CHARLES S. GOODMAN

* Charles S. Goodman, "Do the Poor Pay More?", *Journal of Marketing*, Vol. 32 (January, 1968), pp. 18-24. Reproduced by Special Permission.

Recent BLS studies attempting to determine if food chains were charging higher prices in low-income areas than in other parts of the same city found that this frequent allegation was not supported by evidence in any of the several cities studied.[1] The same studies noted, however, that small independent stores as a class tend to have higher prices than the supermarket chains and that small independents represent a large proportion of the store population in low-income areas. This observation and the wide publicity afforded allegations of high prices being charged by stores in low-income Negro areas have led some people to conclude that the poor pay more for their food than those of greater means. Thus Capolvitz' findings that New York poor families paid higher prices than the well-to-do for consumer durables were believed to hold for food as well.[2] Such allegations cannot be fairly appraised without knowledge of the purchasing practices of the families involved, including particularly the stores which are *actually patronized* for the major part of food purchasing by these groups.

An opportunity to test the hypothesis that the poor pay more for food and to explore their purchasing behavior was presented when the Philadelphia City Planning Commission was faced with the need of determining the desirability of including new supermarkets in redevelopment areas. In the belief that such a policy might be needed to overcome an unsatisfactory high-cost retail food situation, provision was made for inclusion of such a market in the West Mill Creek Redevelopment program. The presence of such an ordered plan of change of retail facilities furnished an opportunity to study current purchasing practices of residents and to note changes that emerged with the introduction of the supermarket. This article summarizes the "before" situation. It deals with the following questions:

Do the poor pay higher prices for food than the well-to-do? If so, why?

What kinds of stores do lower-income families patronize and why?

To what extent do lower-income families use various services such as credit and delivery from stores and home delivery by routemen?

How well do lower-income shoppers perceive price and other differences among stores?

Nature of the Study

Two related surveys were conducted in the summer of 1965: (1) a consumer survey of food purchasing practices, and (2) a study of prices prevailing in 12 stores used by these consumers.

The Survey Area

The survey area encompassed (a) the West Mill Creek Urban Renewal Area, a 120-acre project based on selective rehabilitation, demolition, and redevelopment; (b) the Philadelphia Housing Authority's Mill Creek Public Housing Project comprising 444 dwelling units; and (c) and unredeveloped area similar in many respects to the West Mill Creek area lying east of that area and north of the Mill Creek Project. (Figure 1)

There are no large or modern food retailing facilities within the survey area. As part of the redevelopment program, a new food supermarket is to be installed at 48th and Brown Streets in what is at present the mixed industrial-residential section. The location is about one-half block from the site of a slaughterhouse demolished in redevelopment. It will be closer to virtually all of the residents of the area than any existing outside supermarket.

The Consumer Survey

The food purchasing practices of residents of the survey area were obtained through field interviews. Because location within the area was considered likely to affect the stores which would be patronized, a 20% sample was drawn from each of the 79 blocks. A random starting point was selected for each block and every fifth dwelling unit thereafter selected for interview. The total sample consisted of 651 units. Repeated call-backs were used to obtain responses from those not at home on the initial visit. A total of 520 usable interviews were obtained.

Respondents were asked a series of questions about the store in which they did most of their food shopping. In addition, questions were asked about other stores sometimes patronized to determine respondents' perceptions of store services, quality, and prices.

The Respondent Group—Reflecting the predominatly Negro character of the area, only 6% of the respondents were white. Based on the 1959 median family incomes for the tracts involved, the completed interviews were: 18.5% in tracts in the eighth decile, 42.3% in tracts in the ninth decile, and 39.2% in tracts in the tenth decile of all tracts in the City of Philadelphia. Demolitions and public housing construction since 1959 may or may not have altered these relationships significantly. The median family income reported by respondents was between $4,000 and $5,000.

Classification of Stores—In addition to being classified as supermarkets or non-supermarkets, all stores were assigned a code indicating their location with reference to the area being studied:

Zone A—Stores within the boundaries of the 160-acre interview area:
There are approximately three dozen of these stores, of which 21
were mentioned by three or more respondents as being used as
either primary or secondary sources. There are no supermarkets in
this area.

Zone B—Stores within a band extending out one-half mile from
the boundaries of the area.

Within this area are seven chain supermarket outlets, some
medium-sized independents as part of an old string-street

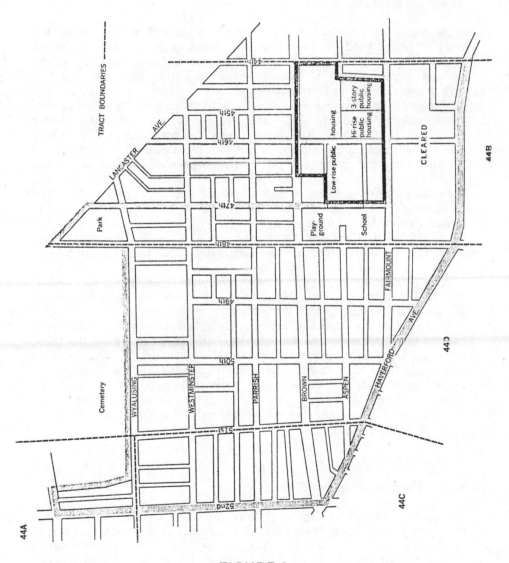

FIGURE 1

Map of survey area. West Mill Creek redevelopment area within heavy black line.

development along Lancaster Avenue, and a number of smaller stores. All of the supermarkets and eight of the nonsupers were reported by three or more respondents as being used as either primary or secondary food sources.

Zone C—Stores more than one-half mile from the boundary of the area.

Eight stores beyond the one-half mile band were listed by three or more respondents. All were chain supermarkets.

The Price Survey

A study of basic food prices was conducted to determine the relative prices paid for food items by families included in the study and to determine if there were differences in food costs dependent on the store or type of store at which a family primarily shopped either from choice or from necessity.

Selection of stores—Prices were sought from three types of stores: supermarkets, medium-sized independent stores, and small corner (mom 'n pop) stores. The stores selected for pricing were those which the consumer indicated to be the most commonly patronized within each of these classes. All of the supermarkets and two of the four medium-sized independents were located outside of the consumer survey area but within one-half mile of its boundaries. The remaining two medium-sized independents and all of the corner stores were within the survey area itself.

Selection of Items and Determination of Prices—The foods priced were the 72 items used by the Pennsylvania Department of Public Welfare in its pricing work. This list is divided into 11 nutritional classes (for example, milk and milk products, leafy green and yellow vegetables, fats and oils). Department of Welfare weights were used to obtain an average price for each store.

Conversion to Market Baskets—Weighted prices for nutritional groups were converted to food baskets through the use of the table of nutritional standards used by the Department of Welfare. This table sets forth the quantity of a nutritional class deemed adequate for a person of a given age and activity group; for example, 12 ounces of leafy green and yellow vegetables per week for a girl aged 13 to 15.[3] A market basket was calculated for each of three hypothetical families.

Shopping Practices

Stores Used for Principal Shopping

Despite the availability of a large number of small stores within the survey area, more than 92% of the residents went outside of the "A" zone for their principal grocery shopping. As may be seen in Table 1, 420 (81%) of the 520 families did their principal grocery shopping at chain supermarkets, all of which lie outside the area. Another 60 (12%) went outside the immediate area to patronize other stores. Of these 60 families, 33 patronized one or the other of two medium-sized independents in zone "B," whose prices were studied and found to compare favorably with those of the supermarket chains.

Table 1

TYPE AND LOCATION OF STORE USED FOR PRINCIPAL FOOD SHOPPING BY 520 FAMILIES

Location	Number of Families		
	Supermarket	Store	Total
Survey area "A"	0[a]	40	40
Fringe area "B"	336	49	385
Outside "C"	84	11	95
Total	420	100	520

[a]No supermarkets in survey area.

Eleven of the 40 families who did their principal grocery shopping within the "A" zone used Max & Jeanne's, a store which our price survey found to be the lowest priced of the 12 stores studied. No more than a half-dozen of the other 29 families used any one store as its principal food source. Presumably these few families placed a high value on store proximity.

Transportation Used in Shopping at Principal Store

Fewer than one-half of the families walked to do their regular shopping at their principal store. Automobiles were used by 45%; and additional 14% used public transportation. As might be expected, the automobile was used more commonly where the store is more remote, although even a few patrons of stores within the "A" zone reported using one.

A surprising finding is that one-seventh of the respondents, or one-fourth of those not using autos, used public transportation for principal food shopping, chiefly in patronizing supermarkets in the fringe ("B") zone. Use of public transportation tended to be highest in tract 44C, reflecting the availability of bus service on 52nd Street and the distance to the nearest supermarkets.

The use of an automobile was also affected by income. About three-fifths of those with family incomes in excess of $5,000 used cars. Less use of a car was made by lower income groups, but even at the lowest income level—under $2,000—an automobile was reported as being used by nearly one-fourth of the respondents.

The use of automobiles, and even more emphatically the use of public transportation, for food shoping reinforces the statement made earlier that families in this area exerted effort and some expense to go outside their immediate neighborhoods for food sources they regard as suitable.

Attitude Toward Store Principally Shopped

Respondents were asked their reasons for shopping primarily at the stores which they named. In addition, they were asked to suggest ways in which the named stores could serve them better, thus providing an indication of areas of dissatisfaction.

Reasons for Shopping Principal Store—Price (52%), quality (42%), and location (28%) were the reasons most frequently stated for patronizing a particular store. The most commonly mentioned reason differed among the patrons of different stores. Thus, price was the reason given by more than 75% of the patrons of Litt's, Max & Jeanne's, and A & P, while quality was most frequently mentioned by Penn Fruit customers, and location by patrons of two small "A"-zone stores.

Ways in Which Principal Store Could Serve Better—In-store service factors, especially check-out speed, were mentioned nearly twice as often as product and price factors and about 2½ times as often as the spatial factors, for example, convenience of location or delivery. Some three-fifths of the respondents had no suggestions for improvements and were at least overtly satisfied. Differences in response by income levels were minor.

When asked how stores other than their principal sources could serve them better as their secondary sources, those interviewed mentioned improvements in products and price factors more frequently than they did in evaluating their principal sources (20% as against 10%). In-store service factors were of minor importance (noted by 6.4% as against 17.2%).

Other Sources of Food Products

In addition to the store principally shopped, two other types of food sources were examined: vendor home delivery (peddling) of milk and bakery products, and the use of one or more stores for secondary shopping.

Home Delivery of Milk and Bread—The extent to which home delivery dairy and bakery systems were used is related directly to a family's need for fill-in purchases during the regular shopping interval.

Only 29% of the families obtained milk from a home delivery route, and fewer than 8% obtained bakery products at the door. The use of home delivered milk is lowest in the under $3,000 income class and in the 36-45 age brackets. The purchase of bakery products from a route man does not seem to be income- or age-related.

Additional Stores Sometimes Used—In addition to being selected as primary food sources by more than four-fifths of the respondents, supermarkets receive important mention as "other" stores used.

Indeed, 45% of the respondents mentioned a supermarket first when asked about other stores used.

Supermarkets are rarely used for fill-ins. Ordinarily they serve as alternative stores for weekly shopping trips. More than 94% of those who mentioned a supermarket as their first choice among secondary sources purchased at the named supermarket once a week or less, most commonly less. The principal reasons given for the selection of such stores were prices or specials (50%), location with reference to home or travel (18%), and quality (18%).

About two-fifths of the residents used small stores in the "A" zone as secondary sources. Of those who visited these stores, 37% used them for small or emergency type items. Another 18% used them for bread and milk only, while 5% used them for meat, poultry, or fish, and 15% for one or two other types of items. Less than one-fourth of the patrons reporting use of these stores obtained as many as three types of goods from them. For the majority of residents these stores are thus used as supplementary sources after one or possibly two supermarkets are used for main supplies. The fill-in character of purchases from these stores is also attested by their frequent use. Nearly one-half of the users of this group of stores made purchases three or more times per week from them.

TABLE 2

PRICES, BY STORES

	Price Index (A & P = 100)		
Store	Family #1 Man 21-40 Woman 21-40 Boy 10-12 Child 7-9	Family #2 Man 21-40 Woman 21-40 Child 4-6 Child 1-3	Family #3 Man 65+ Woman 41-64
Supermarkets			
A & P	100.0	100.0	100.0
Food City	101.8	101.4	101.1
Penn Fruit[c]	103.4	103.0	103.1
Acme	103.7	103.7	103.8
Medium-sized Independents			
Max & Jeanne's	92.8	92.8	91.8
Litt's	95.2	95.2	94.0
Eddie's[a]	98.2	98.1	97.5
Lee's	107.2	107.2	106.9
Small Stores			
Cy's[b]	101.6	101.9	101.4
Miller's	105.5	105.7	105.0
Frank's	107.8	107.8	107.5
Orlando's[c]	114.3	114.4	114.5

[a] Produce not carried.
[b] Processed, but no fresh meat carried.
[c] Eggs not carried.

In sharp contrast to the reasons for using supers, the overwhelming reason for the use of "A" zone stores is convenience of location. Eighty-three percent state this as their reason.

Nonsupermarkets outside of the "A" zone (except those used as the principal food source) are most heavily used for perishables. Eighty-nine (55%) of the 163 persons reporting use of a nonsuper outside the "A" zone as a secondary store used the store solely for meat, fish, or poultry. Quality is stated to be the principal motive for patronizing these stores (39% of mentions), followed by prices or specials (33%), and location (19%).

Use of Delivery and Credit Services Offered by Stores

Both credit and delivery services are available in the area, but their usage is limited.

Delivery Services—Although some of the nonsupermarkets in both the "A" and "B" zones offer delivery services, less than one-fifth of the residents of the area ever make use of them. In fact the total (18%) is not much larger than the number (14%) who, lacking an auto for food shopping, use public transportation. Daily or other frequent deliveries by the grocery boy appear to be a thing of the past in this area. Even among the 18% of the families who used delivery services at some time, only about one in eight used it as often as twice per week.

Charge Accounts—Little use of charge accounts is made by residents of the survey area if what they report about themselves can be relied upon. The allegation that lower income groups are forced to buy groceries on credit does not seem to apply to this area. Only 1% of the respondents used charge accounts regularly, although an additional 4% reported using them occasionally. In addition to the very small usage of charge accounts, only 13% of the residents believed that such service was available.

Price Differences, Price Perceptions, and Store Offerings

Price Differences Among Stores

Prices of three of the four medium-sized independents averaged below those of the supermarket chains. As Table 2 shows, one of the independent stores, the promotionally-oriented Max and Jeanne's had prices about 7% below those of the A & P. Two other stores, Litt's and Eddie's, were observed to have prices below but close to the A & P level. The prices of the remaining medium-sized independent, Lee's were substantially above those of the supermarket chains.

Prices in the small stores were found to be somewhat higher, but here again differences among stores within the group were observed to be greater than differences among the groups. On the one hand, Cy's prices compared favorably with those of Penn Fruit and Acme although higher than A & P, Food City, and three of the medium-sized independents. As the other extreme, Orlando's prices were substantially higher than those of any other store studied.

Relationship of Price Differences to Patronage

It was reported above that four out of five residents of the survey area used one or more of the supermarkets as their principal shopping sources for food. Of those who did not, the largest numbers used Litt's, Eddie's, or Max & Jeanne's as their principal source. Prices in all of these stores compare favorably with those in the supermarket chains. In contrast, despite the fact that Lee's is located near the center of the survey area and is 2400 feet from the nearest supermarket, not one of the more than 500 respondents reported it as their principal shopping store. Perhaps it may be concluded that Lee's relatively high prices outweigh the convenience afforded. The survival of the high-priced small stores would appear to rest on their use for milk, bread, soda, and emergency items rather than as principal food sources.

Price Differences and Shoppers' Perceptions

The failure of residents to use the local stores seems to reflect their perceptions as to these stores' relative prices, although they may also reflect other considerations such as inferior quality, attitudes or promotion.

Respondents were first asked whether there were differences in prices among stores in the area. No comparison of specific stores was requested, though stores were often named. The 439 (85%) who indicated that differences did exist were then asked to indicate the store(s) that had higher and lower prices.

Most respondents (266 cases) consider supermarket prices to be lower than those of other sotres. In 21 cases, on the other hand, independent stores were believed to offer lower prices than supermarkets. In 12 of these 21, the lower-priced store named was one of the three stores priced which, according to our price study, had lower prices than A & P.

Respondents who made comparisons among specific independents most often indicated as the low-priced store Max & Jeanne's, Eddie's or Litt's; these are stores which were found to be competitively priced. Twenty-four of the 31 respondents comparing independents named one of these three as the lower-priced store.

In the cases in which respondents compared prices of two supermarkets covered in our pricing survey and showing price differences in excess of 1%, their opinions agreed with those of our pricing survey in 24 cases and disagreed in five cases.

It seems clear that both in their shopping behavior and in their responses to questions shoppers perceive significant price differences quite well.

Item Coverage of Stores

Although none of the stores carried all of the 72 items priced, the supermarkets generally carried most of them. Every super offered complete coverage in at least eight of the eleven nutritional classes and at least 70% coverage in each of the remaining classes.

Max & Jeanne's, the low-priced independent, also had full coverage in eight classes and at least 75% in each of the others. Litt's and Lee's coverage was slightly lower.

Coverage of the other stores was more limited. Eddie's—meat market turned superette—carries no produce. The smaller stores had important gaps. In some cases lines were so limited that a consumer relying entirely on such a store would have no opportunity to buy a substantial proportion of the items listed. Orlando's, the store with the highest prices, had full coverage in only two of the eleven classes and less than 70% of the listed items in seven classes.

Summary of Findings

1. Because they shop at competitive stores, going outside their residence area to do so if necessary, the poor do *not* pay more for food in this area.

2. Despite the large number of small stores within the area, all but a small fraction (less than 8%) of the residents go outside their immediate vicinity for their principal food shopping. With few exceptions, they go to supermarkets (81%) or to competitively priced, moderate-sized stores (8%). Automobiles or public transportation are used to accomplish this.

3. Price and quality far outweigh location as a stated patronage factor.

4. Most families patronize more than a single store. The second store chosen is more likely to be another supermarket or competitively priced independent outside the residence area than a local convenience store.

5. Local convenience stores are used almost entirely as supplementary sources of emergency items or for frequently purchased perishables such as bread or milk. For these latter items, convenience stores take the place of more costly route delivery sources. Less than 6% of the families use a convenience store as their principal food source.

6. Shoppers' perceptions of the relative levels of prices of different stores are generally good, not only as between stores of different types but also as among stores of a given type.

Further Research Needed

This study dealt with an area considered to be sufficiently low income to need public housing and extensive redevelopment efforts. Nevertheless, the median family income of $4,000 - $5,000 might be considered by some to be too high to represent truly poverty-stricken areas. Further studies might well seek to determine if similar behavior patterns exist in neighborhoods with even lower incomes and in other cities. Further studies might also consider one or more areas in which travel to outside stores was more difficult than found to be the case here.

The price comparisons made in the present study were based on those posted, or, where unposted, those quoted by store operators. Further studies may be needed to determine if the quoted prices are those actually charged in the course of daily business and whether they are uniform among customers.

Further studies are needed to sharpen our knowledge of other aspects of differences in store offerings. In particular, it would be desirable to have appropriate measures of and adjustment factors for differences in product quality, especially for meats and produce. While quality evaluation was not a serious handicap in this pilot study, a more extensive study should make provision for de facto quality evaluations and for appropriate adjustments, including adjustments for trim of meats and freshness of produce. There is also a need to provide appropriate indices of service quality, in particular the adequacy of assortments to meet different types of consumer needs. Low coverage ratios suggest not only that the store does not provide for the varied needs of the customer, but also that the customer may find it necessary to accept substitutes having lower utility per dollar of cost, or to incur additional effort or cost to go elsewhere.

Finally, there is an important need to determine how redevelopment programs affect both the behavior and the welfare of consumers. In particular it should be determined how changes in housing and retailing facilities affect how families in these neighborhoods meet their food needs, and how well retailing serves them. Closely related to this is a need to determine how changes in retailing facilities affect the operations of ambient stores.

QUESTIONS FOR DISCUSSION

1. In contrast to the Cameron article, Professor Goodman finds that the poor do not necessarily pay more. How could two authorities differ so much?

2. Professor Goodman made his survey in a newly redeveloped ghetto area. Do you think the findings would have been different had the survey been done in an older, undeveloped slum area? Why?

3. What would appear to you to be the secret of why the group studied in this article seemed to be rather wiser buyers than were those described in the Cameron article?

4. Would you think this favorable trend towards better buymanship in the slum areas to be spreading or declining?

5. What can be done in old slum areas to restore retailing services that have decayed, often to the vanishing point?

FOOTNOTES

1. "Retail Food Prices in Low and Higher Income Areas: A Study of Prices Charged in Food Stores Located in Low and Higher Income Areas of Six Large Cities, February, 1966" in *Special Studies in Food Marketing* (Technical Study No. 10, National Commission on Food Marketing. Washington: GPO, 1966), pp. 121-144.

2. David Caplovitz, *The Poor Pay More* (New York: The Free Press of Glencoe, 1963).

3. The Dept. of Welfare table used was adapted from "Food Plan at Low Cost," Household Economics Research Division, Agricultural Research Service, U.S. Department of Agriculture, March 10, 1959.

* "A Visit to the 'Territory'," Du Pont *Context*, No. 1,
1973, pp. 19-21. Reproduced by Permission.

At the Neighborhood Consumer Information Center in
Washington, D.C., where he is executive director, Joseph F. Smith
got set to visit the Territory.

"I usually wear old clothes," Smith explained, discarding his tie
and unbuttoning his shirt. "I'm more comfortable that way, and the
people are more comfortable with me.

"The Territory," Smith said as he walked to a car, "is a melting
pot of blacks, whites, Puerto Ricans, Mexican Americans and Latins.
They have one thing in common: most of them are poor."

Tall and lean, Smith is a 27-year-old black lawyer. To thousands in
the nation's capital, his face is familiar as the host of a weekly
Consumer Guide-lines show on WRC-TV. To high-ranking
government officials and Washington's press corps, Smith is a
member of the President's Consumer Advisory Council. To
thousands of consumer protection workers—government, private and
quasi-government—across the nation, Smith is a man dedicated to a
cause: helping the low-income consumer.

"This isn't just a black problem," Smith said in the car heading to
the Territory. "We have some 20 million poor people in this
country—whites, blacks, Indians, Alaskan Indians, Aleuts, Puerto
Ricans, Latins, migrant workers, the aged—they're all trapped in this
vicious cycle.

"Most consumer protection activity to date has been focused on
middle-class America," he continued, "but the consumer problems of
the poor are different in kind and in intensity. Poor people aren't
complaining that their power mowers don't work or that they can't
get a serviceman to fix their dishwasher. Poor people are concerned
with basic human needs . . . Will we have enough to eat today, a
decent place to live?

"Food prices are going like this,"—Smith gestured like a plane
leaving a runway—"but their money isn't going like that. How can
they buy the food they need?"

Though he lives comfortably today, Smith knows what it's like to
be poor. Eldest of six children, he grew up in Thomasville, Ga.,
where his father was a laborer, his mother a domestic worker.

"Down there, from a money standpoint, everybody is poor,"
Smith reminisced. "But it's a different attitude; you don't accept
poverty. People work together—that's what my family did to help
put me through college and law school."

In 1968, Smith and other law students at Howard University [Washington, D.C.] founded the Neighborhood Consumer Information Center, a non-profit, tax-exempt corporation funded by the university and the Office of Economic Opportunity [OEO]. Since then, NCIC has developed a broad range of consumer protection and education programs.

"Through our local programs," Smith said, "we've been able to synthesize many major problems, define how they affect people, and develop solutions that can be applied nationally." According to Smith, problems run the gamut from false advertising tactics and housing code violations to shady finance charges and home-repair gyp artists.

Smith drove along 18th St. and paused while he pointed to a row of shops across the street. "The one with the Spanish signs on the window is Ayuda," he said. "That's Spanish for help.

"Ricardo Moreno runs this place with Spanish-speaking law students from George Washington University. He tells me there are about 25,000 Spanish-speaking people in D.C., and about half are at the poverty level.

"Ayuda provides free service to these people in many ways," Smith explained—"advice on everything from warranties, credit reports and house repairs, to food stamps and job training. We need more voluntary groups like this."

Smith drove on. "We really can't solve the problems of the poor," he observed. "Local consumer protection leaders can do it better because the people they work with know and respect them. If it's a Chicano problem, we leave it to the Chicano; if it's a Puerto Rican problem, the Puerto Rican can handle it best.

"But we do provide guidance and practical information. We also try to put local consumer protection leaders from one area in touch with leaders in other areas when they have common problems.

"We try to help wherever we can be useful. For example, we've worked with an Indian reservation out west. The Indian Council negotiates for the merchandise bought for the entire reservation. They wanted some advice about buying and contacted the Bureau of Indian Affairs, who sent a man to see us. Together, we were able to work out solutions for their problems."

The car pulled up to a parking lot and Smith got out. He was now on 14th St., which intersect a blighted area less than three miles from the White House.

"This is the heart of the Territory," Smith said. "It's where the hell is." He continued walking.

"We've also developed consumer protection programs for the Puerto Ricans in New York," Smith said. "And I spent two weeks near Los Angeles training Mexican-Americans who wanted help with their buying club and credit union.

Smith noticed an old, abandoned car at the curbside.

"You can talk to just about any consumer agency in the country and you'll find that one of the major problems of the poor is used cars," he said, striding into an office building.

"These cars aren't just lemons." He pushed an elevator button.

"—they're junk. But shyster salesmen foist them on unsuspecting people so they can collect a fat finance charge and use the holder-in-due-course process." The elevator arrived and Smith entered. "Five weeks later, the transmission may fall out, but the poor buyer is forced to make payments to a third party against whom he has no redress.

"We're working on things like that." The elevator door opened. "And, in some cases, we've been able to show misrepresentation." He headed down the corridor and opened a door marked CHANGE, Inc.

Seated at her desk when Smith arrived was Mrs. Ruth Webster, executive director of the Cardozo Heights Association for Neighborhood Growth and Enrichment.

Smith and Mrs. Webster discussed 30-day eviction notices, recreation for local youngsters, and a recent problem involving escalating prices at a local store.

"It's the old story," Mrs. Webster frowned. "You see an ad in the paper about a sale. You go to the store and find that the products advertised aren't on sale here; they're on sale in the suburbs."

Out on the streets of the Territory again, Smith noticed two old men.

"Some people have worked themselves out of poverty," he said, "but when they become old they fall right back into it."

Smith crossed 14th St. and headed for a residential area. He paused briefly at a playground, where six teen-age youths scrambled for a basketball. Behind them, a wall of graffiti and deteriorating buildings.

"If you could look inside some of these places, you would see real consumer problems: no janitorial services, plumbing out of order, commodes stopped up, dangerous wiring, lights don't work. Often, no heat.

"But," Smith insisted, "it's not just here in the Territory—you can find the same conditions practically anywhere in the country."

The Territory has many alleys and Smith turned into one.

"One time I walked through this alley and these kids—two and three years old—were begging for nickels so their mommas could wash their clothes.

"Middle-class consumers can drive to chic boutiques or department stores for excellent quality clothing. This mobility they take for granted simply isn't available to many poor people. Often, they're forced to buy at ghetto stores, where the quality and choice of clothing are usually low and the price and credit terms high."

As Smith walked the alley, four tough-looking teenagers appeared. One noticed a photographer taking pictures of the decaying houses.

"Hey, man," he shouted. "You taking pictures of these buildings? You're about 100 years too late."

Teen-age laughter filled the alley. That was the best joke of the day.

Smith continued walking along the alley.

"One of the big problems," he said, "is that there is hardly any consumer education material available for low-income people. Most of it is directed to middle-class consumers.

"We have to start at the earliest grade, even at kindergarten. We need to teach poor children the value of money and what money can do for you. We also have to teach them to negotiate—not just to hand over money—and also how to assess product quality."

Smith stopped and leaned against an abandoned car. He described a week-long conference on low-income consumerism which NCIC recently had held in Washington, D.C.

He said some "big names" in consumerism had attended the conclave, first of its kind in the nation. People like Presidential consumer adviser Virginia Knauer, former FTC consumer protection chief Robert Pitofsky, Council of Better Business Bureaus President H. Bruce Palmer, and others.

Hundreds of consumer protection leaders from coast to coast also attended the conference.

"We're pleased with the results," Smith said. "Some business people thought they were going to get raked over the coals but found that wasn't so."

Encouraged, Smith said plans are already under way to hold a similar conference in Washington again next year.

It was getting late. Smith headed back to the car. "Well, you've seen a little bit of the Territory," he said. "You know, millions of people come to D.C. to see the monuments, the cherry blossoms, and the government. They never come here. If they did, maybe we'd solve our problems a lot faster."

PART IV

MALEFACTORS IN THE MARKET

The problem of false and misleading advertising and selling has been with us for a long time. So, also, have critcisms that the promotion process is wasteful. We have examined the latter question in Parts I and II, and will have more to say about misleading promotion in Part VII where we look at new measures instituted to redress and control such malpractices.

In this section, we first look into the question of role conflict. Many questionable practices arise because business leaders and executives feel several strong pulls in quite different directions: First, the executive is expected to make a profit and a good return on invested capital for the owners and stockholders of his concern. To do so, he must not be too sensitive about cutting corners so as to enhance profits and reduce costs. On the other hand, he has his social obligations to behave honorably towards his competitors and not to abuse or deceive the customers of his product or service. Finally, he has his own personal religious and ethical standards that must be reconciled with the rough and tumble of the market. Professors Nason and Armstrong examine this dilemma as it affects the marketing manager, particularly, who most often of the major executives is vitally affected by the conflicting roles.

As social scientists, the authors feel that the "foxes" can be reoriented by suitable social conditioning, involving rewards for socially acceptable behavior and penalties for anti-social policies (e.g., monopolizing a market).

Many readers will be familiar with the conventional attacks on advertising. But the two authors selected for this book have new and fresh insights into this old controversy. Their two articles make good contrasting pieces. Mr. Hobson is a very respected advertising leader in Great Britain, and he writes wittily and well, as do so many of his countrymen. He makes a strong case for the promotion function in our society. Professor Henry takes an unusual angle of attack, the cultural ills engendered by advertising, indeed, by the business ethic generally. It is broad, and he has a most provocative argument, one which should be better known and appreciated by business critics, and the public generally.

Professor Robertson treats a subject of hot current debate: What is the effect of television advertising on our children? Does the naive, credulous young viewer believe what he or she sees on the tube? Are the child viewer's values warped by the distorted picture of life shown there? Dr. Robertson examines the question carefully and comes to some valuable conclusions. Later on, in Part VII, Robert Choate recommends to the Federal Communications Commission certain controls to redress this abuse of the young.

Finally, as an example of an industry which has come in for very heavy "flack", Robert A. Goodman gives a new, fresh appraisal of that old whipping boy, the drug industry. The reader can judge for himself whether all of the heavy criticism is justified from the well-documented evidence adduced by Mr. Goodman. The drug industry, of course, is not the only industry which has been heavily censured by the critics. But the degree of criticism currently faced by the drug people gives good evidence of the vitality of the forces presently at work to reduce abuses against the consumer in this country. It is also a good case as to how an industry can get itself into trouble with many circles of society.

PETER DRUCKER

* Peter Drucker, "The Shame of Marketing," *Marketing/ Communications* (August, 1969), pp. 60-64. Reproduced by special permission.

We have asked ourselves where in the marketing concept consumerism fits or belongs. I have come to the conclusion that, so far, the only way one can really define it within the total marketing concept is as the shame of the total marketing concept. It is essentially a mark of the failure of the concept.

Marketing has been defined as "looking at the world from the seller's end" — and that's one way of looking at it. And that's the way we have been practicing it. But there is another definition of marketing, which is to look at the business from the buyer's end. And that is consumerism, and we haven't practiced it. Or we would not today have it thrust at us as a challenge and a threat and as an attempt to penalize, to restrict economic activity.

A good many of my friends in business have been telling me over the years that consumerism is an invention of the politicians, and that there is no support for it in the marketplace. And I am willing to believe that up to a point. But I've been around long enough to know that politicians don't flog dead horses — they can't afford to. They are in a much more competitive business than we are, and if there is no support for something they go elsewhere very fast.

And I am told by my friends that the various legislative measures proposed by this or that advocate of consumerism are not going to help any; they are going to make things worse — and I've been around long enough to believe that.

I know that if one waits for the politician to find a solution, it is almost always the wrong one because politicians, by definition, react to the headlines. And that's always treating the symptoms and leaving the basic condition untouched. But that also means that the people whose business it is to concern themselves with a problem have simply not lived up to their opportunities and have waited for the politicians to react to " a scandal."

Consumerism means that the consumer looks upon the manufacturer as somebody who is interested, but who really doesn't know what the consumer's realities are. He regards the manufacturer as somebody who has not made the effort to find out, and who expects the consumer to be able to make distinctions which the consumer is neither able nor willing to make.

When I look at our advertising, I know perfectly well why the consumer doesn't trust us. Not because we scream so much, but because we are talking about things that are meaningless to the consumer. Again and again and again I see advertising that says, "Our clever, ingenious engineers have suspended the laws of gravity to bring you a pocket comb." Well, let me say that the housewife ain't no engineer, thank God, but she has been around for a long time and she isn't stupid. And so she says, "If it was that hard to make this gimmick, it won't work anyhow."

It is our job to make things simple so that they fit the reality of the consumer, not the ego of our engineers. I've long ago learned that when most manufacturers say "quality," they use the engineers' definition, which is: "Something that's very hard to make and costs a lot of money." That's not quality, that's incompetence.

We have not realized that the very abundance, the very multiplicity of choices creates very real problems of information and understanding for the consumer. We have not looked at our business from his, the consumer's, point of view.

The great problem today is lack of information. When you talk to the young people, you find that a great deal of their restlessness stems clearly from absence of information about the enormous, challenging and perhaps even threatening variety of career choices available to them, when 30 or 40 years ago there were almost none. And there business has not done a good job.

Very bluntly, we have been craven, timid in taking responsibility for our influence. Several years ago, I sat with the general counsel of one of the big automobile companies, and we went over the then-new automobile safety bill. When we were all through, he opened his bottom drawer, pulled out a folder and said, "You know, that's a bill we worked out here 12 years ago on this problem. There is nothing in the Nader bill we haven't in our bill." I said why didn't you go any further 10 years ago, and he grinned and said, "You know perfectly well why not. We all immediately said we can't possibly acquaint the American public with the fact that there are automobile accidents." Yet the American public had, by 1950, caught on to that fact — or don't you think so?

I am concerned because I know that it isn't true that the American automotive industry didn't *do* anything about automotive safety. They did almost all the work we have on safe-driving training and on safe highways. Ford began in 1948, '49, '50 to install seat belts. When it turned out that the public didn't want them, it rapidly withdrew and dropped them. And now, 15 or 18 years later, the auto industry is the villain.

The public utility companies have for 30 years been trying to get permission from their regulatory commissions to use low-sulfur, low-smoke fuels to free the air from pollution. But the commissions were concerned only with low power rates, and always said, "No, you can't charge extra for the cost of it." And now the power companies are blamed.

In the first place, if one sees a potential problem, one doesn't say there is no public clamor.

And if it means that one starts lobbying for safety legislation, no matter how unpopular this may be in the board rooms in Detroit, that's what one does.

It is simply not true that the politician doesn't listen to the businessman, or that the public doesn't listen to the businessman. This is simply myth. Whenever we have said, "This is a problem, we are the experts, we have thought it through, this is what needs to be done," well, we haven't gotten 100% always of what we sought, but we have gotten 96-1/8%, and that's good enough most times. But if one waits until there is a scandal and then one starts lobbying, one is automatically in poor shape.

We start out with the assumption that government won't let us. We start out with the good old German proverb which, roughly translated, means, "Don't go near your prince unless he absolutely insists on it." There is something to it, but unfortunately we can't hide any more. And if one can't hide any more, then one has to become the prince's favorite courtier. There's no alternative.

Again and again, my friends and clients tell me they can't do this, they can't do that. So I go to Washington and I go to the commission or to the Congressional committee and do you know that I have never yet found a single case where the general counsel of my client and his public relations vice-president were right. Not once. Nine times out of 10 the commissioner down at the ICC looks at me and he says: "That problem, we have never heard of it. We have no rule on it." And I say: "Well, can my client go ahead?" and the commissioner says, "Look, have you read the Organic Act?" and I say, "No" (and he kind of says sadly haven't you, and he's quite right and I now read organic acts before I go down). Then he says "The Organic Act says that we cannot approve anything in the commission unless it's a tested in practice. So you see, as the act says, we can't approve something you haven't done. You go ahead and do it for five years; don't tell us — do it, find out whether the damn thing works and come back and we'll approve it."

Above all, this is true of Congress. Our attitude toward Congress is a very peculiar one. And it is going to be nasty. We have let ourselves be infected with the idea that Congress is a stupid enemy. That is also the arrogant attitude of the Executive Branch.

Even if it were true, it wouldn't be intelligent to act on it because we depend on the Congressmen. But it isn't true. What is true is that, in our very complex world, Congress is understaffed, is underinformed, has an impossible assignment. Compared to the 5,000 research men Mr. McNamara could call into his office with one stab on the button, the Armed Services Committee, which is the most highly staffed Congressional committee, has 18 people on it, and everybody thinks it's highly overstaffed.

Yet, while they are expected to deal with terrifically complex work, they are dependent on the information monopoly of the experts of the Executive Department, and they are therefore more than eager for reliable information. And yet we never go to them until we want something from them.

What do they need from us? There are a great many things they don't understand, questions they have, things that puzzle them in our very complex world. Yet few businessmen have ever said, "I will go and make it my business not to lobby, not to spend a lot of time, but simply to ask 'What can I do for you? Is there anything I happen to know that might help you? Is there anything you might want to find out? Is there anything you don't understand?'" Anyone who has said these things has found that if and when he needed a friend he had one.

In this present world, we have two pulls — very strong. One is the pull of consumption. If you look at the economy these last 20 years, what has kept it going and has prevented major depressions in the developed countries has been the insatiable appetite of the consumer. Again and again and again we slid into what was, by all signs, a major recession, only to find that the consumer today has the affluence to shift a good bit of his income from savings to consumption. They have learned to do it, and by maintaining or ever increasing consumption they have prevented a recession.

There is at the same time today a second pull, among the young people particularly, which is anticonsumer. How serious it is one sometimes doubts when one realizes that anti-consumer folk songs would not be possible without electric guitars. I love those songs against technology played on the newest electronic devices. The freedom of the consumer is the exciting marketing fact of our situation — not, as the kids think, the manipulation of the consumer.

We have an interest in maintaining this freedom, and therefore, we have an interest in a strong and active consumer movement. Don't make the mistake of thinking this is an enemy. This is the most hopeful thing for us around. How do we really use it, how do we really challenge it, how do we really help it? We have to stop seeing the consumer as a threat and look upon him as an opportunity.

We have a similar dichotomy in our attitude toward government. There is that tremendous constant increase of governmental power — but there is also an increase in disenchantment with government. This is true in all age groups, but incidentally it is strongest among the young. It doesn't mean that they are for business, but they are no longer for government. It doesn't follow anymore for them that you're either for government or for business. They can also say, "a plague on both your houses." Let me say that that we have an interest, therefore, in the acceptance of institutions, both government and business.

The great challenge for this generation is how to make institutions perform — not how to tear them down. And therefore our great challenge is how do we make government capable of doing its job — not how do we defend ourselves against it.

I started out by saying that the place of consumerism in the total marketing concept, if any, is the shame of marketing. Let me finish up by saying that consumerism actually should be, must be, and I hope will be, the opportunity of marketing. This is what we in marketing have been waiting for. Let's not be afraid of it; let's use it. If we don't, these things are going to turn against us.

The question is: Can we anticipate and lead and initiate them constructively — or will we have to spend the rest of our lives fighting rearguard actions which one can never win and in which one can only lose more and more and, above all, lose more and more of the excitement of the initiative of the challenge of the work we are in — the work we think is satisfying, the work we know is productive?

QUESTIONS FOR DISCUSSION

1. What does Mr. Drucker mean by "shame of Marketing"? Who is ashamed of what?

2. Do you believe that the consumer movement is an opportunity for marketing people?

3. The auto industry began to alert consumers to the safety problem 15 years ago. Why did it drop the question, at least publically?

4. Why are government officials loath to judge a company's actions ahead of time? Why wait until they have done something illegal before they prosecute them?

5. Another shame is the business man's typical attitude towards Congress. How did this attitude get started? Why is it wrong? What is the real danger to business, according to our author?

6. What are the two great pulls in today's economy? Can they ever be reconciled?

7. What is the great challenge of our generation?

8. What sort of a call to action does Drucker make for businessmen? Do you think it is realistic?

ROBERT W. NASON, J. SCOTT ARMSTRONG

* Robert W. Nason, J. Scott Armstrong, "Role Conflict: Society's Dilemma with Excellence in Marketing," *Wharton Quarterly*, Fall, 1972, pp. 13-16. Reproduced by Special Permission.

In recent years, the American market system has come under increasing criticism from those it serves. Many young people, radicals, members of minority groups and even middle-of-the-roaders are concerned about such things as poor product quality, poor variety, unsafe products, and misleading advertising. From almost any vantage point, flaws in the American economic system are visible.

The flaws are of such magnitude that many even question the overall value of the market system. For example, in a speech to the Sales Executives Club of New York, marketing researcher Daniel Yankelovich noted that his studies have shown that the public's confidence in business's ability to achieve a good balance between "profit seeking" and "service to the public" has declined sharply from a 56 per cent average in recent years through 1969 to 29 per cent in 1970.[1]

Despite the mounting criticism, marketing goes on as usual. Marketers tend to discard the criticisms as being exaggerated. *Grey Matter*, a publication of Grey Advertising, Inc., extols:

> Among the millions of people engaged in production and distribution there are sure to be *rascals* who seek to prey on the public. The guts issues today are: should the *whole business world* be smeared because of some miscreants? And what does such tarring do to our economy?[2]

Similar pacification is offered by James M. Roche, recent Chairman of the General Motors Corporation:

> ... The dull cloud of pessimism and distrust that some have cast over free enterprise ... makes it urgent that those of us who are in business, who have made business our career, who are justifiably proud of our profession, that we stand up and be counted. It is up to us to reaffirm our belief in free enterprise.[3]

The education of marketers generally assumes that the problems could be eliminated if we would just "try a little harder." Marketing textbooks usually devote their first chapter to the need for considering society as a whole — but this chapter generally has no relationship to the rest of the book where the nature and scope of marketing decisions are discussed.

In this paper we express a point-of-view. It is our basic premise that it is not the free market which has failed; rather, it is the largely premeditated *departures* from the free market which have been the major source of the problems. Furthermore, we shall argue that the major pressure for these departures comes not from outside the system but from within. As Walt Kelly's Pogo once noted, "We have met the enemy and they is us."

The crux of the problem revolves about the role (or the set of prescribed behavior) for the marketing manager. The firm's definition of this role seems to be in conflict with the role as it should be defined to best meet the needs of society. As a result, the marketing manager who attempts to perform well in his role as a marketing manager could be doing overall harm to society. In short, there appears to be a conflict between "excellence in marketing" and the "needs of society."

The conflict between the role of the marketing manager and the needs of society is discussed in the first section of the paper. The major concern of the paper is that this role conflict should be recognized. The second section provides a discussion of how marketing managers often respond to this conflict when they strive for excellence under the current role definition. The third section of the paper provides a brief review of some of the more promising suggestions which have been made to deal with what society considers to be undesirable role behavior by marketing managers.

Understanding Role Conflict

The free market is widely acclaimed as the economic cornerstone of American society and it is closely tied to the ideals of freedom and individual choice. Marketing managers often make public statements about the value of a free market as do government officials. In this paper, we accept the ideology that the free market provides the best solution to the economic problem in the United States. That is, it seems to be the best way to satisfy the needs of those people in an affluent society.*

'While a precise definition of the free market often leads to endless debate, there are certain elements which nearly everyone would agree to as being important to the effective operation of a market system. These include:

Free entry of producers
No collusion among producers
Useful information for consumers
Free choice by consumers

*The term "ombudsman" has been inappropriately used in the public relations efforts of some firms (e.g., Chrysler corporation) to apply to an "assistant-to-the-president."

The need of the people in a society can be met more efficiently, then, when improvement is made in each of these four areas.**

The marketing manager is the chief intermediary between the producers and the consumer. It is the job of the marketing manager then to help in identifying the needs of consumers and to help in meeting these needs in an efficient manner. Since a free market is also helpful in this regard, it would seem that the marketing manager's role should (from society's point of view) be designed to try to promote free entry, to avoid collusion, to provide useful information, and to ensure free choice on the part of consumers.

However, the actual role definition enforces quite the opposite behavior because it is defined to serve predominantly one of the many interest groups in the firm — the stockholder. He is viewed as an agent of the stockholder and his role is to take actions to "maximize profits." In short, the role sub-optimizes from the point of view of society. The narrowness of this role definition should be apparent. For example, consider that about two-thirds of the corporate stock in the U.S. is owned by about one percent of the adults.[5]

What happens then, when a marketing manager takes his role seriously?* What happens when he strives for excellence in his attempt to maximize profits? It turns out that he is rewarded for actions which *reduce* the effectiveness of the free market. He is more successful when he is able to restrict entry of other producers, when he colludes with other producers, when he interferes with the flow of useful information to the consumers, and when he restricts free choice by the consumers.

In short, there is a conflict between the role of the marketing manager, as currently defined by the firm, and the role which would best contribute to the needs of the society. This conflict was documented in the electrical conspiracy case of 1961 which involved collusion to fix prices among GE, Westinghouse, and 27 other firms. Judge Ganey, at the time of sentencing the marketing executives, said ". . . I am convinced that in the great number of these defendants' cases, they were torn between conscience and approved corporate policy, with the rewarding objectives of promotion, comfortable security, and large salaries."[6]

Response to the Conflict

If the marketing manager adopts the current role prescribed by the firm, i.e., to maximize profits, there are two possible strategies for "excellence." These may be referred to as the strategies of the Ox

---

**Berle has conceded that Dodd won the argument. He feels that managers are not limited to working toward maximum profits. Rather they are recognized in law as "administrators of a community system."[21]

*We are, for example, currently involved in some role playing experiments to determine what effects these changes would have on decision making within the firm.[24]

and the Fox. These are presented as "extreme" strategies. We do not wish to imply that all marketing managers pursue such strategies (although it seems that many do). The point is that the strategies of the Ox and the Fox are rational possibilities for those managers who believe that their role is to serve only the stockholders.* An understanding of these strategies may help in isolating effective solutions.

The Ox attempts to increase profits regardless of society's rules and regulations. He accepts the role prescribed by the firm, the yoke as it were, and proceeds directly toward the firm's goal irrespective of legal or moral constraints. Thus, he is willing to break the law whenever there is an advantage to do so. He would be willing to violate the law to restrict entry of other sellers (e.g., the classic case of Standard Oil where prices were lowered in certain areas to drive other producers into bankruptcy;[7] to collude with other sellers (e.g., the electrical conspiracy case mentioned above); to interfere with the flow of useful information (e.g., false and misleading advertising such as Carter's Little Liver Pills which are now Carter's Little Pills since they have nothing to do with the liver); and to restrict the choice of consumers (e.g., where the automobile manufacturers colluded to prevent the introduction of anti-pollution devices on automobiles).[8]

The Ox is moderately successful. His major problem is that he cannot always trust his fellow conspirators (for example, "cheating" on the collusive agreement was found in the 1960 electrical conspiracy case). Seldom, however, is the Ox prosecuted for violation of the law. The penalties imposed by society are very small, implying a "boys will be boys" attitude. And the Ox seems to convince himself that the violations of the law are for the benefit of society. Consider the statement by F. F. Loock, president of Allen-Bradley Co. of Milwaukee, after he had pleaded guilty in the electrical price conspiracy case:

> "No one attending the gatherings (in the electrical controls industry) was so stupid he didn't know (the meetings) were in violation of the law. But it is the only was a business can be run. It is free enterprise."[9]

The above feeling has persisted as indicated by the recent price fixing case of the American Radiator and Standard Sanitary Corporation.[10] This case involved more severe fines and prison terms than in any other anti-trust case since the electrical conspiracy of 1960. Judge Rosenberg pointed out in his refusal to reduce the sentences of the executives, the lack of contrition on the part of the defendants. In fact, the defendants seemed to consider themselves to be the injured party rather than the public.

Unlike the Ox who is only concerned with enforcement and its severity, the Fox is careful to operate within the letter of the law. He attempts to find loopholes in existing laws. If that does not work, he

---

*More precisely, it satisfies the needs for those people with wealth. It does not, however, seem to do a good job of deciding how the wealth should be distributed. But that's another problem.

tries to get the law changed. The position he takes might be something like the following:

> The free market is a wonderful concept. Unfortunately, it sometimes leads to cut-throat competition and this is not only bad for business, but also for the consumer. In our particular situation (e.g., steel, automobiles, education, air travel, mail delivery, milk delivery, cutting hair, helping sick people) — the consumer is not adequately protected by the market. We support Bill No. xxxx which is designed to help the consumer.

The Fox may also take action to prevent the passage of laws designed to help the free market (e.g., truth-in-advertising; truth-in-lending). If he is not successful in stopping passage of the law, he is often successful in rewriting the law "for the benefit of his consumers."

One of the most successful ways in which the Fox achieves his aims to to try to make the government and the public believe that his business is not a business at all — it is a "sport," "a community of scholars," a "non-profit endeavor," a "humanitarian service," or a "necessity for national defense."

Some of the more successful activities of the Fox include:

(1) *Restricting entry of producers* by the American Medical Association in limiting the number of doctors who may practice; by the Yellow Cab Company in restricting the number of taxis available; and by the oil industry with its tariffs and quotas. (The Texaco 1969 Nine Month Interim Report is not even bashful. ". . . Texaco has made its position clear. The domestic producing industry cannot compete on an economic basis with the large-volume low-cost oil produced in many foreign areas. Import controls must therefore be retained.")

(2) *Collusion among producers* by the football industry in their hiring of players; by stockbrokers in fixing commissions; and by the airline industry. The behavior of the American Pharmaceutical Association is a case in point. When the Osco Drug chain attempted to post its discount prices in stores which such posting was legal, the Pharmaceutical Association mounted a massive legal, investigative, and pressure campaign principally through state pharmaceutical control boards.[11]

(3) *Poor and misleading information* may continue thanks to the efforts of industry to delay or to emasculate the truth-in-lending, truth-in-packaging, and truth-in-advertising laws. Further, for some professions advertising is deemed "unprofessional" or "unethical." Restriction of information surfaces in other ways. For example, gas station price signs in Rochester, N.Y. cannot be read from the street due to a city ordinance which limits the size of the numerals which can be used.

(4) *Forced or limited choice by consumers* for the space program, for elementary education, for telephones, for highways, for mail service, and for welfare programs.

Some Possible Solutions

This section briefly reviews some of the more promising solutions which have been suggested for dealing with the problems created by role conflict in marketing. Recognizing that the Ox and the Fox attempt to introduce imperfections into the market, how can these strategies be countered?

Ox-Stoppers: One basic philosophy behind dealing with the strategy of the Ox is to apply punishment. It has been suggested, for example, that the marketing manager be held personally responsible for malpractice. Injured parties could then take legal action against the manager as well as against the company. Should managers be able to purchase malpractice insurance at company expense?

Another suggestion along the lines of punishment has been to make the firm responsible for the performance of its products. The legal system has been moving steadily in this direction. Of particular note is the fact that the value of "privity" as a defense has been greatly reduced. That is, the producer cannot avoid responsibility simply because he did not sell directly to the injured party. This is true for all but eight states in the U.S.[15]

Also, producers cannot rely upon a defense based upon "negligence." That is, it is no longer enough to say that "he tried his best" and is therefore free of blame. The trend is towards holding the firm responsible for insuring that its products and services perform satisfactorily.

Class-action suits by consumers would provide an extremely effective way to hold the producer accountable for its product in situations where the cost of a lawsuit would be prohibitive for an individual consumer.[12] There is currently much interest in enabling legislation which would help to make class action suits effective. They are currently not effective for marketing problems. (Rheingold says he is not aware of any class action suits in product liability[13]).

The effectiveness of the punishment philosophy could be improved also by an increase in vigilance by people within the firm. Everyone in the firm *should* be concerned about stopping illegal and unethical activities. The marketing manager is in an especially advantageous position to observe illegal and unethical activities. If unethical actions not in society's interest are observed, the individual could try to remedy the situation within the firm. If that fails, he could publicly "blow the whistle." The power of the whistle blower is surprisingly large. Some examples[14] include Jacqueline Verrett, a biochemist with the Food and Drug Administration who angered her superiors by appearing on television to warn that cyclamates might cause birth defects; A Dale Console, a former medical director of E. R. Squibb & Sons, who testified before congressional committees about allegedly corrupt practices in the drug industry; John Gofman and Arthur Tamplin, two scientists employed at an Atomic Energy Commission laboratory, who have charged that existing radiation standards will allow thousands of needless deaths; William I. Steiglitz, who resigned as engineering consultant to the National Traffic Safety

Agency because he considered safety standards "totally inadequate"; A. Ernest Fitzgerald, who lost his job as an Air Force efficiency expert after he disclosed cost overruns on the C-5A jet transport to a Senate Committee; Ralph Stein, a former Army intelligence specialist who reported the extent of Army surveillance of civilians; and Edward A. Gregory, a General Motors inspector who complained about faulty exhaust systems in Chevrolets for more than three years before the company finally recalled some 2.4 million vehicles to fix the problem. It should be noted that false exposure can damage innocent firms and individuals but this is a risk which coexists with more accurate information and the freedom of speech.

The big problem with the whistle-blower is that his commitment to society is likely to cost him and his family severe hardship. He gets to make only one major contribution since the behavior which he is protesting is usually sanctioned by the organization. Baumhardt[16] surveyed executives and concluded from his study that the behavior of one's superior was the most important cause of unethical decisions within the firm.

An example of what happens to the whistle-blower is provided by the case of Henry Durham, an executive for Lockheed. For a number of years, he attempted to resolve a number of billing and management irregularities associated with the production of the C-5A aircraft internally within the company. However, it was not until the futility of this effort was obvious through snubs, demotions, and transfers that he took the matter to Senator Proxmire. This action invoked the wrath of his company, his church, and his town.[17]

A recent innovation for this country may help to prolong the life of the whistle-blower. This is the establishment of the office of "ombudsman." The ombudsman represents all interest groups. He is *outside of the formal organization* and does not report to the president or to the board of directors. He works on a fixed-term contract and his contract derives its power from the joint consent of all interest groups.*[18] The ombudsman is in a position to follow up on unlawful or unethical actions which are being taken by a firm or by an industry. The identity of the watchdog can be protected much as the shop steward protects the employee in labor complaints. Ralph Nader has supported an organization whose function is similar to that of the ombudsman. This organization will handle problems for any industry.†

The above ideas represent only a partial listing of ways in which society can stop the Ox. All of these counter forces are to some degree currently being used and have the advantage of not requiring major institutional changes. The use of these counter forces seems to be growing.

**It is possible to construct theoretical arguments where progress on these dimensions would lead to a reduction in welfare.[4]

†"The Clearinghouse for Professional Responsibility, P.O. Box 486, Washington, D.C. 20044.

Re-orienting the Fox: Rather than finding ways to stop the Fox, it seems more fruitful to try to re-orient his goal. In other words, an effort could be made to change the rewards rather than to use punishment.

In the early 1930's, there was much discussion over the role of the manager — e.g., see the exchange between Berle[19] and Dodd.[20] Berle claimed that the manager is and should be held responsible only to the *stockholder.* Dodd, on the other hand, suggested that perhaps the law should return to the original notion that the manager is responsible to all of the *stakeholders* in the firm — i.e., to the employees, stockholders, consumers, creditors, suppliers, and local community.** Though there will be conflicts between the groups, on balance, such a change would bring the role of the marketing manager more into agreement with the role which is oriented towards the needs of society. Thus, there would be less pressure for the manager to use the strategy of the Fox.

There has been little progress since the 1930's toward the stakeholder role. However, there seems to have been a recent revival of interest. An organization known as the Project on Corporate Responsibility was successful in getting a proposal before the General Motors stockholders which would have placed representatives of various interests groups on the board of directors. While this proposal lost by a substantial margin, it did receive much favorable interest among the general public. And in 1972, the Banking Committee of the U.S. House of Representatives was examining the possibility of "legally mandated standards for effective representation on corporate boards of stockholder, consumer, general public, and other interests."[22] Such representation is a step in the right direction but it must be recognized that current boards are often weak.

A related proposal which might also contribute to changing the role of the marketing manager is that firms should develop a system for "social accounting." This would involve an attempt to objectively measure the impact of the firm not only upon its stockholders but also upon the other stakeholders in the firm. Social accounting would be useful in helping to focus more attention on those non-financial goals of the firm. It would give more attention to the concerns of the various stakeholders. While social accounting is not a new idea (a discussion can be found in[23]), it is one which has been receiving a fair amount of attention recently.

Certainly there are other suggestions which might help to improve the effectiveness of the marketing manager. However, we feel that the related ideas of a reorientation toward the stakeholders' role and the use of social accounting are especially worthy of further consideration.*

---

*Some marketing managers do not live up to their role. They try to maximize their own welfare rather than to maximize profits. This simply compounds the negative effect on society.

*This is usually rationalized by saying that the market will protect the other groups affected by the firm.

Conclusions

The most important point in the paper is that there is a conflict between the role of the marketing manager as currently defined by most firms and the role which would seem most beneficial to society. We think that the society would be served more effectively if the marketing manager were punished rather than rewarded for actions which sabotage the free market. Even better, it would seem useful to reorient the role of the marketing manager so that he is rewarded for actions which improve the operation of the market — actions which would promote free entry of other producers, reduce collusion among producers, promote the flow of useful information to consumers, and increase the freedom of choice by consumers. Until this role conflict is recognized, there will remain a dilemma between excellence in marketing and the needs of society.

QUESTIONS FOR DISCUSSION

1. What is meant by the term "role conflict"?

2. What kinds of pulls does the typical manager encounter in his job? From what directions?

3. How does the average marketing manager resolve these pulls in opposite directions?

4. Explain the analogies of the ox and the fox. How common do you think these two sorts of business men are in real life? Do you know persons who would fit one or the other of these categories?

5. How can we stop the ox? The fox?

6. Would building an ombudsman system into a company deal with these specimens?

7. What do the authors advocate to reorient these two animals? Do you think this solution is the best? What would you recommend?

FOOTNOTES

1. *Wall Street Journal*, (November 24, 1971), 14.

2. *Grey Matter*, Vol. 42 No. 7, (July 1971), 1.

3. Roche, James M., *New York Times*, (April 11, 1971).

4. Lipsey, R. G. and Lancaster, K. "The General Theory of Second Best," *Review of Economic Studies*, 24 (1956-7), 11-32.

5. Lampman, Robert, *The Share of Top Wealth-holders in National Wealth 1922-1956*, National Bureau of Economic Research, Princeton, N.J., Princeton University Press, 1962, 209.

6. Brooks, John, *Business Adventures*, New York: Bantam Books, 1969, 188.

7. Tarbell, Ida M., *The History of Standard Oil Company*, New York, McClure, Phillips & Co., 1904.

8. Mintz, Morton and Cohen, Jerry S., *America, Inc.* New York: Dial, 1971, Ch 8.

9. *Wall Street Journal*, January 10, 1961, 10.

10. *Journal of Marketing*, (October 1971), 78-79.

11. *Consumers Reports*, Vol. 27 No. 3, (March 1972), 134-140.

12. *Congressional Quarterly*, Vol. 38 (March 13, 1970), 747-750.

13. Rheingold, Paul D. "Problems in Multiple Party Litigation," in Selma Arnold (ed.) *Products Liability*. New York City: Practicing Law Institute, 1971, 171.

14. Boffey, Philip, "Nader and the Scientists: A Call for Responsibility," *Science* (February 12, 1971), 549-551.

15. Prosser, William L., *Handbook of the Law of Torts*, St. Paul, Minn., West Publishing Co. 1971, 655.

16. Baumhardt, Raymond C., "How Ethical Are Businessmen?" *Harvard Business Review*, 39, (July-August 1961), 156.

17. Knoll, Edwin, "The Education of Henry Durham," *The Progressive*, (January, 1972), 19-24.

18. Gross, Edwin J., "Needed: Consumer Ombudsman", *Business and Society*, Vol. 8 (Autumn 1968), 22-27.

19. Berle, A. A., Jr., "Corporate Powers As Powers in Trust," *Harvard Law Review*, 44 (1931), 1049-1074.
＿＿＿＿＿＿＿＿, "For Whom Corporate Managers Are Trustees," *Harvard Law Review*, 45 (1932), 1365-1372.

20. Dodd, E. Merrick, Jr., "For Whom Are Corporate Managers Trustees?" *Harvard Law Review*, 45 (1932), 1145-1163.
＿＿＿＿＿＿＿＿, "Is Effective Enforcement of the Fiduciary Duties of Corporate Managers Practicable?" *University of Chicago Law Review*. 2 (1935).

21. Berle, A. A. Jr., "Foreword" in Edward S. Mason (ed.) *The Corporation in Modern Soceity*. New York: Antheneum, 1969, XXI.

22. *Wall Street Journal*, January 3, 1972, 4.

23. Bowen, Howard R., *Social Responsibilities of the Businessman*, New York, Harper & Brothers, 1953, 155.

24. Armstrong, J. Scott and Majoros, Walter A., "Marketing Decisions and Social Responsibility," Paper delivered at the Institute of Management Sciences Meetings, Houston, Texas, (April 1972).

JOHN HOBSON

* John Hobson, "The Social and Economic Context of Advertising," *Journal of the Royal Society of Arts*, July, 1964, pp. 1-10. Reproduced by special permission.

John Hobson was senior classical exhibitioner at Rugby School, and subsequently gained a double first in classics at King's College, Cambridge. He also played in the college rugby and tennis teams. In my view this is an ideal background for a person who was destined also to play one of the most distinguished parts in British advertising to-day. In a recent article in *The Observer* he was described as probably the leading expert on marketing in Great Britain. His company, which is no doubt well known to you — Hobson, Bates and Partners — is a result of a merger with Bates of New York, and that enables it to draw on a very wide experience not only in this country but also in the U.S.A.

I am delighted that the Royal Society of Arts have thought fit to make Advertising the subject of these three Cantor Lectures. Not only is advertising one of the most notable areas where the arts, industry and commerce meet. It is also the outward and visible sign of one of the most important social phenomena of the mid-twentieth century in this country — backstreet abundance, the percolation to the mass level of a substantial purchasing power. Certainly advertising would not exist without that mass purchasing power; but I venture to assert, too, that backstreet abundance would not exist without advertising.

I am the Chairman of an Advertising Agency; so you will not expect me to be other than biased in favour of my occupation. I am fascinated by its creativity; its techniques; its vast range of human, social and industrial interest. But I can see that it is open to some question and even some criticism, and I shall try to put a fair and honest appraisal of the subject in front of you. I am going to confine my remarks largely to mass consumer goods advertising. The £225 million of mass consumer advertising is the area in which discussion is most needed and most challenging.

Lastly by way of preamble, I must remind you that inevitably I am speaking in the context of the society and the economics that exist to-day in Britain; where an individual is rightly accorded a measure of free will and free choice, some opportunity to be right or wrong in his own decision; where there is free competition and a drive for profits. If you prefer an authoritarian society and economy, in which some authority decides for everyone what his tastes should be, what is best for him, what profits he should make, and what the limits of his objectives should be, then you alter the terms of reference and you would not necessarily want advertising in exactly its present shape; you might not even want it at all, though I rather doubt the latter.

Before I launch into my main topics, I need to clear away two common confusions about advertising. First, advertising is not (as some people seem to imagine) something in its own right, some separate estate of the realm, like civil administration, or the Services, or law. Advertising is an integral and essential part of industry — its projection into the vital department of selling. This misconception is so widespread that, at the Labour Party Conference last autumn, one delegate could talk of 'curtailing the power of the Advertising Industry'. He should rather have said, 'curtailing the power of industry to sell its products'.

There are indeed advertising specialists serving industry just as there are engineers serving ships. But their sailing orders come from the bridge, and on the bridge are the captains of industry. Advertising reflects industry's intentions and will, its strengths and weaknesses. Indeed, it does more than reflect them — it projects them on to the biggest screen possible. For the most part British industry's intentions are honest, honourable and fair. Most manufacturers believe implicitly that they have succeeded in making products that are better than competitive ones in properties, performance or value. They may sometimes be mistaken, but their belief is honest. This confidence they translate into their advertising, and their advertising technicians are advocates of that confidence. When, however, competition drives or sheer survival demands, industry will signal from the bridge to the engine-room to increase the power, quicken the pace, or change the direction, and advertising is in no position to refuse.

The second misconception I want to clear away is about the true function of advertising. Advertising is selling. Nicholas Kaldor in an important article in the *Journal of Economic Studies* some years ago attempted an interesting appraisal of advertising; but since he started with the wrong premise that the function of advertising is to inform, he produced some notably erroneous conclusions. The object of advertising is not basically to inform, but to inform for the purpose of selling. The information given will be that which is calculated to help the proposition. No one is going to pay large sums of money to give information which hinders his proposition. Often the amount of information is valid; sometimes it is minimal because there is no new information to give. Advertising neither is nor can be a disinterested service of consumer information. It is salesmanship on a mass scale and it is well to start this discussion with all the cards face upwards on the table.

That advertising is a vital part of modern economics is proved by the fact that it exists and thrives in every country where the economics of abundance apply. You cannot have production without consumption. It is absurd to have a National Productivity Year and official NEDC targets of production increase, without the means of stimulating consumption. Or are we to be for ever bedevilled by that typical British fetish that production is *'good'* but consumption is *'bad'*? We live in a society in which the mass of the people already have more than a sufficiency of necessities, and where the extra consumption must take the form of optional benefits ranging from necessary extras to sheer luxuries. The old models of the classical economists are out of date: the models which assume a certain level of demand for bushels of wheat or tons of coal, and play around with supply and price variables. In the context of consumer buying, such cosy, arithmetical factors as price-elasticity in a market are of far less importance than the elusive subjective factors of intensity of want. This always baffles and irritates the old-fashioned economists. An automatic demand does not exist for the types of extra production now coming forward; it has to be created.

Professor Galbraith in *The Affluent Society* pointed out that the economic objectives of the last century have been the increase of production. He believes they should be changed, but for the moment they are so; and while they are so, production has got to find a complementary consumption. We *must* create an acquisitive society if this extra production is not to pile up in the warehouses.

In a recent speech Lord Robens referred to the NEDC target of a 4 per cent increase in production. After eliminating the increase correlated with growth of population and of exports, he pointed out that we shall need *each year* a 2.8 per cent increase of domestic consumer production — compared with a 2.1 per cent growth in recent years. This represents an annual increase of £500 million in domestic consumption and it is an accepted Government target. He added that it cannot be achieved without the power of advertising to stimulate consumption. 'Industry', he said, 'must not have one hand tied behind its back.'

There may be other ways of disposing of increased production, such as giving it to backward countries, but the present state of public opinion and domestic politics admits only of marginal disposals in this way. The rest must be consumed by the home consumer, and the consumer must *like* consuming it. It is the job of advertising and salesmanship on behalf of industry to make the consumer *want* to consume more. Or is this necessary consumption to be a frigid, joyless process without preliminary wooing?

This brings me to the service which advertising performs for the industry which pays for it. Let us be clear that industry does not spend £225 million each year on advertising in order to see its name in the papers. It does so because advertising performs an indispensable service for it. It assures to the manufacturer the mass consumption necessary to match his mass production. That mass production involves high initial and investment risks, and much of this risk could never be undertaken without the assurance of mass consumption.

However, the process does not merely assure a total demand; advertising can help to stabilize demand. It helps to assure the stability and rhythm of the type of mass distribution needed. It can do much to even out seasonal fluctuations of demand. It can smooth out the turmoil of events which result from dynamic competitive innovations. It can offer the opportunity to exploit new inventions and improvements. It can result in a quicker build up of demand which reduces the pay-off period of new machinery, new buildings, research investment. The assurance of steady demand justifies longer-term contracts for raw materials, and this increases stability and reduces costs all down the line right to the raw material producers.

The growth of quantity production, through constantly improving production techniques, and assisted by the confidence in demand created by advertising, is now in its turn the true cause of backstreet abundance, as I have called it. Mass production reduces the real cost of goods and makes them more and more widely available. The price which has to be paid for mass production is some degree of standardization of products, but it is a small price to suffer for a process which brings more and more utilities, pleasures and recreations within the purchasing power of the mass of the population. The rise in the mass standard of living, the competitiveness of industry which results in better and better products coming forward each year, and the stabilization of full employment, these are the fruits of mass production assisted by mass salesmanship which is advertising. Poverty, maybe, still exists here and there, but it is a relative word. Sufficiency and abundance are seen everywhere.

In this context may I touch on the cost of advertising. Advertising is one of the selling costs of a product, like packaging or running a sales force or paying a retail margin. In this sense the public pays for the advertising, as indeed it pays for the costs of ingredients, or the production costs, or the other costs of selling comprised in the ultimate buying price.

But in a much more real sense advertising helps to lower prices: because mass production assuredly lowers unit costs and advertising is indispensable, in a free economy, to mass production. Like the installation of a wonderful new very efficient production machine (which no one would query in principle), advertising *pays for itself*, and more, out of the savings in the unit cost through quantity production. If advertising ceased to exist, most consumer goods would in the long run, or most likely the short run, go up in price.

The main criticism of advertising in its economic aspects, I think, is that there is more of it than is needed to fulfil the economic and industrial function required of it. Much has been made of an old, old saying of Lord Leverhulme about 'half my advertising is wasted but I do not know which half'. There is thought to be wasteful competition. There is a general imputation of slap-dash spending of very large sums of money. This leads to suggestions of restriction and even of taxation.

The figures show that, expressed as a percentage of the Gross National Product, expenditure on advertising is at just about the same level now as it was in 1938. Of course, just after the war the percentage was lower, but at that time the need to stimulate consumption was not so great. The stability of this percentage in pre-war and recent post-war years suggests that as far as the British market is concerned the process has found its level and is unlikely to increase or decrease much.

Modern methods of assessing results from advertising are far more efficient than those of the pre-war or early post-war period. They are not yet perfect but they are improving every year; Lord Leverhulme's saying is no longer true in any major degree. The industrialists who spend large sums on advertising are no fools.

The idea that competitive advertising of brands in the same market is wasteful, is not true in practice. Although it might seem to an outsider that they are merely spending to take business away from each other, this is not in fact what happens. What happens is that their joint spending widens the total market for the product group and both advertisers are well repaid for their efforts. I have seen it happen over and over again.

Of course, there are times when new products are launched ill-advisedly, or extra spending is put into existing products unsuccessfully. There are the occasions when excessive or stubborn optimism overrules good judgement and when, to put it plainly, the manufacturers make a mistake. But unless one envisages a government bureau to decide what shall be sold, and who shall be allowed to progress, and what new initiatives may be undertaken, such misjudgements are unavoidable. They are a normal price of progress.

A restriction or tax on advertising must be a restriction or tax on initiative and on development. If we need more consumption then we must not inhibit the initiatives or the investment in securing it. The industrialists may surely be left to decide for themselves what initiatives and what volume of activity are compatible with running a sound business.

To return to my main theme. Increased production presupposes increased consumption. But increased consumption cannot be achieved merely by making an increase of goods available. It can only be achieved by making the products *wanted*. This raises the question of salesmanship, which, on a mass scale, is what advertising is. Incidentally, advertising is accused of creating wants. This is not a true picture: advertising evokes and activates latent wants, which people never realized they had the means of satisfying. The failures of marketing almost always reside in the failure to assess rightly whether a true want exists. You cannot create a want which does not exist.

The economic phenomenon of abundance at mass level has a natural complement in what historians will, I think, recognize as one of the social phenomena of the century — the rise in importance of salesmanship. In the eyes of a limited intellectual and upper class minority — but I suspect this audience will include such people in a substantial majority — salesmanship is not quite respectable. In the eyes of the great majority of the public it presents very little problem. On the whole, you know, people enjoy being sold things.

In 'salesmanship' I comprise two separate elements. First, the whole complex of activities by which a cornucopia of goods and services and pleasures is spilled out in front of the mass consumer; by which his every next want is assessed and provided for; and of which advertising is the most obvious and ubiquitous outward and visible sign. The consumer is king; his wants are law; and the whole host of specialists is studying how best to cater to them. The impetus of the development derives from two forces that cannot be resisted: the new mass spending power and the democratic expectation of being allowed to exercise choice and free will.

Second, the techniques of salesmanship. These are of course the more tangible of the two elements, and they are therefore used as the main target.

A powerful new force such as salesmanship naturally meets fierce resistance from those elements in society whose existing power it is diminishing. We have seen the same resistance to 'trade' as an occupation as late as at the turn of the century. But the clock cannot be turned back and there is ample evidence that the new generations in the Establishment, in industry and in commerce are recognizing and accepting the new force.

However, the rearguard of conservative social forces have one relatively easy target. Advertising magnifies each day on to a huge projection the difference between the accepted ethics of everyday life and the true philosophical or religious ethics to which each of us in our best moments aspires. For example, by its nature advertising deals in partial truths, not in whole truths. It claims the favourable aspects of the truth about the product it sells, and is silent about the less favourable. It is content if what it says is true for some people on some occasions, even if it cannot be universally true. In short it behaves as ordinary people behave, and I think you would have to be very self-righteous to blame it for that.

The law in its ancient wisdom has accepted that this is permissible in selling, and it is recognized as common practice and common sense. Indeed, the simple words and images comprehensible to the mass market could not possibly comprise the universal truth. Moreover, selling is accepted behaviour in a vast range of other contexts: selling political or social ideas; selling projects across a Committee table; selling one's own personality in every phase of personal relations; and so on. Selling is as old as human relations and it has been accepted as common practice. The advocacy of ideas, it seems, is applauded; but the selling of goods is rejected. Yet good goods are as valuable as good ideas; and, assuredly, bad ideas are far more dangerous than bad goods.

The real problem is that what is accepted common practice in private, or on a small scale, can easily be subjected to criticism when shown up in the limelight of mass proportions.

What is vital therefore is that the beneficial power of this new force of mass salesmanship should neither attract fair criticism nor overstep acceptable limits by being allowed to become misleading or irresponsible. In its earlier phases advertising was often irresponsible and occasionally it still is. The best safeguard lies in the attitude of the industry that sponsors it and the people who practice it. The license of salesmanship must not be allowed to develop into licentiousness.

What then are the reasonable safeguards that the community must have to channel this dynamic into its most beneficial direction? There is a strong movement nowadays in the name of 'consumer protection'. This movement says, 'If the powerful voice of advertising is merely representing the favourable aspects of its products, should not the public have the right to full and precise information on the pros and cons of these products alongside the advertising claims?' The theory is fine; the practice is virtually unworkable. The average public would far rather invest a few shillings to find out whether a product lives up to its claim than read some elaborate objective evaluation. Nor do people really trust the rounded-off 'best buy' pronouncement of some remote, unseen authority. Their own experiences, or the say-so of friends or relations, are far more convincing. The great majority of consumers would not use this kind of protection, if it were provided.

In my judgment and experience there are three great safeguards of the buyer in relation to salesmanship through advertising.

The first is that (unlike the salesman at the door, for example) the advertiser depends on repeat selling, not on a single sale. If his propositions are extravagant or misleading, and his product on its first purchase fails to live up to the promises in its advertising, he will suffer a serious loss.

The second is that people who see and hear advertisements are well aware that they are being sold something, and they discount a large measure of what is said. Talk to them and they will say 'I never believe what the adverts tell me'. By this they mean they mentally prefix to the reading of each advertisement the thought 'the advertiser says . . .'. They distil out of it instinctively as much as they can believe might be true for them personally. Some people worry that children may be over-credulous on exposure to good advertising. This is possible. It is a worry best met, as one of my colleagues said in a speech recently, by *teaching* children to put that mental prefix to each advertisement 'the advertiser says . . .'.

The third safeguard lies in all that has been done during the last sixty years to prevent misleading claims from irresponsible advertisers. Not only have industry and its advertising technicians adopted higher standards, but there has been legislation like the Merchandise Marks Act. However, legislation itself is not the right answer — it can never be watertight. Recently the sections of industry and commerce concerned with advertising have consolidated into a single code, 'the British Code of Advertising Practice', the various existing rules governing advertising claims, and have adopted — with the agreement of the principal media — the sanction that advertisements which offend these standards are debarred from publication. The governing body is called the Advertising Standards Authority, formed half from advertising and half from non-advertising interests, with an independent Chairman. The executive body is called the Code of Advertising Practice Committee, which sets up the codes and deals with the cases arising under them. Then there is the Advertisement Investigation Department of the Advertising Association which investigates the validity of claims, and there are experts available on most subjects to advise on the facts. It is a system which is as watertight as it can be. It may not prevent some fly-by-night advertiser from offering spurious wares in some obscure local medium but it will go a long way to preventing serious abuses. Let me only add that, although this new and elaborate machinery has only recently been established, the responsible media have for years done their utmost to check on advertisement claims, especially on television, which is a special case because of the provisions of the Television Act. For the most part those checks have been successful in eliminating false claims; but the system will now be tighter.

My own appraisal therefore of this whole issue is that the balance of strength between the drive of the seller for more sales, and the natural caution and resistance of the buyer (which is in fact the current balance, and which has grown up in a free society over many centuries), is still the best system, and cannot be replaced by externally imposed limitations on either the buyer or the seller. In this balance of strength, salesmanship and advertising, which is mass salesmanship, play their part on behalf of the seller; and caution, inertia and habit as well as judgement, play their part for the buyer. No one should ever underrate the capacity of the British public to devine and assess the true values of what is offered. It is erroneous as well as patronizing to think it can easily be fooled. The public is very adult and can be treated as such. This is not to say that within this pattern there is not a case for every reasonable limitation on unfair selling and every possible protection for incautious or ignorant buying — and these precautions are being more and more devised by all concerned in the business. But we know this pattern works; all the alternatives are untried.

There are other arguments brought against advertising in its social context: that the whole overwhelming pressure of expert communication to sell things is tending to create a materialistic outlook and an 'acquisitive society'; and secondly, that it debases taste.

To the first of these propositions I must reply 'Yes, the effect of advertising volume is to concentrate people's minds on the pleasures of acquiring, owning, enjoying materialistic benefits.'

We are dealing with a subject which is very much a matter of point of view. Our politics, our economics, our whole basic drive, whether from industry or the trade unions, from the City or from the Labour Party, has been to raise the material well-being of the masses of the population. Who is to say that is is right to ensure that people have a sufficiency of bread and meat, but wrong that they have a variety of attractive foods to choose from? That it is right for women to be released from drudgery, but wrong for the process to go as far as offering them washing machines, mixers, frozen peas or gay curtain material? That we should all have holidays with pay but not to be tempted to take those holidays abroad? And so on?

Let us remember all the time that all the needs of production-orientated economics, all the maintenance of full employment, all the progressive discoveries of modern science, and all the drives of past history, have tended to focus on material betterment for people and nations.

The ascetic, the puritan, the idealist may have other views, but I suspect that very often they are essentially egotistic views proceeding from a personal dislike of possessions. They positively dislike and fear abundance, particularly backstreet abundance. I respect these as personal attitudes. But I do not think that they are compatible with the daily activities of 99 per cent of our population who, in the backstreets or the suburbs, are involved in a struggle for material livelihoods and comforts.

Moreover the achievement of a better materialistic standard of living, the struggle out of the slum outlook, in which the drive for self-betterment fostered by advertising plays so great a part, can be the finest foundation for further *non*-materialistic aspirations. In any case we cannot put the economic clock back, to satisfy the ascetics. Modern economics are the economics of abundance, in which the demand for, and the acquisition and consumption of, goods are an indispensable counterpart of more and more efficient and plentiful production.

The second proposition, that advertising lowers literary usage and standards of taste, and produces debased images and motivations, is to my mind an absurd generalization (though there may be a few cases which can be truly cited). It is of course a view heard from a limited minority, and it proceeds from an intellectual and social snobbery resulting from a complete lack of contact between those people and the vast majority of their fellow countrymen. An eminent leader of public opinion, highly regarded in Government circles, and the Chairman of a number of Royal and other Commissions said to me recently that he approved of the advertising found in *The Times*, but totally disapproved on literary gounds of certain popular advertising found in the *Daily Mirror* and elsewhere. Now what kind of human understanding does that remark reveal? The job of advertising is to communicate with the potential market. If we talk to *Times* readers we talk in *Times* language; but if we want to talk to the *Daily Mirror* readers we might almost as well talk in Russian as talk in *Times* language. To communicate with the people we have to accept and to use their vocabulary, their motives and interests, their ideas of fun, their standard of visual images, just as their favourite newspapers do, or their favourite television programmes.

We hear criticisms that the trivialities of advertising smother the means of important communication. It is true that advertising deals mainly with trivialities — the choice between two beers or two toothpastes must rest on trivialities. But if those who thought they had something important to say to the people would only come down off their pontifical high horses and their classical educations, and use the idioms and images of the people — like negro spirituals or Churchill's speeches — they would, I feel sure, find that they were getting the attention they expect.

In its language and its visual images, in the motives or the aspirations it evidences, advertising reflects without flattery the values of the society we live in. Advertising that hypocritically assumed that tastes and motives were higher than they are, would simply fail to do its primary job. Nor is it the province of advertising to educate or uplift; that is for the educators and the preachers. Advertising is the mirror of our society and if the face we see in the mirror is, on occasion, more ugly or illiterate than we hoped, it is no good solving the problem of breaking the mirror.

Now I do not mean to disparage fine ideals and high standards; and I certainly do not underrate the basic problem which lies in the fact that a great and powerful system of communication, with all its capacity for social good or evil, is motivated and governed by industry seeking its own economic ends. This is indeed a paradox which needs deep reflection. But society must expect, and on the whole does find, that its industrialists have a sense of the responsibility this power entails. Society must build up countervailing forces to promote the interests of non-materialistic well-being, because we all of us know that there are vital factors of well-being that lie outside the materialistic areas. But I say that advertising itself cannot be expected to be schizophrenic; it has its job to do, and it must do it, and it is a job of great value to the community.

I recall one incident which seems to me to crystallize the whole essence of the problem of advertising's social context. A well-known and highly respected Quaker industrialist once said to me, as he approved his vast advertising budgets, 'advertising is a necessary evil'. To him as an industrialist advertising was essential; to him as a Quaker it was an evil. Which is the greater good: the prosperity of an industry which ensures the livelihood of thousands of families and meets the legitimate needs of millions — or the very real and honourable convictions of Quaker asceticism?

These words crystallize the paradox of modern advertising. On the one hand we have a system which is indispensable to the health of our consumer industries, to the abundance of our people's standard of living, to the life-or-death struggle for exports in a competitive world. On the other hand we have the creation of a materialistic society, the question of the partial truths of salesmanship, the risks involved in putting a vast social power into the hands of industry seeking its economic salvation.

The solution to a paradox must, I think, be compromise. Salesmanship, and in particular public salesmanship in the form of advertising, must be allowed pressures. But we must demand responsible salesmanship, highly self-critical, conscious exactly of the line of truth and good manners that it must not overstep. This is not a problem for the law or the Government; such matters cannot be handled by written law. It is the job of industry that pays for advertising and governs it, of the technicians who practice it, and of the pressure of public opinion, to exercise the necessary restraint. The minority view of asceticism, the Puritan strain in our make-up, the eyebrow-raising of the out-of-touch intellectual, must not overpower and outweight the majority needs of a better living standard, but neither must they be ignored. We need salesmanship in our society, but it must be *responsible salesmanship*, and this I believe is what modern industry and modern advertising are striving to give us.

QUESTIONS FOR DISCUSSION

1. What does Mr. Hobson say in favor of advertising? Do you agree with all his points?

2. Do you think that the fact Mr. Hobson is a very successful advertising agency head may have colored his arguments?

3. Do you believe that the three safeguards against misleading advertising are sufficient really to protect the consumer? Could you suggest other measures of protection?

4. Do you think that we have developed an overly materialistic society due to the influence of advertising? What implications for our society does materialism have?

5. What is the "paradox of modern advertising"? Are you satisfied with Mr. Hobson's solution to this paradox?

ETHICAL AND MORAL EFFECTS OF PROMOTION *

WILLIAM T. KELLY

* Drawn in part from *The Management of Promotion* by Edward L. Brink and William T. Kelley (New York: Prentice-Hall, 1963). Reproduced by permission of the copyright holder.

Selling and advertising are severely criticized for their ethical and moral effects on our culture. This subject presents difficulties, for it is hard to even define the terms. Also, the issues are so tied up with intangible values that one might argue forever about them, for they involve the ultimate goals, aspirations, and values of society, philosophical questions of right and wrong, materialism versus spirituality, spartan simplicity versus epicurian indulgence — all these have concerned thinking men since the dawn of recorded history, and perhaps before that.

More has probably been written about the moral effects of promotion on society than any other topic with which we shall deal. Since advertising, particularly, is so conspicuous and a convenient target, critics of various persuasions have lambasted it. People feel strongly about the subject and often speak of it in unrestrained, emotional terms. Just what do people object to? To answer this question it will be necessary to classify the major types of criticisms on moral grounds and to discuss each as objectively as possible. However, it is better to first define terms and trace the origins and development of ethical and moral standards in our culture.

Ethics and Morals

The Greek word for *ethics* and the Latin term for *morals* or *morality* originate from the same root, the Greek word *ethos*, meaning custom or a habitual mode of conduct. Ethics is the systematic study of moral ideas and goals, motives of choice, and patterns of good and bad conduct; morals are the study of the actual patterns of conduct. Thus, ethics deals with moral experience, while morals involve the system of conduct in different cultures and at different times.

Sources of Ethical and Moral Concepts

James Henry Breasted points out that moral ideas about religion and ethical relationships originated within the family group. They spread from the family to the groupings of families (tribes and clans) to the state, which appeared in Egypt around 4,000 B.C.[1] Breasted writes:

> The realm of family life reached a high development as a world of tender emotions, inevitably inclining to become those of approval and disapproval, and leading to notions of praiseworthy or reprehensible conduct. Voices within began to make themselves heard, and moral values as we know them are discerned for the first time. Thus, both the organized power of man *without*, and the power of the moral imperative *within* came to become forces in shaping Egyptian religion ... The earliest known discussion of right and wrong in the history of man is embedded in a Memphite drama celebrating the supremacy of Memphis and dating from the Fourth Millennium B.C.[2]

Breasted feels, however, that such ethical and moral concepts, although primarily arising out of family relationships, were solidified by the thinkers of ancient Egypt, rather than by the people. After they ramified into religious doctrine, which was developed by the priestly body of temple thinkers, they gradually diffused from the aristocrats of the royal court and the temple priesthood to first the provincial nobles and then the masses.[3]

McDougall, the founder of the study of social psychology, agrees with Breasted's view, derived from anthropological study, that the ethical impulses in the life of man have grown out of influences that operate in family relationships. He states:

> From this emotion [parental tenderness], and its impulses to cherish and protect, spring generosity, gratitude, love, pity, true benevolence, and altruistic conduct of every kind; in it they have their main and absolutely essential root, without which they would not be.[4]

Any wrong toward a child inevitably produces anger and resentment. This connection between tender emotions and anger is significant:

> For the anger evoked in this way is the germ of all moral indignation, and on moral indignation justice and the greater part of public law are in the main founded. Thus, paradoxical as it may seem, beneficence and punishment alike have their earliest and most essential root in the parental instinct.[5]

Ethical and Moral Effects of Promotion

Ethical concepts have generally been prescribed by organized religion. Those of ancient Assyria and Egypt involved definite moral codes regulating conduct and group attitudes. Judaism, Christianity,

Mohammedism, Buddhism, Confuciansim, and most other religions inculcate moral precepts besides dealing with matters of worship and ritual. Thus, although there are systems of ethics,[6] religion is the embodiment of the moral standards of a culture.

Modern social psychologists have classified group ways of looking at things into detailed categories. The following categories range from behavior patterns ungoverned by social sanctions or coercion to those strongly governed with prescribed punishments for violation:[7]

Coenotropes — physical adjustment patterns to the environment. These are like ordinary habit patterns, e.g., turning up one's coat collar in the face of a gale. Such common patterns of adjustment are completely uncoerced.

Folkways — primarily uncoerced universal customs. These voluntary cultural adjustments are stable and generally followed by the people. Examples in our Western culture are, shaking hands on meeting a friend, eating three meals a day, tipping one's hat to a lady, and wearing shoes. These folkways cover a good proportion of our daily habits and vary from culture to culture. A person who does not follow a folkway may be considered a boor, or a bit eccentric, but society does not punish the deviator. For example, one who does not wear shoes, especially in winter, may be ridiculed, but he is not cast out of society nor thrown into jail.

Mores — socially coerced universal customs. They originated from folkways that had strong ethical generalizations pertaining to social welfare attached to them. Violation of a folkway leads to laughter or at most mild ostracism. Violation of mores results in public resentment and scorn, strong ostracism, or even violent reprisals, such as lynching. Examples are sex behavior, nudism, violation of property rights and violation of parent-child relationship.[8]

Mores are regimented rather than voluntary patterns. Fear of disapproval or ostracism makes people conform. The Amish, for example, call such punishment "shunning." In a small, socially integrated community, ostracism is probably the strongest force; man is so gregarious that he suffers when denied relations with his kind. Even chimpanzees cry mournfully when isolated from their group.[9] Excommunication by the Catholic Church works on the same principle.

Mores change gradually. For example, a woman who used cosmetics and/or smoked cigarettes at the turn of the twentieth century was considered "a brazen hussy." The mid-Victorians were shocked by the undraped human body, but thought nothing of discussing body functions in a manner that would be considered poor taste today.

Institutional Ways — uniform behavior arising from membership in a social organization, political party, business corporation, church, lodge, school or the like. Institutional ways are not universal, but isolated, since they are confined to the institution's membership. Social coercion keeps the members in line. A person may be a member of several organizations at the same time. He behaves differently in each, thereby adhering to the customs peculiar to the organization, e.g., his behavior in church will be different from that at a lodge meeting.

Stateways — administrative and legal functions of the government. These have the power of society behind them and are highly coercive, since they may entail deprivation of life, liberty, or property; sometimes public shame is involved as well. Legal authorities have often pointed out that good laws originate from mores, but not vice versa. When a law carries social sanctions as well, its power is greatly enhanced;[10] but when a law is contradictory to the customs of the majority of the people, it is usually ineffective. Such an enactment weakens respect for the law in general. A good example was the prohibition amendment to the United States Constitution.

Ethics of Promotion

Discussion of the role of ethics in promotion brings up a fundamental ethical issue; namely, the admissibility of persuasion itself in our society. Should the seller be confined to objective fact, or may he properly engage in argumentation? May he "puff his goods"? Flatter them? Put them in their best light? If he does, he is emphasizing the favorable facts and de-emphasizing the unfavorable facts about his merchandise. He is influencing people to think well of it, i.e., he is persuading them.

Borden claims that persuasion is fundamental freedom. The freedom to persuade is equivalent to freedom of speech and freedom of the press. The preacher expounds a religious doctrine and attempts to persuade people to embrace a better life. The teacher expounds a subject — he is persuading his pupils to grasp ideas and concepts. The politician sells a program to voters to persuade them to vote for him. The lawyer persuades judges and juries. The physician persuades patients to take courses of action to make them well. Persuasion is and always has been fundamental to communication. If we are to maximize our freedom, the seller must be granted the right to exercise persuasion in marketing his goods. [11]

Others, however, are not much concerned with the admissibility of persuasion as with the social responsibility of the seller. David M. Potter makes this a key point in his excellent book, *People of Plenty:*

> . . . the traditional institutions (church, schools, colleges, business, and industry) have tried to improve man and to develop in him qualities of social value, though of course, these values have not always been broadly conceived. The church has sought to inculcate virtue and consideration of others — the golden rule; the schools have made it their business to stimulate ability and to impart skills; the free-enterprise system has constantly stressed the importance of hard work and the sinfulness of unproductive occupations. And at least two

of these institutions, the church and the school, have been very self-conscious about their roles as guardians of the social values and have conducted themselves with a considerable degree of social responsibility.

In contrast with these, advertising has in its dynamics no motivation to seek the improvement of the individual or to impart qualities of social usefulness, unless conformity to material values may be so characterized. And, though it wields an immense social influence, comparable to the influence of religion and learning, it has no social goals, and no social responsibility for what it does with its influence, so long as it refrains from palpable violation of truth and decency. It is this lack of inherent social purpose to balance social power, which, I would argue, is a basic cause for concern about the role of advertising. Occasional deceptions, breaches of taste, and deviations from sound ethical conduct are in a sense superficial and are not necessarily intrinsic. Equally, the high-minded types of advertising which we see more regularly than we sometimes realize are also extraneous to an analysis of the basic nature of advertising. What is basic is that advertising, as such, with all its vast power to influence values and conduct, cannot ever lose sight of the fact that it ultimately regards man as a consumer and defines its own mission as one of stimulating him to consume or to desire to consume.[12]

Potter says that advertising is the only real force to educate people into new needs, to alter men's values, and to train them to act as wise consumers, using their newly acquired abundance wisely.[13] Unlike the other major "instruments of social control," advertising has no socially defined objectives, and this is what frightens Potter and other thinkers.

In rebuttal, one may observe that advertising, unlike the other instruments of social control (e.g., church, school), is a young institution. As is shown below, it has already made great progress in raising the low ethical selling standards of "the good old days." Growing as it did from the status of a mere functional tool of business, it could not be expected to acquire social goals willy-nilly. However the authors contend that the promotional fields are evolving a basic matrix of social responsibility, but evolution works slowly. Those who understand the history of marketing are not pessimistic — they know how long it took for promotion to develop any degree of social conscience and are impressed by how far it has come from the shockingly low standards of yesteryear. They are also encouraged by the amount of discussion at present about these basic ethical and moral considerations; this ferment may speed up the evolutionary process, which is by nature turtle-slow.[14]

In conclusion, the admissibility of commercial persuasion has been established in our society. The major ethical question now is, what shall the *limits* of persuasion be? To what *degree* shall the seller be allowed to exercise persuasion? What *kinds* of tactics should be allowed?

The Changing Limits of Persuasion

The ancient limit, which prevailed from Greek to rather recent times, was the doctrine of *caveat emptor* (let the buyer beware). The role of the seller was to get the highest price for the least value of goods; that of the buyer was to give the least for the greatest value of goods. The buyer was assumed to be as knowledgeable as the seller; he expected the seller to flatter the goods, even to misrepresent them. As long as the buyer had the right to inspect the goods, he was expected to use his own judgment. If the seller took advantage of his carelessness, naiveté, or stupidity, it was the buyer's own fault. The trader was a sharp fellow and had to be keen to stay in business.

Richardson Wright gives a picture of just such a trader, the Yankee peddler. He was "a lanky, hawk-beaked youth, an adventurous, brave, mercenary fellow, who had a rare understanding of human nature, and a ready tongue. His most effective salesmanship was the 'soft sawder' of flattery. He was accused of purveying wooden nutmegs and cucumber seeds, oak-leaf cigars, shoe-peg oats, polyglot Bibles, and realistically painted basswood hams. He always left his customers convinced and satisfied with their share of the bargain, but he usually managed to clear out after finishing the deal."[15]

His social status was far below that of the settled, more respectable retailers of the early nineteenth century.[16] Yet a peculiar attitude prevailed among the people of the period. They expected the trader to try sharp practices and considered dealing with him a challenge. When he outwitted them, their compatriots ridiculed them. "Instead of any particular odium attaching him (the peddler), for having cheated you, you got heartily laughed at for having suffered yourself to be imposed upon, while he escapes with the fruits of his imposition and the general remark, "I guess it was only a regular Yankee Peddler trick.' "[17]

The modern view has changed. The courts and the public expect the seller to be honest; the situation has almost switched to *caveat venditor*. There are several reasons for the decline of the doctrine of *caveat emptor*:

(1) *Increased power of the seller.* The seller is often wealthy while the buyer is poor. It is immoral to take advantage of the poor.

(2) *Better knowledge of the seller.* The seller is now a specialist in his line of merchandise; the buyer is an amateur.[18] Buyer and seller are no longer on equal footing as they were in a more primitive era. Since the seller has an unfair advantage over the buyer, society has imposed higher standards of conduct upon him.

(3) *Proliferation of goods on the market.* The buyer of an earlier age purchased a narrow range of necessities. He or she could take the

time to be informed about them. Since today's consumer must make thousands of choices in the marketplace, he cannot be expected to be as well-informed.

(4) *Growth of hidden qualities in goods.* The simple farm wagon of the nineteenth century has changed to a complicated piece of machinery, the automobile. The simple cotton textile that every mother taught her daughter to judge has turned into a synthetic man-made fiber. The consumer can no longer evaluate goods by sight, touch, smell, or another simple method. He must depend on the reputation of the manufacturer to supply him with what is proper and of good value. This has enhanced the role of advertising in creating a favorable corporate and brand image.

(5) *Change in the goals of business.* The modern firm plans for longrange survival.[19] It cannot expect to make money by outwitting the public and withdrawing from the market. Its investments in buildings, machinery, and the like are too great. Also launching a new product on the modern market would cost too much money and time. Profits depend on repeat business, and the latter is built on fair dealing. Thus, enlightened self-interest has helped raise levels of business ethics.

(6) *Growth of opposing economic ideologies.* The followers of socialism and communism are quick to criticize business conduct if the opportunity arises. Business cannot afford an adverse public image, either at home or abroad.

(7) *Growth of horizontal structure of industry.* Trade associations, Better Business Bureaus, and trade practice conferences under the auspices of the Federal Trade Commission have all aided in formulating improved ethical standards.

(8) *Increased role of the government.* Business has been controlled by laws and regulations of governmental bodies.

(9) *Organization of consumers.* Consumers are educated by home economics courses and other instruction in better buymanship and can get information from consumer rating agencies.

The above factors have helped create a higher standard of ethical behavior expected of business. Business has come a long way in just a couple of generations, but there is still need for improvement.

What Criticisms are Levelled at Promotion by the American Public?

The American Association of Advertising Agencies in 1964 commissioned a study of consumer response to advertising. It was accomplished by the Opinion Research Corporation, using a sample of 1,846 respondents. A number of interesting findings were uncovered by the survey: general attitudes of typical consumers towards advertising, frequency of exposure to advertisements, and features liked and disliked with reasons for the reactions. The survey gives us a valuable insight into what the recipients of promotional messages think about them, and the degree to which they feel they transgress their standards of morality. Let us examine each of the major areas in turn.

General Feelings About Advertising

The American consumer is by no means hostile towards advertising in general. A survey sponsored by *Redbook* magazine in 1959 showed that 75 percent of all respondents said they like advertising, and 65 percent said that things would be more difficult for them if all companies that now advertise decided not to advertise any more.[20]

The AAAA survey of 1964 confirmed this finding: An overwhelming proportion (86 percent) of the respondents said they believe in advertising and think that it aids in bringing them better products. However, most people interviewed had some general and specific criticisms. Amongst the general criticisms were these:

1. Less than one-half of the consumers believed that advertising reduces the cost of goods. The rest either were undecided, or believed that the cost of goods was raised by the advertising expense incorporated in the price to them.
2. About half of the respondents criticised advertising on the grounds that it sometimes makes one buy things he ought not to buy.
3. Most consumers said they would like more information from their advertising.
4. Consumers rejected strongly unreal advertising — that which did not square with their own experience.
5. The majority interviewed believed that advertising practice has improved in recent years.[21]

It is interesting to note that amongst the 14 percent found to be unfavourable towards advertising as a whole in the AAAA study were respondents twice as likely to report having seen an advertisement that was offensive or annoying as the rest. Thus, a generally unfavourable attitude seems to make the consumer especially sensitized to advertising, to be much more on the lookout for "bad" advertising than is the typical reader or viewer.

Exposure and Awareness

All kinds of estimates have been made relating to the total number of exposures to advertisements in all media to which people are exposed. They generally involve astronomic figures. For example, Roger A. Frost of Young and Rubicam, Inc. estimates that the average household is exposed to more than 1,600 advertising impressions per day in all media.[22] Be that as it may, the four A's study found that the average consumer is aware of, or "sees" 75.8

advertisements per day on the average. Of these, 12 bring forth a definite reaction,[23] either positive or negative. Thus, 16 percent of advertisements perceived leave a mark; 84 percent do not.[24] The consumers are neutral towards the latter. They may influence them, but they do not evoke feelings sufficiently strong to be reported to the interviewer.

Positive and Negative Reactions

The study established that, when the consumer was led to react one way or the other by the small proportion of advertisements perceived (16 percent), the majority of the advertisements were remembered because they were liked: The average person daily sees or hears about four and one-half advertisements that inform him, about four that entertain him, less than three that annoy him, and about every other day he hears or sees one that he considers offensive. Thus, out of 12 ads noticed per day, only 3½ evoked negative reactions, a little more than one ad in four.

Highlights of Positive Reactions

Informative reaction — a good majority (59 percent) of the respondents found an advertisement informative because it was product related: It told about a new product; it explained the functions, purposes, effects or advantages of a product. Respondents also designated an ad as informative if it engendered a favorable general image of the product, that of a "good" product.

Entertaining reaction — over half (54 percent) of the people found an advertisement enjoyable because it was "pleasing", "eyecatching", "funny", "liked the music". Others referred to it as "just a good ad"; registering liking but not being able to tell exactly why they felt that way. Curiously, one in five of the interviewees said the ad was enjoyable because product related — they liked to read or hear about its features.

Negative Reactions

Offensive reaction — the most severe degree of negative response was evoked for a variety of reasons. It is interesting to note that respondents frequently gave more than one reason for disliking the ad[25] — it seems that when one dislikes an advertisement he can usually find more than one reason for it!

The most frequent criticism was that the product should not be advertised (38 percent). Here, respondents objected to the product itself on moral or ethical grounds — in their opinion, the consumption of liquor, cigarettes, certain drugs and personal

products should not be encouraged by advertising them. In this case,
the advertisement itself may be all right; they simply object to the
product sponsored.

In another 37 percent of the cases, the advertisement was deemed
to be in bad taste; in 34 percent of the cases the respondent resented
the ad, because of no interest whatever in the product. They thought
that the intrusion of the ad on their consciousness was a waste of
their time, and they tended to view this quite seriously.

Another 34 percent resented the advertisement because it was an
insult to their intelligence; 28 percent because it was unduly
exaggerated; 25 percent seemed to be untruthful.

Annoying reaction — in this category, too much repetition led the
pack (36 percent), followed closely by ads that are exaggerated (34
percent) and boring and monotonous (31 percent). Some
respondents considered ads insulting to one's intelligence (20
percent) or relating to a product having no interest (20 percent), to
be annoying rather than offensive.

Summary: The 4 A's survey found the attitude of the typical
American to be generally favorable towards advertising. People like
advertising and feel that it helps inform them. Only a small minority
of advertisements to which they pay attention bother them; in such
cases, they find most of these annoying rather than offensive. Mr.
Weilbacher sums up these negative feelings:

> Bad taste and concern because some products should
> not be advertised are major reasons for offense. The fact
> that ads are heard or seen too often, or are boring or
> monotonous are major reasons for annoyance.
>
> But there are similarities in response patterns, too.
> Exaggeration can cause either offense or annoyance. Ads
> for products which consumers are simply not interested
> in buying also can cause either offense or annoyance. The
> advertiser who insults the customer's intelligence also
> risks either offense or annoyance.[26]

In respect to the latter point, an interesting finding came out of
the study. Psychologically consumers often appraise an
advertisement with the questions: Does this ad imply that the
advertiser believes I am stupid? Does it imply that the advertiser
believes I am gullible? The reader or listener believes that the
advertiser considers him stupid or gullible when he encounters: (1)
use of "false" illustrations, "phony" demonstrations or gimmicks;
(2) being "talked down to"; (3) obvious exaggerations; (4) silliness or
childishness in ads; (5) excessive repetition of product claims; (6)
failure to accept the fact that consumers *do* compare quality and
prices.

Consumers obviously expect to be treated as adults. They often
consider an advertisement as an intrusion on their valuable time; they
want entertainment or useful information in return for that time.
They resent communications that waste their time and treat them as
stupid or gullible.

The 4 a's survey collected information on differences in people's attitudes towards advertising in the various media. A somewhat larger proportion of objectionable advertisements were found in the television and radio media, than in the print media. This is probably attributable to the superior attention getting and holding powers of the broadcast media. That is, commercials make a more lasting impression, and are better remembered as being good or bad than are advertisements in the other media.

However it is interesting to note that media seemed to have little influence on overall attitudes toward advertising.

> While there is a slightly higher proportion of people with unfavorable attitudes among those who prefer broadcast media rather than print, both groups have the same porportion of people favorable to advertising, and the print preferers are more likely to have mixed attitudes.

> The suggestion is fairly strong that while media exposure is a factor in the type of ads one reports as having seen or heard, this circumstance bears no patterned relationship to his long-run overall attitudes toward advertising.[27]

Bauer and Greyser sum up the salient findings of the Report:

> These responses tell us that although Americans react neither favorably nor unfavorably to a very substantial proportion of the ads of which they are consciously aware, nonetheless when ads do make a particularly favorable or unfavorable impression it is most likely a favorable one. This is true of ads during the day or the evening, for men and for women, for young and for old, for rich and for poor, for those with much education and little education.

> However, there are differences in the way ads are classified depending on the media in which they occur, the product being advertised, and the relationship of the individual to the product and brand advertised. Also, people tend to make evaluations of ads which fit with their overall attitudes toward advertising.[28]

Let us now consider in some detail the various sorts of unethical practices found on today's market place.

Kinds of Unethical Practices Found in Promotion

Fraud

Fraud involves clear-cut misrepresentation, a lie by the seller about a product, with the intention of deceiving. The buyer relied on the statements made or expected the seller to reveal material facts, such as defects, which the seller did not do. The buyer. on the other hand, is expected to exercise prudence and diligence in seeking out facts. If he does so, and material representations are untrue, then the buyer has been defrauded. This is a matter of law and is controlled like any other crime.

Misrepresentation and Exaggeration

These are the gray areas of promotion. False and misleading selling and advertising are not easy to apprehend, even more difficult to prove. These practices fall into the following categories:

Phony Testimonials. It is a basic freedom to express opinions and everyone should be free to commend a product he likes in public places and media, if he wishes. This right has been widely abused. Endorsements have been sold on the open market under conditions where they could not possibly be the honest opinion of the writer. For example, since 1945 a New York organization, Endorsements, Inc., has brought together 8,000 celebrities for approximately 4,500 separate products, such as apparel, household appliances, cosmetics, beverages. food, tobacco, jewelry, and automobiles. The combined cost of media space and time from 1945-57 was more than $700 million. The fees of the celebrities probably were $7 million.[29]

Another example involves the screen star, Constance Talmage. Since she was about to leave for Europe, her agent brought a variety of products to her hotel room. Photographers took Miss Talmage's picture with everything from beds to radios to soaps to toasters to pianos. In fact, during that busy day, several poses were taken with Miss Talmage pointing to nothing: later a product could be inserted into the picture in case something was overlooked![30]

The Federal Trade Commission attempted to end the racket in 1930. It ruled that when a company had paid for a testimonial, the fact had to be printed in the advertisement in type as large as that used for the copy. Unfortunately, this provision was overruled in 1933 by the U.S. Circuit Court of Appeals, which held that a paid endorsement did not have to be so labeled as long as it was truthful and reflected the true opinion of the writer. The authors believe the original F.T.C. ruling was a good one and hope that the same ruling will be made again; the courts would probably sustain the order today.

Misleading Trademarks and Labels. A trademark may be misleading if it suggests the origin or contents of a product falsely. For example, the trademark Lemon Soap was held misleading because the product in fact contains no lemon; neither did cigars called Half-Spanish contain tobacco from Spain.[31] Scotch whiskey, it has been held, must be made in the country, Scotland; although made in the United States by exactly the same process as employed in Scotland, the product would be misbranded if termed "Scotch" whiskey.

Another type of deception occurs if one trademark is so similar to another that it is confusing to the ordinary shopper. For instance, Cycol was held confusingly similar to Tycol; Oxol to Oxydol; Mel-o to Jello; Air-o to Arrow; Ex-ol to Rexall.[32] The ban also falls on deceptive place names. For example, a watch could not adopt the trademark, Lucerne, unless it were made in that Swiss city.

Outright counterfeiting of trademark, package configuration, and label has occurred. The Food and Drug Administration has had trouble with fly-by-night producers of pharmaceuticals who counterfeit the products of reliable houses; often the product is substandard. Some foreign manufacturers have duplicated the identity of well-known American firms abroad, much to the latter's detriment, for the goods are usually shoddy and poorly made.

Almost as bad as outright counterfeiting is the common practice of less well-known competitors to approximate the package, label, and trademark of a reputable, dominant competitor. For example, many competitors have duplicated the distinctive blue color and general configuration of the package, including the trademark of a little girl under an umbrella, of Morton's Salt. Since a color cannot be pre-empted as a trademark and the competitors do not technically duplicate the name or trademark, the company cannot take action, even though they have evidence that many hasty buyers grab the competing package with the mistaken idea that they are obtaining Morton's Salt.

Superlatives and Hanging Comparatives. Examples of this poor advertising practice are: "Best nickel candy there is," "Blank's soap gets clothes whiter than white," and "Acts four times faster." Such silly claims lead consumers to doubt all advertising, for the customer thinks, "If they will make claims like that, how can you believe anything they say?" Indeed, a whole industry may find that nobody pays any attention to its advertising. For example, the moving picture people used superlatives with little restraint for so many years that the public came to believe little or nothing. They called inferior, Grade B pictures "super colossal, stupendous, gigantic, greatest spectacle ever made"; then they had no way of telling the public when a superior picture in fact came out. Subsequent surveys on the influence of their advertising showed that the public was primarily influenced by word-of-mouth communication of other members of the family (especially teen-age girls), friends, and neighbors; opinions of movie reviewers in the local newspaper were the second important influence. Scarcely anyone was influenced by the advertising. The unrestrained making of sensational claims, use of superlatives and the like, bring about "semantic depreciation," which causes loss of efficiency in the symbols of communication.

Claim Qualities That Make No Difference to the Utility of the Product. The cigarette manufacturers have also used this kind of deception. It is true that they have few differentiating features to point to regarding their brands of cigarette; one cannot tell them apart on a blind smoking taste test. However, this is no excuse for the low level of ethical performance of that industry in the past.

The Federal Trade Commission has had a series of cases against cigarette manufacturers. Lorillard cannot say its cigarettes "contain less nicotine, less tar and resin" or "are less irritating to the throat." Reynolds cannot advertise that Camels "encourage the flow of digestive juices, increase the alkalinity of the digestive tract" or help digestion in any respect; that their use "relieves fatigue, or creates, restores, renews, or gives or releases bodily energy; that they do not affect or impair the wind or physical condition or athletes; that the smoke from Camels is soothing, restful, or comforting to the nerves or that it protects from nerve strain; and that Camels never leave an after-taste.[33]

Completely False Claims. A classic of its kind is the following case, which speaks for itself:

> The foregoing claims, statements and representations are grossly exaggerated, false and misleading. In truth and in fact respondent's product, All-Winter Antifreeze is not a high-quality "antifreeze" solution as it is composed of a calcium chloride base and is inferior to solutions containing glycerine or alcohol bases. Said product will not prevent seepage and corrosion. It is not safe and dependable for use as recommended and is not a superior type of antifreeze. It does not protect the cooling system of engines against corrosion, rust, or other deterioration. Use of said product causes and has caused rust, corrosion, clogged passages and other serious damage to engines, radiators, ignition wires, spark plugs, hose connections, and to the exterior finish of automobiles. Said product evaporates and will clog passages in the cooling system.[34]

Creating Erroneous Impressions

An advertisement may make no factual misstatement but still create a false impression. For example, a young enterpriser ran an advertisement, "Hurry, send in your dollar before it's too late!" and gave his name and address. He received thousands of dollars from this ad. Those sending in their dollars got nothing back and complained to the authorities. The latter did not know how to proceed, since the advertiser had offered no product or service, had promised nothing.

Debasement of Cultural Values

Advertising has been criticized on this ground for a long time. For example, John Ruskin, in his speech to the manufacturers of Bradford about 100 years ago, had this to say:

> Whatever happens to you, this, at least, is certain, that the whole of your life will have been spent in corrupting

public taste and encouraging public extravagance. Every preference you have won by gaudiness must have been based on the purchaser's vanity; every demand you have created by novelty has fostered in the consumer a habit of discontent; and when you retire into inactive life, you may, as a subject of consolation for your declining years, reflect that precisely according to the extent of your past operations, your life has been successful in retarding the arts, tarnishing the virtues, and confusing the manners of your country.[35]

Another example of the same kind of thinking is that of the famous historian, Henry Steel Commager. Writing in the *Christian Science Monitor*, he stated:

Or look to another manifestation of public morality, one closely connected with the press, advertising. Who can doubt that the appeal of advertising is in very considerable part ot the wrong rather than to right motives, and that the basest, not the best instincts of men are exploited?

To what does a good part of our advertising appeal? To fear, jealousy, envy, licentiousness, and material interest. By reiterating that everything is to be considered from the point of view of private enhancement, it corrupts much of what it touches.

Friendship is perverted to the techniques of getting ahead in the job. Love of wife or husband becomes a contest in popularity or in sensual appeals. Pride in parents comes to depend on the right automobiles or the right television or the right drinking habits. Distinction is a matter not of character but of liquor or of haircuts or of the kind of silver one uses when company comes to dinner.

It may seem a minor matter that automobiles or cigarettes should be advertised not so much on their merits as on the degree of pulchritude of some model. And in any one case, it is a minor matter; we take all this in our stride after all. But who can compute the long-term effects of recommending almost everything for the wrong reasons?

And what shall we say of the systematic corruption of the judgment of our people by appeal to illogic rather than to logic? What shall we say of the cumulative effect upon the next generation of the picture of American social and moral standards — of family relations, of the relations of the sexes, of the relation of men to their work that emerges from much of our advertising?[36]

Many more similar quotations could be given from the pens of equally impressive authorities. They essentially focus on two criticisms: use of emotional appeals rather than rational appeals, and the consequent distortion of values; and the use of material that offends the critic's good taste.

Use of Emotional Appeals Instead of Rational Appeals. Critics do not approve of catering to the more primitive drives of man instead of to his rational faculty. The problem, as pointed out in the section of the book on psychology, is that human beings insist on responding to life emotionally. In a comfort economy, especially, they prefer to buy psychological satisfactions rather than material utilities. As Walter Taplin says, "Most of the things we buy are not material but mental. We want states of mind."[37] Mr. Taplin continues:

> The advertiser, beginning with a material object which is to be sold, suggests the states of mind which may be achieved by the purchaser. This face powder, he says, will make you more beautiful, this armchair will not merely support your weight in physical comfort but put you in a relaxed and restful frame of mind, this ship will not merely carry you from point A to point B, but introduce you to the romantic atmosphere of foreign lands.
>
> The search for unsatisfied wants goes on; they are found; the customer pays to have them satisfied; he then discovers he still has other wants; the attempt to meet them is made; they are met — and so on, without, to the great joy of the advertisers, any prospect of an end.
>
> This is the process — a process as long and as complicated as life itself. There is no need to stop to be glad or sorry about it. You can either rejoice that human beings have wants, and that other human beings try to satisfy them and be paid for their trouble; or you can deplore the nature of humanity. You can argue, . . . over the reality or unreality, the merits or demerits, of the part played by advertisers in their attempt to add by words and pictures to the range of refinement of wants and to suggest available satisfactions. But the first thing to notice is what goes on in the real world, — to recognize the enormous, endless, range and complexity of wants . . ."[38]

Thus, people do not like to think. They respond emotionally to life. They have a multitude of wants which they derive emotional pleasure from satisfying, and they like to read about satisfying those wants in terms of sensory gratification, sex, social relationships, and the like. The critics cannot change human nature.

Distortion of Values. Child and Cater say, "The advertiser must accept some responsibility for the confusion of values that is a symptom of our time of troubles, Words such as character, faith, belief, integrity are used to commend the quality of beer and pills. If you buy a certain car you are 'exalted, exultant, magnificently at ease.' "[39]

Many have commented on this debasement of values. It is always a matter of concern when the "semantic currency" is debased. Perhaps it is a national trait to exaggerate — Americans have a heritage of being tellers of tall tales. They expect and discount hyperbole. It must seem strange to those of other cultural backgrounds, especially our British cousins, who are masters of understatement. Since Americans expect and discount hyperbole, it may not distort our values as much as critics claim; only when it gets completely out of hand, as it did in moving picture advertising, does it do great damage.

Use of Appeals and Illustrations that Offend the Critic's Sense of Good Taste. Many criticise selling's emphasis on bodily functions. The advertisers of Ban Deodorant thought they were in the best of taste, being very subtle, when they illustrated areas of body odor on Greek Statues in television commercials. They were surprised when they received thousands of letters vehemently protesting. Other people criticize broad humor or overemphasis on sex.

Good taste is a highly subjective matter. Canons of what is good and bad taste are not uniform within a given culture; they change over time. They also vary with circumstances; for instances, advertisers have found newspapers a more permissive medium than radio or television.

The foremost historian of taste, Russell Lynes, comments on how standards of taste, of what is fit and proper, have altered greatly since the Victorian era.

> It is easy, for example, to trace from 1890 to the present the course of social informality, not only by what garments (or lack of garments) appear acceptable in ads, but in how close the male and female may be joined in embrace. The female nude from the back is acceptable today; the male is not. The breast, as long as the nipple is concealed, is acceptable now, though in some ads of the Victorian era the outline drawing of the female nude, nipples included, was evidently considered all right, though that was an era when a lady scarcely dared show her ankle in the parlor. Children can get away with saying things that adults for reasons of "good taste" cannot. "Mummy, they have a lovely house, but their bathroom paper hurts." That appeared in an ad some years ago. Nobody today, however, can say "toilet paper." It's not *toilet* that now is unacceptable, but *paper*! Tissue, however, is in "good taste." No one today would think of using the word "bowels" in an ad, but how to talk about their functions in glorious circumlocutions is a major intellectual challenge to the "creativity" of the copywriters.
>
> These are the sort of switches in social acceptability that delight the historian of taste. How is it, he wonders, that as life becomes more informal, and "gentility" gives

way to casualness in manners, as we discuss in the living room topics not so long ago taboo even in the bedroom, we devise the most elegant coynesses and euphemisms for these same topics in advertising? We laugh at our forebears for never using the word "legs"; even pianos had limbs a century ago; but while we expose and advertise and promote the female breast, we wouldn't think of calling it by its first name in public print. And yet, as we all know, "It's what's up front that counts."[40]

There is no definitive answer to this problem of taste. The advertiser or salesman must be sensitive to prevailing standards of what is fit and proper. Advertisements in bad taste may attract attention; they also arouse anger, resentment, and even disgust. These negative emotions never help to sell a product and must be avoided as a matter of self-interest, not to mention the advertiser's broader duty to be a good citizen in his society.

Materialism

Critics charge that advertising and sellg emphasize the materialistic aspects of life at the expense of spiritual values. F. P. Bishop, who calls it "consumptionism," points out that the conflict over materialism has been an issue not only with the moralists and social philosophers of today, but with much of the teaching of wise men of all ages. Great religious leaders, such as Buddha, Confucius, and Jesus, have all emphasized that morality begins with self-restraint and self-denial. Gibbon in his great *Decline and Fall of the Roman Empire* attributed the decadence of Rome mainly to the overindulgence in luxury by the Romans of the Empire. Observers of the contemporary scene have pointed out that selling and advertising have stirred up the consumer and driven him to enlarge his material desires by calling attention to new wants or refinements in gratifying extant wants. This, they argue, must inevitably be at the expense of manliness, consideration of others, and weakening of the moral fiber.[41]

Others say that selling and advertising create discontent among the masses. By dangling luxurious goods before the eyes of the common man who cannot possibly afford them, they frustrate him and make him unhappy with his lot. Such discontent may in turn cause social unrest and sow the seeds of revolution.

There is absolutely no way to prove or disprove that spiritual values are being destroyed. Nationwide church membership is at an all-time high;[42] book publishers report a tremendous increase in sales in the past decade; attendance at operas, symphony concerts, and art museums is greater now than any time in history,[43] more children are being educated than ever before in our history; and attendance in adult classes is also at unprecedented levels.[44] According to *Fortune*, American taste has improved remarkably since World War II.[45]

Whether these facts, just a few of many of similar purport, will be accepted as sufficient evidence that our culture is not completely materialistic is not too important. The cold, hard fact, based on historical evidence, is that the masses have *never* in any culture been interested in spiritual values. Their interest has *always* been centered on things of this world: on keeping body and soul together; on getting ahead materially; on acquiring goods that will symbolize new and better social status. Advertising has done little to create this state of affairs.

Promotion people may be "merchants of discontent," but a certain amount of discontent is an important mainspring of human progress. The cave man eventually became dissatisfied with living in damp, dark caves, and set about learning to build houses. Thomas Edison was dissatisfied with the dim light given by candles, oil lamps, and gas lights, and he invented the electric light. Indeed, discontent is the divine spark which activates progress.

Does the discontent engendered by promotion become so intense as to cause frustration? It may in some people who are maladjusted and pathologically jealous of the better fortune of others, but there is no evidence that advertising or selling frustrates the normal person more than he or she is frustrated by a great many things — job, family, friends, and others. Promotion undoubtedly stimulates people to work harder for the beautiful goods pictured so enticingly in their magazines, over their television sets, or in store windows and displays. Since the normal man *is* materialistic, these goods give him the incentive to take risks, try out new and better production techniques, and work harder and more efficiently.[46]

Effect on Formal Channels of Communication

To what extent does advertising influence freedom of expression by the different media of public communication; it is undeniable that the advertiser is in a position to influence these media. Table 19.1 shows that advertisers contributed hundreds of millions, even billions of dollars per annum to each major communication media.

In England an average of 59.2 per cent of total revenues of newspapers comes from advertising; 52.8 per cent of the revenue of all periodicals comes from the sale of advertising space.[46] In this country 60 to 80 per cent of magazine revenues comes from advertising, and 70 to 90 per cent of a newspaper's income has the same source. *All* the income of our vast radio-television industry originates from the sale of time to advertisers.

Advertising Income of the Major Media — 1970

Medium	Millions of Dollars
Newspapers	5,850
Magazines	1,321
Television	3,660

Advertising Income of the Major Media — 1970 (Con't.)

Medium		Millions of Dollars
Radio		1,278
Business Papers		714
Outdoor		237
Miscellaneous	6,655	
Total		19,715

Source: *Marketing/Communications*, March, 1971.

Ethical and Moral Effects of Promotion

Do advertisers take unfair advantage of this great potential power? The evidence is quite conflicting. One German authority, writing in the 1930's, said they do:

> Especially in recent years British newspapermen and politicians insist that Great Britain and the United States of America are countries where the Press is absolutely free. This might be warranted to a large extent if "the freedom of the press" meant its freedom in relation to the State. But the claim is absolutely unfounded if one takes into consideration the strong degree of economic dependence in which the modern British Press finds itself. The economic success of an English newspaper is so overwhelmingly dependent upon its advertising columns that the advertiser has been able to develop into a Press dictator who, as such, plays a part far more dangerous than that of the State, since in the majority of cases his influence is secret, entirely selfish, and not susceptible of control. [48]

Henry Wickham Steed, who cites the above passage, feels that the criticsm is overstated, but he claims ". . . it contains criticisms which no fair-minded observer can dismiss as wholly unwarranted."[49]

Bishop dismisses the probability of direct control:

> It is nonsense to talk about any business group being able to "control" the press, and the newspaper of today is not a byproduct of anything. Yet, obviously, advertising has a considerable influence on what goes into the paper day by day, and it is important that the extent and nature of that influence should be understood, so that the newspaper reader can allow for it, without entertaining exaggerated fears about the alleged adulteration of the news and opinions served up to him.[50]

The extent of that influence is controversial. The British P.E.P. report on the Press said that, as a rule, newspapers put the interests of their readers before those of their advertisers.[51] In the United States, the Commission on Freedom of the Press concluded that only the weak newspapers were likely to be greatly influenced:

The evidence of dictation of policy by advertisers is not impressive. Such dictation seems to occur among the weaker units. As a newspaper becomes financially stable, it becomes more independent and tends to resist pressure from advertisers.[52]

The situation is probably similar with magazines, industrial and trade papers, and broadcasting. The weaker magazines and radio stations are most likely subject to a great deal more dictation than the strong ones, just as many advertising abuses tend to be concentrated among the weaker media. The more ethical publications take great pains to completely separate the editorial and business sides of the enterprise. This was illustrated by the experience of one advertiser, a manufacturer of canned soup, who ran an advertisement for his mushroom soup in a great picture magazine. It was placed in the magazine opposite an account of how 65 participants at a Sons of Italy picnic in California were made violently ill by picking and eating toadstools which they had thought were mushrooms. The protests of the company advertising manager brought the response from the magazine; "This shows you how completely divorced our business side is from our editorial side." A few years ago, General Motors canceled all advertising in the *Wall Street Journal* because the latter had run some drawings of new models ahead of the grand introduction. When the *Journal* asserted its right to print anything that was news, the Company quietly dropped the matter and restored its advertising. Specific examples of attempts at direct interference are rare.

Mr. John Cowles, publisher of the *Minneapolis Star* and the *Minneapolis Tribune*, recognizes that a conflict between the editorial and business sides exists, even in the case of a great metropolitan newspaper. But he minimizes its importance.

"These apparent conflicts are rare, but they stem from two sources. First, from some advertising customers who occasionally may try to put pressure on a newspaper to suppress or minimize or distort some news story with a veiled threat that they may reduce or eliminate their advertising patronage if the newspaper does not comply, and, second, from organized pressure groups, whether economic, political or religious, who threaten that large numbers of subscribers will stop taking the paper or boycott its advertisers unless the paper adopts the editorial position or follows news practices that the pressure group favors, or refrains from printing editorials criticising it.

"Fortunately, both types of pressure have steadily decreased over the years.

"I have been in the newspaper business since 1920. Two or three or four decades ago, there was much more pressure for news suppression or distortion than exists today. This is true not only in Mineapolis but throughout the country. This stems partially from the fact that those newspapers that have survived are numerically fewer but economically stronger than was the case twenty or thirty years ago, and so better able to withstand pressure. Also, standards of professional integrity have steadily risen over the years, and now the great majority of newspapers pursue the same policies that we have long followed at the *Star* and *Tribune* — namely, that whether or not a company or an individual is a large or small advertising customer makes no difference in the handling of news about him or his business.[53]

Mr. Cowles gave examples of the kinds of pressures a publisher is under to suppress the news. The paper ran names and addresses of all arrested for drunken driving by the police — there was tremendous pressure from politicians, family and friends of merchants and other local advertisers, not to run specific names, but the paper persisted in doing so. When the Surgeon General's report on cancer linkage with smoking came out, it received front page treatment, despite veiled threats from cigarette advertisers that it had better be played down. Chemical companies expressed their anger when the paper serialized and published Rachel Carson's *Silent Spring*. Movie house owners often are irritated by adverse reviews of current movies by the movie critic of the paper, and they threaten to withdraw their advertising.

However, the modern metropolitan daily is so affluent and powerful itself, it can afford to resist such pressures positively and courageously. A generation ago, major advertisers expected to control the editorial policy of their local papers — it was a prerequisite of wealth. This is now no longer true. So, the consolidation of newspapers, so lamented by certain critics, has had the effect of making them less subject to interference by outsiders, if they want to withstand such pressures.

Mr. Cowles answered the question that often arises: "Don't one newspaper towns have a monopoly of the news, so that the inhabitants get managed news?" He points out that news monopoly is just about impossible in this day of many communication alternatives. The publisher of the paper faces competition from the weekly and suburban papers surrounding his city and from other metropolitan dailies that are shipped into it; from local radio and television stations that broadcast national and local news; from news magazines such as *Time*, *Newsweek*, *U.S. News and World Report*, etc. Moreover, the paper publishes columnists that often have radically different viewpoints from those of the publisher. Therefore, Mr. Cowles concluded that no medium could effectively suppress, alter or monopolize the news in this day and age. And that goes for market areas in which one interest owns competing media, say the local paper, radio and TV stations. The outside media, such as the national newsmagazines, will soon pick up news about some local scandal and publish it, for no single business interest could ever own and control *all* competing media.

Still, observers also criticize the trustification of many important media. In both England and America, from 1900 on, the number of newspapers was steadily reduced by failures and amalgamations. They also cite the attrition of the small "literary" magazine edited for quality rather than circulation. The survivors were usually conservative upholders of the *status quo*. Being wealthy themselves, the "press lords" took a narrow, conservative viewpoint and voluntarily censored anything that was anti-business or against the interests of their important advertisers. Identity of interest made outside pressure from advertisers unnecessary.[54]

A second development is a corollary of the first. Newspapers and magazines needed big circulation to survive, because advertisers were impressed by mere numbers and advertised only in media guaranteeing "coverage of the mass market." To build circulation, publishers had to edit their organs to suit the greatest common denominator of interests; thus the rise of the "yellow press," the tabloid, and the pulp magazine, which emphasized crimes of violence, sex, gambling, and other degrading stories to attract the ignorant and semi-educated. The desire for volume also led to the degradation of programing on radio and, later, television. The media owner is caught in a vicious circle: to get advertising he must have mass circulation; to get mass circulation he must produce material with mass appeal. Magazines and newspapers must also have low subscription rates. There is increasingly less time or space to communicate matters of interest to minorities — articles addressed to thinking readers and programs of interest to listeners who appreciate culture. What is the effect of this? Potter says:

> . . . the newspaper feature, the magazine article, the radio program do not attain the dignity of being ends in themselves; they are rather means to an end; that end, of course, is to catch the reader's attention so that he will then read the advertisement or hear the commercial and to hold his interest until these essential messages have been delivered. The program or the article becomes a kind of advertisement in itself — becomes the "pitch" in the telling language of the circus barker.
>
> A year or two ago an English critic complained of American periodical writing that it "fixes the attention but does not engage the mind.[55]

To attract a maximum number of readers:

> They must suppress any controversial or esoteric aspects of the item and must express it in terms of the least common denominator. But these terms are usually emotional ones rather than rational ones, for the emotional impulses of a large group of people are much more uniform throughout the group than are the mental processes of various individuals in the same group.[56]

Since common experience is essential to communication, the greater the number to be reached, the simpler the communication must be.

These factors of simplification, of intensifying the feeling while degrading the significance and of fixing the attention of the mass audience are all related to one basic condition of the media, namely, that they are concerned not with finding an audience to hear their message but rather with finding a message to hold their audience . . . it must not diminish the audience either by antagonizing or by leaving out anyone.[57]

Potter sums up the problem.

In the mass media we have little evidence of censorship in the sense of deliberate, planned suppression imposed by moral edict but much evidence of censorship in the sense of operative suppression of a great range of subjects — a suppression imposed by public indifference or, more precisely, by the belief of those who control media, that the public would be indifferent.[58]

This situation should concern every intelligent person in our society. Although it is grave, it is not hopeless. Post World War II opulence has elevated millions of American families to an economic position in which they can afford cultural amenities and have the leisure to enjoy them. *Fortune* points out that this new class-mass market has created an unprecedented demand not only for standardized luxuries but also for "special interest" items. People soon tire of the standard accoutrements of the good life. They learn to appreciate good art; better design in furniture, houses, appliances, classical music; unusual leisure time occupations (skin-diving, flying). These interests provide a broader economic base to support such former class interests as *avant-garde* art, modern classical music, functionally-oriented architecture and furniture, and the like. With better education, these people are becoming aware of the limitations of the conventional news magazines and newspapers,[59] the fare of popular music on radio and cowboy and "private eye" shows on television.

There will always be the mass press and mass broadcasting, but new channels will be set up to satisfy the demand created by the rise of "special interest" markets. These channels may aid in further educating the masses to appreciate the better things of life. Advertisers are beginning to recognize the vitality and purchasing power of people interested in the special interest products and services, and they are putting more money into the specialized media.[60] In time, we may secure diversity.

FOOTNOTES

1. *The Dawn of Conscience* (New York: Charles Scribner's Sons, 1933).

2. *Ibid.,* p. 19.

3. *Ibid.*, P. 20.

4. W. McDougall, *An Introduction to Social Psychology,* rev. ed. (Boston: John W. Luce & Co., 1909), p. 74.

5. *Ibid.*, p. 75.

6. Nicomachean (Aristotle), Epicurean (Epicurus), Stoic (Zeno, Seneca, Marcus Aurelius), metaphysical (Spinoza), Utilitarian (Mill, Bentham,), and others.

7. Daniel Katz and Richard L. Schank, *Social Psychology* (New York: John Wiley & Sons, Inc., 1938), pp. 14-25.

8. Advertisers are sometimes shocked by the enraged outcry that comes when they violate one of our society's mores, such as interference with the parent-child relationship. For an excellent case, see S. R. Bernstein, "Good Taste in Advertising," *Harvard Business Review,* May 1951, pp. 42-50.

9. Norman L. Munn, *Psychology* (London: George G. Harrap & Cok., 1946), p. 222.

10. Sociologists say that one major reason for the startling increase in urban crime and violence is the weakened social cohesiveness of the slum dwellers. Punishment by shame and ostracism does not follow violation of mores. Indeed, such mores as there are among such minority groups are diametrically opposed to those of the majority, i.e., criminality and violence are admired and emulated — they are symbols of virility and social protest.

11. N. H. Borden, *Advertising in Our Economy* (Chicago: Richard D. Irwin, Inc.), 1945.

12. (Chicago: University of Chicago Press, 1954), pp. 176-77.

13. *Ibid.*, p. 175.

14. A good example of this ferment is the theme of the Annual Convention of the American Marketing Association, December 1961: "The Social Responsibilities of Marketing."

15. *Hawkers and Walkers In Early America* (Philadelphia: J. B. Lippincott Co., 1927), p. 22.

16. The ethical standards of the typical retailer of 1850 were not very high either. A business historian says: "Misrepresentations of quality, short measure, and other sharp practices were frequently encountered, and selling prices almost everywhere depended upon the customer's ability to bargain with the salesman." Ralph M. Hower, "Urban Retailing 100 Years Ago," *Bulletin of the Business Historical Society,* XII, No. 6, 1939, p. 93. A standard joke of the period cites the grocery retailer who calls to his son in the cellar, "Sand the sugar, water the vinegar, and get upstairs for evening prayer."

17. Wright, *Hawkers and Walkers in Early America,* p. 22.

18. This is true of the consumer goods field only. The purchasing agent of a business is trained to know all about the goods he buys. He sometimes knows them better than the seller.

19. Oswald Knauth, *Managerial Enterprise* (New York: W. W. Norton & Co., Inc., 1948), pp. 20-21.

20. *Grey Matter*, Grey Advertising, Inc. (New York, February, 1965), p. 3.

21. *Ibid.* p. 2.

22. *Advertising Age* (April 1, 1968), p. 1.

23. Four dimensions of reaction were distinguished in the survey:
> Offensive — vulger, morally bad advertisements which the advertiser should be stopped from using.
> Annoying — a weaker reaction than "offensive". Such ads are thought of as irritating because in poor taste, so frequently repeated, or silly and stupid.
> Entertaining — enjoyable and pleasant for any reason whatever.
> Informative — ads from which one obtains information that he is glad to learn about.
From: William Weilbacher, "Text of the 4 A's Exploratory Study of Consumer Judgment of Advertising", *Advertising Age* (April 29, 1963), p. 124.

24. "Preliminary Report: A AAA Study on Consumer Response to Advertising", Broadcasting (November 16, 1964), pp. 29-30. Subsequent data cited in this section are drawn from this source, and from Raymond A. Bauer and Stephen A. Greyser, *Advertising in America, the Consumer View* (Boston: Division of Research, Graduate School of Business Administration, Harvard University, 1968).

25. Therefore percentages will add up to more than 100 percent in this and in the following section, "annoying reactions".

26. *Broadcasting, loc. cit,* p. 30.

27. Bauer and Greyser, *op. cit.,* pp. 257-8.

28. *Ibid.,* p. 337.

29. W. H. Freeman, *The Big Name* (New York: Printers' Ink Books, 1957), p. 37.

30. *Ibid.,* pp. 23-25.

31. Otto Kleppner, *Advertising Procedure,* 4th ed. (Englewood Cliffs, N.J.: Prentice-Hall, Inc., 1950), p. 127.

32. *Ibid.,* p. 128.

33. C. A. Sandage and V. Fryburger, *Advertising Theory and Practice* (Homewood: Richard D. Irwin, Inc., 1938), p. 65.

34. All-Winter Antifreeze Case, F.T.C. Decisions, 1946, pp. 302-303.

35. Quoted by Arthur Schlesinger, Jr., in *Printers' Ink,* August 11, 1959.

36. August 20, 1952, 2nd sect., p. 7.

37. *Advertising, A New Approach* (London: Hutchinson & Co., Ltd., 1960), p. 33.

38. *Ibid.,* pp. 33-34.

39. Marquis W. Childs and Douglass Cater, *Ethics in a Business Society* (New York: Mentor Books, 1954), pp. 168-69.

40. *Printers' Ink,* February 2, 1962, p. 44. See also Russell Lynes, *The Tastemakers* (Ner York: Grosset & Dunlap, 1954), for a fascinating discussion of the history and place of taste in the American culture.

41. *The Ethics of Advertising* (London: Robert Hale, Ltd., 1949), p. 29.

42. There were 124,682,000 church members in the United States in the mid 1960's, according to the National Council of Churches of Christ, *Statistical Abstract, 1968,* p. 41.

43. Since the mid 1950's, the amount spent each year on classical records exceeded that spent for popular numbers; attendance revenues for symphony concerts and operas exceeded total admission income for sporting events in 1959.

44. Total school enrollment was 43.0 million in 1966, *Statistical Abstract, 1968,* p. 121.

45. Among indicators to prove this is the decline of "borax" furniture sales cited in *Markets of the Sixties* (New York: Harper & Row, Publishers, 1960), Chap. 7, "How American Taste Is Changing." This chapter cites convincing examples of how American taste is becoming more refined, even among the masses.

46. It is true that primitive people will often work less hard when given a higher income. When our Air Force built an airfield in Labrador during World War II, it hired a number of the simple fishermen at wages more than twice what they had been accustomed to earning. They simply worked three rather than six days a week. Due to low economic goals they preferred leisure to more goods. People have to be informed about the higher material standard they might enjoy through greater efficiency and application. They will not work for altruistic motives, for the good of society. This has been proven by the failure of various utopian societies. The Allied Control Authorities learned this from the coal miners of the Ruhr after World War II. The Authority was trying to restore the productivity of the coal mines and carried on a big propaganda campaign telling how coal was needed to keep people warm, provide fuel so they could be employed, and the like. Wages were raised well above the average to no avail, since goods were scarce and the miners could not buy much with the money. Production stayed low until the Authority pumped a lot of consumer goods into the region and relaxed rationing; then coal production soared, for the workers could now secure a material reward for their efforts. People who ignore this basic fact of human nature are likely to make serious miscalculations when they formulate practical economic or business policy.

47. F. P. Bishop, *Ethics of Advertising* (London: Robert Hale, Ltd., 1949), p. 151.

48. Max Grunbeck, *Die Presse Grossbritanniens,* 1936.

49. *The Press* (Harmondsworth: Penguin Books, Ltd., 1938), pp. 174-75. Steed fails to show to what extent advertiser control *is* practiced, however,

50. Bishop, *Ethics of Advertising,* p. 168.

51. *Ibid.,* p. 170.

52. Commission of Freedom of the Press, *A Free and Responsible Press* (Chicago: University of Chicago Press, 1947), p. 62.

53. Speech before MBA Club, Harvard University.

54. Many have deplored the demise of papers reflecting a multitude of different opinions. According to A. J. Leibling, [*The Press* (New York: Ballantine Books, 1964), p. 3.] of 1,461 American Cities with daily newspapers, all but 61 were one-ownership cities. In England, the London papers have a strangle-hold on national news and opinion. A good example of how identity of interest works is the fact that bulletins of the Better Business Bureaus exposing frauds and sharp practices seldom receive publicity in many great cities. The media obviously are afraid of losing prospective advertising revenue by offending the companies cited by the BBB. For a good discussion of this identity of interests between publishers and advertisers in the magazine field, see editorial in *Journal of Advertising Research* (August, 1970), p. 46, by William S. Blair, publisher of Harper's magazine.

55. Potter, *People of Plenty,* pp. 181-82.

56. *Ibid.,* p. 183.

57. *Ibid.*

58. *Ibid.,* p. 184.

59. *The Reporter, Atlas,* and *American Heritage* are three examples of media whose main support and surprising circulation volume are attributable to this new, more sophisticated class-mass market.

60. The health development of F.M. broadcasting in the early 1960's may be a harbinger of this, since F.M. programing contains much "special interest" material: good music, opera, panel discussions, public events, and the like. Advertisers began to see the value of these media in 1962 and now most F.M. stations are operating in the black. Even television, that great mass medium *par excellence,* is showing signs of fragmentation by special interest with the opening up of UHF frequencies in numerous market areas. Advertisers are beginning to question the large waste circulation delivered by the generalized media, and are using media that "rifle in on qualified prospects reached by specialized media, rather than employing the "shotgun" approach.

THOMAS S. ROBERTSON

* Thomas S. Robertson, "The Impact of Television Advertising on Children," *Wharton Quarterly*, Fall, 1972, pp. 38-41. Reproduced by special permission.

The subject of children as consumers has recently come into open debate in public policy circles. The Federal Trade Commission, for example, held public hearings in late 1971 on the impact of advertising on consumers and extensive testimony was devoted to the particular effects of television advertising addressed to children. As part of this testimony, it was proposed by a consumer advocate organization, Action for Children's Television, that all television advertising to children be banned. The National Association of Broadcasters in January of 1972 established a lower recommended limit on commercial messages on children's prime-time television — a 25 per cent reduction in commercials from sixteen minutes to twelve minutes per hour. The recommended prime-time limit for adult programming is six minutes per hour.

The implications of this debate are rather far-reaching for the marketing management community — particularly those marketers directly engaged in advertising products and services to children. Some advertising for inexpensive and child-relevant products, such as candy, may be explicitly addressed to the child as purchaser. However, most advertising to children is meant to stimulate sufficient desire on the part of the child that he will request the product from his parents. This means that a good deal of children's advertising is fairly "hard sell," in that it must stimulate actual behavior; that is, it must be so persuasive that the child will ask his parents to purchase.

The thrust of the allegations by consumer advocates against advertising to children and the most typical marketing management responses are summarized in Table 1. Essentially, these arguments are centered on: (1) advertising's ability to persuade and manipulate children; (2) advertising's effect on intra-family processes and the level of conflict generated; and (3) advertising's impact on the socialization of the child and the development of his value system. These points will be discussed in turn, together with some available research evidence. The curious paradox, however, is that the marketing field is almost devoid of research on the behavior of children as consumers and this places the marketing representative in a rather disadvantageous position to coherently answer the critics' claims.

Advertising's Ability To Persuade Children

In large measure the critics' claims are that advertising can unduly persuade and manipulate the unsophisticated child who lacks the cognitive defenses to resist persuasive messages. In testimony before the Federal Trade Commission, for example, representatives of the Action for Children's Television group alleged that: "Sophisticated advertising techniques are often used to deceive, cajole and exploit the youngest and least knowledgeable members of our society" (ACT, 1971, p. 3). Robert Choate, in his attacks on the breakfast cereal industry, has claimed that children are "programmed" and "counter-educated" by advertisers to prefer sweetness in cereals and to ignore nutrition (Choate, 1970, p. 7).

The typical marketer response to these allegations has been to deny, of course, that advertising manipulates children and to cite research evidence, such as that of Klapper (1960), which demonstrates that advertising serves mainly to *reinforce* existing attitudes and opinions. Another response, represented by Banks (1971), is to cite the fact that parents remain the key factor in the child's cognitive development and that television plays a complementary role. After reading some of the statements by representatives of the marketing community, it is logical to wonder why advertising is addressed to children at all, since its "effectiveness" is so disputed by the very people who make use of it.

Advertising is designed for the purpose of *persuasion*. An initial question is whether the society wishes to suscept its children to media persuasion. Our society has so far answered in the affirmative or, perhaps, has somehow never explicitly addressed the issue and its ramifications.

Beyond persuasion is the issue of manipulation. When, in fact, does persuasion become manipulation? This would seem to depend on the marketer's ability to predict and control response, which is related to the sophistication level of the audience.

Evidence for advertising inability to manipulate in the adult arena is frequently centered on new product and advertising campaign failures, which demonstrate lack of predictive ability due to the complexity of human response processes. But what about advertising's ability to manipulate when the consumer is a child — supposedly lacking in sophistication and in the development of defense mechanisms to resist persuasion?

The Federal Trade Commission has recently leaned toward a posture that children may represent a special category of the population, who deserve additional protection because of their lack of sophistication. This is the thrust, for example, of some recent cases against toy manufacturers who may, it is alleged, be in a position to unfairly take advantage of children if the reality-fantasy distinction is confused.

The ability of advertising to persuade and potentially to manipulate is not by any means a new subject of discussion. What is new is the context of children as consumers. The critics' arguments

Table 1

Views of Advertising's Effects on Children

	Critic's View	Marketer's View
Persuasive Processes	Advertising can unduly persuade and manipulate the unsophisticated child.	Advertising mainly reinforces existing opinions. Parents have the key role in what a child believes.
Intra-Family Influence Processes	Advertising encourages the child to pressure his parents to buy. This can be damaging to the parent-child relationship.	Advertising may result in a positive interaction between parent and child and an occasion for learning about consumption.
Socialization Processes	Advertising may imbue undesirable values, such as materialism and the need to consume. It also encourages irrational consumer decision making.	Advertising only reflects the value system of a society and prepares the child for his role as a consumer.

regarding advertising's effects on children smack very much of a stimulus-response model. It is assumed that message reception leads to purchase request. This is a viewpoint which was fairly well disproven emanating from research by Berelson, Bauer, Klapper, Katz and Lazarsfeld, and others, which demonstrated that mass media serve mainly a reinforcement function.

This point of view is expressed by Klapper (1960) in terms of the following generalizations:

> Mass communication is generally not a necessary and sufficient cause of effects, but operates through mediating factors.

> Mass communication is most often a "contributory agent" in a process of reinforcing existing conditions.

> When mass communication does serve to change, it is because the mediating factors are inoperative or are themselves favoring change (p. 8).

The effects of media on children may, however, be quite another matter. What may be critical is not mass media's ability to *change* attitudes but rather to *develop* attitudes. Mass media may, therefore, serve an important function in the creation of children's consumption attitudes and preferences. Furthermore, Krugman's (1965) model of communication learning effects under low involvement conditions may be more relevant to television advertising than the media campaign evidence cited by Klapper (1960). Television may be highly instrumental in learning based on years of exposure and repetition — especially for product preference formation, since this is a relatively low salience aspect of a person's life and, therefore, subject to less critical questioning and cognitive resistance.

Unfortunately, there is very little research evidence to cite focusing on the ability of advertising to persuade young children. This allows the proponent of a particular point of view wide latitude in his pronouncements. For example, Littner (1971) bluntly states his "personal views," with absolutely no empircal support, that:

> Misleading or false TV advertising is readily recognized as such by the average child. . . . Misleading or false TV advertising probably has less effect and impact on children than it does on adults. . . . A warm, secure home and satisfactory peer-group relationships provide a highly effective and complete antidote to any potential harm that might come from the child's viewing of TV commercials. (pp. 2, 4).

The more subtle effects of non-misleading advertising are ignored and we can only wonder about the effects of television advertising when a warm, secure home and peer-group environment are not present.

What research evidence is available cautions us that there may be undesirable effects of advertising to children under certain circumstances. Young children may be particularly persuasible and unable to cope with advertising messages. The simplicity of a very young child's view of reality is reflected in research by Lehmann (1971). He concludes that:

> Very young children tend to view products unidimensionally on a simple like-dislike scale. The development of a multidimensional view of products occurs over time and is probably hastened by exposure to television advertising. While some feel this increased 'consumer sophistication' is beneficial, the desirability of its occurring at a very young age can be debated. (p. 8).

Similarly, Ward, Robertson and Wackman (1971) find important differences in the effects of television advertising depending on the age of the child. Older children (11-12 year-olds) pay less attention to commercials than younger children (especially 5-7 year-olds) and exhibit more negative and sophisticated reactions to television advertising. They also talk more than younger children during commercials but make fewer comments about the product or commercial; and, when they do discuss the product or commercial, negative comments are more frequent. If attention is a necessary prerequisite to influence, then young children would seem to be potentially more persuasible.

The profile which emerges from the Ward, Robertson and Wackman study is that older children become jaded to commercials and pay less attention to them. They seem to develop an immunity which allows them to resist involvement in the form of lower attention levels and more critical reactions to advertising messages. Younger children (5-10 year-olds) are not as well immunized and would appear to be potentially more persuasible. Although there is no indication that younger children are unable to distinguish between program and advertising fare, there is less resistance to commercial interruptions. The television medium is much more of a "massage" for younger children and they play a more passive role.

Intra-Family Influence

Advertising to children is based primarily on encouraging the child to initiate a purchase request. This, claim certain critics, may encourage an unhealthy family relationship — particularly in low income homes where the parents must deny a disproportionate number of requests. Stated differently by members of the Action for Children's Television group: "In the case of children's advertising, the purpose is to use the child as a surrogate salesman to pressure the parent into buying the product. This is unfair to the child . . . this is unfair to the parent . . . and this can be damaging to the parent-child relationship." (ACT, 1971, p. 3). This is basically the same view adhered to by Frederick C. Green of the Office of Child Development, Department of Health, Education and Welfare: "The child, then, is put in the position of an inexperienced soliciter; and the parent, an experienced though unsolicited buyer. When the parent denies the child's request for an advertising product he may feel guilty or resentful at being repeatedly placed in the position of having to say 'no'." (1971, p. 4)

Contrary to this view is that of certain spokesmen for the marketing community who claim that advertising may result in a positive interaction between parents and child, whereby the child learns about consumption and the realities of life. Banks (1971), for example, suggests that "a spirited give-and-take within the household or even an occasional exchange of open hostile interaction between parent and child may actually facilitate the child's ability to cope with the realities of independent living. . . ." (pp. 7-8).

Exactly what happens in consumption-related interaction between parent and child is not known. The particular outcome of this interaction and the role and relative influence of television advertising is probably a function of many factors, including social class, the child's position in the sibling order, the age of the child, the degree of role integration between parents, and the parental discipline style. For example: general research on intrafamily interaction processes finds that middle-class parents rely more on intellect and reasoning than on authority position and are, therefore, more open to interaction and suggestion from their children. (Berkowitz, 1964).

Research by Ward and Wackman (1972) has explicitly considered television advertising and the processes of children's purchase requests and parental yielding. Their findings are that purchase requests decrease with age of the child while parental yielding increases with age of the child. In addition, conflict level between parent and child is related to purchase requests but not to yielding. Finally, the greater the parental restrictions on television viewership, the less yielding to children's requests (although the level of requests does not change).

Research by Berey and Pollay (1968) concludes that the mother is a strong "gatekeeper" in regard to the purchase of ready-to-eat breakfast cereals. Their findings are that yielding by the mother is not significantly related to either the child's assertiveness or the mother's child-centeredness. This leads these researchers to a conclusion which reminds us of the mother's direct influence on the child's brand preferences. "Given that the mother is not only a purchasing agent for the child but also an agent who superimposes her preferences over those of the child, it is clear that a lot of advertising would be well directed at the mother." (p. 72).

Advertising as a Socialization Agent

Socialization refers to the process by which children learn a particular role and the requisite values and requirements for performance of that role. One such role in our society is that of consumer. The importance of mass media (including television advertising) as an agent of socialization hardly requires demonstration, but very little is known about the dynamics of mass media influence and its relative effects compared to other agents of socialization.

The long-run effects of television advertising on the consumer socialization process are not always considered beneficial by consumer critics. Some of the undesirable effects alleged are: that advertising instills undesirable values; that advertising encourages materialism and the need to consume; and that advertising does not teach rational consumer decision-making. Perhaps the most reasonable response by marketers to these charges is that advertising only *reflects* the existing values of the society and does not create these values. Furthermore, advertising performs a vital function in preparing the child for his role as a consumer.

Mass media is not an independent means of socialization and is generally of less importance than family and peers — although this depends on the age and circumstances of the child. The ghetto child who is deprived of a meaningful family context and who has been exposed to television as surrogate guardian and babysitter may be unduly influenced by this medium. The relative effect of mass media is recognized by Maccoby (1963) who suggests, based on research, that movies have greatest influence on children who have limited previous exposure to the kind of people portrayed in movies. Such children are then likely to form more stereotyped impressions of movie characters. Similarly, lower class children who lack relative exposure to consumer models may form stereotyped impressions based on media and learn a limited value system regarding consumption. This is based on the assumption that advertising depicts a fairly homogeneous value system — the great suburban middle class way of life.

The relationship and interdependency between the mass media and the family as agents of socialization have been explored to some extent. Research by Ward and Wackman (1972) reveals that the more a mother sanctions television viewership (by watching television herself), the greater the number of purchase requests by the child and the more likely she is to yield to these requests.

Research with adolescents by Ward and Robertson (1970) has tended to support the notion that (at this age level) television advertising is a complement to intra-family communication about consumption. Commercials sometimes provide a basis for family communication and their impact may be related to family values and goals. Adolescents from homes characterized by high levels of intra-family communication about consumption hold more favorable attitudes toward advertising and are more "materialistic" in orientation than adolescents from homes with limited amounts of communication about consumption.

Conclusion

The research data base to asses advertising's impact on the consumption behavior of children is limited and our conclusions must be quite tenuous at this point. Advertising does not have a stimulus-response effect on children but it may have highly persuasive effects when the child is unsophisticated or relies on television for his view of reality. Advertising's potential ability to persuade may be especially high among young children who lack cognitive defenses and among ghetto children who are deprived of a balanced socialization experience. Advertising may also be instrumental in processes of attitude and preference *formation* among young children.

Management and public policy decisions in this area are hampered by the lack of definitive evidence. More research and conceptualization is necessary — particularly longitudinal research which will chart effects of media advertising over time. The effects of advertising on children seem to be exaggerated by the consumer critics and underestimated by marketing practitioners. A more balanced point of view documenting specific effects under particular conditions (for example, middle class versus ghetto children as consumers) could advance policy decisions for both management and public sector agencies.

Research is now underway at the Wharton School on the persuasive effects of television advertising addressed to children. This research is being conducted in coordination with both government and industry in order to enhance objectivity and to address the most salient policy issues. There is considerable room for further research on consumer socialization in general and the effects of advertising on parent-child relationships. This would seem to be a critical area requiring research design and development in the decade of the 1970s.

QUESTIONS FOR DISCUSSION

1. Do you think that television advertising is an especially bad influence on the children? Is the content of the commercials any worse than the effect of the program material?

2. Looking back on your own experience, do you think that television commercials did you any harm? In what way?

3. According to Professor Robertson's findings, is the influence of the family and the child's associates more or less powerful than the influence of television on them? Why should this be?

4. Do you think it a good thing for society to suscept its children to media persuasion?

5. According to the author, what kind of child is most susceptable to television persuasion? Would attempts to protect these children justify abolution of all television advertising to children, in your opinion? What other measures would be better?

6. What controls over television would you impose? (See Robert Choate's article).

BIBLIOGRAPHY

ACT, "Testimony of Action for Children's Television, Inc., before the Federal Trade Commission," November 10, 1971.

Seymour Banks, "Statement in Behalf of Joint ANA-AAAA Committee before the Federal Trade Commission," October 28, 1971.

Leonard Berkowitz, *The Development of Motives and Values in the Child*. New York: Basic Books, Inc., 1964.

Lewis A. Berey and Richard W. Pollay, "The Influencing Role of the Child in Family Decision Making," *Journal of Marketing Research*, Vol. 5 (February 1968), pp. 70-72.

Robert B. Choate, "Testimony before the Subcommittee of the Consumer Committee on Commerce, U. S. Senate," July 23, 1970.

Frederick C. Green, "Testimony before the Federal Trade Commission," November 12, 1971.

Joseph T. Klapper, *The Effects of Mass Communication*. New York: The Free Press, 1960.

Herbert E. Krugman, "The Impact of Television Advertising: Learning Without Involvement," *Public Opinion Quarterly*, Vol. 29 (Fall 1965), pp. 349-356.

Donald R. Lehmann, "An Exploratory Analysis of the Effect of Television Advertising on Children." A working paper, Columbia University Graduate School of Business, 1971.

Ner Littner, "Television Advertising and its Psychological Effects on Children." A statement appended to Seymour Banks' statement before the Federal Trade Commission, October 28, 1971.

Eleanor Maccoby, "The Effects of Television on Children," in *The Science of Human Communication*, ed. Wilbur Schramm. New York: Basic Books, 1963, pp. 116-128.

Ralph H. Turner, *Family Interaction*. New York: John Wiley & Sons, Inc. 1970.

Scott Ward and Thomas S. Robertson, "Family Influences on Adolescent Consumer Behavior." A paper presented to the First Annual Conference, Association for Consumer Research, Amherst, Massachusetts, August 1970.

Scott Ward, Thomas S. Robertson and Daniel Wackman, "Children's Attention to Television Advertising," *Proceedings, Association for Consumer Research*, ed. David M. Gardner, 1971, pp. 143-156.

Scott Ward and Daniel Wackman, "Television Advertising and Intra-Family Influence: Children's Purchase Influence Attempts and Parental Yielding," in press, *Journal of Marketing Research*, 1972.

ROBERT A. GOODMAN

Robert A. Goodman

The ethical drug trade probably has more dimensions and implications for today's consumer than any other single industry in this country. Consequently there are many problems and areas of concern both at the manufacturing and retail level that should be examined. But I have been constrained by time and resources to direct my attention to a few key issues that have the most relevance for consumers. In my research I have discovered many interesting stories ranging from quinine cartels to placebo distribution. Some areas such as mail order prescriptions, labeling, physician dispensing, Rx advertising, deceptive promotion, patents, recalls, substitution laws or monopoly interests could each independently provide excellent topics for a research paper. However, I decided to approach the paper from an industry level with a broader focus on the basic issues of price, safety, and effectiveness.

Examining price first, it must be understood that a complete economic analysis of the pricing policies of the pharmaceutical manufacturers is a massive undertaking and beyond the scope of this paper. The question of "administered prices" and monopoly interest were first seriously raised at the Kefauver hearings back in 1959. Thousands of pages of testimony and exhibits on a wide range of subjects relating to drug economics and to the nature of competition within the pharmaceutical industry were produced. But nothing was resolved. Subsequently, there have been many other investigations and hearings, and the debate surrounding these issues has continued into the present Congress. In May 1967, the Senate Subcommittee on Monopoly of the Select Committee on Small Business began its own examination of the nature of competition in the drug industry. For nearly five years the Subcommittee has conducted hearings. A long list of witnesses from industry, government agencies, universities, hospitals, and private practice have testified. To date, the Subcommittee, under the chairmanship of Senator Gaylord Nelson has produced over 8,000 pages of printed testimony and exhibits concerned with many of the same issues examined at the beginning of the last decade.

Exposed to the shock of public scrutiny, the drug industry understandably attempts to justify their position. Much of their testimony is devoted to demonstrating the existence of competition. In their defense, the industry points for example, to the rapid displacement of one product on the market by another, the result of intense competitive research efforts on the part of rival firms. The industry spokesmen argue further that such competition introduces into the pharmaceutical industry a high degree of risk, and that this risk requires a favorable rate of return in order to attract the capital to underwrite it, if progress is to be sustained. Industry spokesmen also point to other evidence which they believe demonstrate the competitive nature of the drug industry. For example, spokesmen argue that there are few industries which exhibit the low degree of market concentration found in the pharmaceutical industry.

In short, the industry holds the view that the American pharmaceutical industry is a highly competitive enterprise. Industry spokesmen emphasize the need to look at the industry as a whole, and maintain that to evaluate the industry's competitive performance on the basis of one criterion — price competition alone — produces a distorted and unfair assessment of the industry's contribution to the free enterprise system.

The critics of the industry's performance in the marketplace reject as "competition" those forms of activity found in the industry which have the effect of raising drug costs, rather than reducing prices. The critics argue that the legal-economic conditions found in the drug industry work to preclude effective price competition. It is important to note that the economists who criticize the industry do not apply an orthodox concept of price competition in evaluating the price behavior of drug products. The orthodox concept — in which every firm would attempt to enhance its profitability by increasing efficiency and cutting costs in order to undercut its rivals in the market, and thereby expanding sales by lowering prices — is not applicable to the pharmaceutical industry. There are few economies of scale to be gained and the nature of the consumer (from the standpoint of sales, this is the physician, not the patient) makes price-cutting a largely ineffective means of commercial progress. The economist critics will charge, however, that prices which are established frequently bear little relationship to costs, and that even where identical or comparable products are available in the marketplace at substantially lower prices, such products are unable to compete on the basis of price.

Commenting on the industry's position that competition takes place in a wide-variety of activities, Dr. Henry Steele, an economics professor at the University of Houston, testified:

> Spokesmen for the industry habitually refer to the intense degree of competition among firms. Unfortunately, however, the "competition" referred to is of the type which raises costs instead of reducing prices. This category of activity is generally referred to by economists as "rivalry" rather than "competition" since the latter term is usually reserved for the economically beneficial activity, specifically of price competition.[1]

The critics argue that it is more than a defnintion of terms which separates their views from those of the industry regarding the nature of competition within the drug industry. The critics argue, for example, that ineffective price competition results from the presence of a number of undesirable characteristics found in the industry: high degrees of market concentration among a few firms in any given therapeutic market; the presence of high entry-barriers to potentially competing firms, created by large-scale advertising and promotional efforts; and duplicative research efforts which are designed to get around patent or other arrangements which protect a competitor's position in the market. Dr. Leonard Schifrin, an economist at the College of William and Mary, observed:

> . . . The absence of effective competition in most sectors of the drug industry must be recognized. . . The larger firms in this industry have acquired an economic power incompatible with our conception of a free market economy; opportunity is severely limited for the many small firms in the industry, and the purchasers and consumers of ethical drug products are denied the benefits of competition in the manufacture and sale of these products.[2]

The price issue revolves to a large extent around the generic vs. trade name dispute. Pharmaceutical products for human use can be identified in a number of ways. The "active" ingredients, whether in bulk or in a particular dosage form, may be identified by a chemical name. This name is frequently lengthy and known only to those with training in chemistry. A common name, official name, or "generic" name is also assigned to these "active" ingredients. This name is generally shorter in length, considered by some as easier to use, but usually does not aid in identifying the chemical structure of the substance. A trade name, or more accurately a trademark, is also frequently assigned to a drug product by the manufacturer. This name refers to the particular formulation of the active ingredients, is usually somewhat shorter than even the generic name, and is intended to facilitate promotion of the product. The trade name has little or no information which aids in identifying the chemical formulation, and may or may not aid in identifying the generic name of the product.

The pharmaceutical industry defends the use of trade names in a number of ways. First, it is argued that trade names help physicians identify a reliable, high-quality product on which a manufacturer stakes his reputation. Second, by specifying a trade name on a prescription, the physician assures himself that the product of a specific manufacturer will be dispensed. Prescribing "generically" — that is, identifying only the active ingredients — places in the hands of the pharmacist the choice of particular product to be dispensed. Third, the industry spokesmen point out that physicians find utility and ease in using trade names to specify drug products. Finally, they argue that trade name promotion is consistent with marketing practice and encourages competition by allowing manufacturers to call attention to their products.

The first industry argument to support the use of trade names is that trade names help assure the physician of a reliable, high-quality product — not simply because a trade name is assigned, but because the particular trade name points to a particular manufacturer. Mr. C. Joseph Stetler, President of the Pharmaceutical Manufacturers' Association, explained the industry's position:

> For the physician and pharmacist who cannot conduct his own tests and inspections, manufacturer identification of drug products has proven itself the most practical and reliable measure of consistent quality. Approximately one billion prescriptions are dispensed by the nation's retail pharmacists every year in the United States. Surveys have shown that more than 90 percent of them signify a particular drug product of a specific manufacturer. Once a physician has identified a particular manufacturing source for a particular drug product which he considers on the basis of his own recurring experience, as best for a particular patient, he can have the highest degree of certainty that each succeeding prescription of the same drug product from the same source will carry the same built-in therapeutic performance.[3]

The critics, however, raise two kinds of arguments concerning trade name drug promotion. First, some of the medical and pharmacy witnesses argue that trade names are a source of confusion, that they do not identify the manufacturer, and that such promotion of names can represent a danger in prescribing. One of these critics, Dr. Walter Modell, Director of Clinical Pharmacology at Cornell's School of Medicine observed:

> ... there is a real danger, a danger in confusion, when trade names are used because often these names of drugs are utterly without meaning. Many are made up by Madison Avenue before the drugs are discovered. They have no connection with the meaning of the action or the chemical nature of the drug. Use of trade names is just support of a practice of ignorance and intellectual laziness... Some drugs, for example, methanphetamine, are sold under 30 to 35 different trade names. It would be quite a feat of memory for a physician to remember, amongst other things that he has to remember, all the trade names for methamphetamine if he had a patient who was sensitive to it and had to be properly warned.[4]

The second argument of the critics relates to the impact of trade name promotion on the larger issue of competition. The critics emphasize that the success of advertising-achieved product differentiation depends, in large part, on the degree of uncertainty in the minds of the purchaser about the merits of competing products. They argue that choosing between chemical compounds having the same active ingredients and purportedly doing the same thing creates this uncertainty. The proliferation of trade names for products having identical active ingredients, some critics also suggest, add to uncertainties are made even more acute by the doubt which the industry casts upon the performance of products which are supposedly identical. Trade names facilitate efforts to differentiate among similar or identical products. The critics argue that the use of trade name promotion helps only to raise costs and stifle price competition, without improving the drug selection process. Elimination of trade names altogether would not, according to the economists, eliminate efforts to differentiate drug products, but it might reduce the intensity of such efforts. Dr. William Comaner, an economic professor at Harvard, discussed the relevancy of trade names to drug promotion:

> One route, in some sense an easier route, would be to provide information to the doctor which would reduce the impact of trade names and heavy advertising outlays. . . One might argue that their (the manufacturers') ability to differentiate their products on this basis (using the generic name with the company designation) would be less than it is currently, and as a result, we might find a higher degree of price competition. This is not an all-or-nothing situation; it is clearly a matter of degree. While some measure of product differentiation would remain, and might even be disirable at a small level, it would not lead to the high prices which currently exist and the very high rates of return.[5]

The HEW Task Force on Prescription Drugs, at the direction of President Johnson, undertook an extensive review of the problems connected with including the cost of prescription drugs under medicare, and arrived at the following conclusion:

> The Task Force finds, therefore, that the use of low-cost generic-name counterparts can yield important savings, especially in the case of patients with cardiovascular disease, kidney disease, arthritis, and mental and nervous conditions, and the use of such products should be encouraged wherever this is consistent with high-quality health care.[6]

Intimately related to the generic vs. trade name dispute is the question of "therapeutic" equivalency. The industry argues that the physician has the right to prescribe in any manner he sees fit — by trade name, generically, or by combining the generic name with a manufacturer designation. The industry spokesmen also maintain that where a physician finds two products, manufactured by different concerns, to be of the same quality, and that each produces the same therapeutic effect in his patients, that he should prescribe the least expensive of the two products. However, the industry argues that merely because two products have an identical generic name — supposedly identifying identical active ingredients — there is no guarantee that the products will produce the same therapeutic effects in the patient. In short, generic equivalency is not the same as therapeutic equivalency. Mr. Stetler describes the industry's view of the matter:

> As has been pointed out in papers by a number of leading physicians and pharmacologists and in previous testimony before this Subcommittee, the term "generic equivalency" refers only to the name of a drug product and does not necessarily connote its safety or therapeutic effectiveness. Although two drug products can contain, or are supposed to contain, the same amount of the same active ingredient, this provides no assurance that both products will produce the same clinical effect in any particular patient.[7]

Industry witnesses argue that the quality of a product and assurance of reliability are a function of the quality control efforts made by reliable manufacturers. They contend that not every product placed on the market will perform as expected. The industry representatives conclude that maximum quality and reliability can only be built-in by the manufacturer. They also note that the research-oriented firms are geared to such quality control programs, and that these are the firms which usually market the majority of their products under trade names.

Industry critics see the comments from industry spokesmen as an effort to disparage the quality and performance of products which are usually marketed by smaller manufacturers under generic name designations. By emphasizing this issue, the industry, according to the critics, is helping only to create additional doubt in the minds of physicians about the reliability and quality of products in competition with those of large manufacturers, but available at substantially lower prices. Dr. Edward Feldman, Director of the National Formulary, told the Subcommittee:

> ... from a technical standpoint, there is really no such thing as complete "drug equivalence" — whether we compare two drug products sold under their non-proprietary, or generic name; or whether we compare a generic name drug product to a brand name drug product; or whether we compare two brand name drug products or even if we compare two batches of the very same drug product of a single firm ... Information available in the published literature reveals only isolated case histories, and very few scientifically performed studies, which demonstrate substantial difference in "therapeutic equivalence" between two comparable drug products...[8]

Dr. James Goddard, former Food and Drug Commissioner, supported a similar position. "At the present time, our feeling is that only in a limited number of drug categories will two products with the same active ingredients not produce clinically equivalent results."[9]

Despite all the industry arguments about high risks, heavy research and development costs, and large capital investments, the drug and medicine companies were by far the most profitable in 1970, according to a Federal Trade Commission report released this summer on rates of return in selected manufacturing industries. The comprehensive report which analyzed profit data from 1961 to 1970 for more than 250 firms in 35 industries, shows that drug and medicine companies realized a rate of return on stockholder's investment of 19.6 percent in 1970.[10]

Most recently, Senator Nelson made some startling remarks before the Senate.

> Mr. President, for many years the American people have been forced to pay high and discriminatory prices for drugs. These prices are borne by those people in our society who are least able to afford them — the sick, the poor, and the aged. Moreover, a substantial share of this burden is borne by State and Federal governments — in the form of welfare payments, reimbursable aid programs, and substantial direct purchase for use in community and military hospitals.

> The extent of this discrimination has already been documented by the Monopoly Subcommittee of the Senate Small Business Committee and the Department of Health, Education and Welfare. The price of 100 tablets of propozyphene, Darvon, sold by the Lilly Co. to the druggist in the United States is $7.02, but the price charged by the same company for the same product in Ireland is $1.66, and in the United Kingdom is $1.92. Bristol charges $21.84 for 100 tablets of ampicillin in the United States, but $9.31 in Ireland; Ciba charged $3 for glutethimide, Doriden, in the United States, but 92 cents in Ireland, $1.23 in New Zealand, and $1 in the United Kingdom. The Pfizer Co. charges $20.48 in the United States for oxtetracycline, Terramycin, but $4.63 in Brazil and $3.68 in New Zealand. These are only a few examples of discrimination against the American people.

> . . . There is considerable evidence that the high price of many drugs is due to a large extent to the existence of patent monopolies. Hearings of the Monopoly Subcommittee of the Senate Small Business Committee have indicated 20-to-1 and 10-to-1 differentials between prices for the same drugs, with and without patent monopolies.[11]

Charging that "the American people, who are paying higher prices for drugs than anyone else in the world, are being subjected to monopolistic exploitation," and that it is "a gross abuse of the American patent system to permit such oppression of the public," Senator Nelson has introduced a bill to make drug patents available to all applicants under certain market conditions. Under the bill, the

Federal Trade Commission, with the concurrence of the Surgeon General, would be authorized to require that patents be made available for general licensing whenever it has reason to believe that:

> (1) the average price of a drug to consumers or users is more than five times its production costs or more than its foreign price;
> (2) its annual sales have been $1 million for three or more years;
> (3) a patent on the drug is a substantial contributing factor to the high price of the drug.[12]

This bill, by making the patents of hundreds of widely used drugs available to other manufacturers, would be expected to lower prices through the resulting competition.

Whether prescription drug prices set by the major manufacturers are "too high," "reasonable," or "too low" is obviously a problem which cannot be resolved to the mutual satisfaction of all manufacturers and all consumers. Wyndham Davies, a British scholar, states the situation well.

"There has been a traditional dispute between the industry and its critics. This consists in one side accusing the other of profiteering, while the latter argues that its profits are justified because it has to invest in research. This argument is interminable and irresolvable."[13]

It is just not possible to suggest something simple and dramatic that Congress or the FDA or the industry can do to reduce drug prices. One must face the fact that the drug lobby is one of the most powerful in Washington. Undoubtably the controversy will rage on for years.

Turning to the other areas of safety and effectiveness, the thalidomide affair pointed up the great weakness in the American drug safety system. The Drug Amendments of 1962 (the Kefauver-Harris amendments) were like the 1938 Act, enacted in law following a serious drug incident, the thalidomide disaster. But drug legislation to achieve many of the objectives for which the 1962 Amendments were enacted had also been before the Congress when the thalidomide incident occurred.

Briefly, thalidomide was a supposedly safe sedative that had been available without prescription in Germany since 1957 and in England since 1958. New drug applications for marketing the drug in the United States were filed with the Food and Drug Administration in 1960. While the applications were being processed, Dr. Frances O. Kelsey, the reviewing medical officer, learned of reports that use of the drug for extended periods in pregnant women was associated with the development of neuritis. This raised the question in Dr. Kelsey's mind of possible harm to the developing fetus as well as to the mother. In the absence of any data to support safe use under such circumstances, the applicants were given the alternative of producing such evidence before the drug could be approved for marketing or else to place in the labeling a warning that safety in pregnancy had not been established. Early in 1962 reports from

Europe of infants born with deformed limbs or no limbs at all terminated all clinical trials of the drug as a sedative in the United States, although it later was introduced as an investigational drug in the treatment of cancer and leprosy.

The changes brought by the 1962 Amendments relating to controls over investigational new drugs did, in large part, stem from the experience revealed by the thalidomide story. Thalidomide in the United States was, at the time the incident broke, an experimental drug. However, it was widely distributed with assurance of its being safe. Investigational studies were not controlled, few reports were made on the findings of the manufacturer, inadequate records were kept, and other serious procedural deficiencies in the safety procedures used in the United States were brought into sharp focus in the case of thalidomide.

Unlike the 1938 Act, however, the Drug Amendments of 1962 did not represent an entire revision of current law or the drafting of a completely new proposal. Instead the legislation extended, expanded, and strengthened the regulatory authority of the Food and Drug Administration. These amendments included the crucial requirements that a new drug must be shown to be effective as well as safe, provisions for a more rapid withdrawal of approval of drugs found to be hazardous, and much more stringent controls over investigational drugs.

Under the resulting law are the following important provisions:

(1) All drug factories are to be inspected at least biennially.

(2) Drug manufacturers must maintain quality by following good manufacturing practices, as defined by the FDA.

(3) The Administration can forbid the testing of drugs on humans if it finds that clinical testing on animals has not been adequate.

(4) A physician must get the consent of his patients before giving them experimental drugs, unless he decides that this is not feasible or not in a patient's interest.

(5) All antibiotics must be tested, batch by batch, for strength and purity.

(6) A manufacturer applying for approval of a drug must prove not only that it is safe but also that it is effective.

(7) No drug can be put on the market until it has been specifically approved by the FDA.

(8) Drug manufacturers must keep records on clinical experience with the use of drugs and report on this upon request.

(9) Drug labels and advertisements must contain information on injurious side effects.

(10) They must present the generic names of drugs in type at least half as large as that used for their trade name.

(11) The FDA is authorized to review all generic names and establish simpler ones where they are needed.
(12) The FDA may summarily remove a drug from the market if it has evidence that it carries an imminent threat to health.[14]

In short, under the 1938 statute the manufacturer had the burden of proof that the product was safe, while the government had the burden of proof to disprove efficacy. The 1962 Amendments now required the manufacturer to show both safety and efficacy, and the question of burden of proof shifted to the manufacturers in doubtful cases.

As it used to be, we assumed the burden of proof and if we couldn't prove it was dangerous, we couldn't take it off the market. Now the burden of proof passes back to the manufacturer and he has the burden of continuing to prove it is safe if we question it.[15]

Prior to 1962, the manufacturer was also under no obligation to report any adverse information or findings, after the product was introduced into the market, that would cast doubt or disprove the safety of the product. The 1962 Amendments now required the manufacturer to keep the FDA advised of adverse experience and other data which would shed light on the status of the manufacturer's product.

An important feature of the 1962 Act were those provisions which enabled the Food and Drug Administration to apply tests of effectiveness to every product which was subject to the new drug provisions of the 1938 Act. As a direct result of the drug efficacy provisions of the 1962 amendments, the FDA contracted with the National Academy of Sciences — National Research Council in 1966 to survey the approximately 3,600 drugs marketed through the new drug procedures between 1938 and 1962 to determine whether they are effective. The most recent development in this regard occurred on October 12, 1972. A federal district judge ordered the FDA to remove from the market within a year more than 100 drugs that have been found ineffective. The judge also gave the FDA a timetable of four years to complete action on its review of the effectiveness of the 3,600 prescription drugs. The agency is still only partly through its review and argues that lack of money and manpower and legal challenges from drug companies have hampered its action. Much of the delay stems from the need of drug companies to complete additional testing of their products. Dr. Henry Simmons, director of the FDA's Bureau of Medicine, said the ruling will mean that the FDA will no longer routinely give drug companies time to complete tests on questioned products, before taking regulatory action. Previously the agency has delayed decisions on many drugs judged to be only possibly or probably effective to let pharmaceutical concerns conduct trials to gather evidence of their efficacy. Dr. Simmons predicted the FDA could complete its task within four years if the drug industry doesn't tie up the agency with legal actions. FDA experts give the following summary of the status of drugs under the review:

Ineffective: So far 493 products have been judged ineffective. Of these, 341 have been removed from the market, nine have been reclassified as having a greater degree of effectiveness and 143 remain on the market. Much of the delay in halting the sale of these products stems from the need to consider data submitted by the manufacturers in their defense and to issue a final formal decision.

Possibly effective: 723 products have been evaluated as possibly effective; 113 of these have been removed from the market, 17 upgraded to effective, and 508 remain on the market. The rest are over-the-counter drugs being examined separately.

Probably effective: 197 drugs have been judged probably effective. Of these, seven have been removed from the market, 14 upgraded to a higher classification and 176 remain on the market.

Effective, with reservations: 150 drugs are in this category, which consists mainly of combination drugs. The FDA still has to issue an initial evaluation of their effectiveness.

Effective: 1,978 drugs have been judged effective, but many have some claims which have been judged less than effective. Judge Bryant gave the FDA four years to complete action in requiring companies to relabel products and eliminate excessive claims.[16]

The FDA, like most other large governmental agencies today, is not without its share of critics. Probably the most notable and outspoken is Morton Mintz. In true muckraking fashion his book, *The Therapeutic Nightmare*, assails the pharmaceutical manufacturers and the FDA. The scope of the subject is considerable though, ranging from the pricing practices of the drug industry to physicians' ownership of pharmacies. His stated aim is the reporting of "how and why it came about that drugs went on sale which had not been thoroughly tested, had not been demonstrated to be safe, were worthless, and were irrationally prescribed."[17] To achieve this he presents criticisms of organized medicine, federal regulatory agencies, and the prescription drug industry. Such sweeping indictments of so many cannot be entirely true or false. More recently concern has been raised relative to both the structures and procedures of the FDA in terms of its ability to discharge its responsibilities effectively. Also, the rulings of the FDA have increasingly been attacked as inconsistent, outdated and excessively long in the making.

The problem is to evaluate all the rhetoric. Somewhere between all the charges and counterclaims lies the real truth. I am in no position to pass final judgment. I can only say I respect the work of the FDA but recognize much more still must be done. I sympathize with their position and realize that their role in Government is bound to be a lonely one. Dr. Charles C. Edwards, FDA Commissioner, expresses it well.

> We're directly in the middle. We are on the one hand criticized for being 'soft' on industry and on the other called repressive, the enemy of free enterprise. . . We're expected to deliver on the promises of complete safety made by others, but when the time comes to take action we find ourselves standing alone.[18]

In regard to the question of safety and efficacy it must be understood and accepted that there will continue to be great problems attached with the marketing of modern drugs. One can not place too much faith in the FDA.

> Indeed no set of regulations can get around the great dilemma that confronts medical science, the industry, and government in the testing and introduction of new drugs. It is impossible to determine definitely whether a drug is free from harmful effects unless it is tried widely on humans — and that inevitably means risking lives. . . The only way this situation can be improved is by a better fundamental understanding of the mechanisms of the human body and disease, and of the biologic actions of drugs on both, so that nasty jolts can be foreseen and forestalled. There are still large gaps in knowledge of drug action and of the body's complex reactions and interactions. Even if all reactions were known and coded into a giant computer, it would still be impossible to predict every chance effect or disaster. For the human is a highly mixed breed, genetically. No two individuals ever respond in exactly the same way to a drug, and a joker or two is always lurking somewhere in the genetic deck. In truth, the giving of a drug, old or new, is always an experiment. In this immensely complex situation more knowledge, rather than more politics or regulation, is urgently needed.[19]

But to fully understand, it is also important to have a realistic perspective on the development of new drugs and an appreciation of the situation.

> From conception through all the intricacies of research and development, the odds on developing a new, safe, and efficacious drug have been estimated at about 1 to 30,000. To test the flood of new compounds adequately, swiftly and safely, the pharmaceutical industry long ago had to work out, by necessity and later by law, a system for clinical testing. Indeed, organization of clinical pharmacology as a separate discipline has been more a commercial art than a science up to now. It is a system still developing, still imperfect and chaotic, open to abuse and to criticism. But the leading reputable

pharmaceutical companies, large and small, generally have pursued high standards. In fact, their research and production techniques have set most of the quality and control standards there are. . . [20]

Business Week sums up the situation very well:

Essentially, drug testing remains an inexact science subject to all the vagaries of human and animal reaction to foreign substances. The companies know it; doctors know it; and the FDA knows it. Thus any absolute and radical reform of the present system remains a long shot.[21]

QUESTIONS FOR REVIEW

1. Do you think it unfair to single out the drug industry as a case of malpractice in the market? What other sorts of business should also be examined, being just as guilty, in your opinion?
2. Why do people feel so keenly about alleged mal-practices in the drug industry?
3. What is there about this industry from economic, social, and psychological viewpoints which has particularly invited criticism?
4. In view of the facts and charges brought forth by Mr. Goodman, what do you think should be done? Would you nationalize the industry? Make it into a public utility? Or what?
5. Do you think that proposals to regulate this industry much more stringently would be fair? Better protect the consumer?
6. Do you think the Food and Drug Administration has been effective in testing patent medicines for safety and efficacy? How about the ethical pharmaceuticals (prescription drugs)?

FOOTNOTES

1. "Competitive Problems in the Drug Industry," *Hearings before the Senate Subcommittee on Monopoly*, (Washington, D.C., U.S. Government Printing Office, 1968), Part 5, p. 1809.

2. *Ibid.*, Part 5, p. 1889.

3. *Ibid.*, Part 4, p. 1418.

4. *Ibid.*, Part 1, pp. 290-291.

5. *Ibid.*, Part 5, p. 2061-62.

6. *Task Force on Prescription Drugs Final Report*, (Washington, D.C., U.S. Department of Health, Education, and Welfare, Office of the Secretary, 1969), p. 37.

7. "Competitive Problems in the Drug Industry," *op. cit.*, Part 4, p. 1417.

8. *Ibid.*, Part 1, pp. 410 and 413.

9. *Ibid.*, Part 2, p. 797.

10. Baily Morris, "Drug Firms Lead Profit Race in '70," *Washington Star*, (July 24, 1972), p. 6.

11. *Congressional Record — Senate*, (Washington, D.C., U.S. Government Printing Office, September 29, 1972), p. S16336.

12. *Ibid.*, p. S16342.

13. Wyndham Davies, *The Pharmaceutical Industry*, (London, Pergamon Press, 1967), p. 140.

14. Marian D. Hall, *Summary of Major Federal Consumer Protection Laws, 1906-1968*, (Washington, D.C., U.S. Government Printing Office, 1969), pp. 4-5.

15. *Hearings before a Subcommittee of the House Committee on Government Operations on Drug Safety*, (Washington, D.C., U.S. Government Printing Office, 1964), p. 174.

16. "Court Gives FDA Year to Take Off Market Over 100 Drugs Judged to Be Ineffective," *The Wall Street Journal*, (October 12, 1972), p. 4.

17. Morton Mintz, *The Therapeutic Nightmare*, (Boston, Houghton Mifflin Co., 1965), p. xx.

18. "Behind the Crackdown on Food and Drugs," *U.S. News and World Report*, (February 21, 1972), p. 60.

19. Lawrence Lessing, "Laws Alone Can't Make Drugs Safe," *Fortune*, (March 1963), p. 123.

20. *Ibid.*, p. 125.

21. "Storm Breaks Over Drug Testing," *Business Week*, (February 19, 1966), p. 34.

PART V
THE IMPACT OF CONSUMERISM ON INDUSTRY

It is still much too early to tell how deep and lasting the impact of the new consumerism will be on industry generally. In the next part (Part VI), we look at what business is doing in response to the new consumer movement: How it is organizing to cope with it; what specific policies are being formulated; and what the consequences have been thus far in the way of added cost, bother, and personnel needed to handle complaints.

In this section, we observe what the effect has been on two important industries, cereals and cigarettes, of strongly impelled consumer reactions. Did the Surgeon-General's report harm the cigarette industry, and if so, in what ways? Then we look at the effect of Robert B. Choate's attack on the cereal industry.

It is hoped that the reader will be able to draw distinctions between these two industries in respect to the effectiveness of consumer criticisms in curing deficiencies and eliciting responses favorable to the consumer interest. What characteristics of these two areas made reactions widely different?

From these two early cases, the reader may deduce whether similar exposes in the future are likely to elicit favorable responses from the corporations concerned.

WHAT WAS THE IMPACT OF THE CHOATE STUDY ON THE CEREAL MARKET?

ALBERT J. ZANGER

Introduction

Ready-to-eat cereal producers comprise a $900 million a year business. Receiving such a sizeable amount of society's wealth, the industry should be obligated to present a "quality" offering. It is to this area that I have directed my investigation.

The purpose of this paper is to evaluate the effects of the Choate Study on the cereal market. In doing so, I will analyze the cereal market before the Study, describe Choate's findings, and determine the extent of the industry's response. Advertising claims, sales levels, and a product analysis will all be included. I will also look at the present FTC anti-trust suit, which deals with many important issues. Let us turn now to a description of the market.

The Cereal Market Before The Choate Study

The cereal industry is highly concentrated with three major companies accounting for 85 percent of sales.[1] Brand loyalty is low, while company loyalty remains high. The multitude of brands, the high level of advertising required to promote a new brand's success, and the considerable amount of capital required for production all make entry into the cereal industry a costly and foreboding task. Realizing these facts for the last few years, the FTC has leveled an anti-trust suit at the big four companies. Furthermore, the suit charges the cereal makers are advertising with deception.

A Brief Look At The Market

Six major firms vie for shares of the ready-to-eat cereal market: The Kellogg Company, General Mills, General Foods, Quaker Oats, National Biscuit, and Ralston Purina. According to "Barron's" these six accounted for 98 percent of the 1970 dollar market. The big four: Kellogg's, General Mills, General Foods, and Quaker Oats — rake in 90.7 percent of the dollar market.[2] Kellogg's 45.2 percent clearly takes the industry lead, followed by General Mills 20.4 percent, General Foods 16 percent and Quaker Oats 9.1 percent.[3] In spite of the high degree of consumer company loyalty, only six percent of cereal buyers can be rated as feeling strong brand loyalty.[4] One brand's gains generally come at another's loss. In the battle for market share, product proliferation is an attractive weapon. The National Commission on Food Marketing supports this contention by finding that three out of every five consumers purchase the most popular brands less than four times out of ten.[5] In addition to the number of company brands vying in the competitive ring, another determinant of a producer's market share is the number of brands it has in each segment. If a company can imaginatively disperse a wide variety of brands among many segments, then chances are that company loyalty will prevail over the high level of brand switching. Segmentation is undertaken on a wide variety of bases, including age, nutritional awareness, and weight consciousness. Kellogg's Corn Flakes leads all brands, followed by General Mills Cheerios, and Kellogg's Rice Krispies and Sugar Frosted Flakes. The current emphasis on vitamin and protein charged cereals promises further gains for such brands.

As a whole, the cereal market has been practically devoid of growth in recent years. Price increases have caused dollar sales to continue to rise. Bowermaster, a package goods expert at Batten, Barton, Durstine, and Osborn, stated in 1968 that after 50 years of growth, the ready-to-eat cereal market had reached the saturation point.[6] Over half of the newly introduced brands fail. Success cannot be hoped for without large promotional outlays centering upon considerable television exposure. Seventy-five of the 100 brands on the market in 1968 had less than a one percent market share.[7]

Three main factors have been responsible for this continuing market stagnation. Firstly, the children's market has been shrinking. The National Industrial Conference Board estimates that the population's age group of 17 and under, which consumes 70 percent of cereals, will decrease from 70.7 million in 1970 to 69.4 million in 1980.[8] Secondly, breakfast is no longer a formal, family meal. Most housewives find it impossible to feed their families what they consider an ideal breakfast.[9] Hurried schedules and various waking times often result in poor breakfasting. A large portion of dieting housewives also find that skipping breakfast is a relatively painless slimming technique.[10] Thirdly, stiff competition from breakfast drinks and toaster pop-ups has eaten into the cereal bowl. Introduced in 1965, Carnation's Instant Breakfast has been a quick gainer among breakfast foods. However, many of the cereal companies who complain of such competition have themselves introduced the aforementioned products. Lack of supermarket shelf space also enhances the difficulty of new brand success.

Advertising Claims Puffed With Deception

> Back in 1906 when W. K. Kellogg came up with a corn flake, he did not shout eureka. Instead, he laid out a rather fantastic sum of $90,000 so that the advertising media for the day would shout eureka for him, and he gave away a few million boxes of his flaked corn product so that consumers could yell eureka at each other.[11]

Enormous amounts of money are spent annually for cereal advertising and promotion. $90,000 was a rather fantastic sum to spend on media advertising for corn flakes in 1906. Similarly, $2,780,000 is a rather fantastic sum to spend for advertising in 1969, especially when spent on only one medium — television, for only one brand — Cheerios.[12] According to *Advertising Age*, the cereal industry places 18.2 percent of annual sales into media advertising. The largest television users in the food industry, cereal makers plunge up to 86.3 percent of every advertising dollar into the tube.[13] One can easily see that television advertising is essential to a new brand's success. The National Commission on Food Marketing found that the industry often relies on advertising to force distribution of its product. Because of the consumer demand fostered by advertising, retailers have little choice but to stock the products that are heavily promoted.

One commonly used television strategy which enables companies to promote brand uniqueness and insulate themselves against price competition is the bifold approach.[14] On one hand, this approach directs low-key, logical appeals that may stress nutrition to the purchasing agent — mother. On the other hand, Saturday morning advertising aimed at capturing juniors' heart will stress wackiness, fruitiness, or cruncheability, to mention a few more honest appeals.

One should not readily dismiss the effects of cereal ads. Can a small child sit back and evaluate the claims presented before him? Supporting evidence tends to answer with an emphatic "no". "Marketing Communications" states that a family may quickly plunge into trauma when their little son finds out the hard way that Apple Jacks really don't keep the bullies away. Studies have shown that young television viewers develop a marked cynicism upon learning that products do not live up to what was promised on television.[15] This cynicism might also grow toward teachers and parents.

Extra Dollars For That Sweet Crackle And Pop

According to Sidney Margolius, ready-to-eat cereals exhibit the most widespread case of disproportionate pricing in the food industry. While cereal usage has increased significantly up to 1969, so have cereal prices risen about twice as fast as overall food prices.[16]

The addition of sugar to cereals results in distinct price rises. For example, Margolius states that ordinary corn flakes come to 42 cents a pound. A ten ounce box of Sugar Frosted Flakes at 39 cents comes to 62 cents a pound. However, presugared corn flakes contain about 45 percent sugar compared to the ordinary kind's 12 percent. Consequently, for the sake of convenience (or child catering), the housewife pays 22 cents for about 3.3 ounces of additional sugar, or 1.07 a pound. If the housewife buys the "treat pack" (six individually packaged portions) for a total of five and one-fourth ounces, which comes to 94 cents a pound, she pays for the sugar at a rate of 1.92 per pound.[17] It is debatable whether costs warrant such an exorbitant price increase.

Margolius points out that new ingredients often sound attractive, but do so at the expense of nutritional quality. Post Honey Comb cereal costs 6 cents an ounce or 96 cents a pound. Despite its name, that sweetness is mostly ordinary sugar. Listed by quantity, Honey Comb's ingredients are: corn flour, sugar, oat flour, soy flour, salt, honey. There is even less honey than salt. Reduced nutritional quality is even more serious. Sugar coated puffed oats contain only 1.9 grams of protein per ounce, and sugar coated corn flakes only 1.25. This compares with 3.4 grams from an ounce of plain puffed oats, 2.25 from an ounce of plain corn flakes, and 4 from an ounce of oat meal. Flavorings and shapes similarly jump the price surprisingly.[18]

If air is added, as in puffed cereals, price skyrockets to luxury levels since a large box contains relatively little weight. A recently discovered method of puffing grains to an even greater volume has resulted in puffed wheat and puffed rice prices ranging between $1.00 and $1.14 per pound.[19] For these brand name products, the consumer is paying either for purer air, the box, or the name, since private supermarket brands of puffed cereals in bags cost only 50 cents a pound.[20]

FTC Intervention

The FTC has been well aware of cereal maker antics. By May 1970, the Commission had undertaken an extensive study to show that in highly concentrated industries, price and profitability vary with advertising expenditures. Such outlays are alleged to be decisive advantages for dominant companies in highly concentrated industries. When a few companies control sales, the FTC says they have considerable latitude in such decision making activities as price, output, and other matters. Interdependent behavior easily emerges.[21]

In August 10, 1970, the "Anti-Trust Law and Economic Review" charged that breakfast cereal prices are 25 percent higher than they would be if the industry was more competitive, and that at least 10 percent of this extra cost reflects a level of advertising that can exist only in a concentrated industry. Concentration in consumer industries produces rising advertising expenditures, which in turn lead to further concentration.[22] Almost a year in progress, the FTC study took up the "Anti-Trust Law and Economic Review's" case by charging the cereal industry with boosting prices 15-25 percent to allow for high profits and high advertising expenditures.

After abandoning efforts for a negotiated settlement, the FTC formally charged the top four cereal companies with "illegally monopolizing the market and thus forcing consumers to pay artifically inflated prices."[23] The FTC claims that Kellogg's, General Mills, General Foods, and Quaker Oats have achieved a shared monopoly through such devices as brand proliferation, intensive trademark promotions, artificial product differentiation, restrictive allocation of shelf space, and the use of ads which mislead adults and children on the merits of the product. The top four companies utilize heavy advertising outlays to emphasize and exaggerate trivial differences. These large ad expenditures, alleged to restrict competition, have enabled the big four to introduce 150 new brands from 1950-1970, thus achieving 91 percent of the market. [24] The case lists specific questionable claims and challenges the truthfulness of cereal ads.

The FTC does not claim that the companies conspired in the "classic sense," thus making it the first to determine whether market structure in itself is evidence of illegal monopoly. The Commission would like to see Kellogg's and General Mills divest themselves of certain brands and production facilities. These two were singled out since each one's physical separation facilitates breakup. The Commission hopes that competition will be enhanced and that prices will eventually fall. If successful, the case could greatly expand the legal weapon available to the FTC and other anti-trust prosecutors. Seventy-four separate industries comprising 21 percent of the economy display profiles which are nearly as concentrated as the cereal industry. [25]

The cereal companies did not take these charges lightly. Much criticism was leveled at the FTC charges, including arguments in support of company advertising. All four major cereal makers issued statements of reply, and the most comprehensive rebuttal came from the producer with the most to lose — Kellogg's. Finally, economics professor Brozen charged that the FTC violated its own principal of substantiation.

A cereal industry spokesman initially replied that the companies must spend more on advertising than other food companies who deal directly with supermarkets since cereal makers work through independent wholesalers, and consequently don't have the opportunity to offer specials, deals, or other services directly to the supermarket. Thus, the supermarket can't offer periodic savings to the consumer. Furthermore, since supermarkets don't promote cereals in their own ads, this puts the entire burden of advertising on the manufacturers. [26]

General Mills took exception to the criticism that advertising to children is wrong because it doesn't stress nutrition, asserting,

> Kids aren't really turned on by the idea of vitamins, so no amount of vitamins will do them any good if they don't eat them. We appeal to children in a way that will interest them in a product and then run nutritional information on packages. [27]

General Foods is convinced the industry is competitive, asserting, "We should know, we struggle there every day." [28]

Quaker Oats queries: "How can our hard-earned nine percent market share constitute a basis for a monopoly?" [29]

The Kellogg Company denied the charges of monopoly and unfair competition and stated that they merely seek the most effective methods of marketing and distribution for their products. The Company labeled the suit as dangerous not only to cereal marketers but to other industries as well. According to Kellogg's public relations manager Joseph Thomas, "To determine the competitiveness of an industry simply by counting noses is like saying a football game is less competitive than a golf tournament." [30] (Kellogg's must certainly be aware that the FTC considered more factors than a mere "nose count") In reply to the chief supplier of shelf space charge, Kellogg answered that it offers a computerized space management program to retailers as a service. The program is based on both the existing brands and individual store statistics. It is entirely voluntary, and final stocking and space decisions are left to the store managers. As for price increases, Kellogg's says that all companies usually hike at the same time since cost increases are also felt concommitantly. In reply to brand proliferation charges, the contention was made that all brands are not the same, but cater to consumer needs. [31]

Yale Brozen, economics professor at the University of Chicago, charged that the FTC may be violating its own principle of substantiation. Admitting that some form of control must be exercised against false and misleading advertising, he said that the FTC's clumsy approach to this situation is an example of the cure being more deadly than the disease. Noting that the FTC is calling on more industries to submit documentary proof of ad claims, Brozen said that perhaps the FTC should be forced to substantiate its claims before issuing press releases which greatly mislead consumers. For example, he cited the FTC's claim that through its action, prices could be reduced 25 percent, and he asserted that this contention cannot be substantiated. If advertising were cut, costs of cereals would force higher prices. Advertising is not simply an addition to cost passed on to the buyer, but instead enables cereal makers to economize on other costs. Brozen criticized the contention that advertising is a barrier to new products and company entry. If it were, we would expect low product turnover in industries with high levels of advertising, but we find exactly the opposite; the more intense the level of advertising, the higher the product turnover. Advertising is used as a means of entering a market, not barring entry. [32]

Ralph Nader issued a statement praising the FTC action as "one of the most important developments in anti-trust enforcement in the last decade. Shared oligopolies cost consumers $23 billion a year in overcharges." [33]

The Choate Study

Robert B. Choate first came to Washington in 1966 to work against poverty. He soon became interested in malnutrition, and his activities as a nutrition advocate were first financed through his engineering practice in Phoenix. Choate came from a wealthy and prominent New England family who first published the Boston Herald. Step by step, his growing expertise in the field of nutrition made him a regular consultant and witness to Congressional studies. He currently operates a consulting firm, Robert B. Choate and Associates, with a staff of one assistant. Choate is presently writing a book to show how little the food industry is doing to provide good nutrition.[34]

On July 23, 1970, the 47 year old crusader told a Senate Subcommittee that two-thirds of dry breakfast cereals stocked on grocery store shelves are nutritionally worthless. These are the products that are so intensely pushed at children on Saturday morning television shows. Choate called for changes in cereal industry marketing strategy and government food policy. According to the breakfast table crusader, children are deliberately being sold the sponsor's less nutritious products, children are being programmed to demand sugar and sweetness in every food, and children are being counter-educated away from nutrition knowledge by being sold products on a non-nutritive basis. In Choate's words, "It is apparent that in this first of several food industry analyses that we humans are viewed not as beings to be nourished but as suckers to be sold."[35]

Choate said the cereal industry could be made more responsible to consumer needs. Some nutritious cereals are only advertised to adults. Others could be made nutritious if the government requested. Research departments are capable of producing better products, but sales departments inhibit this upgrading lest it upset the established profit makers. Choate asserted that consumers have a right to be free from misinformation and a right to correct data about nutrition. People are entitled to an explanation of sales techniques that are used to urge products to their table and housewives should understand what is being done to their children. [36]

Ranking sixty cereals in terms of the percentages of daily recommended requirements of nine different nutrients, Choate found that forty of the cereals were primarily caloric in content. They fatten, but do little to prevent malnutrition. Among the 20 top cereals, three — Kellogg's Product 19, General Mills Kaboom and Total — were clearly best. Six were nutritionally meritorious: Nabisco 100% Bran Flakes, Quaker Life, General Foods Fortified Oat Flakes, Kellogg's Special K, General Foods' Super Sugar Crisps, and Kellogg's Sugar Smacks. Others were shown to have redeeming features. Choate noted that even with milk, most cereals failed to provide one-third of the daily minimum requirements of nine nutrients.

The worker for nutritional reform specifically singled out the industry's advertising and promotion practices. None of the top ten brands advertised on television made the top ten in nutrition, and only two made the top twenty.[37] The importance of the visual aspects of television advertising was explained. Even when ads do not specifically claim that cereals contain muscle building ingredients, the flexing of biceps and the lifting of heavy weights while the cereal is being spooned from a bowl conveys that the product will transform one's physique.[38] Heroes are often displayed to convince the child of the cereal's worth. Choate points out that the television message generally avoids verbalizing specific nutritional merits, but stresses repeatedly: sugar, energy, sweetness, chocolate, vigor, frostedness, action, alertness, and prizes.[39] Milk is seldom mentioned. Nine out of nine Kellogg's cereals touted to children stress sweetness or contain sugar.[40] Some sample messages include the following:

> ". . .gives you lots of energy, good wind.
>
> . . .makes breakfast taste like chocolate.
>
> . . .walking stopping, digging, crawling, jumping high and never falling . . . Corn Flakes takes you all the way.
>
> . . . colorful cereal circles, sparkling with sugar crystals."[41]

Consequently:

> A child watching 73 spots in a total of 200 minutes of Saturday television would gather: 1. that cereals with sugar are great energy sources, 2. that energy and action are equivalent to happiness, and 3. that ability and health are a product of eating ready-to-eat cereals, and preferably sweet cereals. Is this true?. . .[42]

Furthermore, Choate found that the most heavily advertised on Saturday morning television were also the lowest ranked in nutrition. General Mills' Cheerios, ranked 25th out of 60 in cumulative nutrient merit, was the most heavily advertised cereal in 1969 with an annual television budget of $5,404,800 out of General Mills' $29,425,000 television total. Ranked 39th in nutritional merit, Kellogg's Rice Krispies was the second most heavily advertised cereal with a television budget of $3,609,200. Kellogg's Sugar Frosted Flakes, 58th in nutrition, was third in advertising with a television outlay of $2,780,000.[43] Tony the Tiger has been called today's anti-Popeye, since Sugar Frosted Flakes contains no vitamin A, C, or D, and is deficient in other nutrients.[44] Judging from available data, Nabisco 100% Bran Flakes looked like a best buy. The brand is ranked fourth in nutrition with a lower price per ounce than other leaders, 2.4 cents. However, it receives relatively little advertising support and claims only a .5 percent share of the market.[45] Choate does not contend that all the better brands are not advertised; they are, in magazines and periodicals.

Choate also decries industry labeling practices:

> The seduction of the innocent encompasses more than sugar coating. Hundreds of millions of cereal packages are

"billboards" used to hawk such items as knives, pen sets, racing cars, and the like. [46]

Labeling policy reforms are in neutral gear, and will continue to be backward until comparative nutritional values are stressed. Nutritional foods must be appropriately labeled and advertised, and the consumer must be sufficiently educated to seek them out.

The industry leaders all voiced their displeasure at Choate's findings. General Foods issues the following statement:

> Naturally, we disagree with Mr. Choate's unique approach to breakfast cereal nutrition. He has for example, totally ignored the very important factor of taste preference. You cannot force a youngster to eat a breakfast cereal he does not like, no matter how loaded it might be with nutrients. It is most important to get children to taste products, and thereby provide nutrition for them. [47]

Kellogg classified cereals among some of the best breakfast buys at the grocery store. General Mills stated that Choate's findings are in contradiction to the findings of many competent and responsible scientists.

General industry expert Frederick B. Stare, of Harvard, termed the Choate arrangement "grossly misleading" and "absolutely meaningless."

> In nearly forty years of studying nutrition, I don't recall of having seen or heard of an arbitrary scale comparable to Mr. Choate's cumulative nutritional content. A breakfast of any cereal and milk, along with some fruit, a couple pieces of toast, some poly-unsaturated margarine, and a little jelly or jam is just as nutritious as a bacon and egg breakfast with fruit, toast, and something on the toast. It doesn't make much difference which cereal you eat. [48]

Senator Moss, head of the Senate Subcommittee, said that for people who eat only cereal for a breakfast, and many do, the differing nutritional content of various cereals becomes quite important.

The Market After The Choate Study

In general, Choate's efforts have stimulated long needed, significant consumer benefits. Forty-five of the sixty rated cereals have improved their formulations at least modestly. [49] Although a temporary switch from lower to higher rated brands occurred immediately after the study, sales have since rebounded to former levels. Cereal makers are well aware of the crucial issues, and advertisements have shown modest improvement. Premiums have become a widespread promotional element.

Back to the Old Brands

A considerable amount of brand switching occurred for a few months after Choate's nutritional attacks, but consumers have since returned to their original brands. A survey of supermarkets across the country indicated that alert store managers and consumers instigated a healthy run on the brands touted most nutritious. Grand Union Markets checked 250 of their stores in the New York Metropolitan area and found that sales of five top brands — Product 19, Kaboom, Total, Fortified Oat Flakes, and Life — increased 85 percent during one week in mid-September against a comparable week in July.[50] The study also found that sales of the five brands at the bottom of the nutritional list decreased 18 percent. Others remained the same. Foreseeing the profitable trend, sharp store managers devoted extra shelf space to the higher rated brands. Sudden consumer nutrition consciousness was proven short lived. As in 1969 and 1970, the top four brands of 1971 remained: Kellogg's Corn Flakes, General Mills' Cheerios, Kellogg's Rice Krispies and Sugar Frosted Flakes. Although Cheerios and Sugar Frosted Flakes have been nutritionally upgraded, Corn Flakes and Rice Krispies, two of the most heavily advertised brands, remain as deficient as ever. Throughout 1971, the more nutritious brands experienced slight gains in market share; but on the whole, this trend was insignificant.

Cereal Makers Respond To Nutritional Demands

Skepticism surrounded all hopes of cereal improvement for about a year after the Choate study. According to "Marketing Communications," none of the 1970 introductions were positioned as super-nutritional. By late June 1971, Choate himself admitted that his crusade had as yet made no lasting impact. He reluctantly said, "I can't compete very well with $47 million in annual cereal advertising."[51]

By November, the long awaited changes had come. Choate pointed out that the industry had been upgrading its formulations, with Kellogg taking the lead by fortifying several of its previously low ranked brands. Of the forty brands receiving the worst nutritional marks, thirty-six have been improved.[52] The nutrition advocate said these changes refute company paid nutritionists who tried to belittle his remarks.

In late November 1971, Choate stated that six upgraded Kellogg's products could finally be considered reasonable breakfast cereals in terms of nutrient content. These brands were Fruit Loops, Apple Jacks, Cocoa Krispies, Sugar Pops, Puffa Puffa Rice, and Sugar Frosted Flakes. Furthermore, Kellogg announced that it was planning to increase the nutritional fortification of nine more of its cereals, including Rice Krispies and Corn Flakes.[53] General Mills upgraded all eight of its previously deficient brands, while General

Foods brought all seven of its lowlies into respectability. Quaker Oats improved two out of five deficients.

New cereals have been quite responsive to the fortification demands. In 1971, Quaker Oats unveiled King Vitamin, which contains 100 percent of daily minimum requirements. General Mills has introduced five new brands in the past two years, all fortified to some degree. Protein Plus has been recently test marketed by General Mills and will be positioned as the highest protein cereal in the field.

Advertisements On The Road To Responsibility

Promotional appeals are gradually moving in the right direction. Although many ads still leave much to be desired, advertisers are beginning to stress nutritional awareness. Even if admen want only to thwart further government intervention, specific ads show that advertisers are well aware of their critics expectations.

Choate also blasted cereal ads when he announced widespread fortification in November, 1971, "Ads continue to use grossly misleading adjectives to describe protein claims, energy claims, and vitamin and mineral fortification, even when comparing products in the same category."[54] For instance, he cited Quaker Oats' Life and General Foods' Fortified Oat Flakes as being vastly superior to General Mills' Cheerios, but this fact is disguised by Cheerios advertising claims. Saturday morning television ads still feature crazy cartoon characters, say a lot about cruncheability, and emphasize colorful cereal designs. Some sample television messages:

> ". . .So crispy you almost have to eat them with your fingers in your ears.
>
> . . .Tastes like a bowl of noisy fruit.
>
> . . .A frootful snootful."[55]

In all the crunchy, crackly, yummy, chewy, colorful cereals paraded before children's eyes, some people wonder where the eggs, milk, meat, potatoes, fruits, and vegetables are that should be basic to any diet. Many new commercials now show the advertised cereal along with bacon, eggs, fruit, juice, and toast. Some include voice-over lines like, "Good breakfast, featuring Post Sugar Crisp."[56] Kellogg's has recently stated that their advertising is becoming more nutrition oriented. An ad for Corn Flakes shows the bowl of flakes with milk, fruit, and the headline, "Some of the good things you can't see or taste in a bowl of Kellogg's Corn Flakes and milk."[57] Crawler lines are drawn from the bowl to copy and list various nutrients including amounts with and without milk. Special K ads have shown a breakfast of cereal with milk, juice, and coffee; and claim that if one is weight-watching, then Kellogg's has breakfast figured out for them.

General Mills' new Protein Plus has taken the biggest nutritional stance. Scheduled for recent distribution, the brand has just been test-marketed. Ads are planned to show athletes performing their feats, and then move to ordinary family situations, all the while stressing, "In the way we move, feel, look, think . . . protein is the name of the game."[58] Most important of all, print ads and packages of the cereal list the protein contents of the top products in that area. Protein Plus naturally comes first (25%) followed by Kellogg's Special K (20%), Quaker Oats Life (18%) and General Foods Fortified Oat Flakes (18%).[59] General Mills does not expect any difficulty from the FTC, since commercials depict the average person doing everyday things.

Promotional gimmicks have become important persuaders. One ad agency man has related,

> When you have two or three brands on the shelf that are
> all equal, then what is going to pull one off the shelf?
> Premiums, that's what is going to charge up the kid. [60]

Premiums are now used more than ever before. Games on or inside the box are popular, along with deals that involve mailing in boxtops. Some ads spend considerable time stressing these premiums instead of the cereal. Wacky names such as Sir Grapefellow, Count Chocula, Frankenberry, and Freakies have also been popular. According to the New York Times, General Mills employed the wackiest names of 1971 and also increased their market share the most.

Conclusions

Robert B. Choate's efforts have been instrumental in making cereal companies more responsive to consumer needs. Consumers have the right to expect cereals to contain minimal nutritional benefits, and a vast proportion of cereals have now been made more nourishing. To what extent fortification is desirable is a question calling for future research. Choate has declared that there is such a thing as overfortification, and has described a few cereals as calorie-connected vitamin pills. In addition, a few industry executives have expressed reluctance to upgrade their cereals since they feel that excessive fortification may result in their being charged with deception by trying to pre-empt the nutrition of other meals. Such criticisms and apprehensions can be cleared up by the FDA. In December, 1971, the FDA announced that it would set nutritional guidelines for a number of foods, including cereals. The guidelines would include maximum as well as minimum standards.[61] Such rules would clearly define what is expected of cereals nutritionally, and would prevent companies from using cheap chemical fortifiers instead of the more expensive natural kind. Choate asks, "If Canada can establish guidelines for a product's protein worth, why can't we?"[62] Hopefully we will. If properly enforced, these regulations would force companies to upgrade such brand leaders as Kellogg's Corn Flakes and Rice Krispies. Consumer responsiveness would thus be placed before apprehension of profit disturbance.

A decision regarding the anti-trust suit requires the introduction of further evidence. Often, governmental regulation and interference appears to be a hindrance for all concerned. The costly monitoring of output and the possibility of lengthy law suits are certainly unattractive to industry executives. However, if empirical evidence shows that cereal company breakup will result in consumer savings of 25 percent, then the scales are greatly tipped in favor of the FTC. If this proves to be the case, then similar action should be taken against other oligopolies. Bigness alone is surely an unfair criterion for breakup. Yet, when this bigness leads to prohibitively large advertising expenditures used to promote a wide variety of brands which insulate against the evils of brand switching, then competitive entry is indeed hindered.

In addition to upgrading cereal nutrition, Choate's findings have also spurred ads toward consumer ends. The increasing advertising emphasis on nutrition is evidenced by the comparative protein ratings used by General Mills' new Protein Plus. Due in general to Choate's request for more nutritional appeals, admen now clearly realize what is expected of them. Our children should not be taught to value fictitious cereal benefits. If cereal advertising men do not shoulder the burden, regulating efforts such as those suggested by Dr. Mayer, White House Nutrition Adviser, should be undertaken. Dr. Mayer asserts,

> When broadcast advertising is directed at children and pertains to their health and nutrition, it should be closely monitored by the FCC either through a committee where nutritionists, physicians, and educators constitute a majority, or through delegation to the FDA or other appropriate HEW body. [63]

As one industry executive sarcastically put it, "Nutrition does not crackle or pop." Through the efforts of Robert B. Choate, nutrition will now be a breakfast reality.

QUESTIONS FOR DISCUSSION

1. What were the characteristics of the market for dry cereals? Is there great brand loyalty? Company loyalty? Is the industry expanding or contracting in sales volume? Why?

2. Why did the Federal Trade Commission intervene in the cereal industry in 1970? What makes this cereal case different from the anti-monopoly case?

3. Do you think the FTC had a good case? What did Dr. Brozen think about it?

4. What charges did Robert B. Choate make aginst the cereal industry? Against its advertising? Against nutritional claims?

5. What happened to the cereal market as a result of Mr. Choate's exposures? Why do you think this happened? Did anything good come out of the expose?

6. What reaction amongst the cereal manufacturers took place? Do you think this was all of much protection to the consumer?

FOOTNOTES

1. "Report Indicts Ads as Cause of Oligopoly Pricing," *Advertising Age*, 41:16 (August 10, 1970).

2. Maxwell, J. C., "Scoreboard for Cereals, Major Brands Post Gains," *Barron's*, 51:18, (July 26, 1971).

3. *Ibid.*

4. Nelson, R., "Cereals, Nutrition doesn't Crackle or Pop," *Marketing Communications*, 219:38 (March 1971).

5. "Cereals Multiply as Ads Push Novelty, Don't Create Loyalty, Report Asserts," *Advertising Age*, 37:1 (July 4, 1966).

6. "Ready-to-eat Cereal Market Reaches Saturation Point, says Bowermaster," *Advertising Age*, 39:4 (April 1, 1968).

7. *Ibid.*

8. Nelson R., "Cereals, Marketing's Survival School," *Marketing Communications*, 298:32 (March, 1970).

9. "Changing Taste in Breakfast," *Financial World*, 130:13 (August 7, 1968).

10. Nelson, R., "Cereals, All Popped Out,: *Marketing Communications*, 296:35 (July, 1968).

11. Nelson, R.C., "Cereals, Capitalizing on the Swing of Youth," *Printer's Ink*, 294:7 (June 23, 1967).

12. Cohen, S.E., "Hefty Ad Efforts Back Non-Nutritious Dry Cereals, Choate Tells Senators," *Advertising Age*, 41:3 (July 27, 1970).

13. "Cereals Multiply as Ads Push Novelty, Don't Create Loyalty, Report Asserts," *Advertising Age*, 37:1 (July 4, 1966).

14. Zalasnick, S., "Fight for a Place at the Breakfast Table," *Fortune*, 76:128, (December, 1967).

15. "Five Weeks of Hearings Strengthen FTC's Determination to Continue Aggressive Regulation of T.V. Ads," *The New York Times* (November 22, 1971), p.3.

16. Margolius, Sidney, *The Innocent Consumer Vs. the Exploiters*, (New York, 1967), p. 117-22.

17. *Ibid.*

18. *Ibid.*

19. *Ibid.*

20. *Ibid.*

21. Cohen, S. E., "FTC Finds Ads Boost Profits but also Foster Monopoly," *Advertising Age*, 41:1 (May 11, 1970).

22. "Report Indicts Ads as Cause of Oligopoly Pricing," *Advertising Age*, 41:16 (August 10, 1970).

23. "Ready-to-eat Cereal Market Reaches Saturation Point, says Bowermaster," *Advertising Age*, 39:4 (April 1, 1968).

24. "Cereal Product Multiplicity Key Issue in FTC's Charges," *Advertising Age*, 43:1 (January 31, 1972).

25. *New York Times* (January 30, 1972), Sec. IV, p. 2.

26. Giges, N., "Cereal Men Reformulate warily as talk of FTC Report Persists," *Advertising Age*, 42:3 (January 28, 1971).

27. *Ibid.*

28. *Ibid.*

29. Giges, N., "Kellogg Calls FTC Order Devastating," *Advertising Age*, 43:8, (January 31, 1972).

30. *New York Times* (January 30, 1972), Sec. IV, p. 4.

31. Giges, N., "Kellogg Calls FTC Order Devastating," *Advertising Age*, 43:8 (January 31, 1972).

32. "FTC Substantiation is Missing in Attack on Cereals: Brozen," *Advertising Age*, (March 6, 1972).

33. "Cereal Monopoly by Four Top Makers charged by FTC," *The New York Times* (January 25, 1972), p. 1.

34. "Choate, Robert, Jr., "Gadfly Buzzes around Breakfast Table," *Business Week*, p. 116 (September 26, 1970).

35. Cohen, S. E., "Hefty Ad Efforts Back Non-Nutritious dry cereals, Choate tells Senators," *Advertising Age*, 41:2 (August 10, 1970).

36. *Ibid.*

37. Nelson, R., "Cereals: Nutrition doesn't Crackle or Pop," *Marketing Communications*, 219:38-42 (March 1971).

38. Furuhashi, Hugh Y., and McCarthy, Jerome E., *Social Issues of Marketing in the American Economy* (Columbus, Oh.: Grid, Inc., 1971), p. 74.

39. *Ibid.*

40, Cohen, S. E., "Hefty Ad Efforts Back Non-Nutritious Dry Cereals, Choate tells Senators," *Advertising Age,* 41:3 (July 27, 1970).

41. Furuhashi, *op. cit.,* p. 74.

42. *Ibid.*

43. Cohen, S. E., "Hefty Ad Efforts Back Non-Nutritious Dry Cereals, Choate tells Senators," *Advertising Age,* 41:3 (July 27, 1970).

44. *Ibid.*

45. Nelson, R., "Cereals: Nutrition doesn't Crackle or Pop," *Marketing Communications,* 219:38-42 (March, 1971).

46. Cohen, S. E., "Hefty Ad Efforts Back Non-Nutritious Dry Cereals, Choate tells Senators," *Advertising Age,* 41:3 (July 27, 1970).

47. *Ibid.*

48. Cohen, S. E., "Industry Witnesses Hit Cereal Nutrition Critics, *Advertising Age,* 41:2 (August 10, 1970).

49. "Breakfast Cereal Critic Cited Widespread Improvement," *New York Times,* November 5, 1971, p. 40.

50. "Cereal Critic Aids His Targets," *Business Week* (October 3, 1970), p. 59.

51. "Sales of Dry Cereals Brisk Despite Warning of Empty Calories," *New York Times* (July 4, 1971), p. 29.

52. *New York Times* (October 22, 1972), Sec. 3, p. 1.

53. Kingman, Merle, *"Top 100 National Advertisers Hike Ad Total to $4.9 Billion"* (August 28, 1972), p. 1.

54. "26 of 40 Cereals Upgraded since Choate Study," *Advertising Age,* 42:1 (November 29, 1971).

55. *New York Times,* October 22, 1972, Sec. 3, p. 1.

56. *Ibid.*

57. Giges, N., Cereal Men Reformulate warily as Talk to FTC Report Persists," *Advertising Age,* 42:3 (June 28, 1971).

58. "General Mills into Test with Protein Plus Cereal Entry," *Advertising Age* (September 25, 1972), p. 14.

59. *Ibid.*

60. *New York Times* (October 22, 1972), Sec. 3, p. 1.

61. "Another Look at the Cereal Debate," *New York Times,* December 19, 1971, p. 62.

62. "26 of 40 Cereals Upgraded since Choate Study," *Advertising Age,* 42:1 (November 29, 1971).

63. "Cereal Ads Come Under Fire," *Broadcasting,* 79:28 (August 10, 1970).

KEITH A. HANSEN

Success of the Cigarettes

The popularity of the cigarette can be contributed to a number of factors. The first is the vast advertising campaigns of the cigarette industry, second the switch by soldiers to easy-to-carry cigarettes during the two World Wars, and the fast pace of life which began during the twenties.[1] The quickened tempo of the times also broke the social barriers against cigarette smoking by women, so much so that out of the millions of smokers today, 40 percent are women. Also cigarettes are a milder form of tobacco and do not emit offensive odor to women as do cigars. Table 1 shows the per capita consumption of cigarettes as compared to cigars for various years. One may note also that while the pounds of tobacco per capita used for cigarettes have increased, the pounds for cigars, smoking tobacco, chewing tobacco and snuff have decreased. The increase in sales of cigarillos and small cigars since 1959 has caused the per capita pound consumption of cigar tobacco to decrease even though per capita consumption of cigars has increased.

In order to get some ideas of the cigarette industry's sales significance and of its ability to sponsor huge advertising campaigns, we may consider the data in Table 2, which shows consumer expenditures for tobacco products in the United States from 1934 to 1963. An estimate of the 1962 advertising budget of the cigarette industry was around $150 million.[2] The reason the cigarette companies are capable of spending this much is a new cigarette machine which came out around 1919 was able to make more than 2,000 cigarettes per minute with only one operator.

With 70 million American smokers in the United States, 66 million of them were cigarette smokers. So the state of the cigarette industry was a healthy one at this point.

In 1962 stirrings were caused by the President Kennedy appointment in 1962 of a group to make a study of the smoking health problem in the United States. His action was in response to the pressure from such medical groups as the American Cancer Society and the American Heart Association.[3] Also in 1963, the Advisory Committee to the Surgeon General of the Public Health Service was compiling a prodigious work on the subject of smoking and health. Adverse publicity against the cigarette industry began to be more common in 1963. The tobacco industry knew what the committee was working on but seemed to believe that nothing serious would ensue when its report was issued. Just before publication of the anticipated Surgeon General's report, Howard Cullman, President of the Tobacco Merchants Association, expressed

TABLE 1

CONSUMPTION PER CAPITA OF TOBACCO PRODUCTS IN THE UNITED STATES (INCLUDING OVERSEAS FORCES) FOR SPECIFIED PERIODS[1]

Year	Per Capita 18 years and over			Per Male 18 years and over			
	Cigarettes[2]		All tobacco products[2]	Large cigars and cigarillos[2]		Smoking tobacco[3]	Chewing tobacco[3]
	Number	Pounds	Pounds	Number	Pounds	Pounds	Pounds
Average 1925-29	1,285	3.56	9.68	177.4	4.10	4.15	5.03
Average 1930-34	1,389	3.78	9.00	125.2	2.96	4.40	3.15
Average 1935-39	1,779	4.81	9.22	120.9	2.89	4.39	2.48
Average 1940-44	2,558	6.97	10.88	118.9	2.87	3.67	2.34
1945...	3,449	9.48	13.02	112.3	2.71	3.41	2.34
1946...	3,446	9.43	12.58	120.4	2.93	2.12	2.21
1947...	3,416	9.12	12.11	112.8	2.78	2.06	1.92
1948...	3,505	9.42	12.36	113.7	2.80	2.09	1.85
1949...	3,480	9.45	12.22	109.3	2.50	2.08	1.71
1950...	3,522	9.54	12.29	107.8	2.53	2.03	1.67
1951...	3.743	9.94	12.59	110.7	2.56	1.89	1.62
1952...	3,884	10.44	13.10	115.0	2.72	1.80	1.58
1953...	3,702	10.36	12.95	115.5	2.72	1.62	1.55
1954...	3,544	9.58	12.11	112.8	2.64	1.55	1.48
1955...	3,595	9.48	11.98	112.8	2.60	1.47	1.44
1956...	3,647	9.34	11.64	110.8	2.41	1.30	1.36
1957...	3,751	9.20	11.38	112.9	2.28	1.27	1.29
1958...	3,949	9.45	11.66	117.3	2.34	1.37	1.23
1959...	4,071	9.45	11.64	125.0	2.36	1.31	1.20
1960...	4,172	9.65	11.77	124.7	2.28	1.30	1.13
1961...	4,266	9.85	11.94	122.9	2.27	1.30	1.13
1962...	4,265	9.69	11.72	121.9	2.24	1.24	1.10
1963[4]..	4,345	9.76	11.81	124.5	2.30	1.22	1.10

1. Includes Alaska and Hawaii for all years.
2. Unstemmed processing-weight equivalent.
3. Finished-product weight.
4. Preliminary

Source: U.S. Department of Agriculture, *Annual Report on Tobacco Statistics,* 1963 table 26.

TABLE 2

CONSUMER EXPENDITURES FOR TOBACCO PRODUCTS AND AVERAGE RETAIL CONSUMER EXPENDITURES FOR TOBACCO PRODUCTS

Year	Cigars	Cigarettes	Chewing and Smoking Tobacco and Snuff	Total-all Tobacco Products
		Millions of Dollars		
	(1)	(2)	(3)	(4)
1939	$261	$1,207	$299	$1,767
1940	265	1,316	302	1,883
1941	284	1,518	306	2,108
1942	305	1,773	303	2,381
1943	358	2,024	295	2,677
1944	402	2,025	290	2,717
1945	443	2,208	321	2,972
1946	542	2,656	280	3,478
1947	547	3,044	278	3,869
1948	548	3,319	288	4,155
1949	520	3,463	289	4,272
1950	514	3,626	292	4,432
1951	526	3,934	283	4,743
1952	545	4,326	282	5,153
1953	560	4,537	268	5,365
1954	552	4,406	260	5,218
1955	549	4,544	257	5,350
1956	553	4,843	242	5,368
1957	557	5,267	240	6,064
1958	581	5,564	255	6,400
1959	625	6,036	279	6,940
1960	647	6,384	292	7,323
1961	633	6,635	303	7,571
1962	646	6,788	320	7,754
1963	660	7,100	320	8,080

NOTES: Columns 1, 2, 3 and 4 are estimates prepared by the U.S. Department of Commerce, Office of Business Economics, as published by the U.S. Department of Agriculture, *Annual Report on Tobacco Statistics*, 1963. They include Federal, state, and local sales and excise taxes. Data prior to 1939 are not available.

Source: *Cigar Manufacturers Association Statistical Record*, Exhibit 23.1.

his confidence in the cigarette industry's ability to overcome sales resistance caused by a possible cancer scare when he said, "After the British report of the Royal College of Physicians in March 1962, sales temporarily declined, but, at the end of the year they were above the preceding year."[4]

So it appears the cigarette companies worried little about the cancer scare in the beginning.

THE CANCER SCARE

The Surgeon General's Report

For over three centuries tobacco has been a subject of medical controversy. In 1604, James I, King of England, allegedly wrote in *A Counterblaste to Tobacco* that tobacco is "a custom Lothesome to the Eye, hatefull to the Nose, harmfulle to the Braine, dangerous to the Lungs, and in the black stinking fumes thereof, neerest resembling the horrible Stigian smoke of the pit that is bottomlesse."[5] Those who defend tobacco have been equally as vehement. A Scottish physician once wrote in a sonnet to a lady friend:

> "Some do this plant with odious crimes disgrace,
> and call the poor tobacco homicide.
> They say that it, Oh what a monstrous cace!
> Forstalls the life, and kills man in the seed.
> It smoketh, blacketh, burneth all the braine . . .
> Good Lady, look not to these raving speaches,
> you know by proof that all these blames are lies,
> Forged by scurvy, lewd, unlearned leeches . . . "[6]

What the physician mentioned above meant "by proof" is not known: But even with the publication of *Smoking and Health* by the Royal College of Physicians of London in 1962, and of *Smoking and Health* by the United States Public Health Service in 1964, there are still some who are waiting to see the "proof" that cigarette smoking causes lung cancer and other harmful diseases. In considering the most comprehensive "proof" available today, we shall first summarize the U.S.P.H.S. report, then make a few comments about the marketing opportunities and problems for the cigar industry which emanate from the report, and finally, give a brief resume of the arguments directed against it. We shall conclude this chapter by discussing who is right in the controversy and how people have reacted to prior cancer scares.

The highlights of the U.S.P.H.S. report are given in the following quotations:

"In 1962, over 500,000 people in the United States died of arterioschlerotic heart disease (principally coronary artery disease), 41,000 died of lung cancer, and 15,000 died of bronchitis and emphysema."[7]

"Lung cancer deaths, less than 3,000 in 1930, increased to 18,000 in 1950. In the short period since 1955, deaths from lung cancer rose from less than 27,000 to the 1962 total of 41,000. This extraordinary rise has not been recorded for cancer of any other site. While part of the rising trend for lung cancer is attributable to improvements in diagnosis and the changing age-composition and size of the population, the evidence leaves little doubt that a true increase in lung cancer has taken place."[8]

"Cigarette smoking is associated with a 70 percent increase in the age-specific death rates of males."[9]

"Cigarette smoking is casually related to lung cancer in men: The magnitude of the effect of cigarette smoking far outweighs all other factors. The data for women, though less extensive, point in the same direction."[10]

"The risk of developing lung cancer increases with duration of smoking and the number of cigarettes smoked per day, and is diminished by discontinuing smoking. In comparison with non-smokers, average male smokers of cigarettes have approximately a 9- to 10-fold risk of developing lung cancer and heavy smokers at least a 20-fold risk."[11]

"Cigarette smoking is much more important than occupational exposures in the causation of lung cancer in the general population."[12]

"Cigarette smoking is the most important of the causes of chronic bronchitis in the United States, and increases the risk of dying from chronic bronchitis and emphysema."[13]

"Death rates of cigar smokers are about the same as those of non-smokers for men smoking less than five cigars daily. For men smoking five or more cigars daily, death rates were slightly higher (9 percent to 27 percent) than for non-smokers in the four studies that gave this information. There is some indication that this higher death rate occurs primarily in men who have been smoking for more than 30 years and in men who stated that they inhaled the smoke to some degree. Death rates for current pipe smokers were little if at all higher than for non-smokers, even with men smoking 10 or more pipefuls per day and with men who had smoked pipes for more than 30 years."[14]

"On the basis of prolonged study and evaluation of many lines of converging evidence, the Committee makes the following judgment: Cigarette smoking is a health hazard of sufficient importance in the United States to warrant appropriate remedial action."[15]

Criticisms of the Report

Whereas the number of magazine and newspaper articles of explaining or praising the advisory report has been large, the number of articles criticizing the report has been large, the number of articles criticizing the report has been few. One cigarette industry spokesman, Joseph F. Cullman III, President of Phillip Morris, Inc. criticized the report on several counts:

1. The report did not present any new material and it was the culmination of old research.

2. A West German pathological study had tended to exonerate cigarettes as a cause of cancer and claimed that cancer was due to air pollution.

3. No study was made regarding the experience of filter and nonfilter smokers.

4. The study did not consider the advantages of new types of cigarettes and did not present a discussion of filters.

5. Finally, "Our scientists and consultants have devoted a great deal of study to the Advisory Committee's report. They do not feel the prime conclusion is justified on the basis of available scientific knowledge and evidence."[16]

Another skeptic is Dr. Milton B. Rosenblatt, Chief of the Medical Clinics at the Metropolitan Hospital and Associate Clinical Professor of Medicine at New York Medical College. He said "It appears from the report that the Surgeon General's Committee was greatly influenced by the statistical studies. These studies are predicated on the concept that there has been an increase in lung cancer since smoking became popular. The fact is that we have no evidence of lung cancer during the past few decades is because we have no reliable comparative data."[17]   Included in the same article with Doctor Rosenblatt's statements were the opinions of Doctor Harry S. Greene, Chairman of the Pathology Department at Yale University, and Doctor R. H. Rigdon, Professor of Pathology at the University of Texas Medical School. Doctor Greene said that "all that the Government has are statistics by a statistical association and the statistics don't mean much." He went on to say that "at the present time I don't believe that cigarette smoking has anything to do with cancer. I am in favor, however, of continuing experimentation." Doctor Rigdon said "it has not been proven from a scientific viewpoint that smoking causes lung cancer. I'd like to see, instead of statistical studies, the mechanics of how it is supposed to cause cancer." Others claim such things as virus, individual susceptibility, and personality type are the causes of cancer and that cigarettes are not "the" cause of even "a" cause.

It is possible that some of the above criticisms are justified. Future research might demonstrate that cancer is caused by a virus and not by cigarette smoking. If that happens, the cigar industry may be up against massive cigarette advertising campaigns, directed at everyone and all his needs, real or otherwise.

Who is Right in the Smoking — Health Controversy?

What can we conclude about this controversy? One could make a very long list of eminent doctors and researchers together with a long list of research projects all of which conclude that smoking is a cause of cancer. The number of persons and articles that dispute the evidence which culminated in the Surgeon General's report is rather short. Cigar men are remaining mum concerning the report. They hope the cancer scare will shift people from smoking cigarettes to smoking cigars. Some of the cigarette industry men, like Mr. Cullman of Philip Morris, claim that the report is erroneous in its findings. On the other hand, some of the cigarette industry men concede that there is an element of truth in the findings but hopefully take the viewpoint that as more research is done the agent in cigarette smoking that causes cancer will be discovered and removed. One cigarette industry official has expressed his doubts about the report saying that, "I'm still not convinced by the Surgeon General's report that cigarettes are the cause of lung cancer . . . but I'm willing to do everything in my power to spend every cent we possibly can for research to produce what the Government and the doctors will consider a safe cigarette."[18]   In any case, it appears as if most people do believe cigarettes are injurious to health; but that they really think cigarette smoking causes cancer is open to doubt. No one really can say for sure whether the cancer scare is a legitimate fear or not.

If research discovers the means of removing the cancer causing agents from cigarettes so that people can inhale them with no harmful effects, the cigar industry may lose those people who have already switched over from cigarettes. Just what the cigarette companies are doing in regards to research and trying to sell the people on safe cigarettes will be discussed later. The point here is that the more research the cigarette companies undertake the sooner will be the introduction of safe cigarettes and perhaps the dwindling of the recent upsurge in popularity of cigars.

How People Have Reacted to Prior Cancer Scares

Thus far we have seen that the cigarette industry is in trouble and that the cigar industry stands to gain somewhat. From these facts, sales of cigarettes should have been plummeting downward and sales of cigars soaring ever since the issuance of the *Smoking and Health* report.

Such is not the case. In order to understand something about what has happened to cigar and cigarette sales since January of this year, one has only to look back a few years to 1954 and to 1962, the former, the year of the last big American cancer scare and the latter, the year of the big English scare.

In December 1953, Dr. Ernest Wynder and Dr. E. A. Graham published a paper called "Experiemental Production of Carcinoma (Cancer) with Cigarette Tars." Immediately after the report was issued sales of cigarettes went down 9 and 17 percent respectively in January and February, 1954, from those same months in 1953.[19] Then in May and June, 1954, sales went up 2 and 8 percent. At the end of June, the American Cancer Society's Life

Expectancy Survey came out and late June sales declined. This shows how the sales of cigarettes decline when adverse publicity occurs, but increase when people begin to forget about it.

The year 1954 showed an overall decline in per capita cigarette consumption from 1953 as shown in Table 1. We may note from that table that per capita consumption of cigarettes declined in 1953 and 1954, but began to rise again in 1955. Thus, while in a cancer scare period sales may fluctuate due to adverse publicity, the overall effect is that total sales will be down. That people forget is demonstrated by the fact that the number of cigarettes manufactured in the United States in fiscal 1963 amounted to 543.7 billion units (1954 unit sales were 401,848,000,000).

During the 1953-54 cancer scare period, cigar sales increased slightly and then fell. From Table 1 we see that the per capita consumption of cigars fell from 1953 until 1956. Small cigars, on the other hand, did feel a slight surge. In 1953 small cigars manufactured were 58,320,000; in 1954, 61,245,000 and in 1955, 58,733,000 were manufactured.[20] In 1963 small cigars manufactured totalled 281,351,000.

In other words, the smoking controversy of 1954 did have an effect on both the cigarette and cigar industries. Both experienced declines in units manufactured and in per capita consumption. The rapid increase in sales of cigarettes after 1955, however, proved that people did not take the smoking-health warnings very seriously. As far as cigars were concerned, and they were under almost no medical attack during the 1954 scare, people did not begin smoking more of them until 1959. The controversy of 1954 faded even after Dr. Alexander G. Gillman, of the National Cancer Institute, said in an address before the American Pharmaceutical Manufacturers Association on December 10, 1954, that "it may now . . . be regarded as an established fact that white, male cigarette smokers in England and the United States suffer a substantially greater risk to cancer of the lung than non-smokers."[21]

Some of the smoking-health articles appearing in magazines in 1954 carried the following titles which compare closely to the current titles used in this thesis' bibliography:

"Three Experts Say Cigarettes Definitely Cause Cancer," *New York Herald Tribune*, Dec. 8, 1954;

"Cigarette Makers Mum in Wake of Cancer Report," *Advertising Age*, June 28, 1954;

"Cigarettes Off 4%," *Business Week*, June 19, 1954;

"Battle of the Scientists Gets Hotter," *Printer's Ink*, December 10, 1954;

"The Smoking Slump," *Wall Street Journal*, January 20, 1954;

"Cancer Scare Fails to Slow Cigarette Sales in Britain,"
Advertising Age, November 8, 1954.[22]

Considering how rapidly cigarette sales rose shortly after the cancer scare of 1954, it is no surprise that in 1962, when the *Smoking and Health* report of the Royal College of Physicians of London came out that cigarette sales dropped off from 10 to 20 percent but then rapidly increased to record levels despite all the anti-smoking campaigns of the English government itself.[23] In 1963, cigarette sales in England rose by five percent to a record three billion, with six out of ten adults using tobacco.

After the issuance of the English report, a member of the Ministry of Health said, "The behavior of the public never, perhaps, has been more paradoxical than in the face of the facts about lung cancer and smoking. Earlier this year there were a few cases of smallpox and people queued for vaccinations and hammered on surgery doors in a state of near panic when confronted by the chance of one in many millions that they might contract the disease. Yet the same people in massive numbers continue, day in and day out, to take deliberately and with seeming indifference chances as high as one in nine or worse that they will die of lung cancer."[24] In addition to the above, the *U.S. News and World Report* said that the cigarette industry prior to the release of the Surgeon General's report on Smoking and Health was completely confident that the American people would react in the same manner as they had done in 1954 and 1955, and in the same paradoxical manner that the English had acted after the Royal College of Physicians report was issued.

The cigarette industry despite reasonable fears by many of its members has probably guessed correctly. After the release of the Surgeon General's report, cigarette sales dropped 10 to 20 percent and in some places as much as 30 percent. The decline in cigarette sales continued on into the first part of March, 1964. During March, the Federal Trade Commission's extensive publicity on planned cigarette advertising curtailments was over and so March sales of cigarettes went up. Another explanation for the rise in cigarette sales during March, is that it was during that month that the tobacco industry through the Tobacco Institute began talking about an advertising code.

During April, sales continued to rise. An explanation of the rise in sales in April is that on April 27, the industry announced that it had finalized its code. During May, sales decreased slightly. During June, the FTC declared that the smoking advertising rule would be delayed until July 1, 1965, and this may have been what prompted June sales to increase. July 1964 shipments were slightly less than those in June.

What these facts show is that adverse publicity only temporarily retards cigarette sales. As soon as bad publicity dies down or favorable publicity comes out, cigarette sales increase. We saw this phenomenon occur in the 1953-54 scare.

Thus the picture in 1964 showed that cigarette sales were off about 16 billion units for the first two quarters. Considering that over 500 billion cigarettes were sold in the United States in 1963, a 16 billion dollar loss in unit sales for the first six months (the height of the cancer scare) is not too significant. As happened in 1953-54 happened in 1964-65, that is a loss in unit sales occurred in 1964 and 1965 showed an increase in sales over 1964.

Conclusions

The way the American people have reacted to past scares has occurred again in the 1964 scare. It was just a matter of time before the Surgeon General's report was forgotten and people that gave up or reduced their smoking of cigarettes resumed their old smoking habits.

As in 1954, 1964 showed a decline in cigarette sales over 1963. As in 1955, 1965 cigarette sales showed an increase over 1964.

WHY PEOPLE SMOKE

How Many Smoke and How Much

When Columbus discovered the island of San Salvador in 1492, and observed the Indians smoking "firebrands" which were rolls of tobacco wrapped with tobacco leaf, the seeds of the future American cigar industry were planted. The spread of this unknown plant to the Old World was rapid. By 1531, the Spanish were commercially growing this crop in the West Indies. At the same time, in Europe, the plant was being cultivated for both its ornamental and medicinal qualities. The crop was raised commercially in Cuba and Venezuela as early as 1580. Through trading, the Spanish and English spread tobacco leaf as early as 1600 or 1605 to almost all parts of the world, including Japan, China and South Africa.[25]

In 1615, the American colonists were able to ship to England about 2,000 pounds of tobacco; in 1628, about 500,000 pounds; in 1638, 1,400,000 pounds; and by 1698, 23,300,000 pounds. During the seventeenth century, American tobacco production expanded rapidly, and tobacco became the most important export from the colonies. In 1963, world tobacco production was slightly above nine billion pounds, the United States producing nearly three billion pounds. (See Table 1 in Chapter I for consumption per capita of tobacco products in the United States).

This phenomenal rise of the tobacco industry has occurred, as we have seen, despite several centuries of smoking-health controversies. The question this chapter will attempt to answer, bearing in mind that we are looking for marketing problems and opportunities for the cigar industry, is, "Why do so many millions of Americans Smoke?"

The Effects of Smoking

Very few studies have been undertaken to learn exactly why people smoke. The most comprehensive investigations into the subject so far are the *Smoking and Health* reports of the Surgeon General of the United States and of the Royal College of Physicians of London. The Advisory Report of the Surgeon General sums up its conclusion by saying, "A consensus among modern authors appears to be that smoking, and presumably nicotine, exert a predominantly tranquilizing and relaxing effect. The act of smoking is of such complexity that the difficulties associated with the objective analysis of whether smoking induces pleasure by creating euphoria or by relieving dysphoria renders objective analysis virtually impossible."[26] Some authors claim that smoking is not "predominantly" relaxing. They simply claim that smoking picks people up when they feel depressed and calms them down when they are nervous. Because of the many combinations of psychological and physiological states that may occur when one is smoking, it is impossible to say just what precise effect will be felt. It is possible, for instance, for a person to feel that he needs a cigarette to relax him; but when he starts to smoke he may find that he is even more nervous than before. On the other hand the same person may find that if he smokes one or two cigarettes he does feel more relaxed: But if he smokes say five or six within a short period of time he may feel more nervous than when he first started, even though he felt relaxed after the first one or two.

The Surgeon General's report says that most people who smoke cigars and pipes do so to relax. The report says that this tranquilizing effect may come from the fact that pipe and cigar smokers do not generally inhale. The inhalation done by cigarette smokers might have an effect on the central nervous system which causes some people to say that they were stimulated rather than calmed by the smoking. We know, in a vague way, what effects result from smoking, but we do not know enough as yet to predict accurately just what effects will be felt in a particular instance.[27]

As far as nicotine is concerned, it has been found that it does have definite pharmocological effects on the nervous system and various organs. These are the effects mentioned in the paragraphs above. To say that nicotine is a drug that one can become addicted to is incorrect, however. According to the Surgeon General's report, "Smokers and users of tobacco in other forms usually develop some degree of dependence upon the practice, some to the point where significant emotional disturbances occur if they are deprived of its use. The evidence indicates this dependence to be psychogenic in origin."[28] Smokers, therefore, become habituated to nicotine. The drug does not cause the smokers to become physically dependent upon it.

That the use of nicotine is psychogenic in origin does not mean that smoking can be easily stopped. While there is no specific series of symptoms produced when smokers give up the habit, some people feel "increased nervous excitability, such as restlessness, insomnia, anxiety, tremor, palpitation," and others experience "diminished excitability, such as drowsiness, amnesia, impared concentration and judgment, and diminished pulse."[29]

Psychological and Social Determinants

The psychogenic need for tobacco arises from psychological and social factors. These psychological and social forces are examined next using various demographic variables.

AGE

With respect to age, few children smoke before they reach 12 years, probably less than five percent of the boys and less than one percent of the girls. From the age of 12 on, the proportion of smokers rapidly increases. At the twelfth grade level, between 40 and 55 percent of the young people smoke. At age 25, about 60 percent of the men and 36 percent of the women smoke. The percentage of smokers increases in the late thirties and early forties. After the mid-forties the smoking habit begins to decline. Only about 20 percent of the men and less than 4 percent of the women after 65 smoke.

For years the cigarette industry has been directing its advertising towards young people. Its idea has been that young people are very susceptible to commencing the smoking habit and that once they have started they find it difficult to stop. The cigarette companies as a group, obviously, have been very successful in using this approach.

There are a number of reasons why teenagers start to smoke. During June, 1964, a two day conference called the National Conference on Cigarette Smoking and Youth was held in New York City. The conference, sponsored by the American Cancer Society, the American Public Health Association, the American Heart Association and the National TB Association, was attended by Doctor Terry. It was called to "counteract the ubiquitous social contagion of smoking."[30] At the conference, Doctor Eva J. Salber of the Harvard School of Public Health asked an unrehearsed panel of seven teenagers why they smoked. The seven replies were "feel older; curiosity, then habit; air of intelligence; maturity; maturity and confidence; something to put in mouth; and psychological, gives something to do."

In the report of the Royal College of Physicians of London, *Smoking and Health*, the three most common reasons given by children for smoking is curiosity, wanting to be like others, and that someone just offered them a cigarette.[31] That report also states that parental smoking behavior has a great deal of influence on their children's smoking habits. Studies of both American and English schoolchildren have shown that children of smoking parents are twice as likely to smoke as those of non or ex-smoking parents. Another interesting aspect of young people smoking is that it was found that children who know of the dangers of smoking smoke less than those who do not know anything at all or very little about them. As far as adults are concerned, they continue to smoke cigarettes despite the extensive news which has been appearing for some time declaring that cigarette smoking is injurious to health. Because the smoking habit is something that gets stronger and stronger as one approaches his mid-forties, the Public Health Service intends to aim most of its anti-smoking campaign at very young people.

SOCIOECONOMIC LEVEL

The Advisory Report says that while there does not appear to be any direct correlation between cigarette smoking and income, there tends to be rather consistent evidence that the lower or working classes smoke more and earlier than do the upper classes. This has been found to be true in both the United States and England.

OCCUPATION

Just what principal association exists between occupation and smoking is not known, but it has been found that the unemployed smoke more than the employed and also that smokers seem to change jobs more frequently than do non-smokers.

EDUCATION

Since the studies of occupation and smoking are unclear and occupation is closely associated with education, no definite statements can be made concerning education and smoking.

SEX

As has been mentioned earlier, about 60 percent of the men and 40 percent of the women smoke cigarettes, Very few women smoke cigars and pipes. The Cigar Institute of America estimates that about 60,000 women have joined the ranks of the men cigar smokers.[32] Two of the most celebrated women cigar smokers of today are Greta Garbo and Edie Adams. From statements made by cigar industry men and from my own experience, I have found that most women do not smoke cigars because they think that they have too strong an odor, that the tobacco is too strong, and that they are unfeminine. While a thorough study of cigar smoking and women should be made, women have expressed a great deal about what they think of it. Miss Edie Adams says she used to "contend that cigars should be the last stronghold of the American male. Now it's different — but I do feel that women should wear a cigar like a piece of jewelry — not just like some-well-cigar cigar."[33]

RACE

The proportion of smokers among white and non-whites is about the same.

MARITAL STATUS

According to the Advisory Report, "smoking (of any kind) is most prevalent among the divorced and widowed and least among those who have never been married, except that among persons over 45, never-marrieds are as likely to be smokers as the married."[34]

While certain relationships to smoking as demonstrated above can be found in the demographic variables, no single, overall theory has as yet been extracted from the complex set of interrelationships. Correspondingly, no single smoker personality can be defined. Both the British and American *Smoking and Health* reports mention that such personality traits as extroversion, restlessness, neuroticism, and psychosomatic manifestations, tend to be more characteristic of smokers than of non-smokers. The reports, however, assert that none of the variables found in one group are completely absent in the other. At the present time, therefore, it is impossible to define precisely the smoker's personality as compared to the non-smoker's.

Conclusions

From all of the above, we can conclude that in general young people start to smoke because of such social and psychological factors as wanting to feel grown-up and part of the "mature" crowd. The physiological aspects of oral gratification and the effects of nicotine must also be included. As the person grows older, he becomes habituated to smoking and it becomes part of his way of life. Many who come to depend on smoking to satisfy various social and psychological needs, find it impossible to discontinue the habit, despite such things as health warnings and cancer scares.

Some claims have been made that tobacco is a help towards "good intestinal tone and bowell habits" and also that it reduces the hunger drive (good for overweight people). These benefits of tobacco cannot be discounted, although in a medical sense they are not as consequential as most people think.

Considering all the social and psychological needs, and perhaps some physiological ones as well, that tobacco fulfills, would it not be a proper question to ask, "Ridiculous as it may seem, what would satisfy the psychological needs of the 70,000,000 Americans who smoked in 1963 if they were suddenly deprived of tobacco?"[35] No one knows the answer to that question. In the next chapter we shall examine the ways in which various organizations are trying to reduce, eliminate, or make safe cigarette smoking. From past history as Chapter II has shown, it appears that people are not willing to give up cigarette smoking despite health warnings and cancer scares. As

Chapter III has demonstrated, cigarette smoking plays such an important part in a smoker's social and psychological worlds that he considers the possible harmful effects of it incidental to his overall well-being.

People are going to continue to smoke cigarettes regardless of cancer scares.

ROLE OF GOVERNMENT AND OTHER AGENCIES IN REGARD TO SMOKING AND HEALTH

Thus far in considering whether the so-called cancer scare has created a problem for cigarette manufacturers, we have looked at two aspects of the matter. Both bear particularly upon the question whether smokers who are scared away from cigarettes remain scared or tend to relapse quickly into their old habit patterns. The data given earlier indicate that people are reacting to the 1964 scare as they have done to prior scares. First, when anti-smoking publicity is strong, they reduce their smoking of cigarettes. Then they resume smoking and may even smoke more than they did before as the effects of the publicity wear off. Previously, we saw that cigarettes play such an important part in smokers' social and psychological worlds that only extreme curbs on cigarettes or revolutions in the marketing of cigars or pipes will induce people permanently to stop smoking cigarettes. In the present chapter, we shall take a look at the roles the Government and various other agencies are taking and plan to take in regard to cigarette smoking.

Obviously, whatever was done in the past has not had a lasting effect. We have seen that James I despised the smoking habit. He would not allow anyone in his presence to smoke. Other rulers found that "official objections to smoking were clearly ineffectual,"[36] so they took to decapitating, torturing, and even slitting the lips of smokers.

English Anti-Smoking Campaign

Many years have passed since rulers could be so severe in their punishment of cigarette smokers. Recent governments have, for the most part, only made "official objections" to cigarette smoking. For an example, let us look at the anti-smoking campaign of the British government. In its report, *Smoking and Health*, issued in 1962, the Royal College of Physicians stated that "decisive steps should be taken by the Government to curb the present rising consumption of tobacco, and especially of cigarettes. This action could be taken along the following lines:

(i) More education of the public and especially schoolchildren concerning the hazards of smoking;

(ii) more effective restrictions on the sale of tobacco to children;

(iii) restriction of tobacco advertising;

(iv) wider restriction of smoking in public places;

(v) an increase of tax on cigarettes, perhaps with adjustment of the tax on pipe and cigar tobaccos;

(vi) informing purchasers of the tar and nicotine content of the smoke of cigarettes;

(vii) investigating the value of anti-smoking clinics to help those who find difficulty in giving up smoking.

The report also stated that the dangers from cigarette smoking can be reduced by persuading people to switch to cigars or pipes.

Since the report came out, the English Government has done the following:

1. Passed out a million anti-cigarette posters.
2. Discouraged people from smoking while in hospitals.
3. Dropped cigarette commercials on TV prior to 9 p.m.
4. Sent two film units around to schools to discourage children from smoking.
5. Set up several anti-smoking clinics in a few cities.[38]

The really effective measures of prevention that were recommended by the Royal Physicians included a punitive tax on cigarettes, a strict curtailment and control of cigarette advertising, and the labeling of dangerous ingredients in cigarettes on the packs. These have not been done. Some critics in Britain say the reasons why more effective measures are not being undertaken are the political power of vested interests and also the consequential loss of tax involved. In England nearly 47,000 people are employed in the tobacco industries and $2.5 billion, or 12 percent of the total British revenues, comes from taxes on tobacco products.

We saw previously that in spite of the relatively mild British anti-smoking campaign the English people are smoking more than ever. The only apparent effect that the campaign has had is that it has persuaded most of the people to switch to filtered cigarettes and some even to seek super-filters. Thus, it appears that the English government has in essence done nothing more than raise "official objections" to the cigarette-health problem.

Voluntary Health Agencies

As we noted before, in the United States, only since 1950 have large and definitive studies been made of the smoking-cancer problem. In 1949, the American Cancer Society began to investigate the matter. That organization from 1952-58 conducted an extensive study of the relationship of cancer to smoking. In 1960, the Board of Directors of the Society said that "many studies reported in recent years indicate beyond reasonable doubt that cigarette smoking is the major cause of the unprecedented increase in lung cancer."[39]   On

August 11, 1960, the Society asked the Federal Trade Commission to force cigarette advertisers to put specific information about tar and nicotine contents on their packages. In June, 1961, the Society, together with the American Heart Association, the American Public Health Association and the National Tuberculosis Association, in a letter to President Kennedy asked that a committee be appointed to evaluate and make a decision based on the medical evidence concerning the smoking-health problem, which had been piling up for some time. Under pressure from these groups, the President conferred with the Surgeon General and it was decided to appoint an Advisory Committee to look into the problem.

Thus, before the issuance of the Surgeon General's report early in 1964, many anti-cigarette materials appeared from the organizations mentioned above. In 1963, the American Cancer Society had distributed 25,000 copies of its filmstrip, "To Smoke or Not to Smoke," and 3,500,000 copies of the pamphlet that supplements the film.

Various agencies are working on the state and local levels. In Pennsylvania, kits of anti-smoking materials have been sent to all school districts by the Pennsylvania Department of Public Instruction and the Pennsylvania Department of Health. Included in the kits is a pamphlet called *Resource Unit for Teachers on Smoking and Health*, prepared by the County Superintendent of Schools Office, the Montgomery County Medical Society, the American Cancer Society (Philadelphia Division), the Heart Association of Southeastern Pennsylvania, the Lankenau Hospital, the Department of Health Education, and the Montgomery County Tuberculosis and Health Association.[10] The purpose of the pamphlet is to provide a listing of resources and a lesson plan guide for teaching of secondary schoolchildren about the harmful effects of cigarette smoking.

It is hard to assess just how effective the health agencies have been or are going to be in their drive to discourage youngsters from taking up the cigarette smoking habit. People are now smoking as much as they ever did; but a decline in the number of smokers will appear in a few years if those children who are now being persuaded not to smoke hold to this decision as they come of smoking age. These agencies have not attacked cigars or pipes, but have confined their anti-smoking campaigns to cigarettes. When the author called the Philadelphia Division of the American Cancer Society to obtain information on its stand in the tobacco controcersy, he asked its representative if persons there had given up cigarette smoking. The answer was that everyone was smoking either cigars or pipes. As it appears at this point, the cigarette companies are headed for some trouble from these health agencies, but not too much.

U.S. Public Health Service

The stand of the U.S. Public Health Service came rather late. Not until 1959 did the agency "assess the then available evidence linking smoking with health and make its findings known to the professions and the public."[41] From 1959 until the issuance of the Advisory Committee's report, the Surgeon General spoke out against cigarette smoking on several occasions. The Advisory Report condemned cigarette smoking but did not include any section covering preventive measures by the Government as had the English report.

With respect to preventive measures, the Government's position was made clearer by the Surgeon General himself in an address delivered to the National Press Club in Washington, D.C.[41]   In summary he said that:

1. The Public Health Service plan of educating the American People, particularly teenagers and younger, to stop smoking cigarettes was long range, at least a ten year program.

2. Representatives of the major voluntary health agencies have been contacted by the Service and arrangements were made to reinforce but not duplicate their anti-cigarette campaigns.

3. The childrens Bureau had made plans for a National Conference on smoking and youth.

4. The Federal Trade Commission was planning to curb cigarette advertising and labeling.

5. The Department of Agriculture was setting up a program of research into trying to develop tobaccos embodying a smaller proportion of cancer causing agents.

6. A National Clearing House on Smoking and Health would be established to provide visual aids, pamphlets, and other materials for public and professional education on the hazards of cigarette smoking.

7. The Service expected to spend around 8.5 million dollars during the 1965 fiscal year on anti-smoking campaigns.

Federal Trade Commission

The only action mentioned above that would directly restrict the cigarette companies was action by the FTC. On January 18, 1964, the FTC announced proposed regulations concerning cigarette advertising and labeling.[43] The proposed rules were as follows:

"Rule 1. Either one of the following statements shall appear, clearly and prominently, in every cigarette advertisement and on every pack, box, carton and other container in which cigarettes are sold to the public:

(a) CAUTION: — CIGARETTE SMOKING IS A HEALTH HAZARD: The Surgeon General's Advisory Committee on Smoking and Health has found that 'cigarette smoking contributes substantially to mortality from certain specific diseases and to the overall death rate': or

(b) CAUTION: Cigarette smoking is dangerous to health. It may cause death from cancer and other diseases."[44]

"Rule 2. No cigarette advertisement (or label) shall state or imply, by words, pictures, symbols, sounds, devices or demonstrations, or any combination thereof, that smoking the advertised cigarettes

(a) promotes good health or physical well-being,

(b) is not a hazard to health, *or*

(c) is less of a hazard to health than smoking other brands, except that a specific and factual claim respecting the health consequences of smoking the advertised cigarettes may be advertised if

(1) the advertiser, before making the claim, has substantial and reliable evidence to prove the accuracy and significance of the claim, *and*

(2) all facts material to the health consequences of smoking advertised cigarettes are clearly, prominently and intelligibly disclosed in close conjunction with the claim."[45]

"Rule 3. No cigarette advertisement (or label) shall contain any statement as to the quantity of any cigarette-smoke ingredients (e.e.g., tars and nicotine) which has not been verified in accordance with the uniform and reliable testing procedure approved by the Federal Trade Commission."[46]

When the proposed rules, effective at the end of 1964, were made public in January, the cigarette companies went into an uproar. One of the first questions asked by the cigarette men was, "Does the FTC have the authority to require the cigarette industry to comply with the proposed regulations?" The Tobacco Institute, acting on behalf of the cigarette companies, said that if the regulations were put into effect it would take the matter to the Supreme Court. Bills then went to Congress in order to give the FTC authority to regulate that industry. As will be explained shortly, a court battle is still anticipated.

After blasting out against the FTC and the Public Health Service, the cigarette industry quieted down and cleverly started devising an industry code aimed at softening the FTC's requirements. On April 27, 1964, in their attempt to forestall the FTC, nine major U.S. cigarette manufacturers announced an Industry Code. This code prohibits advertising that makes cigarettes appear to be "essential to social prominence, distinction, success or sexual attraction."[47] The code also prohibits the advertising of cigarettes in college newspapers, the distribution of cigarettes on campuses, the use of models looking under 25 in ads, the use of testimonials from athletes and other people who appeal to teenagers, and statements about health, except as substantiated by "valid scientific data." Penalties up to $100,000 can be levied against a cigarette advertiser if he breaks the code. This industry has set up a group, headed by Robert Meyner, former governor from New Jersey, to monitor the ads and act against violations.

The Value Line Investment Survey has said that "the cigarette industry's code has penalties probably greater than if the FTC regulated their advertising."[48]   Despite the penalties, whether the industry's code actually will discourage youngsters from smoking is highly doubtful since teenagers imitate adults in that respect. In addition, the code obviously softened the FTC's position considerably. Now all that the FTC is requiring is that cigarette smoking is injurious to health. In contrast to what the FTC demanded in January, cigarette companies are pretty much able to say what they want and in the size of print that they want, except that in the words of Paul Rand Dixon, Chairman of the FTC, "The Commission believes that the individual advertisers should be free to formulate the required disclosure in a fully conspicuous manner."[49] Just what the cigarette companies were going to come up with was anybody's guess, but as far as the FTC was concerned, it has given them much more latitude than was previously offered.

Another indication of the softening of the FTC is that on June 24, Mr. Dixon announced during testimony before the House Commerce Committee that the advertising requirement would not be effective until July 1, 1965.[50] The effective date for the advertising rule has been postponed because of pressure from tobacco men and their lobbyists. The FTC has said that until July 1, 1965, it is interested in receiving the pros and cons of the advertising rule from all interested persons. One can argue, if he is cynical enough, that before that time, enough pressure can be brought upon the FTC to modify even more the already mild, health warning advertisement requirement. What will probably result are health warnings that are difficult to find in the ads because of their small print and that really do not tell the smoker that there is a definite risk in cigarette smoking.

In addition to the probability that further softening of the health warning requirements will probably occur before the effective dates in 1965, those dates themselves might be postponed still further. As was mentioned earlier, the Tobacco Institute early this year warned the FTC that it would take the cigarette labeling and advertising matter to the Supreme Court. As regards the possible court fights ahead and extension of the required dates for the warnings, the *U.S. News & World Report* has stated that "Mr. Dixon said the effective dates might be delayed as much as four years by court action. Tobacco-industry officials immediately drafted a suit challenging the legality of the order. The FTC did not spell out specific language for the warnings. The Commerce Committee Chairman, Representative Oren Harris (Dem.), of Arkansas, questioned the FTC's authority to issue the rule. Mr. Dixon insisted that the FTC is empowered under the present law to regulate both labeling and advertising where public health is a factor."[51]

Other Anti-Smoking Elements

So far, we have examined the activities of such voluntary health agencies as the American Cancer Society and the American Heart Association, of the Public Health Service, and of the Federal Trade

Commission. We have seen that the activities of the above to deter cigarette smoking have not been too strong, yet they do provide some marketing opportunity for the cigar industry. Other forces against cigarettes which must be considered are magizines, advertising agencies, and broadcasting stations.

As far as magazines are concerned, the *Reader's Digest* and *Consumer Reports* have been the leaders against cigarette smoking. The Consumers Union says that you should, of course, quit smoking altogether if you can. If you can't, try cigars or a pipe.

Several advertising agencies do not carry cigarette accounts and more might follow not only because of the health issue, but also because of the risks. On February 6, 1965 William Bernbach, President of Doyle, Dane and Bernbach, said that "in view of the recent report by the U.S. Surgeon General, our present position is that we would not accept a cigarette account."[52] Shortly thereafter, Ogilvy, Benson and Mather announced that it would not handle cigarette accounts. An example of the risks involved is provided by the Leo Burnett agency.[53] In 1964 it was hit with a five million dollar suit from a person claiming that its longtime association with Philip Morris cigarettes, advertised as being non-irritating to the throat, was partly responsible for his developing lung cancer.

The broadcasters are taking some notice of the situation also. Leroy Collins, President of the National Association of Broadcasters blasted the American Tobacco Company's Lucky advertising, "Luckies separate the men from the boys but not from the girls."[54] He called that slogan a "brazen, cynical flouting of the concern of millions of parents about their children starting smoking habits. . . ." Since the source of their revenue comes from advertising, and cigarette advertising provides TV with eight percent its annual gross, the three TV networks have remained fairly quiet, although all gave full coverage to the Surgeon General's report when it came out. Because of the National Association of Broadcasters' attack on cigarette ads which encourage young people to smoke and because of the cigarette Industry Code, the American Tobacco Company (Lucky Strikes, Pall Mall) has decided to drop a five million dollar a year sponsorship of exports on TV and radio when present contracts run out. (1965)

The following are several other developments against cigarette smoking:

1. The defense department prohibits cigarette distribution to servicemen or their families while in Government Hospitals

2. Some insurance companies, for example, The State Mutual of America, have raised life insurance premiums for cigarette smokers but not for pipe and cigar smokers.

3. Because of cigarette-cancer scare, some airline companies now allow inflight smoking of cigars and pipes.

4. The House Rules Committee voted against a bill that

would establish a Government research center for the investigation of the cancer-health problem.

Conclusions

When one considers all that has been said so far in this reading he is likely to conclude that the antismoking campaign in the United States has been very much like that in England, and with just about the same results. There has been no significant talk here of prohibiting the sale of cigarettes, not even to teenagers, nor putting a high tax on them, or even prohibiting their advertising, (in 1965). All in all, little more than official objections have been raised despite the power of the FTC, the Justice Department, The Food and Drug Administration, the Public Health Service, and the Department of Health, Education and Welfare. The American anti-smoking campaign has not been able to get off the ground because of the efforts of the cigarette industry and vested interests. Those efforts are examined later.

WHAT THE CIGARETTE COMPANIES DID

We saw that the anti-cigarette activities of the government and other agencies have not been very effective at this point of time. People are back to smoking as much as ever. In order to understand how much the cigar industry might gain from the anti-cigarette campaigns being carried out, it is necessary to examine what the cigarette companies have done and are doing to counteract slumping sales produced in the wake of cancer scares.

Anti-Medical Claims, Councils, Codes

At the beginning of the 1953-54 cancer scare, cigarette companies protested vehemently against the anti-cigarette medical claims. As we saw earlier they vociferated against the findings of the Surgeon General's report when if first touched off the 1965 scare.

After the industry quieted down in 1954, it announced the founding of the Tobacco Industry Research Committee, now called the Council for Tobacco Research. The purpose behind the inception of the Research Committee was to give the public the idea that the cigarette industry was attempting to make cigarettes "safe" for the smoker and such cigarettes would probably be soon forthcoming.

In 1964, the industry announced the formulation of an Industry Code which will be discussed shortly. By showing the cigarette industry's good intentions, both the Council and the Code were devised to relieve the pressure of the anti-cigarette forces.

Filters

In addition to attempting to obscure the medical problem through the creation of the Council and Code, the cigarette industry has further clouded the issue by marketing new, filtered cigarettes. In 1954 Kent cigarette with the micronite filter was introduced. Its filtering qualities were so widely advertised that Kent has become an all-time seller. Since Kent first came out, there has been a rapid increase in the number and types of filtered brands on the market. How filtered cigarettes have increased is shown in Table 3.

CIGARETTE PRODUCTION
(In Billions)

Year	Total Output	Filter Output	Percent of Total
1952	435.5	5.6	1.3
53	423.1	12.4	2.9
54	401.8	36.9	9.2
55	412.3	77.0	18.7
56	424.2	116.9	27.6
58	470.0	213.0	45.3
60	506.9	258.0	50.9
62	535.5	292.5	54.6
63	550.6	319.1	57.9

Table 4 lists the filtered and nonfiltered cigarette brands being marketed after the 1963 scare. The success of the filters stems from the fact that people think that they are safer than the non-filter types.

Filters			Non-Filters
Winston	Tareyton	Lark	Pall Mall
Salem	Raleigh	Paxton	Camel
Kent	Parliament	Montclair	Lucky Strikes
Marlboro	Newport	Benson & Hedges	Chesterfield
L & M	Old Gold	Spring	Philip Morris
Viceroy	Belair	Oasis	York
Kool	Alpine	Life	Wings
Cavalier	Du Maurier	Hit Parade	Some Others

Source: "Cigarette Smokers still Puffing Away," *Business Week*, December 14, 1965, p. 149.

As Kent helped the cigarette industry to find its way out of the crisis of 1953 and 1954, so helping in the 1964 crisis are the charcoal filtered brands. American Tobacco in 1958, marketed the first charcoal filter in its Tareyton brand. Then, in 1963, Liggett and Myers introduced its charcoal filtered brand, Lark, which has been very successful. Charcoal filtered brands introduced since the beginning of this year include Carlton from American Tobacco, Tempo from R. J. Reynolds, and Multifilter Philip Morris from Philip Morris. Thus the barrage of new brands with new filters has given the public the impression that the cigarette industry is constantly improving upon its cigarettes and making them safer all the time.

Cigarette Advertising

What the cigarette companies do primarily, then, is to counteract anti-cigarette publicity by saying that medical evidence does not support the adverse conclusions reached, by establishing research councils and codes to promote their goodwill and get anti-cigarette forces from pressuring them, and, at the same time, by inundating the market with new brands and filters in the hope that people will continue to smoke, and smoke more as the cancer scare dies. All of the above, of course, are reflected in the industry's publicity and advertising.

The companies do not mention anything about health claims, as they did in the forties and early fifties. In 1953, copy appeared such as "Guard against Throat Scratch"[55] (Pall Mall theme) and "For a full year now a medical specialist has given a group of Chesterfield smokers thorough examinations every two months: He reports no adverse effects to their noses, throats or sinuses from smoking Chesterfields."[56]   P. Lorillard, maker of Old Gold, dropped the medical claim gimmick during the 1953-54 scare and used the slogan saying "No doggone medical claims . . . Old Gold is man's best friend for a treat instead of a treatment."[57] Philip Morris was the last of the cigarette manufacturers to drop medical claims; this occured at the end of 1954. After that, the companies had ads implying rather than stating that cigarette smoking brought such things as social success, sex appeal, and a young, healthful, robust physical constitution to the cigarette smoker.

Under the Industry Code cigarette advertising is not supposed to depict cigarette smoking "as essential to social prominence, distinction, success, or sexual attraction." Nevertheless, cigarette ads still depict healthy and good looking, young people (even though 25 or slightly over) smoking cigarettes in meadow scenes with streams rushing by (Salem ads, for example). While the Industry Code is still in effect, therefore, it appears as if the ads are saying everything they always did, although their direction to teenagers has been diverted. This action by the cigarette companies is an evasive maneuver against the government agencies that are attempting to curb cigarette smoking.

Great Charcoal Derby

It was noted earlier that the FTC has dropped its requirement that a cigarette could not imply on its package or label that it was safer than any other. Carlton cigarette, manufactured by American Tobacco, was first introduced in January, 1965, and its tar and nicotine contents were printed on its package. This cigarette has been a big seller probably because people think that since the company has called attention to its tar and nicotine levels then it must be a safer cigarette than the others. Promotionwise, this is a very clever move. Both the FTC and the Industry Code have been circumvented.

Other manufacturers have realized that there are marketing opportunities associated with the charcoal filtered cigarettes and their low nicotine level and tar contents. This realization has touched off what is called the "Great Charcoal Derby"[58]

As far as filters are concerned, the Surgeon General's report said nothing except that "it has been reported that a filter containing special carbon granules removes gaseous constituents which depress ciliary activity."[59] Although no one knows for sure that the "depression of ciliary activity" is a cause of cancer, the improvement of filters was a move in the right direction. Sen. Cooper of Kentucky wrote to the Surgeon General after the Advisory Committee's report came out and asked him to explain the Committee's position in regards to filters. Dr. Terry replied that the "filters in common use do remove a variable portion of tars and nicotine" and that "the Committee felt that the development of better filters or more selective filters is a promising avenue for further development."[60] Because no one knew how effective the charcoal filters were, the cigarette companies were able to use them as a crutch to keep up sales.

Consumers Union's view on the matter is that "there is no filter that removes the potentially cancer causing materials in burning cigarettes."[61] Since the FTC and the Public Health Service have not taken any positive stand on the matter, the cigarette companies apparently have found their golden egg in the charcoal filter.

Research

As far as research is concerned, the tobacco industry claims that the Council for Tobacco Research has made grants "to over 155 scientists in over 100 hospitals, universities, and research institutions. . . . that now total $7,250,000."[62] These are given "to independent scientists who are assured complete scientific freedom in conducting their research" and in "reporting or publishing their findings in the accepted scientific manner. . . " The industry also pledged in 1965 $10 million to the American Medical Association to conduct research. The Public Health Service spends $3,300,000 a year on smoking studies. Doctor Terry has estimated at least 105 research projects were done on this question of smoking and health.[63] In addition to the abovementioned agencies doing research on the problem, various filter and additive companies who have products used by cigarette industry conducted research themselves. (Celanese, Eastman Kodak, Reynolds Metals, and Union Carbide).

Cigarette Industry Participation In the Cigar Market

Of the six largest cigarette companies (R. J. Reynolds, American Tobacco, Brown and Williamson, P. Lorillard, Laggert and Myers, and Philip Morris) only American Tobacco and Philip Morris have had any actual dealings in the cigar market. American Tobacco, as we have seen, makes Roi-Tan, Antonio λ Cleopatra, and La Corona; but since 95 percent of its sales come from cigarettes, it has not said anything against cigarettes in its cigar ads. Philip Morris markets a large cigar under the Benson & Hedges label. These cigarette companies, however, produce the bulk of the cigarette-size cigars being manufactured today. Of the big cigar companies, only DWG Cigar, Stephano Bros. and Bayuk make cigarette-size cigars. Cigarette-size cigars being made by cigarette companies are as follows: American Tobacco — Little Roi-Tan; Philip Morris — Puritan Cigarettos and Benson & Hedges little cigars; P. Lorrillard — Omega, Madison, Between-The-Acts and Erik; and U.S. Tobacco, Little Sano. In addition to the cigarette-size cigars, American Tobacco has introduced Half & Half pipe tobacco cigarettes, and Philip Morris has brought out Puritan pipe tobacco cigarettes.

How successful these new products will be over the next few years is not known, but the more popular cigars become the more the cigarette companies will adjust their facilities to the making of cigars, especially of smaller ones. Therefore, the very success of the cigar might cause the giant cigarette companies to enter the cigar market and produce real competition there.

Political Influence and Vested Interests

Thus far we have seen that the cigarette industry is doing a pretty effective job in winding its way through the anti-cigarette obstacle path set up for it by the cancer scare. Previously, the author stated that in England vested interests and taxes have forced anti-cigarette agencies to yield considerably in their positions. When we analyze the effectiveness of the cigarette companies in maintaining their positions, we must also consider the political influence which they can muster. Just look at what tobacco means to America and consider that the sales of cigars in 1963, were only $660 million.

"Around 70 million Americans in 1963 bought:
More than 523 billion cigarettes, 14.9 billion more than in 1962;
7.1 billion cigars — up 115 million;
69.5 million lbs. of smoking tobacco;
64.8 million lbs. of chewing tobacco;

More than 32.5 million pounds of snuff.

Tobacco users spent $8.08 billion for cigarettes and other tobacco products — up $326 million over 1962.

About 750,000 farm families in 21 states received $1.3 billion for tobacco crops.

Tobacco is the fifth largest cash crop — after cotton, wheat, corn, and soybeans.

More than 4,500 wholesalers handle tobacco products distribution.

More than 96,000 are employed in tobacco manufactoring plants. Their wages exceed $450 million a year.

There are 500 tobacco factories operating in 30 states.

Net assets of publicly-held tobacco companies are $4 billion, with 400,000 stockbrokers.

The United States sells more than 28 percent of the tobacco leaf bought in free world markets — some 505 billion pounds. This was up 36 million pounds in 1962 and valued at $405 million.

The United States is the world's leading exporter of cigarettes, shipping 23.2 billion in 1963, valued at over $105 million compared with $68 million in 1959.

About 1.5 million businesses share in the tobacco trade, supplying equipment, materials, transport, distribution, and merchandising services in every part of the country.

In the fiscal 1963, the $3,317,126 collected in excises on tobacco products — chiefly cigarettes — went to:

Federal government	$2,079,237,000
State governments	1,196,958,000
Municipal governments	40,931,000

The tobacco industry annually uses:

Over 40 million pounds of moisture proof cellophane (following only the bakery and meat industry in volume)

More than 71 million pounds of aluminum foil

Nearly 27 billion printed packs and 2.7 billion cartons."[64]

In addition to the above, consider also that the 750,000 farm families in the 21 tobacco producing states are represented by senators and representatives who do fight when restrictions that might be placed on the tobacco industry by the Federal government are brought before Congress. After the Surgeon General's report came out, Senator John J. Williams of Delaware, introduced a bill in Congress that would have cut out the Federal Tobacco price support program. Tobacco has been a protected crop for 30 years, and in 1963, tobacco farmers received $40 million from the Government.[65] All in all, about 17 million Americans receive all or part of their incomes from tobacco. It is not hard to see why the bill was defeated.

TV and Radio Ban in 1971

Now let us turn to more recent times, the biggest blow to the cigarette companies was the TV and Radio ban in January of 1971.

To see what effects this legislation had, I will turn to the May, 1971 *Business Week* for a complete analysis. "The $10.6 billion cigarette industry is like a kid's bell-bottom punch toy. No sooner is it knocked flat than it is back up again, grinning and ready for another blow."

One of the industry's hardest smacks came in January of 1971 when Congress banned all radio and television cigarette advertising which was then running at about $225 million annually, or 75 percent of the industry's ad budget. The obvious question was: How would this affect sales? In May of 1971 tobacco companies found out, and the answer had them beaming. According to figures released by the Internal Revenue Service, tobacco warehouse shipments reached a record 131.5 billion cigarettes from January 1 through March 31 of 1971, a gain of six percent over the first quarter of 1970. What is more, tobacco companies claim that the momentum has carried into April and May of 1971. The momentum compares with an over-all four percent sales gain for 1970, which followed two straight years of decline.

"I think it's because people are just tired of hearing that practically everything they eat or drink is harmful." says Curtiss H. Judge, president of the Lorillard Div. of Loew's Corp. "Besides they enjoy smoking." Shrugs James C. Bowling, vice president of Philip Morris, Inc., "We never thought that the electronic media were essential to sales anyway." At most, adds William S. Smith, president of R. J. Reynolds Tobacco Co., the broadcast media "merely induce smokers to switch brands," not to increase total consumption. Equally to the point, Kenneth McAllister, president of the Cigarette Division of Liggett & Myers, Inc. pins the industry's strength on "news marketing techniques and promotions".

Strategy

The industry's marketing, in fact, has shifted completely. With no television to promote new brands, only four new cigarettes came on the market in the first quarter: Philip Morris's News Leaf, American Tobacco's Maryland 100's, Liggett & Meyers' Chesterfield Filter, and Reynolds' Vantage Menthol. During the same period last year, there were seven new brands or types. "It's more difficult now to introduce a new brand," admits Reynolds' Smith. "But that doesn't mean there will be no new brands. You just won't be able to get the same great initial awareness."

The industry also chopped its advertising and promotion spending an average of 25 percent to 30 percent and began pumping more money into other media. Billboard cigarette advertising, which grew from 8.9 million in 1969 to 16.2 million in 1970 and $30 million in 1971. Newspaper cigarette advertising was projected at 40-50 million dollars in 1971 as compared to $20 million in 1970. The other big gainer was magizines. In the first quarter of 1971 according to Publishers Information Bureau some 90 measured magazines ran

1,005 pages of cigarette ads worth $26.9 million. This represented a 162 percent increase in pages and 144 percent increase in dollars.

At the same time the industry was moving deeper into special giveaways and promotions. Brown & Williamson Tobacco Corp. is now offering Kool smokers a $119 sailboat for $88. American Tobacco is selling a special "Activated charcoal water filter" for $5; it clamps onto a faucet and permits the Tareyton buyer to "enjoy better-tasting tap water." Philip Morris recently offered a $4.50 dictionary to its Parliament smokers. They also distributed 7.3 million copies of a free 16 page cookbook in *Life* magazine. Another 1.5 million copies were given away in supermarkets.

The industry's biggest single promotion is sporting events. "That's where the smokers are," says Philip Morris' Bowling Team. Besides, adds Daniel Provost, a spokesman for Liggett & Myers, "It sure generates great publicity." Philip Morris is sponsoring everything from auto and ski racing to women's tennis championships.

Liggett & Myers is focusing mainly on auto racing. "From a marketing view" says L & M's McAllister, "We're convinced that racing is a way to go." This year, L&M will sponsor the "L&M Continental 5000 Championship," a series of eight races at some of the country's best tracks and in its top marketing areas. L&M has even hired Jackie Stewart, the 1969 world champion racing driver, and is investing more than $125,000 to enter the L&M car in the Canadian-American Challenge Cup championships.

Today's sportingest tobacco company is R. J. Reynolds, the country's No. 1 cigarette maker. Along with some bowling tournaments, Reynolds will participate in 36 different stock-car races and spend more than $2 million on their advertising promotion and winners' purses. "I like racing," explains Smith. "It's damned exciting. It is also good business." "Like Winston," says Robert Odear, product brand manager for Winston, "Auto racing is particularly strong in the south. Auto racing is male-oriented and so is Winston. The demographics of Winston and auto racing match up, as well, in age and education."

To promote Reynolds' biggest race of the year — The first Annual Winston 500 ($160,000) in Talladega, Alabama, Reynolds put up hundreds of billboards in Tennessee, Georgia, and South Carolina, bought full-page color ads in *Road & Track* and other racing magazines and plastered the area around Talladega with posters, flags, banners and car stickers. Reynolds also saw to it that local cigarette-vending machines were filled only with Reynolds cigarettes, and that they stayed filled. "We make sure the products are around," says Smith. "These people are loyal to racing and products that support racing."

The payoff came with paid attendance of 40,000 at $15 and $25 a head. This compared with 20,000 fans last year, when the race was called the Alabama 500. Thanks partly to a blizzard of press releases and free Winston lighters and cartons of cigarettes, Reynolds also garnered its share of newspaper coverage.

The only place Reynolds did not seek publicity was on television, even though ABC-TV covered the race. Reynolds did not send any press notices to radio or TV stations. "If they covered the race," says Peter Allen, director of corporate communications, "they got it off the wire services. During the race not one of the Winston signs slipped into TV camera range, and the announcer even referred to the race as the Alabama 500. The nearest thing to a tip-off were the crashwall signs reading "W — 500".

Reynolds and other tobacco companies have been playing it closely and cautiously in their publicity and advertising to avoid incurring any more wrath in Washington. Right now, the Federal Trade commission is considering a mandatory decree that a strong health warning be put on all cigarette companies' ads after July 1, 1971. It would read: "Warning—Cigarette smoking is dangerous to health and may cause death from cancer, coronary heart disease, chronic bronchitis, pulmonary emphysema, and other diseases."

To head off such a stiff labeling, most of the nine major U.S. cigarette makers have agreed voluntarily to include a health warning presumably far milder. But this has not placated their enemies.

Senator Frank Moss (D. Utah), prime sponsor of the 1970 law banning broadcast ads, called the industry's first quarter ad increases "shocking". By greatly expanding their print and billboard advertising, Moss said, cigarette makers showed "callous disregard for expressed Congressional intent and public opinion." The Moss comment drew a swift reply from Joseph F. Culman, Chairman and Chief Executive of Philip Morris. Cullman claimed that because of the advertising broadcast ban, total cigarette advertising had been "drastically reduced" — in PM's case, by more than 200 percent — and that magazine figures "give a misleading impression", since relatively little cigarette advertising appeared in magazines prior to the ban.

The industry is also fretting about state and local legislators who are making life miserable by hiking cigarette taxes. Today the country's average cigarette tax per package is 19¢. Besides raising prices and driving an occasional customer, tax increases spur cigarette bootlegging and hijacking. In New York City alone, distributors now claim that more than one out of every five packs of cigarettes sold is either stolen from local distributors or bootlegged from low tax states. "Since pushing drugs interstate has become a federal crime. a lot of the pushers are going into the cigarette business," says Phillip Cheled, a criminal investigator for the Philadelphia branch of the Pennsylvania cigarette tax department. "Cigarettes are light, clean and up till now, not very hard to get rid of." Some courts tend to go easy on violators. Not only have there been no successful prosecutions of cigarette smugglers in Pennsylvania, but one judge prefaced his dismissal of a case with the observation that he felt "sorry that the taxes are so damned high here."

The cigarette industry feels sorry, too. But it is long inured to what it considers harassment. It also takes comfort both in a market that shows few signs of weakening, and in a diversification program that minimizes its dependence on tobacco. Like a smoker who can only take one puff at a time, tobacco men are content to take each crisis as it comes — and meantime go patiently and profitably on their way."[66]

Conclusion

After studying all the facts in putting this paper together, I have come up with one conclusion I believe holds: People will go right on smoking despite efforts to deter smokers by the government or any body else.

The reason I believe this is because of the way people have reacted to past cancer scares; because of their accustomed dependence on cigarettes for psychological and social needs; because of the really clever job the cigarette industry does in the face of cancer scares (including its ability to muster a sizeable force against those who would consider detering the sale of cigarettes). Also, the government has reached what I believe to be the end of the line for harrassing the cigarette industry. There is not much left for them to do except ban sales altogether, which isn't probable.

So cigarettes are here to stay. With a tremendous market, and combat experience against two past cancer scares, there will be no stopping this still growing industry.

QUESTIONS FOR DISCUSSION

1. What is the background of the Surgeon-General's report that linked cancer to cigarette smoking?

2. In your opinion were the Surgeon-General's figures on heightened mortality found amongst smokers convincing? Were the contentions absolutly proven in a scientific sense? Why or why not?

3. What is the psychological basis for smoking? In your opinion are the gratifications obtained from smoking sufficiently intense to justify the risk involved?

4. What reactions did the report evoke from the government? Were they effective?

5. Why did self-policing not work better?

6. As a result of all the controversy, did people stop smoking? How do you account for the paradox? What can we learn from this case which will be useful in controlling dangerous or socially undesirable products in the future?

FOOTNOTES

1. "Teenagers Express Doubt that Ads Dispose them to Cigarette Smoking," *Advertising Age* (July 20, 1964), p. 124.

2. Philip Morris, Burnett, Tobacco Institute, Hit in Multimillion Dollar Cancer Law Suit," *Advertising Age* (July 20, 1964), p. 85.

3. Royal College of Physicians of London, *Smoking and Health in Relation of the Lung Cancer and Other Diseases* (New York: Pitman Publishing Corporation), p. 42.

4. "The Ex-Inhalers," *Business Week* (February 8, 1964), p. 2.

5. Megary, J.D., *The Cancer Scare and Its Effect on the Cigarette Industry* (University of Pennsylvania Press, 1965), p. 109.

6. "Questions, Findings of Smoking Study," *The New York Times* (April 15, 1964), p. 70.

7. U.S. Department of Agriculture, Agriculture Marketing Service, *Annual Report on Tobacco Statistics* (1963), p. 25.

8. *Ibid.*

9. *Ibid.*, p. 31.

10. *Ibid.*

11. *Ibid.*

12. *Ibid.*

13. *Ibid.*

14. *Ibid.*, p. 36

15. *Ibid.*, p. 33

16. Questions, *op. cit.*, p. 49.

17. Steinheuser, Emil J. "But Statistics are Disputed," *New York Journal American* (January 12, 1964).

18. "Crash Effort for a Safer Cigarette," *Saturday Evening Post* (April 18, 1964), p. 21.

19. Megary, *op. cit.*, p. 34.

20. "Cigar Manufacturers Association of America, Inc., *CMA Statistical Record.*

21. Megary, *op. cit.*, p. 14.

22. *Ibid.*, Bibliogrpahy.

23. "Smoking, the Government Report," *Time* (January 17, 1964), p. 84.

24. "Some Facts About the Tobacco Industry," *Tobacco News* (March, 1964), p. 86.

25. U.S. Department of Agriculture, *op. cit.*, p. 1.

26. U.S. Public Health Service, *Smoking and Health Report of the Advisory Committee to the Surgeon General of the Public Health Service* (Washington: U.S. Government Printing Office, 1964), p. 350.

27. *Ibid.*

28. *Ibid.*

29. *Ibid.* p. 352.

30. Teenagers Express, *op. cit.*, p. 8.

31. Royal College of Physicians, *op. cit.*, p. 39.

32. "The Female Puffer," *Newsweek* (March 23, 1964), p. 80.

33. *Ibid.*, p. 81

34. U.S. Public Health Service, *op. cit.*, p. 364.

35. *Ibid.*, p. 355.

36. Brooks, Jerome E., *The Mighty Leaf: Tobacco through the Ages* (Boston: Little, Brown and Co., 1952), p. 76.

37. Royal College of Physicians, *op. cit.*, p. 58.

38. "Smoking, Health, and a Giant Industry," *U.S. News and World Report* (December 2, 1963), p. 86.

39. American Cancer Society, et. al., *Resource Unit for Teachers on Smoking and Health* (1963), p. 1

40. American Cancer Society, *Cigarette Smoking and Cancer* (New York: American Cancer Society, Inc., 1963), p. 1.

41. U.S. Public Health Service, *op. cit.*, p. v

42. Terry, Luther L., Surgeon General, U.S. Public Health Service, Excerpts from address delivered at reception and the club luncheon of The National Press Club. (February 25, 1964), p. 2.

43. Federal Trade Commission, "FTC Announces Proposed Trade Regulation Rules Governing Future Advertising and Labeling of Cigarettes" (News Release, Washington, January 18, 1964), p. 0.

44. *Ibid.*, p. 1.

45. *Ibid.*, p. 2.

46. *Ibid.*, p. 3.

47. U.S. Public Health Service, *op. cit.*, p. 85.

48. "Tobacco Industry," *The Value Line Investment Survey* (July 10, 1964), p. 1214.

49. "FTC Demands Cancer Warning on Labels," *Sponsor* (June 29, 1964), p. 17.

50. "Ahead: Court Fight over Cigarette Warnings," *U.S. News and World Report* (July 6, 1964), p. 11.

51. *Ibid.*

52. "DDB won't Handle Cigarette Client, Bernbach Says," *Advertising Age* (February 10, 1964), p. 91.

53. Philip Morris, Burnett, *op. cit.*, p. 6.

54. "Cigarette Smokers Still Puffing Away," *Business Week* (December 14, 1963), p. 150.

55. Megary, *op. cit.*, p. 61.

56. *Ibid.*, p. 64.

57. Ibid., p. 73.

58. Crash Effort, *op. cit.*, p. 22.

59. "Dangers in Smoking," *Consumers Report Annual 1963-64* (September, 1963), p. 51.

60. Little, Clarence Cook, *Report of the Scientific Director* (New York: The Council for Tobacco Research, 1964), Inside Front Cover.

61. *Ibid.*

62. *Ibid.*

63. Terry, *op. cit.*, p. 2.

64. Some Facts, *op. cit.*, p. 4.

65. American Cancer Society, Cigarette Smoking, *op. cit.*, pp. 56-57.

PART VI
REACTIONS OF BUSINESS
TO THE NEW CONSUMERISM

In this section we examine the ways in which American business has reacted to the new consumer movement.

Business men in the early 1970's must have felt besieged from all sides. A bright, aggressive young lawyer, Ralph Nader, began the attack by accusing the automobile industry of not paying sufficient attention to safety. The scope of his attack rapidly spread to many other areas: the FTC, ICC, Congress, nursing homes, the food industry, and many others. A new species of activist, the consumer advocate, was born, and others followed Nader's lead, mounting other attacks on business and government.

Then, the ecology movement came along in the Spring of 1970, and many businessmen found themselves under attack for being polluters, spoilers, rapacious "grab the money and run" operators who, it was charged, were rapidly depleting our irreplacable resources and were leaving the country a wasteland in the process.

Advertising was attacked: The Federal Trade Commission laid out stricter regulations for truth in advertising claims, made companies file proof of tangible claims, and, where the FTC deemed that false claims had been made in the past, ordered the firms concerned to run a certain proportion of corrective advertising to disabuse the public's mind.

Finally, consumers became truculent about abuses uncovered by the activists. In particular, they deplored what they perceived to be steadily declining product quality. They were suspicious that artificial obsolescence was being built into "durable" products they were buying. This growing resentment towards business on the part of the public resulted in a great rise in complaints and individual damage suits; the specter of class suits rose on the horizon.

In reaction to all this, business hastened to take measures to deal more effectively with the criticism and consumer complaints. This section analyzes the nature and direction of this reaction.

E. B. Weiss surveys methods in which specific companies are dealing with the situation. One method of establishing machinery to handle complaints was through an adaptation of the ombudsman system. Established as early as 1823 in Sweden, this system elicited little attention outside of Scandanavia until the late 1960's. Then, a number of Canadian provinces and countries such as Great Britain and Australia began to establish ombudsman systems as a part of the government process. Business executives, casting about for guide lines helpful in setting up consumer relations departments of their own, adopted the state ombudsman system, modifying it where appropriate.

Therefore, we first look at what a government system is like; the description and analysis published by the Royal Bank of Canada is short, but quite complete. Then Professor Schutte examines how private business enterprises have adapted the system to their needs, and with what difficulties and results. Mr. Sloan's article brings us up-to-date on the matter, and gives us some idea of what the rush to establish consumer relations departments is costing the consumer.

The section closes with a *Business Week* analysis of progress to date in setting up social audits of company activities. The idea of a social audit is quite new, and many businessmen are still uninformed about it.

It is hoped that this progress report will enlighten the reader as to what is entailed by a corporate social audit. He might well ponder "is it worth all the trouble and expense"?[1]

FOOTNOTE

1. For those wishing more information about the social audit, we recommend: Raymond A. Bauer and D. T. Fenn, Jr., *The Corporate Social Audit* (New York: The Russell Sage Foundation, 1972). Limitations of space have precluded deeper examination of the field of corporate consumer relations programs, and those of trade associations. Those desiring greater depth should read: David A. Aaker and George S. Day, "Corporate Responses to Consumerism Pressures", *Harvard Business Review* (November-December, 1972), pp. 114-124.

THIRTY-THREE WAYS MARKETERS ARE COPING WITH THE NEW ERA OF RESTRICTIONS AND REGULATIONS *

E. B. WEISS

* E. B. Weiss, "Thirty-three Ways Marketers are Coping with the New Era of Restrictions and Regulations," *Advertising Age* (November 8, 1971), pp. 119-121. Reproduced by Special Permission.

In the first part of this two-part series on marketing's future under the relentlessly accelerating stampede of consumerism, I recapitulated the social, economic, technological and political innovations that, unfortunately, aided by marketing's social backwardness, will make a mockery of the tradition of free enterprise.

I underscored the inevitability of that conclusion with a quick recapitulation of just a small part of newly enacted or proposed federal legislation and regulation restricting marketing — most of it made compulsory by marketing's foot-dragging in developing products and marketing programs that are socially acceptable to our more intelligent and, therefore, more demanding society.

Now it is time to examine how marketing will re-adjust to its new restrictive environment.

But first permit me to explain that marketing has already lost big gobs of its original freedom. The process began early in the century with the original Pure Food & Drug legislation. But the freedom marketing had lost until recently had largely been the freedom to engage in out-and-out fraud. Only in recent years have legislative and regulatory agencies restricted marketing practices which are really violations of new standards of business morality, rather than fraud in the traditional sense.

As I pointed out in the first instalment, a more knowledgeable public is insisting on a higher level of marketing ethics. This is the sum and substance of consumerism and of marketing's new social responsibilities.

For example, a television commercial using a somewhat misleading demonstration was not considered precisely fraudulent a few years ago. It is today — and can result in an FTC order requiring corrective advertising. This is the great change — a demand by the public for marketing controls that go far beyond fraud in the traditional sense.

Will marketing simply roll over and play dead as restrictions multiply? That is hardly likely. Business has demonstrated time and again that it has 99 lives — and marketing is an integral part of business. Marketing will not be the same in 1975 as it is currently, but bear in mind that currently it is not the same as it was in 1965.

The question to which this instalment addresses itself is: How will marketing innovate in order to achieve, with profit, the new standards that are being dictated by our new society?

An amusing and tiny (yet really quite instructive) example of how advertising will toe the new mark comes out of a recent regulation in New York City that requires the theater, when quoting the review of critics, to present the critic's views accurately. The promoters of the new (and excellent) film, "Sunday, Bloody Sunday," capitalized on that restriction beautifully with an ad captioned: "The critics quoted below have confirmed in writing that the following excerpts are a true reflection of their total review of 'Sunday, Bloody Sunday'."

So, you see, when the "product" is socially acceptable, even restrictive legislation can spell creative opportunity!

On a much broader scale, here is a rundown of the marketing innovations that have surfaced recently as a direct consequence of new legislative and regulatory restrictions:

1. In early 1970, RCA established an Office of Consumer Affairs at the top corporate level. It has far-reaching responsibilities for the safety and reliability of all RCA products and services, plus the authority to ensure that consumer interests receive prompt attention at all levels of the company. A number of other corporations have made similar organizational changes.

This new corporate division tends to organize a program that incorporates all or some of the following characteristics:

a. The formulation of an up-to-date consumerism code.

b. An internal communications program to communicate the code to all appropriate levels of the organization.

c. Formulation of precise objectives and establishment of measurement systems to check performance.

d. A new venture task force to develop profit opportunities in existing and future consumer legislation, including new products.

e. A *genuine* consumer panel that would provide a continuing playback on marketing programs. It would also provide a listening post that would help to anticipate potential consumerism trends.

f. Programs for working with the various consumer organizations — national, state, local.

g. Reorganization of the scientific-technological function so that it becomes more responsive to the demands of our new society.

h. Finally, formulation by top management of a clear statement of profit policy for marketing in the new era.

2. Now turn to General Mills. That corporation and its subsidiaries spent $54,000,000 for advertising in fiscal 1971. In a statement of corporate responsibility, the company said: "Recognizing the power and importance of such amounts to the corporation and to society," making this perhaps the first time that a large advertiser has acknowledged the social implications and obligations of a huge advertising budget. (It is not merely a coincidence that "the power and importance" of such amounts of advertising constitute one of the serious questions about advertising that our new society — especially on campus — has been debating.)

General Mills' report to stockholders then makes this additional significant point of policy: "Any competitive or comparative statement to be made about any product or service must be supported. Each manager responsible for a product is also responsible for the preparation of claims and the development of adequate substantiation for them where necessary."

Again, it is no coincidence that Congress and the FTC, as I reported in the first instalment of this series, have clearly embarked on a program that will require from advertisers full substantiation of product and advertising claims.

3. George W. Hosefield, group vp, research and development at Pillsbury, reports that highlighting the nation's nutrition needs has required amassing extensive data on the nutrient content of foods. "Thanks to our early involvement with the computer, a very high percentage of all this information is mechanically stored for almost instant retrieval and use," he said, but added that these requirements "should slow the pace of new product introduction."

4. Another example: The current furor over ecology has spawned a new family of electric housewares products at Westinghouse, whose portable appliance division unveiled a line of four Ecologizer products — two for air and two for water. These are the nucleus of an Ecologizer group that will eventually encompass 12 models.

Westinghouse labels this program "Homecology," and specifically declares that it is sparked by the consumer revolution. Westinghouse is also studying how it can modify existing products, or develop new ones, to satisfy Homecology requirements.

5. Hunt-Wesson Foods has announced that it will not advertise products on the basis of minor differences which have little relevance to product value. Here, again, you see a direct response to FTC's and FDA's mounting concern with advertising that exploits insignificant differences in a product. These moves by FTC and FDA, in turn, reflect a growing public awareness of, and complaints about, advertising exaggerations for identical products.

With respect to contemplated new products, Hunt-Wesson is now asking: Is it useful rather than wasteful or superfluous? Is it flexible rather than forcing a permanent change in the environment to accommodate it? Does it enhance life rather than contributing to strain and discomfort? Does it serve real needs, rather than those which have been artificially induced simply to create a market? Does it escalate the dehumanization of society through speed, noise, size or power?

Who in marketing would have asked such questions even three years ago?

One more example from Hunt-Wesson: In response to the rising public insistence on open-dating of product life, Hunt-Wesson has established its own standards on shelf life, and now is engaged in pulling various products off the shelf to see how company standards hold up.

6. Whirlpool has instituted a 90-day test program in Los Angeles and Philadelphia which, in effect, extends its warranty to

unconditional satisfaction or refund of purchase price, or replacement with a comparable model at no additional cost, within 60 days.

The new Whirlpool warranty, which has rocked the industry, stems from its highly successful "hot line" program under which 75% to 80% of the telephone service calls are handled to the customer's satisfaction right over the telephone.

7. A major appliance consumer action panel, which will serve as a "Court of Last Resort" for consumer complaints, is a major innovation being tested by the Assn. of Home Appliance Manufacturers and the Gas Appliance Manufacturers Assn. with the support of the American Retail Federation.

Consumer complaints will go to MACAP after retailer and manufacturer contact has failed to resolve the problem. MACAP intends to analyze the manufacturers' complaint handling procedures, recommend improvements, and, when justified, make recommendations as to final disposition of individual cases. If the consumer is not satisfied with the policy of the dealer, service organization, or manufacturer, then the Court of Last Resort is MACAP.

8. After about a year of planning, the National Advertising Review Board is now functioning. The public is invited to get in touch with one of the 140 or so local offices of the Council of Better Business Bureaus (which are now spending millions to update telephone equipment) to lodge a complaint. The bureau will then try to work out a solution between the shopper and the advertiser. If one can't be found, either the bureau or the advertiser may refer the matter to the review board.

The board will then select a five-man panel from its pool of 30 advertiser representatives, ten agency execs and ten from the public sector. Then, after a thorough review, including the testimony of witnesses, if the advertiser is found in violation of review board standards, he will be warned that if he doesn't change his erring ways, the case will be turned over to the appropriate government agency, and the board will release a statement to the press.

9. The American steel industry has organized a major drive to recover and recycle used steel cans. The eventual aim is to put all of the 60 billion such cans used each year by American consumers back into steel-making furnaces. (The industry conceded that it was motivated partly by the possibility of legislation to ban all non-returnable packages.)

The American Iron and Steel Institute has begun a print and spot radio advertising program with copy that states: "All cans are recyclable. Steel cans most of all," and "Every day is recycling day in a steel mill." The advertising will also refer to the 78 can collection centers "to help collect used cans, all kinds of cans, and to recycle all the steel cans it can get."

10. Coca-Cola is abandoning "king," "giant," and "family" from package size descriptions. The adjectives have "lost much of their meaning," the company declared.

Actually, these terms have *more* meaning today than years ago, but the meaning currently is more negative than positive. In other words, millions of consumers have learned that these terms do not always signify a better value. There have been examples of "giant economy sizes" that are priced higher per ounce than the regular size. Here, again, we see a direct marketing response to a new public awareness and, of course, a direct response to the attention FTC is giving to these terms.

11. Turn again to the food field, which, not only for cereals, but over its broad spectrum of foods, has been under attack for nutritional deficiencies in the product and for misleading advertising claims of superior nutrition.

For cereals the response has been that cereals and cereal advertising have become much more nutrition-oriented. Kellogg's Corn Flakes advertising shows a bowl of corn flakes with milk and fruit. Crawler lines drawn from the bowl to copy list various nutrients and amounts with and without milk. Note that well, since one of the criticisms of some cereal advertising has been its failure to point out the nutritional contribution of added milk.

General Mills has introduced four new cereal products in the past year — all fortified to some degree. (Remember Choate's cereal expose of about a year ago?)

"Where do the food companies go from here?" asked AD AGE recently, and went on to report: "We're not really sure which way to go," said a food marketing exec. "We realize we must do something, but we must consider how the government will look at what we do."

But what the new order demands of marketing is not a study of "how the government will look at what we do," but a study of what the consumerism activists amont the public (and their number is now legion and growing daily) are currently demanding. Congress, the FTC and the FDA are responding to demands made for articulate segments of a more sophisticated shopulation — not leading the public into these new shopping concepts.

In marketing, a corporation will routinely field test a product to make sure it performs its primary function. The same company will market test the product to ascertain whether it will sell. Now research will increasingly check the consumer or the community to determine not only what the adverse side effects may be, but also to make certain that the new product and its marketing program conform with the preferences, not to mention insistence, of our new society.

12. At Quaker Oats top level social policy is summed up this way: "The really significant business solutions to public problems will come when middle managers with a direct profit responsibility see that they can reasonably meet that responsibility while directly serving social purposes."

13. A year ago, at the National Packaging Forum sponsored by the Packaging Institute, a color presentation was made by Reynolds Metals Co. The film explored several methods that packaging can use to reduce its 13.3% share of municipal and industrial solid waste.

14. A National Center for Solid Waste Disposal, headed by Donald M. Kendall, president of PepsiCo, has been organized. It will have a 25-man board of top executives from food, beverage, packaging, government, labor, public and academic fields. The purpose will be to create orderly coordination of solid waste disposal proposals and systems, and to forestall an estimated 300 bills (national, state and local) due to be proposed within a year to tax, ban or otherwise restrict non-returnable containers.

15. The National Curtain, Drapery and Allied Products Assn. is readying the fire resistancy test for acceptance by the American Society for Testing Materials. That test will then be submitted to the Products Standards section of the U.S. Department of Commerce for approval. Once the ASTM approves the test, the association will recommend its acceptance by its members. The aim of this program is to set standards before the U.S. Department of Commerce decides to write its own.

Other associations — take heed!

16. The Proprietary Assn. has added six new advertising recommendations for the advertising of medications. Note how these six points correspond to the demands of the consumer activists:

a. Depiction of consumers continually relying on medicines as simplistic solutions to emotional or mood problems should be avoided.

b. Advertising for proprietary medicines should avoid representations by word or illustraton which, in reasonable construction, are commonly associated with the "drug culture," or which imply a casual attitude toward the use of drugs.

c. Exaggeration or dramatization which misrepresents the product's capabilities should be avoided.

d. Claims of product effectiveness should be supportable by clinical or other medical evidence or experience through long use.

e. Proprietary medicine advertising directed toward young children and encouraging them to use such medicine should be avoided.

f. Advertising of proprietary medicines on programs or in publications which are specifically directed toward young children should be avoided.

Also, the president of the Proprietary Assn., aware of the new attitude of FDA toward combination drugs, stated: "Certainly, there would be some combinations disqualified under any rational plan. But I think those most likely to be disqualified would be the so-called Christmas tree formulations that we all recognize as irrational and redundant. I would strongly urge members of this association to think seriously of reformulating or removing some of these particular drugs from the market on a voluntary basis."

17. Commissioner Kirkpatrick of the FTC has suggested that the FTC and trade associations might work together to develop programs of self regulation which would leave enforcement in the hands of government. Said Kirkpatrick: "A key role today for trade associations may be to help the government regulate their industries

in a manner that will insure a minimum degree of government interference." He urged trade associations to assume the role of monitors of their industries, detecting unfair and deceptive practices. "Wherever such practices are found to exist," he said, "the association might then assume the role of applicant to the FTC, informing the commission of all the facts and circumstances which the association believes warrants commission actions."

18. In a move to blunt criticism about the quality of new cars, General Motors unfolded a new national program under which it will reimburse dealers for inspecting and making any repairs *before* the car is delivered to the buyer. (GM promptly raised prices an average of $20 a car to "cover costs.") All of the auto makers have special programs of this type in Wisconsin, Mississippi and Massachusetts to comply with new state laws that require manufacturers to compensate their dealers for pre-delivery repairs. (Can a federal law be far behind?)

19. General Motors and five of the auto dealers conducted a two-month pilot test project designed to retrieve junked and abandoned cars. Civic groups and individuals in Traverse City, Mich., who know the location of abandoned cars, have been asked to alert one of the five GM dealers, who will record the car's location and, if known its ownership. At the request of the GM dealer, local law-enforcement officials will check the car and certify that it can be disposed of. The dealer will then make arrangements to transport the vehicle to a local auto wrecking yard at no cost to the owner or possessor of the car. (About 800,000 cars are abandoned in the U.S. annually.)

20. In its September, 1971, issue, *Grocery Manufacturer* reports that "Open-dating pressure is building in Washington . . . The FTC is feeling heat from consumer activists . . . Associations like the Grocery Manufacturers of America and National Assn. of Food Chains are pressured by some members to work out a practical voluntary system before bureaucrats get into the act."

21. The prestigious National Academy of Engineering is formulating a role for engineers in the consumer movement. "Some members of the engineering community still remain partially isolated from real-world consumer complexities and needs," said the academy. "If some aspects of product designs are to be improved and higher consumer benefits obtained, then communication barriers must be identified and removed."

22. Lees Carpets has launched the Joanne Lees program. It tells the trade: "An educated consumer will make all of our jobs a little easier — ours, and yours. It's part of our new consumerism campaign. Each month our ads will be answering the kind of questions women ask before they buy a carpet.

"We tell people where to write if they have any questions or problems about carpeting . . . The consumer will get the same kind of knowledgeable answers that you've come to expect from the Lees salesmen."

23. In the first instalment of this series, I referred to the

FTC-FDA restrictions on "cents-off" deals. This is compelling some marketing executives to consider:

a. Deals involving buying one at regular price and getting a second at half price.

b. Adding an extra amount to the regular size package.

c. In-pack or on-pack coupons (for example, offering "cents-off" on food items other than the promoted item — or offering a free sample).

d. In-pack premiums (a la Cracker Jack).

e. Contests (subject, of course, to the new FTC restrictions).

24. Owens-Corning Fiberglas is capitalizing on the inflammability issue by promoting the fire resistance qualities of glass fiber draperies in a "Decorating with Safety" program staged in major department stores. Also, Owens-Corning now has a "Consumer Consultant for Fire Safety."

25. At the retail level, the most significant example of progressive consumerism programs comes from Migros — the hugely successful and highly socially-aware Swiss cooperative federation.

Migros prints the day and the month at which the product is to be taken off the shelf. It also prints a description of recommended home storage techinques, and how long the product will remain fresh at home under these conditions.

Migros introduced an egg called M-48, M standing for Migros and 48 signifying that the egg is no more than 48 hours old. After the eggs have passed the 48-hour limit, the M-48 sticker is removed, revealing the regular Migros date sticker with the normal pull dates for eggs.

Migros also has an open pull date program for products that are not usually considered to present "freshness" problems to the consumer. This includes batteries, photographic film and wristwatches. It returns the merchandise to the manufacturer to be refurbished or reconstituted after the pull date.

Migros has ten items in the flower department that are packed in gas-filled plastic bags. The bags are dated to tell the customer how long the gas will preserve the flowers.

26. Giant Food, in cooperation with the Food & Drug Administration, has been testing nutrition labeling on ten Giant brand items in the chain's 93 stores. The label information will show clearly the nutritional value of the food, as well as lack of it. For the first time, a food label will tell the shopper not only what's in the package, but what is not in it. For example, a proposed pork and beans can label shows that the product contains no Vitamins A or C or Riboflavin.

Giant Food has also hinted it may run advertising explaining why it refuses to stock certain items!

27. King Soopers, a 31-store Denver chain, put up collection centers on its parking lots for recyclable materials. Community Pride, a new non-profit organization, will direct the collection and disposal of the scrap deposited.

Through full-page ads, King is asking for volunteer groups such as Boy Scouts, Campfire Girls, church groups and garden clubs to man the centers. Benton Billings, Community Pride head, said there has been a "fantastic" response from groups wanting to participate in these center projects.

28. The Albertson food chain has begun using only biodegradable trays for meat and produce. In disclosing the switch to sterilized natural-fiber trays, Albertson advertised: "We not only care about the quality of food we package for you, we care about how the package can be disposed of after you've emptied it. It is our contribution to combating pollution of our environment."

29. Prominent shalf labels indicating low-fat foods as well as foods with questionable cholesterol content have been posted throughout a consumer-owned market in Chicago in cooperation with the Chicago Heart Assn. American Heart Assn. logos (a torch framed by a heart) were put near all products judged "appropriate for a fat control diet" by a "nutritional awareness committee" of the CHA. Green question marks appear next to products whose labels do not state cholesterol content.

30. Bohack — a 174-unit chain — is eliminating all packages which it believes are deceptive by value standards, as well as those which create a proliferation of size situations. Bohack is accepting no deals on one size of a product if the deal makes a larger size more expensive on a per measure basis.

31. Alexander's Markets in Los Angeles has a seven-point ecology program that:
- Marks the phosphate content of soaps and detergents with shelf signs.
- Marks other items that are ecologically better than competing items, such as glass instead of plastic, returnables instead of non-returnables, paper plates instead of plastic ones.
- Removes Shell N-Pest strips, and also labels pesticides without DDT as ecologically-preferable.
- Urges its customers to write their congressmen about ecology, and offers an 8½" x 11" letter form printed on its bags.
- Replaced plastic egg cartons, produce trays and meat trays with 100% biodegradable virgin pulp trays.
- Installed collection bins for old newspapers in parking lots.
- Devotes a half-page of ad space each week to ecology information.

32. The Revco drug chain has a number of "consumer affair counselors" to handle consumer complaints (all called Mrs. Alice Bixby).

33. Ralph's food chain has nine women (trained by Hunt-Wesson) who function in the store as "shoppers' guides."

My conclusion? Well, I think honesty really can be profitable! Extraordinary perhaps, but true.

In this connection, I note that Profile bread may spend more than 25% of its budget on corrective advertising — obviously because the new Julia Mead messages seem to be memorable, penetrating, convincing. Commented AD AGE on Oct. 4: "If, indeed, it turns out that honesty sells (the thought boggles the mind), we can visualize advertisers standing in line begging the FTC to make them run corrective advertising. And then FTC's big weapon might be to require advertisers to continue to run their old hard-sell stuff as a penalty for their misdeeds."

But I conclude, nonetheless, that marketing will continue to lag behind the demands of the new public and therefore eventually wind up as deeply regulated as transportation and banking.

QUESTIONS FOR DISCUSSION

1. Why does Mr. Weiss think that marketing in 1975 will not be the same as it is to-day? How did marketing change from 1965?

2. Comment on the effect of the following on business:
   (a) ecology
   (b) verification of advertising claims
   (c) safer products
   (d) self-policing through trade associations
   (e) activities of consumer activists
   (f) more consumer information on labels.

3. Do you think business's reaction has gone far enough? Do you think it is sincere or mere "window dressing"?

4. What other reforms would you suggest which are not mentioned by Mr. Weiss' article?

5. Does Mr. Weiss think that the 33 measures which he analyzes will head off further government regulation for business? Why?

* "The Principle of the Ombudsman," The Royal Bank of Canada, *Monthly Letter*, Vol. 52, No. 11, pp. 1-4. Reproduced by Special Permission.

Everybody knows the meaning of "Ombudsman" — he is someone to whom any citizen may take complaints about the actions of people in the government service. The Ombudsman will listen, examine, and try to obtain redress of an injustice or amends for a grievance.

There are many descriptive titles given the Ombudsman. He may be called Citizen's Defender, Citizen's Champion, Defender of Civil Liberty, Parliamentary Commissioner for Administration, or Citizen's Guardian. Whatever his title, it is his duty to keep watch over the way in which government agencies and officials apply the law and regulations in dealing with the public.

Scores of books and hundreds of magazine and newspaper articles show the interest people take in this relatively new office. In May 1968 the American Academy of Political and Social Science devoted an issue of *The Annals* to an exhaustive examination of "The Ombudsman or Citizen's Defender: A Modern Institution." This has become a source-book and a detailed guide to persons investigating the need for such a system of citizen-protection. Much of the information in this *Letter* has been drawn from it.

The need to keep government administrators from abusing the wide powers that have been necessarily given them in recent years demanded a creative innovation. The institution of the Ombudsman went a long way toward providing what was necessary.

Social service reaches into every area of life, and the officials in charge of its many agencies come into contact with every citizen. The purpose of the Ombudsman is to hold the scales so that justice is satisfied, and justice, as St. Thomas Aquinas defined it, "is a constant and perpetual will to yield to each one his right."

Citizens will take their problems and complaints to the Ombudsman because they look upon him as representing the State's conscience. He is not a person bound by legalities, seeking to win a case, but an arbiter who seeks to dispel erroneous notions on one side or the other by setting forth the truth.

Service to Individuals

A review given in *The Annals* shows that there are many different procedures in the carrying out of Ombudsman duties, but his central purpose is always to protect the individual. He is, as was said upon appointment of the Quebec provincial Ombudsman: "to receive the complaints of the public against the government administration, to make investigations and bring to the attention of the authorities the problems that he uncovers."

Many persons who have grievances would find it difficult to go through procedures required under the regulations. They may not know where to start; they may not be able to pay the legal expenses; or their emergency may be of such a nature as to demand quick action. Then, too, a request for review addressed to a government department may be referred to the officer originally involved, and that is not of the nature of a real appeal.

It has been said that if every member of parliament, every member of a legislature, every civil servant, every member of a municipal council, and every member of a school board looked upon himself as an Ombudsman there might not be an opening for a special appointee. People in administrative positions have a tendency to forget why they exist: to serve the people. They can do this effectively by telling people about their rights.

As it is, there is a gap to be plugged. The existence of an Ombudsman, independent of politics and of the bureaucracy, encourages those in authority to consider maturely before making up their minds about legal decisions and discretionary acts.

Some Objections

It was found in Great Britain and in Australia that the strongest opposition to appointment of an Ombudsman came from the legislators, although it is recognized everywhere that the *sine qua non* of effective citizen guardianship is freedom from political connections. A member of parliament receiving a complaint from a constituent would be under obligation to divorce himself from consideration of the political usefulness of the case and address himself to the merits of the grievance.

Events have not shown that the status of parliamentarians has been eroded by appointment of an Ombudsman. On the other hand it is admitted that in countries where complaints must be submitted through a member of parliament the citizens are deprived of the satisfying feeling that a special power — the Citizen's Champion — is working on their behalf.

Writing in *The Annals* about the situation in the United States, Dr. Ake Sandler, Professor of Government in California State College, said: "The average congressman (or any legislator, for that matter) has neither the time nor the inclination to do anything about a complaint other than to put a phone call or write a letter on behalf of his complaining constituent."

To handle a complaint in the detailed way of the Ombudsman's office requires an expenditure of time, and if legislators spend time in following up complaints they are necessarily absent from the House where their legislating duty demands their presence. Their vital governing function benefits by the appointment of an Ombudsman.

There is another point, one of great importance. When individual legislators handle complaints the administration is deprived of the enlightenment given by the accumulation of information about similar cases. What may appear to be a solitary complaint may be one of a large pattern which it would be important to recognize. A number of complaints of the same nature passing through an Ombudsman's office would ring a warning bell, calling attention to a condition that needed investigation.

Community Needs

It is not only in federal and provincial affairs that there is opportunity for exercise of the Ombudsman function. As Hing Yong Cheng, a Colombo Plan Scholarship student at Carleton University and now in the Ministry of Culture and Social Affairs, Singapore, wrote in *The Annals:* "Faced with a huge and complex body of government instrumentalities, an aggrieved citizen may not even know where or to whom to complain."

In a big urban centre citizens may have the opinion that municipal government is remote from them and unapproachable. They doubt their ability to obtain satisfactory consideration of their complaints about many things: taxes, licenses, garbage collection, street repair, snow clearing, welfare assistance, zoning, fire safety, transportation, police, pollution, parking, airport noise, and a hundred other things in the planning or administration of which something goes wrong.

A great number of people in paid and voluntary positions are meeting some of the need. For some months *The Montreal Star* printed a daily column under the heading "The Target is Trouble". Through it the writer, Bruce Taylor, exemplified one purpose of the press, to be the "Voice of the lowly and oppressed, advocate of the friendless, righter of public and private wrongs."

In the *Monthly Letter* of November 1970 it was suggested that "It might be feasible to transplant the Ombudsman idea to the community by setting up a central service providing information about where to apply for help in solving problems, coping with crises, and starting something designed to improve the community." Some community chests have service offices which will tell citizens where they should apply for this and that kind of help: but first the citizen must find out about this office.

There are, too, many community-type Ombudsmen at work in many capacities: clergymen, private social workers, certain service clubs, settlement workers, and police officers specially trained in ombudsman-type work. Some big business establishments have staff members whose job it is to receive complaints and deal with them in the interest of customers.

Government Agencies

Greatest need for the Ombudsman, however, is in connection with government activities. Government as a going concern consists of thousands of officials, agencies and civil servants. Year by year, under the growing pressure of new services and policies, the work of the agencies expands, not only in volume but into new areas.

In fact, as George B. McClellan, the Alberta Ombudsman, said in an article in *The Alberta Municipal Counsellor:* "There is hardly any field of business, manual labour, or other occupation, in which the average person finds himself engaged, where he is not subject to numerous forms of government control."

Complaints are not always of some fault by a civil servant, but result from the confusion a citizen feels when caught in the complexity of the government structure necessary to supply services. As in an expanding business corporation, mechanisms of management become more elaborate, relationships between departments become a criss-crossing maze, duplication of responsibility and work becomes a menace.

When a crevasse of misunderstanding separates an individual and those in authority it causes unhappiness. To bridge this chasm is primarily the responsibility of those in public service. They must be on their guard against out-and-out violation of the rights of citizens, but in addition they need to watch for ways in which they infringe without realizing that they are doing so. They will keep in mind the principle enunciated by the Emperor Marcus Aurelius: "He often acts unjustly who does not do a certain thing; not only he who does a certain thing."

Control of Agencies

One of government's most pressing problems is the supervision of administration in a time of rapidly-expanding public service. No reasonable person expects the agencies or their officers to be without fault in the performance of their duties, but the source of trouble goes deeper than mere mistakes. There can be misuse of power, or fixation on the rules in a book, or neglect of reasonable duties not expressed in the Act that established the agency.

Appointment of an Ombudsman signifies the government's desire to make sure that its administrators are not guilty of any injustice to any citizen; that they be faithful to the government's plans and purposes, and that they refrain from arbitrary acts.

The Ombudsman will go about his task by checking the history of the transaction complained about. *The Annals* suggests some questions. Did the officer have before him all the facts and did he give them balanced consideration? Were the rules applied properly or harshly? Did the officer discriminate, delay, or pass the decision-making to someone else? Was there inattention, unreasonableness or prejudice? By weighing the evidence connected with the alleged fault the Ombudsman will reach an impartial judgment as to the propriety of the complaint.

If he makes a finding that is unfavourable to the agency, the Ombudsman does not then become prosecutor or judge. He has not the authority to reverse, alter or annul a decision, or to take disciplinary action. He uses admonition and suggestion. He may recommend an appropriate change in the law or rule that caused the complaint to be made. His ultimate weapon is his report to Parliament in which he brings the grievance to attention and recommends that it be redressed.

There is another side to the coin. While making sure that the government agencies do not exceed their power or exercise it in an unreasonable way, the Ombudsman's findings protect the agencies against unjustified complaints. In *The Annals* chapter on the New Zealand practice it is said: "The civil service has come to regard the Ombudsman as a defense against unjustified criticism rather than as an enemy."

To win this high regard from both the complainant and the agency complained about, the Ombudsman needs to be an officer free from meddling or pressure. In Sweden, neither the cabinet nor parliament can stop an investigation that the Ombudsman believes to be necessary.

Essential to the proper carrying out of his duties is the Ombudsman's dedication to the principles of equity. In its broadest and most general signification equity denotes the spirit and the habit of fairness, justness, and right dealing which would regulate the intercouse of men with men — the rule of doing to all others as we desire them to do to us: or, as it is expressed by Justinian: "To live honestly, to harm nobody, to render to every man his due." It is therefore the synonym of natural right or justice.

Democracy and Ombudsmen

The countries that have Ombudsmen functioning as Defenders of Civil Liberties are countries dedicated to the principle of democratic government. Alfred Bexelius, Ombudsman in Sweden, wrote in *The Annals:* "It is certainly an expression of real democracy when a society establishes a special institution with the task of ensuring that the other agencies serving the society respect the rights of the citizens."

In the Canadian ideal of society, every person is as completely in charge of his own life as he can be. The individual is the central figure, but he cannot ensure his own aims in isolation. If he lived alone and tried to meet his problems by himself he would perish. The Ombudsman is a connecting link to bring all the resources of society to the aid of the individual and to protect him against wrongful acts.

Amid all the improvements in social services and welfare plans, civil rights must be preserved if democracy is to live up to its meaning.

Every society finds it necessary to frame legislation which is binding upon citizens, but it must observe basic rights. The Ombudsman helps to keep the balance between the increasing encroachment of government administration and the citizen's rights. He contributes much toward establishing citizens' confidence in government because his appointment is evidence of the government's determination to pay regard to the rights of people and to prevent the abridgment of civil rights by administrative agencies.

Justice Is a Goal

The Ombudsman's duty is not merely to act as a buffer between the individual and authority, but to be actively employed in promoting justice. Justice is good in itself, not merely a necessary means of preserving order in a State. As Cicero put it: "Justice is much the most glorious and splendid of all virtues, and alone entitles us to the name and appellation of good men."

The welfare of the people is the supreme purpose of the government. Grievance-handling machinery should be designed so as to provide easily accessible judicial review, flexible disposition of cases, and speedy judgment. But the Ombudsman must not be so just that he forgets to be humane, nor can he be so generous that he neglects to be just. Those who appeal to him should remember that he is not there to dispense favours but to safeguard rights.

The existence of the Ombudsman, though he is not appealed to by a citizen, gives a feeling of security. The citizen knows that should he ever believe that he has a legitimate reason to complain he has a friend at court who will see that attention is given to his complaint. He will have confidence in the government which has appointed this independent officer to ensure the rule of law and the protection of rights. He will find it less necessary to parade and demonstrate to call attention to his grievance.

Simple In Operation

The Ombudsman's activity is simple, informal and rapid. He is a master in discriminating between what is important and what is trivial; he can diagnose new situations because he has wide knowledge of similarities and differences in cases; he can look at both sides of an argument and seek some negotiable point; he puts the relevant facts together for inspection and brings the problem into sharp focus. He fulfils his duty when he advises fully on the evidence put before him, and initiates remedial action if he considers it necessary.

The complaints reaching an Ombudsman cover a bewildering variety of subjects, running the gamut of human error from mere pin-pricking annoyances to complaints of wrongful infringement of liberty. They are all important to the person making them because they affect his life.

While taking every complaint seriously and giving it the needed attention, the Ombudsman has, of course, to tell some complainants that he cannot deal with their grievances. The test is: have the civil rights of the person complaining been interfered with by an agency or an official?

There are people who enjoy making a fuss, and they are annoyed when other people remain undisturbed. The Ombudsman may decide not to proceed with a case if he believes the complaint to be frivolous, not made in good faith, or designed to attack a person rather than to criticize an action. On occasion an Ombudsman has found it necessary to advise complainants to cease groundless attacks on departments or officials.

What Sort of Man?

Who can fill that sort of office? He must be a person with wide knowledge, high prestige, personal merit, great energy, and abundant courage. He must be able to stand against criticism, concerned more about discharging a job of social worth than with personal popularity.

Professor Sandler wrote in *The Annals:* "He should be so carefully selected that there never could be a question of his honesty, integrity, ability or motive. This is indeed to ask for perfection, or pretty close to it. But it should be aimed for. In all the 160 years that Sweden has had its Ombudsman, the *man* has never been doubted."

The character of the man having been taken account of, it remains to lay down the ground rules for his guidance. The Ombudsman is not appointed because of people's lack of confidence in the public service. He will not exercise general supervision or management over the administrative process, but will deal with individual grievances of citizens who complain that they have been hurt or annoyed by the occasional mistakes made by government departments. These are matters which, while of no great public moment and quite unlikely to make headlines, are of very real importance to the individuals concerned.

The Ombudsman is someone who will listen. Just to be able to tell one's troubles to a person of consequence is a relief. But the Ombudsman is in position to do something about these troubles. He can reach the ears of the individual or organization by whom the wrong was inflicted.

Using the Ombudsman

Anybody who feels that he has been unfairly dealt with by a government agency or official may carry his complaint to the Ombudsman. The citizen who believes that he has been given the run-around by the Circumlocution Office (satirized in Dickens' *Little Dorrit*) will find — at least in Denmark — a sign on the Ombudsman's office: *The door is open.*

There is nothing belittling to one in seeking advice, or in asking help from the Ombudsman. People who are big in spirit are willing to ask for, accept, and consider advice. Test your case by asking: "Can the Ombudsman explain my difficulty, solve my problem, enlighten me on this point, or show me the way to get redress for my injury?" The answer you receive from the Ombudsman will be the honest and impartial advice of a clever, honourable and independent man, well versed in the matters he handles.

Keep in mind that the Ombudsman is not a clairvoyant, able to read your mind. He is an intelligent man. It is your duty, and it is necessary to the successful pleading of your case, to give him all the facts and reasons.

Need for the Ombudsman

Many countries and several Canadian provinces have found it logical that as operations of government increasingly affect the lives of citizens, there should be an equal increase in the care taken to make sure that such intervention is carried out with caution.

Dr. Donald C. Rowat of Carleton University, named by Mr. Cheng as the leading Canadian expert on the subject, is author of *The Ombudsman: Citizen's Defender* (University of Toronto Press, 1965). He gave testimony before the 1964 parliamentary committee which recommended appointment of an Ombudsman for the federal government and one for each of the provinces.

It was Socrates, the man who professed not to be wise but to seek wisdom, who said: "Four things belong to a judge: to hear courteously, to answer wisely, to consider soberly, and to decide impartially." That is an excellent description of the ideal Ombudsman, and an argument for his needs.

The Ombudsman is not to be confused with the writer of advice columns in the newspapers. He is a responsible person — responsible to the person he serves, responsible to his parliament, responsible to the agencies with which he deals, and responsible in a really personal way to himself for the decisions he makes and the actions he takes.

QUESTIONS FOR DISCUSSION

1. What is meant by the word "ombudsman"?

2. What purpose does the office of ombudsman serve in countries having one, such as Denmark, Sweden, Great Britain?

3. What sorts of complaints are received? How does the ombudsman handle them? With what results?

4. Can an ombudsman protect government officials from unjustified abuse by the citizens?

5. An ombudsman system may work well for a small country such as Denmark, but do you think it would do as well in a vast country such as the United States?

6. Do you think such a system would work if adapted to the needs of a private company in its dealings with public complaints? What differences in the situation might reduce its effectiveness?

THOMAS F. SCHUTTE

* Adapted from a paper prepared and given at the Public
Policy and Marketing Conference-Workshop held at
Northwestern University, June 12-13, 1972. Reproduced
by permission of the author.

The Corporate Office for Consumer Affairs. While it would be
unfair to indict American business for not establishing the requisite
policies, procedures and organizational structures for expressing
concern for the consumer, the fact of the matter is that while some
firms have exercised concerted action along these lines, the action
may not yet be in the best interests of the consumer.

Some firms have begun attempts to establish offices for consumer
affairs. Some firms have unconsciously developed the sort of offices
that have not absolved themselves of the biases or the vested interest
of the business firm. Other firms have attempted to develop a variety
of approaches for showing or demonstrating consumer affairs interest
through a WATTS line, more aggressive public relations departments,
institutional advertising messages showing "we care about you"
campaigns, or joint advertising campaigns with trade associations to
show the trade, government and consumer how a specific industry is
"consumer-oriented".

In my examination of several offices for consumer affairs, as well
as the modified attempts by corporations to minister more
ambitiously to the consumer, it has become apparent that there are
several problems in establishing a philosophy and office for consumer
affairs:

1. A good number of business firms really want to be more
effective in dealing with the consumer, but these firms and their
leaders are not aware of their very biases which get in the way of
establishing viable consumer affairs policies. In part, the Levitt
notion of preoccupation with the internal environment of the firm is
such that business leaders are not equipped to handle the external
environments.[1]

2. The marketing concept has been so ingrained into the thinking
of the leaders of so many firms that the concept of consumer affairs,
when pursued, is viewed as a very integral part of marketing. Thus, it
is rather subjective to examine or appraise the "balance sheet" results
as a basis for ministering to the consumer, when consumer affairs
management is viewed as a part of the very operational marketing
group that creates the marketing programs. There is a question of
legitimacy and bias when the operational marketing area also

evaluates and controls the results of its own efforts. It is a well-accepted tenet in business organization that the monitoring and control functions should be distinct from the operational management areas. Often, it is the controller or the financial group of the firm that examines the results of the production or marketing operation. Likewise, one would postulate that it is an outside control group, not marketing, that should minotor the consumer affairs results of the company.

3. So much chatter and literature in the area of consumerism has been divergent in subject matter — from the theoretical, to the platitude, to the consumer advocate or governmental threat, to the suggested solution for a specific area like product safety or health hazard — that it has been arduous for the business leader to know exactly what to do. The air is filled with consumerism, but there has been little direction coming from anywhere which provides an operational solution to getting to the root of consumer affairs — organizing and managing consumer affairs within the business firm. Business leaders need assistance. Except for those with the benefit of outside consultants or a management versed in the subject of consumer affairs, the business firm in America has been in a quandry as to what to do and how to go about doing it. It is my belief that the recent headlines, "Chrysler Project Is Called A Hoax," was an example of a major American firm that was unaware of the possible problems, biases and shortcomings in establishing their office for consumer affairs.[2]

The Center for Auto Safety in Washington, D.C., a Nader-sponsored program, charged that the Chrysler "My Man in Detroit" advertising program is a hoax as well as deceptive and unfair. Charges have been filed with the FTC against the company. Chrysler announced on March 3, 1971, that the firm was appointing a top-level consumer affairs officer, at the vice presidential level. The purpose of the office was "to provide the American consumer with representation at the top executive level in any type of consumer question or problem." "The Man in Detroit" ad campaign advised consumers to write the vice president on any question or problem of a consumer nature. The Center for Auto Safety charged that Chrysler "does nothing more than refer complaints through a central office to regional representatives and dealers. . . . This procedure is similar to that followed by other manufacturers who do not have customer ombudsmen. . . . We know of no instance where Mr. Nichols has modified or gone outside the normal chain of command to assist a customer. . . ."

In another vein, the Senate Commerce Committee has recently commenced a study of the *Fortune* Top 200 manufacturing firms to ascertain the nature, if any, of policies and programs for handling the firms' consumer affairs. Hearings will be conducted later in Washington in which corporate heads will testify.[3]

Also, Ralph Nader is currently studying business firms with professed offices for consumer affairs to ascertain whether the offices are indeed established with objectivity, purpose and the consumer in mind.

4. Pressures on a firm, industry or government to resolve a consumer affairs problem has often been generated by publicity in the local newspaper or business trade publication. If Ralph Nader were to conduct a study of the way in which firms handle consumer affairs, there would be a flurry of corporate energies engaged in "shaping up" the way in which the organization manages consumer affairs. If a study were to show that the meat packing industry was manufacturing its products within unsanitary quarters, there would be a rash of action on the part of politicians and businessmen to handle the problem in some manner. In all these illustrations, as soon as the "heat is off" the indicted party or group, consumer affairs concern declines nationally.

5. Cynicism from business about the role of government and consumer advocates meddling in business affairs causes some business leaders to have a difficult time rationalizing the need for establishing an objective approach for handling the consumer affairs area within the firm. Levitt summarizes this point quite well when he observes: "Yet with all this pragmatism, all his unsentimental zeal to junk what is old and decaying, and all his visible eagerness to find and adopt new things for his business he seems to be enormously contradictory when it comes to new ideas about social reform and relations between business and government."[4]

Guidelines for Establishing the Corporate Office for Consumer Affairs. To avoid both the unconscious development of a biased consumer affairs program, and the failure to handle objectively a firm's responsibility in consumer affairs, it might be helpful to examine some of the guidelines a firm might adopt in establishing or reviewing its consumer affairs management program:

1. Contact the industry's trade association(s) to learn if other firms in the industry have attempted to set up a consumer affairs office. If so, it might be possible to obtain a description of the way in which the office was organized. One should be cautious not to thoughtlessly emulate the program of a firm in the industry or fashioned by the trade association. Such programs may suffer from lack of objectivity. However, it is possible to provide program modification.

2. Communicate with the Office of Consumer Affairs as well as the National Business Council for Consumer Affairs in Washington, D.C. The OCA is currently planning or will have shortly a resource person to contact with regard to possible available models for consumer affairs offices. The National Business Council may have a committee currently studying the area so that proper and helpful advice might be available.

3. Establish the office with a clear-cut purpose to avoid the need for a defensive office to abate the threat from a governmental or consumer spokesman's office. The following areas might be considered for inclusion in establishing a firm's purpose in consumer affairs:

a. Measurement of the extent to which a firm's customers are satisfied with the marketing program — its mix of product, pricing, channel practices, and promotional policies.

b. Assessment of all forms of communication between the firm and the customer. This would include all forms of advertising messages as well as letters of correspondence, product label copy, warranties and guarantees, premium program offers, etc.

c. Periodic customer surveys on consumer satisfaction should be communicated to all operating management in such a way that follow-up and policy changes are encouraged and developed where appropriate.

d. Assessment and distribution of all relevant sources of external information from non-customer sources that might apprise operational management of trends and patterns in dealing with customers. News bulletin, new legislation, controversial relevant issues occurring in the industry or the trade are all examples of what might be included in the information system.

e. Publication of periodic internal consumer affairs reports which present the balance sheet of the firm in terms of the quality of ministering to consumers. What is the health of the customer satisfaction, where are the problems, how long have they been occurring and what are the changes that might be made within the firm to handle consumer affairs more viably? These are some of the questions which need to be answered.

f. Monitoring the nature and the extent of the corporate commitment to assuring customer satisfaction of the firm's marketing program.

g. Establishment of a consumer affairs office at the corporate level, outside the framework of marketing management. To place the office in marketing would jeopardize the objectivity of assuring the realization of the goals of the consumer affairs office. It is often difficult for marketing management to create strategies and programs and, at the same time, remain objective for appraising their quality and results, especially in terms of how the programs affect the consumer. To change or alter his strategies or programs may in part cause the marketing manager to tremble at the risk of reduced results in "making the sales or profit goal" for the period. The manager of consumer affairs ought to report to the chairman, president or senior officer of the firm influential in charting the destiny of the corporation but removed from the management of a specific operational area. In fact, more and more, the chief executive officer will be the one responsible for public witnessing of the firm's activities in consumer affairs, whether this be in the form of a public or private hearing or communication with the various publics of the corporation — stockholder, consumer, employee, or general public.

In November 1971, General Mills sponsored an in-house management conference on "Consumer Concerns" in which the firm's two top executives, the Chairman and the President, both went on record as advocating and endorsing the program. In a pamphlet describing the conference, the executives stated:

In September 1971, on recommendation of General Mills'
Task Force to determine the Company's position in

relation to the changing issues of consumerism, it was decided that this Conference on Consumer Concerns be held for General Mills' Management, Subsidiaries and Advertising Agencies.

The program is designed to explore and analyze current consumer patterns of interest and activity from the viewpoints of government, business and the law. Its purpose is to provide updated direction for day-to-day company operations which will reflect the respect and responsibility General Mills feels for the American consumers who buy and use the products we manufacture.

We are pleased to have as our guests the distinguished Food Editors of some of America's leading magazines and the Consumer Relations Consultants of major food chains who can represent our customers to us.

General Mills is grateful to the participants of this Conference who have generously agreed to share their experience and knowledge with us.[5]

Throughout this conference, both executives had significant visibility among the guests and management participants.

h. Communication from the office for consumer affairs to all employees and management of the company is very important to keep them apprised of the workings and activities of the organization on consumer affairs. This communication must first be directed from the office of the chief operating officer. The office should remain highly visible and influential among the firm's management and employees.

i. Where possible, the office for consumer affairs should include considerations for expertise in the area of the law, information systems, marketing research, and communications. There are numerous occasions where potential input data may be derived from "hitch-hiking" more questions to an on-going marketing research questionnaire aimed at a sample of the firm's customers or consumers. It is not always necessary to think of a consumer affairs office constantly generating new survey research beyond what the firm is essentially doing at the present time.

j. The office for consumer affairs, its organization, procedures for operation, and policies, as well as all other portions of the model, ought to be reviewed with a panel of outsiders which might include marketing professors, economists, representative consumers, and selected or appropriate governmental administrators. Too often a firm may judge its need and approach to a consumer affairs office on the basis of all the unconscious biases of the firm's management. Too often, an office for consumer affairs is really a substitute for an extended public relations function or an extra call-in WATTS line for consumers. A consumer affairs office must be operational and not purely a set of verbal or written guidelines that somehow are expected to permeate throughout the company. The consumer affairs office must be more than this.

In conjunction with its conference on consumer concerns, the General Mills organization published a document on "Corporate Responsibility" which outlined the position of the company in a variety of areas, including nutrition, product quality, product safety, packaging and labeling, advertising, premiums and consumer promotions, consumer sensitivity, consumer correspondence, consumer education, compliance with the law, industry leadership, employment, ecology, and so on. It is quite easy to "mean well" and pontificate from the pulpit of the chief operating officer of the company.[6] It is another matter actually to operationally implement these guidelines through an office such as consumer affairs.

The Results of Corporate Office for Consumer Affairs. While it is apparent that the establishment of a formalized office for consumer affairs may be more appealing for those firms large in consumer visibility and branded sales volume, it is hoped that the concept of an office for consumer affairs will not be identified purely with the giant *Fortune* 500 manufacturing corporation, but rather that the concept will spread to a wide variety of industries and business organizations — banks, insurance, utilities, transportation, retailing, and the like. While the "mom and pop" business is hardly large enough to command the resources for a large scale consumer affairs office, there is no reason why an organized attempt cannot be made to assess the degree to which the firm's marketing program is in the best interests of the consumer as measured by the consumer response to the program. It is possible that local universities might be in a position to assist small businesses in assessing the degree to which the consumers served by the firm are satisfied.

In general, the results of the movement for establishing corporate offices for consumer affairs might be as follows:

1. To provide business an opportunity to take the offensive and examine its internal marketing programs which result in the very policies, procedures, and philosophies affecting customer satisfaction.

2. To encourage a preventative approach to satisfying customers to the extent that "acting in the best interests of the consumer as viewed by the consumer" will be a "way of life" in establishing the plans and action for future marketing.

3. To centralize and coordinate all facets of consumer affairs within the firm so that "the left hand knows what the right hand is doing." All too often bits and pieces of the consumer affairs area are scattered throughout the firm. Centralization provides a mandated opportunity for corporate responsibility in consumer affairs.

4. To serve as a communications center for both internal management and outside consumer-customer, spokesmen and governmental groups. For internal management, the consumer affairs office provides guidance, education, and interface opportunities as well as constraints for operational managers who design and

implement marketing programs. For outside groups, the consumer affairs office provides a place where suggestions, complaints and information can be submitted, reviewed and discussed. Also, the consumer affairs office becomes the central agency of the firm for communicating to outsiders what it is the firm is doing in consumer affairs from the viewpoint of policy, procedures and programs.

5. To serve as a vehicle and catalyst for incorporating concern for consumer affairs in all major policy areas of the corporation.

6. To serve as the depository, review and policy recommending body within the corporation, should the National Institute for Measuring Consumer Issues and Problems be established. It is conceivable the consumer affairs office would want to review and recommend ways in which the national data may be researched and/or presented in a manner more compatible to corporate user needs. The office for consumer affairs would determine the extent of additional detailed research data which the corporation may wish from the Institute, at extra cost. It would be the charge of the consumer affairs office to assess the meaning of the national data from the standpoint of modifying the firm's marketing plans, programs, policies, and procedures.

Conclusions. It is hoped that this paper has demonstrated the need and the rationale for responding to the challenge of the consumer movement by setting forth an operational procedure for ascertaining and resolving consumer problems and issues on the basis of having the facts.

It is hoped that the allocation of our public and private resources will be achieved more adequately as a result of knowing the consumer issues and problems and arranging these into a set of national and corporate priorities.

Furthermore, it is hoped that, together, business and government can determine the strategies, guidelines, regulatory action, and approaches for resolving these consumer issues and problems within the framework of a more melioristic and preventative spirit. It is hoped, also, the Levitt-Bauer and Greyser thesis of "business always loses" and "the dialogue that never happens" are more cliche in nature than reality, for there is no alternative to getting to the root of the public policy area of consumerism for government and business than through a program of action.

One business publication added a bit of humor to connote the import of consumerism and its management:[7]

First Banana:	Hey, did you hear about the man who crossed a parrot with a tiger?
Second Banana:	No; what did he get?
First Banana:	I don't know. But when it talks, you better listen!

Whatever consumerism is, it's beginning to look like a tigerish sort of parrot, and business, it seems, would do well to listen.

QUESTIONS FOR DISCUSSION

1. What is a corporate office for consumer affairs?

2. How is such an office generally organized? Analyze the major sorts of activities engaged in.

3. What are some of the road blocks and problems encountered by a corporation in establishing such an office? Can they be surmounted?

4. Some of the early consumer affairs departments have been attacked by the FTC and a congressional committee. On what grounds?

5. What guidelines would prove useful to a company intending to set up an office of consumer affairs?

6. What positive results have been secured by firms having offices of consumer affairs? Are these the kind of benefits you would have anticipated?

FOOTNOTES

1. Levitt, pp. 53-66.

2. *New York Times* (May 19, 1972), p. 58.

3. Conversation with Frank E. McLaughlin, Director for Industry Relations for the President's Committee on Consumer Interests, Office of Consumer Affairs, Washington, D.C., June 1, 1972.

4. Levitt, *Ibid.*, p. 15.

5. From *Conference on Consumer Concerns* (General Mills, Inc., Minneapolis, Minnesota, November 15, 1971), a non-published document.

6. From *General Mills Corporate Responsibility* (General Mills, Inc. Minneapolis, Minn.), 8 pages, a corporate non-published document.

7. "Business Responds to Consumerism," *Business Week* (September 6, 1969), p. 94.

CONSUMERS SPUR
INDUSTRY RESPONSE *

LEONARD SLOANE

* Leonard Sloane, "Consumers Spur Industry Response,"
New York Times (Sunday, January 7, 1972), pp. 49, 72.
Reproduced by permission.

The Whirlpool Corporation spent $45 million in 1972 to run its consumer services operation, including a warranty program, parts replacement and customer complaint servicing.

The Ford Motor Company's budget for consumer service was $10 million more last year than in 1970, the final year before the start of a division specifically charged with studying the cause of complaints and developing programs to minimize them.

General Mills, Inc., spends more than $4.4 million a year for quality-control programs designed to meet not only customer demands but also the standards established by laws and regulatory agencies.

And Pan American World Airways estimates that the expenditures for its consumer affairs center in New York's Pan Am building amount to $350,000, of which 90 per cent is salary and salary-related.

The amounts spent by these companies in such diverse industries as appliance, automotive, food and transportation to maintain better relationships with their customers is indicative of their efforts to meet the challenges of the modern consumer movement. For there is little doubt that the emphasis on customer service at many corporations today is a direct result of the rise of consumerism beginning in the mid-nineteen-sixties.

Of course, the problems that consumers have had with the products and services they buy are not a phenomenon of the last decade. But the impact of the consumer messages of Presidents Kennedy and Johnson, the writings of such social critics as Rachel Carson and Vance Packard and the rising public consciousness of Ralph Nader helped to make consumerism a household word during the last five years or so. As educational and income levels rose, as technology became more involved and as the awareness of the environment developed for many people into a crusade, much greater discontent with the "brush-offs" that had traditionally been given to complaining consumers by some companies and their dealers became widespread among all strata of society. Customers became more vocal, wrote more letters to the president and called more chairmen of the board at their homes.

One result of this activity has been a rash of consumer relations or consumer affairs departments created by American industry to focus on consumer problems and attempt to come up with answers to solve them, both in individual cases and on an over-all basis. The successes achieved by these departments, however, have not been universally hailed. Some consumer activists — and some plain consumers — have described the corporate efforts as more shadow than substance.

The companies themselves cite impressive statistics to support their claims to the effectiveness of their consumer programs. For instance, Motorola, Inc., says that its number of complaint letters (using 100 as the 1966 base) declined from 41 in 1970 to 35 in 1971 and still further last year. The company's consumer affairs personnel and other corporate officials often visit consumers' homes or telephone the customers.

The General Motors Corporation says that its complaints fell from 7.1 per cent of the total of current sales in 1969 to an estimated percentage of 6.4 in 1972.

"Our zone people know when a dealer has an unusual frequency of complaints and they make it a point to discuss this with the dealer," observed Mack W. Worden, vice president of G.M.'s marketing staff.

"We made a survey and found that in excess of 83 per cent of the people who complained were satisfied with the way their complaint was handled," said Lawrence Klinger, director of public responsibility at Swift & Co. "What we primarily attempt to do, though, is to see what most complaints are about and find out what things we can control and what things we can't control."

For many consumerists, however, business is not controlling enough. They see the actions of corporations in establishing new departments, customer "hot lines" and extensive advertising programs to tout their interest in the consumer as frequently being cosmetic rather than real.

"I think there's an awful lot of P.R. in it," said Don Elberson, executive director of the New York Consumer Assembly. "Companies ought to try to cut out conning the public and give us the facts."

Philip Schrag, professor of consumer protection law at the Columbia University Law School, is equally irate about the activities of businessmen in this regard. "The most important consumer issues require Federal legislation but business is doing everything it can to fight it," he said.

"Until the consumer develops his own countervailing power, as he could through a Federal class action bill, then business is not going to take the consumer movement seriously," Professor Schrag added. "If we had the kind of institutional structure in consumerism we have in securities law, with input from the government, private industry and the public, we'd be a lot better off."

Individual consumers, too, sometimes react strongly to what they believe to be deception by manufacturers and retailers whose promises exceed their practices.

"Years ago a manufacturer wanted to give you a good product, but the quality of everything has gone down very much in the last five years," asserted Mrs. Jean Shechet, a Forest Hills housewife. "Companies put a lot of money into lip service and actually they just give you a snow job."

"Nader's trying to do a good job," Mrs. Joyce Hauser, a Manhattan businesswoman, said. "But it's a vicious cycle. Whenever a manufacturer takes one thing off the market, someone else puts another thing back on."

A survey of 1,600 men and women performed last year by Louis Harris and Associates indicates, moreover, that these feelings of anger at shoddy practices are far from rare. Among the findings of this study were that public perception of product quality had continued to decline.

QUESTIONS FOR DISCUSSION

1. What is the range of expenditures by companies today for offices of consumer relations?

2. Does the consumer have to pay for these new services? In your view, is it worth the higher price that the consumer is obliged to pay?

3. Do you think that money has been wasted in the rush of companies to set up these offices? Why?

4. The number of complaints received seems to decline when a company establishes an office of consumer relations. Why should this be?

5. Is it all just a public relations scheme (window dressing)?

6. Is product quality continuing to decline? What evidence do you have to support this idea?

BUSINESS WEEK

*"The First Attempts at a Corporate 'Social Audit' ",
Business Week, (September 23, 1972), pp. 88-92.
Reproduced by special permission.

The hottest — and possibly the fuzziest — new area of controversy in accounting centers on something called "the corporate social audit." Hounded by critics from Ralph Nader to their own disgruntled stockholders, some of the biggest U. S. companies, including BankAmerica Corp. and American Telephone & Telegraph Co., are looking into ways of measuring their performance in activities that affect the society around them or at least assess the true costs of such programs. If normal financial accounting causes debate, as it does today, the corporate social audit is sure to cause even more.

No one even agrees on what a social audit is and on who should do it, let alone on how to set about doing it. To shed some light on what is happening in the field, two professors at the Harvard Business School have just completed a year-long research project, concentrating on a handful of companies that have tried to devise some measures of how well they are meeting their social responsibilities. Their findings and recommendations appear in a new book, *The Corporate Social Audit*, to be published by the Manhattan-based Russell Sage Foundation early next month.

Co-author Raymond A. Bauer says most companies do not know the scope of their present social programs. "When one stops to think about it, this lack of information is not so surprising," write Bauer and his colleague, Dan H. Fenn, Jr.

"There has been little reason or incentive for corporate officials to report such activities or even catalogue them, much less to pass information on their failures up the line," they say. "Since these activities have not been relevant data for evaluation and promotion, they have not shown up in the offices of top management except on a very hit-or-miss basis."

Low risk value. Bauer and Fenn recommend a four-step social audit which they say is "reasonably demanding, but should prove valuable at low risk to the firm." First, the company would make an inventory of its activities that have a social impact; then it would explain the circumstances that led up to these activities; next there would be an informal evaluation of those programs that are most relevant, perhaps by an outside expert; and finally, the company would assess the ways in which these social programs mesh with the objects both of the firm itself and of society.

Bauer and Fenn say that when they began the study a year ago only a handful of companies had tackled anything faintly resembling a social audit. Now, they say, they hear almost every day of another company thinking of assessing its social contribution. Fenn, who also is director of the separately endowed John F. Kennedy Library, singles out two characteristics common to most companies doing social audits: First, they are large companies. Second, "They have pretty lively, imaginative, somewhat courageous leadership."

"It seems to me there's this feeling of being under a certain amount of public scrutiny," Fenn continues. And Bauer muses: "I think that lurking in the back of any one of these guys' minds is this notice: If somebody started clobbering me in that area, how could I answer him?"

Bauer says he first go interested because the whole social accountability area was in such a mess. Talking about the book, he says: "Social audit was a phrase being thrown about, but there was no defined content." In Fenn's view, the social audit is "a cutting edge" and something that has to be worked out if the social responsibility of business is to have any real meaning or bite to it. "I came to feel that in this whole murky, messy area, the social audit was the best handle to grab on to," he told *Business Week*.

Much confusion arises simply from the use of the word "audit," which suggests a set of dollar figures certified by some outside authority. That may come some day in the social area, in much the same way that financial accounting and auditing gradually evolved. But as Bauer and Fenn write: "The notion that somehow social performance will be integrated with financial performance envisions that a baby which has not yet started to crawl will some day run."

Churches and students. The idea of a corporate social audit has captured the imaginations of social critics, businessmen, consultants, and professional accountants alike. Such groups as the Council on Economic Priorities, the National Council of Churches' Corporate Information Center, and the student-led Committee for Corporate Responsibility all have tried their hands at auditing individual companies' social performance in the areas of minority hiring, defense contracting, or pollution. A number of mutual funds, including the Dreyfus Third Century Fund, have been launched with the policy of investing only in what are deemed to be "socially responsible companies," based on the fund managers' assessment of social performance.

On the business front, management consultants such as Arthur D. Little, Inc., and Abt Associates, Inc., have been helping clients work on social audits, as well as undertaking the same kind of audit on their own companies (see box). And just last month, the American Institute of Certified Public Accountants appointed an eight-man committee to help develop "standards and techniques for measuring, recording, reporting, and auditing social performance."

Many a top executive is intrigued, whether he sees it as a way of appeasing outside critics, of satisfying his own conscience and curiosity, or of guiding his company's decision-making. But the few guidelines previously written have been visionary and theoretical, and of little help to a company trying to "measure the immeasurable" — the impact of its social programs in terms of costs, benefits, performance, or even profits.

How One Company Measures Its Social Contributions
Abt Associates Inc. Social Balance Sheet
Year ended December 31, 1971 with comparative figures for 1970

Social Assets Available	1971	1970
Staff		
Available within one year (Note I)	$ 2,594,390	$ 2,312,000
Available after one year (Note J)	6,368,511	5,821,608
Training Investment (Note K)	507,405	305,889
	9,470,306	8,439,497
Less Accumulated Training Obsolescence (Note K)	136,995	60,523
Total Staff Assets	9,333,311	8,378,974
Organization		
Social Capital Investment (Note L)	1,398,230	1,272,201
Retained Earnings	219,136	–
Land	285,376	293,358
Buildings at cost	334,321	350,188
Equipment at cost	43,018	17,102
Total Organization Assets	2,280,081	1,932,849
Research		
Proposals (Note M)	26,878	15,090
Child Care Research	6,629	–
Social Audit	12,979	–
Total Research	46,486	15,090
Public Services Consumed Net of Tax Payments (Note E)	152,847	243,399
Total Social Assets Available	$11,812,725	$10,570,312
Social Commitments, Obligations, and Equity		
Staff		
Committed to Contracts within one year (Note N)	$ 43,263	$ 81,296
Committed to Contracts after one year (Note O)	114,660	215,459
Committed to Administration within one year (Note N)	62,598	56,915
Committed to Administration after one year (Note O)	165,903	150,842
Total Staff Commitments	386,424	504,512
Organization		
Working Capital Requirements (Note P)	60,000	58,500
Financial Deficit	–	26,814
Facilities and Equipment Committed to Contracts and Administration (Note N)	37,734	36,729
Total Organization Commitments	97,734	122,043
Environmental		
Government Outlays for Public Services Consumed, Net of Tax Payments (Note E)	152,847	243,399
Pollution from Paper Production (Note Q)	1,770	770
Pollution from Electric Power Production (Note R)	2,200	1,080
Pollution from Automobile Commuting (Note S)	10,493	4,333
Total Environmental Obligations	167,310	249,582
Total Commitments and Obligations	651,468	876,137
Society's Equity		
Contributed by Staff (Note T)	8,946,887	7,874,462
Contributed by Stockholders (Note U)	2,182,347	1,810,806
Generated by Operations (Note V)	32,023	8,907
Total Equity	11,161,257	9,694,175
Total Commitments, Obligations and Equity	$11,812,725	$10,570,312

The biggest problem of all may well be internal. Bauer and Fenn note that the audit team at one company could not get safety records from one of its divisions, even though regular reports had to be filed with the U. S. government. And Bauer tells of a manager in charge of his company's social audit who is keeping his plans secret from his fellow executives. "I don't dare let them know what we're up to until we get the president to sit all the vice-presidents down and tell them this is the law," he explained.

Where resistance lies. In their book, Bauer and Fenn explain the resistance from the lower echelons: "The process and outcome of the audit might take up their time and disturb regular operations; expose deep political and philosophic differences within the firm; usurp perogatives (who has the right to see personnel files?); create anxiety that new standards of evaluation are suddenly being applied; stimulate debate over tough issues like who should see the data; and reveal findings that may prove embarrasing if exposed to the public either deliberately or unintentionally. ... In some decentralized companies it seems to smack of 'headquarters' meddling and kibitzing."

Fenn says that he knows of one company evaluating its executives on social performance as well as on financial results. Executives do not get bonuses unless they are performing up to standard on such things as minority hiring. But he concedes that this kind of company policy is rare. The book points out that moving into the social audit area entails a certain amount of risk. "And it's not the firm that takes the risk, but some poor bastard down the line," Bauer says.

One key problem lies in reaching an agreement between those who make the audit and those who use it as to what is feasible and useful. "This is a matter of social communication and the establishment of social trust," Bauer and Fenn write. "Considering the state of trust between the business community and the general public, this may be where the problem lies."

In their book, Bauer and Fenn devote much space to the elaborate "cost-benefit" social audit model developed by management consultant Clark C. Abt, whose company published its own detailed, complex "social income statement" and "social balance sheet" in its 1971 annual report to shareholders.

Numerical camouflage. Such a quantitative exercise may be helpful for internal decision making and planning. In Bauer's view, however, putting in the numbers at this point may camouflage what the public is most interested in knowing. "Frankly, we're just skeptical about being able to convert social benefits exclusively into dollar terms," Bauer says.

Many companies are concentrating on the cost side of the cost-benefit equation and are trying to measure what they call the "true costs" of their social programs, as opposed to the merely out-of-pocket costs. For example, a telephone company that recently hired large numbers of unskilled employees from minority groups is trying to determine what its true costs were when its complaint rate soared.

While such measures may be important for internal control, cost-based social audits, such as have been proposed by accountant David F. Linowes of Laventhol, Krekstein, Horwath & Horwath, could be misinterpreted if released to the public. Bauer cautions that such public reports might make an inefficient management appear to be more socially responsible than an efficient management.

"At this stage of the game, we ought to get away from an exclusive concentration on dollar measurements." Fenn insists, "and explore other ways in which some of these measures can be made." The ultimate form of the social audit may look quite different from the form that has evolved for a financial audit, he says. "and we should be willing to accept that fact, rather than try to push (the social audit) into the acceptable financial auditing box."

Two kinds of balance. Some economists have suggested that equal weight should be given to two kinds of balance sheets, the financial and the social. Bauer is skeptical. "The social critics aren't going to give a damn about the financial," he says. "As a matter of fact, if the financial balance sheet looks good and the social looks bad, they're not going to add them. They're going to subtract them"

Other companies are trying their hands at "performance audits," which attempt to measure the progress of corporate programs against well-defined standards. This can work well in the area of hiring and pollution, where local or national guidelines have been spelled out. Bauer and Fenn suggest three other "reasonable candidates" where performance measures might be applied, even in dollar terms: improved recruiting as a result of the company's socially responsible image; improved consumer acceptability; and improved investor acceptability.

But in many areas of social concern, there are no accepted standards against which to measure performance. Even where standards exist, social critics are constantly pressuring companies to do more. As Bauer and Fenn put it: "Social responsibility is a moving target."

Fenn contends that the community at large is not so much interested in the results of various social programs as in the answer to one key question: Is this company really trying? He and Bauer believe that the most effective kind of social audit — one that would get information to the public so it can answer that question — lies in what they call "process audits." Simply put, a process audit is a rather sophisticated, insightful description of what is being *done* through a particular social program, as contrasted with trying to measure what is being *accomplished* and how effective it is, which is the focus of a performance audit.

The GAO joins in. Bauer points to a study that the General Accounting Office made of one particular series of training programs as an example of a "sensible" process audit. "What they did was sit down and say why the hell was this program set up?" Bauer says. And as he describes it, these were the questions that the GAO explored: "What was the supply problem? You know, what sort of people did you have looking for jobs? What was the demand problem? What sort of jobs were available? What sort of programs were set up? How well did they match the demand? Who went in? Did the people go into the various programs in proportions that were reasonably close to what the demand for jobs was? What proportion got through the program? What proportion got placed?"

Fenn says, "We think that the process audit will reveal the nature of a company's effort better than either the dollar figures or performance figures. If you look at what a company is doing," he adds, "and make it possible for people to judge the seriousness with which management takes this, then it's a valid piece of information. They can judge for themselves whether this is a company that is responsible."

Bauer says that he thinks a social audit can be most useful these days when executives sit down and say, "Let's look at what we're doing and how we're doing it." Most companies, he contends, do not even know that.

He and Fenn acknowledge that companies are going to be reluctant to make such reports public if the results are not favorable, but they argue that if nothing but laudatory reports come out, there is likely to be even more of a credibility gap. "I don't think there's going to be any real credibility until companies start reporting things on which they're not doing so well," Bauer says. "People will just look at the report and say, "Well, what didn't they tell us?' "

He urges companies to "get on the learning curve," because he feels that the social audit will be in increasing demand. "Keep it simple enough that you can do it," he advises. "Be reasonably sure that you're going to have a product that's going to be useful when you get through. And above all, be sure that you've started learning.

"I think a number of companies are ready to buy that," Bauer says.

QUESTIONS FOR DISCUSSION

1. What is a "social audit"? How does it differ from an accounting audit?

2. Why should companies set up such a system? What advantages would be gained?

3. What difficulties are met in doing a social audit? How might these be overcome?

4. "If the reports sound too good there will very likely be even more credibility gaps". Comment.

5. It has been argued by critics that only companies having a very good record for social contributions are likely to set up a social audit system. The rest, who should expose their weaknesses, will avoid such an audit. Do you agree?

6. Should the government make an annual social audit of a company obligatory, just as a financial audit?

PART VII
NEW DEPARTURES IN CONSUMER PROTECTION

This section starts out with a special report on consumerism and the advertising industry's reaction to it, by *Business Week*. In this article, the reader is informed of the latest moves to further consumer protection, and their probable outcome is appraised as of mid-1972.

After receiving this overview of the question, the reader next examines certain of the specific laws and remedies passed or proposed to improve the position of the buyer. The Shaffer article notes the rapid increase in lawsuits filed by consumers against companies, and analyzes the reasons and consequences of this growth. The consumer class action remedy, of which so much is expected by some consumerists, is carefully appraised by the next article. Your editor and Etienne Gorse then examine the provisions and efficacy of the latest Fair Packaging and Labelling Act. The reader should note how the original Hart bill was successively whittled down by special interest groups, until what was left indeed provided a disappointing amount of protection, and failed to cure the package size muddle.

An appraisal is attempted on unit pricing by Miss Garland. Again, much store was put on unit pricing when it was being recommended by various consumer advocates. The author objectively examines research evidence as to the effect of unit pricing on the housewife's shopping prowess. The results, it will be noted, tend to belie early enthusiasm about unit pricing.

Finally, Mrs. Myerson tells us about the progress to date of her department of consumer protection in helping the New York City consumer.

If many of the promises of these new departures in consumer protection seem to be unfulfilled, the reader should not be too discouraged. Remember, (1) it is still too early to tell positively whether they have worked; (2) all human progress is slow and painful. Human endeavor seldom pans out as expected. But the significant fact, we think, is that so many things are being tried, that society has become so experimental. Letting things drift along is the worse of all decisions.

It may be that, out of the welter of laws, regulations and new devices, a few will prove their worth. If so, consumer welfare is bound to be enhanced in the long run.

That great experimenter, President Franklin D. Roosevelt, frequently had a cherished plan shot down. Undaunted and ever optimistic, he would shrug his shoulders, turn to his assistants and say: "Well, that didn't work. Here's another plan . . . here's what we are going to do . . ."

RICHARD A. SHAFFER

* Richard A. Shaffer, "More Customers Press Lawsuits Against Firms Selling Faulty Products", *Wall Street Journal* (November 3, 1972), pp. 1, 27. Reproduced by permission.

Not long ago in suburban Dayton, Ohio, Velma Toth was pouring coffee for her husband, Alexander, when the pot cracked and his leg was burned. Although the pot was a year and a half old, Mr. Toth sued the manufacturer, Corning Glass Works, for damages and won. The award, upheld on appeal, was $6,000.

In Seattle, salesman Bob Andersen was struck in the eye and blinded when the plastic stopper prematurely shot out of a bottle of cold duck. Although the accident occurred as he was opening the bottle, Mr. Andersen sued the vineyard, Gold Seal Vinyards Inc., for damages, and he also won — some $70,000.

Such cases aren't as unusual as they may seem. For consumers injured by allegedly faulty products are going to court in record numbers these days. And not only are they winning more and larger victories, they're also setting precedents that make life increasingly hazardous for markers of everything from toys to airplanes.

"Almost everyone is running scared," says W. H. Graham, director of quality control for Johns-Manville Corp.

Products that don't work as they should, which now rival automobile accidents as the nation's No. 1 cause of litigation, were responsible for an estimated 500,000 court cases last year, compared with 100,000 five years ago, and many expect the annual total to reach one million by 1985.

The percentage of cases in which juries rule in favor of plaintiffs has also risen in recent years — to 52% this year from 49% in 1965, according to surveys by Jury Verdict Research, Cleveland. And the amount of the average award has increased substantially, going to $67,290 in 1969 from $11,644 in 1965 in household chemical cases, for example, and to $77,763 from $38,112 over the same period in cases involving automobiles and trucks. Though more recent figures aren't available, Jury Verdict Research says the increases appear to have continued.

"Today, a poorly made product isn't passed off with the remark, 'I got a lemon,'" observes H. D. Hulme, a manager of quality and material control for Westinghouse Electric Corp. "More likely, the words heard are 'I'll sue.'"

The change stems partly from rising consumerism and also from the gradual spread of a legal theory known as "strict liability." Followed now in 20 states, this theory essentially holds the maker of a faulty product responsible for the damage it does, no matter how careful he may have been in making it.

Formerly, the plaintiff collected only if he proved the defendant's negligence or breach of warranty. Now he need only show that the defective item that caused his injury was unreasonably dangerous when it left the factory. As a practical matter, his own negligence is almost unimportant. Strict liability also goes beyond the maker of the finished product and includes subcontractors, assemblers, construction firms, distributors, retailers and leasing companies — in short, everyone along the "trail of sale," as some lawyers put it.

"The claims have reached a condition now that even the salesman, who might be an independent manufacturer's representative, and all he did was to call in an order to send a particular product to a buyer, is being joined in the suit," says W. H. Ungles, a Beverly Hills, Calif., consultant who helps companies assess their insurance risks. He says such salesmen have been known to be forced "to buy their way off or go in and defend themselves, even though they had absolutely nothing to do with the claim."

More and more courts are extending the benefits of strict liability not only to those who actually use a faulty product but to injured bystanders as well.

A recent example is the case of Mr. and Mrs. Frank Codling of Glenmont, N.Y., injured when their Buick was hit by a Chrysler after its power steering had failed. The traditional view would be that Chrysler owed the Codlings nothing because they weren't driving the defective car. But an appellate judge ruled that they could indeed collect from Chrysler — some $350,000 — because, quoting an earlier California decision, "if anything bystanders should be entitled to greater protection than the consumer or user where injury to bystander from the defect is reasonably foreseeable. Consumers and users, at least, have the opportunity to inspect for defects and to limit their purchases to articles manufactured by reputable manufacturers and sold by reputable retailers, whereas the bystander ordinarily has no such opportunity."

Industrial accidents are another increasingly common source of product-liability litigation. Plaintiffs are bypassing the restricted workmen's compensation machinery and bringing third-party actions directly against industrial equipment makers. The case of John McPhee Jr. makes it easy to see why.

Mr. McPhee, a 22-year-old sawyer in Prairie du Chien, Wis., lost his left leg and part of his right when he was pushed through a circular saw used to cut logs. He alleged that he had put the log carrier into neutral gear and crawled inside to remove a sliver that had jammed the machine, when the carrier slipped back into gear. Under workmen's compensation, Mr. McPhee's total payments came to $33,917. By contrast, a federal court jury awarded him $500,000 in damages from the company that made the log carriage.

The rising number of such sizable awards is bad news for insurance carriers. Insurance Company of North America, which says its experience is fairly typical, has lost increasing amounts of money in product-liability coverage since 1967. In 1970, these losses amounted to several millions of dollars, a record, and accounted for 50% of the company's general liability losses, up from 34% only a year earlier.

To offset this trend, insurance carriers have been increasing premiums — sometimes as much as sevenfold. What's more distressing to many businesses, however, is that with several types of especially hazardous products it is no longer possible to purchase complete coverage at any price.

With some products, the deductible — the uninsured amount the business itself must pay — has reached as high as $1 million, says Gerald L. Maatman, president of National Loss Control Service Corp., a Long Grove, Ill., consulting and engineering company that is owned by Kemper Co.

In some industries, such as aircraft manufacturing, product-liability insurance costs have risen so rapidly that they have become important factors in the price of the product, and in an effort to reduce these costs more and more firms are turning to self-insurance through their own so-called captive companies.

Despite all the concern, however, some observers say it's difficult to tell whether, on the whole, the rash of lawsuits is actually resulting in safer products. This question, among others, is being studied by a research group from Carnegie-Mellon and Duquesne universities in Pittsburgh.

"While most business concerns maintain programs designed to eliminate or reduce casualty losses, adequate product-safety programs are fewer in number," according to the Fireman's Fund American Insurance Cos. "Nor do many concerns consider safety responsibility of top management."

The National Commission on Product Safety found that although private lawsuits are increasingly successful in compensating victims, they "seldom cause manufacturers to take preventive measures as a result of adverse judgment."

QUESTIONS FOR DISCUSSION

1. Are lawsuits a good device to protect consumers?

2. What limitations in protection of the consumer are met in ordinary suits-at-law?

3. Why, then, has there been a big increase in lawsuits, both in numbers filed and in the size of the typical award? Is it because products are more hazardous, or that consumers have an increased awareness of their legal rights?

4. What effect has the rise of lawsuits had on (a) the insurance business, and (b) product safety?

BUSINESS WEEK

* "Madison Avenue's Response to It's Critics," *Business
Week* (June 10, 1972), pp. 44-54. Reproduced by special
permission.

Like a slow-moving Saturn V rocket struggling to escape from the
earth's atmosphere as it heads moonward, the advertising business
has shaken off the shock waves caused by the first blast of
consumerism and has moved into a second stage. It is a period of
sober evaluation — or reevaluation in many cases — and it differs
markedly from the initial period when admen reacted by heaping
invectives on the heads of Ralph Nader and the five members of the
Federal Trade Commission.

Now, according to people at both the client and agency level,
corporate leaders are sitting down with agency heads and creative
men, and, perhaps for the first time, are trying to develop mutual
goals that go beyond the mere selling of goods or services. The result
in some instances is advertising that is deemed "more effective." In
other cases, admen themselves may consider their work less effective
in selling products; but they acknowledge a different kind of
effectiveness: the ads draw no ire from consumer groups and
watchdogs of either appointed or unappointed stripe.

"We have literally taken some campaigns from our agencies that
were not what we thought they should be," says Earl Clasen,
marketing vice-president at Pillsbury Co., who feels that advertising
today must have a corporate role equal to that of personnel planning,
legal affairs, and other top-priority functions. "We have carefully
explained our position on this to the agency, and better ads have
come out of it. It takes time — not necessarily money — and policies
and procedures that make sure that corporate philosophies, from the
topmost levels, are reflected in advertising."

An assistant advertising director at a major airline notes that when
a governmental group questioned an ad recently, "our first thought
was one of righteous indignation — 'They're way out of line,' and so
on. But since then, management has made us take a good hard look
at ourselves, and at what we were saying in trying to get business in a
very competitive situation. And some of us have come around to
thinking that maybe a little closer scrutiny isn't all that bad."

A few months ago, that kind of language would have been
considered near-blasphemy on Madison Avenue. Indeed, verbal
brickbats were hurled by their fellows at several admen who seemed
to have defected to the consumerist "enemy" early in the game.

Noted art director and agency president George Lois, for example, was barely appointed to head the New York Art Directors Club when he announced that the organization stood four-square behind a Council of Economic Priorities study that castigated advertisers in *Time* and *Business Week*. The ads, said the CEP, boasted of ecological gains, but the companies doing the boasting were major polluters. Lois' posture drew some angry comments.

So did an address at Fairleigh Dickinson University by Milton Marcus, a vice-president at a small fashion agency, Claire Advertising. Marcus said: "The quality of life in a society is determined by the quality of its culture. Ours is rotten. The advertising industry has helped create it and is continuing to make it worse." Advertising skeptics shook their heads, too, when Arthur W. Schultz, chairman of Foote, Cone & Belding Communications, Inc., tried to find a rainbow in the clouds, and said that if advertising responded *positively* to the consumerism movement, the resultant effectiveness of ads could save all industry $2-billion a year. As people become more confident that ads are truthful, he explained, "there will be a reduction in the numbers and impact, if not the elimination, of many of the charlatans in our business."

The FTC Attack

The word "charlatan" is a dangerous one in an industry where many spokesmen have lobbied over the years for "professional" status similar to that afforded doctors, engineers, and lawyers. But in looking at the aggressive and punitive record of just one body — the FTC — in recent months, even some of the most impassioned proponents of the "good" in advertising might be suspicious of some of its practitioners. Among other things, the FTC has:

Proposed that American Home Products Corp., Bristol-Myers Co., and Sterling Drug, Inc., which spend about $80-million a year to advertise Bufferin, Anacin, Bayer aspirin, and other remedies, spend 25% of their budgets to "correct" claims made in previous ads.

Ordered major makers of cough-and-cold remedies to come up with proof of such claims as "Contac provides relief for up to 12 hours" and "4-Way Nasal Spray works faster than other products." Makers of toothpaste, TV sets, tires and others also have been asked for such substantiation.

Won agreement from cigarette companies to emphasize the Surgeon General's health warning in all print ads. ("We're changing our printing plates now," says a spokesman for a major company whose ads some months after the agreement carried no warning whatsoever, "but it takes time.")

Moved to eliminate some $73-million in ad spending by cereal makers that, according to the FTC, is unnecessary for sales, serves to drive out competition, and is probably fraudulent to boot.

Where there is so much smoke, there can well be some fire — or so the public and numerous admen themselves have come to believe. "I think much of the industry is getting what it deserves," says Harold Levine, who recently brought former newscaster Chet Huntley into his small agency. The new partner in Levine, Huntley & Schmidt — who watched thousands of commercials during his 18 years with NBC-TV — will check out the agency's TV ads from an ethical standpoint. "The clients are delighted," says Levine. And Robert J. Fisher, ad manager at the Ford Div. of Ford Motor Co., endorses FTC interest in advertising: "Their concern has made top management more responsive to pleas for more straightforward, honest ads. It put a damper on some free-wheeling of years past, and it has brought us closer to the guy we should be talking to, anyway."

Such words sound sincere. Yet, under them is a deep-seated fear on the part of many admen that increased governmental regulation of the $20-billion advertising industry would lead to less advertising, fewer product sales, fewer agency commissions.

The fear grew in the past two years as advertising's growth rate, which was about 5.1% annually during the 1960s, slipped to about 4%. General business conditions — the recession — accounted for the slowdown, admen told themselves repeatedly, but in the backs of their minds was another thought: Was the barrage of anti-advertising criticism weakening clients' belief in the value of advertising (and particularly TV advertising) as part of the marketing mix?

The figures tell a yes-and-no-and-perhaps story. Procter & Gamble Co., for example, spent $190.5-million in TV last year, up from $179.3-million in 1970, and American Home Products raised its spending from $67.2-million to $88-million. General Motors Corp. was up, too, from $42-million to $65-million. General Foods, Bristol-Myers, and Colgate-Palmolive all spent less. But did the decreases have economic justification, or had management lost faith in advertising?

Says a General Foods advertising executive: "If we didn't think advertising worked, we wouldn't spend $100-million a year on it." A further indication that the downturn was a temporary one came when the reviving economy caused advertisers' TV investments to surge in the first quarter of 1972: National clients spend about 9% more for network ads than in the same 1971 period, and 10% more for local ones.

Still, admen themselves have increasingly noted that today's advertising is not all that it once was. FC&B's Schultz, for one, recently pointed out that studies reveal that the industry's repetitive blandishments to "buy this" and "try that" have lost 20% of their effectiveness in the past 10 years. At a Washington (D.C.) meeting last month, a vice-president of Quaker Oats Co. said that for the past two decades, advertising has been seriously lacking "in terms of ethics, in terms of contributions to society, and perhaps even in terms of economic efficiency." Quaker's Vice-President Kenneth Mason proved his point with figures from a special telephone survey of TV viewers: The survey showed that 97% of them did not know who had advertised on six high-rated programs they had watched the night before.

The Kids Tuned Out

Economics Professor Robert L. Heilbroner, a longtime critic of the advertising industry, has a ready explanation for the current seeming lack of effectiveness of advertising. Today's young consumers, he says are yesterday's TV-nurtured children, who learned almost in infancy that toy and cereal advertisers "lied" to sell their mommies products which seldom lived up to their on-screen image. Heilbroner, who teaches at New York City's New School for Social Research, claims that admen responded to the first indications of disbelief not by making their ads more honest and informative, but by simply hitting harder and more often with what he calls "calculated prevarication." This served only to bring on increased attacks from consumerists, and growing suspension of belief by the public.

A study released in mid-April by the American Assn. of Advertising Agencies shows how serious the problem is today. Of some 9,000 students from 177 universities and colleges, 53% told the AAAA that they consider advertising "believable some of the time." Some 57% thought — a chilling thought to the admen — that more government regulation should be imposed on the advertising industry.

Reporting on the study, William H. Genge, president of Ketchum, McLeod & Grove, Inc., looks on the bright side. "The students don't want to ban advertising," he says, "they want to improve it. I regard this attitude as healthy and constructive, and it makes their criticism all the more relevant."

The Adman Also Is Responsive

Admen are listening to criticism these days for any number of reasons. For one thing, many of them have accepted "consumerism" as a worthwhile movement, rather than as simply an attack on big business in itself. "I'm a consumer first of all," says Cunningham & Walsh Chairman Carl Nichols, Jr., "and I have a point of resistance to faulty workmanship and products that don't work or do what they're promoted to do."

In some companies and agencies, younger executives are said to be more receptive to discussions of ad criticism. ("I don't buy that," says the ad director of giant food products company. "I know a chief executive who is 62 years old and is more responsive to the whole consumer movement than a lot of kids just out of college.") But a primary reason that attention is being paid to critics of advertising, whether it is admitted or not, is that the industry hopes it can keep the FTC off its back.

The FTC's attacks in the past two years have made some kind of positive reaction mandatory. When Miles Kirkpatrick was brought into head the FTC early in 1970, the agency set out to establish itself as the "hottest" regulatory body in Washington. It almost had to. Kirkpatrick himself had chaired a study by the American Bar Assn. that labeled the commission a "do-nothing agency" blind to the troubles of consumers. An independent study by a group of Ralph Nader's "raiders" had arrived at the same conclusion.

Under considerable pressure from consumers' groups and some members of Congress, as well as from the FTC staff itself, to bolster the commission, President Nixon named Kirkpatrick, a 56-year-old Republican, to shake up the FTC. The new chief appointed a young aide, Robert Pitofsky, to head a new Bureau of Consumer Protection — and the two men swung into action. Among their innovations:

OPENING THE REGULATORY PROCESS TO "OUTSIDERS." For the first time, consumerist lawyers — such as John F. Banzhaf III, who heads an organization called Action on Smoking & Health (ASH) that was instrumental in obtaining the broadcast ban on cigarette ads — have been made aware that the FTC will listen to their pleas. Numerous lawyers have since petitioned for tough anti-advertising action and have clamored to act as a "friend of the court" whenever the FTC considers ad restrictions.

STRETCHING THE CONCEPT OF "UNFAIR AND DECEPTIVE" ADS. Over the years, the FTC has usually attacked claims it believed to be false — Colgate's Rapid-Shave would not help a razor shave sandpaper, Geritol will not cure "tired blood" — but the commission has lately sought to have drug companies and others conduct extensive tests before making any ad claims, even though their products contain individual ingredients that have long been known to be effective.

Although the FTC lost one such case against Pfizer, Inc.'s Un-Burn sunburn pain-killer, it still wants to restrict claims that are not backed up by scientific data. The agency would also bar ads that imply that a product is unique — for example, "Wonder Bread builds bodies 12 ways" — when such claims could be made by rivals with virtually identical products.

LETTING THE PUBLIC ITSELF DO MORE REGULATING. In a number of product categories, beginning with automobiles and continuing through tires, TV sets, cold remedies, electric shavers, air conditioners, and toothpastes (with more to come), the FTC has ordered advertisers to document their claims. The commission's idea is that, by putting the documentation before a skeptical public, the press and consumerists will point accusing fingers at perpetrators of fraudulent claims.

In practice, however, the idea has not worked out very well. Automobile advertisers, for example, flooded the overworked FTC staff with a mass of technical material that has taken many months to evaluate. It concluded that 13 of 75 claims were not supported by empirical data, 21 had incomplete data, and 32 could not be evaluated at all because the terminology was too technical.

Kirkpatrick told Senator Frank Moss (D-Utah), who chairs the Senate consumer subcommittee, that nine of the "no data" claims might be supported by additional data yet to come and that five are being studied by an independent evaluator who also will consider some of the technical claims. Moss has proposed a "truth in advertising" bill that would require advertisers to back each claim in an ad with the proof alongside, but he has not won FTC support thus far. And the commission's plan to continue its substantiation investigation until the end of the year indicates that he will not get backing before then.

The 'Corrective' Ad

These efforts, while troubling to advertising executives at major corporations and on Madison Avenue, are not regarded as overwhelming threats. Experience has shown that cases in which the FTC charges deceit take years to wend their way through the commission and subsequent court tests. Already, one company — Sunbeam Corp. — that was asked to substantiate claims in an electric shave ad, has complained to the FTC of intimidation and a violation of its rights under the First Amendment. Ad men know, too, that in practice, most controversial ad campaigns are ended long before a final decision is reached and a consent order signed. The real FTC challenge that confronts the ad industry, they believe, stems from three "revolutionary" objectives:

To force advertisers to run costly "corrective" ads that supposedly would counteract any false impressions placed in the public mind by deceptive ads in the past.

To force broadcasters (via Federal Communications Commission rules) to provide free air time for "counteradvertising" messages from groups or individuals seeking to refute product commercials, in the way that antismoking forces were given air time to show the dangers of cigarettes.

To win passage of Senate Bill 986 and House of Representatives Bill 4809, which under Title II would give the FTC authority to issue trade regulation rules that could seriously affect advertising, as well as other industries.

The corrective ads proposal has been controversial for about two years, during which time the FTC has tried to apply it to cases involving such products as Firestone tires, Wonder bread, and most recently, Bufferin, Excedrin, Bayer aspirin, and other pain-killers. Admen scoff at the suggestion that a client spend one-fourth of his annual budget on ads that would say, for example: "It has not been established that Anacin is more effective for the relief of minor pain than aspirin . . ." or that "It has not been established that Bayer aspirin is more effective for the relief of minor pain than any aspirin . . ." The language in both instances was proposed by the

FTC, but in the only case thus far in which an advertiser has run "corrective" ads, the wording was left up to the client, ITT Continental Baking Co., and its agency, Ted Bates & Co.

The 'Concerned' Advertiser

To stave off further complaints and action from the commission — which had objected to claims that Profile bread would aid dieters in losing weight — the baking company put TV spokeswoman Julia Meade on the air last August to clarify "any misunderstandings" that viewers might have reached while viewing Profile commercials over the years. The bread, Miss Meade stated, would not help anyone lose weight — but it was tasty. Despite recurrent rumors that grateful viewers appreciated the new approach, Arthur Ostrove, Continental Baking's ad director, recently announced that the ads would be taken off as soon as the one-year penalty period was up. Profile sales in the past year suffered tremendously, he stated — but whether from the commercials or adverse publicity stemming from the original FTC complaint is unknown.

Continental's compliance with the FTC proposal drew fire from other advertisers, who contended that the commission now had a shining example of "an advertiser concerned with truth." And several weeks ago, when a second company, Ocean Spray Cranberries, Inc., agreed to run corrective ads on a claim made in its advertising, *Advertising Age* editorialized vehemently against Ocean Spray President Harold Thorkilsen, who had said the company would have preferred to fight the FTC charges, but "there are times when economics and practicalities dictate that a company compromise on a lawsuit." Such a resonse, said the trade publication, would make it harder for other companies "with legitimate beefs to win their tilts with the government on another day."

Despite the compliance of two advertisers, the industry at large does not view the proposals for corrective ads as a major threat. They have to be made on a case-by-case basis, and the courts are likely to bottle up individual complaints for lengthy periods, should the advertiser fight back.

It is the counteradvertising proposal that is deemed a real danger by most advertising executives — particularly those at TV stations and networks. As they see it, ecologists would demand free air time to attack car advertising on the grounds that cars cause pollution; organic-food advocates could protest chemical additives in frozen pastries, and so on. Various groups and individuals have asked the FCC, which has jurisdiction over the 43-year-old "fairness doctrine" under which broadcasters operate, to open the airwaves to their messages against the Vietnam war, ecological infractions, and other controversial issues. The communications body has been studying most of the proposals on an issue-by-issue basis, but last March the FTC made the startling proposal that the doctrine should be applied to advertising messages for products.

Broadcasters, mindful of the $200-million-a-year they lost once the ban on cigarette advertising went into effect, feel that the antismoking ads which they were forced to put on the air helped bring about the Congressional ban. They doubt that the FCC will endorse the FTC's broad and sweeping proposal, but they realize that it is possible that "counter ad" forces could win out in specific product areas — in detergents, perhaps, or analgesics. And they worry that advertisers might decline to promote their products in the knowledge that someone might get free air time to rebut their claims. Would it not be easier, agency men wonder, for the client to put his budget into newspapers or magazines, where he would not face the counter-advertising threat — since print media has no "equal time" or fairness requirements. And, if so, his total advertising budget — and the agency commissions — would probably be greatly reduced. (The six major cigarette companies cut their spending 28% last year from $278.5-million in 1970 to $200.2-million in 1971, while domestic consumption of cigarettes rose 3.3%).

The FTC Wants to Make the Rules

Most bothersome of all is the proposal to give the FTC legislative rule-making power. Peter W. Allport, president of the Assn. of National Advertisers, says that if the commission gets the proposed authority, "it would no longer need to prove that a given course of conduct or business activity was unfair or deceptive; it could simply issue a rule saying it was, and find you guilty if you violated the rule."

Allport argues that the FTC could issue rules on almost anything: "It could, for example, say that a given advertising-to-sales ratio was unfair, or that advertising to certain markets — children, let's say — was deceptive per se . . ." The bill that, in Allport's view, would permit this is on "the highest priority" schedule of Representative John Moss (D-Cal.), who chairs the House subcommittee that must consider it first. Moss moved up the priority after the FTC suffered a court setback in April, when a judge blocked a commission rule requiring the posting of octane ratings on gasoline pumps. The FTC has taken the case to the Supreme Court, but a decision will not be reached until next year.

Consumerism Is Here To Stay

Much of the FTC activity, advertisers assume (and some FTC lawyers openly admit), is undertaken just to keep the admen on their guard. "What we're trying to do," says Gerald Thain, Pitofsky's director of national advertising regulations, "is get big advertisers and their lawyers to ask themselves, 'Is it worth the risk to try something that may be deceptive?' If the cost of losing is not worth the candle, they are not going to stop."

Thain's phrasing seems to indicate a presupposition that admen normally consider risking a deceptive ad or two. "I've been in the business 20 years," says F. William Free, who created the controversial National Airlines campaign, attacked by feminists for its "Fly me, I'm Barbara" headlines, "and I've never sat in a creative meeting where somebody said, 'Here's an idea I think we can get away with.'" Thomas Dillon, who heads the gigantic BBDO agency emphasizes the same point: "We have 75 clients, a lot of them in very competitive fields. In all the years I've been here, I've watched our competition's ads, and so have all the other people on our accounts, hoping to catch them in a statement that we can take advantage of. We haven't been able to do it. We've never been able to catch Procter & Gamble in a lie."

Dillon's outspoken attitude toward the FTC — he believes many of its actions are simply politically motivated — draws respect, but not always agreement, from other admen. Maurice L. Kelly, vice-president and director of advertising for Eastern Airlines, believes the time for anger and resentment is past. "The consumerism movement is here to stay," Kelly says, "and, frankly, it has accelerated some things that we should have been doing all along."

Specifically, he notes that the airline last fall instituted an "office of consumer affairs" and will open branches at major airports to handle on-the-scene problems. An executive running the office now checks out Eastern's ads, as do the company's lawyers and public relations people. The airline has also moved to clean up its ads, eliminating the asterisks and footnotes that sometimes make it impossible for the average traveler to obtain the advertising low fares.

"Some guys say that if you have to run 'full-disclosure' ads that cover all the restrictions, the ads will be too dull to read," says Kelly. "I don't believe it. There are enough creative people in the business to make an ad interesting, despite any limitations."

Last fall, after dozens of high-level advertising executives trooped to Washington to explain their ways of doing business at an "informational" hearing conducted by the FTC, admen hoped that some of the governmental suspicions would disappear. But, says William Colihan, vice-president of the American Assn. of Advertising Agencies, "admen walked through the valley of the shadow of death and emerged unscathed" — only to find shortly afterwards that the FTC hoped to broaden its definitions of "unfair advertising."

The New Kind of Advertising

Now the admen are hoping that their new attitudes will take off some of the heat. In addition to expressing themselves in speeches and public statements, they are putting a new kind of advertising — for many of them, at any rate — onto the air. Shell Oil Co., for example, which long has advertised the "secret ingredients" that give automobiles better mileage, has adopted a "no claims" institutional approach in which it talks of such things as its expertise in making soles for tennis shoes. "And if Shell can do that," says a typical commercial, "think what it can do in its primary business of making gasoline for your car." A Sunoco TV spot admits that most cars do not need its gasoline blend with an octane rating of 260, "but isn't it nice to know that there's a company that makes it?" Other "no claim" ads are appearing for American gasoline (which uses folksinger Johnny Cash to tell about the glories of the open road), Ford cars ("The Torino just might be more car than you bargained for"), Dash detergent, and numerous other products.

The Move to Self-Regulation

In another move, the advertising associations and the National Council of Better Business Bureaus have set up a new and elaborate self-regulatory system. The idea is to correct potentially deceptive or misleading ads before the government storms in. The new National Advertising Review Board, headed by former United Nations Ambassador Charles W. Yost, has already received some 200 complaints from consumers groups and individuals. "Some of the groups have admitted they are testing us," says William H. Ewen, executive director of the NARB, which assembles panels of five adjudicators to duscuss complaints with offending agencies and advertisers. The five are drawn from a roster of 50 leading executives both inside and outside the industry. "We hold that the ultimate responsibility for advertising is that of the client, not the agency," says Ewen, who notes that thus far the reaction from both has been extremely positive. It had better be: The NARB says that if an advertiser fails to modify an offending ad once the board has ordered it to do so, the board will turn its findings and the complaint over to the FTC or other regulatory body.

As yet, with panels meeting as often as three times a week, such action has not been necessary. Although some Washington officials, including FTC Chairman Kirkpatrick, have lauded the admen's efforts, the FTC recently moved to set up a special task force to study whether industry self-regulation means much as a general rule. A prior staff study revealed considerable doubt.

Another matter of great concern to the advertising fraternity is that the FTC and the anti-advertising crusaders in Washington have not yet let up the pressure, despite the industry's new conciliatory attitude. Howard H. Bell, president of the American Advertising Federation, recently proposed that the various advertising organizations coordinate industry reaction to the numerous attacks that evidently will continue to come from all sides. *Broadcasting* magazine called Bell's proposal a "Battle plan."

The Question of FTC's Priorities

Admen who still want to fight feel that they have plenty of ammunition. BBDO's Dillon, for example, notes that the FTC's own survey of its regional offices shows that only 5.7% of all complaints from consumers were about advertising. Many more were about product delivery, faulty merchandise, and the like. But according to Kirkpatrick, the issue of consumer protection takes up 60% to 70% of the commission's time — and advertising was the prime consumer issue of the past two years. Contemplating the time and money spent by the FTC to criticize Campbell Soup, Wonder Bread, and a handful of other products, adman Bill Free is aghast. "I mean," he says, "that with all the problems facing the country, there must be a priority list somewhere."

NBC and the Television Bureau of Advertising last month furnished what they consider more concrete evidence of the pitfalls toward which the FTC pushes the broadcast industry when it attacks advertising. The commission's belief in counteradvertising, says TVB, could have cost television some $540.4-million of its gross revenues of $3.2-billion in 1970 and would have changed the industry from one that enjoyed $453.8-million in pretax profits to one that lost $86.6-million.

Kirkpatrick, however, shrugs aside the impassioned protests with an observation that the FTC is not asking braodcasters to run a counter-ad each time a controversial product ad is put on the air. Instead, he suggests that a block of time — say, 15 to 30 minutes weekly — be devoted to countercommercials. Already, an organization called The Stern Concern has prepared several commercials — featuring actor Burt Lancaster — that criticize Chevrolet and seven well-known analgesics. The car commercial was made for the Center For Auto Safety, which is now trying to get it on the networks; the Medical Committee for Human rights, a national doctors' organization, will seek time for the anti-analgesic message. And last month, an FTC staff member called on a convention of pharmacists to seek airtime to warn patients about over-the-counter drugs.

Playing Without Any Rules

Despite some signs of dissension within the FTC itself — and the possibility that both Kirkpatrick and Pitofsky might return to private law — admen dare not hope that the commission will soon relax its anti-advertising posture. Most unsettling to advertisers and agencies is the fact that they do not know in which direction the FTC will move, or what it will go after. One month it's cereals, the next it's analgesics, the next it's toothpaste. Last year, Walter Bregman, who heads the Norman, Craig, & Hummel, Inc., agency, looked at FTC activity and said: "Let's face facts — we are scared. Today, the guidelines aren't set, we're playing a high-stakes game, and we don't know the rules."

Since then, many admen has come to feel that there are no rules. In such a game, the safest tack is to join the consumerist movement — even to use it as an advertising theme — and to make ads that have no claims that can be challenged.

One problem with such advertising is illustrated all too well in a remark by Heilbroner. "One of the few ads I've seen that doesn't turn me off," he says, "is that one where they say they're just giving the facts. It's for — uh — a deodorant, I think, called — uh . . . uh . . . hmm . . ."

APPENDIX I
A Tough Adman Sizes Up a Tough FTC

Tom Dillon, president of Batten, Barton, Durstine & Osborn, Inc., is a hero on Madison Avenue these days, as well as a rarity: He scored a singular victory over the Federal Trade Commission when it announced last November that it was withdrawing a charge of false advertising against BBDO and Du Pont's Zerez anti-leak antifreeze. The adman and his client, who had fought the charge for a full year, saw the FTC eat crow when it said, ". . . in the commission's judgment, the demonstration was accurate and not deceptive."

In his ninth floor office, which is actually on Madison Avenue, the grandfatherly agency president shakes his head as he discusses the case. He thinks that some unknown staff member at the FTC woke up one morning, saw the famous puncture-can Zerez commercial on TV, and said: "I don't believe it." The next thing BBDO and Du Pont knew was that the FTC had announced to the news media that it would charge the advertiser with deception. "They did not come to us," says Dillon, "and say, 'We don't believe the commercial. Could we see a demonstration?' We had two inches of documentation. We had already sent the script of the spot to Washington with details of the technical test. We had even changed the script in accordance with their suggestions."

Attention-getter. Dillon measures his words carefully. "I believe the whole thing was the result of a desire to get Du Pont in the headlines," he says.

The agency man firmly believes that getting public attention is as much of a goal of the FTC as it is of Madison Avenue. Prodded by consumerists and legislators anxious to show their constituency that someone is looking out for their welfare in Washington, the commission, Dillon says, has to react strongly. Says he of that reaction:

"Their own survey showed that only 5% of complaints are about advertising, and I'll bet that only a fraction of those have anything to do with network TV. But the FTC does not have the staff or the money to go after all the little guys. They have to go after the highly visible advertisers, and that means attacking network television.

"The amazing thing is that no medium has such rigorous scrutiny as network TV. Scripts and commercials go through agency lawyers, network lawyers, the National Assn. of Broadcasters, the clients' lawyers, and even the FTC in some cases before they go on the air. Newspapers, wire services — nobody else — subjects what they give the public to that kind of scrutiny. But who gets attacked?

"It's difficult to say what the commission should do. They are widening the parameters of their presumed responsibility — they are trying to regulate communication — and I wish journalists were as concerned with their aims as they are about the Defense Dept.'s. We will probably have to get into court to find out if the FTC is empowered to expand into some of the areas it wants to get into — such as the idea that for every positive claim you make, you will have to make a nonpositive one. No one can write something that gives both sides of a picture in all its ramifications — except attorneys, and that kind of language is not communicative to the ordinary person. To avoid that kind of writing, you reach the point where you say virtually *nothing* about the product.

"The FTC has everyone so nervous about accurate depictions that if you do a commercial for a bathtub cleanser, you have to have 18 kids take a bath to produce a realistic ring. And if you have to reshoot, you have to get the 18 kids back again. The FTC has taken the position that everything seen on the screen is a laboratory demonstration, so we're carrying out some of the most absurd things imaginable. There's no question of any consumer benefit being involved.

"And in the final analysis, the consumer pays for everything — all the extra work involved, the legal checks and double checks, the production details. There's a kind of unwritten rule that corporate profits are fixed from year to year, so the increased costs get passed on to the public.

"I think the situation in Washington will get worse. The FTC has found a way to spotlight its zeal. Most people perceive of themselves as victims — it might be a result of the socioeconomic teaching in our schools these days that advertising is an evil, an unnecessary part of the economy. So when someone announces, 'I am your friend and I will protect you from your enemy — them,' it gets attention. It makes headlines. The networks rush to cover you.

"And the amazing thing — to me, anyway — is that the public thinks the Naders and Pitofskys are brave. The public does not know that in most cases you cannot libel a corporation. There is no legal defense against someone who says that General Motors makes its automobile seats out of tissue paper and wicker. You can't haul him into court. He can be the biggest liar, making any allegation that comes to mind, getting headlines everywhere, and you have no recourse. The corporation is appallingly helpless."

Dillon shrugs his shoulders, shakes the thinning thatch of white hair.

"It's not bravery at all."

APPENDIX II
'If Legal Says Change It — Change It'

As the head of eight-year-old Chuck Blore Creative Services in Los Angeles, adman Chuck Blore has turned out some highly creative radio commercials for Chrysler, Coca-Cola, and other clients. Now he says, restrictions caused by fear are making commercials less interesting and — at least in his opinion — less effective.

"In the last few months," Blore says, "the situation has gotten so tight that a new word has come into the business. It's 'legaled.' We used to get a 'client okay' before a commercial went on the air. Now, it gets on only after each part has been legaled. The script is legaled, the tapes are legaled, and so on. The agency people now attend all the recording sessions. They used to wait until we had a tape for them to hear, and they would check with the creative department if there was a word or two that needed changing. Now they check with legal.

"No one questions anything. If legal says change it, you change it. It costs us more money — we make 15 trips to the studio these days to change perfectly innocuous words because lawyers are so trepidatious.

"And as far as the commercials doing a job, more and more the words are turning to plain pap. Less information. Less chance of getting as much response from the public. Our problems are not at the FTC level, really. The client and agency lawyers are the ones who worry. If most of the changes we are asked to make went to the FTC for consideration, they'd laugh at them. But everyone is trying to avoid putting anything into an ad that could conceivably cause trouble. So you end up with legislation by raised eyebrow."

To help matters, Blore says, creative people try to add interest and meaning to the bland words. "You have the announcer caress the words with his voice, or you add pleasurable music," he says. "It sounds good, but it doesn't tell the listener anything about the product. This, to me, is a form of deceit — but I guess it doesn't seem that way to the FTC or a lawyer."

QUESTIONS FOR DISCUSSION

1. What effect have attacks on advertising by consumerists and by government agencies had on the advertising business?

2. Are the resulting advertisements, which are more acceptable to consumerists, also more effective? Why?

3. Mr. Dillon, head of a large advertising agency, charges that the FTC "shoots from the top", moving against advertisers' claims without adequate investigation into the facts of the case. Why did the FTC do this in certain cases? Are there dangers in this tendency?

4. Why was the FTC termed a "do nothing" agency several years ago? What changed this?

5. What is "corrective advertising"? Do you think this is fair to the advertiser? Will it serve to rectify alleged malpractices by advertisers?

6. Are you in favor of giving the FTC legislative rule-making powers? Are there dangers in the exercise of such powers?

7. What types of self-policing organizations have been set up to review and monitor advertising? Judging by the attempts of the cigarette industry to police itself, do you forecast that such bodies will be effective?

8. Do you think the FTC requirement that braodcasters air "counteradvertising" is desirable? Would you be in favor of extending this "fairness doctrine" to print media (newspaper and magazine advertising)?

*Staff Report to the Federal Trade Commission on the Ad Substantiation Program, Washington, D.C., May 1, 1972. Reproduced by permission.

Summary

In July, 1971, the Federal Trade Commission announced its intention to require that members of selected consumer goods industries submit data substantiating their advertising claims and to make the substantiating material available to the public. The advertising substantiation program's primary goals were twofold: education and deterrence. It was hoped that public disclosure of the substantiating material, or its lack, would assist consumers in making a rational choice between competing claims and in evaluating these claims. At the same time, it was believed that public scrutiny of the substantiating data would encourage advertisers to have adequate substantiation before making claims.

In the nine months since the program's inception, the Commission has issued orders to manufacturers and sellers of six product groups: automobiles; electric shavers; air conditioners; television sets; dentifrices; and cough and cold remedies. Substantiation was sought only for objectively verifiable claims regarding such important attributes as the price, safety, performance and efficacy of the advertised product. Responses from the first four groups including 282 claims by 32 different firms have been received, and with the exception of a handful of responses for which confidential treatment was granted, have been made available to the public.

The Commission staff's preliminary analysis yields a number of general conclusions. With respect to those claims that were made, at least 30% of the substantiating material was so technical in nature that it apparently required special expertise, far beyond the capacity of the average consumer, to evaluate. The quality of substantiation varied greatly from company to company, and claim to claim. Many claims were documented in a most impressive manner; on the other hand, serious questions as to the adequacy of data to support the claims they purported to document arose in about 30% of the responses.

Preliminary experience with the responses and the public's use of these responses leads to some tentative conclusions about the advertising substantiation program. Although the returns are not all in, it appears that few individual consumers are likely to request the substantiating material, and those who do receive it probably will not find the material very useful. Given the complexity of the documentation submitted, it seems apparent that the educational function of any such program will be minimal, unless interested consumer groups undertake to analyze the material and translate them into language the consumer can understand. It is understood that various academic and public interest groups are presently engaged in such analytical work, but none has been published to date. Similarly, it is simply too early to judge the deterrent value of placing on the public record an entire industry's substantiation of advertising claims, since most of the ads questioned were prepared before the program was announced.

QUESTIONS FOR DISCUSSION

1. Would you characterize the FTC's ad substantiation program as a success?

2. What, if anything, went wrong with this attempt to protect the consumer?

3. Could anything be done to make the data filed with the government more useful to the consumers?

4. What effect on advertising claims do you think the advertising substantiation program will have if continued? Will this outcome be favorable to consumers?

5. Considering the evidence, would you be in favor of the FTC continuing the policy?

RICHARD D. SILVERSTEIN

For several years, proponents of the consumer class action have argued that it is the solution to the consumer's needs for an effective low-cost court action. They contend that consumers will effectively be able to organize a class suit under court supervision and recover damages from those who perpetrate unfair acts or practices in business. Proponents believe that the complexities of the class action are provided for under Federal rule 23 and that the courts currently have the proper judicial machinery for adjudicating these cases. The consumer class action is structured only to recover from those who abuse the buyer and honest businessmen have nothing to fear from it.

Opponents believe that the consumer class action will present cost and complexity problems for the consumer, the court, and the businessman. They feel that the majority of frauds are perpetrated by fly-by-night operators rather than established businesses and that these operators have nothing to fear from the class action. The burden on the court caused by the number of side issues to be adjudicated in each case and the duration of the class suit itself will render it unmanageable. Opponents contend that the class action will be unrealistically expensive to the consumer and a source of harassment to the businessman.

This paper seeks to explore the class action debate as it relates to the consumer, the court system, and to the business world.

The Consumer Class Action

The consumer class action is a judicial procedure in which one or more members of a numerous class sue on behalf of themselves and all other members of the class with a common interest. The basic advantage of this technique is that most parties participate only as class members while a small group of members act as their representatives in court. The basic disadvantage is the procedural complexity of the action. The class action originated as a part of English Common Law. However, due to requirements that all interested parties be present, the proceedings often would end due to death or inability of one member to face the court. To remedy this, the class action became an equity proceeding. It was brought to the United States but restricted by the early colonists because it deprived potential litigants of their day in court by allowing only representatives of the class to participate. In addition, later judges felt that due process would be violated by binding class members who weren't in court to the final outcome of the proceeding.

Today, there are four basic sources to the consumer class action. Several states still base this right upon the common law principles of equity. Another source is the field code approach whereby each state must pass legislation providing for specific uses of class action. Federal rule 23 (1938), the third source created three classifications for class actions. A true action applied when the named party was indispensable to the prosecution. A hybrid class action contained litigants with a common interest in some property. Spurious actions were commenced by parties who had several rights but a common interest in the questions of law or fact and sought a common relief. The fourth and most prominent source of the consumer class action is the amended Federal rule 23 (1966).

Rule 23 of the Federal Rules of Civil Procedure sets out four conditions to be satisfied for a case to proceed:

1. The class must be so numerous that identification and joinder of every member as a party to the suit would be impractical.
2. Questions of fact or law exist and are common to the class.
3. Claims and defenses of representative parties must be typical of those of the class.
4. Representation will fairly and adequately protect the interests of the class.

In addition, there are three Rule 23 subsection (b) requirements that are important to the class action:

1. Separate suits would subject the opposing party to the risk of inconsistent adjudication; or separate suits would prevent interested parties from protecting their rights.
2. The appropriate remedy is injunctive relief and the opposing party has already acted as though the class exists.
3. The court finds that questions of law and fact which are common to the class predominate over individual questions and the class action is the superior method for adjudicating the controversy.

Current Status

A landmark case in the area of consumer class actions is *Vasquez v. Superior Court of San Joaquin County* where thirty-seven plaintiffs instituted action for fraud on behalf of two-hundred consumers.[1] The case involved the purchase of a freezer and seven month's supply of food under an installment plan. The plaintiff's allegation was that a misrepresentation was made by the door to door salesmen and that this misrepresentation was common to the class because the salesmen memorized a standard presentation and recited it by rote to the potential buyer. The trial court refused the action but was overruled by the California Supreme Court who reversed and allowed the consumer action on the grounds that when the circumstances provide evidence of misrepresentation, direct evidence need not be shown. This case was significant in two ways. First, prior to this case, the court would never allow a class action if the business transactions were separately consummated. Secondly, it created the presumption that if identical misrepresentations are found in a class, then it is presumed that each member relied on the same misrepresentation in purchasing.

A second major case is *Snyder v. Harris* which dealt with the aggregation of small claims to meet legal requirements.[2] Federal courts are limited to cases arising under federal law or cases between citizens of different states where the amount in controversy exceeds $10,000. The court held that the total claims cannot be aggregated to meet this $10,000 diversity of citizenship requirement. Only the parts of each claim held in common with the class could be aggregated. The significance of this decision is that it barred many cases from the federal courts by requiring a $10,000 minimum claim. Lawyers have had much difficulty in bringing class actions under this ruling with the exception of cases in antitrust and truth-in-lending where they have found statutes enabling them to avoid the $10,000 minimum. One advocate has suggested that it is possible to evade this strict construction because only one class member need have the $10,000 claim and this claim can be composed both of compensatory and punitive damages. It should not be difficult in pollution cases to allege, in good faith, combined damages of over $10,000.

At the present time, many state courts are preventing class actions by requiring that class claims arise from the same transaction or occurrence. Most consumer fraud cases arise from a series of separate transactions or occurrences. These courts do not look to the *Vasquez* decision as precedent.

To avoid these inconsistencies, proponents of the consumer class action are seeking federal legislation to open the courts to the consumer. In the Ninety-first Congress, hearings were held before the Senate Judiciary Subcommittee and Commerce Subcommittee resulting in a bill that did not reach a vote before adjournment. In May, 1972, the Senate Commerce Committee resumed public consideration of consumer class action proposals and developed a questionnaire being sent to lawyers who handle these actions. In addition, the Magnuson Bill (S. 984) and the Administration Bill (S. 1222 and H.R. 6315) were considered. Class actions were authorized for breach of warranty under a consumer warranty bill (H.R. 4809) in the House Subcommittee on Commerce and Finance.

Proposals

MAGNUSON BILL (S. 984)

The Magnuson Bill authorizes consumers to bring class actions for relief against suppliers who engage in unfair or fraudulent practices. An unfair consumer practice is defined as an act or practice which is prohibited by section 5(a)(1) of the Federal Trade Commission Act. This section merely states that unfair methods of competition or deceptive acts or practices in commerce are unlawful. In addition, the Magnuson bill states fifteen specific activities that are considered to be unfair consumer practices under the bill:

1. Offering goods or services intending not to sell them (known as "bait-and-switch").
2. Intentionally understocking advertised products or services.
3. Stating that goods, services, or repairs are needed, with knowledge that they are not.
4. Knowingly misrepresenting consumers' rights, privileges, or remedies.
5. Knowingly misrepresenting that used items are new.
6. Knowingly misrepresenting the quality or grade of a product.
7. Knowingly making false or misleading statements about price reductions or price comparisons.
8. Representing that goods or services are the product of a particular company, with knowledge that they are not.
9. Failing to refund deposits for undelivered goods or unperformed services.
10. Knowingly misrepresenting the sponsorship, origin, ingredients, uses, or benefits of a product or service or misrepresenting the affiliation of a person unless the supplier can show that the statement did not take unfair advantage of the consumer considering the consumer's level of knowledge and experience.
11. Taking payment for goods or services intending not to perform or to perform in a manner materially different from that agreed upon.
12. Knowingly misrepresenting the profitability or risk of any home-operated business.
13. Offering prizes or gifts in connection with a sale intending not to provide them as offered.
14. Knowingly misrepresenting a discount for consumer assistance in obtaining other sales.
15. Using physical force or threat or undue harassment in dealing with consumers.

A consumer must have at least $10 at stake to become a member of the suing class. The court is required to investigate the reasonableness of the attorney's fees and revise them when necessary.

Due to the complexity and cost of a class action suit, Magnuson's bill includes a provision allowing plaintiffs to recover damages and the reasonable costs of litigation. (including attorney's fees) from the liable defendant. On the other side, defendants are protected from suits without grounds by a provision stating that if actions are brought frivolously, with the knowledge that the action lacked probable cause, and with the intent to harass or intimidate the defendant, then the court has the power to award the reasonable costs of defending the class action to the defendant. Liable defendants bear the cost of communicating settlement offers to the injured class members.

The class must give ninety days notice of an unfair practice to the Federal Trade Commission before actually filing suit. This has the benefit of forcing the government to act quickly to remedy the situation before a full-scale court battle evolves.

Further, if the Federal Trade Commission has already issued a cease and desist order to a supplier for an unfair consumer practice, individual suits or class actions are immediately authorized. Any final order (as opposed to a consent order) given by the Federal Trade Commission to enjoin a supplier from engaging in an unfair consumer practice would serve as prima facie evidence in an individual or class suit provided that the order was based upon the evidence given at an evidentiary hearing. The statute of limitations for these consumer class actions would be three years.

ADMINISTRATION BILL (S. 1222, H.R. 6315):

The Administration Bill allows consumers to bring civil actions in federal court against suppliers who engage in unfair consumer practices only if the Department of Justice had obtained an injunction against the unfair consumer practice or if the Federal Trade Commission has issued a final cease and desist order against the practice. This would serve to limit the insignificant suits that would backlog the courts under the Magnuson Bill. Consent decrees would also serve to trigger the individual or class suits.

Any violation of section 5(a)(1) of the Federal Trade Commission Act would not be broadly interpreted as a deception. Instead, only the list of unfair or deceptive consumer practices would be included in the definition. This will help businessmen understand which actions are considered illegal. Further, the administration bill uses narrower language in defining an unfair practice with regard to the list. Item #12, misrepresentations dealing with home-operated businesses, is deleted from the Administration proposal. Unlike the Magnuson Bill, real property and insurance are excluded from the definition of consumer goods and services.

The Department of Justice is empowered to seek injunctions and civil penalties of up to $10,000 against suppliers who willfully commit unfair consumer practices. Class and individual consumer suits could result in recovery of actual damages, litigation costs, and attorneys' fees subject to approval and revision by the court. Liable businessmen must submit a plan for relief which the court must determine to be adequately funded, fair and impartially administered, and offering consumers adequate notification and a reasonable opportunity to apply for relief.

Any final court decree that a business has engaged in an unfair consumer practice would be given prima facie effect in a consumer suit. Consent decrees entered before the court has heard testimony, and Federal Trade Commission decrees that an unfair practice has transpired will not be given prima facie treatment. The statute of limitations under this bill is one year after termination of the government proceeding upon which the suit is based.

Effects on Consumers — Proponents

The scope of deception perpetrated upon the American consumer is enormous according to proponents of the class action legislation. Philip Hart, Chairman of the Senate Antitrust and Monopoly Subcommittee has estimated that 30 percent of all consumer spending does not buy product value.[3] Further, criminal price fixing has caused an increase in costs of goods of 15-35 percent over competitive pricing.[4]

> All the available evidence suggests very strongly that the loss to the consuming public from deception at the manufacturing level by these big TV advertisers greatly exceeds any losses caused by the petty retail crooks. . . .

> False advertising of soap, detergents, aspirin, bleach and a half-dozen other major products on television doubtless inflates prices to the consuming public by more than all the retail frauds put together. . . . [5]

Proponents believe that estimates of deception running into the millions of dollars yearly are accurate. When fraud is calculated and committed on such a large scale a mass remedy, such as the consumer class action, is appropriate.

There is no safeguard to prevent smart operators from cheating thousands of consumers out of their money according to class action advocates. A University of Pennsylvania study notes: "In many instances fraudulent operators avoid cheating individuals out of large sums of money because they realize that 'no one bilked out of fifty dollars is going to pay a lawyer to get his money back',"[6] The economic reality is that the successful claimant may win the suit, recover damages, and still lose out in the long run because of the magnitude of his attorney's fees. Since United States courts do not normally require the loser of a lawsuit to pay the winner's attorney's fees, most claimants are subject to this reality. Further proponents note that it is the rule rather than the exception: "the number of consumers having no redress because the amount lost is not commensurate with the attorney fee constitutes the vast majority."[7]

The fact that the smaller the claim is, the more difficult it is to find a lawyer who will take it to court hits hardest at those with insufficient funds (poverty areas) and those without access to subsidized legal services (middle class consumers whose income is too high for legal subsidies but who could never afford to bear the costs of a court suit individually). President Nixon recognized this problem and brought it to the attention of Congress in 1969 stating:

> "Present Federal law gives private citizens no standing to sue for fraudulent or deceptive practices and state laws are often not adequate to their problems. Even if private citizens could sue, the damages suffered by any one consumer would not ordinarily be great enough to warrant costly, individual litigation. One would probably not go through a lengthy court proceeding, for example, merely to recover the cost of a household appliance."[8]

Even if a consumer can show that he was intentionally deceived, that he relied upon the misrepresentation, and was damaged by the deception, he may not be able to recover. In Eisen v. Carlisle and Jacquelin, the court dismissed a class action brought by Eisen on the grounds that "no lawyer of competence is going to undertake this complex and costly case to recover $70.00 for Mr. Eisen."[9] The court did note, however, that where this denial, due to small claim and high expense, leads to the "death knell" of the action, review should be allowed.[10]

Proponents feel that these economic realities are prohibiting consumers from combatting the mass deceptions of which they are the victims. They demand that the consumer be given a voice and believe that the class action will prove to be a powerful weapon in combating deception. President Johnson recognized this need in a speech to Congress stating that: "What is new is the concern for the total interest of the consumer, the recognition of certain basic consumer rights: the right to safety, the right to be informed, the right to choose, the right to be heard." [11]

Consumer class actions provide the most viable form of challenging unjust and fraudulent practices. Without the class action, the consumer has four basic choices. The buyer can abandon the claim, retain an attorney, personally represent himself, or contact a government agency. Abandoning the claim is certainly not a solution, for it leaves the culprit in an enriched position and fails to discourage him from furthering his deceptive practices. Retaining an attorney entails high legal fees and possibly time in court in exchange for a small recovery (in most cases) and possibly court costs. As opposed to this, the class action enables the litigants to spread the legal costs over a large number of small claims. This removes procedural obstacles and creates an economy of scale in prosecuting liable parties. The third option is for the plaintiff to personally represent himself. Class action proponents believe that this technique will fail due to the complexity of the action and the fact that the defendant has probably been in court before and is more familiar with legal procedures than the average consumer. In addition, there is no requirement that the defendant waive his right to legal counsel merely because the plaintiff is representing himself. The class action would promote private initiative and action by allowing the consumers to participate in the proceedings as a member of an organized group with qualified legal assistance. Finally, there is the question of government regulation. Consumer class action advocates prefer it to regulation because it is not subject to funding and manpower constraints as are the regulatory agencies. Proponents see these agencies as being overworked already and wish to avoid the political considerations that often create a better friendship between government and business than between government and the consumer.

Advocates are convinced that the class action will be given first priority among the several remedies because it applies to mass deceptions and would be used far more frequently than criminal sanctions. In their estimation, the more certain the remedy, the greater the deterrent. In addition, this may be the only consumer remedy with no built-in institutional obstacles to its use that still threatens the cheater with serious consequences.

In response to the use of small claims courts as an appropriate forum for consumer grievances, class action supporters contend that these courts are incapable of deterring fraud on a mass scale. Too few consumers are aware of their rights and these courts would only hear the cases of those familiar with legal machinery. With the class action, the overall cost to society will be diminished because it is less expensive to utilize an existing court system to try similar claims in one process than to use a system of small claims courts to adjudicate individual claims one at a time. Attorneys will be stopped from initiating class actions without merit by being placed under court supervision. This will further reduce the societal costs of the class action.

Proponents believe that all guilty businesses will be caught by the consumer class action because smaller, less well-funded companies are often joined in litigation once there is a reason to believe that they were part of a mass deception perpetrated by larger operations.

Mrs. Virginia Knauer, President Nixon's head of the White House Office of Consumer Affairs, notes that the lack of a means to combat deception has implications for the respect of the law in this country:

> Consumer fraud is an insidious economic cancer which
> eats at the very vitals of our society. The fact that it
> continues to the extent it does erodes the respect of the
> individual, especially the poor, for the law. It rots their
> faith in the equal application of the law to the
> white-collar fraud robber and to the family who cannot
> pay for shoddy merchandise they were tricked into

buying by that self-same operator. It withers our moral fiber. It misdirects our economic resources. It saps the strength of our free enterprise system. [12]

Advocates favor a broad definition of an unfair or deceptive practice. They believe that the Magnuson Bill is the minimum protection that should be offerred to consumers and ask that class actions cover product-related accidents, negligence or omissions by manufacturers and sales people and warranty problems such as product durability promises. Some favor no minimum claim requirement because this could act to defeat the purpose of the class action. A small overcharge on an item would not reach the minimum claim requirement for an action, but if this small overcharge is on a nationally distributed product, millions of dollars might actually be involved. In one case, Montgomery Ward lost a class action over deceptive practices in offering credit life insurance to charge customers. Only $3.50 to $6.00 was recoverable in merchandise certificates per claimant but approximately 1.8 million customers were involved. [13]

Supporters of the Magnuson Bill claim that the Administration Bill is too weak and relies too much upon governmental action. Plaintiffs must wait for the government to commence action before they may seek redress. Birch Bayh remarks: "General Motors does not have to wait for approval from Washington before it goes to court. Why should individual plaintiffs whose claims are just as meritorious although smaller in dollar amount — have to wait for approval of their suits from some government office in Washington?" [14]

There is no guarantee that the governmental agencies will be able to initiate actions on all valid claims. Testimony during hearings revealed that due to backlog and understaffing, only the significant cases will be adjudicated — not all cases that have merit. [15]

The final danger with dependence upon governmental prosecution is the time factor. In the case of *In Re Holland Furnace Company*, the federal government required twenty-nine years to reach a successful conclusion. [16] Under the Administration Bill, a consumer plaintiff could not initiate suit during those twenty-nine years. His ease could easily collapse or the defendant could have made himself judgment-proof in the interim.

Effects on Consumers — Opponents

Opponents of the consumer class action believe that the magnitude of the consumer fraud problem has been exaggerated by its advocates. They cite estimates by some advocates of $200 billion per year or one-quarter of all consumer expenditures as proof of their claim that the fraud problem has been grossly overstated. Class Action critics believe that most fraud is the design of small fly-by-night operators who realize that they can cheat a few individuals out of their money and safely disappear. Because, in their opinion, most complaints arise from individual circumstances rather than mass deceptions, the critics feel that the class action is an ineffective means to remedy the consumers purchasing problem.

A fly-by-night operation is highly mobile and normally has little financial backing. A class action would be ineffective against this operation because the perpetrators of the fraud would be difficult to find and recovery of lost expenditures would be minimal by the time the offenders are brought to court. The here-today-gone-tomorrow business has no reputation to worry about nor does it have any commonly identifiable trade name to be damaged by a lawsuit. Since the class action would be ineffective in justly punishing this offender, critics contend that other, more effective means be developed. They suggest civil penalties and criminal fines and imprisonment to deal with the fly-by-nighter. In their estimation, the possibility of criminal action will deter the fradulent operator because cheating the consumer for several hundred dollars will not be worth a jail sentence.

With respect to court actions, opponents cite the high legal costs arising from a complex class action. If the class is small and the case is complex, the legal expenses may exceed the recovery. Professor Handler notes in a New York Times article:

> The realities of the class settlement are reflected by one antitrust suit brought last year in behalf of 460,000 lifetime members of the Playboy Club in California. Each member of the class recovered an $8.00 chit redeemable over a two-year period. The attorney's fees — modest by antitrust standards — came to $275,000. It is obvious that in such a case it is the attorneys, not the class members, who are the true beneficiaries and the real parties in interest. [17]

Opponents feel that the opportunity to collect very high legal fees will create a desire by lawyers to turn false claims into class actions or organize individual claims in such a way that they might be deemed a class group by the court. This could affect the consumer's legal rights because an improper class action could be rejected by the court and the consumer might not be permitted to bring the identical suit to court as an individual.

Class action critics contend that the complexity of the method creates more problems than it will solve. The larger the class becomes, and proponents speak of classes in the millions, the more difficult it will be to locate absent class members, verify claims and disburse damage funds. Computers and large staffs will be required just to determine who is a member of the class. The problem of notifying the consumers will be massive. Class representatives could find themselves liable for the notice costs. One critic commented:

> A problem inherent in any class action is finding someone to finance the initial cost. Attorneys need advances, filing fees must be paid, litigation expenses are incurred, and

disbursements must be made to provide notice to class members. The problem is greatest in a suit like the typical consumer class action where the party plaintiff cannot bear the financial cost of suing. In that case someone else must be found to provide the initial capital. Funds from other class members and the attorneys representing the class may not be available, however, unless there is a substantial likelihood of success after litigation on the merits.[18]

Opponents believe that the Magnuson Bill will create high litigation costs by allowing individuals to create a class group and initiate a court action at their discretion. The Administration Bill would be more pallatable because it requires prior government action which would better, and presumably more narrowly, define the injured consumers.

The complexity and resulting high costs of the consumer class action will prevent ghetto and other lower income groups from utilizing it to prevent the unfair acts and practices of which they are so often the victims. Further, the action is so complex that members of economic groups may never understand how the action functions. The inherent danger is that the lawyers may be able to stir up controversy and bring actions to court that, although untrue, will create problems for business. The businessman's additional costs will be passed onto the consumer in the form of higher prices.

Another problem arises as the consumer group grows in size. The attorney gains more and more control over the action and the litigants. There is no guarantee that his interests will not be placed before those of the consumer. Procedural safeguards in the form of court supervision of attorney's fees and practices would be another burden placed on the court particular to the class action.

Additional problems result from the duration of a consumer class action. It is not unusual for those trials to last for five to six years. The consumer will be tied up in court for that period of time and be denied the speedy satisfaction of his claim. Presently, it takes a considerable amount of time for a civil case to reach trial. Large class actions would take even longer than most civil actions to process causing the consumer to lose both efficiency and money.

Opponents contend that there are too many side issues particular to this action which will have to be adjudicated for this approach to be useful. For instance, what will be done with unclaimed damages? Inaction of class members to recover damages means dilution of the deterrent effect of large recoveries from guilty defendants and unjust enrichment of those defendants. In this instance, crime will pay.

Under rule 23, the consumer class suit, must be superior to all other methods of recovery in order to be allowed. Critics believe that individual actions will generally be more effective and that this, coupled with the prospect that a substantial portion of the consumer class will not share in the recovery makes the superiority of the class action doubtful. In lieu of this, some critics believe in using the small claims courts to deal with the individual problems of consumer abuse. Others suggest better mediation and arbitration procedures for quick satisfaction of consumer grievances.

The issue of economics is a final problem cited by opponents as limiting the effectiveness of class actions. Since these actions are very costly and time consuming and much of the recovery is not claimed, critics assert that the social expense is a waste of resources. In their opinion, social welfare economics dictates that when the cost of decreasing risk exceeds the cost of the risk itself, society should leave the risk where it falls. Also, as damage suits increase in frequency, the costs of doing business will increase and the consumer will be faced with a long run prospect of justifiably higher prices.

Others argue that the market mechanism is an efficient mechanism for settling consumer grievances because it will deny unfair operators repeat business. Faced with diminishing markets these operators will either reform their practices or close their doors. Even if large businesses perpetrated a fraud, the economic power of the large operation would render the class action ineffective by forcing members of the class with whom they deal to drop out or face refusals for further dealings, reciprocity pressures, and unfriendly trade communications.

Effects on the Courts — Proponents

Proponents contend that the class action will not have an adverse effect upon the workload of the court system. In their estimation, the court system already has the procedural and administrative safeguards necessary to distinguish valid from invalid claims. They believe that, from an economic standpoint, the consumer class action is more efficient per dollar of recovery than any other method because it involves only one suit rather than several individual suits. Because the cost of maintaining an individual suit is so high that it will discourage potential plaintiffs from filing for damages, consumers will effectively be denied their constitutional right to sue. This right is so important that even if the action adds to the courts' workload, it should be allowed for it carries a higher priority than many of the other cases being adjudicated.

Among the procedural safeguards cited to protect the courts is Federal Fule 23, which requires the court to decide on the appropriateness of the class action as soon as possible. In some cases, the courts may require that a preliminary evidentiary hearing be held and that the consumer class must show a "substantial possibility" of winning their case.[19] Unmanageable lawsuits and phony claims will be removed from the docket before any considerable time is wasted upon them. Advocates note that Rule 23 was the result of three years of detailed consideration by judges and attorneys handling civil procedures. Before this rule is criticized, its history and reasonableness should be carefully reviewed.

The purpose of the law is to deter offenders from committing a crime. Strong consumer class action laws will deter businessmen from using unfair and deceptive acts or practices upon the unwary consumer. The long run effect of stiff penalties in this area will be to lessen the offenses and thereby decrease the number of class actions needed. If more class actions are filled than anticipated, proponents contend that it will prove that the remedy was needed that much more than expected. If this creates needs for more judges, then it is more socially desirable to hire judges than deny consumers their legal rights.

Consumer advocates point to the fact that the state and federal courts have not been excessively overburdened with class action so far and Rule 23 has been in existence since 1938. Four methods of minimizing the burden on the courts have been suggested by class action proponents. State and federal courts could be given concurrent jurisdiction enjoining various litigants more efficiently. The minimum on aggregated class claims for federal cases could be raised to $25,000. The suits could be limited to cancellation of future obligations (as in installment recision) and compensation for money paid. Finally, damage money could be awarded to those who claim their share and the remainder could be given to consumer action groups or some other cause.

The organization of a consumer class action is not as impossible a task as critics would like to believe. The U.S. Code provides for judicial panels on multidistrict legislation to transfer class actions from different parts of the country but with common interests to one court.[20] The fact that this procedure is available supports the contention that the class actions belong in federal court. Also, state courts do not have the capacity to deal with a nationwide dispute. Since most business today is conducted by large corporations who have nationwide markets for their goods and national marketing and distribution systems, federal involvement is a necessity.

Once the consumer class action is sustained, the courts have tested methods for organization. The court could separate the class into subclasses, limit the issues to liability, determine only total class damages, or appoint a master to oversee disbursements.[21]

The final question as to the viability of the class action is one of damages. Proponents feel that the determination of damages will be no more difficult in the class action suit than in bankruptcy or receivership proceedings which the courts handle routinely. The Magnuson and Administration proposals eliminate the problems that arise from the defendant's right to a jury proceeding on each individual claim by making the defendant liable for the cost of the proceeding. No defendant, once liable, will increase his costs by demanding a jury trial for every consumer class member. Although diminishing the class size or requiring better documentation of transactions could prevent unjust enrichment of the defendant by more clearly identifying the claimants, these methods would probably place too great a strain upon the sales systems of American businesses. The cypres method of distributing damages would distribute the remedy to members who collect their shares, to the state (either to a general fund or to consumer groups) or through the market (in situations involving price fixing, damages could be applied to lower the price of the product for a period of time).

Proponents cite *Illinois Bell Telephone v. J. Slattery* as proof of the fact that damages can be awarded to consumers through the class action. The sum of $18,798,000 was awarded to successful class action plaintiffs and 2000 people were employed for over three years at a cost of $2,700,000 in order to effect the refund for illegal rates.[22] So, it can be done, and consumers can have the redress to which they are entitled by law.

Effects on the Courts — Opponents

Opponents of the consumer class action believe that there is no question that these actions will increase the burden on the court system. Their complexity and cost will create inefficiencies that will make much more work for the court system and result in an economic burden to society in the long run. There are so many variations in the buyer-seller transaction that a problem common to a group of consumers will be a rarity. Fair and efficient adjudication will be impossible without losing the economy of scale that proponents claim to be an economic benefit of the class action. Allowing federal jurisdiction over these individual frauds will expand the role and power of the federal government into any area that is primarily of local concern. Since state governments have been acting to correct these unfair and deceptive acts and practices, federal involvement will halt the state's progress by imposing sanctions from Congress which may not be applicable to local situations.

Opponents contend that both the Magnuson and the Administration Bills will alter the legal definition of fraud by not requiring proof of reliance upon the misrepresentation by the buyer. This will alter the buyer-seller relationship and make recovery easier for the buyer. Recovery will also be aided by Rule 23 which will place the defendant at a psychological disadvantage because his lawyer will almost have to admit to him that the class action will be found to be proper. With the easy requirements for the class action and the large recovery possible, the defendant, guilty or not, may be scared into making a settlement.

Critics assert that the numerous side issues, most of which will be particular to each case, can bog the court down to the point where more time is spent preparing for the case than adjudicating it. A preliminary trial might be required to determine the merits of the case and could become a costly and complex affair. There are only 402 federal judges for the entire country and during May of 1970 alone, over 1300 small claims were filed in the District of Columbia courts.[23] Statistics show that a substantial number of these claims could go into the Federal courts under the Magnuson Bill.[24] In

Morris v. Burchard, the court addressed itself to this problem: "Class action, so instinct with benefits, is also fraught with mischievous effects, capable of overwhelming the judicial machinery and of imposing unfair burdens and untoward pressures on the participants." [25]

Before the court adds judgeships to hear the consumer class action cases, it should reduce its present backlog of cases. Critics argue that there is a question of judicial priorities inherent in this issue of class actions. Should a $50.00 case of fraud prevent a $10,000 auto accident case from being adjudicated? Critics think not.

Another problem with the consumer class action is notification of absent class members. Under rule 23, absent class members are bound to the outcome of the class action unless they notify the class representatives that they wish to exclude themselves. This reverses the traditional practice of requiring affirmative action before the plaintiff is considered a part of the lawsuit. Because each member must have the right to exclude himself under due process, critics note that individual notice rather than mass advertising or other more economical means must be employed. This creates enormous costs and since most plaintiffs will not be able to finance the notification, the court will be burdened with the job of devising means of lowering notification costs and providing financing. This increases court costs and expends time. In the *Pfizer* antibiotics antitrust case, the cost of notice alone amounted to approximately $300,000. [26]

If the plaintiff should lose the case, the class representatives, the entire consumer class, and even the government through the courts may have to bear the notification cost. A preliminary probable cause hearing could remedy this by forcing the plaintiff to drop the case or finance notification if he lost and requiring the defendant to bear the cost if the plaintiff should prevail. The problem with this is that it takes time and adds to the cost of the overall litigation. By the time the preliminary procedures are dispensed with, the defendant may be judgment proof.

The task of deciding damages and their distribution is too painstaking under the class action method and renders the action untenable. The defendant is constitutionally guaranteed the right to a jury trial on individual damage claims once the action is decided against him. To circumvent this right, class actions proponents propose that the defendant be required to pay the court costs of each of these individual actions. The high cost involved will effectively deny him his constitutional rights to the jury trial. If the liable defendant is permitted the trial, the economy of scale that proponents claim to be a benefit of one large action would be lost. Further, the consumer class action is subject to abuse in damage collections. Plaintiffs could allege a class suit for large damages thereby scaring the defendant, then withdraw the suit and settle individually for more than they would have received had they filed individually. Also, some members of the class could settle out of court but the class action could still be maintained. For the court to police these procedures, additional time and expense would be required.

Effects on Business — Proponents

Proponents of the consumer class action feel that honest businessmen have nothing to fear from the action. The businessmen who are deceiving the public will hopefully be exposed to all consumers. This will aid honest businessmen by protecting them from unfair competition and insidious business tactics used to gain an increased share of the consumer market. Business will lose its negative connotations by exposing guilty parties thereby creating consumer good will and bringing many of the intelligent young people back into its folds, rather than losing them to other, more socially desirable fields. Businessmen will find it easier to complete a sales transaction because an adequate remedy in law will serve to reduce the consumers' perceived risk of purchase by allowing him to have some control over his position. By bringing the consumer into equilibrium with his attitudes as to what is fair, and reducing post-purchase cognitive dissonance by providing an adequate means of redress, the businessman will find it less difficult to consummate the sales transaction.

The magnitude of the potential recovery will have a positive effect upon business by making deceitful business practices highly profitable. If the principle of vicarious liability is imposed then the seller's assignee will be liable for frauds perpetrated by the seller. This will further benefit the business world by causing manufacturers to more carefully investigate their distributor's sales practices. The safer the consumer feels in making a purchase, the greater his psychological happiness and the more content he is to consummate the sale.

Proponents believe that both fly-by-night and blue chip companies are involved in consumer fraud. Fly-by-nighters as well as the big business offenders could be taken to court for defrauding the consumer. The mass small frauds whose remedies do not usually justify expenses can be prosecuted under the consumer class action. When a fraud is stopped the whole of society benefits by increasing the prestige of the business world and the effectiveness of society in handling its problems.

The class action is no more susceptible to abuse by lawyers than any other procedure. The courts supervise the attorney's fees and control of the suit. Defendants will face less litigation by being party to one large class action rather than multiple suits throughout the country. This decreases costs of litigation for the business world.

The businessman will be able to recover the costs of defending against "strike suits" by self-seeking attorneys under the Magnuson Bill. Frivolous suits can easily be dealt with via motions for dismissal and summary judgment. The defendant may bring actions for malicious prosecution, malicious abuse of process, and disbarment. Further, proponents feel that the widespread publicity that usually accompanies nuisance suits will be played down once the consumer class action becomes a normal litigation proceeding.

Effects on Business — Opponents

Opponents of the consumer class action assert that it is a means to harass businessmen primarily for nuisance value. It is designed to recover large amounts of money from business concerns that have the ability to pay. No one would bring an expensive class action against a fly-by-night operator with no financial backing; so the class suit discriminates against those firms from which recovery is possible. Critics demand a very narrow interpretation and specific list of unfair acts and practices. Businessmen should not be sued for damages when they could not possibly know how the court would construe the very broad definitions of deception under the Magnuson Bill. Another problem with a broad definition of deception is that it will stifle competitive innovation because new product offerings and development are frequent sources of controversy and people may not understand their intended use.

Class actions by consumers will have a high cost to the business community. Whether or nor a case is valid, bad publicity will result from a suit brought by thousands of consumers against a firm because people will naturally tend to identify themselves with the consumer rather than the business. This publicity could be so injurious as to cause the company, liable or not, to settle out of court and end the negative image effects of bad publicity. High costs will also be incurred by defendants who will have to pay for the expensive discovery proceedings prior to the preliminary hearing stage of the action. These costs will be incurred regardless of whether or not the suit is dismissed before it actually goes to court. If vicarious liability is permitted, costs of doing business will increase because companies will need to hire staffs to police sellers. Critics believe that this additional cost will be greater than the proportionate losses to consumers by a few fraudulent operators.

At the same time that advocates are broadening the definition of fraud to eliminate the need for evidence of reliance upon the misrepresentation, they are withdrawing the right to a jury trial by making it economically unfeasable. Opponents of the class action feel that unjust enrichment or a material misrepresentation on the part of the businessman should be proven before he is required to pay damages.

Businessmen will be in great jeopardy if the class action is permitted to be directed against them in some cases. One class action proceeding with a large damage claim could make a small retailer subject to the involuntary liquidation of his business. If this is to be permitted, then the cost of doing business for a small operator will skyrocket. Further, who will be the arbiter of which business is to be annihilated? Businessmen want the right to remedy any consumer grievances before an action is filed against them in court which could destroy their image, depress their stock prices, and dry up their markets.

The Future of Class Actions

Schemes to bilk the consumer are endless variations on old themes with a few new twists added over time. These schemes include fictitious pricing, home-improvement frauds, bait and switch devices, phoney correspondence schools, mail solicitations which resemble bills for merchandise, and phony franchise schemes. Ralph Nader had claimed that much of the unfair treatment given to consumers is a result of the marketing policies of some of the largest corporations in the country. As corporations grow in size and consume smaller operators, there must be an effective means to control operations on a mass scale. Virginia Knauer, Presidential Advisor for Consumer Affairs testified:

> We believe that the private bar is the sleeping giant of the consumer protection field; that no governmental agency could do the job of aiding consumers as well as an aroused bar properly motivated. Given proper motivation, we are convinced that thousands of private attorneys will answer the call in their new role of representing consumers. This is why we wholeheartedly support the principle of consumer class actions. . . . [28]

Consumer class actions are being employed in truth-in-lending and antitrust cases presently. Proponents have discussed their utility in welfare frauds, stock corporations, securities, installment frauds, false and deceptive advertising as well as product deficiency cases. Some feel that their economic viability will be greatly enhanced in the future as fewer individuals are being denied access to federal and state courts over fundamental rights due to economically discriminatory laws. This is merely an extension of the ever-expanding rights of indigent defendants in criminal cases onto the civil case equivalent. Currently, 23 states have provisions allowing indigents to proceed in civil courts without payment of fees.[28] It is hoped that the class action statutes will one day be deemed economically discriminatory and the financial requirements will be waived so that all consumers can utilize the action.

Another possibility for the future is the public class action led by an attorney general under a state consumer fraud act. The New Jersey Supreme Court has allowed a broad definition of consumer fraud and permitted the state to prosecute under a public class action stating: "The purpose of the act was to broaden the scope of responsibility for unfair business practices. . . (and) the lawmakers (have) accepted the premise that the market bargaining process does not protect ordinary consumers. . . " [29]

Under the premise of this act, the attorney general would be empowered to bring action for individuals or as a consumer class with a common interest because private remedies do not adequately protect the consumer's interests.

Whether the consumer class action takes the form of a public action led by an attorney general or a private action led by an attorney under court supervision, most legal authorities believe that the class action will evolve into a necessary weapon in the consumers arsenal against unfair acts and practices. "The interrelationship of all facets of consumer trust constitutes a new 'ecology' which literally affects each of us, because we will all wear the hat of a consumer. We will be heard." [30]

QUESTIONS FOR REVIEW

1. Why did traditional suits-at-law over product deficiencies, breach of warranty and the like prove to be unsatisfactory protection for the buyer in certain cases? What sorts of cases?
2. Is the consumer class action suit a new idea?
3. What are the main provisions of the Administration Bill? The Magnuson Bill?
4. Which bill do you favor? Why?
5. What are the main criticisms levelled against the consumer class action idea? How valid are they in your opinion?
6. Do you think that class action suits would harass businessmen?
7. Do you think the lawyers would support the proposed system?
8. Would you support a class action bill if you were a legislator? Give your reasons.

FOOTNOTES

1. 4 Cal. 3d 800, 484 p. 2d 964, 94 Cal Rptr 796(1971).

2. 394 US 332 (1969).

3. Newberg, "Federal consumer class action legislation: making the system work," *Harvard Journal on Legislation*, 9, 219.

4. *Ibid.* p. 219.

5. *Ibid.*, p. 221.

6. "Translating sympathy for deceived consumers into effective progress for protection. *University of Pennsylvania Law Review*, 114, 409.

7. *Ibid.*, p. 409.

8. American Enterprise Institute, "Consumer Class Action Legislation," *Legislative Analysis*, 92, 11.

9. 52 F.R.D. 253 (1970)

10. *Ibid.*

11. "Translating Sympathy," *University of Pennsylvania*, p. 450.

12. Enterprise Institute, "Class Action," p. 12.

13. Kegan, "Consumer Class Suits — Righting the Wrongs to Consumers," *Food-Drug-Cosmetic Law Journal*, 26, 136.

14. Bayh, "Consumer Class Actions — S1378", *Pennsylvania Bar Association Quarterly*, 43.30.

15. Leete, "Right of Consumers to bring class actions in the federal courts — an analysis of possible approaches," *University of Pittsburgh Law Review*, 33, 44.

16. 341,F.2d, 548(7th Cir) 391, US 921(1965).

17. Enterprise Institute, "Class Action", p. 17.

18. "New York City's Alternative to the Consumer Class Action: The Government as Robin Hood," Harvard Journal on Legislation, 9, 230-31.

19. Dolgow v. Anderson, 43 F.R.D. 472(1968).

20. 28 US Code, Section 1407.

21. Enterprise Institute, "Class Action," p. 20.

22. 172 F. 2d, 58(7th Cir.) (1939).

23. B. Wilson, "Consumer Class Actions — S1222," *Pennsylvania Bar Association Quarterly*, 43.25.

24. *Ibid.*, p. 25

25. Morris v. Burchard 51 F.R.D. 530, 536(Sdny 1971).

26. Enterprise Institute, "Class Action", p. 26.

27. Bayh, S. 1378", p. 30.

28. Ashe, "Class Action: solution for the seventies," *New England Law Review*, 7, 22.

29. "Consumer protection — public class actions — new hope for defrauded consumers," *"Dickinson Law Review*, 76, 347.

30. Kegan, "Righting Wrongs," p. 140.

WILLIAM T. KELLEY AND ETIENNE GORSE

INTRODUCTION

Consumer Problems have attracted more and more the attention of the American public to the point of becoming a political issue. This is a relatively new development. Although consumer's unions and cooperatives have been in existence for years, it is the first time that consumers' complaints have been voiced with such success. After the investigation of alleged deceptive labeling and packaging practices by the subcommittee on Anti-trust and Monopoly of the Judiciary Committee of the United States Senate,[1] also called Hart Committee by the name of its chairman, a law called the "Fair Labelling and Packaging Act" was voted in 1966.[2]

In this article we propose to look at the various kinds of deceptive practices investigated by the Hart Committee, analyze the 1966 labelling and packaging law, and critically assess the impact of this law during the five years in which it has been in existence.

Importance of Packaging to the Consumer

Some 50 years ago a housewife could still go to the corner's grocery store and buy a pound of any item such as rice, potatoes, eggs or fifteen cents worth of fat or butter. The buying decision was not a very difficult one because only one variety of each item was the rule. Sometimes but rarely, she could buy green or black tea, mocha or java coffee, or any combination of the two, but that was all. In her decision to buy or not to buy, it is safe to assume that price was the most important variable. The decision was made easier by the fact that she probably knew the grocer personally and that most of the goods on display were not packaged. She could see or smell them and sometimes touch them. Of course, items like canned or dehydrated soups, cake mixes, frozen foods, TV dinners, etc., did not exist. Everything had to be processed at home, and it was sometimes a hard, long and tedious task. But if kitchen chores were harder, shopping was rather simple. It usually only implied rather straight-forward choices.

Now, things seem to have been reversed. Kitchen chores have been simplified a lot by the use of modern kitchen appliances (refrigerators, washing machines, dishwashers) and by the increasing variety and convenience of goods available at the supermarket. But on the other hand, the shopping decision has become more and more complex and perplexing. The customer does not now see what she buys, except for very rare exceptions. She has no way to assess the quality of what she buys, before she starts using it. On the other hand, she cannot ask for a specific measure of this or that item; for instance a pound of flour or a quart of oil. She has to take what is available in pre-packaged form. Neither can she get direct information on the goods she buys from a presumably friendly and honest grocer. Although the great variety of goods on the shelves is an advantage, it can also be very confusing. There is now an average of 7,500[3] items on display in supermarkets. The shopping housewife can easily get lost in this maze. Indeed, it becomes more and more difficult, in these conditions, to make a rational decision. To quote Mrs. Sarah Newman,[4] member of the board of directors of the National Consumers League, "In spite of all the nonsensical propaganda about the dominance of the consumer's wishes. . . the net result has not been to make it easier for her to make intelligent choices, but in fact, the very opposite."

The only information shoppers can rely on is provided by the package and the label. In a self-service system, the label replaces the grocer or the shop assistant, of the past. Instead of the family grocer's advice, the customer has to rely on these "silent salesmen". In the words of Dr. Persia Campbell, Chairman of the Department of Economics, Queens College, City University of N.Y., "What we have now is a product-buyer relationship rather than a seller-buyer relationship." In addition to its protective and handling aspect, the package has a promotional aspect. To quote Dr. Persia Campbell once more, "Packaging is in part a method of handling goods for convenience, cleanliness, and product protection; it is also part of the expanding "demand creation apparatus". . . . Sizes and shapes, colors and materials, pictures and symbols are intended to carry a message to the consumer-buyer, a persuasive message." This is why it is important that the label be accurate and reliable.

If they are not, the consumer is deliberately misguided and deceived. Deceptive practices do not only have ethical consequences. They also have very important economic consequences.[5] In a free-market economy, the allocation of scarce resources is determined by the structure of demand. In the words of Professor Colston E. Wayne, President of Consumers Union of the United States, Inc., "The assumptions that lie behind our free-enterprise system rest on a single, vital, pivotal point, namely the belief that the ultimate consumer, through his free and informed choice, will steer production toward the socially desired goal of the greatest good for the greatest number."[6] The idea of the "greatest good for the greatest number" may seem rather vague. But if one believes in a free economy, there is no doubt that misleading the consumer or manipulating demand in any other ways impairs the efficiency of the economic system, and brings about a waste of scarce resources.

There is also another reason why misleading and deceptive packaging can have adverse economic effects. These practices usually increase costs without really improving the quality of the services provided to the customer, and therefore, in a period of rising costs and prices, contribute their share to inflation.

Last, but not least, the tendency to increase the size, the number and the variety of packages aggravates the difficulty of disposing adequately of household wastes.[7] Deceptive and misleading packaging also brings its contribution to the pollution problem of the United States and increases the country's social costs.

DECEPTIVE PRACTICES IN LABELING AND PACKAGING

Obscure Labeling Information

Information such as weights designated by law in avoirdupois ounces and pounds, or in liquid measurement by fluid ounces, pints, quarts or gallons, should be clearly visible on the label. Cases of "invisible labeling" were reported by consumers and consumers' organizations.[8] Either the type was too small, lost in a clutter of printed matter, or sometimes, it was printed on such material and in such colors that it was very difficult for a customer to find the information he was looking for. Cases where the background of the label does not contrast distinctly enough with the printed matter are reported by J. L. Littlefield, chief of the Foods and Standards Division, Michigan Department of Agriculture, before the Hart Committee: "We find considerable difficulty with labels on the aluminum foil-type wrappers and on pliofilm bags. Have you ever tried to read pale yellow printing on such wrappers?"[9] As far as this problem is concerned F. J. Schlink, President and Technical Director of Consumers' Research Inc., has this to say: "Rigid rules should be established regarding type size, type style, contrast of color, and location of labels as to net weight and likewise as to ingredients of food and beverage products."

Oversized package or slack-fill.

A package should reasonably reflect its content. No customer should be deliberately led into believing she buys more than what is actually in the package. Innumerable cases have been reported by consumers of detergent, cookies, candy or cereal packages which contained one-fourth, sometimes a one-third of empty space (slack-fill). A few examples will be sufficient to illustrate this practice. F. J. Schlink, already quoted above, reports in an article in the *Consumer Bulletin*, 1962, that 35 brands of cereal of nine different manufacturers, purchased in two eastern states, had an average filling shortage of 25 percent with a range from 12 percent to 68 percent. Another case was reported in the mint candy industry. Thomas P. Wharton, President of Packaging Consultants Inc., reports to the Hart Committee (p. 82 and 199) how a mint chocolate manufacturer, instead of increasing the price of the product, just reduced the number of candies and replaced them with filling. Other cases have been reported of excess or perfectly unjustified intracontainers and internal paper foils designed to make the item appear much larger than it actually was. Rather than go through a tedious enumeration of these practices, we refer the reader to the Congressional hearings. Although each particular gimmick may bear testimony to the manufacturers ingenuity and inventiveness, they all have the same purpose: to deceive the customer as to the actual size of the item.

Multiple package sizes.

The increasing number of different package sizes and weights makes it difficult for the consumer to make a rational choice between brands, especially as most of the time manufacturers put different weights into same size packages.

Packaging to price.

This is a trade term to describe the introduction of new packages which are the same size and the same price as before, but which contain less product and which do not provide an easily visible statement of content reduction.

Odd size Packaging or Odd Fractional Weights.

This term describes the packaging of items in fractions of weight units, making price comparisons virtually impossible. Mrs. Sarah H. Newman, Member of the Board of Directors of the National Consumers League, in her statement to the Hart Committee (p. 14) described this type of practice:

> What is the per ounce cost of this tomato sauce which contains 7-3/6 ounces and sells at 2 cans for 17 cents or this 9-1/6 ounce can at 63 cents? ... Or take these crackers varying from 8 ounces to 8-1/2, 9-1/2, 9-3/4 and 10 ounces. Instead of being able to decide by just comparing package price, I have to first work out the per ounce cost of each package separately. Such simple concepts as the pound and half pound have been thrown overboard and one can only wonder why.

Use of misleading art on packages.

This term describes the practice of putting in the label an image of the product much more attractive than the product actually is. A good example is the manufacturer of strawberry pies who puts a dozen strawberries on the label image of the pie, while the actual pie only has eight. Apparently this practice was quite widespread.

Misleading Label Information as to the Number of Servings in a Food Containers

Misleading Nutritional Information

Here again reference is made to Jerry Voorhis' statement to the Hart Committee:

> Many nutritional claims are misleading and capitalize on people's fears of not being well nourished. Examples: (a) Advertising claiming *power protein* in breakfast cereal when a large service (one ounce) of oat cereal will only provide six grams of poor quality protein, or less than six percent of the recommended daily allowance for an average man... (b) *Hi-C* used as a brand name for fruit drinks which are usually more than two-thirds water and rather than being high in vitamin C, as implied, contain only 40 percent as much vitamin C as canned orange juice.

Further on, Voorhis concludes; "The situation is so bad that I tell people not to believe any nutritional claims unless they have some proof it is true."

F. J. Schlink, already quoted, gives the example in his statement to the Hart Committee of a "clear instant chicken soup" without any chicken! (p. 52 of Senate Hearings).

Misleading Cents-off Promotions.

Usually one never knows on what basic-price the costs are off; cases have been reported where for years there has been the same cents-off promotion.

Misleading quantity terminology such as "jumbo half quart", "super giant", "king size", "economy size".

We have referred to the practice of applying to the product adjectives such as "jumbo", "giant", etc., which try to induce the consumer into believing that the item has something special that others do not. Although the legal definition of the pound is 16 ounces, manufacturers kept refering to the "full pound" or the "jumbo pound", implying falsely that their item weighted more than others. J.L.L. Littlefield, already quoted, has taken the trouble of counting in just one daily paper (one morning and one afternoon edition), the number of such misleading terms and statements: He finds at least 36 of them (p. 156 of Hearings.) In Senator Maurine B. Neuberger's words, "I am looking forward to the day when the "jumbo half quart" is bigger than the "full half quart" or "a big 16 ounces" or "16 large ounces" is more than the "king size half quart" or the "quart size half quart."

THE STATE OF LEGISLATION BEFORE THE HART HEARINGS

A description of the Legislation in existence before the passage of the Fair Packaging and Labelling Act, 1966.

It would be wrong to assume that the Hart Bill came from a complete legal void. Legislation and regulation on packaging and labeling practices has been in existence ever since the beginning of the century. In particular, the following Acts dealt more or less, in some of their sections, with packaging and labeling:

Meat Inspection Act
Poultry Products Inspection Act
Standard Container Act
Virus-Serum Toxin Act
Aviation Regulations, part 103
Transportation of Dangerous Articles Act
Food, Drug and Cosmetic Act
Caustic Poison Act
Alcohol Administration Act
Dangerous Cargo Act
Tariff Act, 1930 (as amended)
F.T.C. Act, 1916
Wool Products Labeling Act
Textile Fibre Products Act
Fur Products Labeling Act
The Postal Service Act

Some ten different agencies or departments were charged with the administration and enforcement of this legislation. We shall not go in detail over the responsibilities of each of these agencies and departments. This would lead us into some legal niceties which would only be of interest to a corporate lawyer. For the information of non-lawyers, though, we refer the reader to a short but convenient table published in the "Modern Packaging Encyclopedia" of 1971, which gives the name of the agencies or departments responsible for the enforcement of each different Act. (See Table I)

Table 2

Federal packaging regulations and the agencies that enforce them

Federal enforce-ment agencies	Products covered by packaging and labeling regulations				Federal Act and Code of Federal regulations title number		
	Foods including meat, poultry & soft drinks	Alcoholic products & tobacco	Drugs & cosmetics	Chemicals & related products	Act and date	CFR title number	Part number
DEPT. OF AGRICULTURE	Meat, meat products				Meat Inspection Act, 1906, 1907; Wholesome Meat Act, 1967	9	301-320
Consumer & Marketing Service	Poultry, poultry products				Poultry Products Inspection Act, 1957 Wholesome Poultry Act, 1968	7	81
Agricultural Research Service			Biologics for animals		Virus-Serum-Toxin Act, 1913	9	101-123
DEPT. OF HEALTH, EDUCATION & WELFARE	Foods, includ-ing pet unless otherwise stated	Alcohol in drug prod-ucts	Drugs, cosmetics	Food and color additives	Food, Drug, Cosmetic Act, 1938 (with amendments, including Food and Color Additives amendments)	21	301-390
	Enforces regulations designed to prevent deceptive and unfair trade practices, including deceptive pack-aging and labeling				Fair Packaging & Labeling Act, 1966	21	1
Food & Drug Administration				Hazardous household substances	Hazardous Substances Act, 1967; Caus-tic Poison Act, 1921; Child Pro-tection Act, 1966; Poison Preven-tion Packaging Act, 1970	21	191
FEDERAL TRADE COMMISSION	Enforces regulations designed to prevent deceptive and unfair trade practices, including deceptive pack-aging and labeling				FTC Act, 1914 Wool Products Labeling Act, 1939 Textile Fibre Products Identification Act, 1951 Fur Products Labeling Act, 1951 Cigarette Labeling & Advertising Act, 1965 Fair Packaging & Labeling Act, 1966 Flammable Fabrics Act, 1967	16 16 16 16 16 16 16	Chapter 1 300 303 301 - - - 500-503 302
Environmental Protection Agency				Pesticides	Pesticide, Insecticide, Fungicide, Roden-ticide Act, 1964	7	4
TREASURY DEPT.		Alcoholic beverages			Internal Revenue Code	26	173, 194, 198, 201, 211, 231, 240, 245, 250-252
Alcohol, Tobacco and Firearms Div.					Alcohol Administration Act	27	3, 4, 5, 7
		Tobacco			Internal Revenue Code	26	270, 275 285, 290, 295, 296
		Industrial spirits			Internal Revenue Code	26	201, 211, 250, 251
				Explosives	Internal Revenue Code	26	181
Bureau of Customs	Enforces various regulations regarding imports				Tariff Act, 1930 (as amended)	19	1
JUSTICE DEPT. Bureau of Narcotics			Narcotics		Comprehensive Drug Abuse, Prevention and Control Act, 1970	21	302
DEPT. OF TRANSPORTATION Hazardous Materials Regulations Board	Promulgates regulations pertaining to transportation of hazardous materials				DOT Act, 1967	49	170
Federal Aviation Agency	Enforces regulations pertaining to air shipments of hazardous products				Federal Aviation Act, 1958	14	103
Coast Guard	Enforces regulations pertaining to water shipments of hazardous products				Dangerous Cargo Act, 1940	46	146
Federal Highway Administration	Enforces regulations pertaining to highway shipments of hazardous products				Transportation of Explosives Act	49	170-189
Federal Railroad Administration	Enforces regulations pertaining to rail shipments of hazardous products				Transportation of Explosives Act	49	170-189
POST OFFICE DEPT.	Enforces regulations regarding postal shipments				Postal Service Act, 1960	39	

Source: *Modern Packaging Encyclopedia,* 1971 Issue, Vol. 44, No. 7A, July 1971, p. 80.

An assessment of the legislation in existence before the Fair Packaging and Labelling Act.

Rather than give a full description of each different Act, it would be more to the point to see how the total existing body of legislation deals with the major consumers' complaints.

Obscure Labeling

The principal law dealing with packaged goods is the Federal Food, Drug, and Cosmetic Act of 1938, as amended in 1958. The provisions of this act relating to food packaging and labeling problems are those: (a) Defining certain terms, i.e., "Label" and "Labeling"; (b) Conferring authority on the secretary of HEW (more specifically on the F.D.A.) to promulgate regulations fixing reasonable standards of fill of container; and (c) Prescribing conditions under which a food shall be deemed to be "misbranded".

As far as the label itself is concerned, the Act, as completed by regulation, goes into much detail. A food will be deemed "misbranded" unless "it bears a label containing (1) the name and place of business of the manufacturer, packer, or redistributor; and (2) an accurate statement of the quantity of the contents in terms of weight, measure or numberical count." A food will also be deemed "misbranded" unless the information on the label is prominent enough, that is to say unless the information on the label "is prominently placed thereon with such conspicuousness (as compared with other words, statements, designs, or devices, in the labeling,) and in such terms as to render it likely to be read and understood by the ordinary individual under customary conditions of purchase and use."

Certain other laws referred to above deal with the conspicuousness of the net weight statement but in much less detail (for example, labels for meats, poultry, pet food, wine and distilled spirits, etc. . .) (see Figure 1 for specific labeling requirements).

Oversized packages or slack-fill

Section 401 of the Food, Drug and Cosmetic Act authorizes the formulation and issuance of standards of fill of containers. The Act also specifies that if a food "falls below the standard of fill of container," the label should carry a "statement that it falls below such standards." Reasonable standards of fill of containers have been provided for only a few canned products: peaches, apricots, pears, cherries, fruit cocktail, crushed pineapple, pineapple juice, tomatoes, shrimps, oyster, tuna, pears, corn and mushroom. Slack filled wines are also covered by regulation.

Some basic elements of correct labeling to meet FPLA requirements

Panel most likely to be displayed, presented, shown or examined under normal and customary conditions of display. If more than one principal display panel is created, mandatory must be repeated.

Product name as required by applicable Federal law or regulation; or common or usual name; or either the generic name or a statement of function which appropriately describes the commodity. For drugs, a statement of the general pharmacological category or principal intended action should follow the "established name," common or usual name or proprietary name. The identity statement must be in lines generally parallel to the base on which the package or commodity rests as it is designed to be displayed. The identity statement must comprise a principal feature of the principal display panel and be in such type size and so positioned as to be easily read and understood.

Quantity statement can be left, right or centered; must appear somewhere within the lower 30% of the label. Must be parallel to the base of the package or commodity. Must be separated above and below from other printed matter by height of letters required and on each side by twice the width of the letter "N." Must be in a type size determined by area of side or surface of package or commodity that bears the principal display panel. Type size for this package (area of principal display panel = 108 sq. in.) must be at least ¼ in. for all characters including lower case. Dual declarations — total in ounces and largest whole unit — required for 1-lb. or more but less than 4-lb. packages: "NET WT. 18 OZ. (1 LB. 2 OZ.)" For liquids, 1 pint up to 1 gallon: "20 FL. OZ. (1 PT. 4 OZ.)" For lineal and square measurements, check regulations for specifics. Exempt from requirements: packages with principal display panel less than 5 sq. in., but remember, principal display panel is the determining factor, not label size.

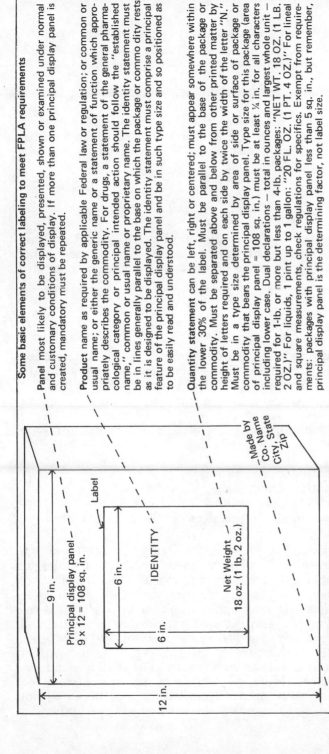

Principal display panel —
9 x 12 = 108 sq. in.

9 in.

Label

IDENTITY

6 in.

6 in.

Net Weight
18 oz. (1 lb. 2 oz.)

12 in.

Made by
Co. Name
City, State
Zip

Manufacturer, packer or distributor. Name and address may appear anywhere on the package. Packer's or distributor's name must be qualified, e.g., "Distributed by ___." Street may be omitted if address is in current city or telephone directory. City, state and zip code must be included. Only standard abbreviations permitted.

Four elements shown here illustrate basic requirements for correct packaging under FPLA. Foods, drugs and many other consumer products commonly found in supermarkets, drug, variety and other retail stores are involved. There are, of course, many variations depending on product and package and some exemptions, but this model will cover most basic situations. For questionable situations, consult FDA for foods, drugs, cosmetics and devices and FTC for all other consumer commodities.

Source: *Modern Packaging Encyclopedia,* 1971 Issue, Vol. 44, No. 7A, July 1971, p. 76.

Multiple package sizes.

No statutory provision or regulation seems to deal with this problem.

Packaging to price.

No specific provisions for this case are found in the law, except for a section of the Food, Drug and Cosmetic Act which specifies that "A food shall be deemed misbranded if its container is so made, formed or filled as to be misleading."

Odd size packaging.

No reference to this practice can be found in the Food, Drug, and Cosmetic Act. Some limitations have been established under other Federal Laws for such products as oleomargarine, wine, and distilled spirits.

Use of misleading art on packages.

The only specific provisions can be found in the Meat Inspection Acts and the Poultry Products Inspection Act as well as in the Federal Alcohol Administration Act for wine and distilled spirits.

Misleading label Information as to the number of servings in a food container.

Misleading nutritional information
Misleading quantity terminology
Misleading "Cents-off promotions
    No provisions for these practices can be found in any
Act.

Although quite extended, the existing body of legislation was obviously not sufficient to plug a great number of holes in consumers' defense lines. Several very important deceptive practices were not even covered by the law. The practices which were explicitly regulated (such as net weight content or the slack-fill in the Food, Drug and Cosmetic Act) did not go into enough detail and depth. Enforcing regulation was too vague and not well developed. Sometimes, like the regulation enforcing net weight content specification on labels, it did not even have the force of law and was only advisory in nature. Moreover, statutory provisions were too dispersed. They dealt with specific problem in specific areas, not with the whole problem. In summary the existing law dealt primarily with deceptive or fradulent practices, which are generally subject to correction only through laborious case by case prosecution.

The Hart Bill

Historical Background

At this point it is necessary to give a short historical background of the Hart Bill. As a result of investigative hearings held by the Senate Antitrust and Monopoly Subcommittee of the Judiciary Committee during late 1961 and 1962, S. 837 was offered by Senator Philip Hart as an amendment to the Clayton Antitrust Act of 1916. The Antitrust and Monopoly subcommittee gave the Bill a favorable report. But, the active support of consumers organizations, such as the Consumers Federation of America, and of Consumers Cooperatives was not enough to overrule business opposition, and the Judiciary Committee declined to act on the Bill. Therefore it died at the close of the 88th Congress in 1964.

In 1965, Senator Hart redrafted the Bill (S.985) as an independent Act rather than as an amendment to the Clayton Act. The new bill was assigned to the Senate Commerce Committee. After further extensive hearings (858 pages of testimony and statements before the Senate Commerce Committee, and 1,169 pages before the House Interstate Commerce Committee), it became obvious that the House Commerce Committee favored a bill less restrictive than S. 985. Public law 89-755, usually called the Fair Packaging and Labelling Act, was the result of a compromise worked out by a joint House-Senate committee.

Public Law 89-755

What Packages are covered by the Act.

The Act covers "Consumer Commodities". Section 10 (a) of the law defines the term "Consumer Commodity" as "food, drug, devices or cosmetic (as these terms are defined by the Federal Food, Drug and Cosmetic Act), and "any other article, product, or commodity of any kind or class which is customarily produced or distributed for sale through retail sales agencies or instrumentalities for consumption by individuals, or use by individuals for purposes of personal care or in the performance of services ordinarily rendered within the household, and which usually is consumed or expended in the course of such consumption or use." This tries to be a pretty wide definition, covering all products customarily found in supermarkets, with the exception of certain commodities (such as meats, poultry, tobacco, prescription drugs, poisons, seeds, etc.) that are subject to federal regulation under other laws. Being wide, the definition is also vague, and will have to be specified by agency regulation.

Which Federal Agencies Administer the Law?

Regulations pertaining to any "consumer commodity" which is a "food, drug, device or cosmetic" as defined by section 201 of the Federal Food, Drug and Cosmetic Act of 1938 will be the responsibility of the secretary of Health, Education and Welfare (H.E.W.). All other domestic packages will be regulated by the F.T.C. Imported packages are subject to regulation by the Secretary of the Treasury.

How is the Act Administered?

The Act provides both for mandatory regulation and regulation by administrative discretion, as did the previous bill. But the items under each heading are not exactly the same.

As part of the mandatory requirements, packages must bear labels specifying (Section 4(a).) (see Figure 1):

a. Identification of the Commodity

b. Name and place of business of the manufacturer or distributor.

c. Net quantity of contents (in terms of weight, measure or numerical count.) The statement of quantity must appear in a uniform location upon the principal display panel of the label.

d. If the package weighs less than four pounds (or one gallon if liquid measure), its weight shall be expressed in both ounces *and* in pounds, with any remainder in terms of ounces or common decimal fractions of the pound. Liquid measure shall be shown in the largest whole unit (quarts or pints as appropriate), with any remainder in terms of fluid ounces or common decimal fractions of the pint or quart.

e. Statements about number of servings must include net weight, measure, or numerical count of each serving.

f. Supplemental statements of net quantity shall not contain any words that tend to exaggerate the net weight statement (such as "Jumbo quarts").

Section 5 of the Law gives the Administrative Agencies authority to establish regulations determining:

a. Appropriate typographic relationships for type sizes.

b. Standards for characterization of package sizes (such as "small," "medium," and "large"). But, in an important restriction, the law states that it "shall not be construed as authorizing any limitation on the size, shape, weight, dimensions, or number of packages which may be used to enclose any commodity."

c. Regulation (but not *prohibition*, as was the case in the proposed Hart Bill,) of the use of such promotional devices as "cents off" or "large economy size".

d. The extension to all products covered, of the requirement that ingredients be listed by their common or usual name, and in descending order of predominance.

e. The interpretation of what constitutes illegal slack fill (slack fill not necessitated by product protection or automatic packaging.)

f. Provision for "undue proliferation" of packages. If the Secretary of Commerce finds that a product is being sold in quantities which make value comparisons difficult for the consumer, he is directed to seek voluntary industry standards for packaging.

Penalties

Any "misbranded" food, drug, device, or cosmetic covered by this Act, if it is delivered for interstate shipment, is subject to seizure or injunction under the federal Food, Drug and Cosmetic Act, but not to the criminal penalties. Manufacturers of "consumer commodities" regulated by the F.D.C. are liable to cease and desist order proceedings.

From the Hart Bill to the Fair Packaging and Labelling Law.

In Senator Hart's own words, "The Fair Packaging and Labelling Act, was pushed, pulled and hammered fiercely before final passage." To what extent was the Hart Bill watered down? The packaging industry was successful first in obtaining provisions for exceptions. Section 5 (b, 6) of the law states that, "If the promulgating authority specified in this section finds that because of the nature, form or quantity of a particular consumer commodity, or for other good and sufficient reasons, full compliance with all the requirements otherwise applicable under section 4 of this Act is impracticable or is not necessary for the adequate protection of consumers", a manufacturer may apply for exemption. Second, several practices which would have been under mandatory prohibition in the Hart Bill ("cents off" promotions), are now under Agency regulation. While the Hart Bill provided for regulation of standards of weight and quantity in which a product would be sold, and gave the agencies the authority to define and prohibit what constituted a deceptive package by reason of size, shape or dimensional proportions, the Bill only provides for the regulation of "slack-fill" and "undue proliferation" of packages, and states very explicitly that the law shall not be construed to limit the number and size of packages. The Hart Bill provided for the regulation of servings standards. The law only specifies that each statement about number of servings must include net weight. Last, but not least, the Hart Bill provision for mandatory prohibition, of deceptive pictorical matter was simply dropped.

The strategy of the packaging industry representatives is very simple. They tried to get as many practices as possible out of the coverage of the law. In this they were not very successful but, at least, they were successful in avoiding mandatory prohibition of several practices and in transferring under Agency regulation these same practices ("cents off" for instance). Thereby, they hoped to gain time, to get out of the public opinion limelight provided by congressional hearings, and to exert leverage on Agency decisions in the future, either by trying to convince them, or by going to the courts. Experience has proven that they were right in their expectations.

Implementing the Regulations

It is our intention in this section to follow the development of agency regulations necessary in order to implement the Fair Packaging and Labelling Act. Althouth the law, signed by the President on November 3, 1966, provided that complementary regulation should be issued by July 1, 1967, additional delays were necessary before this was possible. These delays can be explained by three main factors.

Industry guerilla tactics

The packaging industry used all the means at its disposal to influence the process of regulation and, in case it did not carry forward its point with the agencies, to seek court injunctions. Under the law, regulations enacted by the Agencies is subject to judicial review. The United States Supreme Court even acknowledged the right of packagers to challenge regulations issued under existing Federal Laws *before* the regulations became fully effective as part of the law (Abbot Laboratories Case).

The procedure is as follows. The agency will issue temporary regulations in the Federal Register. Industry will have the time to examine and assess the content of these temporary provisions before they have the force of law. If industry representatives are unable to sway agency decisions, they can still go to courts. This democratic procedure gives citizens full protection against bureaucratic autocracy. It forces the agency and the industry to work in a spirit of compromise and cooperation. It also creates long delays.

For instance, the F.D.A. published the first temporary regulations on food labeling in May and June 1967, just before the deadline set for July 1, 1967. After a great deal of discussion with industry representatives, the F.D.A. came out with a softened version on July 21, 1968. The final version was published in the September 20th Issue of the Federal Register. Regulations were fully enforcable by December 31, 1967 for all new packages, new label designs and label reorders, and by July 1, 1968 for all packages shipped across state lines. In other words there was a delay of about two years before the law could be fully enforced, and only in this part of the law administered by the F.D.A. Delays involving the packaging of cosmetics, toiletries and proprietary drug products were even greater. Final regulations were published in the Federal Register of March 6, 1969, and went into effect on December 31, 1969, a six months rollback from the original deadline of July 1, 1969, and a generous 18 months after the effective date (July 1, 1968) of food labeling regulations.

In the case of the F.T.C., delays were also very long. F.T.C. regulations covering all other households products not covered by the F.D.A. regulations were supposed to go into effect on July 1, 1969, but were postponed because the National Retail Merchant Association (N.R.M.A.) and a number of others asked a U.S. Court of Appeals to step in. The Association sought a preliminary injunction and a declaratory judgment stating that the F.T.C. exceeded its authority when it established lists of commodities to be covered by the regulations. In order to prevent further delays, the Commission changed its definition of "consumer commodity." The new interpretation narrowed the definition of "consumer commodity" by excluding such articles as durable articles and commodities, textiles, items of apparel and paint.

Lack of Congressional and Agency Enthusiasm

Another reason for the delays in implementation is the agencies' inexperience with the new problem they were dealing with.

Chairman Weinberger of the F.T.C., stated before the Senate Consumer Subcommittee in March 1970 that "cents off" regulations for instance had been delayed at the F.T.C., largely from the difficulties inherent in trying to reconcile (1) elimination of fictitious representations; (2) assuring that savings are actually passed on to the consumer; (3) not discouraging manufacturers from passing on real savings to consumers; (4) avoiding the anti-trust consequences of packages control over retailer", and (5) regulating within the limitations of a section of the law which exempts retailers unless they are engaged in packaging.[11]

The F.D.A. Commissioner argues the same lack of substantial background and experience in the pricing field to account for the delays in "cents off" regulations.

The argument rings true. There is no doubt that "cents off" regulations, as well as all the other regulations involved in the Fair Packaging and Labelling Act, are complex, and have to take into account various conflicting factors. Nobody ever claimed that the job was an easy one. However, more than three years would seem to be long enough to acquire the necessary experience. We rather think that the agencies have lacked the necessary enthusiasm and diligence.[12]

In order to be fair to the agencies, one must recognize that they are understaffed and underbudgeted. Enforcing the Fair Packaging and Labelling Act takes people and money. The Agencies have little of either. The F.D.A. for instance says it has only two people assigned to the enforcement of the "truth in packaging" law.[13] It also puts the blame for the delay in the "cents off" legislation on the lack of available funds.

The F.T.C. also puts the blame for delays on Congress's reluctance to appropriate sufficient funds. These delays have brought a great deal of criticism against the agencies. A Senate Subcommittee on Administrative Practices and Procedures, under the chairmanship of Senator Edward Kennedy (D., Mass.) has criticized F.T.C.'s inefficient operations. But the most violent and vocal critics of the F.T.C. and the F.D.A. have been "Nader's Raiders" a group of young lawyers who studied in detail the operations of both agencies. They charged the F.T.C. with rank inefficiency and political corruption. They were not as hard on the F.D.A. The investigating team, led by Ralph Nader, published its findings in A Chemical Feast by James S. Turner, with a preface by Ralph Nader.[14]

The agency is given credit for "occasionally" making well intentioned efforts to upgrade food quality and to promote full disclosure labeling of food products. However, the report continues, those attempts are "continually neutralized by the powerful forces of special interests that include the large, well funded efforts of Washington law firms, massive trade associations made up of the nation's 50,000 food manufacturing firms." In his preface, Nader claimed that "the F.D.A. is unable to exert any meaningful influence on behalf of the food consuming public."[15]

Whether Agency inefficiency and indifference, or Congressional lack of committment, or both are at stake, is unclear at this point in time.

The Impact of the Law

One thing is certain though. There have been very long delays in the enforcement of the law, and to some extent the Act has not lived up to all consumer expectations.

In this section, we propose to examine the results obtained since the passage of the Fair Packaging and Labelling Act and the extent to which consumer expectations were not realized.

Results obtained so far.

Mandatory prohibitions of supplementary words that tend to exaggerate the net weight statement, such as "Jumbo" quarts, have been in force since July 1, 1967. Regulations on Labelling requirements have all been issued although, as we have seen earlier, with great delays. We shall not go in detail about these regulations. Enough has been said on this subject.

As far as "cents off" promotions are concerned, preliminary regulations have been published in the Federal Register of May 10, 1970 for the F.T.C. and of May 21, 1970 for the F.D.A. The period for filing comments was extended until September 1st.

Undue Proliferation of Package Sizes

The enforcement of this part of the law was the responsibility of the Secretary of Commerce, or rather, of the National Bureau of Standards in cooperation with the 4,000 state and local weights and measures officials. The Fair Packaging and Labelling Act gives the Department of Commerce authority to oversee "voluntary" development of package-size standards, and to apply legal leverage only when it becomes apparent that industry is not about to take the initiative.

A certain number of products commonly found in supermarkets have been standardized.[16] With respect to cereals, the number of package sizes has been reduced from 33 to 16 under the industry's voluntary standards. But this does not include variety packs and snack packs (made up of small boxes with individual servings.) As far as detergents are concerned six sizes were authorized for normal density, heavy duty, drug detergents. But three of these sizes are no longer used. These package sizes are 20 oz., 49 oz., and 84 oz. They were picked because distribution curves showed these were the sizes most often produced and displayed. This standardization does not include low suds detergents, light duty detergents for woolens, and other special detergents and soaps, as well as packages in which some premium was included. In the grocery industry, by January 1969, the Commerce Department had a list of 20 grocery product classifications in which industry had voluntary curbed its package sizes. Oil, for instance, came down from a maximum of 15 container sizes to 7 container sizes, with the exception of olive oil. Twenty-eight other industries were working on reducing the number of packages

By January, 1971, 36 product categories had been subject to package size reduction action, involving an estimated $18.5 billion at retail. Perusal of the accompanying table, (Table 2) shows that varying results have been obtained. The most dramatic is the reduction in package sizes in toothpaste, which went from 57 to 5, a 91 percent reduction. Other significant reductions are green olives, 60 percent reduction; vinegar, 67 percent; paper towels, 76 percent; mouthwash, 62 percent; detergents (dry), 73 percent; and adhesive bandages, 73 percent.

In other cases, little or no package size simplification was attained: deodorants; facial tissues, frozen fruits and vegetables, instant coffee, nonfat dry milk. It is discouraging to note that categories in which little or limited progress has been made account for a great deal of retail sales volume and are often important components in consumer household expenditures. Indeed, it is estimated that the 36 categories for which simplified quantity agreements have been developed represent but ten percent of annual expenditures for consumer goods.[17]

Table 2

Package Simplification Program — Status as of May 15, 1971.

Product	Number of Package Sizes		Percent Reduction
	From	**To**	
Adhesive Bandages	37	10	73%
Adhesive and Sealant Products (liquid)	16	16	none
Artificial Sweetners	12	10	17%
Candy	153	728	53%
Cereals, Dry*	33	16	52%
Cheese	22	14	36%
Cookies and Crackers	73	56	23%
Deodorants and Anti-perspirants			
(Aerosol)	18	12	33%
(Cream)	11	8	27%
(Roll-on)			none
(Stick)	88	5	37%
Detergents, Dry	22	6	73%
Facial Tissues			
(1 and 2 ply)	16	13	19%
Frozen Fruits	8	13	0%
Frozen Vegetables	13	13	none
Gift Wrapping			none
Hair Spray	17	14	18%
Instant Coffee	10	8	20%
Instant Tea			
(100%) Type)	12	4	67%
(carbohydrate type)	7	4	43%
Jellies and Preserves	16	10	37%
Macaroni Products	32	16	50%
Mayonnaise & Salad Dressing			
(Spoon Type)	6	5	16%
(Pouring Type)	7	5	29%
Mixed Nuts	66	37	56%
Mouthwash	29	11	62%
Paper Napkins	18	13	28%
Paper Towels			
(1 ply)	33	8	73%
(2 ply)	33	8	76%
Peanut Butter	30	12	60%
Pickles	—	—	35%
Potato Chips	—	—	33%
Pretzels	15	33	none
Refrigerated Dough Products	—	—	24%
Salad and Cooking Oils	15	7	53%
Shampoos, Liquid and Cream	31	17	40%

Package Simplification Program — Status as of May 15, 1971. (continued)

Product	Number of Package Sizes		Percent Reduction
	From	To	
Soft Drinks	—	—	33%
Syrups	—	—	20%
Teabags			
(cup size)	6	4	33%
(quantity service size)	5	3	40%
Toilet Tissue			
(1 ply)	5	4	20%
(2 ply)	11	7	36%
Vinegar	15	10	67%

STANDARDS BEING DEVELOPED THROUGH THE VOLUNTARY PRODUCT STANDARDS PROCEDURE

Green Olives	50	20	60%
Instant Nonfat Dry Milk	9	8	11%
Instant Potatoes	**	**	**
School Paste	**	**	**
Toothpaste	57	5	91%

*Excluding packages of individual serving boxes
**Agreement still being negotiated as of 5/15/71
—No survey made — percentages shown indicate estimates only
In addition to data shown in this table, most agreements contain "quantity patterns"; these are specified increments by which packagers are allowed to increase the size of their packages. It is designed to avoid odd units, percentages and fractions. For example, artificial sweetners not only had the number of package sizes reduced from 12 to 10; the following is found in the agreement:

    1-4 fl. oz. pkgs. = 1 fl. oz. increments
    4-12 fl. oz. pkgs. = 2 fl. oz. increments
    12-20 fl. oz. pkgs. = 4 fl. oz. increments

Nearly every quantity standard agreement has one of these quantity pattern or incremental limitation clauses.

Source: Release of Institute for Applied Technology, U.S. Department of Commerce, Washington, May 15, 1971. Adapted from table entitled "Package Quantity Standards".

Compliance With the Act

Existing level stocks not conforming to the 1966 Act could be used until July 31, 1968; this deadline was extended to June 30, 1969. After the latter date, more than 3,000 firms applied for further extension. All but 14 cases were denied by the FDA. Despite this, by mid 1970, of 5000 packages examined by the FTC, 1,864 different packages were found to be in violation of the new law in some way or another.[18]

A surveillance program was undertaken by the Department of Commerce late in 1970. A total of 205 retail outlets in 40 states was surveyed with the cooperation of state and local officials. A good deal of non-conformance was found.[19]

Enforcement of the 1966 Act got off to a slow start. The FDA had no funds to enforce the Act in 1969; in 1970 it seized 20 branded food items for failure to show mandatory information.[20] Nor did the FTC do much better. From 1967 through 1969, studies were conducted and the FTC collaborated with the FDA in assisting state officials in bringing their packaging laws into conformity with the new Federal law. It was not until 1970 that non-compliance notifications were furnished to 1385 companies, involving 1864 labelling violations.[21]

Consumer Criticism of the Law[22]

By consumer criticism, we mean criticism by representatives of the consumers, such as the President's Adviser on Consumer Affairs, and consumer organizations and cooperatives, such as the Consumer Federation of America. These representatives have been vocal all over the country, and at Congressional hearings. Usually they have been rather severe in their assessment of the law. To the ordinary consumer, the number of packages does not seem to have been reduced very much. Unit price comparisons are just as difficult to make as they were in the past, and some practices such as "packaging to price" (sometimes called by consumer representatives "shrinking packages") have been curbed. Althouth the declaration of ingredients in a package has become mandatory, consumers are bewildered by the complexity of chemical declarations they cannot understand, and feel as frustrated as they were before the law.

A sense of inadequacy and impotence seems to prevail. In a speech to the Consumer Federation of America, in August 1969, Mrs. Virginia Knauer has put these feelings in a nutshell: "We think there are too many packages in the marketplace. We don't think the labeling on products has adequate or clear information. We think something should be done about the Fair Packaging and Labelling Act."

Consumers do not understand all the exceptions to the law nor all the exceptions to standardization procedures. They have the impression that agencies listen more sympathetically to industry complaints than to theirs, a feeling that is illustrated by Ralph Nader's investigations into the agencies' operations. A recent Opinion Research Corporation survey, based on 2,000 at home interviews, indicates that consumers still are not satisfied that government has effective control over business practices, fifty-five percent say more laws are needed to help shoppers get their money's worth. Thirty-four percent want further investigating of packaging and labeling."[23]

Outlook For The Future

What can be done to improve the Fair Packaging and Labelling Act? Everybody, or almost everybody has something to say about that. Most of the time new legislation is proposed to complete or reinforce the F.P.L.A. In this section we analyze the new proposals and industry's response to these new proposals.

New Proposals

Unit pricing is the most important of these new proposals. What is unit pricing? It consists of giving prices per unit of weight or volume or any other measure, in order to make price comparisons possible. Most consumer organizations are clamoring for unit pricing as if it were the remedy for all evils. No doubt unit pricing would provide the customer with extremely valuable information. But he is also interested in quality or convenience. The buying decision is a complex decision taking into account a great number of different variables of which price is only one. A study of the Department of Commerce in Hartford, Connecticut[24] indicates that shoppers do not know what unit pricing means.

After being told what it was, they were favorable, but "indicated by about two to one that unit pricing would not in itself cause them to radically alter their shopping patterns, either as to brands most often used or retail outlets most often shopped." Housewives feel that "they are not solely price shoppers, but rather price-quality shoppers. They have the most confidence in repeat purchases of products known to them as having acceptable quality standards."

Another proposal would curb package shrinkage or packaging to price. Although customers may prefer a decrease in content over an increase in price, this should be made clear. A temporary front panel statement for instance could be added to the package when contents are slightly reduced without change in price.

Instead of simply listing on the label ingredients by order of importance, some consumer representatives would also like to have the percentage of each ingredient, vitamin and protein value, fats and fatty acids and calories. This would be useful to people who have diabetes for instance, and who cannot eat fats. It would also put an end to such practices as marketing butter-flavor cookies that contain no butter, or hot dogs that are more than 50 percent fat.[25] It would also tell Americans how much they consume in way of chemical additives. Very similar to this is the proposal to state the nutritional value of package contents. It has been felt too often that nutritional claims on packages were misleading or unjustified. Making nutritional statements mandatory would help the consumer know exactly what he is eating, and would regulate nutritional claims.

Other ideas have been propounded, such as class-suits for customers in order to allow a group of customers to sue a corporation, and thereby divide expenses. Mrs. Virginia Knauer has been one of the most active supporters of class-suits. She has also advised the creation of local consumer protection offices charged with watching local marketing practices and protecting consumer interests. Finally it was argued that the Fair Packaging and Labelling Act should be the responsibility of only one agency, different from the F.T.C. and the F.D.A., and that a Department of Consumer Affairs should be set up, as in the case of Canada.

Industry's response

How does industry respond to such an abundance of blueprints for reform?

There is of course the negative answer of those manufacturers and manufacturers' associations who believe that consumerism is just another fad fostered by some women's associations or consumers' associations which do not represent anybody but themselves. They do not think consumers are really interested in consumerism and therefore do not hesitate to use some of the delaying tactics, of which we have seen several examples in this study. Unfortunately, it seems that these manufacturers are in the majority and are the most influential. We believe that in the future considerable resources and talents will be pitched against all proposals to complement and reinforce the Fair Packaging and Labeling Law.

Yet, there is some hope. Some manufacturers and retailers, realizing that consumerism is here to stay, have tried to integrate a new strategy for consumerism in their marketing mix. They assume that consumers are interested and that consumers' associations are representative, and they have decided to take these new variables into account. Instead of waiting for legislation to be passed they strive to make the voting of such legislation irrelevent and useless by adopting some of the new proposals for reform.

The Safeway Stores Inc., for instance, have decided to test fully the concept of unit pricing. Tests have been run in two of their Washington D.C. supermarkets.[26] The results have been positive and recently Safeway Stores, Inc. has decided to extend unit-pricing to other stores.

Other manufacturers and retailers, such as the Jewel Cos., Grand Union and Kellogg have engaged in a national nutritional awareness campaign since October, 1970.[27] The drive seems to have little impact so far on consumers, but food executives nevertheless think the effort is worthwhile, "because nutritional programs will help to show our industry's concern for the consumers."

Conclusions

Has there been too much regulation, as industry representatives claim, or is more legislation necessary, as consumers' representatives claim? Too much legislation is sterilizing. It stifles manufacturers' and retailers' initiative and imagination. Too much time and money is spent in law suits and in endless red tape. Yet we seem to be going for more legislation right now because of industry's reluctance to satisfy some of the claims of consumers' organizations. The trend is clear in local and state legislatures. New York City, for instance, made unit-pricing mandatory. This decision was overruled by the courts. But a new bill was voted, giving the mayor legal authority to make unit-pricing mandatory.[28]

In another field, related to packaging — the fight against pollution — local and state legislatures have also led the way. For example, Madison, Wisconsin, has a municipal ordinance that prohibits all non-returnable, reusable containers.[29] This rash of municipal legislation points the way towards future federal legislation. Representative Benjamin Rosenthal (D., N.Y.) and Senator Gaylord Nelson (D., Wisc.) have introduced a bill making unit-pricing mandatory. Senator Nelson has also introduced a Packaging Pollution Control bill. Moreover, a House Democratic Task Force, organized around Rep. Rosenthal, came up with six bills to propose to Congress in order to mend various deficiencies in the consumer protection picture. All of this activity presages considerable changes in the nation's packaging and labelling practices.

Meanwhile, we may conclude that, after five years of experience, the 1966 Packaging Act has given little evidence of improving the protection of the American consumer due to its split jurisdictions, widespread exemptions of items important in the consumer's budget, non-compliance by industry, and non-enforcement by the various responsible government agencies.

QUESTIONS FOR REVIEW

1. Assess the importance of the package.
2. How have packaging and labelling given the marketer more power over (a) his marketing channel, (b) consumer demand?
3. Has packaging and labelling facilitated the consumer's shopping task?
4. What kinds of deceptive practices are found in the field of labelling and packaging? Are these serious abuses, in your opinion?
5. In your view, was the original Hart bill a strong piece of legislation? If passed in its original form, what deceptive practices would it have eliminated? Were there any defects in the bill?
6. What happened to the original Hart bill? Analyze the strategy of the opponents of the bill.
7. What was the impact of the watered-down version that was passed into law?
8. Would you be in favor of the repassage of the original Hart bill (or perhaps even a stronger version)?

FOOTNOTES

1. "Fair Packaging and Labelling, Hearings, Committee on Commerce, U.S. Senate, 89th Congress, 1st Session, Serial 89-28 (Washington: U.S. Government Printing Office, 1965).

2. Public Law 89-755.80 Stat. 1296-1302, 1966.

3. U.S. Congress — Senate — Committee on the Judiciary, 1961, p. 2.

4. *Ibid.*, p. 103.

5. *Ibid.*, p. 166.

6. *Ibid.*

7. *Ibid.*, p. 1050.

8. *Ibid.*, p. 68.

9. *Ibid.*, p. 178.

10. *Ibid.*, p. 543.

11. Hearings, Senate Committee on Commerce, Consumer Subcommittee, January-March, 1970.

12. See *Modern Packaging*, November 1969, p. 143, seq. for arguments supporting this view.

13. *Modern Packaging* (September, 1969), p. 157.

14. New York: Grossman Publishers, 1970.

15. *Ibid.*, p. vi.

16. *Modern Packaging* (January, 1969), p. 107. See also *Advertising Age* (September 1, 1969), p. 1.

17. Statement by Malcolm W. Jensen, Institute of Applied Technology, U.S. Department of Commerce before Senate Interstate Commerce Committee, July, 1970. Mr. Jensen reported that many commodities are felt to be no problem as they are standardized by state law (fluid milk), not felt to be unduly proliferated, or are exempted under the statute. Commodities representing 12 percent of consumer expenditures were being studied and/or proposals evaluated as of mid 1970. The 1966 Act specifically excluded meat and poultry, tobacco and alcohol, seed products, drug products, and economic poisons. Interpretations of the Act by the FTC have resulted in other exclusions from coverage. Eric A. Vadelund estimates that these exclusions cover fully 50 percent of the packaged goods sold at retail. See "The Fair Packaging and Labelling Act: Expectation and Reality", speech presented to the Seminar on Packaging Legislation and Regulations, University of California, Davis Campus, October 19, 1971.

18. Annual Report of the Federal Trade Commission, 1970, p. 13.

19. Annual Report to Congress, January 1971, U.S. Department of Commerce, page 2. The same report speaks of the Department's efforts to get the States to pass a new Model Packaging and Labelling law which brings state law into compatability with the 1966 Act. By January 1971, 16 states had passed this uniform act.

20. Annual Report of Department of Health, Education and Welfare, 1970, p. 241. This scarcely represents a very vigorous enforcement of the law. Before the 1966 Act became effective, the FDA in 1964 made 62 seizures for short-weight or misbranding, 80 seizures in 1965 (HEW Annual Report, 1965, p. 333), and 81 involving 857,694 pounds of food in 1966 (HEW Annual Report, 1966, p. 196).

21. FTC Annual Report, 1970. pp. 13-14.

22. See Hearings, Senate Committee on Commerce, Subcommittee on Consumers, July, 1969 and March, 1970.

23. *Modern Packaging* (June, 1969), p. 173.

24. *Advertising Age*, March 8, 1970.

25. *Advertising Age* (August 2, 1969).

26. *Modern Packaging* (February, 1970), p. 128.

27. *Wall Street Journal* (November 19, 1970), p. 1.

28. *Advertising Age*, September 29, 1969, p. 1.

29. *Modern Packaging*, June, 1970, p. 130.

SUSAN A. GARLAND

Introduction

In the past several years, many changes have occured in food marketing. Not the least of these have been motivated by increasing emphasis on consumerism. One outstanding example is unit pricing, an idea and practice supported by nearly all of the leading consumer advocates, including everyone from Bess Myerson Grant to Ralph Nader. Mrs. Virginia Knauer, special assistant to the President on Consumer Affairs, stated that unit pricing would "... aid our national effort to control inflation. Through unit pricing consumers can better compare prices and quantities of competing items and stretch their food dollar. Consumers can save, and save much by using unit pricing."[1]

But unit pricing has not been without its critics. The first to react to announcements of mandatory unit pricing were the food retailing organizations who feared that it would inflict high costs upon them along with other unfavorable effects. Their opposition was strong and loud. That opposition has quieted considerably and, indeed, many chains are either fully embracing the system or at least seem resigned to make the best of the situation. But one nagging question was present at the conception of unit pricing and still remains today. Is it of any real benefit to the consumer? Did he ever really want or need it and does it affect his shopping decisions now?

History of Unit Pricing

To understand unit pricing's effect on the consumer we must first examine its origins. Unit pricing, which is simply the price per unit measure of a product, is not new in concept. Many housewives claim they have for years performed the necessary computations for themselves and in fact some say they continue to do so now despite the existence of unit pricing. However not all housewives wanted to be their own adding machines and many times the fractions were just too difficult to compute without pad and pencil and time. Mrs. Sarah H. Newman, member of the Board of Directors of the National Consumers League, in her statement to the Hart committee stated,

> What is the per ounce cost of this tomato sauce which contains 7-3/6 ounces and sells at 2 cans for 17 cents or this 9-1/6 ounce can at 63 cents... Or take these crackers varying from 8 ounces to 8-1/2, 9-1/2, 9-3/4 and 10

ounces. Instead of being able to decide by just comparing package price, I have to first work out the per ounce cost of each package separately. Such simple concepts as the pound and half pound have been thrown overboard and one can only wonder why."[2]

The idea of the *store* providing such information was born.

One of the earliest known experimenters is found in Chicago. In 1966, Hyde Park Co-op instituted their own unit price system. They utilized volunteers who labeled over 2000 foods (out of a stock of 12,000 items). The labels contained several items of information including the brand name, product, number of units (i.e. ounces), total price, and price per unit.[3]

Larger stores, including chains, began experimenting with this new idea. In response to rising consumer consciousness and because they thought it would increase consumer loyalty, Jewel Food Stores, also of Chicago, tried their own version of unit pricing called "Compar-A-Buy".[4] They experimented with different methods in three stores. One method was a gialt wheel placed in two or three locations throughout the store for the shoppers to consult. The second was a smaller wheel which was mounted on shopping carts. The third was a similar wheel that was passed out or made available at checkout points. The other method tried was the most practical and least expensive and is the one in largest use today — shelf-ticketing. They couldn't determine immediately whether or not it would produce the desired consumer loyalty but were encouraged by the initial response. They decided to try it on an expermental basis in their stores across the city. Their introduction was accompanied by a large-scale promotional campaign which utilized television and newspaper advertisements as well as massive in-store promotional aids. Their results will be discussed later.

Other stores were not standing idly by. Some at the same time, with others following closely, developed their own version of unit pricing under various names designed to convey one message: "True-Value", "The Actuals", "Chekmate", "Measure Pricing", "Best Buy Pricing", and "Tru-Price".[5]

One retailer, Iowa's Benner Tea Company, looked at Jewel's program and was impressed with the potential for increasing sales and cementing consumer loyalty by presenting themselves as socially aware and active on the consumer's behalf. That is, they were convinced it could be an important merchandising device. The only qualifications were that it had to be computer-based, cover a wide range of items, and was given substantial promotion.[6]

These were all only preliminary probes, however. The real victory for unit pricing was won, not in the supermarket, but in the courts — particularly New York City. Mrs. Bess Myerson Grant, Commissioner of Consumer Affairs for the City of New York, felt that "the proliferation of packaging, with the contents generally in obscure fractions, had turned every supermarket into a Las Vegas casino — and the odds were against the shopper picking a winner."[7] She felt confident that unit pricing was the remedy for that situation.

On September 26, 1969 the Truth-in-Pricing amendment to Consumer Affairs Regulation 49 was first published. The amendment would require all major food chains and independent supermarkets to prominently display the price per unit of the majority of basic food items carried. The first to react was the New York Food Merchants Association who labeled it "socially irresponsible and politically motivated".[8] Their executive director William G. Hildebrand expressed belief that compliance would lead to exhorbitant costs which would be passed on to the consumer in the form of a higher grocery bill (his estimate was $50,000,000 in New York alone).

The original target date for initiation was November 20, 1969 but strong opposition postponed it temporarily for 90 days to February 20, 1970. Food retailers attempted to further delay or kill the plan. Not all of the voices were unreasonable. William Hildebrand of the NYFMA stated that, instead, research should be conducted to find "every conceivable alternative", that in-depth study was needed to find out "just what the consumer wants and needs, and which program could be worked out to satisfy both the food industry and the government."[9] But the Commissioner was not to be denied. After several delays and postponements the bill was passed by the City Council on March 15, 1971, and signed by the mayor on March 30, 1971. The effective date — June 1, 1971.[10]

From the beginning of New York's battle, the activity elsewhere snowballed. Massachusetts became the first state to have a unit price law in August of 1970. Senator James Pearson (R. — Kansas) introduced a bill which would make unit pricing mandatory on a national scale (once again exempting smaller operations). Mrs. Virginia Knauer, Special Assistant to the President for Consumer Affairs, was, and is, solidly behind unit pricing, believing it to be of great benefit to the consumer.[11]

The Mechanics of Implementation

The basic idea of unit pricing is to enable the shopper to determine at a glance the price of an item per unit of appropriate measure, thereby enabling him to make quick comparisons between sizes and/or brands. This was supposed to aid the consumer in buying more intelligently. The implementation for the store is more complicated. The Hyde Park Co-op managed quite well with a volunteer force and hand labels but this was not practical for large supermarkets. When Benner Tea Co. decided to try a unit pricing system they began by compiling, manually, the needed product data such as correct weights or measures for every item, which units of measure to use and how many units of measure in each product size.

All of the information was to be input for the computer. The programming was handled by IBM. They set up eight programs, four dealing with warehouse inventory items and four with direct delivery to the stores. Producing and distributing the labels was the easiest of all. It took only half an hour to run the 4,000 labels needed by each store. The label cost was 2 cents a piece, including the heavy backing to secure them to the shelves. All three steps added up to a $14,000 initial investment for Benner, with estimates of $5,460 per year for system-wide maintenance costs. The programmers felt that the task was a relatively uncomplicated one.

Benner Company found that this system provided them with better internal pricing control, and helped them get a firmer grip on direct deliveries. They felt the cost was almost justified from this aspect alone. The effect of the system on sales was harder to determine. Benner did find, though, that a new brand-name grocery line introduced into the store did quite well, despite strong traditional customer loyalty to another brand, after "Tru-Price" pointed out a savings per ounce (with special promotional material). They also found that when several products were shown to cost more per ounce in larger sizes, shoppers appeared to switch to smaller sizes and the opposite occurred when larger sizes were shown to be more economical.[1][2]

Benner's experience dispelled at least one fear — that unit pricing would be prohibitively expensive to implement. This was important since it meant it would not be so costly to the consumer then, either. But it did not reveal much evidence that unit pricing was fulfilling the goals for which it was formed. In fact, an informal random sample of 25 shoppers at two different Benner stores yielded some surprising results. Twelve said they had used it while thirteen said they had not, and five had not even heard of it, despite heavy in-store and mass media promotion.[13] The evaluation of unit pricing at this point was summed up in *Progressive Grocer* where the author stated it was "a piece of information understood by the leading consumerists, seen as a need by many, and largely misunderstood by the public at large."[14]

The Retailer's Viewpoint

Not all stores were as eager as Jewel or Benner to begin dual pricing. In the spring of 1970, most major food chains and independents were skeptical of unit pricing and slow about implementing it. Ken Partch, marketing director of Grocery Manufacturers of America said, "I don't see how they are going to enforce it (the unit price law in New York). There hasn't even been any research done to see if this is what the consumer wants."[15] An A & P store manager commented that he wasn't sure what it was all about. "I haven't taken it seriously", he said. "I've had no directive from A & P on this. I think it's ridiculous and it just can't be done".[16]

But during the next twelve months an about-face took place. In their annual "Trade Winds Review", *Progressive Grocer* stated that "it was clear by the beginning of the year (1971) that unit pricing. . . was an accepted fact in supermarkets across the country.

Even though repeated studies showed that most customers were blithely ignoring the values of unit pricing — as had been predicted — supermarkets invested time, advertising space, money, and effort to voluntarily, or under the strictures of state legislation, convert their pricing systems".[17] Unit pricing moved onto the shelves of supermarkets across the country "lock, stock, and applesauce".[18]

Stores began to get excited about the promotional possibilities of unit pricing. They knew it was to their advantage to stress consumerism as part of their image. Joseph S. Coyle, managing editor of *Progressive Grocer* magazine, observed that "as prices become an even more intense cause for alarm among shoppers, supermarkets need all the help they can get in maintaining a concerned, economizing image. For some, dual pricing will have come just in time."[19] In addition, there was some speculation that stores were voluntarily complying to ward off additional legislation, especially that of a federal nature. The stores seemed to feel that if they gave the impression that they did not need to be coerced into helping the consumer, Congress would not be so eager to pass more bills that could decrease the supermarket's control over their operations. They succeeded, to a point. The pressure lessened considerably and aside from the initial bills, little action has been taken in Congress concerning unit pricing.

The change of heart produced dramatic results. *Progressive Grocer's* "Thirty-eighth Annual Report of the Grocery Industry" showed that, in 1970, unit pricing was the least favored consumerism program among retailers. While only 30 percent of the chains surveyed even liked the idea in 1970, by 1971 over 40 percent of them had introduced it in their stores. The independants showed the same type of increase, from 13 percent to 33 percent.[20] They had begun to believe, like William Benner, that it could be a positive selling tool. In fact, by the beginning of 1971 there was so much information available for the shopper to consult that it would have been virtually impossible to fully utilize it all. Unit pricing, open coding, nutrition labeling, not to mention Phase II price postings were all present in many stores. "The range and imagination of many of these programs," stated Mrs. Esther Peterson of Giant Foods Co., "demonstrates that the industry has caught on to far more than a lesson in politics. It is true that it all started as a means of heading off restrictive legislation. But it did not take very long for it to turn into a positive competitive tool. One reason is simply that a marketing-centered and promotionally sophisticated business has learned to use what is at hand."[21] However, the original reason for creating unit pricing had been to aid the consumer, not the store's image. How did it fare in that category?

The Consumer Reaction

The motivation behind initiating and spreading unit pricing was complaints by shoppers of confusing package sizes with complicated fractions which made it hard to tell the least expensive buy without using an adding machine. Bess Myerson Grant said that women make mistakes in over 40 percent of their purchases due to inability to compute prices for packages of different sizes.[22] Other studies done produced results claiming that shoppers could save ten percent (ten cents out of every food dollar) by using unit pricing information.[23] A typical unit price example: a 32 ounce jar of Mayonnaise A at 75 cents per quart compared with an 8 ounce jar of Mayonnaise B at $1.20 per quart; the larger jar is by far the cheaper buy.

Mrs. Doris Behre, a representative of a Maryland consumer cooperative, demonstrated before a Senate subcommittee hearing on truth-in-packaging, "I have here two cans of shelled beans. One is a 16 ounce can selling for 2 for 57 cents or 29 cents each. The larger can is 28 ounces for 35 cents. In this case, the smaller can costs 42 percent more than the larger can, but it takes a slide rule to figure it out."[24]

The advantages of a unit pricing system were obvious. If the consumer wanted the least expensive buy, all she would have to do would be compare the unit prices. All this, of course, assumed from the beginning that the shopper would use this information to help in purchasing decisions. There was some reason for believing that this would be true. After all, it seemed to make good sense that consumers would want to know all the pricing information they could get. There is even factual evidence to back up this intuition. A study recently published by the *Journal of Marketing Research*[25] showed that (1) price was relevant in a shopping decision, and (2) when housewives were provided with unit price information, their purchasing behavior was affected.

Unfortunately, the study was not conducted under supermarket conditions where unit pricing does not show a similar impact on buying decisions. Commenting on the prospect of using unit pricing, Rose West, who led the Denver Food Boycott in 1968, said, "We don't want this... Whoever thought this up is someone who has never shopped."[26] She also said she wouldn't pay attention to a price per unit and wanted standardization of packaging instead. The implication was that unit pricing was not the answer to the consumer's dilemma; or at least not the best answer. The consensus was that, while it was theoretically sound, it was worthless for practical purposes. The only way to know for sure, however, was to measure consumer reaction to the actual program.

When asked how unit pricing was faring amongst shoppers, most chain stores kept saying it was too early to tell. Everyone was waiting for conclusive studies to be done and data to be gathered which would finally settle the question of consumer reaction to unit pricing.

Of all the studies done to determine consumer response to unit pricing, there are three which emerge as the most comprehensive and reliable: Jewel Food Store, Kroger Food Stores, and Safeway Food Stores. They all contained a fairly large sample size and were conducted in stores which had some of the better examples of a unit pricing program.

A. Jewel Food Stores, Chicago, Illinois: After a three month trial of unit pricing and much promotional expenditure, Jewel decided to measure the effect unit pricing was having on purchasing decisions. Jewel first introduced unit pricing in their stores in April, 1970. At that time they surveyed about 400 people in their stores to find out their reactions to the new idea. Then from April to June they conducted a massive advertising campaign to inform the public, utilizing full-page newspaper ads, feature spots in regular advertising, and in-store material. A second survey was then conducted with about the same sample size to see if there was any change in response.

Results showed that familiarity had risen from 47 percent to 63 percent among those polled. By June, 41 percent considered it worthwhile and 30 percent said they used it on a regular basis. However, the survey also revealed that only about 5 percent had actually changed a shopping decision on the basis of Jewel's "Compar-A-Buy" program. While customers seemed pleased that Jewel had instituted the system, they nevertheless were not motivated to actually use it to their benefit.

What was Jewel's assessment of their "Compar-A-Buy" experiment? They felt it was successful "in terms of customer psychological response". The shoppers' verbal reactions of interest in the program were positive. Jewel felt, therefore, that it was a good marketing tool since it produced customer satisfaction and helped Jewel's image by assuring shoppers of the store's interest in assisting them by providing helpful information.

However, Jewel also felt that "Compar-A-Buy" had failed to show that it was needed by the shopper. Since the actual performance of customers showed that the use of "Compar-A-Buy" failed to change shopping decisions and no significant shifts in product movement were determined, Jewel felt that it "would seem to indicate that it is not something of essential service need to customers and that its cost could not be justified on that basis."[27] (The cost to Jewel was figured to be about $1,000 per year, per store).

Other interesting findings had to do with who used and didn't use unit pricing. It had originally been intended as an aid for the poor, who would have the need to stretch their food dollars further, so they presumably would be the most interested in such a program. However, the study showed that the opposite was true. Jewel's three test stores were in three different neighborhoods. The one in a white collar neighborhood showed 99 percent familiarity with the "Compar-A-Buy" program and 72 percent said they had used it. The store in a white, blue collar neighborhood showed 68 percent familiarity and 54 percent had used it. But the shoppers in the black neighborhood store in the lower income area indicated only 29 percent familiarity and a disappointingly low usage figure of 14 percent. It was ironic that those for whom it was to have been designed seemed to care so little about it.

B. Kroger Food Stores, New York: The second major study on consumer response to unit pricing was done for Kroger Food Stores under the auspices of the Consumer Research Institute. It was conducted by a team from Cornell University in six Kroger stores over a 16 week period. The results were similar to Jewel's in that they showed a usage figure of around 30 percent; and they also found that changes in buying patterns were negligible (less than 5 percent). Also, although Kroger had used local television and newspaper advertisements plus in-store promotional aids, less than one-half of those polled understood the unit pricing system. The conclusions were all generally negative concerning unit pricing's impact for both retailer and consumer.

They found that most product groups monitored showed no tendencies to shift. "Cold cereal, with a high price-per-unit range, tended toward trading down only slightly, while cooking oil and dried milk, with low unit price ranges, showed an equally small tendency for trading up."[28] There were no mass movements to private brands or particular sizes, as had been predicted.

Also included was the observation that those least likely to understand and use unit pricing were disadvantaged groups i.e. senior citizens and minority groups. In addition, this situation is complicated by the fact that unit pricing costs appear to be excessive for small stores which is where the poor largely shop. The basic conclusion of the team was: "Significant aggregate savings to the consumer are unlikely with dual pricing".[29]

C. Safeway Food Stores: The third study was conducted in Safeway Stores and was co-sponsored by the National Association of Food Chains. They used Monroe P. Friedman from Eastern Michigan University as their academic resource person. Although many of their statistics were similar to the ones found by Jewel and Kroger — Safeway's user percentage was around 31 percent — their conclusions were much more optimistic.

First, they passed off the cost figure by maintaining there was a trade-off in costs, similar to those pointed out by William Benner of Benner Tea Company. But the surprising conclusion was their statement concerning consumer use. Safeway's President Winstead summed up: "Based on experience and testing, we are convinced that our new dual pricing program will be of maximum benefit to our customers".[30] It was, as Mr. Joseph Coyle put it, " . . . one of the warmest statements on the subject by any retailer spokesman."[31]

Analysis of the Studies

How and why are the conclusions so different when the data is so consistently similar? This is not the only question that causes confusion in the mind of anyone who tries to sift through the history of unit pricing. It is a classic example of seeing what you want to see. One possible explanation of the contradiction in conclusions of the aforementioned studies is that the Safeway study was co-sponsored by the National Association of Food Chains which was at first vigorously opposing unit pricing legislation. Perhaps they, like individual store chains, were eager to ward off more compulsory bills

— eager enough to enthusiastically back unit pricing to show Congress they need not rush into anything.

There were others, however, that felt that unit pricing would benefit the consumer, despite the figures to the contrary. Mrs. Virginia Knauer, the President's special assistant on consumer affairs, was one. She blamed the low usage and purchase decision figures on the stores themselves. Her staff conducted a random unit pricing survey in the Washington, D.C. metropolitan area. She was mainly interested in the quality and extent of the unit pricing programs of the stores. Her staff noted many inconsistencies within the same store in addition to those expected among different stores in the same chain and competing chains.

Mrs. Knauer had been concerned with the question mentioned above, that is, why there are different conclusions to similar data. She felt that one possible reason to be optimistic despite negative returns was that the stores had not fully done their part; so unit pricing had not failed, the stores had. She maintained that the programs were not consistent or presented in such a way as to be truly helpful to the consumer. She felt it was necessary to "have a full understanding of what they (the consumers) are reacting to."[32]

The data collected by her staff seemed to bear out her hypothesis. They inspected twelve supermarkets in the area, limiting themselves to those stores who were members of major food chains which had publicly adopted unit pricing policies. The items which were given special attention were (1) presence of some form of unit pricing, (2) extent and uniformity of coverage, (3) presence of some form of in-store promotion, (4) legibility, understandibility, and ease of customer utilization of unit pricing labels. Rating each store in each of these areas, they found wide variances. Some stores would score well in one area but not in others; or stores would score well in all areas but only in certain departments of the store. In addition, differences were noted between stores of the same chain and between chains with regard to labels being clearly and accurately corresponding to shelf items as well as other, sometimes more subtle, discrepencies.

Cleanliness and legibility, particularly on the shelf nearest the floor, were general problems. Frozen food labels were sometimes clustered together at knee level, prohibiting easy reading and comparison. The main objection Mrs. Knauer found, though, was a lack of "prominent in-store promotional or explanatory material to call consumer attention to or aid in utilization of the unit pricing scheme. . . ."[33] She felt this placed the consumer at a great disadvantage with regard to his ability to fully utilize the unit pricing program to his benefit.

Mrs. Knauer summed up her position by stating in a letter sent to Mr. Clarence Adamy of the National Association of Food Chains and to Mr. George Kick of the Grocery Manufacturers of America that:

> These findings lead me to the belief that if the conclusions of the studies conducted by CRI and the various segments of the food industry are based on the

> premise that there is uniformity in the type, degree of implementation, and promotion of unit pricing available to consumers, this is a very shaky premise indeed. . . . if such surveys are to benefit. . . policy makers it is necessary that industry leaders recognize the need to agree on some guiding principles or code upon which these surveys can be based. . . . aimed at obtaining complete objectivity.[34]

Mrs. Knauer thus implied that, while the data on consumer reaction in the aforementioned studies may be accurate, the reason the figures show the consumer to be less than overjoyed with unit pricing is that the stores have failed to do a good job of promoting and implementing it.

This analysis would, indeed, be worthy of much consideration and study and could even be of great significance to the whole unit pricing question had the survey been done in the same stores used for the studies on consumer reaction. Because in those stores, Jewel and Kroger especially, the unit pricing program had not been undertaken half-heartedly and *had* been supplemented by a great deal of in-store and mass media promotional information. Mrs. Knauer can hardly accuse Jewel and Kroger of not wanting unit pricing to succeed after they had spent much time and money and effort on their respective programs. Jewel's president was a firm believer in unit pricing and, if anything, would have wanted the figures to show that it was indeed beneficial to the consumer. Unfortunately, the results indicated a different response.

The consumer indifference to unit pricing goes far deeper than a mere problem of implementation and promotion. Even where the consumers are informed and educated at the values of unit pricing, they do not use it to any great extent. The difficulties of unit pricing are complex and, some feel, insolvable.

Problems of Unit Pricing

Some of the more subtle problems of unit pricing are not apparent until looked at closely. For instance, the price per unit can be deceptive when there are variations in percent of moisture, active ingredients, and bulk density. Unit prices of ice cream had to be changed from per pound to per pint in one instance when a clerk overheard a customer discover that it was really too expensive to buy at all.[35] Concentrated juices if priced by the ounce, appear exhorbitant in cost, but that is because they are meant to be diluted. So grocers take the liberty of figuring out the cost per ounce when diluted, lessening the accuracy. Another example involving concentration and quality is detergents. Some detergents cost more than others but smaller quantities of the higher-priced product are required to do the job. How do you measure this when you determine the price per pound of a detergent?

The question of quality is completely ignored in unit pricing. Admittedly, it is an intangible and undoubtedly hard to quantify, yet it, too, has a large place in the mind of the consumer. Therefore, if what we really want is a program to help the customer shop more intelligently and get the most for his food dollar, we should consider what he wants to know and needs to know. Looked at in this light, unit pricing seems drab, dry, and oversimplified.

Conclusions

There are those who believe unit pricing has failed to cause changes in buying patterns because people don't understand it or know about it so they feel the answer is in more promotion. But recent findings show that increased advertising by stores was a major part (if not all) of the increase in food prices.[36] More advertising, then, would drive prices even higher cancelling out any advantage gained through unit pricing savings. The success of unit pricing would be self-defeating. Alto, it has been previously pointed out that the studies of consumer reaction were done in stores that had already conducted massive promotional campaigns.

The question, then, becomes one of worth. Will the gains experienced by unit pricing offset the cost to consumer and retailer? How much more money should we spend on improving the system before we decide on its success or failure? Bennett Morse of George Washington University in his master's thesis expressed the opinion that, "unit pricing and open dating are, at best, minor consumer benefits as compared to other services that are or could be offered by grocery stores. Consumers do not seek out stores that offer these services when they are well known and widely available. Apparently, very few shoppers use unit pricing when the store they normally shop in offers the service . . . clearly the benefits are not so great nor the consumer needs so urgent that the country should be stampeded into what may prove to be unwanted, ineffective, and costly programs. . . "[37]

Those three words: "unwanted, ineffective, and costly" sum up unit pricing, at least for the time being. There is no question of the need for some type of program to provide consumers with information to make intelligent shopping easier. The poor and disadvantaged as well as the average middle income housewife all want to get more for their food dollar. But evidently there is more to that than just price comparisons.

I believe there are at least two basic reasons why unit pricing has failed on the consumer side. First of all, there was no research done to determine whether or not this was in fact what the consumer wanted. Ken Davis, Jr., Assistant Secretary of Commerce said early in 1970, "There is no substantive body of data on either consumer reaction or the cost of implementing such a system."[38] Had there been such research, chances are it would have discovered the second reason. That is, more price per unit information was not what the consumer wants or needs. Unit pricing is helpful only when price is the lone consideration. There are very few shopping decisions made on price alone; there are almost always other considerations. For example, big boxes may be cheaper, but big boxes go stale.

The longer unit pricing is pushed by consumerists, the longer the consumer will wait for an effective program to come. Some suggested directions are (1) more uniform package sizes, (2) more grading by the U.S. government to aid in quality determination, plus (3) some form of a unit pricing system. In this way, the present unit pricing system is really an enemy of the consumer because it is taking the place of a better program. No more energy should be expended upon a program which will never prove to be more than "a noble experiment". Rather, our efforts should be directed toward finding a program, or programs, which will really meet the needs of today's consumer.

QUESTIONS FOR DISCUSSION

1. Define "unit pricing".

2. When it seemed that federal legislation might be passed, a number of chain stores voluntarily adopted the unit pricing system to head it off. Should Congress, nevertheless, pass legislation compelling unit pricing?

3. Would the compelling of unit pricing throughout the United States significantly raise the price of grocery items to the consumer?

4. What problems for store management are created when they institute a unit pricing system?

5. What does research accomplished to date tell us about the effectiveness of unit pricing where it has been tried?

6. Was it fair, in your opinion, for Mrs. Knauer to blame the stores for the failure of unit pricing? Where did the blame lie?

7. Despite the early discouraging evidence, would you still recommend the adoption of unit pricing (a) on a voluntary level? (b) on a compulsory basis?

FOOTNOTES:

1. Office of Consumer Affairs, press release, April 7, 1972.

2. "The Fair Packaging and Labelling Act of 1966: A Critical Appraisal", William T. Kelley and Etienne Gorse (January, 1972) pp. 9, 10.

3. "Unit Pricing?", *Advertising Age* (April 6, 1970), p. 3.

4. *Ibid.*

5. "Where do we go from here?", *Progressive Grocer* (November, 1970), p. 82.

6. *Ibid.*

7. New York Department of Consumer Affairs, press release, September 23, 1971.

8. "New York Asks Price on Labels", *Advertising Age* (September 29, 1969), p. 123.

9. "Battle Grows Over New York's Price Rule," *Advertising Age* (December 8, 1969), p. 95.

10. New York Department of Consumer Affairs, press release, June 1, 1971.

11. "Dual Pricing Settles In", J. S. Coyle, *Progressive Grocer* (February, 1971), p. 46.

12. "What Cost Dual Pricing?", *Progressive Grocer* (November, 1970), pp. 78-82.

13. *Ibid.*

14. "Consumerisms' Phase II", *Progressive Grocer* (April, 1972), p. 10.

15. "Battle Grows over NY's Price Rule", *Advertising Age* (December 4, 1969), p. 95.

16. *Ibid.*

17. "Consumerisms' Phase II", *Progressive Grocer* (April, 1972), p. 9

18. "Unit Prices Move Onto the Shelf", *Business Week* (June 6, 1970), p. 23.

19. "Dual Pricing Settles In", J.S. Coyle, *Progressive Grocer* (February, 1971), pp. 46-48.

20. *Progressive Grocer* (April, 1972), p. 110.

21. New York Department of Consumer Affairs, press release, January 28, 1970.

22. *Progressive Grocer* (November, 1970), p. 78.

23. "Yes, But How Much Is It Per Pound?", *Business Week* (January, 1970), p. 51.

24. *Journal of Marketing Research* (August, 1972), p. 239.

25. *Advertising Age* (December 8, 1969), p. 95.

26. *Progressive Grocer* (February, 1971), p. 47.

27. *Ibid.*

28. *Ibid.*

29. *Ibid.*

30. *Ibid.*

31. Office of Consumer Affairs, press release, April 7, 1972.

32. Office of Consumer Affairs Survey of Unit Pricing Programs, February 8, 1972.

33. *Ibid.*

34. *Progressive Grocer* (November, 1970), p. 82.

35. *Hot War On the Consumer,* ed. by David Sanford, p. 29.

36. "Unit Pricing May Not Prove Boon, Studies Hint", *Industry Week* (September 13, 1971), p. 18.

37. *Advertising Age* (April 6, 1970), p. 3

CAVEAT VENDOR — OR,
A TALE OF THREE CITIES *

BESS MYERSON

* Bess Myerson, "Caveat Vendor — Or, a Tale of Three
Cities," *New York Times* (Sunday, January 7, 1973), pp.
49, 73. Reproduced by permission.

Our consumer protection is a tale of three cities: Washington,
Albany and New York.

New York does what it can for itself—consumer protection is alive
and kicking here, but only because we treat our aches and complaints
with our own home remedies. But that's not enough. The more
deeply rooted consumer complaints continue to injure us, and they
are beyond our reach.

In Washington, Virginia Knauer says she is "discouraged" about
the prospects of getting consumer legislation through Congress. In
Albany, Attorney General Lefkowitz looked at the 1972 Legislature
from a consumer viewpoint and found it "disappointing." Any
review of the gains achieved and goals remaining for New York City's
consumers must be made within that Washington-Albany framework
of limited opportunity. It's an all too familiar theme for our city.

In December, 1969, the City Council passed and Mayor Lindsay
signed a bill whose key sentence reads as follows: "No person shall
engage in any deceptive or unconscionable trade practice in the sale,
lease, rental or loan of any consumer goods or services or in the
collection of consumer debts."

That authority, in our Consumer Protection Law, has been the
source for the enactment and enforcement of a long list of
hard-hitting regulations issued by our Department of Consumer
Affairs.

These regulations involve consumer credit terms, truth in
advertising, car rentals, mail orders, debt collection, door-to-door
sales, furniture delivery, movie advertising, pyramid sales schemes,
bait-and-switch, short weights, warranties and guarantees, standards
for repair shops and dozens of other consumer areas. The full list is
available to any consumer who cares enough to want to identify a
fraud or misrepresentation *before* he pays for the experience. You
can get a copy of all the regulations by writing to the Department of
Consumer Affairs, 80 Lafayette Street, New York, N.Y. 10013.

Our department is a small one—a staff of 350, including only a
handful of lawyers and only 80 inspectors and an annual budget of
$3.5-million (which, incidentally, is less than the amount of license
fees and fines collected by the agency). Several million dollars are
returned to consumers each year in refunds and debt cancellations.
The men and women of our department work long hours, but the

front line of consumer defense remains the awareness of the individual.

When your calls and letters put the spotlight on a consumer abuse, our lawyers and inspectors check it throughly. If the abuse is prohibited by our existing regulations, it can be resolved promptly. If new regulation is warranted, we invite the responsible members of the industry involved to share their suggestions with us. We also may hold public hearings to which all sides are invited.

A new regulation often begins with an individual complaint that we might not have uncovered until much later if you did not take the time to write or call us. One measure of increased awareness is this number: 964-7777. It is the telephone number of our 24-hour special complaint service — and last year more than 200,000 consumers dialed it.

To shorten the lines of communication between our department and every neighborhood, we have continued our Federally aided program of community complaint offices. We now have five: Forest Hills (107-06 70th Road), Jamaica (90-18 161st Street), Lower East Side (147 Delancey Street), East Harlem (227 E. 116th Street) and West Harlem 248 W. 116th Street.

In the past, many consumers who faced the prospect of court action, either as plaintiff or defendant, in a buyer-seller dispute were at a disadvantage because of the time and expense involved or because they just didn't know their legal rights. In cooperation with Judge Edward Thompson, our department has reclaimed the Small Claims Court for consumers. The department has prepared a booklet, "How to Sue in Small Claims Court," available in English and Spanish on request from either the main or neighborhood offices.

Last January, in cooperation with the Harlem-East Harlem Model Cities Administration and many community leaders, a separate Small Claims Court was opened in the Municipal Building on East 121st Street.

Our New York City consumer effort is in the sum of eight million individual consumer efforts. That was demonstrated last year in two important challenges: Open Dating and Unit Pricing.

Open dating was accepted immediately and widely, because the old secret codes on food products were an obvious and long-recognized abuse. Unit pricing's acceptance has been slower, because the old methods of packaging and labeling and pricing had been convenient if costly. Old buying habits are difficult to change.

Part of the difficulty may have been the original unit-pricing tags—they were different from store to store, a jumble of figures. Our department met with food industry representatives and with neighborhood groups of shoppers, to hear their suggestions for a simpler label. As a result, we have adopted a new unit-pricing regulation which includes the requirement that stores print the unit price on a background of orange.

The number of shoppers beginning to use unit pricing is on the increase, though still a minority. Looking for the unit price is a fine habit for a price-conscious shopper to acquire.

That is a brief overview of consumer life in New York City today. The protection to achieve for ourselves—we have gone ahead to try to achieve. The protection that can come to us only from Washington or Albany — we're waiting for (too quietly, I think). And we have learned that consumer — protection rules that are illusory, meaningless or unenforceable are the greatest abuse of all and should be recognized as such.

We believe that the search for fairness in the marketplace never ends and that everyone who is affected by injustice has a responsibility to try to help make things better than they are.

QUESTIONS FOR DISCUSSION

1. Mrs. Myerson describes what has been done in one city, New York, to better protect the consumer. But other cities have not done as well. What do you think are the reasons for this?

2. Investigate the measures taken to protect the consumer in your own town or city. Are the results as good as those found in New York? Why?

3. Would you favor controlling consumer abuse more at the local level rather than at the national level? Why?

4. Considering the great size of the New York population, do you think that the size of the New York City consumer protection department is adequate enough to do the job?

THE INDUSTRY GETS A
CONTROVERSIAL WATCHDOG *

35

BUSINESS WEEK

* "The Industry Gets a Controversial Watchdog,"
Business Week (May 12, 1973), pp. 130-133. Reproduced
by permission.

The comments might well have come from the most fervent
consumerist or advertising critic on the Federal Trade Commission.
Print and broadcast ads for Kal Kan dog food, they said, were rife
with "unsubtantiated claims" and "false disparagement" of a
competitor. An ad for Nytol, the sleep-aid product of Block Drug
Co., "made false and deceptive use of a medical study."

These and similar charges against such advertisers as Culligan
U.S.A. (water softener)), El Al Israel Airlines, and Emerson TV Sales
Corp. came from the advertising industry's own watchdog, and not
from the offices of Ralph Nader or the FTC. They were made in
recent months by an investigative body and groups of admen and
advertisers who regularly sit in judgment on the work of their
fellows. The National Advertising Div. of the Council of Better
Business Bureaus and a separate "court of appeals," the National
Advertising Review Board, were set up some 18 months ago—but
only since January, when they began to name names, have they
seemed both serious and controversial.

The controversial nature of NADNARB emerges in contradictory
statements from Erma Angevine, executive director of the Consumer
Federation of America, who calls it "a dismal failure," and from FTC
Commissioner Mary Gardiner Jones, who says it "has gone far
beyond the more traditional self-regulatory efforts of industry
groups." A spokesman for Virginia Knauer, President Nixon's Special
Assistant on Consumer Affairs, fence-sits by calling it a "mixed
blessing . . . a step in the right direction."

Impact. To William H. Ewen, executive director of the NARB,
disagreement over the value of the operation is a healthy sign that
someone, at least, is paying attention to its work—while other
self-regulatory and industry groups all too often operate in complete
anonymity. Everyone connected with NAD-NARB, Ewen says, was
aware that critics would label it an apologist for the advertising
industry at first, "but now we think we have changed some minds."

It took time, he admits. The watchdog groups were formed at a
time when the consumerism movement was gathering steam, and the
FTC, along with various legislators, was regularly blasting advertising.
With an eye on potential legislation that threatened to curtail their
industry, the major ad groups—American Assn. of Advertising
Agencies, American Advertising Federation, and the Assn. of

National Advertisers — moved to prove they could handle their own problems. A decision was made to work with the Council of Better Business Bureaus (CBBB), which itself had been under attack by consumerists and had only recently been restructured and revitalized to take a more active consumerist role. CBBB got into the picture when it was reasoned that BBB local offices have long handled complaints against local advertisers, and could also pass on a person's complaint against national advertising to a New York "complaint bureau."

The complaint bureau — the National Advertising Div. — is staffed by about eight people near CBBB headquarters on Third Avenue in New York City. It screens complaints lodged by citizens, consumerists, rival advertisers, and others — serving first in a grand jury capacity to determine if the facts call for a fuller investigation. If so, the NAD calls on the advertiser or agency for comments, substantiation of claims, and other material needed to reach a decision. The NAD has been processing some 12 to 20 complaints a month since it got off the ground. Among them:

> An El Al Israel Airlines ad that featured a "98¢ fare" in what the airline thought was a humorous headline was deemed misleading, and the advertiser agreed to discontinue it.
>
> A Culligan U.S.A. ad boasted of a "$2.75 per month limited offer" without revealing how limited the offer was or that installation charges were extra. Again, the advertiser okayed a change.
>
> Singer Co. failed to note that a case for a sewing machine cost extra. It subsequently included the fact in ads.
>
> Orleans Packing Co. said its dogfood was "the only dry dogfood with real meat in every bite." It agreed to change the line when the NAD said it failed to substantiate the claim.

Of some 511 complaints submitted to the NAD thus far, more than 400 have been processed, and about 150 have been dismissed after consideration. For example, one TV viewer felt that a line in a jingle for Armour hot dogs — stating that they were desired by "even kids with chicken pox" — was dangerous. It might induce a child with chicken pox to demand hot dogs as a cure, said the complaint. The NAD consulted two doctors who saw no potential harm in a child eating hot dogs while he had chicken pox.

Another dismissal occurred when a visitor to the Holiday Inn at Kennedy International Airport found the motel's indoor pool closed and complained to the NAD that an advertisement featured both indoor and outdoor pools. The case was dismissed when the advertiser pointed out that the ad in question was an old one, and new ads did not mention the indoor pool. A question about Johnson & Johnson's baby shampoo, advertised as being non-irritating to a child's eyes, was dismissed when the company provided its test data and an outside medical consultant accepted the results.

Appeals board. If complainants or advertisers are not satisfied with the NAD finding, they can ask for an appeal to the review board. The NARB, independent of the Better Business Bureau affiliation, is headed by Charles W. Yost, former U.S. Ambassador to the United Nations. About 10 cases have gone to the NARB, but they have been the ones that made the headlines in the advertising trade press. The decisions have also pleased some industry supporters of the operation, riled others, and drawn consumerists' blasts.

In the NARB procedure, a panel of five judges rules on the merits of each complaint. The panel is drawn from 50 high-ranking executives on call, 30 of whom are from advertisers, 10 might be considered the ranks of consumers in that they are lawyers, college professors, and the like. Each panel is assembled in a 3-1-1 ratio, and members are called in from across the country so the panel does not have an eastern or Madison Avenue bias.

The NARB panels — which ruled recently against Kal Kan and Nytol but upheld Bristol-Myers Co.'s claim that a deodorant "keeps you drier" — can be difficult to assemble, Ewen says, because the executives are otherwise busy with their own duties. "We met for a half-day," says Dr. Aurelia Miller, director of the Data Center of the National Board of the YWCA, who served on one panel. "For me to get there, it was just a short walk down the street, but others came from long distances."

Slow to act. A typical panel might include Dr. Miller, who has been active in consumer affairs, Ira Herbert, marketing director of Coca-Cola U.S.A. from Atlanta, Robert S. Wheeler, advertising vice president of Best Foods in New Jersey, Claude Jakes, director of marketing communications at Westinghouse Electric Corp. in Pittsburgh, and ad agency head Neal O'Connor of N.W. Ayer & Son in New York. "Just organizing such a group—and then getting the data from the complainant for study and a representative of the challenged advertiser to appear — can take 30 letters back and forth to arrange a suitable date," says Ewen.

The procedure troubles Ms. Angevine of the Consumer Federation. "I used to think the FTC was slow," she says. Of 35 complaints filed by the CFA in the past year, she complains, only 17 have been acted upon — and none has been upheld. "We won't be sending any more complaints," she says. "We simply don't have the time and energy for such a charade."

Dr. Miller notes that there were delays at first, but things are moving faster now. "After we deliberated all morning," she notes, "the chairman wrote the decision in a week." A problem, she adds, is that complaints must work their way through the NAD first, and then be appealed before the NARB panel can be convened. "When something annoys people, they want it settled fast."

Test cases. Ewen believes that numerous complaints submitted to the NAD have been "test cases" tossed into the hopper by consumerists anxious to check the mechanism of the self-regulatory body. "One of 'Nader's outposts' sent in 80 complaints — each of which had to be considered, the ad in question studied, the advertiser asked for substantiation, and so on," he says. The operation was set up originally with a budget reported at $1.2-million, "but nowhere near that has been spent," Ewen adds. "More manpower is not the answer to processing complaints more quickly. It's like the critics who said we would be more effective if there were more 'public representatives' on the panel and fewer agency people. Well, the agency people are consumers, too, of course. Everyone is a consumer."

Working from virtually empty offices with a single secretary — "It's a liaison kind of job," Ewen explains — the NARB director thinks much good has come from the operation. In addition to its role as an arbiter, it recently fostered the first of several consultative panels to study such things as how women are portrayed in ads and whether some ads may cause unsafe behavior. The panels will issue position papers to guide admen in the future. "But already," says Ewen, "along with the FTC and other groups, we have made advertisers and agencies aware that claims they make need substantiation. We have no legal force, we cannot subpoena anyone to come in and defend themselves against a complainant — but they come in to state their case, knowing that we now publish our decisions for everyone to see. It is hard to put a scorecard value on the merits of persusasion vs. legal regulation, but I feel that fewer wild claims are being made these days."

QUESTIONS FOR DISCUSSION

1. What is the relationship between the National Advertising Division and the National Advertising Review Board?

2. From what sources do complaints originate? How are they handled by NAD?

3. What powers do NAD and NARB possess? Are these sufficient to control bad advertising? To discourage it?

4. What are the advantages of self-policing? What limitations are encountered by such bodies as NAD and NARB?

5. Would you have any suggestions for strengthening such voluntary regulation systems?

6. Do you pin your hopes for better standards for advertising on self-regulation, or on governmental and legal regulation?

PART VIII
THE OTHER SIDE: HOW BUSINESS IS ABUSED BY CONSUMERS; WHAT IT DOES TO PROTECT THEM

Debatable questions, like coins, have two sides. We have been quite candid in pointing out the deficiencies of American business. Now it is only fair to examine the other side of the question. Are all businessmen malefactors? Do all of them not care for the customers they are supposed to be serving? Are they all exploiters? Have they no social conscience?

Very obviously the answer is yes and no. Indeed, some are exploiters, the "fast buck artists" who think of their customers as an eagle considers a rabbit. Some have the social consciousness of an alligator.

But not all by any means. Indeed, this writer feels that a very small tail wags a very large dog. Only a small proportion of our business people are dishonest and uncaring. The overwhelming majority are like we are: They try to do the right thing. It is not always clear what the right thing is. They recoil with horror at the charges levelled at business by its most vehement critics. Indeed, they often answer in anger when facts and calm reason would be much more appropriate and effective. But so do we all when we think we are under a savage and unjustified attack.

This section takes a brief look at the other side. How does business itself feel about consumeristic attacks? Is business trying to clean up its own mess? Do responsible firms try to avoid producing dangerous goods? Do they attempt to advertise honestly?

The answer may surprise some readers. For they really do try at least the responsible majority. In evidence of this we look at the statement of Elisha Grey, a recognized business leader who is also highly respected by the consumerists. Mr. Grey regrets that consumers tend to hold it against all business when they are cheated by one malefactor. He also points out that things were not ideal in the "good old days". Indeed, the ethical standards of business have come a long way since then. Grey feels that we tend to get too impatient and clamor for instant results. He feels that consumers are tuning out business when it tries to tell its side of the story, which is patently unfair to business.

Mrs. Knauer gives a fair appraisal of business' response to consumerism, which she thinks to be most encouraging. She shows that responsive firms have found it good business, when consumers become aware that companies are on their side and trying to do better by them. They patronize their products and sales swell.

Getting objective product information to their customers has been a developing occupation of businesses, and we learn how Du Pont has set up their direct channel to the public just as Mr. Grey's Whirlpool Corp. has the "hot line" direct to Benton Harbor to deal with consumer product difficulties and complaints.

Rose de Wolf, a columnist for the *Philadelphia Bulletin*, tells in her delightful style of ways in which consumers abuse business by deceiving businessmen and making false claims about them. This little discussed side of the consumer question should be given more airing. It is obvious that consumers cannot well complain about unfair tactics on the part of business, and then turn around and employ such tactics themselves.

C. Clinton Collins analyzes the attempts of one company, Du Pont, to further protect the public by testing products for safety and reliability before putting them on the market. For example, just to research one new kind of product and to develop flame-resistant fibers, Du Pont spent some $4 million in 1972. This could be duplicated many times over in United States industry. For example, Sears, Roebuck and Company has testing laboratories in Chicago that are larger than those of the U.S. Bureau of Standards in Washington. Sears not only tests new products but constantly monitors the quality performance and competitive value of samples of older products sold by the chain. All of this costs millions of dollars per year. Few critics seem to be aware of these considerable corporate efforts to protect the public and to increase product reliability and value.

Long before consumerism became a household word, Elisha Gray
II not only talked about it but responded to its symptoms. When he
was chairman and chief executive officer of Whirlpool Corporation,
he started several innovative consumer action programs, including the
first nationwide, toll-free "Cool Line" telephone service for
customers with complaints.

Small wonder that when a group of top businessmen in 1970
decided to beef up the nation's Better Business Bureaus they chose
Gray to head up the newly formed Council.

Affectation is not Gray's nature. Most people call him Bud. In his
unpaid role as chairman of the Council of Better Business Bureaus,
Inc., he prefers a spartan approach. At Council headquarters, high
above Manhattan's throbbing traffic at 51st Street and Third Avenue,
Gray doesn't even have his own office. Instead, he settles for
whatever desk space is available during his weekly trips there from
his home in Benton Harbor, Michigan.

Like thousands of executives, Gray is concerned with the declining
reputation of business which, surveys show, is at an all-time low.
Unlike many, he has diagnosed the ailment, spotted what he feels are
the causes, and is busy trying to find a solution.

"You can't persuade a person to believe in the integrity, strength
and importance of business if he just got shafted in some
transaction," Gray says. "A prerequisite to public confidence in the
business system is consumer confidence in the market place."

Gray says consumerism isn't really new. Its functions — buying
and selling — were always present and merchants always were subject
to complaints.

"What has changed," he says, "is the public's expectations of
business, and today they're at an all-time high. With each new and
better product, the consumer's expectations climb to a new plateau
and he immediately wonders what the next new product will be."

To illustrate his point, Gray tells about the telephone call he
received the morning after astronaut Neil Armstrong became the first
man to walk on the moon. The caller had bought a color TV set
made by a Whirlpool subsidiary and was furious because he said he
had trouble with the telecast. The man admitted he saw the whole
show but complained that the color was very poor on the flesh tones.

"I was very sympathetic with him," said Gray. "Not until he hung up did it dawn on me that the telecast from the moon was in black and white only. Obviously, this fact hadn't been considered by the caller either. He had become so accustomed to watching color TV programs that when the astrunauts appeared in black and white he automatically assumed his TV set was defective."

Why do consumers expect so much from business today?

According to Gray, business itself is partly to blame. "By our very accomplishments we have encouraged consumers to expect miracles as routine. They say, 'You can put a man on the moon but you can't fix my automobile.' They want their cars to work perfectly, but cars are complicated pieces of machinery, and there are millions of them out there, and they don't always work perfectly.

"In their enthusiasm to sell, some businessmen promise more than they can deliver, and all businessmen suffer because of it. In addition, the consumer has no way of putting his market problems in perspective. Business hasn't communicated the fact that there are billions of business transactions daily and 99 per cent of them are handled perfectly. Even a 99 per cent satisfied population leaves several million dissatisfied people and is cold comfort to the lady whose monthly bill has been mixed up by a department store computer, or who is sent the wrong article, or who received the right article only to find that it had been broken in shipment.

"The reason the business story has failed to be accepted by the public is because the public isn't listening. Consumers are so fired up about the inadequacies of the marketplace that they tune us out."

As a result, Gray says, many people continue to insist: "They don't make them like they used to.

"That's nonsense," says Gray. "People forget that shirts used to shrink, that colors used to fade and that the paint we used was apt to peel. By whatever yardstick, the performance of business has never been better. Its products, quality and assortments are all better. Today, auto tire and gas performance are better, clothes are made better, and so are appliances and building materials. That camera and film you're using to take my picture (Gray pointed to veteran photographer Werner Wolff) are much better than we had 20 years ago."

Part of the problem as Gray sees it, is the immensity of today's marketplace.

"To serve the demands of our increasing population, we have geared our business operations to mass numbers. In my own company alone, we talk about scheduling 40,000 major appliances a day, and our purchasing people are buying on these scales. It's difficult to suddenly switch gears and think about one woman who is hopping mad because her refrigerator doesn't work. And yet, she's right — it doesn't work, and she couldn't care less about our mass numbers."

The growth of impersonal marketing is another reason why consumers are dissatisfied with business. Says Gray:

"The woman who buys at the supermarket, with its 11 per cent markup, instead of at the little grocery store, with its 30 per cent markup, would like to have the highly personalized service that the little grocer offers plus the supermarket's lower price tag. Of course, she can't have it both ways. This is a changed characteristic of our marketplace. We're wedded to it; there's no going back."

Gray also believes that the gap between business reputation and consumer expectations has widened because consumerism has received so much pulicity lately — most of it at the expense of business.

"It's an easy tag that has been used to cover all the errors that may crop up in the business system," says Gray. "Unfortunately, some people use consumerism as a form of warfare. They ignore the good that business does and rarely mention the increased costs the consumer will have to pay for greater product safety, improved service, more information, and less pollution.

"Some consumer activists are pushing for laws that would force business to produce things that many consumers don't even want. When regulations are passed telling you how many models or what sizes of a certain product you can sell, then you are changing the basic rules of the free enterprise system. And that's what some people would like to see happen."

The philosophy behind much of this thinking, Gray says, is that the customer is a moron, can't think for himself or herself, and needs protection.

"That's ridiculous," Gray asserts. "Consumers are your wife and mine; they are each of us and are very discerning. You're not going to fool the consumer for more than a moment, and you certainly aren't going to do it twice."

Gray feels that instead of taking a defensive posture, more businessmen should recognize that response to consumerism is just good business.

For example, he cites the success that Whirlpool has had with its "Cool Line" since it was introduced in 1967 to improve communications with customers. The telephone service is intended to help customers keep their cool when they have questions about Whirlpool products, parts replacement, warranty information or service centers.

"It's one of the best sales boosters we've ever had," says Gray, "and it doesn't cost that much, either. We receive about 300 calls a day and we have about 20 million units in operation daily.

"The line also provides a quick feedback on quality problems from the field. The problem is that you make a product today and it averages 30 days in your inventory, then it's in the distributor's inventory, then the dealer's. So by the time it's in the customer's home and hooked up, 90 days have passed and you've been building them as fast as you can. If you have a sleeper in there, you're in trouble. So, this feedback can be very important."

Gray feels education is the key to restoring consumer confidence in the marketplace and in business. He would like to see economic education begin at the elementary grade level and go right on through. "Hell, we teach our children about communism, driver training, and how to play in a band, but we teach them appallingly little about the American free enterprise system."

When the Council of Better Business Bureaus was established, Gray launched a 14-point program aimed at making local bureaus more responsive to consumer needs. Consumer education — in the form of books, pamphlets, mobile vans, radio and TV spots on some 3,400 radio and TV stations — is an important part of that effort. Other high-priority projects include a national advertising review board; establishment of consumer councils in major cities for more consumer-business dialog; and the establishment of consumer arbitration panels (65 now with a goal of 120 by May) for quick, virtually free settlement of disputes that cannot be resolved through BBB's mediation efforts.

Gray believes the nation's 136 Better Business Bureaus, which handled more than 6 million calls last year, can help serve as a bridge between the businessman and the public.

"Many of today's consumer wants stem from vital needs, and it's our job to show initiative in filling them. Consumers need business and business needs consumers. They're asking: What have you done for me lately? It's time business began telling them."

QUESTIONS FOR DISCUSSION

1. "You can't persuade a person to believe in the integrity, strength and importance of business if he just got shafted in some transaction." Comment.

2. Do you think the public is unreasonable in its demands on business? Should they reasonably expect miracles?

3. Why are the consumers not listening to the business side of the story? Is this mostly the fault of business? How so?

4. What can business do about this?

5. Do you think self-policing attempts, such as the Council of Better Business Bureaus, are the answer? How about a strong public relations program telling the business position? How about the use of advertising?

6. Mr. Grey is enthusiastic about consumer education. How do you appraise this as a means for furthering consumer welfare?

VIRGINIA KNAUER AND FRANK McLAUGHLIN

*Virginia Knauer, Frank McLaughlin, "Consumerism is Good for Business," Du Pont *Context*, Vol. 2, No. 1, (1973), pp. 16-18. Reproduced by Permission.

At her sixth-floor office in the New Executive Office Building, Mrs. Virginia H. Knauer, Special Assistant to the President for Consumer Affairs, sat at her desk. Behind her, a picture of President Nixon, the American flag and a bouquet of flowers. To her left, a large window framing the top half of the Washington Monument.

Seated in a chair facing Mrs. Knauer was Frank McLaughlin, Director of Industry Relations for the U.S. Office of Consumer Affairs. Behind him was a wall lined with pictures, mostly political friends of Mrs. Knauer, and reprints of magazine covers on which she has been featured.

Before she was appointed to her present position in April, 1969, Mrs. Knauer was director of the Pennsylvania Bureau of Consumer Protection. In 1960, she was the first Republican woman elected to the Philadelphia City Council.

Is consumer discontent still on the rise in the U.S.?

Mrs. Knauer: It really accelerated during the last five years, but I think it is leveling off now.

Why?

Mrs. Knauer: Because consumers and business people have learned to speak with civility to each other and are beginning to cooperate with each other.

Didn't they do this before?

Mrs. Knauer: When I took over this job four years ago, many business people had the attitude that consumer complaints were coming from a lot of old ladies in tennis shoes . . . the nuts and kooks who are always demanding something that business can't supply. But that attitude has changed now, especially in the past year.

Why has this changed?

Mrs. Knauer: Well, for one thing, the really smart businessmen now recognize that consumerism is good for business. They've seen their sales go up as they've responded more to consumer needs.

Mr. McLaughlin: There are two new elements that weren't present before. First, there's a strong recognition today among consumer groups that they needn't rely on legislation every time they're calling for a change in the marketplace. Instead, they've found that by touching the competitive instincts of business, many consumer problems can be solved literally overnight.

Mrs. Knauer: I think the key to this is the appeal being made to the really progressive business leaders—selling them the idea: why not do it yourself? If not, Congress just might do it for you.

Who's selling this idea?

Mrs. Knauer: We certainly are, and so are consumer groups.

To what types of business?

Mrs. Knauer: To all types. This is what we did with unit pricing in the food industry. When Jewel Tea, Safeway and Giant adopted unit pricing voluntarily, we kept talking about them as leaders, and they got great publicity. Soon, there was a domino effect. Others had to adopt it to stay competitive. That's why today nearly 90 per cent of all major food chains have some unit pricing.

Mr. McLaughlin: We did the same thing with open dating on foods—first with the food chains and later with the meat packers. All it takes is one or two business leaders to start responding to consumer complaints and their competitors will soon follow. That's what's happening more and more now.

What industries are giving you the most resistance?

Mrs. Knauer: Strangely, there's very little resistance. We had some problems at first with the cosmetics industry. They argued that they couldn't put their lipstick ingredients on a label—trade secrets, you know. But we pointed out that any chemist can tell exactly what's in any lipstick, and they backed down on this. They're now registering their formulations with the Food and Drug Administration. We're still urging them to share their adverse data and they don't like that. But they're coming along.

What is the second element you mentioned?

Mr. McLaughlin: Today, consumers are much more involved in the decision-making process. They're no longer content to sit by and leave decisions to some government administrator, or to the administrator and business. The Department of Agriculture heard from thousands of consumers on bacon packaging; cosmetic makers have heard from thousands on the issue of cosmetic safety and labeling. The same applies to insurance and other industries. And in many cases, consumer involvement is changing business programs and government regulations.

Are consumers complaining today about the same things as when you took office?

Mrs. Knauer: No. When I came here our greatest complaints were about household appliances, in terms of the warranties, the high cost of repair and the length of time you waited for service. That was both in brown goods [such as radios and TVs] and white goods [such as refrigerators and washers]. Today, for every complaint we get on major appliances we get about five on automobiles. We average about 100 complaints a month on major appliances and about 400 to 600 on cars.

What specifically are car owners complaining about?

Mr. McLaughlin: We get some complaints about warranties and unethical practices but the vast majority are about repair service. People bring their car in repeatedly, but it doesn't get fixed. More people now recognize that their time is money.

Mrs. Knauer: What we have zeroed in on is a lack of standards.

Mr. McLaughlin: Right. There's a lack of standards for measuring the competency of the mechanic, a lack of standards for the amount of service space in proportion to the number of cars sold, a lack of standards for diagnostic equipment.

Is anything being done about this problem?

Mrs. Knauer: Yes. The auto companies and the independent garages are making efforts to aid the consumer. Recently, they established a National Institute for Auto Service Excellence, which is an organization for setting standards to measure the competency of mechanics. Individual dealerships also have done some interesting things, but there are still no standards across the board.

Mr. McLaughlin: Some states are moving into this area. California has a statute; so do Rhode Island and Connecticut.

What about the costs of consumerism? Some business people say improving quality, service, safety and providing more information about products increases costs. They say these costs will have to be passed on to consumers who already are complaining about rising prices.

Mrs. Knauer: But the consumer already pays for those rejects that are knocked off at the end of the assembly line because of shoddy workmanship.

Mr. McLaughlin: And he pays for the inefficiency of markets.

Mrs. Knauer: When people buy a product that fails, they have to pay to have it repaired or replaced. Consumers are asking: Why don't they make it better? They're willing to pay for it. Why don't they make it right in the first place?

Do you feel the same way about label information?

Mrs. Knauer: Absolutely. We got a bunch of flak—business people saying, "Ohhh, we can't do that. We would have to tack this cost on to consumers." Nonsense! Companies update their labels regularly. As long as they're going to change a label, why not put all the information on it that consumers want and need?

What about the suggestion that the Federal government establish a consumer authority with real power, such as the Consumer Ombudsman in Sweden?

Mrs. Knauer: This may be working well for the Swedes but they don't have a Federal Trade Commission like we do; nor do they have a Food and Drug Administration similar to ours. The solutions for them are not necessarily the same for us.

What about the proposed new Consumer Protection Agency? Twice in the past three years, Congress has killed the idea, but now it has been revived again. Will we have such an agency in 1973?

Mrs. Knauer: That's in the lap of the gods. I think there's a good chance but, of course, I've said that for four years.
What is the real significance of the new Product Safety Commission?
Mrs. Knauer: For the first time, a government agency will set safety standards for consumer products. I think this is great.
Mr. McLaughlin: It also will make existing programs more visible. The average consumer really has no way of knowing that the responsibility for possible radiological hazards of tv sets and microwave ovens is lodged in the FDA. It's going to make hazardous substances labeling more visible, even if the agency itself doesn't have the authority to deal with the subject.

APPENDIX
Du Pont's Product Information Service

One complaint of many consumers is lack of information about products. Information about Du Pont products is as close as the nearest telephone.

Du Pont has long maintained a company-wide, 24-hour-a-day inquiry handling network, with headquarters in Wilmington, Del. (302-774-2421), and contact points in eight major metropolitan centers: Baltimore, Boston, Chicago, Houston, Los Angeles, New York, Philadelphia, and Washington, D.C.

When someone calls with a question or a complaint (only a small percentage of the calls involve complaints), a product information expediter connects the caller with a person who can provide the answer. More than 1,000 Du Pont employees with thorough knowledge of certain products or product lines have been designated to assist the expediters. They perform this service in addition to their regular jobs.

Du Pont plants and sales offices across the country also offer consumers help in getting product information, during normal working hours. Abroad, Du Pont subsidiaries in Europe and Australia have product information expediters.

Providing product information is a big job in Du Pont. Last year, the U.S. inquiry handling network received 161,000 calls, a record.

QUESTIONS FOR DISCUSSION

1. Do you really believe that consumerism is good for business?

2. What argument does Mrs. Knauer use to prove this point?

3. Mrs. Knauer says that her office is receiving many more complaints about automobiles than before. Does this indicate that the auto producers should be ashamed?

4. Does Mrs. Knauer feel that her federal office will be continued? Should it be?

ROSE DEWOLF

* Rose Dewolf "Consumers Aren't All Angels Either,"
Du Pont *Context*, Vol. 2, No. 1, (1973), pp. 9-10.
Reproduced by permission.

Oh, I know whose side I'm on . . . I'm a consumer. I bow to no one in my antagonism to useless warranties, fraudulent claims, garbled instructions, hidden flaws, and ridiculous computers which threatened to have me arrested if I don't pay $0.00 right away. If I feel affronted, I can holler for Ralph Nader as loud as anyone. And yet . . .

Every once in a while, much as I try to fight it, I feel a twinge of sympathy for merchants, manufacturers, and provider of service. Every once in a while, though I feel like a traitor, I want to jump up and say: "You know, consumers can be pretty rotten, too."

Consumers are not all angels. They include in their numbers those who would quite cheerfully cheat, steal, lie and/or behave with incredible stupidity. There, I've said it and I'm glad.

Take the "switchers," for example. Those are the people who take the price tag from a cheap item and put it on an expensive item before taking the expensive item to the salesclerk. They hope the clerk will be too busy to notice and will sell the goods at a "bargain" price the store hadn't really counted on.

Switchers are everywhere. I once saw this very dignified-looking gentleman craftily switch the lids on a jar of cashews. The prices, you see, were stamped on the lids. The man intended to buy his cashews, quite literally, for "peanuts."

And I have seen a dear little housewife slip a pound of butter into an oleomargarine box, assuming that the check-out clerk would never check. She assumed wrong. All check-out clerks know that trick.

One time I merely mentioned the word "consumer" to a friend of mine who works for a supermarket and the poor guy went bananas. [On special, that week.]

"Consumers!" he wailed. "I'll tell you about consumers. They buy magazines, take them home and read them, then return them for a refund claiming their husband bought duplicates . . . they demand to get five cents back on the five-cents-back coupon without buying the product first . . . they finish off bars of candy or bottles of soda while they walk through the store and then don't mention it when it comes time to pay. . ."

Did you know that baby food manufacturers deliberately seal their jars so they'll open with a loud "POP". That, says my friend, is so that a consumer who gets a jar that opens only with a little "poof" knows it has been opened before. Seems some mothers want to taste the food at the store to make sure little junior will like it, but then don't want to buy the jar they tasted.

Do you know why most cereal manufacturers don't give away prizes in the cereal boxes anymore? That's because so many women used to pry open the package, snitch the prize, and leave the unsalable torn box on the shelf. Nowadays, if you want to get that super-spy ring your kid has been crying for, you have to buy the box, clip the coupon, and send 25 cents in coin.

Suburban stores tell of women who "buy" a fancy dress on the Friday just before the Country Club dance and then return it ["I just changed my mind."] on Monday. They get indignant if the clerk says the dress looks as if it had been worn.

There are those who carry on loudly when the billing computer makes a mistake and claims they owe a bill they know they don't owe—but keep awfully quiet when the computer gives them credit they know they don't deserve. That makes it tougher for the store to straighten out the error.

Don't we all know people who brag about how they got the "whole car fixed" on the insurance of the guy who merely dented a fender?

My local laundryman claims that if he ever loses a shirt [Heaven forbid], it invariably turns out to be [a] "very expensive" and [b] "just purchased."

"How come I never lose last year's cheap shirt?" he asks. "No. Those are the ones I manage to return. Right?" He is skeptical.

There are, of course, those who cheat the stores even more forthrightly. Shoplifting is at an all-time high. Do you know why manufacturers often pack such little items as batteries, pencils and razor blades in plastic bubbles attached to huge pieces of cardboard? That's because the cardboard is larger than the average consumer's pocket where many batteries, pencils and razor blades used to just disappear.

People who deal with consumers sometimes lose patience with them not because the consumers are greedy or dishonest but because they sometimes simply cause problems for themselves.

A local weights and measures inspector told me of pulling a surprise raid on a local butcher shop where the butcher was suspected of resting his elbow on the scale while weighing meat. Did the consumers appreciate the inspector's arrival? They did not.

"They were angry because it was close to dinner time. They started yelling at me," the inspector said. "They said I was holding them up . . . they had to get home to start cooking. They called me a city hall drone. They said I was annoying the butcher who was their friend. Some friend!"

Consumers can be funny. Recently, a spokesman for a national meat canning company told a convention of food editors that consumers persist in sending an open can of meat back to the company to illustrate whatever complaint they're making. The fact is, that after days of travel in the unrefrigerated mail, the product *always* looks awful and smells worse. How can the company possibly tell if the complaint was justified in the first place?

Consumers complain about high food prices and then insist on buying every convenience food on the market. They yell about too loud commercials and then don't buy the products advertised on soft ones.

The government says motorists will be safer if their cars buzz until the safety belts are fastened. But car-buyers by the hordes are threatening dealers with mayhem unless the buzzers are unhooked. [The dealers are prohibited by law from complying.]

Consumers are just not always happy with what is being done *for* them. Frankly, I have to admit that I was a lot happier before packages of hot dogs had to admit right out in public that they contain ground-up cow's lips. Ycchh. Do we have to know EVERYTHING?

I'm not trying to say that the fact that the consumer can be, in his turn, greedy, dishonest, unappreciative, and just plain stupid, in any way excuses commercial interests for being the same. As my mother used to say, "Two wrongs don't make a right."

Still, fair is fair and somebody had to speak out. And now that I have gotten that out of the way, I can get to all these complaint letters I'm preparing for Ralph, and Virginia, and my local office of Consumer Affairs.

QUESTIONS FOR DISCUSSION

1. How do consumers abuse businessmen?

2. Do you think that this is a new tendency, or have some consumers always been dishonest?

3. If consumer dishonesty is increasing, what reasons would you deem are responsible for the increase?

4. Do consumers really want to be protected? How about the examples given by Rose de Wolf?

5. Should business be tougher with dishonest consumers, just as consumers are calling for a tightening up on business malpractices?

6. What could be done to discourage such dishonesty?

G. CLINTON COLLINS

* G. Clinton Collins,"An Extra Dimension of Care," Du Pont *Context*, Vol. 2, No. 1 (1973), pp. 11-13. Reproduced by permission.

Products of the Du Pont Company have a profound effect on the everyday activities of the average consumer.

Du Pont's technical innovations include the first moisture-proof packaging film, the first true synthetic fiber (nylon), the first quick-drying lacquer, and many more.

But these technological contributions are only part of the story of Du Pont's relationship to the consumer. The rest of the story involves an extra dimension of care and effort.

The Laboratory That Rejects New Products

The Haskell Laboratory for Toxicology and Industrial Medicine was established by Du Pont near Wilmington, Del., in 1935. Its sole function was—and is—to make certain that Du Pont products can be manufactured and used safely. At the time it was founded, Haskell was a pioneering venture in American industry.

Today, its 85 staff members carry on a wide range of studies to determine possible toxic effects of some 300 new materials each year. Extensive tests make certain that prospective new products will not cause allergic reactions or other harmful effects when used as intended. Animal studies involve inhalation, injection, skin and eye contact, and feeding. (Studies that determine whether a substance will persist in or be harmful to the environment are also done, but not at Haskell.)

The diversity of Du Pont's 1600 products and product lines means that studies are done on everything from paint to crop protection chemicals, with emphasis on textile fibers, which account for more than a third of the company's sales. Before any new or modified synthetic fiber is introduced, its potential toxicity and psssible environmental problems must be determined.

Elsewhere in this article is a description of Du Pont's efforts to develop effective flame-resistant fibers. One candidate that showed excellent flame resistance recently underwent a battery of 13 different and extensive tests ranging up to 22 weeks in length. Rats, quail, rabbits and guinea pigs were used in these tests, and patches of the fiber were applied to the skin of 200 volunteers to test for irritation.

The result: rejection. The new fiber posed a potential toxicity problem, and evidence indicated a disposal problem due to persistence in the environment.

It was back to the drawing board—with, as described later, more success.

Textile Fibers and the Consumers

A complex of fabric mills, clothing, tire and home furnishing manufacturers and retailers forms a link between Du Pont and the consumer. Consumer benefits are the company's primary yardstick in developing new products and modifying old ones. Du Pont's well-known technical triumphs — nylon, "Dacron" polyester fiber, "orlon" acrylic fiber, "Lycra" spandex fiber, "Qiana" nylon — all offer one or more consumer advantages. In many cases, the technical breakthrough brought the price of high performance down within the means of more consumers.

The development of safer automobile tires parallels the development of stronger and more durable fibers from Du Pont. A new level of safety and performance was achieved with introduction of nylon into tires in the '50s.

Now, Du Pont has introduced DP-01* (Fiber B) — so strong that in belts of radial belted tires one pound of this fiber does the work of five pounds of steel wire. This heat-resistant fiber is engineered to stand the severe conditions it encounters in tires, thereby providing safety along with a good ride.

In developing the fiber, Du Pont built 1500 tires at its Textile Research Laboratory near Wilmington. Performance was established by lab tests and nearly 10 million miles of road tests. More than 100,000 tires with this fiber have been produced to date. All major tire companies are evaluating it, and two large U.S. companies have announced plans for commercialization of radial passenger car tires with belts of DP-01.

Beyond the Technical Triumph

Responding to consumer needs, however, is not just a matter of research and testing.

Three years ago, Sears, Roebuch and Company recognized a need to offer boys' jeans much stronger than the conventional permanent press type. A survey of mothers confirmed that what they wanted most in boys' pants was durability. Sears sought Du Pont's help in building a "super-jean." What Du Pont's fabric development experts came up with was an innovative blend of three fibers — nylon, "Dacron" polyester and cotton. Lab tests showed the new fabric to be one-and-a-half to three times stronger than coventional permanent press material.

Test jeans were made. At a children's home in Chicago they were worn and washed 100 times without significant fabric failures, fading or loss of permanent press. And so "Toughskins" high durability jeans were born.

"Today, 'Toughskins' are extremely well-accepted," says Ira Quint, Sears' national group merchandise manager for children's wear.

Sometimes, Du Pont works directly with consumers. Last year, on textile fibers alone, the company conducted 65 research studies involving panels of consumers.

The Textile Research Laboratory mentioned earlier is further evidence of Du Pont's concern with the end-use performance of its fibers. Contained in this laboratory are "minature industries" — equipment with which Du Pont can make tires, tuft carpets, make hosiery; and weave or knit fabrics, finish and dye them and fabricate them into garments.

Fabric Flammability

An issue that has received a lot of publicity recently is the search for flame-resistant fibers. Much of the attention focuses on new Federal standards being written for garments and home furnishings. The first standard for garments is the small children's sleepwear flammability standard. By July 30 this year, all children's sleepwear (sizes 0-6X) must meet the standard.

While Du Pont's conventional nylon and polyester fibers show good flame resistance, they will not consistently pass the strict test in a wide range of fabric constructions. Therefore, it has been necessary to develop fibers that will pass. Du Pont now has four fibers that, in properly made fabrics and garments, consistently pass the test. One, "Nomex" high temperature resistant nylon, has been on the market for some 10 years. However, it is not likely to be used extensively in ordinary apparel soon, since it costs about six times more than conventional nylon. It is used primarily in high-hazard applications such as military uniforms and suits for racing car drivers. "Acele" acetate Type FLR is commercially available. "Dacron" FLR polyester and "Orlon" FLR modacrylic Type 775 are in the final stages of evaluation before being commercialized.

Last year alone Du Pont spent some $4 million on development of these four flame-resistant fibers.

Wide Range of Products

This story has focused on textile fibers. With Du Pont's vast range of products, similar stories abound in many other areas. A sampler:

Precious metal pastes for microelectronic circuits that revolutionized the electronic products industry . . . A fungicide that inhibits brown rot to help keep fruits from spoiling on the store shelf or during home storage . . . Plastic pipe for natural gas transmission that cuts pipe installation costs and minimizes torn-up streets and roads . . . A bonded fiber sheet used in operating room gowns as a superior barrier against bacteria to lessen the chance of infection . . . A brand new household interior enamel with up to 25 per cent greater hiding power and excellent stain resistance . . . A new system for prepackaging frozen red meat to help cut food costs . . .Neoprene latex foam used in mattresses in institutions such as nursing homes because of its inherent long-lasting fire resistance.

The point is that response to consumer needs is a complex matter that can involve anything from booklets on sewing to highly sophisticated laboratory research. Du Pont's aim is to maintain its good record in all these areas.

QUESTIONS FOR DISCUSSION

1. "It is all right for a big firm such as Du Pont to spend all that money on product testing and research. They can afford it! How about the little businessman who can't afford all that?" Comment.

2. Should product reliability and safety standards be relaxed for the small producer who cannot afford them? If not, and he is forced out of business, what then?

3. Despite all the product research and testing done by large companies, consumers seem to complain all the more about product defects, certainly more than a generation ago. To what do you attribute this seeming paradox?

4. Should the results of product tests done by the United States Bureau of Standards and other government bodies be made freely available to the American consumers? Develop the pros and cons of this issue.

5. Would you be in favor of extending compulsory product standards (such as the Federal Auto Safety Standards), to all products? What main difficulties would be met by this policy?

6. Are you for compulsory grade labeling?

FOOTNOTES

*Temporary designation assigned by FTC pending action on petition for a new generic name.

PART IX

THE NEW SOCIAL RESPONSIBILITIES OF BUSINESS

The idea that business has a social responsibility beyond providing goods and services and making a profit if it can is indeed new in the history of ideas. Until recently, little attention was paid to business's role in the public welfare. But with increasing attention being paid to the problems of our ecology, and to the idea that firms making products should make safe products, of good utility and performance; more and more discussion has taken place as to the new social responsibilities of our business establishment.

Traditionally, business was successful if it maximized profits, provided good conditions and security for employees, and supplied customers with products or services at a price they were prepared to pay. Something new has been added, according to T.G.P. Rogers:

> In today's environment, business must add a fourth responsibility — to society in general. This is an obligation on the national company to meet the needs of society in that nation; there is equally an obligation in the multinational company to respond to the needs of society in each of the countries in which it trades.
>
> The fourth dimension is a recognition that business cannot ignore or separate itself from the social and economic problems of our day. It has to help meet the needs of society.
>
> Today there is an increasing acceptance in business that what society expects of it is changing, and the extent to which companies are willing to respond to these expectations may well determine the survival of individual companies and indeed the survival of the private enterprise system itself."[1]

In view of the obvious importance of this fourth dimension of business responsibility, it behoves us to examine thoroughly this question of corporate social responsibility.

The White House Conference on "The Industrial World Ahead," held in 1972, addressed itself in part to this vital question. Highly qualified experts mirroring every shade of opinion presented papers. These interesting statements are reprinted in this section. Your editor will not try to comment on the positions held by each of the authors. But it is hoped that the reader will analyze each position, and will be able to build up his or her own opinion as to the proper role of business in the world ahead. For such collective attitudes will indeed themselves shape the kind of society in which we want to live.

Identification of the various authors is made on the first page of each article in this section, rather than in the acknowledgments, Needless to say we are most indebted to these thoughtful persons for their significant contributions to this new social issue.

FOOTNOTE

1. "Partnership with Society: The Social Responsibility of Business", *Management Decision* (Vol. 10, Summer, 1972), p. 137. Mr. Rogers is Director of External Affairs for IBM (UK) Ltd.

AN OVERVIEW ON THE SOCIAL RESPONSIBILITY OF BUSINESS *

ROY AMARA

* *A look at Business in 1990*, White House Conference on the Industrial World Ahead, Washington, 1972, pp. 77-84. Reproduced by permission.

Rapid social change has increasingly become a way of life. Such change produces a variety of new social forces impacting on all our social institutions. As a result, new responses and new social mechanisms are required to adapt successfully to the future environment that is thereby created.

In the present context, "social responsibilities of business' are defined as expectations arising from the transactions between a corporation and the following principal societal claimants: shareholders and bond holders, employees, consumers, government, public, suppliers, and competitors.

The Changing Environment

I shall consider how the increasing velocity of social change might affect the size, form, structure, and internal and external relationships of the corporation. To answer such questions, the characteristics of the most relevant societal changes can be aggregated into four environmental trends.[1,2,3]

Economic toward Social
Industrial toward Postindustrial
Technological toward Posttechnological
National toward International

In some instances these trends are mutually reinforcing, in others they are conflicting. Technology has created an environment in which it is both necessary and possible for society to shift its concerns from predominantly economic ones toward social ones. However, the amount and kind of technological development required to satisfy social concerns may be at variance with that required to meet growing international challenges. As a whole, these four key trends may be seen as representing a transition from one type of society to another.

Economic toward Social — No simple phrase can capture adequately the changes in values and expectations that are taking place in society. They are characterized by such descriptions as youth culture, new "consciousness," equality of opportunity, and quality of life. The manifestations are also many: decreasing emphasis on materialistic, achievement-oriented pursuits; shifts from growth-motivated to person-centered orientations; concern with quality of physical environment; abandonment of the puritan ethic of hard work as an end in itself for stress on human self-fulfillment and the concept of leisure as a right; diversity of value systems; and so forth.

These changes are made possible in large part by present and expected future economic affluence (about 40 percent per decade growth in per capita real income).[4] They are not restricted to the young nor is their effect likely to dissipate. Rather, they are expected to intensify because they represent, in many cases, basic shifts in value systems that underlie much of the attitudinal and belief structure of large segments of society. As a result, their societal effects can be expected to be fairly pervasive and fundamental. In particular, such shifts are at the root of the growing list of social and public concerns in contrast to prior emphasis on economic and private ones.[5]

Industrial toward Postindustrial — The economic history of the United States can be characterized by three distinct periods of economic activity. The agrarian period was featured by the dominance of agriculture as an economic pursuit with a correspondingly low per-capita income. The industrial age, beginning with the Civil War, and fueled by the development of the west, was characterized by the preponderance of workers employed in manufacturing and a moderate standard of living. The postindustrial age, which is now emerging, portends a much higher standard of living, a decline in the importance of manufacturing, and the rise of service-oriented and knowledge-oriented activities. Among its more important features are: the expanding role and importance of education as a generator of wealth; greater individualization in access to and dissemination of information (now done through the mass media); the dominant role of computer and communication technologies in business and industry as well as in societal interactions; and the increased capability for citizen participation and feedback in political processes.

The growth of postindustrial applications of technology and the growth of channels of communication imply basic redistribution of influence and power — where more real power will now be exercised by better-informed citizen groups, consumer groups, students, and the like. Ultimately, this will create basic changes in institutional forms. The full effects of such changes — particularly in politics, government, and education — are only now beginning to be felt through increased public awareness, growth of public participation in defining social issues, and in an increasing public insistence on reappraisal of national priorities. Virtually no sector of society will be left untouched by the effects. The end result may be a well-educated, leisure-oriented, informed society of highly interacting and participating citizenry.

Technological toward Posttechnological — It is being increasingly recognized that technology should be developed and applied with somewhat more deliberation than in the past, for the effects can be detrimental as well as beneficial. It has contributed to problems of population growth, threat of nuclear warfare, pollution, congestion, and so forth. Similarly, it has made possible an increasingly higher standard of living throughout society.

In the pase, whenever technology has become available, it has been used without much forethought as to its long-run consequences — the urge to use it has normally been overriding. Private decisions to employ a new technology have generally been based on a short-run economic gain. The growing understanding that it is not technology per se that is at fault, but rather the way in which it has been applied or not applied will have widespread consequences.

The more balanced and discriminating application of technology, which characterizes the posttechnological age, will require the assessment of the secondary and higher order effects and costs of technology.

This is because the complexity of technology is accelerating at a rate so rapid that it causes instability in institutional relationships. This concept relates to the management principle operative in a cybernetic system, by which a system grows, exhibits stability, adjusts, adapts, and evolves. When the laws of self-regulation and self-organization are no longer operative the behavior governed by the dynamic structure of the system is no longer viable and the system self-destructs.

Solution of this situation will in part require introducing into the decision-making process an analysis of the possibly negative social costs of technology. It will also cause more research and development funds to be channeled into areas having high social value in the long run but may cause unfavorable economic costs in the short run.

National toward International — Clearer than almost any other change in the environment of the corporation is the extent to which societal interactions have become international and global. Communications, transportation, production, and distribution systems are bringing nations closer and closer together. Obsolescence of traditional political, economic, and ideological boundaries is occurring because of population growth, decreasing costs of transportation and communication, and emergence of new patterns of economic interaction.

The world has thus become increasingly dependent on the resources of the entire planet. As a result of this increasing interdependence, there is a growing interlocking of economies, technological development, and social progress. Some of the most important problems resulting from this emerging international environment are the increasing gap between developed and less-developed countries; the decreasing ability of the United States to compete in low-technology industries such as textiles, leather goods, and clothing; and the increasing dependence of the United States on foreign raw materials and fuels. Perhaps the most visible example of this trend is the growing importance of the multinational corporation.

Meaning for the Corporation

Resolution of the central problem, a definition of the social responsibilities of business, can be accomplished through the integration of the conflicting demands on the corporation created by the emergence of the four environmental changes. This can be achieved when the demands of the constituencies of business (shareholders, employees, consumers, the public, and government) are integrated into a new and internally consistent pattern.

The impact that the four environmental changes will have on the five constituencies of business can be illustrated in a matrix, Table 1. The entry, at the intersection of each row and column, illustrates in summary form some of the possible effects.

A broad outline of a possible scenario that might emerge is as follows:

The corporation will have been led to a reexamination and reformulation of its basic goals and a restructuring of its basic form. As a result of political and legislative processes, and spurred on by increasing public awareness and desire to redefine the corporate role in society, several private-public sector legislative and administrative guidelines and incentives will be formulated. Such guidelines and incentives will reflect national objectives, provide mechanisms for greater corporate involvement in the public-sector goods and services market, encourage a balanced development of new technology, reflect a more sophisticated understanding of manpower planning, and facilitate international trade.

Two other major groups will be more involved in the corporate enterprise: consumers and employees. Consumers will play a major role in influencing product planning and design; employees, in influencing basic changes in corporate structure, goals, and work environment. The next result will be a shift by the corporation toward greater involvement in public-sector goods and services. This shift may aggravate problems of raising corporate capital and problems of meeting increasing foreign competition; ultimately it may lead to restructuring, or public-sector financing, of some basic industries (e.g., transportation, steel, power, and so forth). Opportunities for foreign investment and the increasing role of multinational corporations may also accelerate these processes. In short, the corporation will exist increasingly in a "fish bowl" environment where the public, government, consumers, and employees participate with shareholders in setting corporate objectives.

TABLE I
SOME POSSIBLE IMPACTS OF
SOCIAL TRENDS ON THE CORPORATION

Corporate Constituents	Economic toward Social	Industrial toward Postindustrial	Technological toward Posttechnological	National toward International
Shareholders	Encourage corporate social involvement but retain largely economic concept of profit.	Encourage gains in productivity through applications of information-related technologies.	Seek mechanisms for sharing costs with government for development of new technologies.	Encourage development of new technology to meet foreign competition. Look to multinational investment opportunities
Employees	Seek meaningful work. Seek a less-structured work environment.	Seek voice in corporate affairs. Seek shorter workweek and increased fringe benefits.	Seek means for hedging against delays, uncertainties and additional costs of new technologies.	Seek mechanisms for easing dislocations to employees from foreign competition.
Consumers	Press for useful, safe, reliable products that serve genuine consumer needs.	Demand publication and dissemination of production data. Seek voice in corporate affairs.	Insist on thorough assessments of new technologies affecting consumer.	Encourage trade measures for reducing costs of consumer products.
Government	Reexamine and reformulate national goals to reflect public-sector priorities. Provide legislative guidelines and financial incentives to stimulate private initiative in public-sector areas.	Revamp manpower planning programs for retraining, for mid-career changes, and so forth. Encourage productivity gains.	Encourage balanced development of new technology.	Facilitate international trade.
Public	Seek redefinitions of corporate objectives to reflect increasing role in social goals.	Seek mechanisms for greater public involvement in corporate boards.	Demand that corporations understand environmental effects of new technologies.	Support measures for balanced development of international trade.

Some Alternative Initial Adaptations

In attempting to paint a representative and plausible picture of impacts on the corporation, some important details have been omitted. These details concern the differences in responses or adaptations that may be made by individual corporations and industries. For some, the changes may be minor, and the present market mechanism for allocating resources may continue to be used. For example, this is likely for such activities as retailing and personal services, where the impacts from postindustrial, posttechnological, and international developments may be minimal. For others, the changes may be extreme, and basically new corporate public-private forms may emerge in housing, education, and health services. Diversity will be the end product, while incremental trial-and-error rather than grand strategic planning or comprehensive conceptual theories will show the way.

Many difficulties concerning underlying corporate purpose may arise in seeking adaptations to environmental changes. Many of these have been eloquently described by a number of authors, but perhaps Milton Friedman[6] captures the essence most effectively. His central theme is that the proper business of business is economic profit. Unresolvable dilemmas arise if we veer away from this basic principle, for we are then asking the agents (managers) of corporate owners (shareholders) to make social choices by allocating private capital for public purposes. Such agents are neither qualified nor authorized to do this. The result will be an obfuscation of roles and, ultimately, perhaps the demise of the most efficient mechanism known to man for allocating scarce resources — namely, the corporate enterprise.

Such difficulties must be squarely faced. One way is to explore how expected environmental changes may suggest redefinitions of corporate purposes and roles. For example, it is unlikely that the solution to the steady degradation of the quality of our public-goods and services sector will come from dependence on voluntary assistance from the private sector operating under present ground rules. So far, such efforts can be considered miniscule by any measure. It is unjust and unwise, as Friedman says, to expect individual corporations to hasten their possible demise through such efforts. In the short run (e.g., less than five years), government, reflecting societal desires, must specify through legislation and administrative guidelines the requirements for meeting societal responsibilities, be those in the fields of pollution, minority employment, or consumer goods. This will provide a common frame of reference for each corporation. In addition, incentives — financial and otherwise — must be provided to make some socially important markets economically attractive. There is no reason why essential corporate purposes, including economic profit as a central objective, may not be retained as some corporate resources are redirected toward the public sector. In these adaptations, government will play a key role.

In the longer run (e.g., 5 to 10 years), however, some basic changes may take place as a result of impacts on the other claimants of the corporate organism. For example, already some signs have appeared that particular institutional and individual shareholders will invest only in those corporations that pass some minimum social audit.[7] Also, consumers directly influence the corporations through their "votes" for consumer products; as dissemination of product information and consumer coherence increase, the effect will become even more pronounced. But perhaps the most important influence will be registered by employees, particularly those destined to assume management positions. The signs are already fairly clear that the new breed of future managerial talent is oriented differently from his present-day counterparts. This may be the single most important and most sustaining factor influencing corporate adaptation.[8] Finally, the general public exercises its influence through its general awareness of corporate activities. A recent case study brings this forcefully into focus. The study suggests that corporations in a particular industry that rank high in social concern (i.e., concern for pollution) also are the most profitable.[9] The conjecture is that the correlation is due not only to reduced operating costs from health insurances, maintenance, and taxes, but also to reduced costs in raising capital and marketing its products (i.e., projection of a "clean company" image).

In any case, however impacts are ultimately felt, and, however each individual corporation adapts, a number of public- and private-sector mechanisms can be considered for making some initial adaptations. Six are described as follows:

Responses to New Social Demands

Human-Resource Planning

Changes in career requirements are becoming so rapid at every level that virtually no one is immune from job obsolescence. This problem will intensify as the shift to a postindustrial, posttechnological, international-oriented society continues. One urgent need is for government to revamp completely its manpower forecasting and planning policies. A supplementary approach is the development of a scheme for voluntary career insurance, supported by the employee, the employer, and perhaps government.[10] Under this scheme, as an individual approaches job obsolescence, he would be provided with career counseling, retraining and, perhaps, income maintenance during the period of transition. If the posttraining position were at a lesser income rate than the original one, the income maintenance might be on a sliding scale to account for the difference in income levels. In fact, such plans may become agenda items in union-management negotiations in the near future.[11]

Technology Assessment

Technology assessment is the evaluation of the second and higher order consequences of new technology before it is developed and

applied, so that a more effective balance can be made of total benefits and costs.[12] This function must be performed far more effectively than in the past. A search for improved mechanisms for technology assessment is under way, largely in the public sector. The basic
problems center on performing this function objectively and without
raising further the risks of new technology development so that it
becomes, as has been admonished, "technology arrestment."

To date, industry has not taken full cognizance of the
responsibilities it has in future assessments of technology. It is likely
that industry may need to develop its own assessment capability to
minimize its own risk in new-product development. If this is not
done, the prospects of increasing government intervention in product
innovation, increased costs of product development, and loss of
public confidence may be materially increased.

Voluntary Associations

Buried in the backwaters of corporate relationships are a number
of dormant mechanisms that may be revitalized to serve future
socially related purposes. One of these is the industry trade
association.[13] The attractiveness of using such a mechanism is that it
already exists, involves the possibility for joint industry action, and is
based on private initiative.

The list of areas in which such associations can be effective social
agents is almost endless. They can set safety and performance
standards; they can act in concert on pollution abatement, hard-core
hiring, public-private partnership forms; and so forth. Antitrust laws
may have to be redefined, but this should not be a major obstacle.[14]

Social Auditing

There appear to be few, if any, standards to determine how well a
corporation is responding and adapting to socially related demands
being placed on it. In view of the variety of more or less suitable
responses that can be made, such assessments are extremely difficult
to make. Various attempts to devise relative rating systems have been
suggested,[15] but, at best, these efforts can be considered only
exploratory.

Ultimately, the social-audit function may be performed by
independent nonprofit corporations operating under a set of
independently determined and continuously refined criteria. Other
approaches related to social auditing are possible. One is the creation
of a Staff Corporate Ombudsman,[11] perhaps chosen by the staff and
reporting to the president. The position might be filled by a fairly
young staff member for a period of, say, two to four years.

New Public-Goods Divisions

It has been suggested that business skills and resources will not be turned to the public goods and service sector unless business begins to view it as a normal risk-taking, profit-making enterprise.[14] At least two broad approaches can be taken. In the first, a detailed analysis may be made of the opportunities present, the roles possible, the risks involved, and the incentives required. Preliminary work in this area indicates that a number of unexplored opportunities exist in housing, education, health, and possibly transportation. Using another approach, a search can be made for social and technological inventions that might meet high-priority needs. Among the areas suggested for research and development are: nonharmful and inexpensive substitutes for food additives now thought to be harmful; inexpensive power sources; freshwater production and distribution systems for irrigation; and fertilizer production methods for use in developing countries. To promote such areas, patent laws might be amended to allow patent life to exceed the normal 17 years, and special cost allowances may be given to support research and development by corporations.

New Public-Private Partnerships

At some point, the interaction of corporate and government initiatives can lead to entirely new public-private partnerships. Although much has been written about such possibilities and some attempts are being made (e.g., Postal Service, National Corporation for Housing, COMSAT), little is known about the ways in which they should be structured or the conditions under which they operate best. In the future, the possibilities for new public-private intersect organizations will increase. This increase will reflect greater corporate involvement in unprofitable but socially useful public-sector activities.

The basic notion in such a partnership is that government assumes a major role in financing, policy-making, and planning; the private sector, on the other hand, provides the technological, managerial, and marketing expertise.[16] In principle, it seems workable; in practice, some hard thinking still remains to be done.

One of the key problems is the definition of the circumstances under which private corporations are both competent for, and willing to enter into, such partnerships.[17] Included among the principal requirements are: a clearly defined and specified task; available technology and supporting systems; unambiguous methods of performance measurement; and adequate financial incentives.

The absence of any one of these conditions can lead to failure. For example, the "improvement of community health services" is too broadly defined to be useful; "reducing incidence of drug use" is too difficult to tackle given our state of knowledge; "improving the appreciation of music" is hard to measure; and "building of low-income housing" may not offer sufficient return in view of the attendant risks. Nevertheless, a number of experiments is under way — particularly in teaching reading and arithmetic skills to public-school children — that are being closely watched. Although the results are not all in and some difficult problems remain to be solved, such "performance controls" may well be harbingers of similar partnerships in other fields.

Selection and Integration

Some of the adaptive measures described may blossom into useful forms for helping to shape the social responsibilities of business; at best, however, they cannot be expected to be more than small pieces of a larger mosaic that can only be dimly perceived at this time. In the long run (10 to 30 years and beyond) the accuracy with which we can project the nature of the social responsibilities of business becomes negligible.

Perhaps one way in which we can begin to focus this image is to examine our unique societal strengths from the longer perspective. Three such strengths stand out as potentially central to shaping future policies influencing the role of the corporate enterprise. These are: uses of technology; societal diversity; and a new image of man.

Uses of Technology — It may at first be surprising — in this day of deepening public disappointment in, and distrust of, technology — to identify the uses of technology as a key force in the future development of our society. And yet, a large measure of our success will depend critically on how well we learn to use it. Technology provides the economic base for meeting social needs, the resources for contributing uniquely to international trade,[18] and the leading edge for realizing the benefits of a postindustrial and posttechnological society. Without its continuous development, all our social goals become infinitely more difficult to achieve.

Our ability to apply technology in the past has made an enormous difference in our economic and social progress.[19] In recent years, we have fallen badly behind when measured in terms of per-capita patents and the fraction of civilian man-power employed in research and development. A real danger facing us in the next several decades is that the present disenchantment with technology will lead us to shun it, rather than to use it to serve us more effectively.

This hazard is particularly worrisome since it is becoming clearer that we are now, and have been, underinvesting in the kinds of technology that are most directly coupled to industrial output. This situation has been aggravated by the rates of expenditures in defense and space. Notwithstanding the differences in absolute levels of expenditures, most European countries and Japan allocate more than 20 percent of their government research and development for civilian outputs, whereas the corresponding figure for the United States is less than 6 percent.[20]

The impact of this misallocation is felt ultimately as reduced productivity. When the growth rate of productivity falters, as it appears to have done recently, the growth in standard of living falters, and all our social goals are in jeopardy, both domestically and internationally. Thus, instead of using technology less, we must learn to use it more, gearing it to meeting our social needs. Such considerations have important implications to long-range business planning in terms of investments in research and development, in new-product planning, and in capital equipment.

Societal Diversity — The second factor is societal diversity. In recent years, it has become increasingly recognized that our society is an amalgam of separate cultures rather than a melting pot. This fact of existence is two-edged, for it can be a great source of strength as well as a source for division and conflict.

One of the hazards we face is strife, divisiveness, squandering of our material and intellectual resources, and eventual decline. Few countries span the diversity of groups, subcultures, and factions that exist in the United States today. What does this all mean? Among other things, it means we will have to live in a society of unprecedented social diversity. To do so requires steering a course between anarchy on the one hand and repression on the other.

The need to encourage diversity, pluralism, differentiation, and experimentation is overriding. Simple cultures are characteristics of simple societies; societies as complex as ours is and will be must include diversity as a hallmark. From this diversity usually emerge the most useful social adaptations — hammered out through the open competition of ideas. This is the social analogue of the economic marketplace.

Thus, what could become a disabling malady can become, instead, a source of great strength. This is because the drives for diversity are not governed, in most instances, by blind allegiance to some political, economic, or religious ideology. Rather, the drives stem from the desire to discover and realize new sets of social values and goals, as summarized by the transitions described in an earlier section. The implications of all this to business are fairly clear. Among other things, business will have to learn to become an even better listener to the variety of voices, a better integrator of conflicting demands bearing on it, and a better responder to the range of publics it will need to serve. More importantly to both business and society, out of this diversity can emerge a new image of man.

New Image of Man — As a society, we are beginning to understand more clearly how to balance the social with the economic, the technological with the environmental, and man with nature. Out of this heightened understanding can develop a more satisfying relationship of man to the society that he creates and in which he lives.

The corporate form represents the most efficient producer and allocator of goods and services that we know. The new challenge facing this system is the question of its adaptability in meeting the emerging economic and social needs of an increasingly interdependent globe. At present, no one quite knows how this is best done. Nevertheless, if business assumes a major role in searching for new social forms and new social responses, then a great step forward might be made toward the person-centered society" of Mumford, the "learning society" of Hutchins, and the "self-actualizing society" of Maslow — where man increasingly learns to realize his noblest aspirations by using the productive capacity at his disposal to serve his most basic human needs. If it cannot, we may face a period of considerable uncertainty and, eventually, decline.

The vitality of the American business system will be a measure of our flexibility in marshalling these three fundamental strengths and will largely determine the eventual structure of our private enterprise system. For these unique qualities hold the answers to the ultimate questions and challenges that will be thrust on business in discharging its social responsibilities in the future.

QUESTIONS FOR REVIEW

1. What is meant by a company's "social responsibilities"?

2. Explain the following environmental trends to which business must adjust:
   (a) Economic Toward Social
   (b) Industrial toward Postindustrial
   (c) Technological toward Posttechnological
   (d) National toward International

3. Has technology itself been at fault or is it the way it has been applied?

4. What does the emerging post-industrial age portend for the average American?

5. "When the growth rate of productivity falters, as it appears to have done recently, the growth in the standard of living falters, and all our social goals are in jeopardy, both domestically and internationally." Explain.

6. What "new image of man" is the author postulating? How may man achieve it?

FOOTNOTES

1. Theodore J. Gordon and Robert H. Ament, *Forecasts of Some Technological and Scientific Developments and Their Societal Consequences*, Report R-6, Institute for the Future, Sept. 1969.

2. Raul de Brigard and Olaf Helmer, *Some Potential Societal Developments — 1970-2000,* Report R-7, Institute for the Future, April 1970.

3. Earl B. Dunckel, William K. Reed, and Ian H. Wilson, *The Business Environment of the Seventies: A Trend Analysis for Business Planning,* McGraw-Hill, New York, 1970.

4. Fabian Linden, "The Decade of the Seventies," *Consumer Economics,* June 1969.

5. Committee for Economic Development, *Can We Afford Tomorrow?* Jan. 23, 1971.

6. Milton Friedman, "A Friedman Doctrine — The Social Responsibility of Business Is to Increase Its Profits," *New York Times Magazine,* Sept. 13, 1970.

7. Marge Speidel, "Investor Firm Adopts Social Concern Outlet," *Palo Alto Times,* Palo Alto, California, Aug. 9, 1971.

8. Samuel A. Culbert and James M. Elden, "An Anatomy of Activism for Executives," *Harvard Business Review,* Nov.-Dec. 1970.

9. John Cunniff, "Study Indicates Pollution Control and Higher Profits Linked," *Palo Alto Times,* Palo Alto, California, Aug. 6, 1971.

10. Theodore J. Gordon, et. al., *A Forecast of the Interaction between Business and Society in the Next Five Years,* Report R-21, Institute for the Future, April 1971.

11. Joseph A. Beirne, *New Horizons for American Labor,* Public Affairs Press, Washington, D.C., 1962.

12. David M. Keifer, "Technology Assessment," *Chemical and Engineering News,* Oct. 5, 1970.

13. Clarence C. Walton, *Business and Social Progress,* Praeger, New York, 1970.

14. William J. Baumol, et al, *A New Rationale for Corporate Social Policy,* Supplementary Paper No. 31, Committee for Economic Development, 1970.

15. Clair W. Sater, "A Supplement to the Bottom Line: Rating Corporations on Social Responsibility," *Bulletin,* Summer 1971.

16. Committee for Economic Development, *Social Responsibilities of Business Corporations,* A Statement by the Research and Policy Committee, June 1971.

17. James Q. Wilson, "The Corporate Role in the Community," *Boston Globe,* Boston, Massachusetts, Oct. 3, 1971.

18. "The U.S. Searches for a Realistic Trade Policy," *Business Week,* July 3, 1971.

19. Myron Tribus, "Technology for Tomorrow versus Profit for Today," Winter Annual Meeting, American Society of Mechanical Engineers, 1970.

20. J. Herbert Hollomon and Alan E. Harger, "America's Technological Dilemma," *Technology Review,* July/August 1971.

ARJAY MILLER

* Arjay Miller, "The Social Responsibility of Business,"
A Look at Business in 1990, White House, Conference on
the Industrial World Ahead, Washington, 1972, pp.
85-89.

Business Should not pretend to be something it is not. More bluntly, a business is a business, not a philanthropy. Its actions should be justified essentially on business grounds, on enlightened self-interest; not on abstract moral or ethical grounds. To try to do otherwise will only increase the credibility gap from which business already suffers. Business leaders should therefore avoid the temptation of promising too much, because some in our society already have an exaggerated notion of what business alone can do. Dr. Kenneth Clark has said, "Business and industry are our last hope. They are the most realistic elements in our society. Other areas in society—government, education, churches, labor—have defaulted in dealing with the Negro problem. It is now up to business." A black militant in Detroit put it even more bluntly when he told a group of business leaders, "If you cats can't do it, it's never going to get done."

Business, of course, can do much more than it is now doing. However, it is no more reasonable to expect business to do everything than it is to expect government to do everything. If the general public becomes too unrealistic in its expectations, and business, in turn, loses sight of the limitations of what it can accomplish working alone, we could experience a backlash of opinion that would be hurtful to the limited but important role that business can legitimately be expected to play.

Proper Role of Business

What, then, is the proper role of business? At one extreme, Adam Smith maintained that the businessman pursuing his own self-interest would be guided "as by an unseen hand" to do more good for society than if he consciously set out to do so.

That was a simple concept, but for nearly 200 years it worked remarkably well. In fact, until the 1960s, most businessmen continued to believe that their exclusive function was to make the biggest profit they could, with only minimal attention to the world outside the business arena. Furthermore, society by and large accepted—even applauded—this concept.

This view still has its champions among some respected economists. Milton Friedman is one. In a recent article entitled "The Social Responsibility of Business Is to Increase Its Profits," Friedman contends that businessmen who believe they are defending the free enterprise system by saying that business is not "merely" concerned with profits but also with promoting desirable social ends are "preaching pure and unadulterated socialism."

At the other extreme is a large number of vocal critics who blame business for virtually all of the ills of society, and demand a much more restricted role for business. In their view, this society will survive only if business control is taken from private hands and placed for the most part in government—or in their willing hands, if that be needed. They argue that because of the constant focus of business on profits, it cannot be trusted to do what is right and just.

Critics holding this view fail to understand that profits are a necessary cost of production, as even Iron Curtain countries are being forced to recognize. President Nixon addressed himself to this question some months ago when he said, "It is only through profits that industry can buy the new plants, the new equipment that will make our workers more productive and therefore more competitive in the world . . . I am for more profits because I believe that more profits mean more jobs."

Without adequate profits business has no way to undertake and sustain new efforts to meet pressing social needs. We must *earn* social progress, in a literal sense.

Our approach during the decades ahead must be somewhere in between these two extremes. Neither promises to do too much, nor fails to do what can be reasonably expected of us, either alone or in cooperation with government and other segments of society.

Business Now in a New Ball Game

The central fact of business today is that we are in a new ball game. We cannot return to the old, familiar ground rules. It is really too bad, in a way, that Adam Smith and Milton Friedman are not right. Life would be so much simpler if our only task and our only responsibility was the narrow pursuit of profits.

As it happens, however, tremendous new demands are being made on this society, and these in turn are causing tremendous new demands on business. We need mention only the insistent pressures for a cleaner environment, for better housing, for improved education at all levels, for greater traffic safety, and so on through a long list. The key question is, what share of the responsibility should business undertake?

For several years the federal government has encouraged business to perform an increasing variety of social tasks that were formerly regarded as almost exclusively governmental responsibilities—training disadvantaged persons, rebuilding the ghettos, helping blacks and other minority—group members establish their own enterprises, and many more. Because these involve special added costs for most of the companies involved, the government has offered special inducements to encourage business participation.

Is this the way of the future? The final returns are not yet in, because efforts to date are largely experimental, leaving many questions still to be resolved. But some ideas are taking root that should serve us well in the years ahead.

One of these tenets is that society will be best served if each of its major institutions concentrates on what it does best, and does not waste time and resources on tasks it is poorly equipped to handle. Business, for example, can increase the hiring and training of minority-group persons, introduce new technology and increase the level of job skills, improve the quality and serviceability of essential products, and eliminate as quickly as possible harmful air or water pollutants resulting from its operations. On the other hand, some jobs it can tackle only in cooperation with government; still others it should not attempt.

In sorting out the proper assignments, we should recognize that many of our most serious and urgent current demands are in the area of public, rather than private, goods. People want cleaner air and water, safer streets, less traffic congestion, better education systems, and so forth. These demands cannot be satisfied in the traditional private marketplace. You cannot buy clean air or a lane of your own on the highway between home and office.

Need to Establish National Goals and Priorities

Since the output of public goods cannot be determined automatically by the expenditure pattern of individuals, therefore, how should we approach the problem? What is needed first, in my opinion, is a much clearer statement of our national goals and the priority we assign to each. We as people cannot continue to "muddle through" as we have been doing—starting and stopping, making piecemeal efforts wherever the pressure is greatest and, in general, having no real idea of what the ultimate cost of any particular program will be. We must improve our decision-making process if we are to make the kind of solid, sustained progress we desire.

Decisions as to what we as a people propose to accomplish are and must remain, of course, a part of our normal political process. In a democracy, only elected representatives of the people will be entrusted with the establishment of national goals and priorities.

At present, however, neither the Congress nor the Administration can make sound decisions about far-reaching social goals because they lack adequate financial and other facts that are critical in determining how far and how fast we should go. Too often Congress does not know the ultimate costs of legislation. How much, for example, will the Clean Air Act and its amendments cost? $10 billion? $100 billion? No one really knows.

It seems to me essential that we know the costs of present and pending legislation because of the increasingly severe crunch on our resources, which is not generally recognized. In testimony before the

Joint Economic Committee of Congress last February, I reported that the National Planning Association had estimated that the gap between accepted national goals and our ability to pay would reach $150 billion annually by 1975. In my opinion, recognition of new social needs, plus inflation, would now make that figure much larger, and the gap will certainly continue to increase in the years ahead.

Probably the most significant figure in such a report would be the gap between the total cost of our national goals and our ability to pay. General recognition of this gap would in itself be valuable, because it would open the eyes of those who believe that our problem today is overproduction or failure to divide properly what they call an "economy of abundance." It also would throw into perspective such recurrent questions as the shorter workweek and technological unemployment. As long as so many recognized needs remain unsatisfied, we are facing—along with the remainder of the world—what can only be called an "economy of scarcity" requiring more work, not less.

Focusing attention on the gap between what we want and what we can afford also underscores the importance of increasing output per man-hour because increased output is the basic source of all economic progress. And unless we make the unrealistic assumption that individuals will work harder, higher output per man-hour can be achieved only through technological advance. In measuring technological progress, however, we must make certain that *all* costs are recognized, not merely the short-term direct effects.

The annual reports prepared by the proposed National Goals Institute would have no binding or direct authority. They would simply point out directions and possibilities, and provide a factual basis for enlightened public discussion and decision making. Our concern would be to make available the kind of information that we as a people must have if we are to be able to see clearly the various alternatives open to us and to choose rationally from among them.

In all of this kind of planning—defining goals, allocating resources and shaping specific programs—a clear need exists for business participation. Business must get into the planning process early and bring its experience to bear *before* programs are baked into law. If business does not cooperate in such planning, we can be sure that others will move ahead without us, leaving it to business to pick up the check, which will be larger than it might otherwise be.

It is unrealistic today to contend that business must be free to pursue its own goals without reference to the broader needs and aims of the total society. All of us in business must recognize and accept the necessity for an expanded government role in our economic life. We must make the most of the situation by cooperating fully in setting the new ground rules.

This could mean, for example, that we must be prepared to disclose certain kinds of information that have, up to now, been considered confidential. This need not be a harmful development if it is done in such a way as to protect the confidentiality of the figures of any single company. As a case in point, the automobile companies have been supplying safety and pollution cost data to the Bureau of Labor Statistics for some years without prejudice to their own individual competitive situations. The Bureau has used these data to compile average industry-wide cost increases, which are then released to the public and reflected in the Cost of Living index.

Before leaving the subject of national goals, I would like to emphasize that the establishment of goals by government need not restrict the important role business can and should play in the attainment of those goals. In some cases, such as air and water, the government role can be essentially limited to the establishment of standards that everyone must meet. Each individual firm can proceed in the most efficient manner to meet the standards, safe in the assumption that in so doing it will not place itself in an untenable competitive cost position.

Government Incentives

In many cases, however, government financial support will be required to attain established goals. In the case of low-cost housing, for example, private business is unable to make a more significant contribution at present because the families with the greatest need do not have sufficient funds to enter the market. What is needed in cases like this are government-provided incentives adequate to "turn-on" the private sector.

The type of incentive to be used should depend on the particular need to be met. In housing, for example, both rent supplements to low-income families and subsidies to building contractors are appropriate. In other cases, such as the procurement of goods and services, more use can be made of direct negotiations and contracts with private firms. As an underlying principle, maximum reliance should be placed on private enterprise and the effectiveness of management techniques that have proved so successful under our free enterprise system.

For special situations, however, we should be willing to create new institutions, such as COMSAT, Amtrak, and the new Postal Service. Where neither private nor public resources alone can get a job done, there should be no hesitation at joining both to whatever extent is required to achieve the desired results.

Specific Suggestions for Corporation Executives

I will offer six specific suggestions to corporation executives as to the social responsibility of business in the next twenty years.

First, *I urge that executives integrate social objectives into the basic fabric of their company*, treating them just as they would any regular corporate activities. Although there is a role for a staff "Director of Public Affairs" or some such, the task of responding to new social needs must be accepted by all layers of management in all components throughout the entire organization. The general manager of a division or a subsidiary, for example, should feel the same responsibility for meeting established corporate social objectives as he does for meeting profit objectives.

This means that "reporting" and "scorekeeping" for both sets of objectives must be subject to the same internal accounting procedures. Also, to be consistent, the reward system must be structured so as to penalize a manager for failing to meet either kind of objective.

Does all of this sound like too much to expect of a typical business firm? On the contrary, I believe it represents a minimum kind of effort, and one that we cannot avoid if we are to gear our operations to the needs of our time.

Second, in establishing social objectives for the corporation, use a rifle, not a shotgun, approach. Here it would be best to *have the line and staff managers participate in the setting of specific, measurable objectives*, including the time period over which each goal will be met. Although the objectives and time periods would vary from industry to industry and from company to company, they migh typically include:

Hiring objectives for minority-group persons and women expressed as a percentage of new hires, and projected perhaps five years ahead.

Equally important, objectives for the upgrading of minority-group persons to higher levels of skill and responsibility, with specific numbers targeted in each of the higher salary grades. Where qualified new employees are not available, this would require in-house training programs aimed at increased upward mobility.

Quotas for the purchase of goods and services from minority-owned firms, again with specific year-to-year dollar targets. This might require special help and encouragement for potential suppliers, but some firms are now doing this successfully. Much more can be done. For example, a letter from the business firm promising to make a substantial deposit would be helpful in starting a minority bank. Or, perhaps you would justify a long-term contract to a struggling new minority-owned advertising or consulting group.

Use of minority-owned firms to the extent possible in your distribution or sales network.

As a third suggestion, I recommend that corporate executives, as individuals, *participate actively in public organizations of all kinds* at local, state, and national levels. One plant manager who is active in local organizations puts it this way: "Being a member of these groups enables us to keep a finger on the community's pulse, and lets us feel how residents think about whatever might come up . . . And we get out in the shop and tell the people to get involved in whatever interests them, to lend a hand where they're needed."

Fourth, I urge businessmen to *speak out more on current issues*. You have something to say, and you will be listened to. But I offer two cautions: Do not speak up only when you are *against* something. Be positive and constructive. Be honest and candid when the chips are down. Do not add to the credibility gap that has hurt much of business in recent years.

Fifth, where a company finds that it cannot tackle a worthy program or correct some problem on its own, I suggest that it *make greater use of its trade association or some other voluntary grouping* to achieve its purpose. Representative ones are the National Alliance of Businessmen, which has helped many companies in the minority-hiring area, the Better Business Bureau, the Urban Coalition, and other groups that are ready to help individual companies on a collective basis do what a single company might not be able to undertake on its own. Do not be afraid to cooperate with academic organizations. At the Stanford Business School, for example, I have been impressed with the sincerity and purpose of a student-organized Committee for Corporate Responsibility that cooperates with business firms in seeking positive approaches to common problems.

As a sixth and final suggestion, *accent the positive*. Businessmen have for too long been stereotyped as men who always react negatively to any kind of social progress that interferes with traditional ways of doing business. This need not be so. People have demanded a small, low-pollutant automobile and we are now fast approaching that goal. We *can* do more to clean up our environment through the recycling of cans, bottles, and waste papaer. We *can* clean up our lakes and other waterways through more careful planning and through the introduction of new systems and methods. We *can* relieve congestion in our cities and make better housing available for more people. We must endeavor to find ways to get them done, either acting alone or in conjunction with government, rather than in explaining why they cannot be done.

We must not be satisfied simply to react to pressures. How much more can be done, at less cost and with less pulling and hauling, if we make up our minds to anticipate trends and problems, and then devise a strategy to meet the situation.

The industrial world ahead—or in broader terms, the very destiny of this nation—depends in large part on how this country's businessmen respond to the new environment. Is optimistic that our business leaders will both recognize the importance of their role and carry it out in a bold, constructive manner.

QUESTIONS FOR DISCUSSION

1. Is it reasonable to expect busines to do everything to cure our social and economic ills? Why?

2. What is the proper role of business in our achieving society? What sorts of things can it do best? Which activities should it avoid?

3. Dean Miller, like Dr. Schutte, says that we must determine our national goals and set priorities better than we have in the past. What does the author propose? Do you believe it to be a good idea?

4. The author says that businessmen have always been accused of reacting negatively to any kind of proposed social progress. Do you think this is a valid charge? Can you think of examples to the contrary?

5. What specific actions does Dean Miller say are immediately feasible for business to undertake? Would you add any to this list?

6. Is the author optimistic or pessimistic regarding the willingness of business to behave in a more socially responsible manner in the future?

APPENDIX

Proposal for a National Goals Institute

I proposed to the Congressional Committee that, as an aid in working out realistic and enduring social programs, a National Goals Institute be established by law. It would have four major tasks:

Estimate the general magnitude of future increases in national output—in other words, how much new money will be available for spending.

Project the cost of presently established programs—education, health care, roads and so on—over a 10-year period.

Project the cost of attaining additional generally recognized goals over a similar 10-year period.

Publish annually a listing of all our national goals, together with estimated costs and the resources available to meet them.

CLEO W. BLACKBURN

*Cleo W. Blackburn, "Short on Time, Long on Space," *A Look at Business in 1990*, White House Conference on the Industrial World Ahead, Washington, 1972, pp. 90-91. Reproduced by permission.

Remarks by Cleo W. Blackburn, President, Board for Fundamental Education, Indianapolis, Indiana.

The American man has historically been short on time and long on space. The great question, however, remains: can the values and virtues that were used to win this continent sustain us as a nation? Until now we have been able to run away from our problems. We could move west of the mountains, across the river, over the plains to the great Pacific Northwest, and more recently to the suburbs.

We must now stand and face the problems, which are neither simple nor suddenly created. They do not lend themselves to categorical answers. One has to see our problems in terms of wholes. We must see that neither this nation nor its people experience life in neat little categories. People or nations cannot classify their needs into neat little packages, such as research, housing, health, education, employment, or productivity in terms of per-man output, wrap it up into a neat little package or index that we call GNP, correct it for certain known and unknown factors, and predict what will happen to the business community or to America, for that matter, in 1990. We must consider all the factors that go into the production of a great nation, because we experience life as a people and as a nation in one unified conflicting whole. We must somehow combine our economics with great moral and social concerns on the part of the entire American community, and then apply all of today's knowledge, technology, and understanding to the task of human development.

No one doubts the great strength of American technology and production. We have demonstrated that we can make war through the power of atomic energy and all the other forms of technology used so successfully in the space program in landing a man on the moon.

All these somehow alone are inadequate. As we think about the social responsibility of business, may I suggest a third force. Another power man possesses has not yet been fully explored. Yet it perhaps contains the seed or the possibility greater than all the power we have yet realized or achieved through technology, vast communication and management procedures, which have eliminated time and space. I believe that if somehow we are to survive, we have to discover this third power, the power of human spirit. You cannot see it. You cannot measure it, but somehow we know without it and without the results that it can produce, all of the so-called technological advances we now possess cannot sustain us as a nation.

Coupled with this rapidly changing society is American impatience with problems that do not lend themselves to instant solutions. The public demands instant gratification, instant tea, and instant coffee. Legislators and various other governmental and industrial consultants have yielded to public pressure and promised instant housing and instant economic stability. Hence, the credibility gap has widened to a credibility chasm.

Hindsight now illuminates the fact that backing into the future is costly. Piecemeal or "micro" solutions for overwhelmingly complex issues are "hit-and-run" approaches involving crash programs, duplication of efforts, and waste of precious resources.

Anticipate the Import of Change

A good case in point can be seen in the simple example of a great corporation that decided to develop the cotton picker. It was originally intended to be in the field by 1947, but it did not get full acceptance until 1953. Agricultural economists and rural sociologists, among others, began in 1947 to call attention to the people in government, at all levels, and in business that this one piece of equipment would release some three and a half million people from the cotton industry and a cotton culture with no plan. "What is to become of the people?" Nobody paid any attention. It was not until 10 years later, when people began to migrate into Los Angeles County at a rate of 10,000 a month, and into Chicago, Detroit, and other cities, that the problem was recognized. The already overcrowded urban communities of the South, North, and West could not absorb three and a half million people who lacked the knowledge and skills for making a life or living in industry.

Not until 1964 did the holocaust begin to break loose. Then everybody became concerned and became what I call 'For God's Sakers" and began to say, "Gosh, our town is in a hell of a mess. For God's sake, let's do something about it." And the For God's Sakers usually end up doing the wrong thing at the wrong time for the wrong reasons. This has been characteristically America.

The great challenge before us is to foresee opportunities, and to anticipate the impacts and cross-impacts of today's decisions on tomorrow's society. We shape the world of tomorrow by the way we handle the decisions of today.

The fact is that the business world of 1990 begins in 1970. The ability to assess direction accurately is a management tool essential to the task of shaping the future and making change. If we are to avoid what Toffler so accurately defined as *Future Shock* we must deal with the phenomenon of change.

We must define the pace and scope of change, and must harness it—else we will be destroyed through obsolescence. In a recent industrial study, people at different job levels were analyzed in terms of their attitudes toward change. The startling finding was that even among scientists and engineers only 20 percent was enthusiastic of change while 70 percent was apathetic.

Changing Values

Awareness is growing that we are indeed at the end of an era. No longer must we expand and invest in international commitments, when at home we have pollution, inadequate housing, an obsolete transportation system, and high unemployment. Research and development expenditures in housing lag a quarter of a century behind comparable expenditures in other industries. Two voters in three assign responsibility for a minority problem to business, labor, and government leaders. Awareness and concern for consumer protection have increased sharply. Seven voters in ten now favor new laws to protect public health and safety. Eighty-one percent favor legislation to guarantee truth in lending. A strong trend exists, especially among the young, toward an antibusiness stance. Business finds itself in a precarious position. If it does not consider its social responsibility it must face up to more government control and regulation. If business relies on profits based on consumer buying it must take responsibility for assuring itself of consumers.

Like it or not, the distinctions between the private sector and the public sector are becoming increasingly blurred. America stands on the brink of revitalizing its economy through a solid commitment by industry joining with the government to rebuild and reclaim our human resources, to reverse our past method of operating to be long on time and short on space—as we did when we committed ourselves to the space race.

We are a nation of mighty giants who need only to "get the spirit" as in the old Negro spirtiual. As we begin to revitalize and expand all the traditional economic indicators, such as GNP, capital expenditures, and worker productivity, let us invest in our human resources, and tap the margin of profit called people.

QUESTIONS FOR DISCUSSION

1. What does the author mean by "short on time, long on space?"

2. What "third force" does the author think is needed if we are to survive?

3. "Backing into the future is costly". What, then, does the writer suggest?

4. What changing values does the author see to be evolving? What differences will these make to business in 1990?

THE PARADOX OF CORPORATE RESPONSIBILITY *

43

HENRY G. MANNE

* Henry G. Manne, "The Paradox of Corporate Responsibility," *A Look at Business in 1990*, White House Conference on the Industrial World Ahead, Washington, 1972, pp. 95-98. Reproduced by Permission.

Remarks by Henry G. Manne, Kenan Professor of Law, University of Rochester, Rochester, New York, and Visiting Professor, Stanford University Law School.

Corporate social responsibility occupies a peculiar role in business intellectual history. It is peculiar because the underlying idea persists in spite of the absence of any rigorous justification of the concept. It has never been integrated into a coherent theory of economics or human behavior, and few of its scholarly proponents have ever analyzed the real economic implications of the idea. Yet this idea provided significant intellectual fuel for the Populist movement, the Progressive era, the New Deal, and the present antibusiness movement, sometimes euphemistically termed consumerism. It is likely to be with us until at least 1990.

It might be instructive to inquire into reasons why the idea of corporate social responsibility persists before we examine the merits of the notion. Probably some private interests are being served by the perpetuation of the concept, apart from whether it has any effect on corporate behavior. This, at least, is the hypothesis I shall examine.

The Support of the Corporate Social-Responsibility Concept

Americans seem to enjoy being told that business has a personal responsiblility to them outside the marketplace. Perhaps this provides a sense of power and comfort to millions of people who cannot comprehend a complex market system no matter how well it performs. Furthermore, the successes of the capitalist system provide little opportunity for the political gore mass audiences seem to favor. Little is to be gained by those seeking either large audiences or political power from trying to explain the dull concepts of economic cost and competitive markets to the citizenry.

Government officials are maximizers just as much as are investors or industrialists, and their own utility is generally served by increases in governmental power. The concept of corporate social responsibility suits them almost perfectly. Today, as in years past, much new legislation is vaunted as making business more responsible to the public and as controlling the venal instincts of the capitalists. In fact, our political system is such that these regulatory provisions are often beneficial mainly to the politicians while carrying a high price tag for the public.

It is easy for politicians to take credit for vanquishing polluters while making no disclosure to the public of how much the cleanliness will cost them. And if for these and other reasons prices rise, then obviously price controls must be needed to guarantee socially responsible behavior by the corporations. The concept of corporate social responsibility is truly ideal for government officials who wish to claim credit for all public benefits and accept no responsibility for increased costs and long-run antisocial effects.

American intellectuals of the left have also found happy hunting in the realm of corporate social responsibility. From Veblen and Ripley to Berle, Galbraith, and Nader, we have long been treated to one strained explanation after another of why free markets are not good for us. The alleged assumptions of the free-market model are derided; the myth of growing monopoly is constantly repeated; and the free market's inability to cope with certain externalities and social problems is blown out of all proportion.

The idea of a social responsibility fits all the liberal intellectual's predilections. It makes a moral issue out of business behavior; it accentuates the monopoly issue, since without some monopoly power, nonprofit-oriented behavior is unlikely; and it fits snugly with the recently discovered ecological crisis. The idea of corporate social responsibility becomes a convenient peg on which to hang every hackneyed criticism of business conduct and even a few new ones, like the lack of democracy and due process in dealing with employees, customers, or the community. We are, I might add, still awaiting the serious intellectual defense of all this.

Still another group who enthuses about corporate social responsibility is businessmen, particularly some prominent executives of large corporations. Several explanations can be given for this phenomenon. First, businessmen as a group are at best only slightly more expert in economic theory than the general population. And, like others, they espouse popular ideologies regardless of the underlying implications even for their own behavior.

Further, the concept of corporate responsibility flatters businessmen that they are the divine elect, as Andrew Carnegie would have had it. They are not only merely responsible for producing diaper pins or corrugated sheet metal or rock crushers, but also they are obliged to look after us lesser beings. It is thus easy for some businessmen to believe that universities would collapse, the air become unbreathable, and civilization be lost if they did not thrust out their chins, flex their muscles and do good according to the gospel of business statesmanship—without even spending their own money.

Justification for Corporate Social Responsibility

But I do not believe that business advocacy of corporate responsibility is principally a matter of ideology or psychology. I think that it is economic. Corporate responsibility is good business because it is good public relations. Certainly in the economic propaganda war that has been waged for so long now, business would be ill advised to let politicians and consumerists claim all the credit for taming the corporate beasts—at least so long as the voting public thinks that corporations are beasts that must be tamed. One has only to look at the public pronouncements of General Motors since the Nader-inspired Project on Corporate Responsibility began its Campaign GM. Parts of the annual report now read like chapters from a corporate activist's text, implying that management operates the company as a public-service institution devoted to improvements in social welfare but not to profits.

But the talk may have consequences. As public expectations are built up both by politicians and businessmen, it becomes more and more difficult to do nothing when a new problem is identified. Then business must engage in otherwise unwanted behavior so as to stave off even more onerous political or regulatory burdens. If by these actions the public can be made to believe that business is already operating in a socially responsible way, the political threat may be defused or moderated at a relatively low cost. Better yet, the situation may be turned to positive business advantage if the situation can be used to gain "self-regulation" for the industry. The phrase is widely recognized today as meaning that potential competitiors may, under a variety of ruses, be excluded from the market. But businessmen who covet this status claim that it will maintain ethical standards of business for the public's protection.

And if specific regulation ensues, that too will inevitably affect one group of firms in an industry differently than it does others. Typically the larger firms are the ones preferred. They can normally accept new regulatory costs with less effect on their total average cost because their volume is higher than that of smaller firms. And again we can see the possibility of some significant anticompetitive implications of corporate-responsibility proposals.

These then are some of the reasons why arguments for corporate responsibility continue to be made, and some of the substantive arguments against the concept. Other objections exist as well. For instance, cleanliness, safety, and nondiscrimination do not come free. Yet the ultimate incidence of the costs of these goods is rarely known. Costs can be passed forward to consumers or backward to suppliers of labor, goods, or capital. But there is nowhere else they can go. No entity called the corporation can be made to suffer or bear ultimate costs. Only people bear costs. If the costs cannot be shifted, they rest ultimately on the shareholders of the company. But only the most hardened capitalist-baiter can take satisfaction from that. Most of the shareholders will have bought their shares for prices that did not discount these new costs. Thus the financial burden will fall on those who did not receive the economic benefits of the misdeed now being corrected. And even where that is not true, the effect is still that of a tax arbitrarily placed on certain individuals to provide a general social benefit.

Many of the goals specified for corporate largess cannot be accomplished satisfactorily by firms acting individually. This may be because competitive pressures will not allow the altruistic corporation to survive, as has been claimed by some steel companies; or because the do-good firms simply are not large enough to solve the social problem on their own, as may be the case with minority hiring; or because other firms will simply continue to dirty the water or the air even if one or more stops voluntarily. A solution then will require either collective decision making by all firms, which is normally illegal under our antitrust laws, or government regulation.

Thus government has a special role in most of these areas, whether it is in determining acceptable levels of pollution, training the unskilled, or making foreign policy by outlawing trade with certain nations. But to talk of corporate responsibility for such issues does no more than muddy the water by suggesting that there is some effective way to reach the desired goal without government action. Literally no evidence can be found that voluntary corporate altruism has ever made a significant dent in any but the most insignificant problems addressed.

Latitude of the Corporate Manager

Perhaps, indeed, the most crucial question about this subject is the extent to which nonmarket-oriented discretion is actually available to corporate managers. Berle, Galbraith, and others have long claimed that managers of large corporations are autonomous, self-perpetuating oligarchs who are free to use corporate funds in almost any way they see fit, whether it be for the shareholders, society, or themselves. Until recently this idea was widely accepted. But careful investigators have begun to test this thesis empirically and have found it strangely wanting in substance. Even Galbraith has admitted fundamental error in this regard.

No one should have been surprised by this discovery. If an industry is fully competitive, significant nonprofitable behavior is, of course, impossible. A firm insisting on such behavior would be unable to survive and function at all. We know, however, that competition is rarely this stringent, and that some surplus may be available for social-welfare purposes in large corporations. Such firms should thus find it possible to engage in some limited but significant amount of nonmarket-oriented activity without depriving the shareholders, the managers, or anyone else of their market rate of return. But, in fact, this is still not the case unless such a corporation is personally or closely held, in which case the owners are simply giving away their own money through a corporate conduit.

If public shareholders exist and without significant legal barriers to takeovers, mergers, or proxy fights, managers who actually engage in nonprofitable activities will soon be displaced. This time the market forces that will discipline the managers will not be those of the product market in which the company sells, as with competitive firms, but rather of the capital market. A stock price will decline just as quickly whether corporate funds are given to charity, expended on social-welfare projects, stolen, or simply used inefficiently in the business. And when stock prices decline sufficiently, a takeover of some sort by individuals who will manage the company in a different fashion becomes inevitable. The stock market is ruthless, objective, and without social conscience. And for that we can all be thankful.

For good public-relations reasons, corporations must continue their efforts to buy political and social goodwill by asserting noncapitalistic values. Even if everyone understood the tremendous social benefits to be derived from competitive capitalism, no individual firm could profit from voluntarily advocating the traditional values and ethics of the free enterprise system. Gain comes only from promising something for nothing.

The late Joseph Schumpeter argued, in his *Capitalism, Socialism and Democracy*, that as corporations grow and become bureaucratized, business executives cease to think and act like entrepreneurs, and therefore, cease to defend capitalism. Schumpeter may have been correct for the wrong reason. Contrary to his view, businessmen still behave precisely as classical economic theory prescribed. But today's maximizing behavior includes advocating the nonmaximization of profits. So, it is true that businessmen have largely ceased to defend business, but only because that was the businesslike thing to do.

Probably businessmen will continue, along with intellectuals and politicians, to advocate a second-rate economic system and to denegate a better one. The saving grace, at least for now, is that what businessmen say and what the market constrains them to do are two completely different things. The danger is that ultimately the talk will have so much political effect that the market system will be destroyed. When that process is complete, the only cry heard in the land will be for social responsibility from an all-powerful, overwhelming government.

QUESTIONS FOR DISCUSSION

1. Is consumerism an "anit-business movement"?

2. Why should the politicians favor increased corporate responsibility? How can this enhance their own power?

3. Why do certain businessmen "enthuse" about increased corporate responsibility?

4. What does Professor Manne mean when he says: "A stock price will decline as quickly whether corporate funds are given to charity, expended on social-welfare projects, stolen, or simply used inefficiently in business"?

5. "Many of the goals specified for corporate largess cannot be accomplished satisfactorily by firms acting individually". Is, then, collective action by companies illegal? Why?

6. Do you agree that corporate actions to enhance public welfare are merely public relations gimmicks?

7. Are we in danger of becoming a "corporate state"? (see W.M. Batten's statement)

APPENDIX I

Corporate Responsibility Paradox

We find several phenomena surrounding the issue of corporate social responsibility. One is the large amount of talk on the subject. Another is the support of this notion by corporate executives, including support of government programs in no sense conducive to competitive capitalism. And still another is the meager amount of truly charitable behavior we actually witness in the corporate world. Herein lies the paradox of the corporate-responsibility notion.

APPENDIX II

Role of the Corporation In The Economy
W. M. Batten

The role of the corporation in the economy has not enlarged in recent years. As an owner of tangible wealth of the economy, the corporate sector's share has remained stable at around 28 percent during the past half century. Over the past 20 years, rewards going to the corporate sector in the form of profits (before taxes) have declined from 16 percent to 11 percent of the national income, while the rewards of employees in the form of wages and salaries have risen. In addition, government's share of the wealth has been expanding at the expense of other sectors. The profit-seeking corporation is, indeed, a vital institution, but the United States is not, nor is it becoming a "corporate" economy. By most measures, the corporate sector has maintained a stable relation with the remainder of the economy for at least a generation.

REDEPLOYING CORPORATE
RESOURCES TOWARD NEW PRIORITIES *

HAZEL HENDERSON

* Hazel Henderson "Redeploying Corporate Resources forward New Priorities," *A Look at Business in 1990*, White House Conference on the Industrial World Ahead, Washington, 1972, pp. 99-104. Reproduced by permission.

Remarks by Hazel Henderson, writer, lecturer, and consultant on current social problems.

The new "postindustrial values" transcend the goals of security and survival. They are, therefore, less materialistic, often untranslatable into economic terms and, in turn, beyond the scope of the market economy. They constitute a new type of "consumer demand," not for products as much as for life styles.

New Social Values

Ironically, these new values attest to the material successes of our present business system. They represent validation of a prosaic theory of traditional economics that holds that the more plentiful goods become the less they are valued. For example, to the new postindustrial consumers, the automobile is no longer prized as enhancing social status, sexual prowess, or even individual mobility, which has been eroded by increasing traffic congestion. Such a consumer has begun to view the automobile as the instrument of a monolithic system of auto, oil, highway, and rubber interests, and client-group dependencies, which has produced an enormous array of social problems and costs. These include decaying, abandoned inner cities, an overburdened law-enforcement system, an appalling toll of deaths and injuries, some 60 percent of air pollution, and the sacrifice of millions of acres of arable land to a costly highway system.

While such consumer sentiments are often discounted as those of an affluent minority, many other postindustrial values held by the affluent groups are also being expressed by the poor and less privileged. Some groups, whether welfare recipients or public employees, less-powerful labor unions, or modest homeowners andd taxpayers, seem to share a demand for greater participation in the decisions affecting their lives and disaffection with large bureaucracies of both business and government. For example, we have witnessed the real suspicions of the labor movement expressed in the charges that President Nixon's New Economic Policy was tailored much more to the liking of business interests than it was to labor. Similar charges were made by consumers, environmentalists, minorities, and the poor concerning the unfairness of tax credits "trickling down" from business rather than "trickling up" from some form of consumer credits to create instant purchasing power.

Further, environmentalists who are sometimes viewed as elitists have found themselves agreeing with labor and minorities that human-service programs, which also tend to be environmentally benign, should have been expanded rather than cut. They believe that a federal minimum-income program is more needed than ever. Such a program would create purchasing power for instant spending on unmet basic needs, such as food and clothing. It would permit the poor greater mobility to seek opportunities in uncrowded areas, thereby relieving the overburdened biosystems of our cities. Or, to recast the disenchantment with our automobile-dominated transportation system, we may note the different but equally vocal objections of the poor. Some one-fifth of all American families do not own an automobile. This decreases their mobility and narrows their job opportunities, while the decline in mass transit and increased spatial sprawl permitted by extensive use of the automobile worsen the situation, and the relentless construction of new highways continues to ravage their neighborhood.

New Challenges to Industry

The middle-upper-income, postindustrial consumers represent a new and different challenge of vital concern to corporations. Their opinion-leadership roles and trend-setting life styles will continue to influence traditional consumer tastes as they have in several important respects, such as: the new anarchism and casualness in clothing fashions; the popularity of bicycling; the trends away from ostentatious overconsumption toward more psychologically rewarding leisure and life styles; and the astounding growth of encounter groups and kindred activities. Their increasingly skillful political activism and acceptance of concern for social injustice is already producing new political coalitions. Their growing confrontations with corporations over their middle-class issues, such as the environment and peace, have led them to discover the role of profit-maximizing theories in environmental pollution, and the role of the military-industrial complex in defense expenditures and war. These insights are leading to convergence with other socio-economic group interests so much in evidence in the movement for corporate responsibility.

Many of the corporate campaigns have been concerned with peace, equal opportunity in employment, pollution, the effects of foreign operations, safety, and the broadest spectrum of social effects of corporate activities. Campaign GM was typical. It sought representation on General Motor's board of directors for minorities, women, consumers, and environmental concerns. The same convergence is evident in the newly formed Washington-based Committee to Stop Environmental Blackmail, composed of labor unions and a cross section of environmental groups. It is pledged to oppose the growing number of corporations that attempt to prevent implementation of pollution-control laws by raising fears of unemployment, plant shutdowns, or even relocating in more "favorable" states or other countries. Labor unions and environmentalists view such tactics as more often power plays and bluffing, or poor management, than bona-fide cases of corporate hardship.

This growing understanding of the political nature of economic distribution has naturally focused on the dominant economic institution of our time: the corporation in both its political and economic role. Nothing displays the political power of our large corporations more vividly than their own managements' concepts of the corporation as power broker, mediating the interests of virtually all other constituent groups in the entire society! Such an all-encompassing role is traditionally ascribed to popularly elected governments in a democratic system such as ours, rather than to private, special purpose organizations. Acknowledgment, by both businessmen and their critics, of the overriding social power of the large corporations points up the fallacy of Dr. Milton Friedman's argument that corporations do not have the right to make social decisions, but only to maximize stockholders' profits. The reality is that corporations in pursuing their profit motives regularly make ipso facto social decisions of enormous consequence.

One might conclude, therefore, that if our corporations remain as powerful as they are today, we might also expect them to collide more extensively with other social forces. This will lead to unprecedented challenges to corporate activities that are based on traditional economic theories. We can expect greater numbers of confrontations with citizens who become more radicalized as they are more affected by corporate efforts to expand, apply new technology, increase production, or move into new areas such as large-scale agri-business op rations with specially severe social repercussions. It is to be hoped that these confrontations, whether boycotts, picket lines, or politicizing annual meetings and proxy machinery, will eventually find civilized channels for expression, and will lead to new structures of social mediation.

Technology Assessment

Technology assessment will surely advance beyond today's rudimentary stage. As technology-assessment methods improve, become democratized, and institutionalized at every level of government by public demand, we can expect that these former areas of management prerogative will give way to a more open, consultative public-decision-making process.

Similarly, we can also expect currently stepped-up funding to produce workable sets of social indicators of human well-being, as well as better documentation of social and environmental diseconomies generated by current production. These indicators must take into account data on depletion of resources and other environmental capital, the social health and welfare costs passed on to taxpayers by corporate automation, relocation, or various standards for employee occupational health and product safety. They must be sensitive to subjective data concerning states of relative satisfaction with quality of life as perceived by the citizen. These might be based on polling techniques, or monitoring citizens' complaints funneling into government agencies or city halls, and using them as inputs into social indicators of the gap between expectation and performance of government.

As macrolevel social indicators are developed and begin to reformulate and enhance the accuracy of current narrowly defined economic indicators, the information on which individual companies base their decisions will also change. As social and environmental costs are factored into the GNP, company decisions will be framed in terms of a much more slowly growing "net national product." As these externalities become more explicitly quantified and publicly disseminated, pressure will increase to internalize these formerly unacknowledged costs of production and add them to the market price of products. The definition of profit will necessarily change to apply only to those activities that create real added wealth, rather than private gain extracted by social or environmental exploitation.

At the microlevel, community groups are already asking their local chambers of commerce penetrating questions concerning their euphoric development plans. Some communities already demand that exhaustive cost/benefit analyses be prepared on a broad range of development options, including the option of *not* developing at all.

Public-Interest Economics

As a result of all this reassessment of economic concepts and qualification methods, one would expect to see the growth of "public-interest economics groups" to join those in public-interest law and science. Such groups will eventually find foundation and other institutionalized support as citizens' groups learn that they must have their own economists present testimony on such matters as the diseconomies of one-way bottles to counter the testimony of the container companies' economists at public hearings. Similar insights will lead to demand for interest-group representation on all governmental economic decision-making bodies, such as the Federal Reserve Board, the Treasury, and the President's Council of Economic Advisers, on which consumer, environmental, and minority groups have already sought to expand for this purpose.

Corporations will find similarly stepped-up demands for interest-group representation on their boards of directors. It is likely that other corporate publics, particularly stockholders, consumers, and environmentalists will organize themselves into coherent negotiating blocs, and engage in annual bargaining with corporations just as labor unions today.

Meanwhile, efforts are under way on Wall Street to broaden traditional security analysis to cover the social and environmental performance of corporations, following the pioneering work of New York City's Council on Economic Priorities, of which I am a director. The Council's bimonthly *Economic Priorities Report* counts among its subscribers a growing list of banks, brokerage houses, mutual funds, and other institution and individual investors, and citizens. It publishes comparative information about the social impact of corporations in various industry groups in five key areas: environment, employment practices, military contracting, political influence, and foreign operations. The need for this type of corporate analysis is highlighted by the fact that there are now no less than six new mutual funds whose stated purpose is to invest only in those companies with superior social and environmental performances.

A report on an in-depth study of pollution in the pulp and paper industry, by the Council on Economic Priorities, disputes the widely held contentions that a) pollution control is achieved only at the expense of profits, and b) that pollution control is a close function of profitability. On the contrary, many companies in that industry with excellent environmental performance were shown to also have superior profitability. Several possible explanations were advanced: better management; lower cost of capital, which a favorable corporate image can sometimes command through marginally higher stock prices and lower borrowing costs; and lower operating costs in labor, health insurance, maintenance, taxes, and particularly in the cost of pollution control itself, when it is an integral part of the design of manufacturing equipment, rather than added later This suggests the U.S. capital markets are becoming more sensitive to socially related aspects of business performance. Social-performance ratings sheets on companies will be common in the future as are those rating traditional performance today.

Changes in Corporation Operation

If this kind of future domestic environment is a likely scenario for the U.S. corporation, then it will have to change considerably so as to maintain its current broad mandate, or embark on a restless search overseas for short-run advantages in politically or economically prostrate nation states willing to provide sweated labor and resources, and a blank check to pollute. Some U.S. corporations, driven by profit-maximizing imperatives, are already eyeing such less-developed nations. Japan has already declared its intention to transfer its own labor-intensive, high-energy, polluting industries to such areas of the world.

Corporations choosing such a strategy will surely gain their short-term, narrowly defined profit objectives, but they will incur social and environmental debts that will eventually lead to further social conflict both in the United States and in international relations. Meanwhile U.S. labor unions, fearing the further export of jobs, are themselves going multinational. Consumer and environmental movements are gaining strength in the industrialized nations of Europe and in Japan. Therefore, let us assume that companies will refrain from such a destructive course, and, instead, attempt to modify their policies and practices so as to bring them more into harmony with emerging social goals and the diminishing resources of the ecosystem on which they and society ultimately depend.

New Definition of Profit

One of the most vital and far-reaching new corporate strategies must be that of learning to live with the new definition of profit, and with the internalizing of the full social and environmental costs of prodiuction. This will alter markets and production as it more rationally assigns such costs to the consumer, rather than the taxpayer. For example, in the face of the coming energy squeeze, current promotional rates for electricity will likely be restructured to include external costs and remove subsidies from heavy users, such as the aluminum industry. One outcome might be the wholesale replacement of aluminum in many consumer products; another might be the disappearance of the throwaway aluminum can. A more realistic definition of profit would also result in the discontinuance of many consumer items whose production is profitable only with formerly hidden social or environmental subsidies. As resources become scarcer, we would see the gradual replacement of high-energy/matter-input goods with low-energy/matter-input goods, and the continued growth of services in the public and private sectors that is already evident.

All of this may be initially inflationary while readjustments are occurring, and may cause many American products to face even stiffer competition in world markets. However, this is disputed by Professor James B. Quinn[1] who believes: that the new environmental costs will eventually be sold as value added in products; that the new pollution-control processes will result in raw-materials savings; and that the possible initial disruption caused by foreign competition may be offset by rising ecological awareness in other nations; added exports from a growing domestic pollution-control industry; and other factors.

The only possible avenues for future profits seem to lie in four general areas:

Better energy-conversion ratios—For example, we will no longer be able to afford the thermal inefficiencies of the current genreation of light-water, nuclear-fission reactors or the internal-combustion engine. Only by developing inherently more efficient energy-conversion systems, such as fuel cells or nuclear fission, can we hope to achieve actual economy and environmental benefits.

Better resource management and rehabilitation—Production loops must be closed by recycling. However, this will probably not be in the current mode of volunteer recycling of bottles and cans, because it does not constitutee a valid negative feedback loop for the container industry, and permits them to continue externalizing the severe costs of collection.

Better "market-failure research" into needs for basic consumer goods unmet because of inadequate purchasing power. Some 10 million families with incomes of less than $5000 per year, as well as those with annual incomes between $5000 and $10,000 per year, represent one of the greatest challenges to our business system. These will require conceptual breakthroughs as far reaching as the invention of consumer credit, federally underwritten home mortgages, or the G.I. Bill's massive investment in human resources. All these families, even those below the poverty line or on welfare, have explosive aspirations for better housing, education, vacations, and consumer goods so widely advertised.

One obvious strategy for corporations is to support an adequate national minimum income, not only for humanitarian reasons and to prevent further erosion of our human resources and to equalize the unfair distribution of welfare costs among our taxpayers, but also to irrigate our economy with instant and much-needed purchasing power. For those families in the annual income range between $5000 and $10,000, corporations and labor unions alike should explore the strategies of building purchasing power by broadening of corporate ownership by cutting employees in on "a piece of the action" after the style of Louis O. Kelso's Second Income Plan Trusts, which has already proved effective in many corporations and has also reduced labor strife and increased motivation. These employee stock-ownership trusts permit corporations to finance new capital equipment with tax-deductible dollars, while apportioning out newly issued shares representing the expansion to the workers, without payroll deductions.

Better "market-failure research" into those areas where individual consumer demand is inoperable unless it can be aggregated, i.e., the potentially enormous public-sector markets where the backlog of unmet group-consumer needs is greatest. Examples are such services as mass transit, health care, clean air and water, education, retraining, parks, and all kinds of public amenities. Many of these needs might well become coherently aggregated with a little corporate support of the necessary political activities of coalitions of potential consumers now working to underpin them with government appropriations.

Strategies for Public-Service Needs

If corporations can lobby to procure government contracts for military and space products, they can also learn the methodologies of the new multistage public-sector marketing. Companies interested in developing new markets in the public sector must first contact citizens' organizations pushing for new priorities in public spending and assess which new needs they are best equipped to serve. Only these grass-roots coalitions of potential consumers can create enough genuine political steam to capitalize these new economic activities. Corporations must learn to see these groups as indispensable allies instead of enemies. Companies must then determine the citizens' expectations for the performance of the new public-sector goods and services. Then, together, they can begin to formulate the design criteria and functional goals, with the companies providing technical and other supporting services to develop more detailed plans.

These processes are particularly vital in such areas as the design of mass-transit routes and facilities, so as to include the greatest number of riders. The size and shape of the total market must be measured by extensive polling and interviewing. New technology for social choice is now in the experimental stage, which has proved capable of increasing citizens' motivation and participation in articulating such new demand, assessing and formulating community goals, and then used to analyze and profile the resulting feedback.[2] For example, using computers and television, we might model all the alternatives for a town's transportation mix and assess outcomes for such options as: do nothing and permit continued ad hoc growth of highways and auto use; make more provision for safe paths for short trips on foot or cycle; build mass-transit lines for high-density areas, based on route desires of potential riders; start a dial-a-bus-on-demand system with computerized dispatching; or designate open lanes for express buses on major freeways so as to lure commuters out of their cars with the faster trip. All the variables can be plotted and simulated on television as "games." Audience feedback can be profiled to change the plotting of the diagrams on the screen as the "votes" are recorded. Currently corporations hoping to serve the incipient mass-transit market are circling and waiting, or developing expensive hardware designs that they will try to put across with lobbying efforts, instead of becoming involved with all the clamoring civic groups demanding such facilities, so as to learn their needs and thereby design systems that they will use.

Finally, corporate-marketing men should begin to sell these groups of potential consumers on the merits of their systems or services, and then join with them in lobbying efforts to pass legislation or bond issues necessary to create the market for these big-ticket items.

The new consumers are not Luddites; they are realists. They do not reject technology. Rather, they seek an end to the gross, wasteful, "meataxe" technology that has characterized our receding industrial age. They envision a second-generation technology, more refined, miniaturized and organically modelled along biological analogies. For instance, we might deemphasize the high-energy transportation side of the coin of human interaction and increase the communications side. This could mean decentralizing of population into smaller, more organic-sized communities, managed locally by cable-TV-based "electronic town meetings," all linked by mass media. Likewise it might mean decentralizing corporations by breaking them up into more functional units, while somewhat more costly, can be offset by lower transportation, distribution, and inventory costs. It could also mean a renaissance of grass-roots capitalism, with small entrepreneurial groups providing local day-care and other community services, or cooperatives for cable-TV or apartment-building ownership and operation.

The new consumers are aware of how narrowly based economic decisions control current allocations of resources, and that large corporations and the business system in general are a predominant force in our society and much of the rest of the world. Therefore, they also understand that they must deal with this system and work within it because they are, in reality, within it and a part of it. But they also believe that with sufficient creative, vigorous, and uncomfortable public pressures, the productive forces within capitalism can be adapted to the needs of the immediate present as well as the next two decades.

QUESTIONS FOR DISCUSSION

1. What does Hazel Henderson see will be the characteristic social values and life styles in the post-industrial society?

2. Do you agree that human-service programs should be expanded? Which should have top priority?

3. How can individuals, whether poor, labor union members, modest homeowners, etc., expect to have more control over decisions affecting their lives and at the same time expect society collectively through government to provide these vital benefits?

4. "Corporations in pursuing their profit motives regularly make *ipso facto* social decisions of enormous consequence." What social decisions are referred to?

5. What "confrontation" with other interests does the author anticipate that business will encounter? Are there dangers to the corporation in these confrontations?

6 "Social performance rating sheets on companies will be as common in the future as are those rating traditional performance today" Explain. (Compare with "The First Attempts at a Corporate Social Audit" in Section VI).

7. The author states that many companies doing most for social welfare and the ecology are also the most profitable and best performing firms in their respective fields. What are the reasons ascribed for this? Does it tend to refute Professor Manne's position?

8. What more realistic definition of profit does the author advocate? Do you think this is a realistic definition? Could it be reflected on the conventional corporate balance sheet?

9. Of what use may electronic computers be in social planning?

FOOTNOTES

1. Of the Amos Tuck School of Business Administration in the Harvard Business Review, Sept.-Oct., 1971.

2. See "The Computer in Social Planning: A Chance for the Little Man to be Heard," H. Henderson, The MBA, Dec. 1971.

THE NEW ENVIRONMENT
FOR BUSINESS *

45

PAUL N. YLVISAKER

* Paul N. Ylvisaker, "The New Environment for Business," *A Look at Business in 1990*, White House Conference on the Industrial World Ahead, Washington, 1972, pp. 105-106. Reproduced by permission.

Remarks by Dr. Paul N. Ylvisaker, Professor, Public Affairs and Urban Planning, Princton University. (Dr. Ylvisaker has since become Dean of the Graduate School of Education, Harvard University.)

The next 18 years for business (i.e., industry) — as for all of us — will be exciting all the way. Exciting in the sense of precarious. The main preoccupation of all of us will be survival.

The principal threat will be a general retreat to social Darwinism, one form of it being a temptation to those having control over capital to build fortresses of privilege across an international landscape flooding with restive populations. The prime social responsibility of ·business during this period will be to confront honestly the "reciprocals" of its own self-interest, and to negotiate rather than shoulder its way through the wearying maze of these other interests.

The numbers and complexities of these other interests being what they are, and the international competition for capital being what it is, business cannot expect to avoid growing public scrutiny of its performance as the public becomes increasingly concerned with the basic ground rules by which the search for profits goes on and the industrial resources are allocated. The publics of this country and the world are not likely to be satisfied with tokenism, self-regulation, or other responses that are left to the discretion of individual firms.

Industry's self-confidence and political standing will be shaken by the growing realization that its competence does not easily extend to the concerns and problems that the general publics are restive about: viz., the redistribution of income and the acquisition of public goods and services — a better and better quality of life for more and more people.

The performance of American industry on this score has not been impressive. Discretionary giving for charitable purposes has been only one-fifth what is allowed under the tax code. It has not done well with multipurpose ventures that involve multiple consents, e.g., the building of new communities, the renovation of old communities, even housing.

The employment it offers is heavily involved with manufacturing. Because of automation, this sector of employment is not expanding, certainly it will not increase the number of jobs this country will need to absorb its vast growth in labor force between now and 1990. Jobs in the service sector are subject to strong inflationary trends, tied to the monopolistic tendencies of the guilds that provide them. Industry is used to a simpler logic of efficiency and growth than prevails in the public-service sector.

Industry has not been notably successful in providing the critical services essential to a quality of life and the creation of sufficient jobs to ensure full employment, health, education, etc.

As industry becomes more involved with international activity, it will also be caught in crossfires of conflicting social responsibilities with relatively less feeling of responsiblity, or option to be responsible, to the immediate interests of the United States with its high labor costs and standard of living. One can therefore expect most of the "action" to move toward the service sector, toward the public sector, and to the process of arbitrating competing social demands. The prime skill and the most in demand will be that of weighing diverse and even incompatible interests.

Also on the rise will be buffering and packaging organizations and the public-development corporation, responsible for building and rebuilding cities, for designing, building, and maintaining public infrastructures, for structuring and financing critical public services, such as health and education. Ideally, these could be joint ventures. But the probability is that the rate of return on capital invested in these public services and social goods cannot ever reach the levels expected and obtainable on the free capital market. Public allocations of capital will be made at lower rates of return. Stormy debates will occur over those allocations.

Ideally, the same qualities of enterprise and social responsibility will permeate both the private and public sectors— and certainly everything should be done to achieve a growing community of shared values. But the realities of the coming decades will be too harsh to expect the process of mediation and balance to be entirely or even predominantly rational and humane. The intervening years will be full of conflict and confrontation—a good deal of it violent.

The temptation will be to rely on force to resolve these tensions. But force by itself is counterproductive. The better answers are continuous negotiation, continuous change and adjustment. We should hope that an international pluralism will grow rapidly, so that no one, or single set of polarizations can develop or last for long. We are moving from one level of complexity (the industrialized nation) to an even greater order of complexity (the multinational corporation and denationalized society). Our fear should be that the transition will not come quickly enough; and we should be ready if not willing to take some rough riding so as to accelerate our way to survival.

The most encouraging prospect for survival is the exploding awareness of the public and especially the younger generation who have developed a tolerance and capacity for rapid change. Both industry and governments can count on accelerating public acceptance of accelerating change. The challenge will be for government and industry not so much too lead as to keep pace.

QUESTIONS FOR DISCUSSION

1. Industry has not been successful in providing the critical services essential to a quality of life and the creation of sufficient jobs to ensure full employment, health, education, etc." Comment.

2. What is a "public development corporation"?

3. "The intervening years will be full of conflict and confrontation" Why? Do you think that mediating influences will prove to be stronger than Dean Ylvisaker predicts?

4. Do you think we shall achieve a "de-nationalized" society by 1990? In your opinion would this be a good thing?

5. Willingness to accept rapid change, the author says, is the key to the successful evolution of the new post-industrial society. Do you feel as opitmistic as the author that people will be willing to accept radical change? What dangers exist in this situation?

6. Pulling together all of the rather diverse arguments found in Section IX, give your own thoughts as to what the world will be like in 1990.

PART X

CONSUMERISM, 1990

We now come to the end of our examination of the New Consumer Movement by looking into the future. What will consumerism be like by 1990?

To answer this question, we first analyze two forward-looking proposals by two well-known consumer advocates. Robert B. Choate urges that something be done about the blatant selling of the child by our television industry. He makes two proposals, interesting in themselves, but more broadly indicative of the sort of corrective action which business may expect in future decades. Mr. Choate very obviously pins his hopes on self-regulation rather than relying on further incursions by the government.

Dr. Thomas F. Schutte is worried about establishing priorities. To do so properly he recommends that we set up a national institute to measure consumer issues and problems. By so doing, he feels that we shall be able to deploy society's resources more effectively. Indeed, his arguments are part and parcel of the broader issue: Has the United States economy outgrown the old "shoot-from-the-hip" cowboy tradition of wasteful squandering of our resources? In the post-industrial world, must we reconcile ourselves to more forward planning? More careful management of our resources, human and material? More social control? More careful decision-making on national priorities? This writer predicts that we shall inevitably see these tendencies become very strong by 1990 if we are to survive and prosper as a viable society.

Finally, Aaron S. Yohalem, in a carefully constructed paper, looks at the probable changes which consumerism will bring by 1990. As the reader will note, he foresees some major impacts on our present way of life. But his thesis is not by any means pessimistic. He envisions a rise in the quality of American life, if only we can manage the necessary changes efficiently and with cool reason. Your editor joins Mr. Yohalam in his belief. Progressive evolution affords us the best chance of attaining a really good, just, caring society.

ROBERT B. CHOATE

Testimony Given before the Federal Communications Commission, January 9, 1973. Mr. Choate is Chairman of Council on Children, Media and Merchandising.

We are now in the 35th month of deliberations by the Federal Communications Commission in the matter of Children's Television Proceedings. The petition submitted by Action For Children's Television (ACT) which precipitated still another round of debate over the rights and needs of children *vis a vis* the airwaves has ended up swamped in a morass of opinions weakly supported by hazy facts.

Several Commissioners have already indicated that they are not inclined to ban commercials from Saturday and Sunday morning television even though a large segment of those under 12 watch many of the programs.

The ACT petition has revealed the commercial lenses through which broadcasters regard children. The public has not yet been told this story; the stations themselves have done little to add factual opinion to a very emotional public debate.

Today I will draw to the Commission's attention other related opportunities, short of an outright commercial ban, which could improve programs while diminishing the hardsell of a child-oriented television ad. There are a number of things which this commission can do which will meet the sense, if not the substance, of the ACT. It is time that the Federal Communications Commission make some decisions; they *can* be made within 60 days.

I will offer two large scale reforms; I will then suggest seven commercial corrections. Were these to be enacted, together with some of the other suggestions made in these hearings, both the broadcasters of this nation and the FCC could be said to have dealt more fairly with children under 12. Let me address the two broader reforms before I move to the specifics.

F.C.C. And Department of Justice

In a truly competitive situation, quality usually suffers. The logger who strips the forest can usually undersell the forester who cuts selectively. The manufacturer of heavily advertised fragile junk toys can win, in the beginning, a large share of the market from the producer of quality goods with a lower promotion budget. So it is with broadcasting. The young public has become accustomed to low grade programming. Children will continue to turn the knob to the least challenging material, while responsible broadcasters tear their hair out over a program that deserves a bigger audience.

There is something in all of us that continually seeks a lower and lower denominator. Today, while competitive networks and syndicated independents note the excellence of a rival's program, it may well pay them to maintain their present programming, rather than go to the expense of countering with a first rate production. Thus the broadcaster who has opted for excellence may watch his audience desert him for drivel, and his per viewer costs mount out of sight. The rivals win sponsors and viewers away from the competitor's quality. This will continue while low grade programs compete with quality shows for a child's mind.

In a situation such as this, it is the responsibility of those in government to help create a corrective process.

If the FCC wishes to change today's television for children it can start by creating two corrective processes: a Children's Television Broadcast Center and a Children's Television Code Board.

The former would be designed as a quasi-public corporation, with a mixed public/private board of directors.* It would be funded by a mandatory tithe on all national sponsors who advertise on regular commercial shows where the under twelve audience exceeds one million. The tithe would be scaled to the audience size. The corporation would finance and make available at nominal fee quality programs for broadcast on any network, any chain or any station. Unions would be asked to invest in the corporation on a basis of a percentage of the guild fees and residuals incurred in both programming and advertising to children. The Telephone Company would be asked for a percentage of its longline charges. Credits to the Center's backers would be institutional credits, and could accompany the program. As a public service, twice each night in prime time, the broadcaster would air institutional mention of the backers who had financed the improved programs for children. He would mention the names of the programs, their age focus and their time of airing, and he would invite parents to join their children in watching the show. Advertising of ordinary products would be limited to four advertisements per hour during the hours when the Center's programs were on the air. With FCC direction, various Center programs could be run simultaneously on competing stations. Thus, quality would start to compete with quality, and the lower grade programs would be left to compete with each other. I would suggest that this format should start with one hundred hours of Center programming the first year, and build from there.

The cooperative nature of this effort, together with the planned simultaneous air schedule, will require certain waivers from antitrust proceedings by the Department of Justice. There are precedents for this cooperative action; the Department of Agriculture and the Department of Commerce are familiar with the leadership required by governmental agencies when minimum standards or quality standards are established. Inasmuch as the "message" of these programs would remain in private hands, the potential of political messages would be minimal.

A Children's Television Code Board would also require some involvement of the FCC with the Department of Justice. No self-regulation code can have real teeth today unless the FTC and the Department of Justice condone it. A Children's Television Code should be able to set minimum standards for all commercial programs as well as for commercials themselves. Violation of the Code should be met with continuously aired disclaimers that the program or the commercial has not met the Code Board's standards. I fear that nothing short of this will work. The National Association of Broadcasters Code Authority today is an industry front. The new National Advertising Review Board is a farce. Leaving self-regulation exclusively, or almost exclusively, in the hands of those who broadcast or advertise is, as Paul Stevens has described it, "kind of like leaving the goat to mind the garbage."[1] (I speak from experience. I approached the NAB Code Authority 20 months ago to establish a Code for Advertising Edibles to Children. They gave me a formal hearing and took it under advisement. They still have not acted.)

The Commission must realize that it is moves of this magnitude which can improve the giant called children's television. The average child is watching over 1,000 hours of television per year; it is a controversial force in a child's development.[2]

It is also quite fitting and proper that the FCC initiate actions of this magnitude. You have given the broadcasters two years to improve children's television, Mr. Chairman. They have let you down. They have indicated they cannot do it alone. They need your help. You need not fear you are trammeling with the private enterprise system in some unethical way. The private enterprise system can be compared to a superb automobile engine. When you build the engine bigger and stronger, the brakes and clutch have to be tougher too. Raw power in automobiles, and in the private enterprise system is frequently self-defeating. The philosophers in the upper echelons of American business realize the benefits brought to them by governmental oversight. The Ward Quaals of this world are either naive, or are kidding you. Thirty million children cannot await the second 25 years of Mr. Quaal's television tree growth.[3]

You can make the private enterprise broadcast system work; you can help build the profits of those who perform honorably and you can help protect the profits of those who experiment with improvements. This is a proper role for an FCC. And today the broadcaster needs you to act, not postpone decisions, for the pressures on him are building daily.

F.C.C. And Advertising

Now for areas of FCC specific interest.

Much has been said about whether advertising is proper for young children. Some feel that the tough, hard sell of the private enterprise system should not intrude on the minds of children under twelve. Some say advertising is educative. Some say it is misleading. Some say it is the only thing that keeps the programs on the air. Some say children are being warped by television. All of this is part truth, part lie. The trouble is that no one really knows.

I have conducted an extensive search for those who really can tell us what advertising does to children's behavior, attitudes, cultural traits and family tensions. I have been referred to numerous experts and to many books and reports. Commissioners, while television the entertainment medium has been studied from a hundred perspectives, television the carrier of commercials has been studied scantily, badly and erratically. A few studies have been made to support industry theses. Very few studies have been made to judge children's credibility. Now in television's 27th year, we find the moderate TV watching child views over 25,000 commercials each year. The federal government and the private foundations have spent hardly a cent to judge the impact of this massive message. If a child really starts to watch the tube at four, that means that the child of fourteen will have seen a quarter of a million commercials — a quarter million "scientifically" designed persuaders. Individual parents know something is happening, but they cannot pin it down.

As we look further, we find that industry has been carefully recording children's reactions to commercials. Motivational research houses, complete with one way mirrors, hidden microphones and psychological interrogation have been finding out a child's innermost thoughts about specific ads. This information is kept secret in agency files and sponsor desks. It is not shared with the public. It is not entered into the body of research information that child psychologists refer to as they seek to explain why our younger generation is changing its attitudes toward families, parents, homes and the very private enterprise system.

Thus, when witnesses come before you claiming that TV is evil or TV is great, your instant reaction should be, "How do they know?" And your second reaction should be to ascertain how much this Commission knows. When this issue first arose in the 1960's the FCC should have written publicly to the National Institute of Mental Health, the National Institutes of Health, the National Science Foundation, the Office of Child Development, and every major private foundation and major university interested in children, asking them to provide all available evidence of the effects of television commercials on children.

Noting the Chairman's admission last October 2nd that children's television "has . . . not been really studied by this agency at least", I have been telephoning the FCC for a week trying to find out if the FCC has done anything to to stimulate this type of research, since children's television has been under consideration by the Commission. The longer I look for positive FCC action in stimulating such research, the more I confirm that the FCC knows very little about children.

We cannot now wait another three years for the FCC to learn about the subject at hand. I do recommend that the Chairman write to the officers in charge of the governmental and private entities familiar with children's learning processes, and invite them to enter into or fund studies which will inform all of us — regulators, broadcasters and critics — of the real impact of television on children.

It may interest you to know that Federal Trade Commission Chairman Miles Kirkpatrick, concerned over the $400 million plus spent each year in selling to children, is exploring who knows what about the subject.

If the FCC wishes to change today's television for children, it must lead the country's research institutions into short and long term unbiased research in this field. This is area number one for improvement.

Congressional Oversight

Today, evidence of advertising impact is held primarily in secret by the country's biggest sponsoring companies and agencies. Congress has every right to ask both the FCC and the psychiatric profession why it is so ignorant in these matters. If sponsors and agencies, holding most of the presently available data, will not work to make the deliberations of the FCC and FTC more factual and meaningful, then Congress has every right to call for legislation to bring out of company secret files the data which reveals who is being influenced by which of the industry's techniques.

Commercials and Children

There are some areas of advertising to children where common sense calls upon the FCC to act now *if it wants to change today's television for children.* Area number two is hazardous products.

ACT has suggested all Saturday and Sunday morning ads be removed. We and they think clustering ads at other times would help the child. But this does not clothe the child under twelve with the wisdom to perceive advertising as it exists in a private enterprise society. The preoccupation of the ACT petition with Saturday and Sunday mornings masks the fact that many television shows which attract the biggest under twelve audience appear in the early evenings.

This past fall, over five million youngsters watched each of the following shows each week:

The Partridge Family	Emergency
The Brady Bunch	Adam 12
The Wonderful World of Disney	Bridget Loves Bernie
All in the Family	The Waltons
Room 222	The Mary Tyler Moore Show

It may interest you to know that among the products advertised on these shows, the following products appeared:

*Geritol Tablets	*Arrid Extra Dry
*Anacin	*Alka Seltzer
*Dristan	*Bayer Aspirin
Cheer Super Detergent	Hi-C Fruit Drinks
Neo-Synephrine Nose Drops	Tang
Neo-Synephrine Nose Spray	*Gillette Soft & Dry
*Lysol Deodorizing Cleaners	*Foot Guard Foot Spray
*Mennen E. Deodorant	Pam Coating Spray
Tums	Yardley Lip Gloss

I point these products out to you to dispell the notion that kids are protected by today's broadcasters and the N.A.B. Of the above list, the starred items carry on the labels of the bottles or packages a warning to the effect that they should be kept away from children! Exhibit A, attached to this testimony gives visual evidence of the warnings. There is no warning as we sell these products to children; knowing familiarity breeds contempt, we have not had the common sense to include the warning in the advertisement when over five million children under 12 can see the product sold each week. The prime responsibility rests on the FCC; surely the FCC using the cooperation and support of the FDA and FTC, can act today, *if it wants to change today's television for children.*

Area number three is the FCC's similar responsibility to act in en masse, or generic, advertising situations. Broadcasters have become the confluence of varied advertising practices — and in this confluence, an unbalanced commercial situation emerges. The case in point is advertising on cartoon programs. The spectrum of products advertised during these periods is very limited. Repitition is common. The food industry is particularly visible.

The moderate TV watching child of today sees over 5,000 food ads per year, 80,000 by the time that child is 16 years old. The foods sold to children are not the meats, fruits, vegetables or dairy products we all respect. The contrived and processed foods, some with, but many without nutritional merit, dominate the air-waves. In most advertisements of foods to children, nutritional ABCs generally are displaced by emphasis on sweetness, color and shape. (I do not consider mention of fortification a nutritional ABC.)[4]

The en masse message to children inevitably deprecates natural staples such as fruits, vegetables, or meat and legume protein sources. The avoidance of such mention leaves a child with a preoccupation for processed foods.[5] Some advertisements go out of their way to ridicule nutritional awareness.

Since at certain times of the year food product advertising may constitute 82 percent[6] of the sales message to the Saturday and Sunday watching crowd, a child's nutritional wisdom and the relationship of good eating habits to health must be considered.

I do not really expect food to disappear off children's airwaves, but I do think we have a right to expect some balancing nutritional

The table below indicates that on network television during the week ending April 11, 1971, on programs directed at adults and generally family audiences, 25 percent of all the ads were for foods and beverages. The other 75 percent of the ads were spread over several categories of products, with toilet items, detergents, cleansers and medications predominating.

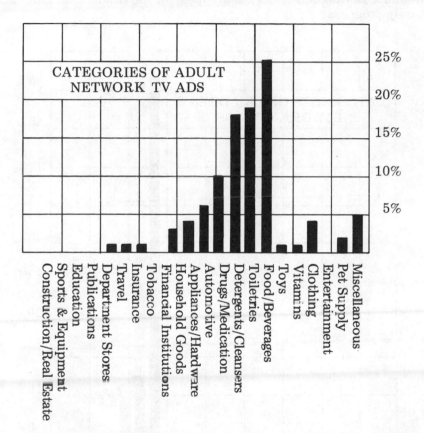

messages on children's time mixed in regularly with the mass of food commercials. Since the sponsors have not maliciously designed the 82 percent edible mix, (but seem to delegate nutritional education to buyers of dog food), it falls to the broadcaster, the man at the confluence of these messages, to bring balance to his broadcasting. It is unfair to the child, and unfair to the parent trying to inculcate nutritional wisdom, for television to spend so much time telling a child the other side of the coin. *If the FCC wants to change today's television for children,* it can require broadcasters to weigh the en masse commercial message to children for its ommissions and mis-emphasis, and to air corrective messages to keep the child on a prudent path.

During the same week, the ads on programs directed specifically at children were much more limited. The chart below shows that over 50 percent of the ads on children's programs that week were for foods and beverages, and another 28 percent were for toys.

Also note that 10 percent of all ads on children's programs were for vitamins, as opposed to less than 1 percent for vitamins on adult and family programs.

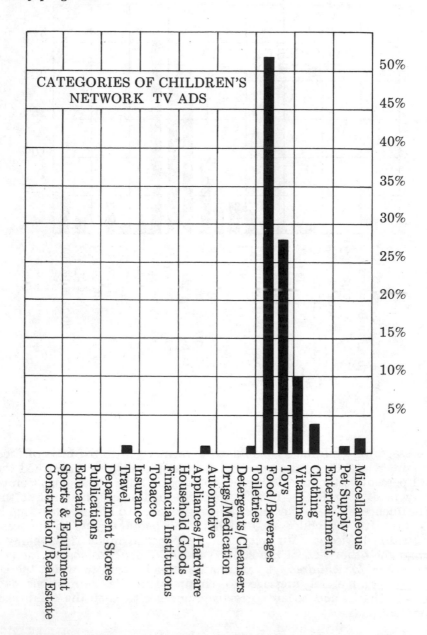

CATEGORIES OF CHILDREN'S NETWORK TV ADS

Data is from Broadcast Advertisers' Reports, Network TV, Week Ending April 11, 1971.

* Food and beverages includes drive-in restaurants.

F.C.C.'s Own Knowledge of Children's Television

Area number four concerns itself with the paucity of information available both to the FCC and to the public as to what constitutes children's television.

Your past station renewal forms seem not to ask one single question about children's television. There are no questions which single out for special scrutiny the policies of the broadcasters during those hours when the under twelve group can be expected to watch the most. You do not ask what Public Service Announcements are aired in those hours. You do not ask how many and which promotions are run. You do not even ask how man hours of programming are run for the under 12 group, or when they are run, or what age group they serve.

You do ask stations to justify at renewal time why they exceed the promises made in the last renewal application. Since none of the questions are related to children, it would appear the FCC was disinterested in the frequency of commercials at renewal time. There are wild swings in the number of commercials aimed at children.[7]

I suggest that the whole process of judging once every three years how a station performed on the basis of seven composite days taken out of 1,100 days is a shallow and belated effort to judge a station's commitment to service to the public.

I understand the renewal process is being redesigned. *If the FCC wants to change today's television for children* it can make station logs available the year around, require detailed explanations of the station's programming and advertising policy toward children, require self-documentation within 60 days of any policy violations or changes, require detailed descriptions of the PSAs aired as well as the promos, and ask for promises of discussion of television-the-children's-medium on prime time. The FCC can even declare a children's prime time. It can ask questions relating to tie-ins and local issues. In short, the FCC can improve its own, and the public's knowledge of what a station has aimed at the under 12 audience. Only when this material becomes available will parents be knowledgeable enough to exercise the local parental authority that your broadcasters seem to wish would take the monkey off their back.

FCC and PSAs and Promos

While we are talking about PSAs, I wonder why the FCC shows so little interest in them. Why does a national censor like the Advertising Council seem to have a grip on national PSAs? (Stations often use this as a justification for rejecting non-Ad Council ads.) We reject the present policy of dumping PSAs into children's programming when a void appears. PSAs for adults should be aimed at adults. PSAs for children should be aimed at them.[8] If a void appears in commercialand, the children should be permitted to benefit from the drop. PSAs of a local nature also deserve more attention, but I doubt that the FCC knows station policy on national versus local PSAs.

Promotions are still another area for FCC attention. Promos make up much of the clutter on television, particularly children's television. A promo is an invitation to keep watching, or to be in front of the set at a later date. Promos are broadcaster influences on the child not to heed his parent's admonition to turn the set off. Promos are also the extra dividend for a heavy sponsor. They are the continuity commercial for a station afraid to lose even the under 12 audience. Promos, interestingly, seem carefully screened for the age group they seek to recruit. I suggest Area No. 5 is an FCC policy on PSAs and promos, particularly to children.

We interject here a comment on the appropriateness of certain Public Service Announcements. They are usually produced at considerable expense by non-profit organizations or agencies sponsoring a message of public importance. They are developed with an audience in mind. They are sent to stations with a request that they be aired. The station can accept or reject them; it need not notify the sponsor as to the time or frequency of airing. One would hope they were handled in a responsible manner to serve society.

Instead, we find that PSAs frequently are handled as a filler item to be dumped in anywhere there is a commercial lag. Stations know they have to run a certain number. The count is more important than the placement.

ABC and NBC provided an interesting example of this on Saturday, January 6, 1973. The myriad toy manufacturers had pulled back their Christmas ads. Rather than fill the time with informational or educational materials, ABC and NBC decided to dump PSAs into the void, irregardless of the appropriateness of the message. Thus we saw on ABC that children were being advised that the Council on Special Education said you can be a teacher of the handicapped; that the Social Security Office offered protection for a child's future; that the National Alliance of Business Men wanted to get all men working; that people should give to the United Negro College Fund; that drug laws overseas were tough; that ACTION needed volunteers; and that the TB Association advised one not to smoke.

NBC advised children Saturday morning that religion keeps marriages going; that the Army wants young men in ROTC; that the March of Dimes needs volunteers; that dogs and cats should be spayed; that parents should keep children exercising; that religion in America was good; that Savings bonds were good; and that seat belts were for safety.

While several other public service announcements with relevance for children were interspersed among these messages (CBS having the most relevant), one can gather that PSAs are dumped wherever a void appears, and children's programs are a natural dumping spot.

F.C.C. and The Local Parent

Let us look at the role of the parent to whom your earlier panelists gave so much responsibility. Conservatives frequently state that local control is better than federal control. In the matter of communication and the airwaves, the courts and Congress have restricted the regulation of the airwaves to the Federal establishment. The public thus is left with no alternative to dealing with you. You have no counterpart in Tucson, Chicago or Nashville. Critics of children's television thus become frustrated when you, to whom the power of decision has been given, will not act. Congress and the courts have deprived us of local influence; you have deprived us of a national decision.

The irate parent in Tucson, who wants to correct the broadcast material at the source, can only go to the perpetrator, or to you. The local broadcaster will frequently cite the networks or the NAB as a reason why local broadcast materials should not be changed. He shunts the critic off his back while keeping him in the dark as to his rights and responsibilities. He sends the parent to a nebulous executive in New York who hardly represents local control. It is time for the FCC to make some programming, commercial, and balanced presentation decisions, for local as well as national reasons. Your lack of decisions on children's television is, in effect, a decision to maintain the status quo. You have given the broadcasters and the networks two years to clean their own shop, Mr. Chairman. They have let you down. If the broadcasters believed in the parent as the ultimate responsible restricter of television, he would have shown it.

I have never seen a local station broadcast a message telling the viewer that the station logs are available for inspection. I have never seen a station advise parents to meet with the station managers to improve children's television. While many stations carry the Public Service Announcement, "It's __ o'clock. Do you know where your children are?", I have never heard a station ask parents, "Do you know what your child watched on TV today?"

It is time this nation recognized that television has become an extra parent within the home. The weaker the family structure, the more important "Uncle Television" becomes. He offers candy and cake, music and laughter; he sings and dances, has animals and child actors. Uncle Television can be turned from one subject to another with the flip of the dial; he seldom lectures and never punishes. Uncle Television is an ever present companion, so the other parents find it handy to be elsewhere, or wrapped up in other things.

If Uncle Television told children and their parents that these hearings were going on, parents would be stimulated to find out more about the responsibilities that broadcasters have assigned them. If broadcasters staged programs where kids and parents could discuss what television means in their lives, parents would awaken to the responsibility they have abdicated to the set. Do networks do this? Do stations? During your last three day hearings, your panelists discussed with occasional merit the characteristics of the 26 year old television industry. *Not one network carried one word of the subject of these hearings on their major news programs.* "Silence is Golden" is more than the name of a new cough syrup; it is the pervading censorship policy of the broadcasters to keep children's television out of public debate.

The FCC and Parent-Child Conflict

The repetitive advocacy to children that they "stay tuned" or "remember to tune in" is but one manifestation of a broadcaster inviting tensions and dissent in the home. This unstudied area of television is also pertinent in the heavy promotion of toys to the child of poverty; both the child and the parent may end up frustrated by their inability to respond.

Topics such as this cannot be dealt with by individual psychiatrists. The audience is too large. It is a whole class of people who are affected. To resolve feelings of incompetance, inferiority or inability to manage one's children in television matters, a public discussion is in order. It is a matter of critical public importance similar to taxes, schooling, or war. One would think that broadcasters would realize that if we are to have television as a positive force in our lives, television the medium needs living room discussions. Television could put it there; television could help children put it there. Does it? No! The heavy hand of censorship lies everywhere in the electronic media. Examples abound of where stations and networks have evaded, ducked or hidden issues of importance to the viewer/consumer audience. The very deliberations of this Commission should be a matter of public knowledge. If children's television has elicited the mass of comment that Chairman Burch and ACT have referred to, certainly the public is entitled to know the issues, the suggested solutions, and the role parents can play in improving television for their child.

Area number six for FCC attention is an FCC rule opening the airwaves to public discussion of the airwaves, particularly that affecting children.

Perhaps the FCC can go further. If parental cognizance of the "other parent" role television frequently now plays would be healthy, I suggest "parental promos" on public service time asking parents to monitor what their children see and feel as a result of TV.

FCC and A Child's Advertising Education

Area number seven for immediate FCC attention is the obvious unfairness of a sponsor using $50,000 to hire script writers, editors, musicians, photographers, psychological analysers, sound effects experts, paid laughers, and other children to create a message of supreme sophistication to persuade a child to buy an item or become a salesman within his own home.

The four, five and six year old cannot read disclaimers. He probably grants credibility to every commercial phrase. Even the older child, while skeptical, continues to urge his mother to buy.[9]

If we recognize that children will see commercials, let us prepare them so the tug of war for their compliance is done on a fairer plane. *Let us educate children about advertising.*

For the youngest watchers, let us flag ads so the child knows the message has changed. By audio or video techniques, we can set the ad apart from the program. A "frame", much like a picture frame, if labelled "advertisement," would quickly cue a child to the fact that he was watching a commercial message.

For the child of seven or above, we recommend a program which tells children about advertising. I do not mean a puff type program that speaks only of sweetness and light; I mean a program that draws upon the insights of advertising such as those expressed in Bauer's *Advertising in America — The Consumer View*; Mayer's *About Television*; Buxton's *Promise Them Anything*; Stevens' *I Can Sell You Anything*; Scott Ward's NIMH report; Wilbur Schramm's *Television In the Lives Of Our Children*; and Morris' *Television's Child*.

If the FCC wishes to change today's television for children, it can facilitate the airing of a joint advertiser-consumer education program in short PSA segments for those hours of the week when the under twelve group watch TV the most. This perhaps would be the ultimate compensatory commercial, for it would educate the child to become a prudent consumer before he became a burned skeptic. The responsible sponsor would gain credibility. The responsible broadcaster would experience less guilt. The responsible parent would gain an ally. The child might gain respect for our commercial system.

SUMMARY

I have suggested to you that while you consider banning commercials Saturday mornings, the FCC can act tomorrow on a number of fronts to improve programs while diminishing the commercial onslaught to children. Let me repeat them as I close.

The FCC can:

A. Form a Children's Television Broadcast Center for jointly sponsored and simultaneously aired shows.

B. Established a Children Television Code which puts the public in charge of what their children are to see.

and

1. Stimulate research into children's reactions to television commercials.

2. Ban or Require Warnings on hazardous substances advertised to Children.

3. Define station responsibilities on en masse commercial distortions.

4. Correct FCC and parental ignorance of present broadcast patterns.

5. Define more tightly correct broadcaster policies on PSAs and promos.

6. Stimulate electronic media discussion of the electronic media.

7. Facilitate an advertiser/consumer education program on the air to help children become prudent consumers.

QUESTIONS FOR DISCUSSION

1. Do you think that commercials should be banned from television shows seen by quite young children? (Especially those aired on Saturday mornings)?

2. What are the two large scale reforms proposed to the FCC by Mr. Choate? Would you be in favor of them?

3. "There is something in all of us that continually seeks a lower and lower denominator." Comment.

4. What would be the mission of a Children's Television Center? Do you think it a good thing? Would it work?

5. Are you in favor of instituting a Children's Television Code Board? Would it be compulsory or self-regulatory? Can you see any serious weaknesses in this recommendation?

6. Do you think the FCC should have put more effort into researching the effect of television commercials on the children? How about on researching the effect on the children of the program content?

7. To what extent do the authorities feel that television warps the child's viewpoints and values? How? Is there any differences on the listener if he or she is older (say in the early teens)?

8. What happens when the angry consumer wants to complain about something on television. Would Mr. Choate's recommendations aid this situation?

9. If you approve of Mr. Choate's plan, what should be done to get it adopted?

FOOTNOTES

* *Not* made up as Ruth Handler suggested in her October 4, 1972 FCC appearance.

1. Paul Stevens, *I Can Sell You Anything* (Peter H. Wyden, 1972), p. 149.

2. Martin Mayer, *About Television* (Harper & Son, 1972), Chapter 6.

3. See testimony of Warren Quaal, October 4, 1972, before the FCC.

4. See Robert B. Choate presentation to the NAB, May 26, 1971.

5. See Joan Gussow testimony before Senate Commerce Committee, Subcommittee on Consumer Affairs, March 2, 1972.

6. On Saturday morning, January 6, 1973, 96% of CBS commercials were for edible products.

7. Between December 9 and December 23, 1972, because toy commercials withdrew, the number of PSAs used as "fillers" on Saturday mornings jumped 100 percent on the three networks.

8. On January 6, 1973, CBS promos and PSAs seemed child oriented; most of NBC's were not.

9. Professor Scott Ward, *Effects of Television Advertising on Children and Adolescents* (Harvard Business School, June, 1971).

THOMAS F. SCHUTTE

* Paper presented at the Public Policy and Marketing Conference/Workshop, Northwestern University, June 12, 1972.

Introduction. In an assessment of the plethora of public policy issues and problems confronting the marketing decision-maker, none confront and perplex the marketing decision-maker so much as the consumerism movement. Needless to say, the subject is ominous and the rhetoric pervasive.

No matter which way one turns, it seems, there is some public in our society with another comment, viewpoint, theory, proposed regulation, solution and so on.[1]

Just examine some of the subjects of the academician, business leader, or governmental bureaucrat. The Aaker-Day reader provides an insight into some of the topical areas.[2]

Subjects or topics include regulation of advertising, consumer credit reform, the consumer as king, deceptive packaging, *caveat emptor*, product warranties and guarantees, branding on trial, gyps, consumer protection, consumer information, faulty product design, consumer legislation for the poor, exploitation of disadvantaged customers, product liability, self-regulation and the public interest and so on. One could scan the many trade and professional publications only to observe these and similar titles pervading. And one could examine the countless speeches being made by executives about what their firms are doing in the interest of the consumer. Or one could examine the annals of the Congressional Record and the numerous speeches of governmental representatives to observe all that is being said and done. Too, one could examine the recent publication of Virginia Knauer's Office of Consumer Affairs which describes 128 agencies and departments of government that provide some role in offering services and protection to the American consumer.[3]

One can examine the numerous professional associations and organizations throughout the United States that have selected, as a thematic, the consumer cause for study and evaluation. But nowhere have we come to grips with the pragmatism needed for operationally conquering the specific issues and problems of the consumer and the controlling needed save through the vehicle of the law. We think of laws and more laws!

Purpose of the Paper. The purpose of this paper is propositionary in nature. I should like to urge that government and business cease endless uninformed theorizing on consumer needs and concentrate on establishing policies, procedures, and organizational structure for getting at the heart of what's wrong with the consumer movement, today. This is not to say that some firms and agencies of government have totally neglected the pragmatics of "action" in the consumer affairs area. We've got to avoid the "clutter of chatter" and "cosmetics" of doctoring organizational programs and get to work!

More specifically, I propose, that with the joint aid of marketers and government, a National Institute for Measuring Consumer Issues and Problems be established and housed in an appropriate or on-going agency or office, whether it be the Office of Consumer Affairs or the National Business Council on Consumer Affairs or some other area. Secondly, I propose that with the joint aid of marketers and government, corporations establish full-fledged offices for consumer affairs.

National Institute for Measuring Consumer Issues and Problems. It is absolutely incredible that government and business have no accurate measures of the specific issues and problems confronted by consumers and how these issues affect differing groups of people. What is more incredible is that marketers have voiced concern for patching up the gap that exists between business and government interaction. Levitt tried to explain why business is so defensively oriented in opposing change through governmental regulation. He showed how preoccupied business leaders were with the internal environment of battling competition, improving performance, and struggling to get to the top of the organization as leaders.[4]

Despite this business apathy, we have witnessed governmental initiation of consumer interest departments in Washington, D. C., such as the Office of Consumer Affairs and more recently the National Business Council for Consumer Affairs. Business and government have not taken the lead in any aggressive way for working out a joint program of action for monitoring consumer problems and issues in the country. There is some evidence this joint action may accrue through the new National Business Council.

Bauer and Greyser charge that business and government have more recently shown evidence of providing spokesmen to contribute dialogue between the two groups for the "reduction of friction and the advancement of the general good . . . yet, too often, this is a dialogue that never happens," for it is often in the form of a hearing where there is "equal time".[5]

Aaker and Day explain that the area of consumerism requires further research so that the proper public policy commitments can be made.[6] Too often poor legislation evolves before research provides important input and bases for determining the viable form of legislation or solution to a public policy problem or issue.

The Need for a National Institute for Measuring Consumer Issues and Problems. In reality, there are some universals or common denominators of consumer affairs that a number of publics share in terms of data necessary for dealing more effectively in solving consumer problems and establishing more consumer-oriented programs. For example, Virginia Knauer should want to know more precisely what are the specific consumer issues and problems in the United States. She should desire to know the demographic breakdown of those consumers who voice concern for certain problems and issues. She should want to know which issues and problems seem to be on the increase or the wane. She should want to know whether or not her programs of governmental action are helping to correct some of the on-going issues and problems. She should want to know more about those consumer problem areas where regulation may be required before legislation is recommended.

So too with business. Business needs to know what are the critical issues and problems of the consumer. Business should care to know whether their firm or company has any bearing on the issues or problems. Is the firm's product or service an area where the consumer voices some unrest or dismay? If so, in which markets are these consumers distressed? What is the shopping behavior of those consumers who appear to be dismayed? For how long has a particular issue been surfacing? And so on.

Professors of marketing have a critical need for information which pinpoints the specific issues and problems voiced by consumers at varying points in time. The professor may direct classroom and research efforts in areas where the issues and problems are important or where there appears to be a trend upwards or downwards. Lectures, discussions and student projects may be more focused or encouraged in these areas. Points of view, recommendations for change, and guidelines may be established by the probing professor in his research and classroom activity.

Presently, government derives its information relative to consumer problems from a variety of sources: (a) periodic public opinion polls or surveys conducted by professional research organizations, (b) testimony by government and private groups, (c) violations or reported injustices from governmental regulatory bodies, (d) observations from the consumer public through news-worthy events such as debates and reactionary groups, and (e) the complaint "mail bag" from consumers.

The Office of Consumer Affairs conducts a periodic survey of its mail bag of complaints. While such a survey is laudatory as a probing and informational device, it in no way represents, with any degree of accuracy, the representativeness and intracacies of issues and problems of the consuming public. In the July 1971 study, it was found that automobile and appliance repair and warranties were the most critical complaint areas.[7] But do we know that these areas are really representative of American consumers' perceptions?

However, the researcher could raise many questions about the "mail bag" technique. To what extent were those who responded cranks or the constantly querulous? How representative were the complaints as a cross section of Americans? What was the distribution of the various demographics by each complaint category. What do we know about the buying behavior and values of those who registered complaints? Were those who complained more highly educated in consumer matters because they knew to whom to write their complaints? Are there other complaint areas more critical in scope even though these problems are not communicated as manifestly as perhaps the appliance and automobile areas?

Periodically, professionally-recognized research organizations conduct survey research for various offices of the government in order to learn what the critical consumer issues and problems are. However, the research is tailored for the specific department or agency of government and may not be as detailed as necessary for the diversity of those making policy decisions on consumer affairs — business leaders, other agencies of government, professors, consumer groups and the like. Often such research is sensitive information and not available to other than public agencies or special committees. In fact, some may question whether tax dollar-supported consumer research can and should be classified as "top secret." Some of the research seen in recent publications of one research group "picks at" the consumer affairs area, but not as fully as the businessman of a specific company might require. Some sample topics include:

> "Consumer Protection: The Consumer Steamroller Rumbles On — Mid-May 1970

> "Consumer Well-Being: Public Reaction to President Nixon's Economic Policies" — Mid-September 1971

> "Consumer Protection: Which Products and Services are the Chief Targets of Consumer Complaints?" — Mid-June 1970

> "Consumer Protection: How Widespread are Consumer Complaints about Safety Hazards?" — End November 1971

> "Ideological Trends: The Public is Critical of American Business" — End December 1971

> "The Changing Consumer" — December 1962[8]

Unfortunately, these studies, as well as others conducted by other firms, represent focused research projects geared to specific client needs. For purposes of confidentiality, as well as financial reasons, it is not viable to expand these projects and findings may not be available to the public.

Often, government action is motivated by the interest area of a governmental agency. For example, the Federal Trade Commission conducted a study of supermarket advertising practices in San Francisco and Washington, only to learn that a significant percentage of advertised products were not on the shelves or were mispriced.[9] Such a study prompted the FTC to develop some guideline principles for curbing the abusive practices of supermarkets. Had there not been a governmental study conducted in this area, consumers would not have received the possible benefits of potential improvements in this area. With the National Institute for Measuring Consumer Issues and Problems, formal measurement of consumer issues and problems would have uncovered whether or not supermarket selling prices represented an issue, and, if so, how significant and for whom. With such a study, it might have been found that supermarket selling practices, while important to control, might not have been the most critical area for the FTC to allocate its resources. Another problem area could have proved to be of far greater importance, affecting more people in more serious ways. However, to date, we have no central measurement group to apprise the country of the issues and problems.

While numerous business organizations conduct marketing research, either through contractual or in-house facilities, business firms may not conduct the kind of research that would provide the insight into unresolved consumer problems. Business firms tend to conduct research that serves its own best interests — optimizing financial returns and increasing or maintaining its share of market. If one believes in basic economics one can make a case for consumer surveys and departments as long-range profit optimization tools.

Definition of the National Institute for Measuring Consumer Issues and Problems. Dean Arjay Miller of the Graduate School of Business at Stanford has proposed the establishment of a national institute on priorities to determine those areas of the political, economic and social sectors where government should allocate its resources in given priorities. Similarly, I propose the establishment of a research institute at the national level whose principal task would be ascertaining national consumer affairs priorities by conducting and analyzing periodic studies of how a representative sample of the American public perceives consumer issues and problems. While there are a number of methodological considerations to examine and observe for a meaningful study, I am not at all concerned about such techniques. These can be resolved, for these technical skills are abundant.

A National Institute for Measuring Consumer Issues and Problems might also incorporate the idea or concept of Professor Cohen, who has strongly recommended that the Federal Trade Commission establish a new organization within the framework of the FTC to be called the Bureau of Behavioral Studies. She suggests that the main thrust of the bureau would be "to gather and analyze data on consumer buying behavior relevant to the regulation of advertising in the consumer interest."[10]

Such a study should pinpoint the problems and issues perceived by the American consumer as well as the extent to which these problems exist — especially when correlated with a multiple number of demographics (age, sex, family size, position in household, income, urban, suburban, rural, etc.) and characteristics of buying behavior and values (chain store buyer vs. small mom and pop store buyer, once a week shopper vs. two or three times a week, heavy users vs. light users, strong religiously conservative values vs. liberal, etc.).

Studies dealing with the disadvantaged or poor in America might lead one to believe that as far as consumerism goes, the majority of deep-rooted issues fall in this income group. The truth of the matter is that the problems of the poor may not be the problems of the middle income or higher income groups. The problems of the higher income or more affluent or more educated might be quite different from the problems of the poor in the area of consumer issues. It is about time that America and her corporations awaken to the fact that the area of consumer affairs and the crises of consumerism will be deepened if we do not begin to focus our survey research on all the population in order to single out the specific issues and problems by market segments, demographics, psychographics, buying behavior and the like. It is unfortunate that we seem to peg the consumer affairs or consumerism issues with the disadvantaged!

Furthermore, with the conduct of periodic studies, trends can be ascertained: Government and business can determine the extent to which changes in government and business practices (*e.g.*, new marketing decisions to improve certain kinds of services to consumers, or a new FTC guideline to help curb deceptive packaging practices) have abated or abetted a problem area. Periodic studies will permit the data user to help lessen problems in the "bud" stage.

Index numbers could be developed for purposes of simply describing the extent to which distinct issues and problems exist. It is also possible to develop an overall weighted index of consumer issues and problems after the conduct of each study. Such an index might be popularly presented to the American public much as the consumer price index or the pollution index in the local daily newspaper.

There is no end to which computer cross-tabbing and correlations could be developed by the national institute.

The National Institute for Measuring Consumer Issues and Problems (NIMCIP) would be funded totally by government. Possibly, a partial contractual arrangement might be developed with the Institute's heavy users. The Institute's charter would call for the periodic conduct of analysis and communication of consumer issues and problems. NIMCIP would publish these findings through a public newsletter at a nominal subscription fee. All governmental agencies and bureaus would have access to the NIMCIP data. In addition, trade associations, business firms, and research groups could contract with NIMCIP for more detailed "break-out" data tapes, at cost, from the government. Such specific data could involve detailed industry-product-demographic-buying behavior-value data.

The Results of the National Institute for Measuring Consumer Issues and Problems. A few guidelines to simplify some of the results of having NIMCIP as a governmentally based and sponsored operation are as follows:

1. All governmental agencies and bureaus of government would have detailed consumer data from which more optimal allocation of budget resources could be accomplished. Agencies and bureaus like the OCA, NBC, FDA, Commerce, etc., could establish priorities for attacking consumer problems and providing for their resolution. This would reduce the tendency for agencies and bureaus to "shoot from the hip" in determining which consumer problem areas to study.

2. Business firms would have a set of representative data which would describe the kinds of consumer problems perceived and

experienced by the consumer. Further print-out or specific data could be purchased by the business firm at a nominal price. All business firms would have equal opportunity for obtaining quality research data. As a result, business firms and leaders of marketing may be more encouraged to generate internal policies for reducing or eliminating consumer problem areas that relate to their markets, products and consumers. Furthermore, the quality and nature of the data may provide an encouragement to engage in a preventative program for satisfying customer needs and expectations regarding all facets of the marketing mix.

3. University, consumer, research and other groups would have access to the same data as governmental and business firms. Not only would the data be current, but nominal in cost (if more than general information was needed). These groups might use these data as a base from which to do more exploration, theory building, hypothesis development or empirical research, all of which might help resolve the consumerism struggle in this country.

4. The availability of the NIMCIP data would be in keeping with the possible evolution of a national institute on priorities, as developed by Dean Arjay Miller at Stanford. The importance of consumerism, as measured by NIMCIP, would be arranged in our national system of priorities. Also, the partial or full incorporation of the Cohen concept of the Bureau of Behavioral Studies might well be included in the NIMCIP operation.

5. Consumers per se would benefit from the communication of the NIMCIP data in terms of an educational gain. Consumers would become more cognizant of the need for more rational buying behavior, as well as problem-solving opportunities.

6. Social action groups, governmental and non-governmental, might benefit from the availability of the NIMCIP data. Special forums, courses or classes in consumer education might benefit from this information.

7. A common set of research data could enable governmental, business, and academic leaders to engage in dialogue "in the same tongue" instead of "different tongues". The hearing technique where government prepares its own set of empirical data and business prepares its set would no longer be necessary in consumerism.

To conclude, it is possible that the newly-established business committees of the National Business Council for Consumer Affairs could be engaged in examining the viability and procedures for establishing the National Institute for Measuring Consumer Issues and Problems. It was the President's intention that the National Business Council would work on resolving consumer affair problems through the concerted efforts of industry. The NBC might engage representatives from the American Marketing Association and government to further explore the NIMCIP proposal.

QUESTIONS FOR DISCUSSION

1. In view of the fact that some 128 agencies and departments of the government are supposed to play a part in protecting the consumer, why, then, is the consumer not protected adequately? What is wrong with the system?

2. What is the purpose of the Institute recommended by Dr. Schutte? Why is a "playback loop" from consumers to government and business needed?

3. What do you think of the "mail bag" method of assaying consumer opinion? Is it an accurate gauge?

4. What is wrong with the surveys conducted by private research organizations?

5. What would be the purpose of a national institute on priorities?

6. What advantages would occur if NIMCIP were established? Can you foresee any limitations or difficulties?

FOOTNOTES

1. For example, see David A. Aaker and George S. Day, "Introduction: A Guide for Consumerism," in Aaker and Day, editors, *Consumerism: Search for Consumer Interest* (New York: Free Press, 1971), pp. 1-22. Or see "Business Responds to Consumerism," *Business Week* (September 6, 1969), pp. 94-108.

2. Aaker and Day, *Ibid.*, pp. 1-442.

3. Virginia H. Knauer, Director, Office of Consumer Affairs, *Guide to Federal Consumer Services* (Washington, D.C.: United States Government Printing Office, August 1971), 151 pages.

4. Theodore Levitt, "Why Business Always Loses: A Marketing View of Government Regulation," *Marketing for Tomorrow ... Today* (American Marketing Association, June 1967), pp. 14-19.

5. Raymond A. Bauer and Stephen A. Greyser, "The Dialogue That Never Happens," in Norman Kangun, *Society and Marketing: An Unconventional View* (New York: Harper and Row, 1971), p. 35.

6. Aaker and Day, *Ibid.*, p. xviii.

7. Unpublished study conducted by the Office of Consumer Affairs, Summer 1971. However, the mail bag analysis is now occurring on a more regular basis.

8. These reports are part of a "Report to Management" program sponsored by ORC Corporation in Princeton, N.J.

9. Federal Trade Commission, *Economic Report: On Food Chain Selling Practices in the District of Columbia and San Francisco* (Washington, D.C.: United States Government Printing Office, July 1969), 47 pages.

10. Dorothy Cohen, "The Federal Trade Commission and the Regulation of Advertising in the Consumer Interest," *Journal of Marketing*, XXXIII (January 1969), p. 42.

CONSUMERISM, 1990 — ADAPTING TO TODAY'S VALUES FOR TOMORROW'S IMPERATIVES *

AARON S. YOHALEM

* Aaron S. Yohalem, "Consumerism, 1990 — Adapting to Today's Values for Tomorrow's Imperatives," *A Look At Business in 1990*, White House Conference on the Industrial World Ahead, Washington, 1972, pp. 107-110. Reproduced by permission.

Remarks by Aaron S. Yohalem, Senior Vice President, CPC International, Inc.

Our technology and industrial performance has all too palpably lacked clear, resolved, and balanced social perspectives. It has lacked a critical sense of itself; lacked an awareness of the social context in which it operates and the social impact it necessarily generates. In many major areas of our economy we have had a kind of mindlessness for which we are paying high costs.

Thus far, we in industry have not even questioned, let alone attempted to direct or control our technology, production, and distribution with a view toward consciously maximizing the public weal while minimizing public risk. Not that individual companies have not been mindful of this defect, for they have. But insofar as industry-wide or business-wide consciousness is concerned, our performance has been nonexistent.

Listen to the New Winds

The traditional cost/benefit factor, the short- and long-term profit orientation are seen as motivation and the foundation of our economic system. But the myths of business-as-usual, and the market-will-right-itself simply will not suffice in the face of the consumerism of today, let alone 1990. Nor will our own long-term best interests, including our profitable well being, be served.

We in industry can anticipate, of course, that as we seek to adapt to changing values, the very process of adaptation will impact on those values and alter them, bringing about the need for still further industry readjustments. But the inexorable vigor of the consumer movement permits little room for leisurely contemplation on an optimum course of action. It is clear that if business does not get moving well ahead of the consumerism train, we shall see one of the biggest wrecks in our economic history.

The potential threat, in my view, is that corporate lethargy, married with political timidity, may procreate unworkable alterations in the economic system. This would needlessly frustrate the nation's existing capacity to meet totally legitimate consumer demands, as well as other national imperatives.

The existing system of free markets and open competition is not immutable. Although it excelled in meeting yesterday's demands for economic growth, and for abundance at reasonable prices, those achievements are widely regarded today as insufficient. Today's concern is increasingly with "quality of life." There is a disquieting lack of public confidence as to the capacity of the industrial system to add this new requirement.

To be sure, today's consumer shops for products and services with a flinty eye on the price tag. But that is only one consideration. Now the consumer is likely to ask questions about such matters as the safety of the product, completeness of the information provided about it, its performance, the recourse if it does not perform well, hiring practices of the manufacturer, pollution created in its manufacture or use, and its social relevance.

Surveys of consumer attitudes reflect the depth of these concerns. Over half the public approves of Ralph Nader, an eloquent symbol and summary of consumer aspirations. Two-thirds want Congressional legislation assuring consumers of better value.

Consider, also, the attitudes of today's students. Researcher Daniel Yankelovich, a specialist on the restless generation, notes that: "What is new is not the presence of a small group of radicals on the campus but the mushrooming growth of a much larger number of students who agree with the radicals' diagnosis of what is wrong with America, even though they do not endorse their tactics. This larger supportive group is estimated at a whopping two out of five college students."

Their overriding concern, and the growing concern of many of their parents, is that the country's institutions, especially its business institutions, are indifferent to social needs — and incapable of voluntary change. This concern is highly emotional, often not susceptible to intellectual argument. It has taken a totally *political* turn.

This development is also reflected in the society at large. In just the last eight years, more than two dozen federal consumer laws have been passed. But they fall far short of what consumer activists find desirable. Consequently, they are pressing aggressively and effectively for personal involvement and for reform through the judicial system.

So long as the business community retains any appearance of ignoring the revolution in consumer values, the consumerism train will gain speed, trip another series of political signals, and the consequences may tangle our economic tracks to the satisfaction of no one — with the exception of a handful of committed extremists. Probably the most articulate expression of industry's social responsibility — embracing employees, stockholders, communities, and suppliers — would be to respond imaginatively to consumer demands.

Need for Consumer-Trend Analysis

This suggests to me the need for industry to study the new dimension of consumerism with the same scale of investment in time, money, research, and analysis that it devotes to a major new service or product line prior to its introduction. Individual corporations, in the interest of improving on the best of the competitive system, should:

> analyze the demographics of consumerism as they affect their specific operations
>
> define those areas where consumer segments are correct or misinformed
>
> make the adjustments necessary to meet legitimate complaints
>
> undertake the communication effort required to alert the public, and its elected leaders, to the adjustments made and to areas of public misunderstanding or misinformation.

This is not a simple assignment. I suggest the only choice is to grasp the nettle. The question we in the business community must ask ourselves is: Are we smart enough to see what is happening? Have we the will to work at it in a methodical, professional way? Particularly, do we have the good sense to open up our communication channels to listen to, and learn from, even the most militant of the groups who oppose everything we believe in?

Are we in business and industry prepared to question the eternal validity of the GNP? Will we sit still to consider the arguments of the ZPGers and the ZEGers — respectively, the Zero Population Growth and the Zero Economic Growth advocates? Will we be able to derive any insight from the concept of static growth as opposed to dynamic, purely one-dimensional, linear growth?

I trust the answer will be a positive one; it had best be.

It is essential to realize that consumerism has long ago ceased to have the circumscribed limits of customary marketing concerns. Consumerism has a far more comprehensive, sophisticated relevance to our society as a whole. Consumerism further encompasses such controversial issues as:

> The use of stockholder proxies to propose resolutions affecting corporate policy, including public representation on corporate boards
>
> How to determine, and who to charge for, the cost of "negative externalities," such as air or water pollution
>
> "Product performance insurance" — and its effect on freedom of choice and the living standards of the poor
>
> Meaningful methods for auditing the social accountability of business
>
> The role of advertising and other promotion forms as they affect society's best interests

The social obligation of investors, individual and institutional

"Nationalizing" private systems, or "commercializing" public systems or both

And the federal chartering of publicly held corporations

I am trying to emphasize that the complexity and intensity of the consumer movement cannot be overestimated. It is only a part, if a large part, of a pervasive public concern with increasing the social responsibility of business. Consumerism will not just go away. Coming to grips with it will inevitably take the form of a new but operative aspect of management responsibility.

While this movement is not new to our nation, it has never enjoyed more favorable conditions for nurturing it to full and robust bloom. To underscore the point, consider an extreme example: Bangladesh, which is light years from any concern over slack-fill, unit pricing, or grade labeling. Its single consumer demand is at the first plateau of Maslow's tier of hierarchial values: survival. America's consumers, on the other hand, are concerning themselves with his highest plateau: self-actualization and spiritual or humanistic rather than material considerations.

The consumer movement is today riding a flood tide characterized by a fundamental shift in national attitudes toward legislation affecting private enterprise. Historically, government has sought to proscribe those things that institutions *cannot* do. Today, however, government increasingly seeks to circumscribe those things institutions *can* do.

Clearly, then, if industry wishes to affect the shape of consumer legislation, the time is now, not the '90s, to take an introspective look at business performance as against new consumer attitudes toward "quality of life." Will we have the wisdom to recognize that the dollars involved in rearguard movements and holding actions normally exceed those required to bring about solutions?

Industry cannot, nor should it, undertake all the initiatives in seeking a rapprochement among business, government, and the consumer movement. Nor have I the naive hope that consumerists will ever be totally satisfied, which, indeed, would impede social progress. But I do believe, given the kind of industry-wide effort required, that the business community can introduce The Rule of Reason to the consumer-industry dialogue. It will not be possible for each of the diverse elements striving for a better consumer society to have its own aspirations fulfilled, *totally*. Each will have to succumb to the rule of reason and make some accommodation to the needs of others. This, after all, is the definition of society.

The rule of reason demands that all of the sectors involved listen with comprehension — not merely take turns talking. It demands that we seek, in our own self-interest, to share understanding of common problems so that we do not exhaust our energies on the impossible or, unwittingly, the undesirable. It demands, too, that we distinguish carefully between our own point of view and the genuine insight of others, and that all of us accept the democracy of man's frailities. It may behoove us to consider some of the role reversals, that, if society is to be properly served by industry, might possibly occur.

While the public utterances of industry on the matters of consumerism are encouraging, words hardly constitute actuality. I am concerned with its performance; that it matches its words. More to the point, I am concerned that our performance responds to the demands and needs confronting us. Only with performance can we begin to build a credibility that is today sorely missing, but which is a necessary foundation for the future.

Along with our own corporate committees on the environment, minority employment, the cities and the like, we must make certain that we maintain in industry the most realistic kind of self-criticism. We need, in effect, to maintain some form of corporate counter-culture or sub-stratum thereof that will make its business the task of continuously keeping us disabused so the better to keep us on our toes and performing credibly.

Business necessarily has to become more involved socially and more responsive to business in society. Business must be able to detach itself from its own myopic traditions. It must seek out, not automatically reject, reasonable critics. It must anticipate, indeed provide, progressive leadership in the march of consumerism to the 1990s.

The question remains: Not, do we have the foresight to understand the future, but, do we have the courage to change it?

QUESTIONS FOR DISCUSSION

1. What is Mr. Yohalem arguing for?

2. What dangers does he see in the "business-as-usual" and "the market-will-right-itself" attitudes?

3. What new elements in a product besides its price will the consumer of the future require information about?

4. Why do you think many students feel that the corporation is indifferent to social needs? Are businessmen indifferent, in your view?

5. Mr. Yohalem argues that all parties must pay renewed attention to the "quality of life". Explain.

6. He says we need some form of "corporate counter-culture". What is meant by this?

7. What do you think consumerism will be like in 1990? How about the form of the corporation?

APPENDIX I

Society Will Determine the Corporate Form
Elisha Gray II

Remarks by Elisha Gray II, Chairman, Finance Committee, Whirlpool Corporation.

It should be perfectly clear to any thoughtful businessman that the *form* of the enterprise system in the final analysis will be what our society thinks it should be. The corporate charter is not the Holy writ.

The public has been modifying the original free-wheeling character of the institution of business for three centuries or so — particularly since the Industrial Revolution began. Since the turn of this century the process of change has accelerated until now the regulations affecting business cover everything from whom they may employ to what words they may use in selling their wares.

This process of change shows no sign of tapering off and our challenge is to try to forecast what will be expected of us 20 years hence.

APPENDIX II

Possible Results to Response to
Society's Objectives

The consumer movement itself should be prepared for still higher prices and even deeper employment dislocation if it seriously expects all of its demands to be met immediately.

Labor leadership should prepare itself for the possibility that consumerists will one day ask what unions can do to encourage improved workmanship and to retard inflation.

Perhaps organized labor will concern itself not only with wages, hours, and working conditions but also with such issues as balance of payments, currency convertibility, quotas, production/cost ratios, and the impact of protectionism.

Government, on its part, should be prepared to resolve the present incompatibility between consumerism and antitrust policies. It is virtually impossible for industry to develop an effective program of cooperation or self-regulation to resolve consumer or environmental problems without violating antitrust, as currently interpreted.

State governments will be asked to share their sovereignty by supporting, when and where needed, federal preemptive legislation in the consumer field. National or regional companies cannot offer maximum savings or service to consumers when they are forced, as now, to meet varying and even conflicting state requirements.